INTRODUCTION

At the request of the publisher for a volume of records for persons with Presbyterian ancestry, I began searching for a body of information which would be useful to a large number of researchers. Since most session records available are for a limited number of families, a denominational newspaper seemed the logical choice. The *Charleston Observer* was the answer. The notices in this newspaper surpassed my expectations for the number of persons mentioned and the wide territory covered.

Obviously, the *Charleston Observer* was exchanging with several papers and copying notices appearing in them, especially in the early years. Though often abbreviated, these notices are extremely valuable since some issues of these other newspapers are not extant. The notices from North Carolina, Georgia, and Alabama are a welcome addition to vital dates now in print in addition to notices from all over South Carolina. Used in conjunction with the volumes already published on the *Southern Christian Advocate* and the *Lutheran Observer* and *Southern Lutheran*, this volume can help pin down some rather obscure persons and prove family connections not otherwise ascertainable.

Brent H. Holcomb, C.A.L.S.
Columbia, South Carolina
October 6, 1979

Issue of January 20, 1827 (Volume I, #3)

Departed this life on the 11th ult., the Rev. Thomas Osborn for several years the greatly respected and esteemed Rector of Trinity and St. Stephen's Churches, on Edisto Island.
Died, at Augusta (Geo.), 10th inst., Mr. Benjamin T. Duyckinck, formerly one of the Editors of the Augusta Chronicle, in the 53d year of his age.

Issue of January 27, 1827

Died, in Exeter, Miss Anna Rogers, aged 78, daughter of Rev. Daniel Rogers, of Exeter, who died in 1787, who was son of Rev. John Rogers of Ipswich, who died in 1745, who was son of Rev. John Rogers, President of Harvard College, who died in 1684, who was the eldest son of Rev. Nathaniel Rogers, who came from England in 1636, and settled in Ipswich, and died in 1655, who was son of Rev. John Rogers of Dedham in England, who died in 1639, who was grandson of the Rev. John Rogers of London, who was burnt at Smithfield in 1555.

Issue of February 10, 1827

Died, at Mount Zion, Georgia, on the 23d of January, Mrs. Elizabeth Reid, in her 87th year. Mrs. Reid early embraced the gospel of Christ.... Some years since she divided her property among her children, reserving what she conceived enough for her own maintenance, and this at her death was bequeathed to the Presbyterian church of that place, of which she was a member.
On the next day in the same neighbourhood, Mr. Moses Wiley aged rising 80. Mr. Wiley had also been a member of the Presbyterian church for many years. He had the satisfaction of seeing all his children in the bosom of the church....
At his residence rear Darien (Ga.), on the 2d instant, James Nephew , Esq., an Elder in the Presbyterian church of that place. ... He founded the Nephew scholarship in the Theological Seminary of Princeton....

Issue of February 17, 1827

Married by the Rev. David Humphreys, on the 18th ult., Major John W. Hooper, Attorney at Law of the State of Georgia, to Miss Sarah A. Word, daughter of Robert Word, of Laurence (sic) District, South Carolina.
Died on the 6th inst., Mr. John James Fowler, at the early age of 20 years and 3 months. (eulogy).
in Augusta, William Hogan, Attorney at law--late from Charleston, and formerly of Philadelphia.
In Ohio, on the 25th ult., in the 34th year of his age, the Rev. Samuel Davis Hoge, Professor of the Natural Sciences in the Ohio University. The deceased was the son of Dr. Moses Hoge, late President of Hamden Sidney College, Virginia
In Tekbunah (missionary station among the Indians,) on the 13th November last, Lucinda Wright, wife of Mr. David Wright, and daughter of Colonel Asabel Washburn, of Montpelier, Vt., aged 25 years.

Issue of March 3, 1827

Married on the 21st ult., by the Rev. Mr. Hanckel, Mr. Robert Barnwell Smith, to Miss Elizabeth W. Burnett, late of St. Bartholomew's Parish.

In Sparta, Ga., on the 15th inst., Archibald Stokes, Esq., Merchant of Petersburg, to Miss Catharine Paton, of Woodbridge, N. J.
On the 2d Jan. last, by Q. L. C. Franklin, Esq., Col. Aaron W. Grier of Warren County, Ga., to the amiable and accomplished Miss Elizabeth Perry, of Wilkes Co.
On the 5th ult., Richard Stockton, Esq., Attorney General of Mississippi. At Pittsfield, Mass., Thomas Gold, Esq., aged 67. In Baltimore, Jacob Nurser, a German, aged 114 years, 87 of which he passed in America.

Issue of March 10, 1827

Died, at Pottersville, S. C., 23d ult., Mr. Ranson Milton, aged 27. At Decatur, Ga., on the 16th ult., Mrs. Ann Reynolds, 76. In Philadelphia, Charles W. Peale, founder of the Museum of that city, 86. At Contonment Clinch, near Pensacola, Captain W. Armstrong, of the 16th regt. U. S. Infantry.

Issue of March 17, 1827

(Died) in this city on the 9th inst., Mr. John P. Young. On the 14th Mr. John Schirer. At Combahee, Mrs. Susannah Addison, consort of Mr. Wm. Addison. In Savannah, Alex. Hunter, Esq., Surveyor of the Port, aged 38. In Wilkes co., Ga., John Hood, a revolutionary soldier, and for 30 years an esteemed member of the Baptist church, 68. At Augusta, suddenly, Mr. John King, of Clark county. Near Boston, Hon. Christopher Gore, formerly Governor of Massachusetts and a Senator of the U. States. In Concord, N. H., Rev. Asa McFarland, D. D. 58.

Issue of March 24, 1827

Married on the 28th ult., Dr. Henry Towns of Greenville Dist., to Miss Lucretia Ann, daughter of Mr. Wm. Calhoun, of Abbeville dist. At Camden, Mr. James B. Berry, to Miss Elizabeth Childers. At Albany, N. Y., Dr. P. H. Wilson, of Savannah, to Miss Mary W. Morris, granddaughter of the late Robert Morris, Esq., of Philadelphia. At Augusta, Mr. Richard J. Thomas, of Burke co., to Mrs. Ann Appleton.
(Died) in this city, on the 14th ult., Dr. Samuel Wilson, 64. On the 20th, Mrs. Simons, wife of Mr. Keating Simons. On the 15th, Mrs. Ann Ross, for 58 years a respectable resident of this city.
At Savannah, on the 16th inst., Charles Harris, Esq., a distinguished citizen of that place. At Saratoga, N. Y., Abijah Lee, aged 94. He was a soldier under Wolfe, at the capture of Quebec, and was also in most of the actions on Lakes George and Champlain during the French war. He sent four sons to the field during the revolution, one of whom fell at the capture of Burgoyne. At New Durham, N. H., Stephen Webster, 87, one of the few individuals who escaped the massacre at Fort Wm. Henry, in 1757, and a soldier of the revolution. At Athens, Ga., Mrs. Narcissa, wife of Mr. Z. Beall. On board the British ship of war Revenge, off Naples, in Nov. last, the Marquis of Hastings, formerly Gov. Gen. of India, aged 71. He was known as Lord Rawdon, in the Revolutionary War, and made himself conspicuous in the Southern States. He died Governor of Malta.
In Culpeper co., Va., Maj. Gabriel Long, 76. He was the last surviving officer who commanded a company in Col. Morgan's celebrated Rifle Regiment, and was engaged in no less than eighteen actions. He led the advance at Saratoga...saved the life of Lieut. White, now Judge White of Virginia....

in London, Wm. Gifford, Esq., translator of Juvenal and for many years editor of the Quarterly Review....

Issue of March 31, 1827

Married in Laurens dist. by the Rev. J. Foster, the Rev. David Humphreys to Miss Rebecca, daughter of Samuel Cunningham, Esq. In Savannah, Abram D'Lyon, Esq. to Miss Hannah Sheftall. In London, on the 6th Feb. the Rev. Joseph Folk, Missionary to the Jews, to Lady Georgiana Mary Walpole, fourth daughter of the late, and sister of the present Earl of Oxford.
 (Died) on John's Island, on the 26th Feb., Mr. Franklin Paine Mackey, aged 29, son of Dr. John Mackey, of this city. in Lexington Dist., Mrs. Lavinia Taylor, relict of Wm. Taylor. On the 18th ult., Mr. John Boyle, a respectable planter of St. Paul's Parish. In Pendleton Dist., Capt. Jehu Orr. In Savannah, Mr. John Forsyth.

Issue of April 7, 1827

Married in this city on the 29th ult., Mr. James Chapman to Miss Isabella Brown. Mr. John Douglass to Miss Martha S. Williams.
 In Savannah, on the 15th ult., Maj. Jonathan Thomas to Mrs. Mary Ann Houston, both of McIntosh county. At Columbia, Mr. Wm. Ancrum of Camden, to Miss Julia Arthur. In Pendleton D., Mr. Geo. W. Liddell to Miss Rebecca Harris. Mr. C. P. DuPre to Miss Mary E. Crane. Mr. John Hallum to Miss Frances Hamilton of Clarkesville, Ga.
 (Died) in this city, Mrs. Rachel, wife of Mr. Isaac Harby. On the 1st inst., Mary, youngest daughter of the late Mr. F. A. Willman.
 In Havana, on the 25th ult., Mr. George Hoffman, of this city. In New York. Dr. Cheve Felch, one of the Editors of Coram's Champion. Lieut. Charles A. Budd, of the Navy, who acted a gallant part with McDonough at Plattsburgh.

Issue of April 21, 1827

Died at St. Petersburgh, on the 26th January, Eleanor Isabella, second daughter of Henry Middleton Esq., Envoy Extraordinary of the U. S. to the Court of Russia.

Issue of April 28, 1827

We stop the press to announce the painful intelligence that Mrs. Judson, one of our Missionaries at Burmah, is no more....
 At New-York, on the 15th inst., James Freeman Dans, M. D., Professor of Chemistry in the College of Physicians and Surgeons of the U. of N. Y., aged 34....

Issue of May 5, 1827

Married at Savannah, Mr. John Mallory to Mrs. Hestor Ann Sherman. In York Dist. Mr. Robert Lindsay, to Miss Margaret Ann Lattimer. In St. Paul's Parish, Julius M. Martin, Esq.,of Yorkville, to Mrs. Emma Coturier. In Milledgeville, Rev. S. Olin, of Athens, Ga. to Miss Mary Ann Bostick.
 Died near Terrysville, Abbeville District, S. C., on the evening of the 15th April, Mrs. Sarah Patterson, wife of Josiah Patterson, Esq., in the 50th year of her age...member of the Presbyterian Church...left a husband, two aged parents (of whom she was an only daughter) and an only daughter....

Died, in Salisbury, N. C., on the 10th of April, Miss Elizabeth, daughter of Thomas L. and Elizabeth Cowen, aged seven years and three months....
　　In Concord, N. C., Mr. Philip Corss, a soldier of the revolution. In Gates co., Wm. M. Harvey, Esq. In Camden co., Enoch Sawyer, Esq., Collector of Customs, to which office he was appointed by Gen. Washington, aged 70.

Issue of May 12, 1827

　　Married on the 30th of January, by the Rev. E. J. Mills, Mr. Jacob Mills, to Miss Ann Rose, only daughter of Thos. Rose, Esq., of Sumter District.
　　In Pendleton Dist., Mr. John B. Proctor to Miss Eliza Ann Hallum. In Chester Dist. Mr. John Bigham to Miss Nancy McDill. in York Dist., Gen. Richard D. S. McLean of N. C. to Miss Jane Adams. In Savannah, Mr. Horace Blair to Mrs. Rebecca L. Wiseman, both of Augusta.
　　Died in New York, on the 29th ult., the Hon Rufus King, in the 73d year of his age. (eulogy). In Malta, Mrs. Temple, wife of the American missionary on that island. In Pendleton Dist., Captain Wm. Perkins. In Greenville Dist. Rev. Lewis Rector, Pastor of the Baptist Church at Brushy Creek. At Georgetown Capt. Paul Cartwright, 75.
　　Died on the 6th day of January in the 78th year of his age, Mr. William Mills, of Sumter District. (eulogy)

Issue of May 19, 1827

　　Married on Thursday evening last, by the Rev. Mr. McDowell, Mr. Alfred Y. Walton, of the house of Tho. Flemming & Co. to Mrs. Elizabeth Flemming, of Philadelphia.
　　(Died) in this city, Maj. Robert M. Head, a revolutionary officer, who for some time commanded the escort of Gen. Lafayette. Near Harrisburgh, Mr. Stephen Webb, of York District, killed by a fall from the saddle horse while descending a hill with his wagon. In Christ Ch. Parish, Mrs. Rebecca S. Legay, aged 70. At Farmville, St. John's, Frederick Laurens, Esq. At Columbia, (drowned) Mr. John Lofton, a member of the Senior Class, S. C. College. In Halifax, Wm. Drew, Esq., late At. Gen. of N. C. In Sharon, Ms., Mrs. Deborah Garnett, 67. This woman was a heroine of the revolution, having enlisted in one of the Massachusetts regiments....the mother of a respectable family of children....

Issue of May 26, 1827

　　Married on Tuesday evening last, by the Rev. Dr. Gadsden, Fisher Gadsden, Esq., to Miss Laura W. Michau, both of this city.
　　(Died) in Kershaw Dist., Col. Adam Wilkie, aged 60. In St. Luke's Parish, John Frampton, a soldier of the revolution, 77. At Rowley, Ms., Robert S. Coffin, the "Boston Bard." In Providence, Lieut. P. M. Whipple, of the Navy.... At the Sandwich Islands, George Tamoree, son of the King of Taui. He was educated at the foreign mission school in Cornwall.... On the 30th of January last, at Syra, Mr. W. H. Potter, formerly of the Navy, and second son of John Potter, Esq. of Charleston, S. C. Mr. P. volunteered his services in the cause of Greece, and sailed from N. York in the ship Hope.

Issue of June 2, 1827

Married in Camden, Major John Walker to Miss Margaret McRa. in Columbia, Col. T. H. Elmore of Walterboro', to Miss Harriet C. Taylor, daughter of Gov. Taylor.
Died in Liberty co., Ga., Mrs. Julia Ann Martin, aged 19. in Augusta, Mrs. Amelia Main, 25. At Chesterville, Hannah, youngest daughter of John Kennedy, Esq., In Mecklenburgh co., N. C., Capt. John Gilmer, 63.
in Winnsborough, Fairfield District, on 4th ult., Mrs. Nancy McCreight, consort of Col. Wm. M'Creight, 52....(eulogy)

Issue of June 9, 1827

Married in Savannah, C. S. Henry, Esq., to Miss Sarah R. Aborn, of Rhode Island.
Died in Matanzas, where he had gone for the benefit of his health, Israel Pickens, late Gov. of Alabama. In Boston, Wm. Philips, Esq., late Lieut. Governor of Mass., 77. in Lexington, Ga., Hon. John M. Dolly, for many years Judge of the Northern Circuit. In Fishkill, N. Y., Gen. Jacobus Swartworth, 93. When very young, he commanded the body guard of Gen. Amherst; and in the war of the Revolution, was alternately a Legislator and a Soldier. In Georgetown, S. C., Mrs. Clara E., wife of Mr. Francis R. Shackelford, aged 24. In Savannah, Miss Mary E. Darby, daughter of the late Capt. R. A. Darby of this city, 21.
Died of the consumption, in Salem, Sumter District, the 20th May, Capt. John McFaddin, in the 34th year of his age....

Issue of June 23, 1827

Departed this life on the 10th inst., at Union Village, S. C., Mrs. Nancy Gage, consort of John Gage, jun. On the 7th ult., she was delivered of three children, a son and two daughters ....
A correspondent, in announcing to us the death of George Kennedy, Esq., Post Master of Chesterville, S. C. remarks: "This old and respectable citizen departed this life on the 8th inst., in the 63d year of his age...."

Issue of June 30, 1827

Married in this city, 26th inst., by Rev. Mr. McDowell, Dr. Benjamin B. Strobel, to Miss Mary J. Stewart.
In Augusta, 12th inst., James Terry, Esq. of Edgefield District, to Miss Ann S.Hutchinson. On the 10th, Capt. Allen Craig, to Mrs. Mary Luther. At Santee, 21st inst., Mr. Isaac J. Singletary, to Miss Mary C. Michau, of Williamsburgh District.
Died in Pendleton, Mr. Josiah Wright, 50. Mr. Elijah Sprigg, 36.
At Ebenezer, Ga., Miss Mary M. Cooper, aged 17. In Clinton, Ga., Mr. Peter Pease, 30. In Savannah, Mrs. Sarah Cline, 46. in Augusta, Alexander Gibson, 21. Francis B. Coquillon, aged 79, formerly a planter of St. Domingo.
in Covington, Ga., Thomas T. Cureton, Esq., formerly a respectable citizen of Newbury (sic) Dist. in Spartenburgh (sic) District, Dr. Hugh Davitt, 38.
Died in consequence of a most distressing accident in St. Bartholomew's Parish, on the 8th ult., Barkley Ferguson, in the 52d year of his age. The deceased left his residence in Prince William's Parish in his usual health in the morning to procure a dwelling house, to locate a minister of the Gospel for Saltcatcher church...for many years a respectable member of the Legis-

lature. City Gaz.
In Hadley, Ms., Mrs. Sybil Smith, aged 101 years....

Issue of July 7, 1827

Married at New-York, Brockholst Cutting, to Ann Markoe, daughter of William Heyward of South Carolina.
On the 28th ult., by the Rev. E. J. Mills, Mr. William Pressley, to Miss Elizabeth Gamble, both of Williamsburgh District.
In Hancock Co., Ga., on the 21st ult., by the Rev. Mr. Stiles, John H. Walker, Esq. to Miss Emily H., only daughter of Rev. John Brown, D. D.
In Milledgeville, Mr. P. D. Sarye, of Montgomery, A. to Miss Caroline V. eldest daughter of G. R. Clayton, Esq. Mr. Anthony Newsom to Miss Lydia Pierce.
Died in this city on the 4th inst., Mr. John B. Payne, 38. Mr. Wm. H. Capers, of St. Andrew's Parish, 24. At Walterboro', Mrs. Mary Sprout, 26. At Mount Pleasant, Mrs. Ann C., wife of Dr. R. S. Bailey, 34.
In Edgefield Dist., on the 22d ult., Miss Emeline Youngblood. At Elberton, Ga., Isaac Anthony, formerly of N. York, 42. At Tallahasse, Hon. A. B. Woodward, Judge Sup. Court for Middle Florida. In N. York, Gen. T. Worthington, late U. S. Senator from Ohio. In Danbury, Ct. of an inflammation of the lungs, Rev. Carlos Wilcox, in the meridian of life.
Died at Walterborough, on Friday, 29th June, William, son of the late General Oswald, of St. Bartholomews Parish, aged 18 years and 3 months. (eulogy)
In Tunis, in May last, her highness Lilli Fatima, only consort of the Bashaw Bey. At her funeral, 1500 slaves received their freedom.

Issue of July 14, 1827

Married in this city, by the Rev. B. Gildersleeve, Mr. Henry A. Cohrs to Miss Sarah A. Broer.
At Richmond Bath, Col. Samuel Dowse to Miss Abbey E. Sturges, both of Burke Co., Ga.
Died in this city Mrs. Mary A. E. Cogdell, 69. Mr. Frederick A. Geyer, 25. Mr. J. T. Cowan, 27.
On board ship Othello, on her passage to New-York, Margaret B., third daughter of Rt. Rev. Dr. Bowen, of this city, aged 6 years, 7 months. In Columbia, Mrs. Jane, wife of Dr. Elias Marks, 39. In Cheraw, Wm. W. Brown, 63. In Georgetown, Major General Thomas Carr.
In Hancock Co., Geo.,Rev.Gideon Hagood. Walter Hamilton, Esq. In Augusta, Mrs. Mary Coghlan, 48.

Issue of July 21, 1827

Married in Pendleton, 5th inst., by the Rev. A. Foster, Capt. Joseph J. Pickens to Miss Ellenor Frances Keys.
Died on the morning of the 18th inst., Mrs. Maria H. Brown, wife of the Rev. Joseph Brown, of this city. Mr. Charles S. Tucker. Mrs. Ann Hutchinson.
In Christ Church Parish, Mr. Thomas Allan, aged 72, a native of England, but for 61 years a resident of Charleston and vicinity, and a soldier of the Revolution. In St. Thomas Parish between the 23d ult and 9th inst., Margaret Honour, aged 3 years, Thomas Mason, 5 and John Wesley 15 months, children of Mr. John Page, late of this city.
In Pendleton, Mrs. Caroline O'Riley, late of this city, 39.
In Abbeville District, Martha Jane, eldest daughter of Col.

Joseph Grisham, of Pendleton, 13. At Varennes, Pendleton, on the 17th ult., Mr. James Dobbins, one of the most efficient members of the Church at Varennes.... In Sumter Dist., Capt. Matthew S. Moore, a highly respectable citizen. In York Dist., (drowned) Mr. Matthew Biggens.
In Augusta, Mr. Austin Woolfook, 40. In Chatham Co., Ga., Mrs. Martha Spiers, 62. In Bryan Co., Mary T. Maxwell. 25.

Issue of July 28, 1827

Married in Savannah, Mr. Stephen Mitchell to Miss Harriet S. Seabrook, of S. C. in Columbia, Mr. Charles Brenan to Miss Eliza Smith.
Mrs. Maria H. Brown whose death was mentioned in this paper last week was a native of Rindge, N. H. She was the only child of her parents, who are both still living. In Oct. 1821, she was married to Rev. Joseph Brown and came immediately to South-Carolina...left one child with her husband. (eulogy)
In this city, Capt. Joseph B. Paine, late of the Army, aged 38. At Edgefield, Miss Ellen H. Carroll, 16. In Cheraw, James Coit, Esq. in P. William's Parish, Dr. C. W. Grayson, 23. In Columbia, Mrs. Susan Arthur, 51. Mrs. Eliza Snowden.
In Augusta, by a fall from a window of the mansion-house, Wm. Overstreet, of the firm of Wm. Overstreet & Co. of this city. In Moore co., N. C., Dr. Archibald McQueen, 27. Near Pittsboro', Roderick Cotton, Esq. 56. Capt. George King, 30.
On board the frigate Constellation, at Norfolk, midshipman Edward Worthington, a young officer of high promise, a native of Ky. At Madbury, N. H. Israel Tibbets, 50, probably the largest man in America. His weight exceeded 450....
In Spain, Don Onis, late minister to this country.

Issue of August 4, 1827

Married in this city, Mr. Elbridge Bainbridge, of Boston, to Miss Anna Eliza Johnston.
In Greenville District, Mr. Nathan Davis, to Mrs. Elizabeth Cureton. In York District, Mr. Samuel B. Knox, of N. C. to Miss Cynthia Pettus. In Columbia, Dr. Edward Sill to Miss Carolina M. Greenwood.
Died in this city, Wm. Dewees, sen. Mr. John Warner. Mr. Frederick A. Jenks. Mrs. Mary Taggart, 37.
On Thursday last, Mrs. Sarah Hibben, aged 56. (eulogy) At Sullivan's island, of a wound caused by the accidental discharge of his fowling-piece, Edward Mortimer, Esq. of this city.
In Georgetown, James M. Grier, Esq. in Pendleton, Mrs. Elizabeth Joudon, 51. Julius H. Walker, of Wilmington, N. C. 33.
in Wilkes co., Ga.,Mrs. Harriet L. C., wife of Andrew Rembert, Esq. of Abbeville dist. In Warren co., Ga. on the 4th ult. John Torrence, Esq. a soldier of the revolution....
in Charlotte, N. C., Mrs. Elizabeth, wife of James Alexander. at Williamburgh (sie) Va., Rev. Dr. Wilmer. In New York, suddenly, Dr. William Chambers. In Edgarton, Mass. Rev. Joseph Thaxter, the last of the revolutionary chaplains, 83. In Havana, George Teimarsch, formerly of Charleston. At the Trenton Falls, near Utica, Miss Eliza M. Suydam, 17...belonged to one of the most respectable families in the city of N. York.
In England, Rev. Leigh Richmond, author of the Dairyman's Daughter, and other excellent Tracts.

Issue of August 18, 1827

Married in Winnsboro', by the Rev. Mr. Rennic, Rev. Richard

B. Cater, of Abbeville, to Miss Jemima M., daughter of the Rev. Samuel W. Yongue. At St. Mary's by the Rev. Mr. Pratt, Dr. C. A. Watkins, of Tallahasse, F. to Miss Martha Ann, daughter of Judge Gibson. In Stokes co., N. C., Mr. R. D. Golding to Miss Mary Bitting. In Mecklenburgh, Maj. John Montgomery to Miss Mary B. Wylie.
  Died in this city, Mrs. Rachel Alexander, aged 70. Mr. Flavel Loomis, of East Windsor, Con. 27. Mr. John R. Gitzinger. Mrs. Jessy Rosalia Furman, 26. Mr. E. D. Ingraham, of Maine, 18 (of yellow fever). Mrs. Margaret Passman, late of N. York. Mr. John W. Black, late of Columbia, of yellow fever. Mrs. Elizabeth Robertson.
  in York Dist., Mr. John Currence, 80, one of the heroes of King's Mountain. In Abbeville, Mrs. Elizabeth Steed Miller, 59. In Georgetown, Mrs. Nancy Jayroe, 24.
  In Savannah, 9th inst., Hon. John Elliott, late a Senator of the U. States, 55. Mr. E. while administering to his sick slaves in Liberty co. 12 of whom died of dysentery, was seized with the same complaint....
  In Petersham, Vt. Mrs. Lydia Beckham, 45....
At Harrisbrugh, Pa., suddenly, Rev. Robert Little, pastor of the Unitarian Church, Washington city.

Issue of August 25, 1827

  Married in this city, John G. North, Esq. of Georgetown, to Miss Jane G., eldest daughter of James Petigur, Esq. of Abbeville District. William Lloyd, to Miss Mary Rebb. In Greenville Dist. Mr. Willis Wells, to Miss Eliza Stokes. Mr. John Stennis, to Miss Mary Paden. In Charlotte, N. C. Mr. Hugh McMurray, of Lancaster S. C. to Miss Nancy Walkup.
  Died in this city at the residence of Mr. J. C. Hanahan, on the 13th instant, after a short but painful illness of 5 days, Mr. Elias C. Roberts, aged 40 years and 5 months. He was a native of Newark (N. J.) but for 7 years a resident of this city....
  In Savannah, Mrs. Henrietta B. Williams, aged 34. In Twiggs Co., Ga., Rev. Theophilus Pearce, 60. At Athens, Ga. Miss Dorothy Randolph, of Wilkes Co., aged 20, daughter of Capt. Richard Randolph.
  In York Dist., Mr. James McKenzie, 59. In Yorkville, Miss Jane Walker. In Lancaster, Mr. Mathew Sims. In Camden, Mr. Wm. Cook.
  In Mecklenburg, N. C., Mrs. Lecy Abernethy, 21. Mrs. Mary Dinkens.
  On board the ship Louisiana, on her passage from New-Orleans to New-York, 31st ult., Dr. Horace Holley, late President of the University of Kentucky.

Issue of September 1, 1827

  Married in Hancock Co., Mr. James Harris, of Warrenton, to Miss Sarah N. Andrews. In Twiggs Co., Ga., Rev. John M. Gray of Monroe, to Mrs. Mary Hill. In Savannah, Mr. Charles J. Brown to Miss Susan G. Carr. In Pendleton, Mr. John Gassaway to Miss Sarah McDow.
  Death of Miss Elizabeth Robertson, of this city (long eulogy) Died in this city, on Saturday 25th inst., Mrs. Sarah Faber, in the 23d year of her age, wife of Henry Faber, Esq. On 28th inst., Edward Hollinshead Chitty.... On the 19th inst., Alexander Grant, in the 54th year of his age, born in Murray or Eglinshire, in Scotland...left a widow and four children in England.
  Died in this city on Sunday last, the 26th ult., Mr. James M'Kenzie, a native of Scotland, in the 36th year of his age, leav-

a widow and two children.... (eulogy)
On Sullivan's Island, on the 20th inst., Mary Ann, eldest daughter of Mr. Daniel Macaulay, of this city.
In Edgefield, Col. Frank Butler, 34. In Pendleton, Mrs. Elizabeth, wife of Mr. Thomas Johnston, of this city, 41.
In Hall Co. Ga. Mr. Joshua Denton, a veteran of the Revolution. In Jackson Co. Mr. John M. Bacon, 18.
At Brunswick, Mineral Springs, Col. Joseph Hawkins, Comptroller of the State of N. C. In Jones Co., Rev. Wm. Jones, 23.
Died on Wednesday the 19th July, Mrs. Eliza Jane Snowden, wife of Mr. Gilbert T. Snowden, merchant of Columbia, aged 20 years and 11 months....

Issue of September 8, 1827

Married in Morgan Co., Ga., Mr. Samuel Walker of Putnam, to Miss Mary Shepherd, In Beaufort, Mr. Wm. Morcock, of Savannah, to Miss Susan A. M. Aggnew. At Cheraw, Mr. Drury Thomas to Miss Emily Saltonstall.
In New York city, Rev. A. Stephen Mealy, pastor of the Evangelical Lutheran Church in Savannah, to Mrs. Catharine A. Brasch.
Died in this city, Dr. Mathew Irvine, an aged and respectable physician, and an active Whig of the revolution. Of Yellow Fever, Thomas G. Buswell, 27, a native of Gilmantown, N. H. He was a candidate for the ministry in the Protestant Episcopal Church in the Diocess of S. C. James A. Blackman, a native of Virginia, 25. John Magarth, 35. Mr. Thomas Broughton, 19.
In Fairfield District, Mrs. Martha F. Rogers, wife of John Rogers, aged 30. At Red Bluff Spring, Julianna Ellen, daughter of Mr. J. H. Alston, aged 6.
In Bullock Co. Ga. Stephen H. Stocking, a native of Hartford, Ct., but for some years a resident of Savannah. In Hancock Co., Ga., Gen. Epps Brown, for many years a Senator in the Georgia Legislature. Col. Andrew Danielly. Mrs. Louisa, wife of Mr. Pleasant Stavall, of Augusta. Near Macon, Mr. James Bozeman, 42. In Wilkes Co., Mrs. Hannah Clark, relict of Gen. Elijah Clark, aged 90. In Scriven Co., Rev. Thomas D. Howell, of the Methodist Church. In Savannah, Abraham Delamater, 25.
In Surry Co., N. C. Col. Joseph Williams, a well known and distinguished officer of the Revolution, 80.
Our friend Carlos Tracy has fallen asleep inJesus'....on Wed. the 15th ult....   Beaufort, Aug. 15.

Issue of September 15, 1827

Departed this life on the 30th August, Mr. Thomas Broughton, only son of Philip Porcher Broughton, Esq. of St. John's Berkeley, deceased, in the 19th year of his age. (eulogy)...returned from Yale College....

Issue of September 22, 1827

Married in Georgetown, Mr. John G. Wilson to Miss Rachael Pigott. In Savannah, Mr. James W. Sims to Mrs. Margaret Sims. In Boston, Rev. John T. Kirkland, D. D., President of Harvard University, to Miss Elizabeth Cabot, daughter of the late George Cabot, Esq., of Boston.
Died in this city on the 10th inst., Mrs. Sarah consort of Mr. Joseph B. Rivers, of James Island, 31.
In Georgetown, Miss Ann Bond, 53. Mrs. Tabitah Avinett, 46. Mr. Richard Green, 73. Mr. Wm. Shackleford, jr. Mr. Thomas Westbury, 52. Near Winnsboro, Col. Jesse Havis, a revolutionary soldier. In Lexington dist. Mr. Elisha Daniel, 51. In Edgefield,

Mrs. Sophia C., wife of Mr. John Johnston, 27. Col. Leontine Butler, 25. Miss Elizabeth J. Bonham, 18. Maj. Charles Goodwin. In Yorkville, Mrs. Mary Ann, wife of Andrew M'Whorter, Esq. In Savannah, Mr. Henry Champion, a native of W. Springfield, Mass. 33. In Lawrenceville, Major Benjamin Baker, 29. In Effingham Co. Joseph C. Truetlin, 29. Near Augusta, James W. Holcombe. At White Hall, N. C. Rev. Humphrey Hunter, aged 74, Pastor of Steel Creek Church, and for nearly 40 years, an ardent and devoted Minister of the Gospel. In Mecklenburg, James McKnight, senior, 64.
G. Laurens, son of Wm. and Elizabeth Smith, departed this life on Friday Morning, 7th inst., in the 13th year of his age.... Beaufort, Sept. 17th,1827.

Issue of September 29, 1827

Married in Pendleton, James C. Griffin, Esq. to Miss Drusilla Edmonson. Near Morristown, N. J., Mr. Charles M. King, of Savannah, to Miss Caroline E. Parsons. At Lexington, Ga., Mr. Wiley Sledge, of Athens, to Miss Martha Lyons.
Died in this city, of Yellow Fever, Rev. Godfrey Sheehan, aged 32, of the Catholic Church. Andrew Hubbell, 27, a native of Connecticut.
On the evening of the 19th inst., Mr. Jacob Mills, of Sumter, late of Williamsburgh district, in the 25th year of his age.... leaving an affectionate companion and many friends....
On Black River, Thomas M. Blount, 37. In Cheraw, John McMillan, merchant, 29. In Georgetown, Benjn. D. Green, 19. In Pendleton, Dr. Henry W. Davis, 32. In Richland Dist., Miss Nancy Parrot.
In Wilkes Co., on the 18th inst., Capt. Mathew Talbot...presided for many years in the Senate of Georgia.
In Macon, Ga., Mrs. Lucy V. Powledge, 22. In Laurens Co. Wm. Fullwood, Esq. In Savannah, Thomas Hathaway, a native of Mass. 25. Near Augusta, on the 23d inst., Major Freeman Walker, a distinguished lawyer and esteemed citizen. At Athens, Dr. Edmund T. King, 23.

Issue of October 6, 1827

Died in Walton co., Ga. Mrs. Orra Jackson, 26, consort of Col. Samuel Jackson. In Savannah, Mrs. Matilda Ann, wife of Joseph Cumming, Esq.... Geo.

Issue of October 13, 1827

Married in Greenville, Mr. Nehemiah Tankersley, to Miss Frances Tarrant. In Georgetown, Mr. Thomas Wilson to Miss Elizabeth Thompson. In Columbia, Alexander Herbemet, Esq. to Miss Martha D. Bay. In Iredell co., N. C. Mr. Milas Dobbins to Miss Fanny Campbell. Mr. George H. Snow to Miss Tirza McConnell. Mr. Thomas Evans to Miss Polly Mason. Rev. Henry N. Pharr to Miss Amanda D. King. Mr. Z. Summers, to Miss Sally Burnett. In Rowan co., N. C. Mr. Richard Peack, to Miss Sally Hendricks. In Keene, Rev. Artemas Boies, of S. Hadley, Mass. to Miss Susan Lamson.
Mrs. Elizabeth Badger, late of this city, departed this life at Orangeburgh, on the 25th Sept....
Also, at the same place, on the 3d inst., Elizabeth R. Hahnbaum, aged 13 months, infant daughter of Dr. Thomas A. Elliott.
Died at Sullivan's Island, Lieut. C. G. Smith of the army. In Edgefield, Mrs. Sabra J. Randolph, 21. John B. Price, 21. James D. Brown. Capt. John Ryan. Miss Eliza Drisdale. In Macon, Ga. Maj. Joel Rushin, 40. At Savannah, Mrs. Sophia Gildon, 45.

In De Kalb co., Mr. John Reid, 30. In Wilkes co. Captain Wm. F. Hay, 28. Near Athens, Mrs. Rebecca Daugherty, 61. In Fayetteville, N. C. John B. Moss, of Randolph co., 25. In Cumberland co. Mr. Duncan Wright, a native of Scotland, aged 103 years! In Richmond co., Wm. P. Leak, Esq. In Iredell co., Lawrence Trexler, 70. Michael Peeler, 60. In Lincolnton, Silas McBee. In Rowan, John W. Linster, 45. In New-York, Mr. George Ryerson of Savannah.

Issue of October 27, 1827

Married in Greenville, Mr. Daniel F. Wheaton of Raleigh, to Miss Grace Benson. At Columbia, James L. Clark, Esq. to Mrs. Martha S. Scott. Col. Esek H. Maxey to Miss Elizabeth C. Dinkins. In Lexington, Mr. John I. Rawls of Columbia to Miss Ann G. Gieger. In Edgefield Francis W. Pickens, of Ala. to Miss Margaret Eliza, daughter of Col. Simkins.
At Watumpkah (the new village at the falls of the Chatahoochie, Ga.) Mr. Zechariah Durell, merchant late of Cahawba to Miss Nancy Day. This is the first marriage at the village since its settlement. In Macon, Robert Colman, Esq. to Miss Mary B. Taylor. In Bibb co., Ambrose Edwards, of Monroe to Miss Emily J. Gaulding. At Forsyth, Mr. Pitt W. Millner, to Miss Adeline M. Putnam. Mr. Jonathan Johnson to Miss Susan Milner.
In Lincoln co., N. C. Mr. Jacob Huffman to Miss Susan Shook. In Rowan Co., Mr. Bryson Moore, to Miss Nancy Hutson. In Mocksville, Col. Wm. T. Kelly to Miss Sarah Ann Gaither. In Raleigh, Mr. Henry Ward, printer, to Mrs. Mary Ann Reeks, formerly of Chatham county. In Guilford co., Mr. Wm. Rankin to Miss Tilla McCalin.
Departed this life on Thursday 25th inst., Susan Adeline Gready, aged 26 months and 22 days, daughter of Mr. A. P. Gready.
Death of Mrs. Caroline Amelia Bulow, wife of Major John J. Bulow, and second daughter of Col. Thomas Lehre, all of this city (eulogy)
Died near Winnsborough, on 2d Sept., Mrs. Margaret McCreight, in the 76th year of her age. (eulogy)
In Baltimore, Col. John Eager Howard, late Governor of Maryland, a distinguished officer of the Revolution, and one of the heroes of the Cowpens and Eutaw....

Issue of November 3, 1827

Married in Pendleton, Mr. H. S. Liston to Miss Emily Benson. Mr. James Yeatman to Miss Minerva Mayhon.
In Chatham N. C. Mr. Joseph Palmer to Miss Eliza McQueen.
Died in Pendleton, Capt. Wm. McGregor. Mr. Jonathan Watson. In Georgetown, Mrs. Henry Joseph, 26. Mrs. Ann C. Mariano, 20.
In Savannah, Edward S. Seabrook, Esq. of Rockbridge, Va. On the 28th, Mrs. Maria B. Carter, wife of the Rev. Abiel Carter, and daughter of the Rev. Dr. Beach of N. J. In Putnam co., Ga. Mrs. Nancy H. Dixon, wife of Robert H. Dixon. In Macon, Capt. Peter Lequex, late of the U. S. Army. In Oglethorpe, Miss Martha W. Milner.
On the morning of the 24th October, in Lexington Geo., Mrs. Ann Baldwin, wife of Doctor William Baldwin, in the 27th year of her age...member of the Presbyterian church.
In Cantonment Clinch, 4th ult., Capt. J. J. Clinch, late of the Army, and a native of Nash co., N. C.
In New York, at an advanced age, Rev. Freeborn Garreston, a contemporary of Wesley.
In Philadelphia, Mrs. Sarah Telfair, widow of the late Edward Telfair, formerly Gov. of Georgia, aged 70.

in Williamston (Mass.) Schuyler Putnam, Esq. youngest son of Maj. Gen. Israel Putnam, of the Revolutionary army. He accompanied his father in his last campaign.

Issue of November 10, 1827

Married in Columbia, Mr. Geo. A. Hillegas to Mrs. Mary Williamson. In Savannah, Mr. Elisha Willy to Miss Eliza Cooper. In Houston co., Ga. James N. Bozeman, Esq. of Milledgeville, to Mrs. Salina Ann Glass of Savannah. In Salisbury, N. C. Dr. R. C. Neagle of Lincoln, to Miss Albertine Utzman. In Iredell co., Mr. Hiram L. Sloan to Miss Sarah Brevard. Mr. James Johnson, of Mecklenburgh to Miss Nancy Torrence.
Died in this city, Mr. Cashal F. Pritchard, 20. In Barnwell, Mr. Charles R. Stone, formerly of this city. In Covington, Ga., Mrs. Naomi J. Stewart, In Jones co., Mr. Washington Dawson, 22. In Augusta, Mr. Jos Tuttle, a native of N. Jersey. Mr. Samuel G. Starr, a native of Con. In Columbia co., Miss Martha Anthony, 11. In Houston co. Mr. Wm. Miles. Near Salisbury, N. C. Miss Margaret Krider, 16. In Warren co., Mrs. Sarah Cornelia Coleman, wife of Mr. Nath. T. Greene, 18. In Richmond, Gen. B. H. Covington, Clerk of the Senate of N. C. In Montgomery, R. Peacock, Esq. 26.
In Baltimore, Rt. Rev. Bishop Kemp. He was present in Philadelphia at the ordination of the Rev. Dr. Onderdonk, as Assistant Bishop....
In Kentucky, Hon. D. P. Cook, late a member of Congress from Illinois.

Issue of November 17, 1827

Married in Walterboro', Rev. David Erving Campbell to Mrs. Maria Pinkney Girardeau. At Beach Island, Mr. Luthern Roll, of Augusta, to Miss Susan Torrence.
In Lincoln, N. C. Mr. John Sipe, to Miss Mary Holler. Mr. Daniel Pope to Miss Polly Deal. In Charlotte, Mr. M. T. Polk of Ten. to Miss Laura T. Wilson. In Iredell, Mr. Jacob Tipps to Mrs. Mary C. Cowan.
Died in Columbia, Dr. John W. Robeson, 23. In Georgetown, Christopher Rich. Near Augusta, by a fall from his sulky, Mr. Wm. Pelot, of this state.
In Savannah, Hermon D. Greene, 32. In Augusta, Basil Lamar, sen. In Washington, Ga. E. B. Candee. Miss Avis Minton. In Coweta, Henry D. Beman. In Hancock, John Daniel, Esq. 50. In Gwinnett, Richard Medlin.

Issue of November 24, 1827

Married in Edgefield, 8th inst., Rev. Winborn A. Laughton, of Beaufort dist. to Miss Lucinda, daughter of the Rev. J. Landrum. In Abbeville, Rev. B. Huckaba of Georgia, to Miss Caroline A. Power.
In Richmond co., Ga. Mr. A. Livingston, to Miss Angelina T. Womble.
In the Forks of the Yadkin, N. C. Mr. Joseph Wyatt to Miss Irena Parker. In Iredell, Thomas M. Wilson, Esq. to Miss Catharine Caldwell. Dr. Sheldon Lemmon to Miss Eliza Hall.
Died near Columbia, Mrs. Mary T. Hopkins, 58. In Pendleton, John Gage, Esq. 77. In Williamsburgh, David McClary, Esq., 55, Ordinary of that Dist...a member of the Presbyterian Church.
In Barnwell Dist., Mrs. Elizabeth E. Wilson, wife of the Rev. James Wilson. (eulogy)

At Whitterville, Buncomb co, N. C. Dr. Robert B. Vanie, late of the Congress of the U. States, 30. Dr. V. was mortally wounded in a duel with Seth P. Carson, who is now a member of Congress, and survived but one day. (The name should be Vance-BHH). Near Charlotte, John G. Alexander, 39. James Potts, 50. In Savannah, Pierre Stoy. At Fort Hawkins, Ga., Nathaniel Cornwall, of the firm of Cutter & Cornwell. In Burke co., Mrs. Sarah Mathews, 71. In Clinton, Pheldon R. Snow, 24, late of Mass. In New York City, Thomas Addis Emmett, an eminent Counsellor, aged 65.

Issue of December 1, 1827

Married in Camden, by the Rev. Mr. Powers, Dr. Alexander Williams of Sumter, to Miss S. E. Craig, of Chesterfield. In Augusta, Mr. George R. Rountree to Miss Parmelia W. Woolfolk. Died in this city on the 29th ult., Mrs. Abigail H. Gilman. In Savannah, Margaret Wallace, 33, youngest daughter of the late John Wallace, Esq. of that city. In Salisbury, N. C., Mrs. Margaret, wife of Mr. James E. Todd. In Montgomery co., Rev.Jos. Clark, of Randolph, of the Methodist E. Church.

Issue of December 8, 1827

Married in Edgefield, Mr. Henry Mims, to Miss Susan B. Reed. In Greenville, Dr. Wm. Robinson, to Miss Maria Earle. In York dist., Maj. J. W. Hamilton of N. C.to Miss Jane Sadler. In Union, Abner Benson, Esq. to Miss Elizabeth Dawkins. In Salisbury, N. C., Mr. Aaron Woolworth to Miss Mary Hampton. In Hillsboro, Dr. Samuel Studwick to Miss Elizabeth Nash. In Warrenton, Mr. B. H. Stammire to Miss Elizabeth H. Powers. In Rowan, Mr. Thomas A. Hague to Miss Sarah Waddell. Near Charlotte, Mr. A. A. Kennedy, to Miss Jane Sloan.
In Washington, Ga., Mr. Ernest L. Wittich of Madison, to Miss Eliza C. Baird. At Athens, Mr. James L. Jones to Miss Eliza Johnson. In Walton co., Mr. Wm. H. C. Mills of Augusta, to Miss Jane E. Evans.
Died in Barnwell, Reuben Boyd, 59. In Edgefield, Elias Blackman, 71. In Augusta, Alexander Bertram, 32. At Beach Island, Mrs. Mary Ann Gray, 80. Her parents came from Switzerland in 1730, and were among the first settlers of B. I. of which Mrs. G. was a native.
In Mecklenburgh, N. C., Mrs. Margaret Morrison. In Orange, Capt. Wm. Hicks. In Raleigh, Mrs. Altona H. relict of the late Rev. Anthony Foster, of Charleston. John Haywood, Esq. for 41 years the faithful Treasurer of N. C., 73. In Burke Co., Ga., Col. Thomas Jones.
In Ipswich, Mass., Rev. Joseph Danan, D. D,a fellow graduate of Mr. Jefferson, Harvard Col. 1760. In Boston, Samuel Danforth, M. D., 89. In Bradford, Ct. Capt. Samuel Baldwin, 88. He was an officer in the Revolution and a soldier under the then Major Putnam in the old French war....

Issue of December 15, 1827

Married on the 6th inst., Thomas Legare Jones, Esq., to Miss Mary E., daughter of the late Richard Fishburn, Esq., of St. Bartholomews. In St. Mathews Parish, Lewis Fielder to Miss Mary C. Wolfe.

In Savannah, Henry W. Stoy to Miss Sarah Harrison. Thomas M. Sanders to Miss Elizabeth A. Lanchester. John R. Shadd, of Wilmington Island, to Miss Eliza Butts, of South Hadley, Mass. In Augusta, Gary F. Parish, to Miss Mary Ann Sarah White. In Twiggs co., Henry G. Abernethy, Esq. to Miss Mary A. K. Guerry. In Monroe, Abner F. Bison of Clinton, to Miss Caroline Pope.
In Mecklenburgh co., N. C. Aaron A. Kennedy to Miss Jane Sloan.
In New York, on the 20th inst., M. M. Noah, Esq., Editor of the Enquirer, to Miss Rachel Jackson.
Died in Augusta, Miss Caroline A. Porter, 15. In Rowan N. C. Jacob Clutts, 70. Mrs. Frierny Cauble. In Cabarras co., Mrs. Sarah Corl, 25. In Mecklenburgh, Mrs. Hannah Stevens, 51. In Granville co., Mrs. Betsey K. Martin, the last surviving child of Hon. Nathaniel Macon, 44.

Issue of December 22, 1827

Married on Tuesday evening, by the Rev. Dr. Palmer, Felix Long, of Cheraw, to Miss Martha Bennett, daughter of the late Henry Bennett of this city.
In Savannah, Frederick S. Fell, editor of the Republican, to Miss Mary C. Shick. In Crawford co., Ga., Samuel Vining, to Miss Jane McBride. In Monroe co., Young F. Tigner to Miss Sarah F. Tinsley. In Newton co., Peter Scott of Hancock, to Miss Nancy Rogers. In Wayne co., Benj. F. Cater of St. Simon's, to Miss Anne Armstrong. In Burke co., Dr. B. F. Green to Miss Sarah Harlow.
In Mecklenburgh, N. C., Robert C. Barnett to Miss Margaret Weeks.
In Natchez, Miss., Col. Wm. H. Sparks, formerly of Eatonton, Ga., to Mrs. Maria A. Carmichael.
Died on the 23d ult., at her residence in St. Luke's, Mrs. Susan Baker Dupont, widow of Mr. Charles Dupont. At St. John's Berkeley, at the residence of Thomas Broughton, Esq., James Burchard of Lima, N. Y.
In Yorkville, Robert R. Beatty. In Beaufort, by a fall from his horse, John Hennis.
In Norfolk, Martin Oster, 87, Ex-Vice Consul of France for the State of Virginia.

Issue of December 29, 1827

Married in Barnwell, John J. Boyd, Esq. to Miss Rebecca Dunbar. In Pendleton, by the Rev. D. Humphreys, Wm. McCoy to Miss Mary McMahen. Samuel Warson to Miss Peggy McCorley. Enos Massey to Miss Rebecca Dobbins. James Stewart of Pendleton, to Miss Elizabeth Wingfield of Abbeville. James Baskin to Miss Rebecca Amanda Caldwell, both of Abbeville dist. In Columbia, Robert Wilson Gibbes, of this city, to Miss Caroline Guignard.
In Augusta, Hays Bowdre to Mrs. Harriet E. Young. In Jones Co., Ga. Austin Ellis, to Miss Caroline Rice. In Oglethorpe, Ephraim S. Hopping to Mrs. Parmelia Stewart. In Athens, John Kirkpatrick to Miss Malvina Witter.
In Wilkes co., N. C.,Major L. Hickerton to Miss Amelia Gwyn. In Surry, Nathan Craft of Stokes, aged 70, to Mrs. Polly Padget, 25. In Stokes, Col. Wm. Poindexter to Miss Ann Eliza Nelson.
Died in Columbia, Gen. J. J. Faust. In Pendleton, 17th inst., Sarah Ann, daughter of Wm. Brewster, 12; and on the 18th, her mother, Mrs. Margaret B.
In Augusta, Levin Erwin of Morgan co. Nathaniel Clarke, formerly Editor of the Georgia Courier, 35. In Hancock co., Mrs. Sophia, wife of Col. Thos Hudson, 37. In Laurens, Mrs. Eliza,

wife of Dr. N. Tucker.
In Surry, N. C., Moses Day, Esq., 35.

Issue of January 5, 1828

Married in Columbia, Thomas Waul to Miss Jane D. Dudley. In Macon,Ga., Lemuel Newcomb, late of Savannah, to Miss Martha Snow.
In Lincoln N. C., Capt. Wm. M. Grier of Meck'n to Miss Minerva Hays.
In Selma, Ala., Wm. Thompson of St. Clair, to Miss Martha Jones. In Montgomery, Malakiah Edwards to Miss Maria, eldest daughter of Thomas Reeves, Esq. In Erie, Philip T. Beasly to Miss Mary R. Crawford.
Died in Augusta, Col. Thomas F. Wells, formerly Attorney General of Georgia.
In Montgomery, N. C., James Atkins, 93.... In Mecklenburgh, Mrs. Mary Whiteside, 70.
In Greenesborough, Ala., Mrs. Sarah Hillhouse, 72. All her seven children stood around her; all her children by marriage and all her grand children were present...a member of the Presbyterian Church for 41 years.

Issue of January 12, 1828

Married in Savannah, Wm. Hogan, Esq. to Mrs Lydia Garner. In Morgan co., Wm. H. Cooper, to Miss Eliza J. C. Fall.
Died in Columbia, James C. Keith, a student of S. C. Col. Near Powelton, Ga., Mrs. Martha T. wife of Thomas Seals. In Washington co., Capt. Cato Riddle, 76.
At Mount Vernon, Rowan, N. C. John Young, Esq. 56. Thomas Brown, 21. In Burke, Col. A. Baird, 66. Mrs. Mary, wife of Rev. R. J. Miller, 66. In Raleigh, William Shaw, 65.
In Northampton, Mass. Solomon Stoddard Esq, 91. He was sheriff of the county of Hampshire under the King of G. Britain, at the commencement of the revolution.

Issue of January 19, 1828

Married on the 27th ult.,by the Rev. E. J. Mills, Jas. A. Mills of Williamsburgh, to Miss Mary Stuart, of Darlington D. In Georgetown, John Coachman, Esq. to Miss Charlotte A. Alston. In this city, by the Rev. Mr. Bachman, Wm. Stoll to Miss Caroline E. Crask. In St. Paul's Parish, Rev. Daniel K. Whitaker, of Cambridge, Mass. to Mrs. Mary H. Firth.
In Baldwin co., Ga. Capt. Wm. F. Scott, to Mrs. Elizabeth Reynolds. In Hancock co., John W. Rabun, Esq. to Miss Harriet A. Hagnod. At White Bluff, John B. Bacon of Sunbury, to Miss Jane E. Adams.
In Salisbury, N. C. Peter M. Brown to Miss Elizabeth Pool. Near Mocksville, Jesse A. Clement, to Miss Malinda Nail. In Davidson co., Charles Walk to Miss Lydia Rothrock, In Randolph, Dr. W. W. Turner to Miss Eliza B., daughter of J. B. Moss, Esq.
In Greene co., Aa., Dr. Ricard Inge to Miss Rebecca E. Brownlow. Near Selma, George G. Brooks, Esq., to Miss Margaret Cathey.
Died at Ebenezer Academy, Mrs. Jane Agnew, wife of the Rev. Eleazur Harris, 18.
In Hancock co., Ga., Col. Isaac Birdsong, for several years a member of the Legislature.
In Rowan co., N. C., John Adams, 75. At Indian Land, Miss Margaret P., daughter of Gen. Davies Hartt, 16.
In Greene co., Ala., Thomas J. Anderson, 54.
In Portsmouth, N. H., P. C. Schaeffer, a native of Germany, 95,

a doctor of music, and instructer to the present royal family.

Issue of January 26, 1828

Married in this city, by the Rev. Mr. Buist, Alexander Gordon to Miss Jane, second daughter of Daniel Bruikshank, Esq.
In Williamsburgh Dist., on the 10th inst., by the Rev. R. W. James, Dr. John R. Witherspoon, to Miss Esther Louisa M'Crea. In Columbia, by the Rev. Mr. Rennie, Samuel Ewart to Miss Louisa H. Laval of Charleston. In Pendleton d. by Rev. Mr. Humphreys, James Dobbins to Miss Mary Stevenson; Wm. Carr to Miss Sarah Dollar. In Abbeville, by the same, Isaac Carlisle to Miss Jane Crosby; Wm. Hutchinson to Miss Betsy Lindsay. In Louisville, Ga., John Murphy to Miss Martha G. Carter.
Died in Surry, N. C. Thomas Allen, 85.
In Tuscaloosa, A., Thos M. Davenport, late editor of the Mirror, and formerly editor of the Anti-Monarchist in this State.
At Harper's Ferry, Va., John McKenny, 25. He was the 5th husband of a lady yet under the age of 29.

Issue of February 2, 1828

Married in Mecklenburgh, N. C., John Weeks, Esq. to Mrs. Nancy Roberson. John Fox, to Miss Agnes Alexander. In Burke co., Hugh A. Tate, to Miss Fatima E. Forney.
Died in Savannah, Alexander M. Kerr, Esq. In Morgan co., Ga., Mrs. Mary, wife of Gabriel Johnson, 28. In Lawrenceville, Dr. Philo C. Hall, formerly of Fairfield, Con. In Macon, Capt. Thos A. Gillups. In Burke co., Amos P. Whitehead, 35.
In Wilkesboro, N. C. Jefferson Maston, 26.
In Alabama, Dr. Asa Thompson, late of Elbert co., Ga.
At St. Augustina, Lieut. Horace Smith, of the 1st regt. U. S. Artillery, a native of N. York.
In N. York city, Mrs. Grace, wife of the Hon. Daniel Webster... left husband and three children. Her remains were removed to Boston for interment.

Issue of February 9, 1828

Married on the 6th inst., Benj. Fuller, Jun., Esq. to Miss Ann E. Miles. James Robertson, Esq. to Miss Ellen Atkins.
in Greenville, Richard Burnham, to Miss Theresa Vickers. In Hamburgh, Alfred R. Lattimer to Miss Augusta L. Spann. In Barnwell, Edward W. Peyton, Esq. to Miss Mary Furst. At Beach Island, Richard Prior to Miss Barbara T. Nail. In Fairfield, George Owen to Miss Nancy Montgomery; Washington Yarbrough to Miss Debby Ann Hodge; Barnet Buchannan to Miss Hannah Welsh.
In Savannah, Wm. Quarterman of Liberty co., to Miss Mary Dawsey. In Hancock Co. John W. Ely, to Miss Virginia Baugh. At Morganton, N. C. on the 24th ult., by the Rev. Mr. Silliman, Mr. James W. Patton, merchant of Ashvill, to Miss Jane Clarissa, eldest daughter of Thomas Walton, Esq. of Morganton.
At Edgefield, Joseph Samuel, 22. Charles Deloach of Beach Island, 47. In Crawfordsville, Ga., Samuel Robards, a native of Massachusetts, 38. In Charlotte, n. C., Daniel Gillespie of Rowan, 30. In N. York, Catherine Ann Louisa, wife of Capt. Charles W. Morgan of the U. S. Navy, and daughter of the late Gen. Read of Charleston. In Philadelphia, Rev. Joseph Eastburn, the "Mariner's Friend," aged 80.

Issue of February 16, 1828

Married in Pendleton, David Moore, jr. to Miss Fanny Lord. In Edgefield, Taliaferro Erskine, of Ala. to Miss Sophia B. Butler. In York Dist. Wm. Glover to Miss Elizabeth P. Barnes. James Simmerl to Miss Vilet Simmerl.
In Milledgeville, Ga., Charles Bulloch Esq. of Macon to Mrs. Eliza A. Grantland. In Macon, Capt. Wm. J. Danelly to Miss Ann Eliza Slade, formerly of Warreton, N. C. In Twiggs Co., Wm. M. Tarver to Miss Hannah Slappey. In Pike Co., Charles R. Wynn to Miss Elizabeth Milner.
at Nassau Florida, Rev. John L. Jerry, Methodist Missionary for St. Augustine, to Miss Jane J. O'Neil.
Death of Mrs. Sarah Legare, relict of Joseph Legare, Esq., of St. James' Santee, who died on Friday morning last, in the 75th year of her age...(eulogy).
Died, in Columbia, Christopher Barnillon, 64. Greuman Tidwell, 32.
In Mecklenburg co., N. C. Xerzes H. Cushman, formerly editor of the P. Advocate, Yorkville.
At Montgomery, A. Milton Cooper, Esq.,formerly of Eatonton, Ga.

Issue of February 23, 1828

Married in Pendleton Dist. Willis Geer to Cynthia Hall. Thos Hanks to Elizabeth Means. Russell Shipley to Lydia Prater. Samuel McQuerne, to Caroline Keys, Dobson Warnock, to Sarah Emberson.
In Macon, Ga., Isaac B. Rowland to Miss Frances Campbell. In Houston co., Major Michael Barnwell, a native of France, aged 70, to Mrs. Anne Goss, a native of Switzerland, aged 75. In Clinton, Wm. Moughon to Miss Ellen E. Mitchell.
In Lincoln, N. C. Elisha Perkins to Miss Elizabeth L. Sherill. On the 27th ult., Rev. Paxton Cunningham of Ten. to Miss Priscilla E. Davidson, of Heywood co.
Died in Fairfield, John W. Starke, a revolutionary officer, 66. On board the steam boat Marion, Capt. Gamaliel Darling, master. In Lancaster Dist., James Rodgers.
In Macon, Ga., Mrs. Anna D. Bates, wife of Thos G. Bates, Esq., 22. In Covington, Mrs. Louisa, wife of Col. John N. Williamson. In Jasper co., Wm. Lebetter (sic), 42.
In Rowan, N. C., Mrs. Nancy, wife of B. Howard, Esq. In Iredell, John M. Morrison, 46. In Mecklenburgh, Thos Greer, Esq., 85. In Sampson co., Rev. Fleet Cooper, 79, and for more than 60 years a Minister of the Baptist Church.
In New-York, Miss Henrietta Eckford, aged 19, daughter of Henry E. Esq. (account).
In New Castle, Delaware, Hon. James Booth, Chief Justice of the Court of Common Pleas of the State.
At the University of Va., Dr. Henry Wm. Tucker, late of Charlotte co. In Harrison co., Col. Benjn. Wilson, 80, an officer of the Revolution.
At Lucknow, in India, the venerable native Minister of the Gospel, Abdool Messeeh, 55....

Issue of March 1, 1828

Married in Columbia, by the Rev. Mr. Peixotta, M. C. Mordecai, of this city, to Miss Isabella Lyons. the Rev. Rt. Adams, Capt. H. Macon, of Sumterville, to Eliza D. Russell, of Columbia. James E. Williamson, of Richland, to Eliza Ann Kennedy, of Lexington. In Pendleton District, Saml. Starke of Abbeville, to Deen

17

Rutledge. Britain Hanna to Lotta Johnson.
In Salem, on Thursday 4th Feb., by the Rev. R. W. James, Mr. James Edmond Witherspoon, to Miss Susan Elizabeth, daughter of Hugh Wilson, Es q., all of Sumter District.
In Mecklenburg, N. C., Alexander Gillespie, to Elizabeth Robinson.
Died in Augusta, Ga., Noah Parker, formerly of Fayetteville, N. C. Aaron Kellogg, a native of New-York, 30. Richard Bush, Esq. 61.
At the Sand Hills, Alexander M. Edwards, of Nassau, New Providence.
In Mecklenburg, N. C. on the 8th ult., Wm. Lees, sen. On the 19th, Jas H. Simison, attorney at Law.
Death of Gov. De Witt Clinton of New York...born in Orange Co., N. Y., in March, 1769.

Issue of March 8, 1828

Married in Camden, Mr. Eugene Coley to Miss Elizabeth C. Allen.
In Watkinsville, Ga., by Rev. A. Church, Mr. George W. Shaw, of Athens, to Miss Mary P. Jackson, of Watkinsville.
In Montevallo, Alab., Mr. John Dougherty to Miss Olive Ann Echols.
Died in this city, Mrs. Susanna M. Benjamin, 35. Capt. Thomas Paine, harbour-master. William Broadfoot, Esq., 50.
At Augusta, Ga., Mrs. Elizabeth Olivia Germany, 17.
Near Sumterville, Mrs. Sarah Eugenia Knox, 32.
At Spring Place, Cherokee Nation, Rev. John Gambold, the Moravian minister of the Gospel to the Indians at that station....
At Durham, Mass., Rev. Federal Burt, editor of the Hampshire Observer. He was graduated at Williams College in 1812.

Issue of March 15, 1828

Married in Union district, Rev. G. W. Davis, to Miss Jane Black. In Chester District, Mr. Uriah Jordon, to Miss Margaret Robeson, In York District, Mr. Eli O. Alexander to Mrs. Margaret Ellison. In Pendleton, Mr. Andrew Floyd to Miss Esther Shannon, of N. C.
In Baldwin co., Ga., Mr. Bartholomew Ingram to Miss Sarah Grigg.
In Perry co., A., by the Rev. R. Holman, Mr. Joseph Wiley, late of N. C. to Mrs. Mary A. Johnson.
In Mecklenburgh, N. C. on the 15th ult., Mrs. Harris E., wife of Lewis Dinkins, 37. On the 28th Mrs. Lydia Wallace, 76.
In St. Augustine, on the 20th ult., Lieut. Jackman J. Davis, of the 1st Regiment of Artillery.
On the 19th Feb. in Perry co., A. Bryan Boroughs, 20, of Moore Co., N. C.
At Pendleton, S. C. on the 28th ult., Mr. Daniel Symmes, in the 67th year. He was a native of Andover, Mass., but has been for 30 years a resident of this district.
At the Parish of St. Rock, Canada, John Robertson, a soldier in Wolfe's army, 97.

Issue of March 22, 1828

Married in this city, on the 12th inst.,by the Right Rev. Bishop Bowen, Mr. H. G. O. Mills, to Miss Sarah Jane Miller.
In Georgetown, by Rev. Noah Laney, Mr. John Matthews to Mrs. Mary Louisa Taylor.

In Pendleton, Mr. Joseph Brown, to Miss Mary Moore. Mr. Robert L. Robertson, to Miss Rachel S. Williams.
In Abbeville Dist., S. C. on the 12th inst., by Rev. H. Reid, Major Armistead Burt, of Pendleton, S. C., to Miss Martha Catharine, second daughter of Wm. Calhoun, of the former place.
In Newbery N. C. by Bishop England, Rt. Donaldson, Esq. to Miss Susan Jane, daughter of the Hon. Wm. Gaston. In Cabarras Co., Mr. Eli Sherer, to Miss Marg. Duke.
At Two Runs, in the Cherokee Nation, by the Rev. Mr. Henderson, Rev. James Trott, Missionary of the Methodist Episcopal Church, to Miss Sally Adair, of the former place.
Died in Georgetown, Mr. Joseph Pigot, 46. On the 5th, Master George Jones Rich, 11. On the 8th, Master Asa G. Young.
In Rowan, N. C., Mr. Danl. Webb, sen, 70. In Chatham co., suddenly, John Moring, jr., 38.
In Augusta, Ga., Mrs. Sarah Wateman, a member of the Methodist Church, 58.
In Clarke Co., Ga., Capt. White Rossetter, 55.
In Princeton, N. J., Hon. Richard Stockton, 64.
In Geneva, N. Y., Rev. Orin Clark, D. D., Rector of Trinity Church, Geneva, 41.
At Tellico, Ten. on the 1st Feb., Rev. Richard Nealy, formerly a Missionary of the Methodist Episcopal Church.
At Willstown, Cherokee Nation, on the 18th Feb., very suddenly, Rev. A. Hoyt, Missionary of the American Board of Foreign Missions.
At Coosewattie, Keeltchule, an aged Member of the National Council.

Issue of March 29, 1828

Married in Savannah, by the Rev. Mr. Wyer, Mr. Hugh Rose, to Miss Eugenia Amanda Huguenin. In the German Lutheran Church, by the Rev. Mr. Mealy, Mr. John F. Katchler, to Miss Maria J. Foullen.
In Perry co., Ala. on the 21st Feb. by Rev. R. Holman, Mr. Joseph Wiley, late of N. C. to Miss Mary A. Johnson Curry.
On the 24th inst., by the Rev. P. T. Keith, John Izzard Middleton jr., to Sarah M., daughter of Col. J. A. Alston.
Died lately in Abbeville district, Miss Lucretia T. Finney, daughter of Mrs. Lucretia Finney, in the 17th year of her age. (eulogy).
In Dallas County, Ala., on the 23d Feb., Major David McCord, receiver of the public monies for the Cahawba District.

Issue of April 5, 1828

Married in this city, by the Rt. Rev. Bishop Bowen, Bentley Hasell, Esq., to Catharine De Nully, daughter of the late Nicholas Cruger, Esq.
In Washington, Ga., by the Rev. Nathan Hoyt, Edw. M. Burton, Esq., P. M., to Miss Mary R., daughter of Jas. Wingfield.
Died in Augusta, Ga., Miss Caroline Elizabeth Berry, 8. On Board the staem boat Marion, on her passage from Savannah to Purrysburg, Capt. G. Darling, master of said boat.
At her father's residence in South Carolina, on the 9th March, Mrs. Martha E. Craft, wife of Mr. Hugh Craft. She has left a large circle of relatives and friends....Milledgeville Southron.
On the 23d December, at his residence near the Choctaw Agency, Gen. Humming-Bird, a Choctaw Chief, at the advanced age of 75....
Port Gib. Correspondent.

Issue of April 12, 1828

Married in Orangeburgh District, the 27th ult., by the Rev. S. S. Burdett, Mr. Robert Riley, to Miss Louisa Buzzard, both of that district.
In Salisbury, N. C. on the 5th ult., Mr. John Reimer, to Miss Sophia Schollebarger. In Rowan co., on the 27th inst., Mr. Garrett Pickler to Miss Mary Barringer. In Richmond co., on the 26th Feb. Mr. Whitson H. Chisolm, to Miss Marth Standback. On the 13th ult., Mr. Dawalt Beaver to Miss Martha Simons. On the 20th inst., Mr. Joel Hembree to Miss Eve Fite.
Died in Salisbury, Mr. George Shuman, 45. On 26th ult., Mr. John Bird, jr., about 30.
In Hancock co., Ga. on the 26th ult., Mr. Amos Brantley, in the 70th year of his age. He was a revolutionary soldier.... in Jackson co., 6th ult., Capt. Owen J. Bowen, 64.

Issue of April 19, 1828

Married in this city, on the 9th inst., by the Rev. Mr. Bachman, Mr. Andrew C. Dibble, formerly of Danbury, Con. to Miss Henrietta M. H., daughter of S. J. Wagner, Esq. of this city.
On the 8th by Bishop England, Mr. Lawrence Ryan, to Miss Ann Ball Waring.
In Lexington, Ga., Mr. George Scott, to Miss Mary Ann Moore.
In Pickens District, S. C., Mr. Isaac Judson, to Miss Martha Mitchell. In the village of Anderson, on the 19th ult., Mr. Joseph Drennan, to Miss Phoebe H. Norris. In Anderson district, on 20th ult., Mr. Reuben Burriss, to Miss Deliah Burriss.
In England, Thomas Legh, Esq., P. M. to Miss Turner, only daughter of Wm. Turner, Esq. of Springley Park, Cheshire.
Died in Washington, Ga., on the 4th inst., Mr. John K. M. Charlton, editor of the Washington News, and formerly editor of the Augusta Chronicle, aged 42.
In Monticello, Ga., Col. Nathan Warner, aged 32.... in Columbua, Ga., Jacob T. H. Thomas, 20. In Augusta, on the 8th inst., John G. Cowling, esq. 43.
In Montgomery co., Ala., Wm. Ashley sen., esq., formerly of N. C. At the Falls of Chattachoochie, lately, Mr. Zachariah Dewill, formerly of Cahawba, Alabama.
In West-Cambridge, Massachusetts, on the 27th ult., Mr. Amos Whittemore, aged 69....

Issue of April 26, 1828

Married in this city on the 15th inst., by the Rev. Mr. Gilman, Mr. John Davies Brown, to Miss Caroline H., daughter of the late Isaac Griggs.
In Greenville, 3d inst., by the Rev. Mr. Hutchins, Mr. J. W. T. Holland, of that District to Miss Susannah Brockman, of Spartanburgh Dist.
Died in York Dist., Mr. Daniel Sturgis, sen, at an advanced age.
In Chester Dist., Mr. Samuel M'Neel.
In Savannah, Mrs. Rebecca Hobbs, widow of the late John Hobbs. Edward Pinckney, Esq. of the Bar of Baltimore.
At Pleasant Valley, Ala., Mr. Starkey Hill, at an advanced age.
At the Falls of the Chatahoochie, Ala., Mr. Zachariah Dewell. At Montgomery county, Ala., Mr. Wm. Ashely, sen. Mr. A. emigrated to this state from N. C., about 10 years ago.
In Mecklenburg, N. C., Mr. Andrew McNeely, in the 71st year of his age....

At Mount Pleasant, N. C., Mrs. Ruth B. Porter, 72.
In Windham, on the 12th ult., Rebecca, the wife of Leonard Sackett, late of the Mission family at the Maumee, the daughter of Thatcher and Elizabeth Conant....

Issue of May 3, 1828

Married on Tuesday evening, by the Rev. Dr. A. W. Leland, Mr. J. T. W. Holmes, to Miss Elizabeth Zephryne Amanda, eldest daughter of the late Benjamin Witter, planter of James Island.
In Pendleton, S. C., Mr. John Ariail to Miss Parthena Blasingame.
In Lincolnton,N. C., Mr. Jacob Propst, to Miss Mary McCulloch.
In Rowan, N. C., Mr. Spencer Benson, to Miss Nancy Rice. In Edgecombe co., N. C., on the 27th Feb., Mr. Frederick Mayo, to Miss Manisia Ganer Mcnetta Sylvester Malvina Llewellen Sherrard!
In Augusta, Ga., Mr. Luthern Goodrich of Hartford, Conn. to Miss Eliza Ann Clark. By the Rev. Bishop England, George P. Turpin, esq. to Miss Eloise Therese Bouyer. In Savannah, 22d inst., Capt. Wm. D. Ray, to Miss Mary E. Cope. In Elbert Co., 1st Feb. Col. Thomas J. Heard, to Miss Nancy P. Middleton.
Died near Salisbury, N. C., Henry Hartman, 28. in Rowan Co., Capt. Nathan Neely, 28. In Mecklenburg, Andrew McNeely, 71. In Morgan co., Ga., James Irwin, Esq., 50.
In Augusta, Ga., on the 19th inst.,Mrs. Ann Margaret Clarke, widow of the late Nathaniel Clark, esq., deceased . The day before, her daughter Leonora Agnes.
In Greensborough, Ala., Col. Absalom Alston, formerly of Orange co., N. C. 48.
At Yale College, of the varioloid, Saml. McNeely,of Rowan Co., N. C. a member of the senior class.

Issue of May 10, 1828

Married in Perry co., Ga., Rev. Robert Holman to Miss Maria Carlisle. In Twiggs co., Ga., 15th ult., James Park, esq., to Miss Martha Woddard. In Wilkinson co., Mr. James Hatfield to Miss Elvira Vinson. In Powelton, 24th ult., James W. Fannin, esq. to Miss Minerva D. Fort. In Savannah, 1st inst., Dr. John S. Law, to Miss Jane E. Elliott.
Died on the 28th ult., at Sandy River, Chester district, Mr. Wm. Hall, a native of Scotland. On 24th March, at Sontesville, Greenville district, Master Josiah Kilgore.
Died on the 5th inst., in this city, James Duhun, late Seaman on board the brig Apthorp....Savannah Georgian May 7.
In this city, the Hon. Thomas Tudor Tucker, Treasurer of the U. States, in the 84th year of his age... Nat. Intel. 4th inst.

Issue of May 17, 1828

Married in this city, on the 7th inst., by the Rev. Mr. Hanckle, John Hayward, Esq. to Miss Constantia Smith, daughter of Wm. Pritchard, sen. both of this city.
On the 22d April at the seat of Capt. Alex. Brevard, by the Rev. Henry N. Pharr, Richard T. Brumby, esq. of Sumterville, S. C., to Miss Mary M. Brevard, of Lincoln, N. C.
In Sparta, Ga., 30th ult.,by J. G. Gilbert, Esq. Mr. John Thompson, to Miss Elizabeth Frances Haynes.
Died in Chesterfield dist., on the 26th ult., Mrs. Mary Strother, aged 81.
In Milledgeville, Ga., 13th March, Mrs. Elizabeth C. Anthony, consort of James Anthony, of Jones co., Ga., 40.
In Wayne, Ashtabula co., Ohio, 31st March, Mrs. Lucy Caldwell,

formerly of Hartford, Connecticut, 63.

Issue of May 24, 1828

Married in this city, on the 22d inst., by the Rev. Mr. Gibbs, Mr. John Cleapor, to Miss Mary Cudworth.
In Camden, Mr. Thomas W. Love, to Mrs. Sarah Love. In Richland, on the 4th inst., Mr. Augustus McNeal to Mrs. Mary Carr, of Chester dist.
In Wadesborough, N. C., on the 6th inst., Dr. George W. Dismukes, to Miss Mary S. Pegues.
On the 8th inst.,in Laurens co., Ga., Col. E. B. W. Spivey, to Miss Sarah Georgiana McCall. In Elbert co., Ga., on the 8th inst. Capt. Robert S. Hardway, to Miss Martha Bibb Jarratt. In Milledgeville, Ga., 15th inst., Dr. H. C. Phelps, to Miss Sarah H. Jones, On the 1st inst., in Savannah, Mr. John I. Dews, to Miss Harriet Gugel.
In Tuscaloosa, Ala. on the 1st inst., Dr. James S. Davenport, to Miss Alethe Ann Glover. On the same evening, Mr. William Springfellow, to Miss Brame.
Died in this city, 18th inst., Capt. Robert Burger, in the 23d year of his age.
In Richland, Delanore B. Pasmore, aged 1 year and 6 months. At Mount Zion, Ga., Mrs. Jane Smith, wife of Horace Smith.
In Milledgeville, Ga., on the 12th inst., Mr. Vinson Ellis Vickers, a native of South Carolina. In Coweta co., on the 18th ult., Mrs. Francis Eliza Daniel, 25. In Putnam co., on 10th ult., Mrs. Susan Adams.
In Philadelphia on the 14th inst., Mr. Silas E. Weir, a highly respectable resident of that city....brother-in-law to the late Dr. Henry.

Issue of May 31, 1828

Married on the 13th inst., by the Rev. Francis Callaway, Mr. Wm. D. Sloan to Miss Martha, daughter of Mr. Jabez Jones, all of Pickens district.
On the 13th inst., by the Rev. S. Vandiver, Mr. David R. Brazeal of Anderson district, to Miss Utincy W. daughter of Mr. Silas Holloway, of Greenville District.
In Edgefield district, S. C., 7th inst., Mr. Isaac Redfield, of Barnwell dist. to Miss Eliza Cary.
In Barnwell dist. 14th inst., Major John Aarons, to Miss --- Kennedy.
In Savannah, on the 15th inst., by the Rev. S. A. Mealy, Mr. Augustus Bouyssou, to Miss Lucretia Zipperor.
In Augusta, 15th inst., by the Rev. Mr. Talley, Mr. John B. Harn, to Miss Margaret E. J. Walker. Mr. John Evans, to Miss Martha M. Kennedy, of South Carolina.
In Wilkes, Ga., 15th inst., Mr. Silas Mercer to Miss Ann Thompson.
In Baldwin co., Mr. Homer Howard, to Miss Elizabeth Thweatt. In Jones co., Mr. Henry Jernigan, to Miss Caroline S.M.Gachet.
In Alabama, Mr. James N. Carothers, recently of Union dist., S. C. to Miss Mary Stewart Baskins. Mr. John Petete to Miss Duckett. Mr. Elias Dejarnat, to Miss Lavina Swift.
Died in Columbia, S. C., Mr. R. A. Taylor, formerly of Charleston.
In Richland dist., Mrs. Caroline Anne Brevard.
In Wilkes Ga., Mrs. Sarah Hoxey, aged 67.
In Augusta, Mr. Wm. J. Norris, of Charleston, S. C.
In Macon, Capt. Andrew Jeter, aged 75, soldier of the Revolution.

Issue of June 7, 1828

Married on Sunday evening, April 27th, 1828, in St. Michael's Church, by the Right Rev. Bishop Bowen, the Rev. Thomas John Young, Minister of Prince William's and St. Luke's Parishes, to Miss Ann R. Gourdin, second daughter of the late Major Samuel Gourdin, of St. John's, Berkley.
In Prince William's Parish, on the 22d ult., William Heyward jun, Esq. to Mrs. Mary Augusta Grimke.
In Augusta, Ga., Mr. G. W. Speed, to Miss Mary E. Airey. Mr. Mr. Thomas J. Dasher to Miss Sophia L. Clarke. in Savannah, Mr. Augustus Bouyson, to Miss Lucretia Zipperor. In Newfield, Mr. John Mansfield, to Miss Martha Wakefield.
In Elbert co., Ga. 8th ult., Mr. Robert S. Hardaway, to Miss Martha B. Jarratt. In Baldwin co., Mr. C. Landers to Mrs. S. Stevens.
In the Forks of the Yadkin in N. C., 15th ult., Mr. J. Moore, to Miss Sally Milstead. On the 18th ulst., Mr. Joshua Beeman, to Miss Lydia Moreland. In Rowan, N. C. on the 8th inst., Mr. James Harbin, to Miss Delphia Fletcher. Mr. Fergus Graham to Miss Sarah Baker.
Died in this city, Duncan Leitch, merchant.
In Fayetteville, N. C., Mr. William Shepherd, a soldier of the revolution, aged 87. In Caswell co., Mr. Hiram Turner. In Rowan Co., Capt. John Coleman, 50. At his residnce, 7 miles east of Salisbury, on the 14th ult., Mr. Henry Myers, 60.
In Augusta, Ga.,William Sims, 36. On the 25th ult., Mrs. R. Baldwin, 43. Mr. John M. Doughty, 25. In Richmond co., on the 25th ult., Mr. Benjamin Gipson, 25. In Watkinsville on the 15th ult., Mrs. Elizabeth Heard, 93.
In New-York, Mrs. Troup, consort of Col. G. M. Troup, late Gov. of Georgia.
On the 24th of Feb. last, at Lima, the Hon. James Colley, of the State of Ohio, and Charge d'Affaires of the United States in Peru, after an illness of four days.
The New-York City Inspector reports the death of 78 persons during the week ending on Saturday the 24th ult., viz 16 men, 18 women, 18 boys and 28 girls.

Issue of June 14, 1828

Married in this city, on the 4th inst., by the Rev. Dr. McDowell, Mr. James Ross, to Miss Ann Henry, all fo this place
In Camden, the 20th ult., Mr. Algernon S. Clifton, to Miss Caledonia C. Macell.
In Savannah, on the 4th inst., by the Rev. Hugh Smith, in Christ Church, the Rev. Edward Neufville, Pastor of said Church, to Miss Mary M. Bulloch, daughter of Wm. Bulloch, Esq. On the 24th ult., Mr. Council S. Brian to Miss Cathrine Herb.
In Augusta, Mr. Henry Parson, to Miss Eliza Wilson. Mr. John P. Greiner, to Miss Mary Anna Barney. Mr. Robert T. Walker to Miss Ann Formentin Polk. In Eatonton, on the 22d ult., Mr. John H. McMath, to Miss Margaret Gaither. In Morgan co., 18th ult. Mr. James Ferrill to Miss Eliza Maxwell.
Died in Yorkville, S. C., on the 27th ult., Mr. George Horton. In St. Marys, Ga., on the 24th ult., Mr. Henry Sadler, Sen. In Effingham Co. on the 22d ult., Mrs. Mary Ann Porter, 36. In Jones co. on the 24th ult., John Jenkins. In Macon, Mr. Charles P. Clemence, 24.
In Milledgeville, Mr. Charles Lanos, a native of Normandy, in France. In Warren Co., Mrs. Ally Caroline Loyless, 20.

Issue of June 21, 1828

Married in Philadelphia, on the 4th inst., Mr. John Hoff of this city, to Mrs. Frances H. Tucker, daughter of the late Rev. Dr. Henry Holcombe.
At Byron, Baker co., Ga., on the 29th ult., Isaac Welch, to Miss E. W. Porter. In Richmond co. on the 3d inst., Mr. Henry Parsons to Miss Eliza Wilson. Mr. John P. Greiner to Miss Mary Anna Barnet. In Macon, Bibb co. 5th inst., Mr. Nathan C. Munroe to Miss Tabitha E. Napier. In Augusta, 5th inst., Mr. B. F. Chew to Miss Lucy V. Buford.
At Mobile, on the 27th ult., Gen. William Taylor, to Miss Eliza H. Head.
Died in Jones co., Ga.,on the 2d inst., Mrs. Priscilla King. In Iredell Co., N. C. Mrs. Elizabeth Lackey, aged 47.

Issue of June 28, 1828

Married in Georgetown, Mr. John Daniell, to Miss Lucy Bishop. In Monticello, Ga., Mr. Bailey Goddard to Miss Catharine R. Usher. In Gwinnet co., Mr. Thomas H. Jones to Miss Margaret H. Hoyle.
Died in Greenville, S. C., Mr. Ira Cole, formerly of the State of New-York. In Columbia, Mrs. Mary C. Park, 54. In Richland district, Capt. William Taylor, 71.
At Milford, on the 9th inst., Mr. Charles Pond, a member of the Sophomore class in Yale College, 18.
At Richmond Baths, on 20th inst., Mary Susan Whitehead, 11.

Issue of July 5, 1828

Married in this city, on Wednesday Evening, by the Rev. Mr. Gildersleeve, Mr. Wm. Grierson, to Miss Elizabeth T. Walton.
In Robeson co., N. C., Mr. John Parker to Miss Flora McDonald. In Hancock, Ga., Mr. Augustus Kennon, to Miss Henrietta Alston.
In Savannah, Mr. Joseph Burroughs, to Miss Valeria G. Berrien. In Edgefield, Mr. Daniel D. Brunson, to Miss Sarah Ann Roper.
Died in this city on the 23d ult., in the 94th year of his age, Mr. Solomon Moses, sen. a native of Amsterdam, but for the last 34 years a resident of this city.
In Washington, Ga., Mr. Andrew Ruddell, he was a member of the Baptist Church....
Departed this life at Timber Grove, in Abbeville District, on the 24th June, Mrs. Mary Jack, aged about 76 years....
Near Sparta, on the 19th ult., the Rev. John Simmons, aged 33 years. He was a native of England, but came to America at the age of 14....in Congaree Circuit, S. C.
In Virginia, on the 20th inst., Thomas M. Randolph, esq. formerly Governor of that Commonwealth.

Issue of July 12, 1828

Married in Anderson District, 24th ult., Maj. George Seaborn to Miss Sarah Ann Earle. In Camden, 25th ult., Mr. Francis Cook to Miss Margaret M. Ellison.
In Columbia co., Ga., Maj. Benjamin L. Greenwood to Miss Elizabeth M. M. Scurry. In Warreton (sic), 24th ult., Mr. George A. Dawson, to Miss Martha B. Burt.
Died in this city on the 9th inst., Elijah P., infant son of James B. and Maria F. Russell, aged 12 months and 23 days....
In Camden, S. C., on the 27th ult., Mrs. Rosina Levy, wife of Col. Chapman Levy, 19.
In Abbeville, S. C., 22d ult., Sarah, daughter of the Rev. Henry Reid, aged 8 years, 2 months and 16 days.

In Milledgeville, Ga., on the 1st inst., Jesse youngest son of Mr. John W. Sanford, aged 6 months. In Hall co., Ga.,on the 9th ult., Willis Thurmond, Esq. 48.
Departed this life, the 28th ult., at the Richmond Bath, Mrs. Abbey E. Dowse, consort of Samuel Dowse, Esq., aged 20...a member of the Presbyterian Church.

Issue of July 19, 1828

Married in Columbia, S. C., Mr. Simeon Wheeler, to Miss Rebecca Henson.
In Augusta, Ga., Mr. William O. Kindrick, to Miss Mary McLean. Mr. John T. Wise to Miss Siney Ann Davis. In Monticello, Mr. Asa T. Smith, to Mrs. Mary Ann Yeaman. Mr. James Hamilton Blackshear to Miss Caroline E. L. Floyd. In Monroe co., Mr. Seaborn L. Dean to Miss Charlotte F. Pinckard.
Died on the 22d ult., at Malvern near Statesburg, the Hon. Thomas Waties, one of the Associate Justices of this State.
In Sumpter District, Mrs. Mary Garret, aged one hundred and twenty years!
In Augusta, Ga, Miss Anna Gardner, 14. In Louisville, 27th ult., Reuben Wilkinson.
In Raleigh, N. C., on the 29th ult., James F. Taylor, Esq., Attorney General of that State.

Issue of July 26, 1828

Married in Pendleton, S. C., Mr. Madison C. Livingston to Miss Ariana B. Griffin.
In Savannah, Ga., Mr. Wm. N. Brower, to Miss Susan M. J. Cunningham. In Morgan co., 8th inst., Mr. Mathew J. Pass to Miss Ann Hardman. In Sparta, on 13th inst., Lieut. Thomas S. Twiss, of the U. S. Army, to Miss Elizabeth Sherrill. In Columbia co., 26th ult., Mr. Hilary M. Murray, to Miss Eliza C. Starks.
Died in this city, on Wednesday morning, Mr. Samuel Pilsbury, a very respectable member of the Presbyterian Church, aged 81 years and 6 months.
In York Dist., S. C., on the 8th ult., Col. John Caruthers, 80.
In Salisbury, Rowan Co., N. C. Dr. Robert Moore.
In Savannah, Ga., 22d ult., Dr. Wm. P. Marshall, a native of S. C. On the 15th inst., Mr. P. McDermont, 36. On the 6th inst., Mrs. Mary Antoinette Berthelot, 44. In Augusta, 10th inst., Mrs. Ann Savage, 35. In Macon, 8th inst. Dr. Thompson Bird, 68.
In Spencertown, in this county, 6th inst., Col. David Pratt, 91--a soldier of the Revolution.

Issue of August 2, 1828

Married in Greenville, S. C., on the 17th ult., by the Rev. Mr. Taylor, Dr. Alfred Howard, of Augusta, to Miss Juliana Thomas, of Charleston, S. C.
In Charlotte, N. C., on the 10th inst.,Mr. John Henderson, to Miss Priscilla Porter.
In Hillsborough, Ga., on the 10th inst., Rev. John H. Norment to Miss Mary Ann Spear. In Wilkes co., on the 25th ult., James Edward Henry, Esq. attorney at law, of S. C. to Miss Ann Eliza Jones, daughter of General Edmund Jones, of the former place. In Savannah, Mr. Jesse Furness, to Miss Rebecca Forsyth.
Died in this city, on the 21st ult., Jervis Henry Stevens, esq., aged 79--a soldier of the Revolution. On the 25th ult., Joseph Winthrop, Esq. a native of New-England, but for the last 43 years a resident of this city. On the 29th ult., Mr. John Dunn. On

the 30th ult., Benjamin Elfe, senior. On the 21st ult., Mrs. Jane D. McNish, of St. Luke's Parish, 40.
On Monday 14th ult. in Orangeburg dist., Jane M. eldest daughter of Mrs. E. E. Murchison, and grand-daughter of S. P. Jones, Esq., aged 10 years and 3 months.
In Georgetown, Samuel Smith, Esq., 40.
In York dist., S. C., Mr. Nathaniel Enloe. On the 3d ult., James Stitt, 31.
In Milledgeville, Ga., on the 13th inst., Mrs. Caroline Calhoun, 25.

Issue of August 9, 1828

Married in Columbia, S. C., Mr. David W.Sims, proprietor of the Telescope, to Miss Ann McGowen. Mr. F. W. Green, to Miss Sarah Briggs. In Pendleton, Mr. Joseph C. Eaton to Miss Jane Robinson. Mr. Loton Davis to Miss Mary McKenzie.
Died in this city, Mr. J. Main, 40. Mrs. Elizabeth Grand. Mrs. Mary Ann Green, relict of Christopher R. Green, Esq., deceased, 30.
In Pee Dee, Major John Thompson Green, 77--a revolutionary soldier.
In Walthourville, Liberty co., Ga., Mr. Joseph Hargraves, 65. In Norfolk, on the 26th ult.,Mrs. Sarah B. Kollock, wife of Rev. Shepherd K. Kollock, pastor of the Presbyterian Church in that borough.
In Bucks Co., Pennsylvania, Dr. Isaac B. Snowden, Editor and Proprietor of the Philadelphia Monthly Magazine, aged 36 years and 6 months.

Issue of August 16, 1828

Married in this city, on the 13th inst., by the Rev. Dr. McDowell, the Rev. B. Gildersleeve, to Miss Emma Louisa Lanneau, all of this city.
In Savannah, Mr. Thomas M. Goddard, of S. C.,to Miss Mary C. Dixon. In Milledgeville, Ga., Mr. Henry Darnell, to Miss Nancy Wright. Mr. Arden R. Mershon to Miss Frances Jones.
In Cabarrus co., N. C., Mr. Angus Carter to Miss Jane Martin. At Montpelier, Vermont, Mr. J. P. Miller, the Geek (sic) Agent, to Miss Sarah Arms.
Died in this city, Mr. David White. Mr. Ferdinand Schilpp. Mr. Thomas Caught.
In Rowan Co., Mr. Thomas Ghen, 70.
At Washington, Ga., Col. Duncan G. Campbell, an eminent Lawyer and a pious man. At St. Mary's, Jane Eves Meers, 24.
On the 16th ult. at Fishkill, New-York, Col. William Few, in the 81st year of his age...a Senator of the U. S. from that State from 1799 to 1793, and a member of the Convention which framed the Constitution of the U. S.
In New-Jersey, on the 23d ult., the Hon. Hedge Thompson, a Representative in Congress, for that State.

Issue of August 23, 1828

Married in Greenville, S. C., Dr. S. M. Holloway, to Miss Maria Garrison.
In Milledgeville, Ga., Mr. Ardin R. Mershon, to Miss Frances Jones. In Hancock, Mr. Uriah Battle to Miss Amanda J. Askew.
In New-York, on the 1st inst., Mr. Nathaniel B. Webb, of Savannah, to Adeline L. Osborne.
Died on Santee, Mrs. Desdemona Harrington.

On the 8th inst., at his farm near Hamburg, S. C., Major Thomas Hall, 38.
In Abbeville District, S. C., on the 11th inst., William Henry Parker, aged 33 years and 5 months.
In Crawford Co., Ga., on the 4th inst., Mr. James Jones.
In Milledgeville, Ga., 30th ult., Dr. Harris Graham Jones of Lexington.
In Clinton, Ala., on the 8th inst., Mr. Jenkins D. Weathers.
At Princeton, N. J., on the 10th inst., Mrs. Mary Stewart, relict of the late Robert Stewart, merchant of this city, aged 52.
At Staten Island, N.Y., on the 28th ult.,Mr. Andrew Brown of Savannah, aged 37.

Issue of August 30, 1828

Married in Greenville, S. C. on the 7th inst., Wm. H. Talley to Miss Elizabeth Merritt. In Pendleton, Mr. Larkin Gambrell to Miss Susannah Elenor Douthit. In Orangeburg, Mr. John H. Stephenson, to Miss Lavenia W. Browning.
At Lawrenceville, Ga., Mr. Robert Clark Thompson, to Miss Caroline Hart.
In Rowan, N. C., 7th inst., Mr. Benjamin Beaver, to Miss Mary Cooper.
Died in this city on Wednesday, John T. Robinson of the firm of John Robinson, Son & Co., merchants, in the 26th year of his age.
On the 13th inst., in Anderson dist., S. C., very suddenly, Hon. John Wilson, formerly member of Congress from Greenville and Pendleton.
In Savannah, Ga., 7th inst., Joseph Miller, Esq. In Augusta 20th inst., Mrs. Catharine Maguire, aged 60. In Athens, Mr. Joshua Jordan, 22. In Lawrenceville, 28th ult., Mrs. Louisa M'Keen.
In Montgomery co., N. C. 23d ult.,Mrs. Martha Chisolm.
On the 28th ult., Rev. John M'Farland, pastor of the Presbyterian Church in Paris, Ky.
In Mobile, Ala., Willoughby Barton, Esq.,Attorney at Law, formerly of Augusta, Ga.

Issue of September 6, 1828

Married in Macon, by the Rev. Mr. Hodges, Mr. Jefferson J. Lamar, of Putnam Co., to Miss Rebecca Ann Lamar, of the former place.
Died in Pendleton, S. C., Mrs. Harriet Earle, aged 49.
In Augusta, Ga., on the 16th ult., Mr. Cyprean Sage, aged about 28, a bricklayer, and believed to be a native of Connecticut.
At his residence in Washington County, on the 20th ult., Mr. John Jordan in the 73d year of his age--a soldier of the Revolution.

Issue of September 13, 1828

Married in Georgetown, S. C., Mr. Jacob J. Joseph, to Miss Sarah Emanuel. In Darlington dist., 14th ult., Mr. Charles B. Howard, to Miss Amelia Cannon.
Died at Clifton plantation, Waccamaw, William M. Wilson, aged 23 years and 7 months. At Cat-Island, 28th ult., Miss Elizabeth Kitchings, a native of Washington co., Ga.,aged 15 years and 3 months. On Bever Creek in Kershaw dist.,at a very advanced age, Mr. Arthur Cunningham. In Hamburg, on the 4th inst., Miss Eliza Hammond, aged 17 years.
In Washington Ga., Major Andrew Shepherd.

The Kentucky Argus of the 27th ult says: "We learn that Judge Robert Trimble died on Monday last."

Issue of September 20, 1828

Married in Athens, Ga., on the 26th ult., Henry Clinton Lea, to Miss Serena Roots.
Died on the 16th inst., Lilly, the infant daughter of Mr. James Robb, of this city, aged 20 months and 6 days....
In Sumter District, on the 8th inst., Mrs. Mary M. Plowden, wife of Mr. Wm. Plowden, aged 33 years....left a husband and three children....
Death of Mrs. Mitchell King (long account and eulogy)

Issue of September 27, 1828

Married on Thursday 28th August, Rev. John D. Scheck, pastor of the United Evangelical Lutheran Churches, to Miss J. C. Shepherd, third daughter of the late James Sheppard, all of Newberry District.
In Barnwell Dist., S. C., Mr. James M. Garvin to Miss Caroline E. Cannon.
In Wilkesborough, Ga., on the 4th inst., Whitfield Kerr, Esq. to Miss Maria Louisa Wilson. In Davidson co., 4th inst., Jesse Hargrave esq. toMiss Esther Lindsay.
In Alabama, 2d inst., Mr. John Steele, toMiss Lucy Stoue. On 21st. David Bullock, esq. to Miss Ann Carter.
Died in this city on Thursday morning, 25th inst., Rev. Asbury Morgan, one of the stationed Ministers of the Methodist Episcopal Church in the Charleston circuit.
On the 21st inst., at his pine land residence, St. John's Berkley, James Burn Harleston, in the 34th year of his age.
In York District, S. C., on 7th inst., Robert Hill, aged 72 years. In Greenville, on the 25th ult., Mrs. Eliza Berrien.
On the 11th inst., in Jasper co., Ga., Dr. George Matthews Merriwether, aged 32 years. In Putnam co., on the 13th inst., Mrs. Maria Reid. In Milledgeville,on the 15th inst., Thomas F. Martin , aged 15 years and six months. In Augusta, on the 11th instant, Mr. John Souleay, aged 29 or 28 years, a native of the city of New-York. On the 15th inst., Mr. John Turman. On the 12th inst., Mr. Moses Tebbetts, formerly of Boston, aged 39 years. On the 30th ult. near Milton, N. C. Bartley Yancey, esq. formerly a member of Congress and for many years Speaker of the Senate of the State of N. C. In Raleigh, on the 4th inst., Maj. John G. Blount. At Smithville, on the 20th ult., Thomas Callender, of Wilmington, aged 74.
In Montgomery co., Ala., Capt. James Hays, at an advanced age. At Rye, N. Y., on the 11th inst., Mr. Josiah Penfield, of Savannah, Ga., aged 43 years.

Issue of October 4, 1828

Married at Camden on the 16th ult., Mr. Robert Martin, of this city, to Miss Serena M. Daniel.
In Twiggs co., Ga., Mr. William Solomon, to Miss Susan Smith. In Houston co., Dr. William Crocker, to Miss Louisa J. Stapler. In Columbus, Major Rufus M. Farrington, to Miss Sarah McIntosh.
In N. York, on the 18th ult., James M. Shapter, of Savannah, Ga., to Miss Elizabeth A. Caldwell.
At Morristown, N. J., on the 9th ult., James Burnet, of Columbia, S. C. to Miss Catharine Ann Schenk.
Died in Greenville, S. C., Mrs. Harriet Earle, aged 49.

in Savannah, Ga., on the 25th ult., Mr. George W.Graham, aged 26 years; Sergeant Major of the 2d Regiment U. S. Artillery. On the 22d ult., Mr. George Penny, aged 46; a native of Willington, Surry Co., England, and a resident of the former place for the last 31 years. At White Bluff, Wm. H. Greene, esq.,aged 36 years. In Augusta, Mrs. Eliza Dill. In Jones co., on the 10th ult, Gardner Tufts, 18. In Columbus, on the 11th ult., Samuel Judson Collidge, Post Master at that place, in the 26th year of his age. In Powelton, Dr. T. Meriwether, aged 26. On the 14th ult., Mrs. Susan Callier, aged 34. Near Powelton on the 17th ult., Mrs. Hannah Crowder.
In Iredell co., N. C. on the 2d ult., Mrs. Ruthy Almira Flemming, aged 19 years. In Mecklenburg, N. C. on the 31st ult., Mr. James Dinkins Jr. Onthe same day, Mrs. Ann McKnight. On the 2d ult., Mr. Wm. M. Neely.
At Rye, N. Y., on the 11th ult., Mr. Josiah Penfield, 43., a native of Savannah, Ga.

Issue of October 11, 1828

Married in Milledgeville, Ga., Rev. Charles Hardey to Miss Emily Reynolds. In Macon on the 25th ult., Dr. Thomas R. Lamar, to Mrs. Nancy Fullwood.
In Iredell co., Mr. Charles Churchill to Miss Matilda Johnston. On the same day, H. Young, Esq. of South Carolina to Miss Lucy Young.
Died on Monday evening last, at Sullivan's Island, Capt. Robert Henley, of the U. S. Navy.
On the 10th ult., in St. Mathew's Parish, John Reid, Esq., formerly a resident of Columbia, and for several years a very respectable Tutor in the S. C. College.
At Godfrey Savannah, 4th inst., Mr. Andrew White, 48.
In Lincolnton, N. C. on the 13th ult., Lemuel Moorman, Esq.
At Lexington, Ky., on the 16th ult., Dr. Anderson Watkins, of Augusta, Ga., 54.
In Clinton, Jones co., Ga.,on the 30th Aug., Harris Allen, 49. In Putnam on the 13th ult., Mrs. Mary Ried.
In Anson Co., on Rocky river, near Austin's Gold Mine, on the 17th ult., Mr. Green Deberry Austin, 26. In Montgomery co., Ala. on the same day, Mrs. Chelaty Austin.
At Greenbush, Rensselaer co., N. Y., Gen. John J. Van Ransselaer.

Issue of October 18, 1828

Married in Macon, Ga.,Mr. Angus Gillis, to Miss Margaret H. Allston. In Columbus, Mr. Samuel R. Andrews, to Miss Elizabeth Day. In Troup co., Col. J.W. Kendrick, to Miss Martha Ector.
Died in Georgia, on the 1st inst., Mr. Obediah Potter. In Elbert co., on the 30th ult., Mr. Thomas J. White, 25.
At his seat near New Brunswick, New Jersey, on the 11th ult., the Rev. Abraham Beach, D. D., in the 89th year of his age.

Issue of October 25, 1828

Married in Houston co., Ga., on the 2d inst., Major Robert A. Beall, to Miss Caroline Smith. In Jones co., 21st ult., Mr. William Freeman, to Miss Lucy Kirk. In Wilkes co., on the 2d inst., Daniel Chandler, to Miss Sarah G. Campbell. In Augusta, Mr. Kenneth M. Grant, to Miss Mary E. Clark.
In Autauga co., Ala., Mosely Baker, Esq., Editor of the Alabama Journal, to Miss Eliza W. Pecket. In Perry co., on the 2d inst., Mr. Henry Potts, to Miss Nancy E. Mims.

Died in Cheraw, S. C., on the 6th inst., Dr. Alexander McQueen, 57.
In Richland District, on the 29th ult., Jacob Deleon, 64.
At his residence on Little River, on the 10th inst., Mr. Anthony Pullig.
On the 16th inst.,near Milledgeville, Ga., Dr. Charles Williamson. In Augusta, Mr. W. J. Rayfield, a native of the County of Antrim, in Ireland. On the 30th ult., in Columbia co., Rev. John F. Jeffers, in the 24th year of his age; he was a native of Eneckelon, Ireland. In Augusta, on the 17th inst., Mr. Conrad Liverman, sen. In Savannah, on the 8th inst., Mr. Wm. A. Moore.
At New-Orleans, on the 20th ult, Mr. Charles Mitchell, recently of Augusta, Ga.

Issue of November 1, 1828

Married in Milledgeville, Ga.,on the 2d ult., Rev. Charles Hardy, to Miss Emily Reynolds. Onthe 16th ult., Mr. Philip Augustin Clayton, to Miss Elizabeth Ann Williamson. In Houston, on the 2d ult., Major Robert A. Beall, to Miss Caroline Smith. In Clinton, on the 15th ult., Mr. Simri Rose, one of the Editors of the Georgia Messenger, to Miss Lavinia E. H. Blount.
In Wadesborough, N. C., Mr. Thomas Y. Houze, to Miss Frances Pickett. In Rowan, on the 25th ult., Mr. John Reinhardt, to Miss Sally Boger. In Concord, Cabarrus, on the 7th ult., Mr. George W. Spears, to Miss Caroline Elizabeth Area. In the Forks of the Yadkin, Rowan co., Mr. Henry Guffy, to Miss Elizabeth Walker.
In Alabama on the 1st ult., Mr. Paschall Traylor to Miss Jane Gardner. In Washington, Autauga, Ala., on the 30th Sept., Dr. Wm. Burt, to Miss Caroline Mathews.
In Norwalk, Con. on the 22d Sept., Jacob Chadbourn to Mrs. Isabella Champion, both of Savannah, Ga.
Died in Lincoln Co., Ga.,on the 11th August, Miss Elizabeth Howard Fleming, aged 18 years....
In Columbia, S. C. on the 20th inst., Mr. Samuel Wilson, 26.
In Georgetown, Col. John Porter jun., a Representative in the State Legislature.
In Augusta, Ga., on the 20th ult., Mr. John Campbell, a native of Ballyrobbin, near Antrim, in Ireland. In Columbia co., 20th ult., Reubin Reynolds, sen.
In Rowan, N. C. 9th inst.,Capt. John Stirewalt, 60.

Issue of November 8, 1828

Married in this city on the 15th ult., by the Rev. Dr. Dalcho, Mr. John F. Stock, to Miss Ann H., daughter of the Right Rev. Bishop Bowen. On Wednesday Evening last, by the Rev. Dr. Gadsden, Mr. H. Cogswell, to Miss Esther Susan, eldest daughter of Charles Mouzon, Esq., all of this city.
In Harris co., Ga.,Dr. William A.Culp, to Miss Cynthia W. Smith.
Died in this city on Sunday morning last, Major General THOMAS PINCKNEY, in the 79th year of his age.
In Newberry district, 17th ult., Mr. Noah Simpson Harmon, in the 21st year of his age.

Issue of November 15, 1828

Married in Pendleton, S. C., on the 28th ult., Mr. Benjamin Kirkpatrick to Miss Rebecca C.Stribling. On the 30th ult., Mr. WM. Noble to Miss Caroline Houston.
On the 30th ult. at Skidaway Island, the Hon. T. U. P. Charlton, to Miss Clementine Helen Lefevre.

Near Augusta, Ga., on the 30th ult., Col. John S. Porter, (of the Senate) to Miss Mary Ann Greenwood.
In Athens, Ga., on the 22d ult., Wm. Cronn, Esq., to Miss Doda Glass. On the 25th ult., Mr. James Patillar, to Miss Jane Gurvin. On the 28th ult., Mr. Venon Holmes, to Miss Olivia Wynn.
In Hancock co., Ga., on the 28th ult., Major James Hillsman to Miss Emeline Hudson. In Lincoln, on the 30th ult., Mr. Abram Stow, to Miss Sarah M. BEard. In Jasper co., Mr. Robert C. Beasley, to Miss Elizabeth Byron. In Augusta, on the 22d ult., Mr. Byrd B. Mitchell, to Miss Mary Ann Bagley.
Died in Milledgeville, on the 19th ult., Dr. Lewis H. Kennan, 31.
In Jackson co., Ga., on the 19th ult., Miss Eliza Henderson, aged 15 years and 28 days.
In Henry co., Ala., on the 17th Sept., Col. Wm. C. Watson, a native of N. C.

Issue of November 22, 1828

Married at Paris, Ky., on Tuesday evening, the 4th inst., by the Rev. James Blythe, D. D., Thomas Witherspoon, lately of Williamsburg, S. C., now of Greene Co., Alabama, to Mrs. Sarah W. Lapsley, relict of Rev. Joseph Lapsley, late of Bowling Greene, Ky., deceased.
In Milledgeville, Ga., on the 7th inst., Dr. Benjamin F. Owens, to Mrs. Almira Hargrave. In Gwinnett co., on 28th ult., Mr. Viveon Holmes to Miss Olivia Winn.
In Lincoln, N. C., on the 30th ult., Mr. Abram Stow, to Miss Sarah M. Beard.
Died at his residence near Pendleton district, S. C., Mr. Lewis L. Gibbes, formerly of this city. In Fairfield, on the 1st inst., Mrs. Deborah Anne Yarborough, wife of Mr. Washington Yarborough.
In Greensborough, Ga., on the 1st Nov., in the 51st year of her age, Mrs. Elizabeth Langdon.

Issue of November 29, 1828

Married in this city, on Tuesday evening last, by the Rev. Dr. Palmer, Mr. Benjamin J. Evans, to Miss Martha Perdriau, both of this city. On Wednesday the 26th inst., by the Rev. Mr. Gildersleeve, Dr. Robert Durant to Miss Mary, daughter of Capt. Robert McFaddin, of Sumpter District.
In Mecklenburg co., N. C. on the 30thult., Dr. Amvi Alexander, to Miss Mary Delia Harris.
In Boston, Rev. Nathan W. Fiske, Professor in Amderst College, to Miss Deborah M. Vinel.
In Savannah, on the 27th inst., Mr. Wm. Thompson, to Miss M. A. White.
Died in Pendleton District, S. C., Mr. Alexander Bryce. On the 17th inst., Mr. John Bishop, aged about 30 years.
In Iredell co., N. C. on the 4th inst., Mr. John Witherspoon, 32. On the 29th ult., Joseph Cyers, 80. In Lincoln co., on the 25th inst., William McClean, sen. 73.

Issue of December 6, 1828

Married in Abbeville, S. C., by the Rev. John T. Pressly, on Tuesday the 18th Nov., Rev. Henry Bryson of Lyncoln co., W. Tennessee, to Miss Hannah McMullen, daughter of Mr. Archibald McMullen, of Abbeville, S. C.
In Pendleton, S. C. on the 18th ult., Mr. Williamson Brazeal to Miss Penelope H. Holloway.

In Milledgeville, Ga., on the 20th ult., Maj. A. Richardson to Mrs. Jones. In Athens, Edmund C. Atkinson, Esq., to Miss Sarah E., daughter of the Rev. Moses Waddel, D. D.
Died in this city, Mrs. Elizabeth Bee.
In Pendleton, S. C. on the 18th ult., Mrs. Jane Dalton. In Milledgeville, Ga.,on the 25th ult., Mrs. Mary S. Gorman, in the 22d year of her age.

Issue of December 13, 1828

Married in Washington co., Ga., 27th ult., Mr. Myles W. Cullens, to Miss Ann Henrietta Roe. In Crawford, on the 23d ult., Mr. John B. Lumpkin to Miss Mary Graves. In Macon, on the 25th ult., Major D. Tracy to Miss Susan Campbell. In Augusta, on the 27th ult., Mr. Antoine P. Diliac to Mrs. Sarah Singes.
At Claiborne, Ala., 30th Oct., A. P. Bagby, Esq., to Miss Elizabeth Connell.
Died at her plantation in St. Thomas on the 4th Dec. Mrs. Caroline Olivia Laurens, relict of the late John Ball Laurens.
In Savannah, Ga., on the 27th ult., Midshipman Joseph Arnold of the U. S. Navy, in the 22d year of his age. At Mallow, M'Intosh co., on the 27th ult., Mrs. Barbara M'Intosh. In Milledgeville, on the 29th ult., Mr. T. Williams, 30. At Monticello, Jasper co., 28th ult., Mr. Thomas Grant, aged 72, a native of Virginia, and for 40 years a citizen of Georgia; he was a soldier of the Revolution and a member of the Methodist Church for 42 years....
In Kingston, Morgan co., Dr. Seth Ward.
In Haywood co., N. C.on the 27th ult., Lieut. Samuel Wragg, of the U. S. Army.

Issue of December 20, 1828

Married in Abbeville, S. C. on the 25th ult, Mr. Robert G. Quarles, of Edgefield, to Miss Mary E. Robertson of Abbeville. At the same time and place the Rev. John H. Gray, of Greene, Ala., to Miss Jane B. Robertson.
At Powelton, Ga., 4th inst., Thomas F. Green, Esq., to Miss Adeline E. A. Crowder. In Milledgeville, on the 27th ult., Mr. Miles D. Cullens, to Miss Ann H. Roe. In Morgan co., on the 28th ult., Dr. Edward Delony, to Miss Piannah Shepherd. In Greenesborough, on the 27th ult., Maj. Hugh A. Harleston, to Miss Caroline M. Lewis.
In Lincoln co., on the 27th Nov., Dr. Benjamin Johnston, to Miss Sarah Johnston.
Died in Columbia, S. C., 3d inst.,Mrs. Susan M. Brickle. In Charlotte, N. C. on the 3d inst., at the house of Mr. Robert Watson, Mr. Chauncey Pettibone of Burlington, Con. In Salisbury, on the 24th ult., Mr. Benjamin Cowan, sen. aged 79.
In Clinton, Ga., MIss Eliza Jastice, aged 17. In Jackson, Butts, Ga., on the 13th ult., Mrs. Ann H. Swift.

Issue of December 27, 1828

Married in Savannah, on the 11th inst., Mr. James D. Huguenin to Miss Maria Matilda Law. On the same evening, Mr. William McWhir Maxwell, to Miss Ann Law. In Augusta, on the 15th inst., Charles Black, Esq. of South Carolina, to Miss Janet Joanna, eldest daughter of R. R. Reid, Esq. of that city.
At Trenton, N. Y., on the 2d inst. Mr. Isaac G. Seymour, of Macon Ga., to Eulalia, second daughter of the late Rev. Henry Whitlock, of New Haven, Con.

Died in New-York on the 14th inst., Isaac Harby, Esq. He was formerly editor of the Southern Patriot, and subsequently of the City Gazette.
In Washington, Ga., 8th inst., Dr. Richard W. Worsham. In Putnam, on the 29th ult., Mr. Henry Turner, aged 70. In Athens, 15th inst., Major William Marstern Cowles. In Monroe, on the 1st inst., Mr. John Chappel, aged 63. At St. Mary's on the 1st inst., Capt. James Bentham, Post Master, and formerly of Charleston, S. C.

(No issues have been located for the year 1829)

Issue of January 2, 1830

Married in this (city) on Wednesday Evening last, by the Rev. Wm. Capers, Capt. Edward N. Smith, to Miss Elizabeth Henderson.
In Barnwell District, on Thursday evening, the 17th ult., by the Rev. Mr. Talmage, Dr. Thomas W. Hutson, to Miss Martha L. Hay, late of New-York.
Died in Athens, Ga., Mrs. Sarah, wife of John F. Wallace.
In Liberty county, at the residence of her father, on the 4th inst., Miss Hetty Augusta Dunwoody. (eulogy) Savannah Georgian, 22nd December.
Departed this life in Williamsburgh District, S. C., on the 16th Nov., in the 32d year of her age, Mrs. Mary Ballow...left husband, five children and a sister....

Issue of January 9, 1830

Married near Beeville C. H. on Thursday evening, 24th Dec., by the Rev. Dr. Barr, Mr. John Shelleto, to Miss Margaret McMeens; also Mr. Wm. Smith to Miss Matilda McMeens.
In this city, on Tuesday evening, December 31, 1829, by the Rev. Dr. Dalcho, Mr. James L. Murray, to Miss Elizabeth, youngest daughter of Richard Connolly, Esq. all of this city.
Died in this city on the 5th inst., in the 56 year of his age, William W. Selah, Printer, a native of Fredericksburg, Virginia.
In Columbia, S. C., on the 29th ult., Mr. Benjamin Courson, 43. On the 30th, Joshua James, 20. At Lexington Court House, on the 11th ult., William Jones, Esq. Attorney at Law, and formerly Commissioner in Equity for Lexington district.

Issue of January 16, 1830

Married in this city, on the 7th inst., by Rev. John Bachman, James C. Norris, to Emma C. Hayden. Also, Mr. John B. Bruce, Esq. of Darlington to Miss Elizabeth Newton. On Wednesday 6th, by the Rev. Dr. Palmer, Mr. George Elfe, jr., to Mrs. Mary Jane O'Hara, daughter of the late Stephen Mazyck.
In Screven co., Ga., on the 30th ult., Col. Joseph D. Thomas of Burke co. to Miss Louisa Kittles. In Macon, on the 24th ult., Washington Poe, Esq., to Miss Selina S. Norman.
Died in this city, on the 1st inst., Mr. Joseph Sampson. On the 12th ult., Dr. William A. Herring, of Elbert County, Ga., in the 28th year of his age.

Issue of January 23, 1830

Married on the 14th inst., by the Rev. B. Manly, Dr. Samuel Henry Hambleton, to Miss Susan Matthews, eldest daughter of the late Robert Matthews, Esq. of St. James Goose Creek.
On Edisto Island, on the 12th inst., by the Rev. Wm. S. Lee, Col. George W. Seabrook, to Miss Abigail M. youngest daughter

of the late James Clark, Sen.
　　　In St. Paul's Parish, Colleton District, on the 4th inst., by the Rev. Mr. Williams, John C. Cobourn, to Miss Eliza M., second daughter of the late Job P. Givhan, all of Colleton District.
　　　On the 12th inst., by the Rev. Mr. Jones, at Summerset, the Hon. W. D. Martin, of South-Carolina, to Miss Sally Maria, daughter of the Hon. Clement Dorsey, of Maryland.
　　　Died in this city, on the 10th inst., Joseph Bellinger, Esq., in the 58th year of his age. On the 8th inst., John C. Jones, a native of Germany, but for many years a respectable inhabitant of this city.

Issue of January 30, 1830

　　　Married in Beaufort, S. C.,on the 20th inst., Col. Stephen Elliott, to Miss Ann Habersham.
　　　On the 7th ult., by the Rev Mr. Huphrys (sic), Mr. Thomas McAdams, of Abbeville District, to Miss Margaret Martin, of Anderson. And, on the 14th, Mr. Miles Hardy, of Anderson District, to Mrs. Eliza Speer, of Abbeville District.
　　　Departed this life at Santee on the 14th inst., in the 26th year of her age, Mrs. Louisa Blake Huggins, wife of Charles Huggins, Esq., and eldest daughter of Col. Charles John Steedman, of this city.
　　　Died at his country seat on John's Island,on the 15th inst., James Legare, Esq., aged 67 years and 10 months...at a very early age, received a commission in the continenal Line...subsequently a member of the Legislature...(eulogy)
　　　Departed this life on Friday the 8th ult., Mrs. Elsy Caldwell, wife of Col. Wm. H. Caldwell, of Abbeville District...member of the Presbyterian Church (eulogy).

Issue of February 6, 1830

　　　Married in this city, on the 27th ult., by the Rev. Mr. Bachman, Jacob F. Mintzing, Esq., to Miss Louisa, daughter of Edward Thwing, Esq.
　　　On the 21st ult., in St. David's Church, Cheraw, by the Rev. J. W. Chamber, the Rev. Alexander W. Marshall, to Miss Elizabeth Ann, daughter of Dr. Richard Maynard.
　　　At Andersonville, S. C., on the 26th ult., General Joseph N. Whitner, to Miss Elizabeth Harrison. At Newberry C. H. on the 19th ult., Thomas H. Pope, Esq. to Miss Harriet Harrington. At the same place, on the 21st ult., Major Robert Dunlap, to Miss Sarah Nance. At Edgefield, B. A. Wallace, Esq. to Miss Ellen Rearden.
　　　Died on the 14th Dec., Mrs. Dorcas DuBose, wife of Capt. Jno. DuBose, of Darlington, S. C., aged 38 years...left a husband and family of small children....
　　　At R. Felder's, on the State Road, on the 25th ult., Wm. Fauster, of Laurens District, on his way to Charleston with his wagon.
　　　On the 15th ult., in Putnam co., Ga., Mrs. Martha Cooper.

Issue of February 13, 1830

　　　Married in this city on the 4th inst., by the Right Rev. Bishop Bowen, William R. Smith, Es q., of Virginia, to Mrs. John Middleton.
　　　Near Sumterville, on the 12th ult., by the Rev. Jesse Hartwell, Rev. Staunton S. Burdett, Pastor of the Baptist Church in St. Mathews Parish, Orangeburg District, S. C., to Miss Sophenia Matilda,

second daughter of T. V. Fort, Esq.
On the 21st ult., Jeffrey Palmer, Esq. of Union District, to Miss Elizabeth Martha, youngest daughter of Mr. Thomas Reaves, of Lexington District.
Died on the 20th ult., at her residence on North Santee, in the 22d year of her age, Mrs. Henrietta Hume.
In Greensborough, Ga., on the 1st inst., from an affection of the liver, the Hon. Thomas W. Cobb, one of the Judges of the Supreme Court and late Senator of the United States, from that State.
On the 20th ult.,near Buffalo, N. Y., the celebrated Indian Chief, Red Jacket, aged 80.

Issue of February 20, 1830

Married in St. Lukes, Beaufort, on Sunday Evening last, 14th inst., by the Rev. J. B. Van Dyck, Mr. Fountain R. Floyd, of Jefferson Co., Ken., to Mrs. Mary B. Fitts, of the former place.
On the 3d inst., Mr. Charles Bussy, of Edgefield District, S. C., to Mrs. Bugg.
Died in this city on the 3d inst., Henry Ingraham, Esq., in the 42d year of his age.
At Collins X Roads, Colleton Dist., on the 8th of Jan. last, Miss Frances Wright, aged 18 years....
At Yorkville, S. C., on the 25th ult., Mrs. Nancy Winston.
At Greenville, on the 30th ult., Mrs. Eliza B. THompson. At Beaufort, on the 5th inst., Mrs. Jane Graham, aged 32 years, 1 month and 22 days, consort of Mr. James Graham, Pastor of the Baptist Church of that place, after an illness of about 26 hours.
At the head of Elliott River, Prince Edward island, on the 24th of December, Mrs. Mary Gibbons, aged 107 years.
At Savannah, on Sunday last, Capt. Henry W. Lubbock, formerly of this city. On the 15th inst., Mrs. Jane Shaw.

Issue of February 27, 1830

Married in Thomas co., on the 28th ult., Mr. Lucien H. Raines, of Twiggs co., Ga., to Miss Anne, youngest daughter of the late Edward Blackshear, of Thomas co.
Died in Savannah, Ga., Mrs. C. C. Woodruff. In Jones co., on the 10th inst., Col. Thomas White. In Monroe co., William Culloden, Es. Post Master, at the office known as Culloden's Store.
On Sugar Creek, in Mecklenburg co., N. C., Captain Hugh Parks, a soldier of the Revolution. In Iredell co., on the 28th ult., Miss Sarah Lowrance.
In New-York, on the 17th inst., the venerable Revolutionary character, Col. Henry Rutgers.

Issue of March 6, 1830

Married in this city on the 24th ult.,by the Rev. Mr. Talley, Mr. William J. Gayer, to Miss Mary Bythewood. And on the 25th, Mr. William S.Parsons, to Miss Martha Ann Landershine.
In Walterborough, on the 10th ult., Alexander L. Edwards, Esq., to Miss Rachel M. Ford.
On the 11th ult., Mr. Nelson Carter, of Augusta, Ga., to Miss Martha Hannah Groves, of Abbeville, S. C.
In Augusta, Ga., on the 28th ult., Dr. Augustus Baudry, to Mrs. Eliza S. M. La Roche.
Died on John's Island, on the 18th ult., Micah Jenkins, sen., Esq., in the 78th year of his age.
In Abbeville, S. C., on the 4th inst., Mr. Ira Griffin, aged about 50.

In Columbia co., Ga., on the 20th ult., Benjamin Leigh.

Issue of March 13, 1830

Married in St. Michael's Church, on Wednesday Morning last, by the Right Rev. Bishop Bowen, John Berkley Grimball, Esq. to Miss Meta A. Morris, second daughter of Col. Lewis Morris.
Died in this city on the 27th ult., in the 45th year of his age, William Washington, Esq., only son of the late General William Washington.
At Savannah, on the 26th ult., Mrs. Susan P., wife of Thomas J. Shepherd, and daughter of the Rev. Samuel Leak, of Pike co., Ga.

Issue of March 20, 1830

Married in Edgefield district, on the 7th inst., Mr. Wm. F. Durisoe, to Miss Mary Ann E. Roper. On the 4th Joseph W. Trisdale, Esq., from Mobile, to Miss Mary Amelia Wilson. In Beach Island, on the 7th, Mr. Davis Bottom, of Augusta, to Miss Martha Brooks of the former place. In Rowan, N. C., on the 4th inst., Mr. Matthew B. Locke, to Miss Margaret Gibson.
Died in Sumter District, Maj. William Smith, aged 56. At Milledgeville, 6th inst., Mrs. Sarah W. McCombs, wife of Robert McCombs, Esq., aged 31. In Henry co., Ga.,Daniel Mercer, aged 50. At Columbia C. H., Capt. William F. Wilkins, aged 31. In Riceborough, Mrs. Susan P., wife of Mr. Thos P. Shepherd.
In Rowan N .C.,on the 16th ult., Mrs. Margaret Williams, wife of Mr. John Williams, aged 41. At Jonesborough, in Granville co., on the 15th, Richard Bullock Henderson. In Cabarus co., on the 26th ult.,in the 34th year of her age, Mrs. Jane Harris, consort of Dr. Samuel S. Harris.

Issue of March 27, 1830

Married at Athens on the 17th ult., Dr. W. W. Waddel, to Miss Louisa M. Hilliard. In Darien, on the 11th inst.,Rev. Nathaniel Pratt, to Miss Catharine King.
Died in Sumter, S. C.,on the 4th inst., Maj. William Smith, aged 56.
At Appling, Columbia co., on the 6th inst., Capt. Wm. F. Wilkins, 31.
In Raleigh, N. C., the Rt. Rev. John Stark Ravenscroft, D. D., Bishop of the Protestant Episcopal Church in N. C., in the 58th year of his age.

Issue of April 3, 1830

Married in this city, on Thursday night, by the Rev. Mr. Gildersleeve, Dr. Edward C. Keckeley, to Miss Mary Jane Moore, all of this city.
On the 2d March, by the Rev. D. L. Gray, Captain White, to Miss Catharine Cunningham, both of Spartanburg district. And on the 11th, Wm. Tramble, to Miss M. Howard, both of Union.
In McIntosh co., on the 18th inst., Alexander C. Wylly, Esq. to Miss Elizabeth S. Spalding.
Died in this city, on the evening of the 22d ult., Edwin H. Jones, in the 15th year of his age...left a widowed mother.....
In the neighborhood of Meansville, Union, on the 19th of Feb., Mrs. E. Howard, aged 74. In Laurens district, on the 25th of December last, Mr. John Slone, in the 114th year of his age. He was a native of Antrim co., Ireland, a Soldier of 76.

In Salem, Sumter District, on the 19th March, in the 35th year of her age, Mrs Susan G. Shaw, the consort of John Shaw....

Issue of April 10, 1830

Married in Beach Island on the 7th inst., Mr. Davis Bottom, of Augusta, to Miss Martha Brooks of the former place.
Died in York district, S. C., near Broad River, on the 26th ult., John H. Whishert, 17.
In Monroe co., Ga.,on the 19th ult., Joseph Cotton, 56.
At Mount Zion, on the 25th ult., Mrs. Ann Robertson.

Issue of April 17, 1830

Married at Clarksville (Ala.), 21st March 1830, by Thomas Sanders, Esq., Dr. J. A. Huber of Coffeville (Ala.) to Miss Mary Summers, of Edgefield District, S. C.
Died at Willington, Abbeville, S. C. on the 4th inst., Mrs. Eliza Woodson, consort of the Rev. Dr. Waddel, in the 60th year of her age. In Barnwell district on the 10th inst., in the 49th year of her age, Miss Mary M. Linder.

Issue of April 24, 1830

Died in this city on the 16th inst., in the 34th year of her age, Mrs. Mariette, wife of Rev. Dr. Reuel Keith of Alexandria, D. C., and daughter of George Cleaveland, Esq., of Middlebury, Vt., left husband and brother....

Issue of May 1, 1830

Married in Camden, S. C. on the 15th ult., Mr. Benjamin Cook to Miss Sarah, eldest daughter of George Stratford, Esq. At Mount Elon, Mr. Joseph Fenet, to Miss Rachel, daughter of Mr. Daniel Herron, all of Darlington District.
Died at Walterborough, on the 11th ult., Felix Bruneau Warley, in his 43d year--he served during the late was as Captain, in the 8th Regt. of U. S. Infantry....
At Savannah, on the 23d ult., Richard Gookin.
In Rowan co., N. C., on the 10th ult., John Andrews, aged 58 years and 9 months.
On the 29th March, at his late residence in Georgeville, Miss., Mr. William Gilmore Simms, sen.

Issue of May 8, 1830

Married in Athens, Ga., on the 21st ult., Harris Smith Evans, Esq. of Alabama, to Miss Laurinda E. D. Bouchelle. On the 22d ult., Hugh W. Nesbit, Esq. of Augusta, to Miss MaryW. Harris.
Died at Augusta, Ga., on the 28th ult., Charles Granville.
At the same place, James Moore.
At Tuscaloosa Co., Ala., on the 16th ult., aged 63, Mrs. Elizabeth Foster, widow of the late Col. John Foster, of Columbia Co., Geo.

Issue of May 15, 1830

Married in this city, on the 4th inst., by the Rev. Mr. Bachman, James G. Moody, Esq., to Rosa Adeline, eldest daughter of the late Thos. Cochran.
On the 5th inst., by the Rev. Dr. Palmer, Mr. J. S. Bailey, to Miss Hannah Jane, daughter of Mr. William McElmoyle, all of this city.

Died at Old Fort, Beaufort, S. C., on the 3d inst., Mr. Archibald Smith, of Savannah, aged 75.
In Savannah, on the 26th ult., Mrs. Henrietta Burke, aged 33. At Bethesda, Mr. Wm. F. Ladson, aged 61.
Died in child bed, in Tuskaloosa Co., Ala., on the morning of the 23d of April, in the 22d year of her age, Mrs. Jennet Emeline Frierson, consort of William V.Frierson and only daughter of Thomas Witherspoon, late of Williamsburgh, S. C. (eulogy)

Issue of May 22, 1830

Married on Sunday evening last, by the Rev. Dr. Gadsden, Mr. Michael Arnau, of St. Augustine, to Miss Mary Ann Nickerson, of this city.
In Washington Ga., on the 13th inst., by the Rev. Mr. Hoyt, William L. Harris, Esq., to Miss Frances Semmes, daughter of Andrew Semmes, Esq.
Died at Lancasterville, S. C. on the 9th inst., Smith L. Lewis, a young merchant of much promise of the firm of J. M. Stringfellow & Co.
At Eatonton, Ga., on the 10th inst.,Moses B. Hamilton, Rector of the Academy of that place, and a native of Massachusetts. At his residence near Watkinsville, on the 2d inst., Geo. W. Lumpkin, in the 29th year of his age.
At Greenfield, Mass., on the 1st inst.,Hon. Jonathan Leavitt, in the 66th year of his age....
Major John Alexander is no more...died 9th of May, 1830 at his residence in Lawrenceville, Ga., in the 75th year of his age. ...born 17th Nov 1756 in the county Antrim, from whence his parents emigrated to this country when he was 14 years old... (long account).

Issue of May 29, 1830

Married on Wednesday evening, the 26th inst., by the Rev. Dr. Gadsden, Lieut. Ingraham, of the U. S. Navy, to Miss Harriet Horry, third daughter of the late Henry Laurens.
In Anderson district, by the Rev. D. Humphrys, Mr. James Gray, of Abbeville, to Miss Elizabeth Sadler, of Anderson.
Death of Mrs. Martha Evans, who departed this life on Saturday last, in the 24th year of her age.... (eulogy)

Issue of June 5, 1830

Married in Augusta, Ga., on the 20th ult.,Mr. J. C. Preval, to Miss Martha Harper. On the 27th ult., David F. Halsey, Esq. to Miss Mary M. Flournoy. Mr. Andrew G. Bull, to Miss Ellenor H. Micon.
In Savannah, on the 4th ult., Col. W. H. Dunham, to Miss Mary E. Bond. On the 18th, Mr. Peter T. Shick, to Miss Elizabeth Cline.
In Darien, Ga., on the 6th ult., Dr. Wm. B. Rogers, to Miss Jane H. Holmes.
In Columbia Co., Ga., on the 13th ult., Mr. John N. Baker to Miss Mary Anne Roberts.
In Mecklenburg co., N. C. on the 6th ult., Mr. Samuel J. Neel, to Miss Louisa Ross. In Iredell co., on the 18th ult., Mr. Alexander R. Lawrence to Miss Caroline Sharp.
Died at his residence, Seneca River, S. C. on the 22d ult., Mr. Horatia Reese, aged 45.
In Cheraw, S. C., on the 11th ult., Mrs. Elizabeth S. Morrison, aged 30. On the 20th, Capt. William Ellerbe, in the 68th year of his age. Near Edgefield C. H., Mrs.Susan Ann Butler.

In Augusta, Ga., on the 26th ult., James M. Walker, aged 29.
In Wilkes Co., Mr. George Jones, aged 87.
Near Fayetteville, N. C. on the 7th inst., the Rev. James Vann, local preacher of the Methodist Church.

Issue of June 12, 1830

Married on Tuesday evening last,by the Rev. Mr. Bachman, Dr. William Wilkins, of Purysburg, S. C. to Miss Martha C. Broer, of this city.
In Raleigh, N. C., on the 6th ult., the Rev. Leonidas Polk, to Miss Frances A. Devereux.
Died in this city on the 20th ult.,Mr. John Moore, aged 32 years, a native of Belfast, Ireland, for many years an inhabitant of this city.
In this city on the 24th April, Samuel Bigelow, aged 47 years, a native of New Salem, Mass., well known through N. C., S. C., and Georgia, for the last 19 years, as a teacher of sacred music.
At the residence of Col. Eldred Simkins, near Edgefield village, on the morning of the 22d May, 1830, Mrs. Susan Ann Butler, the wife of Col. A. P. Butler.
Departed this life at the house of Eleazer F. Heard, on the Chattahooche, Dekalb co., Ga., Amos Guthrie, son of James Guthrie, of Union district, S. C.
At the female academy in Sparta, Hancock Co., Miss Sophronia J. Magrauder, in her 15th year.

Issue of June 19, 1830

Married in this city, on Wednesday last, by the Rev. Mr. B. Manly, Mr. John Taylor Bowles, to Miss Ann Catharine Crawford, all of this city.
Died at Washington, Ga., on the 5th inst., Mrs. MaryS. Lane, wife of Mark A. Lane, aged 18..a member of the Presbyterian Church.
At Pendleton, S. C. on the 24th ult., Stephen Chastain, Sen. in his 68th year.
At Sumterville, S. C. on the 27th ult., Mrs. Jane Hawthorn, aged about 90.
Died at the residence of Mrs. Mary Carter, on Black River, Salem County, Sumter Dist., S. C., on the 1st inst., Miss Elizabeth Flemming, at the advanced age of 72. a member of the Presbyterian Church for more than 50 years....

Issue of June 26, 1830

Married on Sunday evening last, by the Rev. Mr. Gibbes, at St. Philip's Church, Stephen P. Monk, Esq., to Mrs. Esther Cripps, daughter of F. G. Deliesseline, Esq.
Died in this city on the 16th inst.,in the 35th year of his age, Mr. Thomas Bridgewood, a native of England, but for the last 8 years a respectable Merchant of this place.
In Union district, on the 5th ult.,Mrs. Louisa Gist.
At Savannah, Ga., on the 19th inst., Edward Duffy. At Augusta, on the 15th inst., Mrs. Kezia Arnold, 98. At Milford, Byron co., on the 13th inst., Mrs. Eliza Footman.
At Washington, D. C., on the 15th inst., JosephWood, Miniature Painter, in the 52d year of his age.
At the Theological Seminary in Auburn, on the 2d inst., John L. Howard, aged 27.

Issue of July 3, 1830

Married in Milledgeville, Ga., on the 22d ult., Mr. Adolphus S. Rutherford, to Miss Susan R. Thweatt.
Died on the 27th ult., in the 82d year of his age, Capt. John Williamson, Merchant of this city. At Johnsonville, James Island, Mrs. Margaret M. Lawton, consort of Winborn Lawton, in the 43d year of her age.
In Savannah, Ga., on the 19th ult., Mrs. Isabella Chadbourn, aged 21 years and 6 months.
At Greensborough, Ala., on the 22d May, Mrs. Nancy Hillhouse, wife of the Rev. James Hillhouse, formerly of this state.

Issue of July 10, 1830

Married in Louisville, Ga., on the 10th ult., Dr. Alexander Lowry, to Miss Elizabeth Stokey. At Macon, on the 24th, David B. Butler, Esq. to Miss Rebecca Ann Campbell in Wilkes Co., on the 24th, Charles S. Burks, to Miss Elizabeth Armstrong. In Athens, on the 27th ult., Mr. John Lasseter, to Mrs. Elizabeth Doyle.
Died at Pendleton, S. C., on the 23d ult., Col. John G. Hunter, aged 25.
In Morgan co., Ga., on the 23d ult., Faulkner Heard, aged about 43. In Madison co., on the 17th ult., Mrs. Mary Saye in her 87th year.
At Columbia co., Ala., on the 9th ult., Col. Thomas D. Carr, aged 27. At the plantation of Mr. George Hill, in Columbia co., on the 24th ult., Mrs. Ann B. Hill, in her 27th year.
in Georgetown, D. C., on 14th ult., Mrs. Margaret Cassin, wife of Com. Stephen Cassin, of the U. S. Navy, in her 41st year.

Issue of July 17, 1830

Married in this city on Sunday last, by the Rev. Mr. Bachman, William Adrian, to Jane Walker.
In Savannah, Ga., on the 29th ult., Dr. Ralph E. Elliott, of Beaufort, S. C. to Miss Margaret C. Mackay, daughter of the late Robert Mackay, Esq.
In Sparta, Ga., on the 1st inst., Mr. Alfred Skinner, Merchant of St. Louis,Missouri, to Mrs. Nancy Skinner, of Sparta, Ga.
At New York on Thursday evening, by the Rev. Dr. Power, Jean Germain Samuel Adams Dannery, Esq., Knight of the Royal Order of the Legion of Honour, Consul of France for the port of Philadelphia, to Miss Marie Alexandrine, eldest daughter of Mr. Durant St. Andre, Consul General of France for the U. S.
Died in this city on the 16th ult., at the advanced age of 78 years and 5 months, Mrs. Ann Hayes Bennett, relict of the late Thomas Bennett.
Drowned on Saturday evening last, Mr. John Potter, of Newport, R. I., acting as Second Mate of the ship Harriet, lying at Fitzsimons' wharf...left a wife and child.
In Darlington District, S. C. on the 29th June, Miss Mary Louisa Sage, in the 21st year of her age.
In Savannah, on the 5th inst., Jacob Read, Esq., eldest son of the late Gen. Read of S. C.
In Iredell co., N. C. on the 22d ult., Mr. David Dunlap, Postmaster at Bethany Church. Mr. Dunlap was a respected member of the Presbyterian Church.
In the city of London, on the 22d of May last, Mrs. Harriet C. Lee, wife of George W. Lee of Boston, and daughter of the late Charles Glover of this city.

In New York, on the 2d inst., the Rev. Charles O. Screven of Sunbury, Ga. He was born in Medway, Liberty co., Ga., in Feb. 1773, and brought to the knowledge...under Rev. Dr. Furman of Charleston, S. C....(eulogy)

Issue of July 24, 1830

Married at Washington, Ga., on the 15th July by the Rev. N. Hoyt, Mr. Lock Weems, to Miss W. F. Shepard. In Laurens county, on the 24th ult.,Mr. John F. Spicer, to Miss Evelina Hampton. On the 29th, Charles S. Guyton, to Miss Elmina Horn. In Morgan co., on the 30th ult., Major Wm. Woods, to Miss Nancy A. Vason. In Washington, on the 8th inst., Mr. Andrew Huling, to Miss Martha A. Smith. On the same evening, Mr. Thomas Kelogh, to Miss Jane Dickens.
Died in Edgefield village, on the 6th inst., Mr. Sabra Jeter, aged 39.
At his residence in Columbia co., Ga., on the 1st inst., Mr. John Sutherland, in the 66th year of his age. In Lincoln co., Mr. William R. Statham, aged 24.
on board the U. S. Sloop of war Peacock, off the Island of Cuba, on the 23d ult., Lieut. William T. Temple (first of that ship) a citizen of Caroline County, Virginia.

Issue of July 31, 1830

Married on Tuesday evening the 29th ult., by the Rev. Mr. Chandler, Col. Augustus Flud, of St. Matthew's Parish, to Miss Matilda M., daughter of Col. James B. Richardson, of Sumpter District.
On the 6th inst., in Laurens district, by the Rev. D. Humphrys, Thomas Cunningham to Miss Nancy A., daughter of Dr. Cammel.
Died of Paralysis, at the house of Gen. David Blackshear, on the evening of the 2d inst., Col. JosephBlackshear, of Laurens co., Ga., in the 55th year of his age. In Fayette co., on the 3d May, Gen. David Dickson.
At Philadelphia, on the 15th inst., the Rev. Noah Davis, an active, faithful and successful Agent of the Baptist Tract Society, aged 28....
in Philadelphia, on the 15th inst., Mrs. Margaret Hoff, in her 83d year, formerly a resident of this city.

Issue of August 7, 1830

Died at Moultrieville, Sullivan's Island, on the 15th ult., Mrs. Bridget Bedford, aged 93.
At Raleigh, N. C. on the 25th ult., Rev. Josiah James Kirkpatrick, pastor of the Presbyterian Congregation at Fayetteville.
Died at his residence in Boston about 12 o'clock, on Sunday night, 26th ult., Hon. Isaac Parker, Chief Justice of the Supreme Court of Massachusetts, aged 63. (account). Boston Recorder

Issue of August 14, 1830

Married at Macon, on the 16th ult., H. W. Hilliard, to Miss Mary Bedell. On the 27th ult.,at Sydenham, Clark co., John Crawford, Esq. to Miss Sarah Eaton Bass.
In Autauga co., Ala., on the 22d ult., Dr. Samuel D. Holt, to Miss Laura Hall.
Died on the 1st inst.,in the 33d year of his age, Mr. Robert A. Paisley.
At her residence in South Carolina, on the 14th of July, Mrs. Mary Ann Lawton, daughter of Mrs. Sarah King of Clark co.,

Ga., aged 27 years.

Issue of August 21, 1830

Married in Rutherfordton, N. C., the 27th ult., Mr. Isaac C. Woodward of Fairfield dist., S. C. to Miss Irena Suttle. A short time since, Mr. Wm. Little of Lincoln co., to Miss Elizabeth Guffey. On the 1st inst., Mr. William Morehead to Miss Betsey Fortune.
Died on the 10th inst., at the house of Mr. William Wilson, in Salem county, Sumter District, Major Josiah Wilson, in the 52d year of his age...a native of the District in which he died. In 1802 he went to Ga. and located himself in Liberty county...settled near Sunbury....
On Sunday morning the 25th ult., near Pendleton, the Rev. Henry Gains, in the 94th year of his age. He was born in King & Queen county Virginia, and removed to this State when about 60 years old. He resided a few years in Newberry and Abbeville, but has been for about twenty years a resident of this neighborhood... more than 50 years a preacher of the Gospel...member of the Methodist Church.
In Milledgeville, Ga., on the 5th inst., Col. Robert R. Ruffin, aged 42 years.

Issue of August 28, 1830

Died in this city on the 5th inst., Mrs. Celia Cohen, in the 75th year of her age. On the 24th inst., in the 31st year of his age, Wm. McKenzie Parker.
On the 10th inst., at St. Augustine, Mr. Andrew Little, a native of Scotland, and lately a resident of this city.
On the 6th inst., in the 53d year of her age, Mrs. Susannah Boyd, consort of Dr. John Boyd of Sumter District.
On the 9th inst., near Greensborough, Ga., Mrs. Elizabeth Randal, aged 20.
Departed this life on Friday evening, the 13th inst., Miss Elizabeth W. Wilson, aged about 25 years, and consort of Capt. James H. Wilson of Middle Salem, Sumter District...left four small children...(eulogy).

Issue of September 4, 1830

Married on the 14th ultimo, at the summer residence of Mrs. Campbell, in Bumcombe county, N. C., by the Rev. Mr. Buist, Mitchel King, Esq. of Charleston, to Miss Margaret Campbell, youngest daughter of McMillan Campbell, Esq., deceased, and Henrietta Campbell, all of the same place.
Died in this city on the 23d ult., Mr. Louis Alexander Edward Moodie, aged 29 yeras and 7 months.
At Edisto Island, S. C., on the 16th ult., Daniel Dowling, Sen., aged 49, a native of the Queen's County (Ireland) but for many years past a resident of this city.
In Wilkes co., Ga., Mr. Robert Harris, 56. Near Macon, 8th ult., Samuel Gillespie, 28. In Hancock co., on the 12th ult., Rev. William B. Smith, a native of Edgefield district, S. C.

Issue of September 11, 1830

Married in Augusta, Ga.,on the 2d inst., Mr. Mathew Nelson, to Mrs. Charlotte Cooper.
Died at Bradford Springs, in Sumter District on the 28th ult., Col. William A. Colclough, of Clarendon, 45. At his summer residence of Mill Creek, on the 4th inst., in the 66th year of his age, Hon. Robert Stark, Secretary of State. Near Sumterville,

on the 19th ult., Miss Mary Ann Chandler, aged 22. At Yorkville, on the 29th ult., the Hon. Robert Clendinnen, Senator for York District, in the State Legislature.
In Augusta, Ga., on the 6th inst.,Mr. George W. Fox, 26.
On the 2d, Miss Mary Ann Clarke. In Twiggs co., on the 28th ult., Col. Roger Lawson, 55.
Died in child bed in Lincoln co., Ga., on the 28th ult., in the 33d year of her age, Mrs. Jane E. Stovall, consort of Stephen Stovall, Esq...(eulogy)
Also on the 23d ult., Mrs. Nancy Jennings (the mother of Mrs. Stovall) aged about 63....
On the 20th ult., at his residence in Greene co. (Ala.), Samuel Archibald, Esq. aged 68 years and 3 months....a native of North Carolina, and when very young an active soldier in the Revolution; and elder of the Presbyterian Church....

Issue of September 18, 1830

Died in this city on the 11th inst.,Mr. Alfred S. Gailard, eldest son of the late Theodore Gaillard, jun. in the 35th year of his age.
In Savannah, on the 6th inst., Mr. Wm. H. Coe, in the 36th year of his age, a native of Springfield (N. J.).
In Twiggs co., Geo., on the 30th ult., Mr. Terril Perry.
At her residence near Lawrenceville, Gwinnett Co., Geo., on the 28th ult., Mrs. Rachel Kenney, aged 53--formerly of Edgefield Dist., S. C.

Issue of September 25, 1830

Married in Columbia, S. C., Mr. Thomas B. Poindexter of Halifax Co., Va., to Miss Mary E. Zimmerman.
In Savannah, Mr. Albert P. Williams, of Providence, R. I., to Miss Abigail M. Stilwell. In WIlkinson co., Robert Hatcher, Esq., to Miss Eliza Ard.
Died in this city, on the 13th inst., Mrs. Thomas L. Jones, in the 23d year of her age. On the 31st ult., John Jacob Schnell.
At the residence of her father, near Manchester, on the 14th inst., Mrs. Mary Rebecca M'Duffie, consort of the Hon. George McDuffie, and daughter of Richard Singleton, Esq.
At his residence in Hancock co, on the 1st the Rev. Edmund Shackleford, aged 49 years, 2 months and 22 days. In Augusta, Mr. John M. Clarke. In Wrightsbo', on the 7th inst., Mrs. Mary Ann White.

Issue of October 2, 1830

Married on Sunday evening last, by the Rev. Mr.Wightman, Mr. John W. Hagood, to Miss Elizabeth B. Martin, all of this city.
In Edgefield, S. C., on the 23d ult., Mr. Thomas Barrett to Miss Mary Savannah, daughter of Gen. Thomas Glascock, all of Augusta.
In Augusta, Ga., on the 21st ult., Dr. James B. Walker, to Miss Louisa Matilda, second daughter of Mr. John Wolfolk, all of that city.
Died on Thursday evening, the 9th ult., Mrs. Margaret Drummond, consort of Mr. John Drummond, aged 31 years and 10 months, a native of this city; leaving a husband and three small children....
In this city, on the 20th ult., Mr. John S. Lynn, aged 31 years.
In Sumterville, S. C. on the 7th ult., Mr. Holloway James, aged about 69.
In Savannah, Ga., on the 23d ult., Mrs. Ann Dixon, 41.

Issue of October 9, 1830

Married in Marlborough district, S. C., on the 9th ult., Mr. Wm. Beverly, to Miss Charlotte Bridges. In Edgefield, on the 26th ult., William W. Guyton, Esq., to Miss Ann Miller.
In Augusta, on the 30th ult., Capt. Benjamin Granger, to Miss Sarah M. Allen. In Jackson co., Ga.,on the 20th ult., Mr. Simon Smith to Miss Mary Lampkin. In Morgan co., on the 22d ult., Mr. Asberry Daniel, to Miss Susan Randle. At Retirement, on the 21st ult., the Rev. Charles Evans, to Mary Walton, daughter of Col. Zachariah Williams, all of Columbia county.
Died in this city on the 4th inst., Julia Augusta, second daughter of Dr. Thomas Y. Simons, aged 7 years and 4 days.
In Augusta, Ga., on the 22d ult, Mr. Lewis Hunter, 83. In Clarke co., on the 17th ult., Mrs. Serena Stroub, 35. In Macon, on the 20th ult., Mrs. Nicey Collins, 25. Near Milledgeville, on the 20th ult., Mrs. Sarah A. Cheney, of South Carolina.
At Mr. Clarke's in Albermarle, Hon. George Hay, U. S. Judge for the Eastern District of Va., and son-in-law of James Monroe, late President of the U. S.

Issue of October 16, 1830

Married on the 13th inst., by the Rev. Mr. Manley, Mr. Galloway Monteith, of Columbia, to Miss Mary S. Hussey, of this city.
Died in this city on the 28th ult., Mrs. Martha F. Washington, relict of the late Wm. Washington.
At Wadmalaw Island, in Charleston District, on the 1st Oct., Dr. Henry Olin Harvey, aged 27.
At St. Augustine, on the 27th ult., Mrs. Lydia Boyce, formerly a resident of this city.

Issue of October 23, 1830

Married in this city on the 13th inst., by the Rev. Mr. Gibbes, Mr. Charles D. Carr, to Miss Margaret Emma Prevost.
On the 14th inst., by the Rev. Mr. Mitchell, Mr. William Allen, of Roxbury, Mas. to Miss Mary Ann Suit, of this city.
At New-York, on the 12th inst., Mr. Hiram P. Woodward, Professor of Mathematics, &c., in the Richland School, South Carolina, to Miss Jane Houghton, of that city.
In Christ Church, Hartford, on the 9th inst.,Mr. Ralph Post, of Cheraw, S. c., to Miss Sibyl H. May, of Hartford.
Died in this city, Benjamin Bonneau, aged 3 years and 6 months, son of Dr. Thomas Y. Simons.
On the 15th inst., at Lewisville, St. Thomas' Parish, of Typhus Fever, Mr. Samuel Wigfall, in the 30th year of his age, Mr. John G. Fordham, a native of this city.
In Columbia co., Ga., Mr. Peter Crawford. In Lincoln, on the 22d ult., Mrs. Elizabeth Hardy, in the 55th year of her age.
At Fort Dearborn, Chicago, on the 29th August last, Lieut. John G. Furman, of the U. S. 5th Infantry, son of the late Rev. Dr. Furman of this city, in the 25th year of his age....
At New-York, on the 10th inst., James Fairlie, Esq. for more than 30 years, clerk of the Circuit Court.
On the 7th inst., George Washington, twin son of Wm. N. and Rebechah M. Thompson, aged 2 years and 8 months....St. Bartholomew's Parish, October 13th, 1830.

Issue of October 30, 1830

Married on the 14th inst., Mr. Joseph Barnes, to Miss Louisa M. Rees, both of Columbia co., Ga.

At Savannah, on the 24th inst., Mr. Thomas Y. Lee, to Miss Ann Zackman.
Died in this city on the 20th inst., Catharine Ann, youngest daughter of Jacint Laval, jr., aged 4 years, 6 months and 4 days. At Walterborough, on the 8th inst., Thomas Boone, Esq., aged 45 years. At Edisto Island, on the 23d inst., Miss Susan Mathews, third daughter of John R. Mathews, Esq. At Beaufort, on the 14th inst., John A. Joiner, Esq., in the 29th year of his age. In Camden on the 9th inst., the Rev. Thomas L. Wynn, aged 39, a minister of the Methodist Episcopal Church. (eulogy)
At New-York, on the 15th inst., Mrs. Elizabeth W. Rose, consort of Arthur G. Rose of this city.
In Edgefield, S. C., Mrs. Rebecca Frazer, aged 36.
At Athens, Ga., on the 21st inst., Cicero Holt, Esq., a highly esteemed and valuable member of society. Also, on the 24th inst., Mr. Wm. H. Hunt, aged 47 years.
In Rowan co., N. C. on the 7th inst., Mrs. Tabitha Pinkston. On the 8th, Mr. Michael Smith, 23. in Mecklenburg, on the 29th of September, Mr. Robert Lindsay, a member of the Steel Creek Presbyterian Church and a zealous advocate in the cause of Temperance.

Issue of November 6, 1830

Married on the 21st ult., Mr. Wm. Sowell of Kershaw district to Miss Mary Blackwell, of Chesterfield district. On the 19th ult., Mr. Thomas Kirkly of Chestrfield district, to Miss Isabell Mercheson of Camden.
At Palmyra, Liberty co., Ga., on the 21st ult., Col. Joseph Quarterman, to Miss Harriette E., second daughter of Major John Stevens.
Died at Athens, Ga., on the 29th October, Mary Frances Gildersleeve, daughter of the Editor of this paper, aged 5 years....
In Lincoln co., Ga., onthe 23d ult., Mrs. Elizabeth Creswell Jones.
In Cincinnati, Ohio, on the 19th ult., William Appleton, Esq., of Amherst, N. H., aged 22 years, son of the late Dr. Appleton, president of Bowdoin College, Maine.

Issue of November 13, 1830

Married in Rutherfordton, N. C. on the 14th ult., Mr. Buffon D. Terrell, to Miss Martha M'Faddin. On the 17th ult., Mr. Thomas Burnett, of Tenn., to Miss Margaret Parter, of S. C. In Lincolnton, on the 12th ult., Mr. William Robertson, to Miss Eliza Dews.
Died near Edgefield village, on the 24th ult., Benjamin Murrill, in the 97th year of his age.
In Charlotte, N. C. on the 8th ult., Mrs. Iby Jamison. On the 22d ult., Miss Margaret McKelvey. In Salem, Stokes co., on the 14th ult., Mrs. Bagge, 52. In Rutherfordton, on the 19th ult., Mr. Owen Forman, from Onondaga county, N. Y., 33.
At his residence in the Territory of Arkansas, on the 16th September, Edward W. Duval, Esq., late Indian Agent for the Cherokees in that Territory, aged about 40 years.

Issue of November 20, 1830

Married in the German Lutheran Church, on Sunday evening, by the Rev. Mr. Bachman, Mr. Simeon H. Patterson of Augusta, Ga., to Miss Ann R. James, of this city.
At Barnwell C. H. on the 21st ult., Dr. Richard C. Fowke, to Miss Harriett S., daughter of the late John C. Allen, all of Barnwell district, S. C.

At Savannah, Ga., on the 3d inst., Mr. W. H. Cannon, to Miss Euphemia Dane, both of Barnwell District, S. C.
Died in this city on the 9th inst., Mr. Samuel F. Seyle, in the 23d year of his age.
In St. James' Santee, the Hon. James E. Jerman, in the 45th year of his age.
In Barnwell district, S. C., on the 25th ult., Robert Dimbar, aged 53. In Lancaster, on the 6th inst., Miss MaryM. Dunlap, aged 26.
At St. Augustine, on the 3d inst., Mrs. Mary Ferguson, consort of Mr. John Ferguson, and daughter ofMr. Daniel Cruickshanks of this city.
At Mobile, Ala., on the 2d inst., Mrs. Rosina Lyon, 27.
In Lexington, Ky., on the 4th of Sept. last, in the in the 27th year of his age, Dr. Lawson Caldwell, of Charlotte, N. C.

Issue of November 27, 1830

Married in Edgefield, S. C., on the 11th inst., Mr. Benjamin F. Nicholson, to Miss Georgiana Brocker. In Williamsburg, on the 16th inst.,Mr. William E. James, to Miss Jane I. Wilson. In Barnwell District, on the 11th inst., Mr. Chs. Dewett, to Mrs. Sarah R. Burton.
Died in this city on the 23d inst., Capt. William H. Miller. On the 14th, Daniel C. Webb, jun. 22. On the same day, Daniel C. Welsh, jr., 23. In Cannonborough, on the 12th inst, Mrs. Martha Simpson, 56.
At his father's residence, North Bend, Ohio, on the 30th ult., John Cleves Symms Harrison.

Issue of December 4, 1830

Married on Thursday evening last, by the Rev. Mr. Manly, Mr. Robert R. Bee, to Miss Mary F. Morrison, all of this city.
On Wednesday evening, the 1st inst., at the Unitarian Church, by the Rev. Mr. Gilman, Mr. Richard W. Hutcherson, to Miss Mary H. Chamberlain, all of this city.
On the 1st inst., by the Rev. Mr. Buist, Mr. Charles T. Haskell, to Sophia L., daughter of the Hon. Langdon Cheves, of this city.
Died in this city, on the 29th ult., Mr. Philip N. Gidiere.
In Savannah, Ga., on the 30th ult., Miss Margaret Cuyler, daughter of Judge Cuyler.

Issue of December 11, 1830

Married on Tuesday evening, 7th inst., by the Rev. Mr. Manly, George Hamilton Dunlap, Esq., of Camden, to Miss Louisa Long, of this city.
In this city, on Thursday evening, 2d inst., by the Rev. Mr. Bachman. Mr. William B. Warren, of St. Bartholomews, to Miss Remalia Louisa, eldest daughter of Col. William N. Thompson, of the same place.
Died in this city, on the 15th Nov., Mrs. Ann D. Perry, in the 55th year of her age.
After a few hours illness at the 32 Mile House, on the Georgetown Road, Mrs. Ann Black, late of this city.
At his Plantation in St. George's Parish, on the 1st inst., Major Seth T. Prior, in the 49th year of his age. He has left a widow and two sons to lament their irreparable loss.
At Monroe, Walton, Ga., on the 16th ult., Col. Samuel Jackson, 54. At Savannah, on the 3d inst., Robert Melvin, Esq. of Quebec, Lower Canada.

Issue of December 18, 1830

Died in this city, on the morning of the 12th inst.,Maria, daughter of Alexander and Maria Berry....
In Fairfield District, S. C., Hannah Beers, aged 67.
On the 6th ult., Mrs. Lydia, consort of John Lawry, Esq., and daughter of the late Capt. James Garvin of Barnwell district, S. C.

Issue of December 25, 1830

Married on the 21st inst.,by the Rev. Mr. Hanckel, Mr. Edward D. Perry, to Mrs. Maria Ann Mauger, all of this city.
At Black Creek, by Rev. John B. Van Dyck, Mr. William Barns, of Port Royal Ferry, to Miss Mary Patterson, eldest daughter of the late William Patterson, jr., of Saltcatcher.
In Alabama, on Tuesday evening 23d Nov., by the Rev. R. W. B. Kennedy, Rev. James Martin, to Miss Nancy R. Gillaspie, youngest daughter of Mr.J. Gillaspie.
Died in this city, on the 15th inst., Dr. Henry Buist, aged 25.
In Columbia co., Ga., on the 3d inst., Mr. Talbot S. Rees.
In Merriwether co., on the 27th ult., Mrs. Sarah Allen, consort of Rev. James Allen.

Issue of January 1, 1831

Married at Armenia, Barnwell District, on the 16th inst., by the Rev. William B. Johnson, the Rev. Elliott Estes of Virginia, to Mrs Elvira A. M'Pherson, daughter of the late Rev. Gideon Hagood.
Died at the house of Esqr. Cunningham (the residence of her father-in-law), in Laurens District, on the 3d of December,in the 21st year of her age, Mrs.Nancy A. Cunningham, wife of Thomas Cunningham, after an illness of four days. She had just returned from her father's (Dr. Cammels)....(eulogy)
At Georgetown, S. C., on the 25th inst., Thomas F.Goddard, Esq.

Issue of January 8, 1831

Married on Thursday evening, the 6th inst., by the Rev. Dr. Palmer, Mr. Benjamin S. Neufville, to Miss Harriet E. Gray, all of this City.
In this city, on the 3d inst.,by the Rev. Mr.Bachman, Mr. Jacob Strobel to Mrs. Sarah Hillegas, both of this city.
In Savannah, Ga., Mr. Wm. F. Sheaver, to Mrs. E. A. Addison.
In Mecklenburg Co., N. C., Mr. Harvey Huie, to Miss Nancy Calder.
Died at Columbia, S. C., on the 25th ult, Mrs. Mary Nutting, aged 48.
At Savannah, Ga., Mr. Samuel Stiles, Mr. Peter Blois, and Capt. Samuel Barns.
Suddenly, in Milledgeville, on the 26th ult., Mr. Chas. Birch, of apoplexy.
Died in Liberty Co., Ga., on the 19th Dec., Mrs. Sarah, wife of Quarterma Way, and daughter of Thos Mallard...(eulogy)

Issue of January 15, 1831

Married at Gillsonville, on the 4th inst., by the Rev. John B. Van Dyck, Dr. John Du Pont to Mrs. Mary Ferguson of St. Luke's Parish, Beaufort District.
In Augusta Ga., on the 4th inst., William Washington Randall, of Westmoreland Co., Va., to Mrs. Eliza W. Brower. On the 6th

inst., Col. Thomas Napier of Columbia Co., to Mrs. Hester Ann Rockwell. On the same evening, Mr. Francis O'Callaghan, to Miss Charlotte(?) Frances Hamill. In Lexington, on the 30th ult., James W. Harris, Esq., to Miss Martha Watkins.
    At Charlotte, N. C. on the 30th ult., Mr. Walter A. Hill to Miss Narcissa Montgomery.
    Died at Sumterville, S. C., on the 24th ult., Mrs. Grace Brown, wife of Wm. S. Brown, in the 68th year of her age.
    In Cheraw, S. C., 19th ult., Mrs. Justina M. H. Taylor, wife of Mr. John Taylor, Jr.
    In Brighton, N. Y., on the 25th ult., Rev. A. Benedict, aged about 50 years.

Issue of January 22, 1831

    Married in Augusta, Ga., Mr. William Wright, to Miss Keziah Dillon. On the 13th inst., Rev. Mr. Josiah S. Law, of Sunbury, to Miss Ellen S. daughter of the late Thomas Barrett.
    Died at his residence in Bryan co., Ga., on the 5th inst., John Vanbrackel, Esq., in the 79th year of his age. In Augusta, on the 8th inst., James R. Allen, 34.

Issue of January 29, 1831

    Married in Camden, S. C., on the 11th inst., Rev. Samuel Wragg Capers, Pastor of the Methodist Church in that place, to Miss Abthiah Harvey, eldest daughter of Phineas Thornton, Esq. In Edgefield, on the 18th inst., Dr. John O. Nicholson, to Miss Elizabeth Julia Threewits.
    In Augusta, Ga., on the 20th inst., Rev. Josiah S. Law, of Sunbury, to Miss Ellen S., daughter of the late Thomas Barrett. On the same evening, James McCallister, to Miss Sarah Ally.
    Died in this city, Mr. J. L. F. Mills,late a member of the Charleston Medical College.
    In All Saints Parish, S. C., on the 15thinst., Stephen Ford, formerly of Marion. At Camden on the 18th inst.,James S.Smith. In Lexington, on the 12th inst., Rev. Jacob Wingard, of the Lutheran Church, aged 28.
    In Washington, Ga., suddenly., on the 13th inst.,Miss Elizabeth Borum, aged 34.
    In Charlotte, N. C., on the 4th inst., Miss Mary D. McDowell, 24.
    At New Brunswick, Rober (sic) Boggs, aged 64.
    In Hartford, Con. Dec. 18th, Mason F. Cogswell, M. D., aged 69. Departed this life on the 4th inst., Dr. Caleb P. Shive, late of Lincoln Co., Ga.,and formerly of Cabarrus Co., N. C., after having been married only 13 days....

Issue of February 5, 1831

    Died in Columbus, Ga., Wm. Walker, Sen., in the 66th year of age, formerly of Putnam Co. He was a member of the Baptist Church for 36 years....
    In Salem county, Sumter District, on the 7th ult., at the house of his brother, H. Wilson, Mr. Robert William Wilson, of Marion District, in the 54th year of his age. Also on the 20th January, Mary N. James, infant daughter of John and Sarah James, aged 8 months.
    Married by the Rev. A. Foster, Mr. George W. Knox, of Pickens District, to Miss Maria, daughter of H. D. Reese, Esq. of Pendleton District.

Issue of February 12, 1831

Died in St. John's Berkley, Miss C. R. Porcher, in the 20th year of her age. In Augusta, Ga., on the 31st ult., Mrs. Louisa Woolfolk, aged 39.

Issue of February 19, 1831

Died at his residence on Staten Island, N. Y., on the 3d inst., David Devose Burger, in the 53d year of his age, a native of this city, but for many years a resident of New-York.
After a protracted illness, Commodore Arthur Sinclair, of the U. S. Navy, many years commanding Naval Officer on this station. Norfolk Beacon, 10th inst.

Issue of Feburary 26, 1831

Married on the 2d inst., on Edisto Island, by the Rev. E. Thomas, Dr. J. Holmes Mathews, to Miss Elizabeth J., eldest daughter of the lateCapt. Wm. Meggett. Also, 15th inst., Dr. F. Yonge Simons, of St. Paul's Parish, to Miss Eliza Ann, second daughter of J. R. Mathewes, Esq.
Died in this city on Thursday last, Rev. Mr. Rolfe, of Massachusetts, who recently came to the South in pursuit of his health.
Near Columbia, S. C., on the 3d inst., Clough Shelton, of Union District, aged 22. Near Granby, on the 17th ult., John W. Hane, aged 31.
At Augusta, Ga., on the 11th inst.,Col. Thomas Pace, aged 38. In Columbia co., on the 24th ult., Lewis Powell, aged 83, a soldier of the Revolution.

Issue of March 5, 1831

Married on Thursday evening, the 24th ult., by the Rev. Dr. Palmer, Mr. Z. B. Oakes, of this city to Miss Margaret F. G., daughter of the late John Christie, Esq., of Boston (Mass.) Also, Mr. James M. Stocker, to Miss Charlotte H., daughter of Mr. Samuel Oakes, all of this city.
In Milledgeville, Ga., on the 17th ult., Mr. Henry Mangham to Miss Elizabeth Barnett.
Died in this city, on Monday last,Mr. James Mitchell, one of the Elders of the Third Presbyterian Church.
In Camden, S. C., on the 6th ult, Malachi Dickson, aged 27, a native of Georgia. On the 21st, Capt. Henry T. Cantley, son of the late Gen. Z. Cantey, aged 37. In Lancaster, on the 2d ult., Dr. Bartlett Jones. In Edgefield, on the 1st ult., John Howard, a soldier of the Revolution.
In Savannah, Ga., on the 21st ult., Mrs. Hetty A., wife of James S.Bulloch, and daughter of the late Hon. John Elliott, 30 years old. In Macon, on the 13th ult., Mr. Thomas P. Carnes, late of Athens.

Issue of March 12, 1831

Married on Thursday evening, the 3d inst., by the Rev. Mr. Bachman, Mr. H. F. Strohecker, to Miss Mary, second daughter of the late Mr. T. Sullivan, all of this city.
Died in this city on Tuesday night last, Mrs. Charlotte E., wife of Joseph L. Enslow, aged 29...member of the Presbyterian Church.
In this city, on Saturday morning last,William Aiken, Esq.

Issue of March 19, 1831

    Married at Brailsfordsville, Prince Williams, S. C., on Thursday evening, 10th inst.,by the Rev. Edward Palmer, the Rev. John B. Van Dyck, to Miss Mary Saltus Christian, formerly of this city.
    Died in this city, on the 4th inst., Rev. Robert Hall,late Pastor of the Presbyterian Church, at Warrenton,Va., aged 39.
    In St. Augustine, E. F. Thomas Murphy, Esq; Edw. M. Walker, of Tryon, N. Y. Nathan Brady jr., of Stewart Co. Near Milledgeville, Wyatt Ford. Near Montgomery, A. Joshua Falconer.

Issue of March 26, 1831

    Married in Macon,Ga., on the 17th inst., Mr. Francis M'Key, to Miss Amanda A. B. Barker. Mr. Amos Subers to Miss Julia A. Crawford.
    In Monroe co., Ga., on the 10th inst., Mr. Benier Pye, to Miss Cuzziahr Robinson.
    Died at his residence near Greenville, S. C., on the 9th inst., aged 44, Dr. Richard Harrison.
    In Baldwin county, Ga., on the 11th inst., Capt. Goodwin Myrick, of Baldwin co., aged 52.
    In Tuscarawas co., Ohio, on the 30th of Jan. last, Mr. William Young, at the advanced age of 99 years 4 months and 16 days. He was twice married, and was the father of 26 children, 9 by the first, and 17 by the second wife.
    Died in Savannah, on the 22d inst., Mrs. S. Lord, wife of Mr. Hezekiah Lord....(eulogy)
    Departed this life at his residence in Coweta Co., Ga., on the 10th inst., Col. John Dickson, in the 64th year of his age. He was for many years a ruling Elder of the Presbyterian Church....
    Died, in Winnsborough, S. C., on Sabbath evening, 13th inst., Mr. John W. Elliott, formerly of this city....

Issue of April 2, 1831

    Died on the evening of the 20th inst., at the residence of Alfred Moore, Esq.,near Yorkville, S. C., Mr. John Hemingway, aged about 25 years, after a very short and painful illness.

Issue of April 9, 1831

    Married in La Grange, Troup County, Ga., on the 17th inst., Dr. Cosmo P. Richardsone, of Savannah, to Miss Margaret C. Bailey, of the former place.

Issue of April 16, 1831

    Married on Monday the 11th inst., by the Rev. Mr. Field, Dr. Charles Wm. Capers, to Miss Adeline Elizabeth Bourquin, second daughter of Wm. H. Bourquin, all of St. Helena Island.
    Died at Society Hill, on the 5th inst., Mrs. Mary Bonneau Lee Hawes, widow of Dr. Oliver Hawes.
    In Rowan, N. C., on the 27th ult., the Rev. Charles A. G. Storke, aged 67.
    At St. Augustine, E. F., on the 30th ult., of consumption, Lieut. J. B. Shaw, late of the U. S. Army.

Issue of April 23, 1831

    Married in Pendleton Dist., on the 12th inst., by the Rev. D. Humphrys, Rev. Wm. Carlile, to Miss Margaret Sadler.

In Edgefield, on the 7th inst., Mr. Joseph Adams to Miss Frances Elizabeth Adams.
Died near the Ridge, in Edgefield Dist., on the 7th inst., Mrs. Helen Lamkin.
In Washington, Wilkes, Ga.,on the 24th ult., Mrs. Sarah Hillhouse, aged 75. On the 4th inst., Mrs. Elizabeth Bruckner.
In Washington, Wilkes Co., Ga., on the 12th inst., Mrs. Eliza Webster, in the 26th year of her age, consort of the late Rev. A. H. Webster, formerly pastor of the Presbyterian Church of this place....
In Franklin Co., Penn., Mr. John Hill, aged 127.
In Bristol, England, on the 7th March, Rev. Robert Hall, a distinguished Baptist Clergyman.

Issue of April 30, 1831

Married on Tuesday evening last, by the Rev. Dr. Gadsden, Mr. Edward C. Tharm, to Miss Arabella Sophia, second daughter of the late Rev. R. S. Symmes, all of this city.
In Gainesville, Hall Co., Ga., on the 7th inst., Henry Lightfoot Sims, Esq., to Miss Emily Clements.
Died in Greene county, Ga., on the 13th inst., Mrs. Nancy More, wife of Mr. William More, in the 21st year of her age...left a disconsolate husband and a larger circle of friends....a member of the Presbyterian Church....
In Cabarrus co., N. C. on the 19th ult., Mrs. Barbara Phifer, relict of the late Col. Caleb Phifer, aged 77. In Charlotte, on the 13th inst., Marshall T. Polk, Esq.

Issue of May 7, 1831

Married in Pendleton, S. C., on the 26th ult., Mr. Francis Burt, jun. to Esq. (sic) to Miss George Ann Hall. In Anderson, on the 21st March, Mr. Robert White, to Miss Mary W. Cobb.
In Savannah, Ga., on the 1st inst.,Mr. Holmes Tupper, to Miss Lydia Maria Crabtree. On the 7th ult., at the Sand Hills near Augusta, Col. Alfred Iverson, of Columbus, to Miss Julia Forsyth, daughter of the Hon. John Forsyth.
Died in Cilumbus, Ga., on the 14th ult., Mrs. Ann Martin, aged 17. On the 29th March, Mr. Alexander Caswell, of Twiggs Co., Ga.
In Bristol R. I. on the 25th ult., Hon. John Howland, for many years Chief Justice of the Court of Common Pleas, of that dist.
At his residence in Halifax Co., Va., on the 21st April, Col. John Hill, in the 55th year of his age.

Issue of May 14, 1831

Married on Wednesday evening, by the Rev. Dr. Palmer, Dr. Thomas Eveleigh, to Mrs. Ann E. Hillard, all of this city.
On the 5th inst., by the Rev. Wm. Crook, Mr. Joseph M. Lawton, to Miss Elizabeth A. Thomson, eldest daughter of Benjamin Thomson, Esq., all of St. Peter's Parish, Beaufort District.
Departed this life, in this city, on the 6th inst., Maria Sophia, consort of Thomas P. Green, Esq., and daughter of Dr. Philip Moser.
In Edgefield Village,S. C. on the 6th inst., Henry W. Lowe, aged 44. On the 1st, Thomas Merriwether, aged 57. In Camden, on the 4th inst.,Mrs. Mary Logan, wife of Tyre J. Logan, aged 20. On the 30th ult., Mrs. E. Berry, wife of James B. Berry.
In Macon, Ga.,on the 29th ult., Mrs. Sarah A. Hill, aged 35. On the 1st inst., near Washington, Ga., Mrs. Lucinda Gresham, aged 25. In Putnam co., on the 28th ult., William Hathorn, aged one

hundred and nine years.

Issue of May 21, 1831

Married in this city, on Tuesday evening, the 17th inst., by the Rev. Mr. Gildersleeve, Mr. John William Sleigh, of Wadmalaw Island, to Miss Amanda Emerson Harrison, grand daughter of the late Saml Pillsbury.

In this city, on the 12th inst., by the Rev. Mr. Bachman, Mr. Wm. T. Hieronymous, of Kentucky, to Miss Mary Eliza, eldest daughter of Mr. John Carson.

Died in this city, on the 7th inst., Rachel C. Steele, only daughter of Mr. and Mrs. Wm. G. Steele, in the 7th year of her age....

On Saturday evening, April 16, at his residence in Canonborough, Capt. George R. Turner, sen. aged 56 years and 3 months, a native of Portsmouth, N. H., but during the last 18 years, a resident of this place.

In Hancock, Ga., on the 25th April, aged 21, Mrs. Julia Ann Ford, consort of Maj. Wm. P. Ford.

Died, in Lower Salem, Sumter district, S. C. on the 10th of May, 1831, Mrs. SArah Witherspoon, wife of Capt. John M. Witherspoon, in the 47 year of her age...for 30 years a member of the Presbyterian Church....

Issue of May 28, 1831

Married on Thursday evening, 19th inst.,by the Rev. Dr. Palmer, William Whittemore, Jr., Esq. of Boston, to Miss Lucinda Sophronia, daughter of John King, Esq., of this city.

In Pocotaligo, onthe 21st April, by the Rev. T. J. Young, Mr. James Bowman, of Prince William's Parish, to Miss Susan E. Burleson, of St. Peter's Parish.

Died at Natches, on the 19th April, Rev. Mr. Alexander Aikman. In Salisbury, N. C., on the 3d inst., John Gardiner, aged 77.

Issue of June 4, 1831

Married in Wilkes Co., Ga., on the 24th, Mr. Jas. S. Griffin, to Miss Eugenia, daughter of Wm. Grant.

Died in this city on the 18th ult., Mrs. Elizabeth C. Toomer, aged 44.

At Washington, Ga., on the 23d May, Maj. William G. Gilbert, aged 69, a very excellent citizen, and a devoted Christian.

Issue of June 11, 1831

Married at Mount Zion, Geo., on the 30th ult., by ____ Dr. Brown, Lieut. William Henry Harford, to Miss Maria M., daughter of Joseph Bryan, Esq.

In Edgefield Dist., S. C. on the 1st inst., R. I. Brooks, of Jasper Co., Geo., to Mrs. Sarah _____, of the former place.

Died in this city, on the 17th May, Mr. William Price,jr., in the 46th year of his age.

In Edgefield Dist., on the 25th ult., James Blocker, Esq., in the 56th year of his age.

At Providence, R. I., on the 28th ult.,Mr. Gershom Jones, formerly a merchant in this city.

Issue of June 18, 1831

Married in Bibb Co., Geo., on the 2d, Mr. Thos M. Ellis to Miss Eliza Cunningham, daughter of Rt. Cunningham, Esq.,of Jones Co.
Departed this life, on the 7th inst., at Pineville, Mrs. Ann Isabella Gibbes, wife of the Rev. Henry Gibbes, in the 34th year of her age.
Departed this life May 30th, 1831, at his residence in Chester Co., Pa., the Rev. Ebenezer Dickey, D. D., on the 60th year of his age, for 35 years pastor of the congregation of Oxford.
In New Haven, Con., on the 26th ult., the Rev. Claudius Herrick, aged 56....

Issue of June 25, 1831

Died on the 6th of June, at his residence, near Eatonton, Putnam Co., Ga., William Flournoy, Esq., in the 57th year of his age.
Death of Rev. Sutherland Douglass, son of Alanson Douglass, Esq. of Troy....New York Com. Adv. 16th inst.

Issue of July 2, 1831

Married in this city, on Tuesday evening, 28th ult., Charles C. Strobecker, Esq. to Miss Agnes Taylor, daughter of Paul Pritchard, Esq.
In New Orleans, on the 13th ult., Mr. John B. Leefe, of this city, to Miss Laura Louisa Baron.
Died in this city on the 24th ult., Mr. Edwin Gibbes, aged 31....
At Salisbury, N. C. on the 11th ult., Miss Margaret Brandon, aged 60.
At Danville, Va., on the 9th ult., Thomas Sparks, a minister of the Methodist Church, and a soldier of the Revolution.

Issue of July 9, 1831

Married on the 21st ult., Edwin R. Andrews, Esq. to Miss Mary Ann McKinley, daughter of Dr. C. E. Haynes, all of Sparta, Ga.
On the 30th ult., Mr. Wm. M. Cozart, of Washington, Ga., to Miss Sarah J., daughter of Col. D. Murray, of Lincoln county, Ga.
In Lincoln co., N. C. on the 26th May, Mr. Josiah Q. Hall, of Tennessee, to Miss Dorcas Sherrell.
Died on the 11th June, at the house of Mr. James Madison Frierson, in Greene County, Alabama, Mrs. Mary Freeman, in the 67th year of her age. She was the second daughter of John and Mary Witherspoon, sen., late of Midway, Sumter Dist., S. C....shortly before the close of the war, married Capt. Daniel Conyers...widowed...married Mr. Michael Freeman, a member of Steel Creek Church in MEcklenburg Co., N. C. They afterwards removed to Caldwell Co., Ky.... (eulogy)
Death of Rev. Nathaniel Dwight, D. M. of Norwich, Conn, the 10th child and 6th son of Honor. Timothy Dwight of Northampton, Mass. Utica Christian Journal
At Pendleton, S. C. on the 17th ult., Robert M'Cann, Esq., aged 68.
In Macon, Ga., on the 27th ult., Capt. Wm. J. Danelly, aged 30.
Died in Williston, Vt.,April 30, aged 70, Mr. Nathaniel Winslow, father of Rev. Miron Winslow, Missionary in Ceylon.

Issue of July 16, 1831

Married in Grafton, Mass., Mr. Joseph Leland, of the firm of J. Leland & Brothers, of this city, to Miss Charlotte Meriam, daughter of Mr. Joseph Meriam, of the former place.
In Monroe Co., on Thursday evening, the 30th ult., Mr. Samuel T. Beecher, to Miss Laura P. Brown, daughter of Dr. George A. Brown.
Died in this city, on the 12th inst., Mr. George Petrie, an officer of the Revolution, and for nearly 60 years a consistent Christian,; aged 75 years.
At St. Mary's, Geo., on the 26th ult., Mrs. Letitia, wife of Dr. Whipple Aldrich, aged 39.
In Macon, Geo., on the 6th inst., Mrs. Louisa C. Smith.
In Zebulon, Pike, Geo., on the 27th ult., Mrs. Mary Ann Neal, aged 19.
At Madison Springs, on 23d, Thomas W. Davies, of Burke Co., 45. At. Judge M'Tyre's, on Thursday night last, Joseph Crane, Esq., 70.

Issue of July 23, 1831

Married on the 13th inst., Philip Henry Echols, Esq. of Monticello, Ga., to Miss L. M. Berrien, daughter of John McPherson Berrien, Esq. of Georgia. In Wilkes co., on the 28th ult., Mr. John B. Kendrick to Miss Sarah Ann Powell.
At Georgetown, S. C. on the 13th inst., Miss Louisa Farley.
At Santee, on the 6th inst., Mr. Samuel Hopkins, a native of Maryland, but for years past a citizen of S. C.
At St. Augustine, E. F., on the 12th inst., Mrs. Mary J. Ashe, relict of Major Richard Ashe, of N. C.
At New Orleans, on the 7th inst., Major Charles Willard.

Issue of July 30, 1831

Married on the 19th of July, Dr. Myron Bartlett, Editor of the Macon Telegraph, to Miss Tabitha Napier Harvey.
In Salisbury, N. C., on the 12th inst., Mr. Alexander W. Buis, to Miss Malinda Fraley. Also, Mr. John Brinkle, to Miss C. Cauble.
Died in this city, on the 24th inst., Mrs. Catharine Futerell, aged 67.
In this city, on the 21st inst., Mrs. Sarah S. Boinest, in the 29th year of her age....
At Beechhill, St. Paul's Parish, on the 22d inst., Philip Girhan, infant son of John L. and Eliza M. Coburn.
At his residence at Spring Hill, Sumter District, Capt. Wille Belvin, in the 44th year of his age.
At Bethlehem, (Penn.), on the 3d inst., Rev. Jacob Van Vleck, a Bishop of the United Brethren's Church, in the 81st year of his age....

Issue of August 6, 1831

Married in Warrenton, Ga., on the 19th inst.,Mr. Vincent E. Riviere, to Miss Francis Wright.
On the 12th ult., Dr. James C. Rudisil, of Mecklenburg, N. C., to Miss Amanda C. Alexander, of Lincoln.
In Erie, Greene co., Ala., on the 19th ult., Mr. Wm. C. McAlpin, to Miss Ann Watson.
Died on the 17th ult., in Longtown, Kershaw dist., S. C., Mrs. Jemima Briggs. In Cheraw, on the 29th ult., Mr. Elisha Parker. At Spring Hill, Sumter District, on the 16th inst., Capt. Wilie Belvin, aged 44.

In Washington Wilkes co., Ga., on the 12th ult., Mr. James M. Anderson, one of the firm of John & James Anderson, aged 29. In Twiggs co. on the 24th ult., Mr. James Guerry.

Issue of August 13, 1831

Married in Meclenburg (sic) Co., N. C. on the 21st July, Mr. Rela F. Helms, to Miss Susan Kissiah. On the 26th July, Mr. N. Harris, to Miss Mary Gilmer.
Died at his residence in Mecklenburg county, N. C. on the 30th ultimo, Rev. John M. Wilson, D. D., Pastor of Rocky River and Philadelphia Churches in the 63d year of his age....(eulogy)
At Edingubrgh, on the 11th June, Rev. Dr. Meiklejohn, minister of Abercorn, and Professor of Church History in the University.
At his residence in the county of Prince Edward, Va., on the 24th of July, in the 81st year of his age, Mr. Thomas Tuggle, a soldier of the Revolution.
At Louisville, Jefferson County, Ga., on the 23d ult., Mrs. Susannah Flournoy (consort of Marcus A. Flournoy) aged 35.
At Columbus, Ga., on the 25th ult., Mrs. Francis Harris, wife of Edmund S. Harris, Esq. of Troup county, in the 30th year of her age.

Issue of August 20, 1831

Married in this city, on the 16th inst., by the Rev. Mr. Bachman, Mr. Andrew Reid to Miss Caroline Ballund, all of this city.
At Savannah, on the 11th, Mr. John Decker, to Miss Mary McLean.
Died in Lower Salem, Sumter Dist., S. C.,on the 25th July, Mrs. Rebecca Ann Rose, consort of Thomas Rose, Jun. and daughter of Capt. John M. Witherspoon, aged 18 years, 6 months and 21 days.
At Savannah, on the 11th inst., Mr. Bartlett M. Dozier, aged 40. In Beach Island, Ga., on the 4th inst., Daniel Savage, in the 41st year of his age.
In Stokes co., N. C., on the 31st ult., Capt. William Ancrum, of Camden, S. C., aged 60.

Issue of August 27, 1831

Married in Macon, Ga., on the 11th inst., Mr. George Wagnen to Miss Louisa Danelly. In Hancock co., Major Alfred M. Horton to Miss Rebecca Holmes. In Clinton, Mr. Thomas Ward, to Miss Emily C. Cam.
Died in Barnwell, S. C. on the 22d July, Mr. Isaac Redfield, aged 36.
In Twiggs co., Ga., on the 24th ult., James Guerry, Esq., 60. In Harris co., on the 7th inst., Dr. John Kennon. In Twiggs co., on the 28th ult., Mrs. Nancy Dupree, consort of Dr. Ira E. Dupree. In Bullock co., on the 4th of July last, Samuel Williams, a Revolutionary Soldier.
In Suggsville, Clark co., Ala., on the 22d June last, the Hon. William Mobley, aged 32.
At Shepherdstown, Va., July 15. Rev. Jacob Beecher, Pastor of the German Reformed churches of Shepherstown, Martinsburg, and Smithfield, aged 32.

Issue of September 3, 1831

Married on the 27th ult., by the Rev. Mr. Rogers, Capt. Edward Candler, of Marblehead, to Margaret, fourth daughter of Mr. Samuel Corrie, of this city.

On the 16th ult., Charles B. Clurkey, to Joanna E. Walsh, daughter of the late Patrick Walsh, of Beaufort, S. C.

On the 18th ult., St. Michael's Church, Trenton, N. J., by the Rev. Beasley, Prince Lucian Marat, second son of Joachim Murat, the last ex-king of Naples, to Caroline Georgiana youngest daughter of the late Major Thomas Fraser, of S. C.

Died in St. George's Parish, on the 17th ult., Mr. David Kittleband, aged 50 years, a native of the State, and long a resident of this city.

At Georgetown, S. C., on the 28th ult., Moses Fort., Esq., Cashier of the Branch Bank of that town. And on the 26th, Mrs. Elizabeth Carson, in the 88th year of her age.

In Augusta, on the 15th ult., Mrs. Kezia H. Russell, aged 36.

In Jefferson co., Ga., Jacob Young, in the 109th year of his age.

Issue of September 10, 1831

Married in Columbus, Ga., on the 30th ult., Dr. James C.Sullivan, to Miss Josephine O. Grinage. In Milledgeville, on the 28th ult., Mr. William R. Scott, to Miss Susan J. Pierce.

In Philadelphia, on the 25th ult.,Mr. R. Penot, of this city, to Miss P. Harriet C. Dauce, of that city.

Died in Beaufort, S. C., on the 18th ult., Captain William Burke.

In Baldwin co., Ga., on the 26th July, Jesse Doles, sen. in his 80th year. In Talbot co., on the 30th July, Col. John P. Blackmon, aged 46 years.

At Newbern, N. C. on the 29th ult., in the 29th year of his age, Charles G. Spaight, Esq. Attorney at Law.

At New-York, on the 25th ult., in the 62 year of his age, Mr. Isaac Moses, a native of this city, but for the last 25 years a respectable inhabitant of that city.

Issue of September 17, 1831

Married in Darien, Ga., on the 23d ult., Anon Kimberly, Esq. to Mrs. Sarah Street.

Died at Camden, S. C., on Sunday morning last,Mr. J. R. Carmell, Printer.

In Augusta, Ga., on the 7th inst., Mrs. Martin, wife of Edmund Martin. Also, Mr. Horace T. Campfield, aged 21, a native of Morristown, N. J. Near Darien on the 25th ult., Miss Ann Hutson, in the 50th year of her age.

At Wooster, Ohio, 27th ult., Rev. Ralph Cushman, general Agent of the American Home Missionary Society for the Valley of the Mississippi.

Issue of September 24, 1831

Married at Philadelphia, on the 13th inst.,by the Rev. Bishop Onderdonk,Robert Purvis, of this city, to Harriet Davy, daughter of James Forten, of that city.

Died in ths Parish of St. Thomas, on the 10th inst., Mrs. Elizabeth Harleston, consort of Col. John Harlestn, in the 32d year of her age. And on the 11th inst at the same place, Col. John Harleston, second son of the late Edward Harleston, Esq., in the 35th year of his age.

At his residence Uxbridge, on Ashley River, Richard Osborn, Esq., in the 48th year of his age.

At Georgetown, S. C., Thomas L. Jones, Esq. a native of this city. On the 15th, Rev. Henry H. Heath, an itinerant minister of the M. E. Church. Mrs. Sarah Hartley, consort of Mr. Thomas Hartley. Mr. Thomas Tarbox (who was drowned....). In Cheraw,

on the 12th inst., Mr. John Donaldson, in the 25th year of his age.
  On the 10th inst., at the Sand-hill, near Camden, Col. Thomas A. Hopkins, aged 28.
  On the 13th inst., William Hart, Esq. Counsellor at Law, aged 28 years. On the 7th inst., Miss Harriet Chesnut, daughter of the late Col. John Chesnut. On the 15th inst., Mr. Dan Carpenter, aged 29. Camden Beacon.
  At Salem, N. C. on the 6th inst., Samuel M'Clary, Esq. The deceased was on his return from the White Sulphur Springs, and was a resident of Charleston, S. C.

Issue of October 1, 1831

  Married in Burke co., Ga., on the 15th ult., Rev. Lawson Clinton, to Miss Angelina Gilstrap. In Greene co., on the 15th ult., Rev. Isaac Waddel, to Miss Sarah Daniel. In Lexington on the 1st ult., Mr. Thomas Wray, to Miss Theodocia Cardwell. In Salem, on the 15th ult., Mr. Wm. Cocke to Miss Sarah Hester. In Jones co., on the 19th ult., Mr. Edward W. Chapman, to Miss Penelope E. Mourton.
  Died in Augusta, Ga., Mrs. Elizabeth Salter, aged 76. On the 15th ult., Mr. David Smith. In Elbert co.,Mrs. Catharine Garret, 64. In Coweta, on the 27th August, Mr. Absalom Tarver, 74. In Twiggs on the 9th ult., Mr. Allen Dormon.
  At Pensacola, on the 14th ult., Lieut. Paul H. Hayne, of the U. S. Navy.
  On Thursday, the 25th of August, Mrs. Madison, in her 18th year, the last surviving sister of Patrick Henry. Bowling Green Ky. Adv.

Issue of October 8, 1831

  Died in Columbus, Ga., on the 24th ult., in the 18th year of her age, Mrs. Martha Lucas, widow of Robert Lucas, deceased.
  In Barnwell district, S. C. on the 21st ult., Miss Lucy J. Williams, aged 18.

Issue of October 15, 1831

  Died in Charlotte, N. C. on the 22d ult., in the 98th year of her age, Mrs. Elizabeth McGinn, a native of Pennsylvania, but for 60 years past an inhabitant of that county.
  In Sparta, Ga., on the 1st inst., John Lucas, Esq.
Died at Decatur, Ga., on the 17th Sept., Mrs. Maria, wife of Daniel Johnson (eulogy).

Issue of October 22, 1831

  Married at New York, on the 5th inst., Mr. Horace Waldo, of that city, to Mrs. Sarah C. H. Montgomery, of South Carolina.
  Died in this city on the 13th inst., Miss Eliza E. Vinyard, in the 17th year of her age.
  In Pendleton District, S. C., on the 9th inst., Mrs. Nancy W. Shand, aged 28, wife of Peter J. Shand, Esq. of this city.
  In Greenville, S. C., Mrs. Louisa M. Manigault, wife of Peter Manigault, Esq. of this city.
  In Burke co., Ga., Mrs. Mary Lavinia Brown, daughter of the late Washington Potter, of this city. Also, Mrs. Elizabeth, wife of Maj. Stephen W. Blount, aged 47. Rev. Wm. Young, Itinerant minister of the Methodist Episcopal Church, in the Oakmulgee Circuit, Ga. In Washington Co., Capt. Reuben N. Hecklin, aged 34.

At Bombay, suddenly, on the 5th Feb. last, Mrs. Mary Allen, wife of Rev. D. O. Allen, Missionary of the American Board of Commissioners for Foreign Missions.
At her residence in St. George's Parish, on the 27th ult., Mrs. Margaret Kittleband....

Issue of October 29, 1831

Married at Gillisonville, on Thursday evening, the 20th inst., by the Rev. John B. Van Dyck, Isaac B. Ulmer, Esq. of Prince William, to Miss Mary Ann Mulheron.
On the 12th inst., Dr. George A. Brown of Monroe co., to Mrs. Eliza Allen, of Milledgeville, Ga.
Died in Columbus, Ga.,on the 1st inst., Edmund Bugg, Esq., in the 37th year of his age. On the 29th ult., James M. Hitchcock, aged 21.
In Fairfield District, S. C., on the 29th Sept. 1831, Mrs. Mary, consort of Mr. John Johnston, Sen in the 64th year of her age (eulogy)
At Barnwell, on Sabbath, the 2nd inst., Samuel, son of W. C. and Eleanor Neely, aged 2 years and 4 months.

Issue of November 5, 1831

Departed this life on Tuesday, 18th ult., Mr. John G. Hamlet, a Mechanic, in the 26th or 27th year of his age. He was born and partly raised in Orange County, N. C., in the neighborhood of the Hawfields. He came into Lower Salem, Midway Congregation, Sumter Dist., S. C., last fall....
In Burke co., Ga., Robert T. Walker, Esq. In Camden co. on the 14th ult., in the 19th year of her age, Mrs. Isabella Melinda Hopkins, wife of Major P. Hopkins, of Darien, and youngest daughter of Gen. John Floyd.

Issue of November 12, 1831

Married on Wednesday last, by the Rev. Dr. Palmer, Mr. Horatio Leavitt, to Miss Maria C. King, all of this city.
Died at his residence Sandy Hill, St. George's Parish, on the 24th September, Daniel Cahill, Esq., in the 71st year of his age. He was a native of New Jersey, but for many years a resident of this state. He has left and widow and one son....

Issue of November 19, 1831

Married on Tuesday the 16th inst., by the Rev. Mr. Hanckle, Mr. F. B. Marion, to Miss Mary Ann S., youngest daughter of the late Elias Smerdon, both of this city .
On Tuesday evening, the 8th inst., by the Rev. Dr. Gadsden, Dr. A. F. Gadsden, to Miss Mary W. Edwards, both of this city.
On Wednesday evening, the 9th inst., by the Rev. Allston Gibbes, Alexander H. Mazyck, to Emma Anna, daughter of B. Gaillard, Esq. of this city.
In McPhersonville, died, on Tuesday 8th inst., Mr. Daniel Heyward, in the 25th year of his age.
At John's Island, on the 1st inst., in the 38th year of her age, Miss Elizabeth M. Sams--and, on the morning of the 5th, her only sister, Ariana H. Sams.
In Georgetown, S. C. on the 13th inst., Mr. Nelson L. Stow, a native of Milford, Conn., aged about 36 years.
In New-Orleans, on the 14th Oct., Mr. Felix L. Annely, a native of this city.

Issue of November 26, 1831

Death of Mr. Robert R. Gibbes, who departed this life on the 13th of October last, aged 62 years and 9 months (long eulogy)
In Edgefield, S. C. on the 17th inst., Col. Eldred Simkins, sen. At his residence on Deep Creek, in Pendleton district, on the 11th inst.,Mr. Charles Webb, aged about 64.
At his residence in Wilkes co., Ga., on the 31st of October, the Rev. William Davis, of the Baptist Church, aged 60 years and 7 months.

Issue of December 3, 1831

Married on Wednesday evening, by the Rev. Mr. Gildersleeve, Mr. Henry C. Tovey, to Miss Julia Ann Vardell, all of this city.
Died in Jasper co., Ga., Mary Rowan, daughter of Thomas Gilham, and the wife of William B. Richards (long account and eulogy)
Departed this life of sin and sorrow, in Newnan, Ga., Joseph Houston, infant son of J. Y. Alexander, aged 19 months. (poem)
Died at her residence, Sandy Hill, St. George's Parish, on the 13th of November, Mrs. Elizabeth Cahill, widow of the late Daniel Cahill, Esq. in the 59th year of her age...left an aged mother, a daughter and two sons....

Issue of December 10, 1831

Died in this city on the 8th Nov., Mr. John M. Tyler, aged 24 years. On the 4th inst.,Mr. Thomas J. Chitty.

Issue of December 17, 1831

Married on Thursday 1st Dec. in Beaufort by the Rev. Mr. Walker, Mr. Charles C. Dupont, of St. Luke's Parish, to Miss Rebecca D. Black, of the former place.

Issue of December 24, 1831

Married in this city on the 13th inst., by the Rev. Mr. Gillard(?), Ramon Leon Sanches, Esq. to Miss Ann S. Darrell.
In St. Luke's Parish, on the 14th inst., Dr. Edward Neufville Chisolm, to Miss Mary Elizabeth Hazzard.
Died in Williamsburg, S. C. on the 1st inst., Mrs. Jane Isabella James, consort of Wm. F. James, in the 18th year of her age...left husband and infant daughter.
At Savannah, Ga., on the 8th inst., Mr. Joseph B. Herbert of the House of J. B. Herbert & Co. And on the 14th Mr. Joseph Habersham. At Athens, on the 8th inst., Mrs. Ann Hull, relict of the Rev. Hope Hull, at a very advanced age.

Issue of December 31, 1831

Married on Monday evening, 26th inst., by the Rev. Mr. Bachman, Mr. Edward Paslay of Laurens District, to Miss Caroline D. Blum, of this city.
In Columbia, S. C. on Wednesday the 21st inst., by the Rev. T. Gouldine, D. D., Mr. Richard S. Gladney to Miss Jane A. McMillan.
Died at the residence of her father, Windsor Hill, Columbia Co., Ga., on Thursday morning, the 15th inst.,Miss Sarah A., daughter of Capt. Henry Gibson....

Issue of January 7, 1832

    Married on the evening of the 1st inst.,by the Rev. M. Gildersleeve, Mr. William Lacoste, to Miss Sarah Grier, all of this city.
    Died at his residence in the parish of Green's Farms, Fairfield Co., Conn., on the 30th Nov., the Rev. Hezekiah Tipley, D.D., aged 89...(eulogy) N. Y. Observer.

Issue of January 14, 1832

    Married at Fayetteville, Fayette co., Ga., on the 22d ult., Mr. Peter D. Mann, to Miss Elizabeth S. King.
    Died at his residence near Church Hill, Abbeville district, S. C., John Cameron, Esq. near the close of his 55th year...member of the Presbyterian Church....
    At Macon, Ga., on the 4th inst., Reuben Turner, a native of Burke county, aged 33 years.
    On the 1st January, in New-York, Mrs. Sarah wife of Drake Mills, formerly a resident of this city.

Issue of January 21, 1832

    Married at Williamsburg, S. C. on Thursday the 29th ult., by the Rev.Mr. McEwin, James G. White, Esq. of Sumter to Miss Mary E. McCrea, youngest daughter of Thomas McCrea, Esq.
    Died in this city on the 14th inst., John S.Rhodus, in the 17th year of his age.
    At his plantation on Ladies Island on the 6th inst., in the 53d year of his age,Isaac Perry Fripp, Esq.

Issue of January 28, 1832

    Married on Thursday 12th inst.,by the Rev. Mr. Osborn, Mr. Wm. H. Houston, to Miss Eliza Martha Emeline, eldest daughter of Moses Whitesides, Esq. of Christ Church Parish.
    On the 17th inst.,at Edgefield Village, S. C. by the Rev. S. K. Talmage, the Rev. Horace S. Pratt, of St. Marys, Ga. to Miss Isabel Drysdale, of the former place.
    Died in this city on the 24th inst., Mrs. Ann Eliza Gilliland.
    At Georgetown, S. C. on the 22d inst., Mr. William G. Palmer, aged about 33 years.
    In Lancaster dist., on the 19th inst., Mrs.Ferriby Royal.

Issue of February 4, 1832

    Married on Tuesday evening, by the Rev. Mr. Gildersleeve, Mr. Thomas R. Vardell, to Miss Amelia A. Tovey, all of this city.
    At Gravel Hill, St. Stephen's Parish, on Thursday, 26th ult., by the Rev. D. J. Campbell, Dr. Peter P. P. Palmer, of St. John's to Miss Harriet Jerman, youngest daughter of the late John Palmer, Esq.
    In Darlington district, S. C., on the 19th ult., by the Rev. N. R. Morgan, John G. Gregg, Esq. of Marion district to Miss Louisa McCall, daughter of Thos. McCall, deceased, of the former place.
    At Columbia, S. C. on the 24th ult., in the Chapel at Barhamville, by the Rev. Dr. Goulding, Dr. Elias Marks, to Mrs. Julia Pierpont Warne.
    Died in this city on the 16th inst., Mrs. Elizabeth Timme, in the 63d year of her age. On the 30th ult., William Neilson Bell, aged 19 years and 1 month.

Issue of February 11, 1832

Married on Tuesday evening the 7th inst., by the Rev. Dr. Palmer, Mr. Samuel L. Bennett, of Santee, to Miss Martha Frances Woolley, of this city.
On the 1st inst.,by the Rev. Mr. Bachman, Mr. George S. Hacker, to Miss Anna Maria Butler, all of this city.
Died on the 3d ult., of Consumption, at the residence of B. R. Johnson, near Landsford, Chester district, S. C., Mr. William Cox Young, of this city, former Editor of the Greenville Republican, aged 36 years.
At White Oak Creek, in Lancaster district, S. C. on the 17th ult., Mr. William Shiver, in the 69th year of his age....served with Marion in the war of the Revolution.

Issue of February 18, 1832

Married on the 9th inst., by the Rev. William Carlile, Mr. Joel H. Berry, to Miss Martha E. Simpson, both of Anderson District, S. C.
On the 13th January, by the Rev. J. Haddon, Mr. John Murphy, to Mrs. S. Carter, both of Clark co., Alabama.
On the 29th January, by the Rev. Mr. Murphy, Rev J. Hadden, of Green Co., Alabama, to Mrs. Martha Bronson, of Claiborne.
In Cincinnati, Ohio, on the 12th ult., Capt. H. L. Branham, editor of the Farmer's Reporter, to Miss Augusta L. Moore.
Died lately at his residence in Rowan Co., N. C., in the 82d year of his age, Mr. John Barr....(eulogy)

Issue of February 25, 1832

Married on Wednesday evening last, in St. Paul's Church, by the Rev. Mr. Hanckle, Frederick A. Porcher, Esq. to Miss Rebecca B. Rhodes, youngest daughter of the late Dr. Nathaniel Rhodes, of Beaufort.
Died in this city on the 15th inst.,Mrs. R. White, consort of George K. White. On the 15th, Mr. John Freer.

Issue of March 3, 1832

Married in the Baptist Church, on Thursday evening, the 23d ult.,by the Rev. Mr. Manly, Thomas Pinckney Harvey, Esq. of this city, to Catharine Burdick, daughter of Henry Tew, of Newport, Rhode Island.
On Thursday evening, the 23d ult., by the Rev. Mr. Balst, Mr. J. Albert Hopkins, to Maria Sutherland, daughter of the late Mr. James Mitchell, all of this city.
On Wednesday evening, the 22d ult., by the Rev. Mr. Brown, Mr. Victor Durand, to Miss Azelie, daughter of Mr. Francis Duboc, all of this city.
Died in Prince Williams Parish, on the 6th ult., Mr. Pphraim (sic) Mikell Mackay, aged 25.
Of Consumption, near Havana, Island of Cuba, on the 13th Jan. last, Dr. Edwin D. Faust, of Columbia, S. C., aged 24.

Issue of March 10, 1832

Died in this city on the 24th of January, Mrs. Ann Eliza Gilleland, wife of William H. Gilleland, aged 40 years, 3 months and 11 days...a native of this city...(eulogy)
On the 23d ult., at the residence of his mother, in Upper All Saints Parish, Mr. Thomas Livingston, aged about 26 years.

Issue of March 17, 1832

Married on Wednesday morning, the 7th inst., in St. Philip's Church, by the Rev. Dr. Gadsden, John Postell, Esq. of Coosawhatchie, to Miss Emma R., daughter of William Payne, Esq. of this city.
On Tuesday evening last, by the Rev. Dr. Gadsden, Dr. Hamilton S. Hawkins, of the U. S. Army, to Miss Ann Alicia, second daughter of Thomas P. Chifelle, Esq. of this city.
On the 13th inst., by the Rev. Mr. Brown, Mr. Jackson McClelland to Miss Amanda Margaret, daughter of the late Peter Murphy, Esq. of this city.
Died at his plantation, Federal Hill, Prince William's Parish, on the 12th ult., James Bowman, Esq.

Issue of March 24, 1832

Married on Thursday evening the 15th inst., by the Rev. Mr. Leadbetter, A. J. Bessent, Esq., Attorney at Law, of St. Mary's, Ga., to Miss Eliza, third daughter of Capt. William Fair, of this city.
Died in this city on the 17th inst., Mr. John T. Elsworth, aged 25.
At the house of Mr. Wm. Thompson, on Wed., 21st inst., Mary M., only surviving daughter of Samuel Allen, of New York... aged 19 years.

Issue of March 31, 1832

Died on the 20th inst.,at the residence of Francis Withers, Esq. on Sampit, Mrs. Mary Warham, aged 74.
In Milledgeville, Ga., on the 17th inst.,Mr. John P. Smith, of the tetanus or lockjaw.
In Leon city, Florida, on the 2d inst., Mrs. Jane C. Randolph, wife of Thomas E. Randolph, U. S. Marshal.

Issue of April 7, 1832

Married on the 21st ult., at Ysclocsy, in the Parish of St. Barnard, La., by the Rev. Mr. Clapp, Daniel Elliott Huger, Jr., Esq., to Miss Carolina Matilda Proctor, daughter of Col. Stephen Proctor.
Died in this city, on the 25th inst., Mr. E. S. Duryea, one of the proprietors of the City Gazette, in the 26th year of his age. On the 1st inst., Mr. Robert E. Cochran, in the 59th year of his age.
In Beaufort, S. C., on the 13th ult., Mrs. Martha Givins, in the 55th year of her age.
At his residence in Columbia co., Ga., on the 29th ultimo, in the beginning of the 37th year of his age, the Rev. Jabez P. Marshall...of the Baptist Denomination.

Issue of April 14, 1832

Married on Thursday morning the 12th inst.,by the Rev. Dr. Palmer, Rev. Thaddeus Pomeroy, of Gorham, Maine, to Miss Harriet R. Ruberry, of this city.
At Carlisle, Pa., on the 29th ult., the Rev. Adam Gilchrist, of Walterborough, S. C., to Miss Mary Blaine, of the former place.
Died at his plantation on Edisto Island, on the 11th ult., Mr. Benjamin Whaley, in the 41st year of his age.
In Philadelphia, on the 1st inst.,Mrs.Alice Izard, widow of the late Ralph Izard, Esq. of S. C., in the 87th yearof her age.

Issue of April 21, 1832

Married on the 12th inst., by the Right Rev. Dr. Bowen, Joseph W. Allston Esq. to Mary K., eldest daughter of the late William Allan, Esq.

Near Winnsborough, S. C. on the 10th inst., by the Rev. Wm. Brearly, Rev. George W.Boggs, Missionary to Bombay, to Mrs. Isabella W. Adger, daughter of Wm. Ellison, Esq.

Died at Petersburg, Ga., at the house of M. Stokes, George Leavitt, only child of the Rev. A. Foster, aged 4 months. They stopped a day at the house of these friends on their way from Pendleton to New Hampshire, and the child died suddenly of the croup. At Athens, Dr. James Nesbit, an Elder of the Presbyterian Church, aged 68.

Issue of April 28, 1832

Married on the 2d inst., at Hartwick, Otsego Co., N. Y., by the Rev. G. B. Miller, Rev. William D.Strobel, formerly of this city, to Miss Emma Cornelia Clark, daughter of Jerome Clark, Esq. of the former place.

Death of James Madison Frierson, who died at his residence in Greene co., Ala., on the 31st ult...a native of Williamsburgh district, S. C. (long eulogy)...left wife and five children.

Issue of May 5, 1832

Married on the 18th ult., by the Rev. Mr. Bachman, Mr. William Welling to Miss Margaret Mary Dawson, both of this city.

In St. Johns Berkley, 26th ult., by the Rev. Mr. Schudy, Dr. William D. Gourdin, to Miss Eleanor E. Gaillard, daughter of B. Gaillard, Esq.

Departed this life in Greenesborough, Geo., on the 22d inst., Mrs. Charity Grimes, consort of Mr. Thomas W. Grimes, in the 55th year of her age...a member of the Presbyterian Church...(eulogy)
E. H. Macon.

Issue of May 12, 1832

Married on the 24th ult., by the Rev. Dr. Palmer, Dr. Thomas Lee, of St. George's Dorchester, to Caroline, daughter of the late Jacob H. Alison, Esq. of St. Bartholomew's Parish, Planter, deceased.

Died in Hall county, Ga., on the 27th ult., Russell Baldwin, Lieut. U. S. Navy. In Augusta, 1st inst., S. C. Catlin, aged 22.

Issue of May 19, 1832

Died on the 9th inst., at his residence near Columbia, Col. Henry P. Taylor, in the 47th year of his age.

Issue of May 26, 1832

Married in Hamburg, S. C., on the 18th inst., Mr. George M. Thew, to Miss Elizabeth G. Mayson.

In Columbia co., Ga., on the 1st inst., Mr. George M. Magruder, to Miss Mary Emily Heggie. Onthe 15th, in Louisville, Mr. John J. Heard, to Miss Cynthia Ann Battey. At. St. Mary's on the 25th ult., Edward Hopkins, Esq. to Miss E. Dufore. In Twiggs co., on the 10th inst., Dr. Joshua R. Wimberly, to Miss Caroline Starr.

Died in Augusta, Ga.,on the 17th inst., Mrs. Elizabeth A. Heard, in the 21st year of her age.

Issue of June 2, 1832

Married in this city on the 22d ult., by the Rev. Dr. Dalcho, Mr. E. Wilmot Walter, to Miss Sarah Pritchard, only daughter of the late Captain William P. Dove.
Died in Mazyckborough, on the 22d ult.,Mr. Richard F. Howard, aged 53.
In Columbia, S. C., on the 18th ult, Mrs. Mary Player, daughter of Gen. Hampton, and wife of Col. Player, of Fairfield.
In Pendleton, on the 17th ult., Mrs. Piety Davis, aged 80.
In Augusta, Ga., on the 20th ult., Col. Samuel Warren Mays, late of Pendleton District, aged 27.

Issue of June 9, 1832

Married on Tuesday evening, the 5th inst., by the Rev. Mr. Ledbetter, Robert Nesbit, Esq. of Georgetown, S. C. to Miss Mary, daughter of John Hamilton, Esq. of this city.
On the 31st ult., by the Rev. Mr. Bachman, William Burn, Esq., to Miss Margaret L. Syfan, both of this place.
Died in Chester, S. C., on the 1st inst.,David Daniel, Esq., aged 63 years.

Issue of June 16, 1832

Died at Philadelphia, in the 71st year of his age, Andrew Bayard, President of the Commercial Bank of that City.

Issue of June 23, 1832

Death of Mrs. Russell, of Charleston. (eulogy)
In this city, on Saturday, the 16th inst., Mrs.Esther Palmer, consort of Job Palmer, aged 74 years, 10 months....
At Montgomery, Ala., William Preston, infant son of Norborne Ratcliffe, late of Walterborough, S. C....

Issue of June 30, 1832

Married on Sunday last, by the Rev. Allston Gibbes, Frederick Smith, Esq. of Manchester (England) to Henrietta Macbride, eldest daughter of the late Dr. James Macbride of this city.

Issue of July 7, 1832

Married in this city on Tuesday 2d inst., by the Rev. Dr. Palmer, Mr. Saml. N. Stevens, to Miss Mary S. Tennent
By the Rev. Mr. Gilman, Mr. T. C. Jenkins, to Miss Amanda Moore, all of this city.
Died on the 18th June, at the residence of her son, Samuel N. Snow, near M'Gil's Hill, Lowndes Co., Ala., Mrs. Margaret Snow, relict of Capt. Wm. Snow, of Williamsburgh Dist., S. C.,aged 81 years and 6 months. (eulogy)

Issue of July 14, 1832

Married in this city, on Monday evening, in the 2d Presbyterian Church, by the Rev. Dr. McDowell, Rev. Thomas Smith, to Miss Margaret M., eldest daughter of James Adger, Esq.
On Tuesday evening by the Rev. Mr. Gildersleeve, Mr. M. P. Walsh, Merchant to Miss Mary Vardell, all of this city.
Death of Major Thomas White, at his residence in Green Co., Alabama, on the 15th June inst., in the 66th year of his age...a native of Union District, S. C.   A. C. Storey

Issue of July 21, 1832

   Died at Wasington, Ga., William W. Smyth, Esq. one of the Editors of the News.
   In Edgefield Dist.,on the 12th inst., Thomas B.Tompkins, a member of the Edgefield Bar.

Issue of July 28, 1832

   Died at Montgomery, Alabama, on the 3d inst., MaryF. consort of Norborne Ratcliffe, late of Walterborough; and on the same day, their son Thomas Campbell....

Issue of August 4, 1832

   Died near Milledgeville, Ga., on the 20th ult., Rev.S. B. Townsend, of the Presbyterian Church, a native of Rhode Island. In Macon, on the 20th ult., in the 35th year of his age, Mr. Mortimer R. Wallis...one of the first settlers of Macon, and held the office of Post Master, ever since the establishment of that place. In Columbia co., on the 24th ult., William A. Carson.

Issue of August 11, 1832

   Died in New-York, on the 1st inst., Mrs. William S. Ogden, of this city, aged 30 years.
   At New-Orleans, on the 27th July, Mary Lavinia, wife of Richard Brenan, Esq. and daughter of the late Joshua Brown, in the 26th year of her age.
   In Norfolk, on the 1st inst., Rev. Saber Munsell, of the Presbyterian Church.
   In New Brunswick, the Rt. Rev. John Cross, D. D., Bishop of the Protestant Episcopal Church, in the State of New-Jersey, in the 70th year of his age.

Issue of August 18, 1832

   Married on the 8th inst., by the Rev. Dr. Capers, Mr. Samuel Burrows, to Miss Martha T., only daughter of Mr. Chrietzberg, all of this city.
   At Barnwell C. H. on the 1st inst., by the Rev. William H. Brisbane, Henry M. Tompkins, Attorney at Law, to Mrs. Carolina W. Hamilton.
   Died on the 2d inst., at Mount Clio, Sumter District, in the 22d year of his age, Mr. Wm. C. Lacoste...a native of this city, and resided her until last January, when he was married and moved to Cheraw, where he formed a mercantile connexion with a brother ....
   At New-York, on the evening of the 7th inst., Mrs. Catharine Clarkson, aged 66 years, relict of the late Rev. William Clarkson, of S. C., and daughter of the late General William Floyd.

Issue of August 25, 1832

   Married in this city, on Thursday evening, 16th inst, by the Rev. McDowell, Capt. William Kerrison, to Miss Henrietta, fourth daughter of Daniel McIntosh, all of this city.
   Died in this city on Sabbath morning, Mrs. Louisa C., wife of Mr. George Pringle, in the 40th year of her age, a member of the 2d Presbyterian Church....
   In this city, on Friday the 17th inst., James Gorden Cogdell, aged 26 years.

Issue of September 1, 1832

Married in this city on Tuesday Evening last, by the Rev. Dr. McDowell, Thomas Waring, Esq., to Miss Lydia Catharine, youngest daughter of the late John Ball, Esq.
At Milford, Jefferson co., on the 16th ult., Dr. James B. Smith, to Miss Susan, daughter of Dr. John J. Jenkins.
Died in Jefferson, Jackson co., Ga., on the 19th ult., Col. Thomas W. Murray, of Lincoln county.
On the 22d ult., on Horse Creek, in South Carolina, Mr. Hezekiah Richardson, a native of South Coventry, Connecticut, who came to the South for the purpose of selling books.

Issue of September 8, 1832

Married at Church Hill, Abbeville dist., S. C. on the evening of the 23d August, by the Rev. Moses Waddel, D. D., Mr. Richard B. Cater, to Miss Jane L. Patterson, both of this place.
Died, on Wednesday morning the 5th inst., in the 50th year of her age, Mrs. Anna Coburn, widow of the late John Coburn, Esq. of Beech Hill, St. Paul's Parish, leaving a numerous family....

Issue of September 15, 1832

Died in this city on the 7th inst., Mr. Jacob Davis, aged 37, a native of Roxbury, Mass., but for many years a resident of this city.
At Bull's Hill, St. Luke's Parish, on the 9th inst., Mr. John Guerard. In St. Matthew's Parish, on the 4th inst., Capt. Abram Felder, aged 77--a patriot of the Revolution.
In Raleigh, N. C. on the 3d inst., Dr. Sterling Wheaton, a native of Providence. At Baltimore, 31st ult., Rev. Saml. Knox, aged 75, for many years President of the Baltimore College.

Issue of September 22, 1832

Died in Augusta, Ga., Mrs. Sarah, wife of John Gulmarin, 40. In Burke co., Mrs. Mourning Wooten, at an advanced age. At Lumpkin, Stewart co., James Wood, Esq., attorney at Law. At Athens, on the 4th Mrs. Isabella, wife of Samuel Galliber.
Near Cincinnati, Ohio, Mrs. Alvira, wife of Rev. David Root, aged 39.

Issue of September 29, 1832

Married in this city on the 20th inst., by the Rev. Mr. Hanckell, Mr. William Washington Ancrum, to Miss Harriet Horry, daughter of the late Laurens M. Dawson.
On Wednesday evening last, 26th inst., by the Rev. Mr. Bachman, Mr. William D. Ellis, to Miss Charlotte J. McIntosh, all of this city.
In this city on the 25th inst., by the Rev. Mr. McDowell, Mr. Henry Morton, of Richmond, Va., to Miss Florinda B., daughter of Mr. Benjamin Wood, formerly of Philadelphia.
At Westborough, Mass., by the Rev. M. Rockwood, Mr. James H. Taylor, of Sunderland, Mass., to Miss Elizabeth Ann, daughter of Joseph Tyler, of this city.
Died in this city on the 23d inst., D. Jennings Waring, Esq. At Clements' Ferry, on the 22d inst., Mrs. Ann Elizabeth Pennington, in the 59th year of her age.

Issue of October 6, 1832

Married in Beaufort, S. C. on the 25th ult., Mr. John G. McCall, of Scriven co., Geo., to Miss Jane Rebecca Dopson, of the former place.

In Macon, Ga., on the 23d ult., Mr. Alfred M. Hobby, to Miss Ann Eliza Danelly.

Death of George W. Cox, at Hawkinsville, on the 22d inst....
Savannah Georgian, 29th ult.

Issue of October 13, 1832

Died at his residence in Beech Island, S. C., on the 1st inst., Dr. Thomas S. Mills, aged about 49 years...member of the Presbyterian Church....

On Tuesday morning, the 18th of September, Mrs. Mary Howe, wife of Rev. Professor Howe, of the Theological Seminary at Columbia, S. C., and daughter of Rev. Jedediah Bushnull, of Cornwall, Vermont, aged 24.

At the residence of her only child, Col. George Walton, of Pensacola, on the 12th of Sept. last, Mrs. Dorothy Walton, relict of the Hon. George Walton, one of the signers of the Declaration of Independence and for several years one of the Judges of the Superior Court of the State of Georgia.

Issue of October 20, 1832

Died, near Robertsville, on the 29th ult., Mrs. Hannah Hunt, the relict of the late Capt. Joseph Hunt, about 65 years of age... gone to spend the summer with an only sister, and whilst on a visit at Major Maner's in the same neighborhood, was taken with country fever...a native of Norwalk Co., but for more than 30 years a resident of Charleston....

Issue of October 27, 1832

Married in this city on Monday evening last, by the Rev. Mr. Manly, Mr. Benjamin J. Evans, to Miss Lydia Ann Perdriau.

On Thursday evening, by the Rev. Mr. Manly, Mr. Wm. H. Bee, to Miss Mary Axson.

In Winnsborough, on the 11th inst., Mr. Felix Long, to Miss Mary A. McCreight.

In Washington, Ga., on the 10th inst., Mr. John H. Dyson, to Miss Emily C. Sneed.

In Macon on the 4th, Mr. Fred. Sims to Miss Susan Wells.

In Savannah, Ga., on the 6th, Mr. A. P. Dauvergne, to Miss Louisa G. Perony.

Died in this city on Tuesday, the 16th inst., Mrs. Catherine Prioleau, widow of Samuel Prioleau, Esq., aged 88.

Died at his residence on Long-cane, in the District of Abbeville, S. C., on the 17th inst.,Major Uel Hill, in the 79th year of his age. He was a native of Caroline County, Va., and a soldier of the Revolution...member of the Baptist Church....

Issue of November 3, 1832

Married on Tuesday evening last, by the Rev. Mr. Manly, Mr. William Hopson Toney, of Greenville District, to Miss Susan Berney, of this city.

On Tuesday evening, 25th ult., by the Rev. Mr. Hanckel, Col. C. G. Memminger, to Miss MaryWilkinson, second daughter of Dr. Wilkinson, of this city.

At Baltimore, on the 23d ult., by the Rev. Mr. Johns, John Macpherson Brien, Esq. of Frederick co., Md.,to Miss Isabel Ann Baron, daughter of the late Dr. Baron, of Charleston.

Died in this city, on the 26th ult., in the 29th year of her age, Miss Mary Smith.

In Edgefield, S. C., on the 6th ult., Stephen Tompkins, Esq., aged 66.

Issue of November 10, 1832

Married on Wednesday evening last, by the Rev. Mr. Gildersleeve, Mr. Peter J. Suder, to Miss Elvira, daughter of Mr. Archibald Whitney, all of this city.

On Sunday evening last, by the Rev. Mr. Mitchell, Mr. Walter Jardoe, to Miss Mary McLelland, all of this city.

At Washington, Ga., on the 25th ult., Major Andrew J. T. Semmes, of Washington, to Miss Antoinette Tait, daughter of Gen. James M. Tait, of Elbert County.

Died at Cincinnati, Ohio, on the 24th ult., Louis J. Gourdin, Esq. Attorney at Law, aged 23 years,formerly of this state.

Issue of November 17, 1832

Married in this city on the 12th inst.,by the Rev. Dr. Dalcho, James Sinkler, Esq. to Miss Margaret Heyward, eldest daughter of John Huger, Esq.

On the 8th inst., by the Rev. Mr. Buist, Alfred Y. Drayton, Esq., to Miss Martha Sommers, youngest daughter of Charles E. Rowand, Esq.

On Thursday evening, 8th inst., by the Rev. Mr. Gadsden, Mr. J.C. Millar, to Miss Anna Booth.

In Milledgeville, Ga., on the 28th ult., Mr. James M. Williams, to Miss Nancy Williams.

In Savannah, Ga., on the 8th inst., Mr. C. C. Bennett, to Miss Thirza Ann Brantley.

In Sutuga, Ga., on the 8th inst.,Major Felix A. M. Sherrod, of Alabama, to Miss Margaret McGran, of Augusta.

Died in Hampstead, on the night of the 6th inst., Master Edward Bounetheau, son of E. W. Bounetheau, in the 14th year of his age.

At Columbia, S. C. on the 20th ult., Mrs. S. Moffat, who had hardly reached the prime of life.

At Pendleton, S. C., on the 24th ult., in the prime of life, Mr. Harvey Drake, of Edgefield.

In the vicinity of Hillsborough, N. C.on the 31st ult., Mr. Martin Palmer, aged 89.

At Savannah, Ga., 8th inst.,Mrs. Adelai Forbs, of New-York.

At Athens Ga., 29th ult., Thos K. J. Adams, aged 29.

At Macon,Ga., 31st ult., Mr. Reuben Burroughs, 49.

Died at Lancasterville, on Sabbath night, the 23d of Sept., Mrs. Sarah C. Dunlap, wife of Samuel Dunlap, Esq.and eldest daughter of Col. J. H. Witherspoon. (eulogy)

Issue of November 24, 1832

Married on the 15th inst., by the Rev. Mr. Trapier, Alexander H. Brown, to Miss Sarah Ann, eldest daughter of the late John Calhoun, all of this city.

On the 15th inst., by the Rev. Mr. Hanckel, Mr. Joseph H. Young, to Miss Caroline, second daughter of Mr. John Howard, all of this city.

In the Circular Church, on the 15th inst., by the Rev. Mr. Taylor, Mr. Thomas P. Green, to Miss Selina K., daughter of the

late Charles Snowden, all of this city.
In Beaufort, S. C., on the 8th inst., by the Rev. Joseph Walker, Dr. Charles Atkins, of St. Luke's Parish, to Miss Mary Nelson Agnew, of that place.
Died at Bradford's Spring, S. C., 11th inst.,Mrs.Lucy C. Bailey, wife of the Rev. R. W. Bailey, aged 32....daughter of the late Hon. Reuben Hatch, of Vermont....

Issue of December 1, 1832

Married on Tuesday evening, last, by the Rev. Mr. Gildersleeve, Mr. Fleetwood Lanneau, to Miss Gracey Windsor, all of this city.
Departed this life at New-Orleans, on the 2d ult., Master William C. Jones, a native of this city....

Issue of December 8, 1832

Married on the 20th ult, by the Rev. Mr. Crook, Mr. Thomas A. Hayden, to Miss Adeline C. Happoldt, all of this city.
In Columbia, S. C. on the 26th ult., by the Rev. Dr. Goulding, Dr. James Postell Jervey, of this city, to Miss Emma Gough Smith, second daughter of the late Dr. Edward D. Smith, Professor of Chemistry in the S. C. College.
Died at New-Orleans, on the 15th ult, Mr. D. H. W. Whiting, turner, formerly of this city.
In Sparta, Hancock co., on the 20th ult., Capt. Duke Hamilton, in the 62d year of his age.

Issue of December 15, 1832

Died in this city on the 21st ult., in the 91st year of her age, Mrs. Margaret Gowdey.
In Augusta, Ga., on the 1st inst.,Mrs. MaryAnn Belinda White, aged 57. In Milledgeville, on the 3d ult., Mr. Horace Steadman, aged 28, a native of Berlin, Conn.

Issue of December 22, 1832

Married on Tuesday evening, by the Rev. Arthur Buist, Rev. E. T. Buist, to Miss Margaret, eldest daughter of Mr. John Robinson, all of this city.
On the 27th Nov., at the residence of Major R. F. Quarles, Greene Co.,Alabama, by the Rev. J. H. Gray. Mr. John N. Waddel, to Miss Martha A. Robertson, both of Abbeville District, S. C.
Died in Florida, on the 8th ult., Richard Morgan, formerly of Milledgeville, Ga.

Issue of December 29, 1832

Married on Monday evening last, by the Rev. Mr. Hanckle, Mr. Joseph Provost, to Miss Elizabeth Dunham, youngest daughter of the late John Simpson, Esq. all of this city.
On Monday last,by the Rev. Dr. Capers, Mr. Stephen Thomas, to Miss Mary Amanda Adeline Lea, of Wilmington, N. C.
On the 20th inst., at St. James' Santee, by the Rev. Mr. Lance, Dr. Charles L. Gaillard, to Miss Anne D. Gaillard, daughter of the late David Gaillard, Esq. of that Parish.
Died in this city on the 22d inst., in the 86th year of her age, Mrs. MarySmith, relict of Roger Smith, Esq.
At his residence, near Greenville, S. C. on the 21st inst., Mr. Rawlins W. Lowndes, son of the late Hon. William Lowndes.
In Columbia Co., Ga., on the 5th inst., Thomas H. Sergeant, aged 30 years.

Issue of January 5, 1833

Married on the 1st inst., by the Rev. Mr. Smith, William Daniel Logan, Esq. to Miss Mary Ann, only daughter of Capt. Joseph Young, of this city.
In Augusta, Ga., on the 27th ult, Dr. Paul F. Eve, to Miss Louisa Sarah, daughter of Maj. George L. Twiggs.
Died in Burke co., Ga., 14th ult., Col. William R. Caldwell.
At Milledgeville, 23d ult., Rev. Thomas Rhodes, of Jasper co., for many years a member of the Baptist Church and a Minister of the Gospel.

Issue of January 12, 1833

Married on Thursday morning 3d inst., by the Rev. Dr. McDowell, Mr. Thomas Jervey of Christ Church Parish, to Miss Angeline, youngest daughter of R. Dorrill, Esq. of this city.
Died at the seat of John Mayrant, Esq., near Statesburg, S. C., on the 3d inst., Mrs. Isabella Myarant, aged 70 years, having been his consort 50 years.
At Washington, N. C., on the 4th inst., John G. Blount, Esq., in the 81st year of his age....

Issue of January 19, 1833

Married on the 27th ult., Richard Allen Gantt, Esq., to Maria Louisa, daughter of Col. Frederick J. Hay, all of Barnwell Dist.
Died on the 29th ult., near Lexington Court House, S. C., Mr. Christopher Fitzsimons, aged 21.

Issue of January 26, 1833

Died on Edisto Island, 17th inst., Miss Anna H. Thomas, formerly of St. Stephen's Parish, in this State.
In Augusta, Ga., 19th inst., Miss Isabella Morrison, aged 26.
In Athens, 10th inst., Mrs. Martha M. Lane, consort of Mr. Benjamin Lane, of Clark co., aged 51.

Issue of February 2, 1833

Married on Wednesday evening the 30th ult., by the Rev. Mr. Gildersleeve, Mr. Peter Lanneau, jr., to Miss Mary, only daughter of Mrs. Elizabeth Johnston, all of this city.
Died in this city on the 24th ult., Mrs. Elizabeth B. Burger, consort of Samuel Burger, Esq.
In Augusta, Ga.,on the 21st ult., Mr. John Marshall, Sexton of the city.

Issue of February 9, 1833

Died, on the 16th Nov. last, Henrietta Amanda, daughter of James S. and Anna Glen, aged 5 years and 6 months. This is the fourth child these afflicated parenst have consigned to the dust in eleven weeks....
departed this life on the 30th ult, Capt. Isaac Fithina... left behind him at Darien, Ga.,a wife and four children and numerous relatives in other places....interred in the burying ground of Trinity Church.

Issue of February 16, 1833

Married at Montgomery, Alabama, on the 7th inst., Mr. Norborne Ratcliffe, late of Walterborough, S. C. to Mrs. Jennetta Edwards,

all of this place.
Died at the residence of her husband, East Florida, Jan. 2, 1833, Mrs. Ann C. Howe, the amiable consort of Charles Howe, Esq., formerly of this city...born in Providence, R. I., August 1800, brought up in Seekonk, Mass., and removed to Charleston, S. C., Nov. 1816, thence to Florida in May 1828....

Issue of February 23, 1833

Died near London, the 29th of Dec., Jonathan Lucas, Sen., Esq.,for many years a respectable inhabitant of this city.
Suddenly at Athens, Ga., Mr. Moses Beard, aged about 80 years, a soldier of the Revolution. At Macon, on the 21st ult., Mrs. Elizabeth Erwin, wife of Leander A. Erwin, Esq. formerly of Athens.
In Salisbury, n. C., Mrs. Elizabeth Hughs, aged 50. In Rowan, on the 16th inst., Mrs. Sarah Long, relict of Wm. Long deceased, aged about 35.

Issue of March 2, 1833

Married on Wednesday evening by the Rev. Dr. McDowell, Mr. James J. McCarter, to Miss Elizabeth, daughter of Jonathan Bryan, Esq. all of this city.
Died in Milledgeville, Ga., on the 16th ult., Mrs. Sarah Ann Daniel, aged 27. On the 14th ult., Mrs. Jane F. Hudson, wife of Irby Hudson, Eatonton.

Issue of March 9, 1833

Married on Monday evening last, by the Rev. Mr. Manly, Mr. Henry H. Berry, to Miss Adelena A. V. Roberts, all of this city.
Died in Milledgeville, Ga., on the 16th ult., Mrs. Sarah Ann Daniel, in the 27th year of her age, wife of John W. L. Daniel, Esq., of that place and daughter of John P. Graham, of Richmond Co., N. C...a member of the Presbyterian Church...left a husband and three infant children.
In Warren co., Ga.,on the 22d Feb., George Cotton in the 70th year of his age, a Soldier of the Revolution....
Near Waynesboro, Ga., on the 23d, Dr. Southworth Harlow, in the 53d year of his age, a native of Plymouth, Mass., but for 28 years a citizen of Georgia...member of the Presbyterian Church.

Issue of March 16, 1833

Married on Tuesday evening last, by the Right Rev. Bishop Bowen, Thomas Leger Hutchinson, Esq., to Miss Lydia Julia, eldest daughter of George Macaulay, Esq., all of this city.
Died in Columbia, S. C., on the 22d ult., John R. Davis, Esq. Near Columbia, after a long illness, Mrs. Ann Hampton, consort of Col. Wade Hampton, and daughter of the late Christopher Fitzsimons, Esq.

Issue of March 23, 1833

Married on the 14th inst.,by the Rev. Mr. Bachman, Mr. George R. Manson, to Miss Eleanor Virginia Hagan, both of this city.
In Sunbury, Ga., on the 7th inst., Dr. James D. Stevens, to Miss Jane Mary, daughter of Mr. Paul H. Wilkins.
Died in the city of New-York, on the 27th Feb., in the 25th year of her age, Mrs. Emma Cornelia, wife of the Rev. Wm. D. Strobel, and eldest daughter of Capt. Jerome Clark, of Cooperstown, Otsego county, New-York.

In Montgomery, Ala., 1st inst., Mr. H. White, a native of Georgetown, S. C., aged 18. Same place, 2nd inst., T. D. Huff, a native of Edgefield District, S. C.

Issue of March 30, 1833

Married on Thursday evening,the 21st inst., by the Rev.A. C. Walker, Mr. John W.Chitty to Miss Julia A. Purse, both of this city.
Died on the 22d inst., in the 34th year of his age,Mr. Chs. Winthrop jr. of the firm of F. & C. Winthrop, a native of this city. On the 17th, Mr. John Haig Blake.
In Greenville, S. C., 15th inst., George Russel, Esq. aged 54.
In Clark co., Ga., 18th ult., Reuben Ransom, sen., a Revolutionary Soldier, aged 79.
In Fayetteville, N. C.,11th inst., Mr. Gilbert Carmichael, aged 68, for the last 30 years a Ruling Elder of the Presbyterian Church.

Issue of April 6, 1833

Married in Augusta, Ga., on the 28th ult., Mr. Wm. M. Adams, to Miss Clemantine C. Broadwater, of Columbia, S. C.
Died in Granville co., N. C., on the 8th ult., Col. William Hunt, in the 76th year of his age. He was a native of Virginia, and a Soldier of the Revolution. Near Enfield, N. C., on the 14th ult., in the 71st year of his age, the Rev. Henry Bradford, a Minister of the Methodist Protestant Church.

Issue of April 13, 1833

Died on Saturday, March 30th, Mr. Charles O'Neal...in the 51st year of his age, at Summerville, a native of Ireland. He early emigrated to this country, and became a resident in Charleston....
Departed this life on Saturday, March 30th, at Granby, Mrs. Narcissa Sondley, wife of Mr. Richard Sondley, of Columbia....

Issue of April 20, 1833

Married at Beaufort, S. C., on the 11th inst., David Wilson, Esq., to Mrs. Jane M. Ellis, all of that place.
In Athens, Ga., on the 4th inst., Rev.Mr. Hampden C. Carter, to Miss Ann D. Cole.
Died at Columbia, S. C. on the 30th of March, John H. Carwile, a member of the Baptist Church in that place. (eulogy)
At Norfolk, on board the U. S. ship Java, on Thursday the 12th inst., in the 22d year of his age,Midshipman John Middleton, of the U. S. Navy, a native of Charleston, S. C.

Issue of April 27, 1833

Died in this city, on Wednesday, Mr. Jonathan Brown, of Utica, New York.

Issue of May 4, 1833

Married on the 27th ult., by the Rt. Rev. Dr. Bowen, the Rev. Paul Trapier, Rector of St. Andrew's Parish, and St. James' Church, to Miss Sarah Russell Dehon, only daughter of the late Bishop Dehon.

On Thursday the 28th March, at Lincolnton, Ga.,by the Rev. J. L. Kennedy, Mr. Francis F. Fleming to Mrs. Susan Ann Beall, both of the county of Lincoln.

Died in this city on the 14th ult., Miss Harriet Lee, daughter of Wm. Lee, Esq.

At Mount Pleasant, in the parish of St. John's Berkley, S. C., on the 24th ult., Francis Marion, Esq., the grand nephew and adopted son of the revolutionary patriot and soldier, Gen. Francis Marion.

In Pendleton, S. C. on the 7th ult., Andrew Liddell, sen. aged about 83. In Abbeville, 13th ult., Major General Edward Ware.

At Wilmington Island, Ga., on the 23d ult., Col. Solomon Shad, aged 74, a soldier of the Revolution.

In Lincoln co., N. C. 17th ult., Rev. Thomas Espey, a zealous Minister of the Gospel in the Presbyterian Church.

In Northampton, Mass., Miss Hannah Drayton, sister of Hon. Wm. Drayton, of S. C.

Issue of May 11, 1833

Died in Augusta, Ga., on the 1st inst.,Mrs. Eugenie Carre, formerly of this city.

At Matanzas, recently, Col. John L. Wilson, a native of this State.

Issue of May 18, 1833

Married on Wednesday evening by the Rev. Mr. Gildersleeve, Mr. Jonah M. Venning, to Miss Elizabeth Bell, all of this city.

On the 7th inst., at Middleton Place, in St. George's Parish, by the Rev. Dr. Adams, Edward J. Pringle, to Maria Henrietta, daughter of the Honorable Henry Middleton.

Died in Abbeville District, S. C. on the 13th ult., Major Edward Ware.

In Morgan co., Ga., 24th ult. Wade Hemphill, Esq. In Warren co., 1st inst.,Major Robert A. Beall, sen. aged 69.

Issue of May 25, 1833

Married in Columbia, S. C. on the 1st inst., in Columbia, S. C., by the Rev. Mr. English, Mr. John Palmer of this city, to Miss Martha Howell McGarrity, of the former place.

In Lincolnton, Ga., on the 9th inst.,by the Rev. J. Leland Kennedy, Mr. Joshua Daniel, to Miss Mary Ann Lamar, all of that place.

Death of Mrs. Rebecca Hertz, consort of Mr. J. Hertz, who died on Wednesday morning, the 15th inst., in the 41st year of her age. (eulogy)

Issue of June 1, 1833

Died in this city on the 7th May, Emily, daughter of Mr. A. P. Gready, aged 16 months and 16 days.(Poem)

Issue of June 8, 1833

Married at Columbia, S. C. on the 30th ult., by the Rev. Dr. Goulding, William Jesse Taylor, Esq. of that place, to Miss Alexina Jessie, daughter of the late William Muir, esq. of this city.

Died in this city on the 26th ult., the Rev. Henry Gibbes, late Rector of All Saints Parish.

Miss Sarah W. Read, youngest daughter of Dr. Wm. Read. Died on the 15th ult., Mrs. Sarah E. Corbett, aged 28 years and 8 months....(eulogy)
In Savannah, on the 2d inst., Mrs. Catharine Bollough, a native of Charleston S. C. in the 72d year of her age.

Issue of June 15, 1833

Died at Columbia, S. C. on the 29th May, Mr. Ephraim Peck, in the 38th year of his age.

Issue of June 22, 1833

Departed this life on the 13th inst., on Edisto Island, Mrs. Mary C. Lee, wife of the Rev. Wm. States Lee, pastor of the Presbyterian Church of that place...left husband and ten children.
In Augusta, Ga., 4th inst., Gen. Robert Tuttle, of Burke Co. in the 30th year of his age.
Near Burnt Corn, in Conecuh co., Ala., 22d ult., Mr. James Salter, aged 66 Mr. S. was a native of S. C.

Issue of June 29, 1833

Married on Sunday evening last, 23d inst., by the Rev. Dr. Leland, Mr. Theodore B. Guy, to Miss Sarah Cudworth, all of this city.
Died on the 17th of May, at his residence in Cannonborough, Capt. Daniel McNeill, in the 87th year of his age...a native of boston, Mass., for many years an Officer in the Naval and Revenue service of the U. S. and for the last 25 years a resident of this city.
Died in Greenesborough, Ga., on the 10th inst., Mrs. Sarah Cummins, consort of the late Francis Cummins, D. D., in the 83d year of her age....
In St. Mary's, Ga., on the 6th inst., Mr. John Bachlot, Sen., in the 74th year of his age--a Soldier of the Revolution.

Issue of July 6, 1833

Death of Mr. John Anderson Mills, on the 7th June, at the residence of Capt. Harris, Sumter district...graduated from S. C. College with distinction. (eulogy) Furman Institution, June 26th, 1833.
On the 1st of June, at Philadelphia, Peter Fayssoux, Esq. of S. C., and formerly of the U. S. Navy.

Issue of July 13, 1833

Married on Wednesday evening, 3d inst., by the Rev. Mr. Manly, Mr. Charles C. Woolley, to Miss Amanda M. Clenette, both of this city.
Died, at his residence in Hampstead, Charleston Neck, on the 12th of June, Mr. Thomas Screven, a member of the Charleston Baptist Church. (eulogy)...in the 59th year of his age.
In Greene co., Alabama, on the 21st of June 1833, Mrs. Jennet Cooper Wilson, wife of Mr. James S. Wilson, aged 21 years, one month,1 day, leaving an infant daughter three days old....
In New York, on the 29th ult., William Elliott Huger, aged 27 years, son of Judge Huger of this city. On the 18th ult., Rev. Girardus A. Kuypers, D. D. in the 67th year of his age, and for 44 years Pastor of the Reformed Dutch Church of New York.

Issue of July 20, 1833

Married on the 3d inst.,by the Rev. Dr. Gadsden, George Edwards, Esq. to Mrs. Henrietta Aiken, all of this city.
Died in this city on the 10th inst., Mr. John Speissegger, Sen. in the 70th year of his age.
At Savannah, Ga.,on the morning of the 4th inst., Mrs. Mary Martha Neufville, consort of Rev. Edward Neufville and daughter of William B. Bulloch, Esq. aged 24 years and 28 days.

Issue of July 27, 1833

Departed this life at his summer residence in Cedar Swamp, Williamsburg District, on Sunday the 21st inst.,Thomas McCrea, Esq., in the 79th year of his age...a soldier of the Revolution (eulogy and account).
Died on the 18th of June, in the 58th year of his age, at his residence near Winnsborough, Mr. William Ellison, Sen. the father of Mrs. Boggs, wife of one of the Missionaries now in India....
On the 12th inst., near Athens, Ga., Mrs. Cynthia Carr, consort of William A. Carr, Esq., aged 33 yeras and 7 months.

Issue of August 3, 1833

Died at Georgetown on the 25th inst., D. V. Berton, M. D., aged 32. At Pickens district, S. C., a few weeks since, the Rev. George Vandiver, a soldier of the Revolution and clergyman of the Baptist persuasion....
In Savannah, on the 11th inst., James Hamden, son of Col. Wm. A. Thompson, aged two years and eleven months.
At New Orleans, on the 17th inst., Edward Bernie, a native of this city.

Issue of August 10, 1833

Died suddenly, on the 21st ult., at his residence in All Saints, S. C., Mr. Lewis Siau, aged 56 years, formerly a resident of Georgeotwn. In Yorkville, 29th ult., Gen. R. D. M'Lean, aged 40. In Lancaster, 25th ult., Mr. Samuel Stewart, aged 27.
At Lexington, Ky., on the 11th June last, Mr. James Bunch, a native of S. C., and for many years a resident of the former place.

Issue of August 17, 1833

Died in this city on the 2d inst., Mar. Caroline Hammett, in the 60th year of her age.
At Pineville, S. c.,on the 4th inst., in the 21st year of his age, Dr. Edward Ravenel.

Issue of August 24, 1833

Married in Augusta, Ga., on the 13th inst.,Mr. Wm. Pritchard, to Mrs. Jane Adelaide Dimon. In Milledgeville, on the 11th inst., Mr. Edward W. Miller, to Miss Pamelia Ann Wilkinson. In Monroe co. on the 1st inst.,Mr. Wm. M. Pledger, to Miss Parmelia J. Nolls.
Died in this city, on the 5th inst., Mr. Charles Lowrey, Sen., aged 51 years and 5 months.

Issue of August 31, 1833

Married on Tuesday the 13th inst., by the Rev. Wm.Carlile, Mr. William H. Harris, late a graduate of Franklin College, Ga., to Miss Mary Ann Caldwell, both of Abbeville District.

Died in York Dist., S. C., 11th inst., Mr. Wm. Rowell. On the 10th, Walter M'Carter, a soldier of the Revolution. Near Edgefield C. H., 22d inst., Capt. John Simkins.

Issue of September 7, 1833

Died in this city, Mrs. Hester B. Merritt, in her 31st year. In the neighborhood of Bradford Springs, S. C., 24th ult., Rev. Joseph B. Cook, a Preacher of the Baptist denomination.

In York, 27th ult., Mrs. Martha M'Cullough, consort of Wm. M'Cullough, aged 55.

Issue of September 14, 1833

Married in St. Luke's Parish, on the 5th inst.,by the Rev. Mr. Walsh, Thomas S. Gillison, Esq. to Miss Mary Julia Brooks, of Savannah.

Near, Abingdon, Va., Mr. Robt. Campbell, to Mrs. Catharine Watkins, both of Augusta, Ga.

Died in Walterborough, on the 1st inst., Mrs. Margaret Ann Ford, consort of the late Malachi Ford, in the 68th year of her age.

In Stewart Co., Ga., on the 14th ult., Rev. Moses Mathews, of the Methodist Church, in the 60th year of his age....

In Liverpool, on the 31st July, Mr. John McDowell, a partner of the house of Andrew McDowall & Co. of Charleston, S. C.... He was accompanied to Liverpool by his cousin, Dr. Porter...Dr. Porter died the day following.

At Pendleton, S. C. on the 1st inst., in the 78th year of his age, Mr. Thomas Ogier, one of the soldier of the revolution, and for more than half a century, an inhabitant of this city...a native of London, where he was born 25th April 1755....(eulogy)

On the 5th inst., in Kingstree, Williamsburg district, on bilious fever, David Ramsay Witherspoon, M. D. in the 27th year of his age.

Issue of September 21, 1833

Died suddenly, in Marion district, S. C. on the road side, not far from his residence, Mr. William Bigham...member of Hopewell Presbyterian Church....

Died on the 5th inst., at Kingstree, Williamsburg dist., S. C., Dr. David Ramsay Witherspoon...left a father and mother.... (eulogy).

In Savannah, Ga., on the 12th inst., Mrs. Sarah H. Preston, sister of the Rev. W. Preston, Pastor of the Independent Presbyterian Church of that city.

At New Rochelle, N. Y., on the 11th inst., Edward B. Weyman, aged 40 years, a native of S. C., and son of the late Catharine Weyman.

Issue of September 28, 1833

Married on Thursday evening, by the Rev. B. Gildersleeve, Mr. Wm. Benson, to Miss Zilpah Locke, sister of Mr. George B. Locke, of this city.

Died in New-York, on the 18th inst., of Paralysis, Mr. Timothy Street, of the firm of T. Street & Co. of this city.

On the 9th inst., in Wilkes co., Ga., Mr. William A. Grant, in the 67th year of his age.

Issue of October 5, 1833

Married in this city, on Sunday evening, 29th ult., Mr. Dexter Leland to Miss Susan E. Smerdon, daughter of the late Elias Smerdon, of this city.

Died near Pendleton, S. C. on the 25th Sept., Mr. John Schulz, of this city.

At his residence in MarionDistrict, on the 11th ult., Mr. Joseph Davis, in the 83d year of his age.

In York Dist., on the 20th ult., William Gazaway, a resident of that District, and for many years, a minister of the Methodist Episcopal Church.

In Georgetown, D. C., 22d ult., Stephen B. Balch, D. D.,Pastor of the Presbyterian Church in that place,aged 87, and for the last 55 years Pastor of that Church.

In Jefferson co., Florida, 5th ult., Mrs. Margaret Skennal, a native of Edgefield, S. C.

Issue of October 12, 1833

Married on Wednesday evening 2d inst., by the Rev. Mr. Walker, Mr. James T. Godfrey of Marion District, to Miss Anges M. Taylor, second daughter of the late Capt. Joseph Taylor, of this city.

On Wednesday evening, 2d inst.,by the Rev. Mr. Walker, Mr. Henry W. Smith, to Miss Adeline S. Taylor, youngest daughter of the late Capt Joseph Taylor, all of this city.

Died on the 1st inst., Dr. Isaac A. Johnson, leaving to lament...an interesting family....

In the village of Pineville, in this State, Charles Stevens, Esq. a gentlemen....(eulogy)

Issue of October 19, 1833

Died at Pineville, on the 1st inst., in the 66th year of her age, Mrs. Catharine Porcher, relict of hte late Philip Procher, Esq., of St. Stephen's Parish.

At Georgetown, S. C., on the 7th inst., in the 19th year of her age, Mrs. Charlotte M. C. Fort, consort of John E. Fort, Esq.

Issue of October 26, 1833

Married on the 16th inst.,by the Rev. Dr. Capers, Mr. David Haig, to Miss Isabella Brown, all of this city.

In Camden, S. C.,on the 16th inst., by the Rev. W. M. Kennedy, the Rev. W. Murrah to Miss Mary S., second daughter of Everard Cureton, Esq.

Died in this city, on leaving the Steam Ship, David Brown, on Wed. morning last,Miss Eliza de Lancey, daughter of the late John de Lancey, of West Chester Co., N. Y. She left the house of her uncle, the Hon. Joseph C. Yates, of Schenectady, in company with J. D. Watkins, Esq. and family of Lexington, Ga....

In this city, on the 13th inst., in the 54th year of his age, Col. Henry H. Bacot, universally respected and esteemed.

Issue of November 2, 1833

Married on the 15th ult., by the Rev. Dr. Capers, Mr. Thomas C. Sheppard to Miss Mary Jane Leefe, both of this city.

At the residence of Col. Eustis, Fort Monroe, Norfolk Harbor, Hon. Joel R. Poinsett, to Mrs. Mary Pringle, both of Charleston.

Died on the 19th ult., in the 56th year of his age, Capt. Samuel Bacot, of Darlington dist., S. C. In Camden, 18th ult., Mr. T. Warren, aged 51, a native of Newport, R. I., but for the last 25 years a resident of Camden. At Silver Bluff, Edgefield Dist., Mr. I. N. Pearson, of Union dist., aged 24.

Issue of November 9, 1833

Married in Beaufort, S. C., on the 31st ult., by the Rev. Mr. Walker, Dr. Thomas L. Ogier, of this city, of this city, to Miss Maria Willard, daughter of the Hon. William J. Grayson.

On the 23d of October, by the Rev. R. W. James, Mr. Johnson J. Knox, to Miss Sarah Ann, only daughter of Robert Witherspoon, Esq., all of Sumter District.

Died on the 21st ult., Mrs. Mary Stillman, consort of Mr. James Stillman, in the 42 year of her age, leaving a husband and five children...a native of Norwalk, Conn, but for the last 18 years a resident of this city.

Died, in Salem, Sumter District, S. C., on the 29th of Oct., Robert Wilson, Esq., in the 68th year of his age...member of Mount Zion Church...(eulogy).

Departed this life at Columbia, S. C., on the 21st Oct., Mrs. Francis Caroline Coe, in the 26th year of her age...a member of the Protestant Episcoapl Church for many years...left husband and four children....

Issue of November 16, 1833

Married by the Rev. R. W. Bailey, Hopkins G. Charles, Esq., to Miss Louisa M. DuBose, all of Darlington, S. C.

On the 22d of October, by the Rev. Mr. Cater, Major Hampdon McCann, to Miss Narcissa Walker, daughter of Wm. Walker, Esq. all of Pickens district, S. C.

Died, on the 9th inst., in this city, at his residence where he had lived for 58 years, Mr. Bazile Lanneau, at the advanced age of 88. Mr. L. was of French origin, whose ancestors were among the first settlers in Acadie, now Nova Scotia. He was born in Balisle, a little town not far from Annapolis Royal about 60 miles from Halifax, as near as he could ascertain on the 1st November O. S. 1745...with an elder brother, mother and several sisters was brought to Charleston....(eulogy)

Death on 22d of Sept of Mrs. Jennet Gladney, in the 76th year of her age...upwards of 40 years a member of Jackson's Creek Church, Fairfield Dist.... (eulogy)

Issue of November 23, 1833

Married on Tuesday evening 12th inst.,by the Rev. Mr. Manly, Mr. William Gray of Columbia, S. C. to Mrs. Maria Eliza Jenkins, of this city.

On Thursday evening, 14th inst.,by the Rev. Mr. Forrest, Valentine Ruger, Esq. of St. Bartholomew's Parish, to Miss Sabina Elliott, daughter of James Turnbull, Esq. of this city.

On Thursday evening, 14th inst., by the Rev. Dr. Palmer, Mr. William H. Ehney, to Miss Susan Pickering Lloyd, all of this city.

Died on the 28th of Oct. last, in Williamsburg district, S. C., Mr. William Wilson, in the 71st year of his age...a Rev. soldier and served under Marion...an elder in the Presbyterian Church.

Issue of November 30, 1833

Married on the 17th inst.,by the Rev. Dr. Capers, Mr. William P. Forbes to Miss Ann Catharine, second daughter of the late Mr. Thomas Sigwald, all of this city.
On the 21st inst.,by the Rev. Mr. Lee, on Edisto Island, B. Rivers Carroll, Esq. of this city, to Miss Eliza Adeline, daughter of Ephraim Mikell, Esq. of Edisto.
At Bridgewater, Mass., Mr. Benjamin Clough of Saubornton, to Miss Carolina Bowers, of B., both deaf and dumb....

Issue of December 7, 1833

Died at his residence, Liberty Hill, in St. John's Berkley, John Frierson, Esq. in the 56th year of his age. On the 21st ult., in Fairfield, Major Joshua Player, in the 52d year of his age. In Pickens district, on the 23d ult., Mr. Samuel Earle, aged 73 years...in the Revolutionary war and was many years a Representative in Congress. At his residence in S. C., on the 14th ult., John David Mongin, one of the last Revolutionary worthies, aged 71 years and 11 months.
At his residence on Pee Dee, on the 23d ult., Major Edward Drayton Perry.
Near Georgetown, on the 21st ult., Mrs. Samuel Green, aged about 60 years.
In Georgetown, on the 23d ult., Mrs. Hannah Tate, in the 70th year of her age.
At her residence on Black River, on the 25th ult.,Mrs. Margaret Ford, aged about 75 years.
On Black River, on the 25th ult., Mr. Francis G. Coachman, aged about 28 years, second son of John Coachman, Esq.
Married on the 26th ult., in St. Paul's Church, by the Right Rev. Dr. Bowen, William Izard Bull, to Gracia C. daughter of the late Robert J. Turnbull, all of this city.
On the 28th ult., by the Rev. Mr. White, Mr. James C. W. Legare, to Miss Lydia Ball, second daughter of Col. John Bryan, all of this city.
On Tuesday evening, 26th ult., by the Rev. Mr. Hanckel, Col. William Yeadon, to Miss Elizabeth Steedman, daughter of Col. Charles J. Steedman, all of this city.
On Thursday 28th ult., by the Rev. Mr. Hanckel, Edward Rutledge Lowndes, third son of James Lowndes, Senr. to Mary Lucia, eldest daughter of the late John Guerard, all of this city.
On Thursday evening, 28th ult., by the Rev. Mr. Hanckel, William Hazard Wigg, Esq. of Beaufort, S. C. to Margaret Euphamia, second daughter of Samuel Patterson, Esq. of this city.
On Monday evening, the 2d inst.,by the Rev. John Dickson, Mr. Henry M. Bruns, to Miss Margaret, third daughter of the late Robert Stewart, Esq.,Merchant, all of this city.
On the 28th ult., at Beaufort, S. C., by the Rev. Daniel Bythewood, Frederick A. Tupper, Merchant, Savannah, Ga.,to Miss Louisa W.,daughter of David Turner, Esq., Post Master of said place.

Issue of December 14, 1833

Married on Saturday evening last, by the Rev. Mr. Bachman, Mr. Peter Ehney, to Mrs. Mary Lowry, all of this city.
In St. Paul's Parish, on the 5th inst., by the Rev. Mr. Gadsden, Mr. Wade Hampton Schutz, to Miss Rosa S., only daughter of John Boyle, Esq., formerly of the same Parish.
Died in Wilmington, N. C., 7th inst., Mrs. A. Brown, aged 44, wife of R. W. Brown, Esq. merchant of that place.

In Philadelphia, 5th inst.,Rev. Dr. E. Fisk, Professor of Ecclesiastical History and Church Government in the Western Theological Seminary.

Issue of December 21, 1833

Married in this city on the 10th inst.,by the Rev. Mr. Hanckell, John B. Guerard, Esq. to Miss Ann, third daughter of the late John Simmons Bee, Esq.

Died on the 21st ult. near Georgetown, S. C., Mrs. Sarah Green, widow of the late Mr. Samuel Green, deceased, in the 65th year of her age...a member of the Presbyterian Church....

Died, onthe 23d ult., the Rev. John McMillan, D. D....Ch. Herald

Issue of December 28, 1833

Married in this city on the 19th inst., by the Rev. Mr. Capers, Mr. James Laurens Frazer, to Miss Elizeth (sic) Martha, eldest daughter of the late Mr. James Mitchell.

On the 18th inst., by the Rev. Dr. Bachman, Mr. Geo. E. Ring, to Miss Eliza R., eldest daughter of A. Bolles, Esq. all of this city.

On the 19th inst., by the Rev. Mr. Gilchrist, James C. A. Johnston, Esq. of Savannah, Ga., to Miss Caroline S. Stevens, daughter of Jacob Stevens, Esq. of Colleton.

On the 12th inst.,by the Rev. Mr. Carlisle, Mr. Thos. C. Harris, toMiss Hanna Caroline Harris, both of Abbeville District.

Died on the 9th ult., at his late residence in Clarksville, Ga., Mr. Thomas B. Cooper, late of S. C.

Issue of January 4, 1834

Married on Tuesday evening, 24th ult., by the Rev. Mr. Manly, Mr. James W. Brown, to Miss Mary Chatburn, both of this city.

On the 26th ult., by the Rev. Thomas Young, Julius G. Huguenin, Esq., to Miss Eliza Louisiana, eldest daughter of George W. Morrell, Esq. all of St. Luke's Parish.

Died in this city on the 12th ult., Mr. Job P. Miller, in the 50th year of his age, leaving to mourn his loss, and widow and other relatives.

Died at Appling, Columbia co., Ga.,on Thursday the 19th ult., Laird Fleming, Esq., in the 34th year of his age...left a widow, an aged mother and numerous relatives....

Issue of January 11, 1834

Married in the Presbyterian Church, John's Island, on the 23d ult.,by the Rev. Mr. White, Mr. I. S. Keith Legare, to Miss Emma Catharine, eldest daughter of Wm. Mathews, Esq.

In Winnsboro, S. C. on Thursday evening last, the 2d inst., by the Rev. Wm. Brearly, Joseph Woodword, Esq. to Miss Malinda R. Bones.

Departed this life on Friday night, 27th ult.,William Jones, Esq., of Columbia Co., Ga.,aged nearly 73 years...(eulogy)

Died on Tuesday the 17th inst.,Mrs. Martha E. Berry, late consort of Joel H. Berry, and daughter of Archibald Simpson, of Anderson District...(eulogy)....

Issue of January 18, 1834

Married on Tuesday evening, the 7th inst., by the Rev. Mr. Hanckel, J. Drayton Dawson, Esq. to Miss Cecelia J., daughter of the late Dr. Richardson, all of this city.
    On the 8th inst., by the Rev. J. Witherspoon, Dr. George Reynolds, Ruling Elder of the Presbyterian Church, in Camden, S. C., to Miss Mary Chesnut, daughter of Col. James Chesnut, of Mulberry Grove.
    On the 9th inst., by the Rev. J. Witherspoon, the Rev. Urias Powers, Pastor of the Presbyterian Church at Cheraw, to Miss Henrietta Perkins, daughter of Benjamin Perkins, Esq. of Pine Tree.
    At New-York, on the 2d inst., Lawrence Kearney, Esq. Captain in the U. S. Navy, to Miss Josephine C. Hall.
    Died in this city, on the 6th inst., after a long and painful illness, Mrs. Jane Peters, in the 60th year of her age.
    At Columbia, S. C. of consumption, on the 1st inst., Miss Jane Arabella Faust, second daughter of Daniel Faust, of that town.
    Died on the 11th inst., at the Park, Prince William's Parish, Mrs. A. F. Gregorie...left a large family....

Issue of January 25, 1834

Married at Accabee Lodge, St. Andrew's Parish, on Thursday evening, the 16th inst., by the Rev. Mr. John Forrest, Mr. James Davidson, to Miss Agnes Morison, all of this city.
    On Thursday evening, 16th inst., by the Rev. Mr. Hanckel, Mr. James Robertson, Esq. to Penelope Bentley, daughter of Dr. Paul Weston.
    Departed this life in Abbeville Dist., on Sunday morning, the 12th inst., in the 22d year of her age, Miss Elmira R. A. Wilson, eldest daughter of the late Robert Wilson....(eulogy)

Issue of February 1, 1834

Married on the 21st ult., Mr. William Bacon, to Miss Mary H. Linton, daughter of Dr. A. B. Linton, all of Athens, Ga.
    Died in the village of Lancaster, on the morning of the 2d ult., in the 48th year of her age, Mrs. Jane Witherspoon, consort of Col. J. H. Witherspoon. (eulogy)

Issue of February 8, 1834

Married on the 1st January, by the Rev. Mr. Alexander at the residence of John C. McGehee, Esq., in Florida, Mr. James E. Broome, of S. C., to Miss Amelia Ann, daughter of Agram Giles Dozier, Esq., deceased.
    Died at his residence on Colonel's Island, Liberty Co., Ga., on the 17th January, in the 63d year of his age, Major Andrew Maybank...a member of Midway Church....(eulogy)

Issue of February 15, 1834

Married in this city on the 6th inst., by Rev. William Wightman, Capt. William Riggs, of Colleton District, to Miss Rachel M. Baily of Charleston District.
    on the 4th inst.,in Union District, by the Rev. J. Harrison, Mr. James Bankhead, to Miss Cynthia Moorhead.
    Departed this life on the 7th inst., Mr. William M'Call, only son of the late Hext M'Call, Esq. in the 20th year of his age.

Died at May River, St. Lukes Parish, S. C. on the 6th inst., Dr. James A. Gray.

Issue of February 22, 1834

Married in this city on Tuesday evening last, by the Rev. Mr. Hanckel, Mr. Aylwin Lawrence Prince, to Miss Mary, second daughter of the late Mr. George Peters.

On Tuesday Evening last, by the Rev. Mr. Bass, Dr. George Hunt, of Orangeburg, S. C., to Mrs. Catherine C. Moore, of this city.

On Wednesday evening last, by the Rev. Mr. Bass, Mr. William F. Anderson, of St. John's Berkley, to Miss Frances Lavinia C. Williams, of this city.

On Wednesday evening last, by the Rt. Rev. Dr. Bowen, Dr. George Haig, to Miss Susan M., youngest daughter of the late William Allan, Esq.

On Wednesday evening last, by the Rev. Mr. Phillips, Mr. Thomas H. D. Potts, of Philadelphia, to Miss Caroline S. N. Boyd, of this city.

Died in this city, Mr. William Hasell Gibbes, in the 80th year of his age--a Soldier of the Revolution.

At Jericho, Port Royal Island, on the 12th inst.,Mr. Robert Oswald, Senr. in the 41st year of his age.

On the 7th inst., at Coosawhatchie, Mr. Nathaniel J. S. Farr, aged 21 years and nine months.

Departed this life on the 13th inst., at the residence of his sisters, in Richmond Co., Ga., Major Abraham Walker, in the 41st year of his age....

Issue of March 1, 1834

Married on the 18th ult., by the Rt. Rev. Dr. Bowen, William C. Murray Esq. of England, to Ann W., daughter of the late James H. Ancrum, Esq. of this city.

On the 20th ult., by the Rev. Mr. Pierce, Mr. P. Cantwell, to Miss Elizabeth G. Sullivan, all of this city.

On the 22d ult., by the Rt. Rev. Dr. Bowen, Mr. Alexander Gilfillin, to Miss Ann E., eldest daughter of William Lindsay, Esq., all of this city.

On the 25th ult., by the Rev. Thos Smith, Mr. Thomas S. Jones, to Miss Elizabeth C. F. Ripley, all of this city.

At Beaufort, S. C., on the 13th ult.,by the Rev. Mr. Walker, the Rev. Charles Pinckney Elliott, to Miss Elizabeth M. Guerard, of Beaufort, daughter of the late Joseph Guerard, Esq.

Died in this city on the 11th inst., Mrs. Agnes Smith, aged 75 years....

Departed this life in Hamburg, S. C.,on the 30th ult., Mrs. Ann C. Moore, wife of Mr. James D. Moore, aged 25 years...member of the Baptist Church.

At Savannah, on the 18th inst., in the 56th year of his age, Mr. Calvin Baker, for many years a residence of that city....

In Raleigh, N. C., 2d inst.,Mr. Jesse Wall, aged about 90, the son of Mr. Arthur Wall, who is now living at the advanced age of 115 years. Mr. Wall was in the Revolutionary war with his father, together with a younger brother.

At New York, on the 18th inst., Mrs. Susan Cameron, aged 28 years and 1 month, wife of Samuel D. Cameron, of Charleston, S. C.

Issue of March 8, 1834

Married on the 20th ult., by the Rev. Mr. Bachman, Mr. John E. O'Dina, to Miss Elizabeth, only daughter of Mr. P. Duval, both

of this city.
Died in this city on the 28th ult., Mr. Andrew Bay, in the 44th year of his age.
In Savannah, Ga., on the 14th ult., Mrs. Martha Daniell, daughter of the late Major John Screven, and wife of Dr. W. C. Daniell, of that place, aged 32 years. In Hall co., 1st ult., Arthur Crawford, a Revolutionary Soldier, aged 85.

Issue of March 15, 1834

Married on Thursday evening the 20th ult., by the Rev. Mr. Gilman, Mr. Benjamin Prince Colburn, to Ann Ashby, youngest daughter of William Matthewes, Esq.
Died in this city on the 4th inst., Col. James E. McPherson, of Prince Williams, Beaufort District, in the 65th year of his age.

Issue of March 22, 1834 (Montreat issue clipped; SCL issue complete)
Married on the 13th ult., by the Rev. J. Harrison, Mr. Wm. C. Dunn, to Miss Mary L., Hughes, both of Union district.
Also, by the Rev. Mr. Harrison, Mr. Richard G. Holson, to Miss Sarah Ann Frances McDaniel, both of Union district.
On the 17th inst., by the Rev. Mr. Thomas Smith, Mr. William Dickson of Quincy, Florida, to Miss Mary Campbell, daughter of Mr. Thomas Johnston, of this city.
To the memory of Mrs. Hannah Simons, who died on the 16th inst.,in the 87th year of her age....(eulogy)

Issue of March 29, 1834

Married on Thursday evening 20th inst., by the Rev. Dr. Gadsden, Capt. W. C. Sally, to Miss Mary Proctor, eldest daughter of A. B. Lord, Esq. of this city.
On Thursday the 13th inst., at St. James' Church, James Island, by the Rev. Mr. Trapier, Edward C. Peronneau, Esq. to Miss Ann S. Parker, all of this city.
Died, at his residence in Sumpter Dist., on the 7th Jan. last, in the 66th year of his age, Mr. William Whilden (eulogy)
In Savannah, on the 16th inst.,Mr. Wm. H. Ferguson, aged 33, a native of S. C., but for several years past a resident of Ga.

Issue of April 5, 1834

Married on Thursday evening by the Rev. John Dickson, Dr. S. Henry Dickson, to Miss Jane Robertson, daughter of the late Samuel Robertson, all of this city.
On the 23d ult., by the Rev. Mr. Bachman, Mr. John H. Gros, to Miss Selena C. Zackman, both of this city.
At Ashepoo, St. Bartholomew Parish, on the 26th inst., by the Rev. Francis P. Delaveaux, Daniel S. Henderson, Esq. of Walterboro, to Miss Caroline R. Webb, eldest daughter of Mr. Charles Webb, deceased.
On the 13th ult., by the Rev. J. Harrison, Mr. David W. Hamilton, to Miss Canzada McCulloch, both of Union district, S. C.
Died in this city on the 18th inst.,Mrs. Elizabeth L. Hutchinson, aged 71 years.
In Pendleton District, recently, Mr. William Noble, aged 90 a soldier of the rev.

Issue of April 12, 1834

Died on the morning of the 30th ult., in the 25th year of her age, Mrs. Mary W. Gadsden, consort of Dr. A. E. Gadsden.
In Greenville, on the 27th of March, Mrs. Ann Ladson Gregorie.
In Lincoln co., Ga., on the 6th ult., Mr. Michael West in the 108th year of his age.

Issue of April 19, 1834

Married on the evening of the 13th inst., by the Rev. B. Gildersleeve, Mr. D. McNarr, Merchant of Cheraw, to Mrs. Sarah E. Lacoste, of this city.
In this city on Thursday evening 10th inst., by The Rev. Mr. Kennedy, Mr. John Gee, of Barnwell Dist., S. C.,to Miss Letitia Jane, eldest daughter of Mr. James Johnson, of Charleston, S. C.
At St. Paul's Church, on Thursday evening, 10th inst., by the Rev. Mr. Folker, Mr. B. Burgh Smith, to Miss Catherine S., youngest daughter of the late Nathaniel Farr.
Died in Sunbury, Ga., on the 3d inst., Mr. Charles G. Hart, in the 40th year of his age, a native of this city, but for many years a resident of that State.
At her residence, St. John's Berkley, on the 9th inst., having nearly completed her 69th year, Mrs. Elizabeth Damaris Broughton, relict of Alexander Broughton....

Issue of April 26, 1834

Married on the 22d inst., by the Rev. Mr. Gadsden, Dr. Wm. M. Brailsford, of St. George's Parish, to Miss Margaret E., second daughter of Col. Charles Boyle, of St. Paul's Parish.
In New Orleans, on the 29th ult., Dr. Thomas Hunt, late of this city, to Miss Agale Carleton, daughter of Henry Carleton, Esq.
Departed this life at his residence near Summerville, S. C., on the 26th ult., Mr. Charles Mayrant...left wife and four infant children.
In Perry, Houston Co., Ga., on Sunday morning, 6th inst., the Rev. Robert Flournoy, aged 37 years...Minister of the Methodist Episcopal Church.
At St. Marys, Ga., Mr. John Sleigh, aged 76, a native of Philadelphia, and a soldier of the Revolution.

Issue of May 3, 1834

Married in this city on Tuesday 22d ult., by the Rev. Dr. Gadsden, William Nelson, Esq. of Frederic County, Va.,to Miss Anne F. Mitchell.
On Saturday 19th ult., in St. Paul's Church, by Rev. C. Hanckel, Dr. A. Darby, to Miss Margaret Thompson, both of Orangeburg, S.C.
Died in this city on the 21st ult., Mr. Patrick M'Gann, aged 89 years--a native of Ireland. He was a resident of this city 48 years.
In Darien, Ga., on the 18th ult., Mr. Marcus T. Peirce, aged 34 years.

Issue of May 10, 1834

Married on the 17th ult., by the Rev. John Bachman, Mr. William A. Nopie, to Mrs. Martha E. Baker, both of this city.
On the 1st inst., by the Rev. Thomas Smith, Mr. Samuel T. Maxey, to Miss Mary M. Burgoine, all of this city.
In Greenville, S. C., on the 22d ult.,by the Rev. Richard B. Cater, Mr. Fountarin F. Beattie, to Miss Emily Edgeworth, eldest

daughter of Elisha Hamlin, Esq. deceased.
   Died in Granville, S. C., 27th ult., Mrs. Rachael Bolan, wife of James Bolan, Esq., aged 35 years.
   On the 10th ult., at his residence in the County of Monroe, Ga., Abraham Womack, in the 91st year of hsi age--a Soldier of the Revolution. At Darien, on the 18th ult., Marcus T. Peirce, Esq., in the 34th year of his age.
   In Tuscaloosa, Ala., on the 19th ult., Mr. F. M. Shingler, in the 27th year of his age, Merchant, formerly of this city.

Issue of May 17, 1834

   Married in this city on Wednesday evening the 7th inst., by the Rev. A. Buist, the Rev. John Forrest, to Miss Sarah J. K. Ogier, daughter of the late Thomas Ogier, Esq.
   In this city on the night of the 1st inst., by the Rev. Mr. Hanckel, Mr. Samuel M. Thompson of Augusta, Geo., to Miss Julia Dunham, only daughter of Mrs. Mary H. Willis.
   On the 1st inst., by the Rev. Mr. Trapier, Col. Isaac W. Hayne, to Miss Alicia Palina, daughter of the late Paul Trapier, Esq.
   On the 8th inst., by the Rev. Wm. M. Kennedy, the Rev. Whiteford Smith, to Miss Martha Ann, daughter of Charles Mouzon, Esq. all of this city.
   On the 1st inst., by the Rev. Mr. Lewers, Mr. Thomas H. Meree, to Miss Ann J., youngest daughter of Moses Whitesides, Esq., of Christ Church Parish.
   In Beaufort, S. C., on the 30th ult., by the Rev. Mr. Walker, Richard Reynolds, Esq., to Miss Margaret McKee.
   In Beaufort, S. C., on the 1st inst., by the Rev. Mr. Walker, Charles Hopkin, Esq., of Georgia, to Miss Mary Givens, daughter of Charles Givens, Esq.
   Died on the 8th inst., at her fathers residence, Prince Williams' Parish, Miss Caroline Sarah Gregorie, aged 7 years....
   On Waccamaw, on the 4th inst., Mrs. Catharine Palmer, consort of L. Palmer, in the 37th year of her age.
   Died, at his residence in New-Jersey, on the 4th inst., the Hon. John Condit....

Issue of May 24, 1834

   Married on Thursday 15th inst., by the Rev. F. H. Rutledge, Julius Lachicotte, Esq., to Miss Mary Gibson, daughter of Cornelius Hamlin, Esq. all of St. Thomas Parish.
   In Williamsburgh, S. C. on the evening of the 30th ult., by the Rev. R. W. James, Mr. James Green, of Georgetown Dist., to Miss Sarah A. James of the former place.
   On Friday evening, the 2d inst., by the Rev. Samuel B. Wilson, the Rev. Jeptha Harrison, of S. C., to Miss Nancy Thompson, of Stafford Co., Va.
   Died at Camden, on the morning of the 11th inst., Mrs. Mary Ray, relict of the late Captain Peter Ray, in the 61st year of her age...a member of the Presbyterian Church.
   Died at Camden, S. C., Mrs. Joshua Reynolds, leaving a family of nine children, and the partner of her life...member of the Methodist Church.
   At New-Orleans, on the morning of the 5th inst., Mr. James Patterson, aged 33 years, a native of Scotland, and for many years a resident of this city...left widow, three children....

Issue of May 31, 1834

Married on Tuesday evening 20th inst., by the Rev. Dr. Gadsden, Mr. John L. Holmes, to Miss Rebecca, third daughter of the late James W. Gadsden, Esq. all of this city.
On Thursday evening, 22d inst., by the Rev. Mr. Bachman, Mr J. A. Duffus, to Miss Louisa, youngest daughter of the late Benj. Leefe, Esq., all of this city.
On Thursday evening last, by the Rev. Mr. Pierce, Mr. William R. Jones, to Miss Ann Eliza, eldest daughter of Mr. John N. Martin, all of this city.
Died on the 10th May, 1834, at his residence in St. Matthews Parish, of which he was Rector, The Rev. Wm. S. Wilson, aged 33 years....
In Pendleton, at the residence of Mr. Samuel Maverick, Joseph T. Weyman, aged 38 years.

Issue of June 7, 1834

Married on Thursday evening by the Rev. Thomas Smith, Mr. E. R. Stokes of Philadelphia, to Miss Helen L., daughter of Mr. James Sweeny, of this City.
On Wednesday evening last, by the Rev. Mr. Gilman, Joseph M. Bourreus, to Elizabeth Ann, second daughter of Daniel Burie, Sen., all of this city.
On Thursday Evening last, in the Town of Beaufort, by the Rev. Joseph R. Walker, Wm. H. Bold, to Miss Emeline S., daughter of the late Stephen Givens.
In Coosawhatchie, on the 22d inst., by the Rev. Mr. Youmans, Wm. M'Farland, Esq. to Mrs. Martha Lancaster, all of St. Luke's Parish.
In the neighborhood of Darien, Ga., on Thursday last, the 29th May, by the Rev. Mr. Pratt, Francis R. Shackelford of Georgetown, S. C., to Caroline S., eldest daughter of Col. James Dunwody.
At Otaheite, Society Islands, Captain Charles Spooner of whale ship Erie, of Newport, to Miss Kingatara Orurute.
Died in Walterborough on the 23d ult., Dr. William Pinckney, in the 27th year of his age.
In Columbia, S. C. on the 24th of May, Miss Elizabeth Francis Pawley, in the 32d year of her age.
On the 14th ult., at May River, St. Luke's Parish, S. C., Mrs. Eliza Gray, aged 37 years.
In Mary's Grove, (his seat), in the County of Burke, N. C., the Rev. Robert Miller of the Episcopal Church, aged 75 years and 10 months. Mr. Miller was a native of Scotland.

Issue of June 14, 1834

Married on Thursday evening the 5th inst., by the Rev. Mr. Hanckel, William Purvis, Esq., of Mobile, Ala., to Miss Ann, third daughter of John Dixon, Esq. of this city.
On the evening of the 29th of May, at Fodgrey, Savannah, by the Rev. Adam Gilchrist, John A. Frayssee, Esq., to Miss Ann Stevens, eldest daughter of Jacob Stevens, Esq. of Colleton Dist.
Died in Cheraw, S. C., on the 1st inst., Mrs. Jane Secress, formerly of this place.
Died at Mobile, Ala., on the 6th inst., the Rev. Walter Monteith...a native of Broadalbin, Montgomery co., in this state....
New York Observer.

Issue of June 21, 1834

Married in this city on Thursday afternoon, 12th inst., by the Rev. C. E. Gadsden, in St. Philips Church, Henry B. Tommer, jr., Esq., to Miss Ann Eliza Price, only daughter of the late Wm. Price, jr., Esq.
On Tuesday evening last, by the Rev. Dr. Palmer, Mr. Peter K. Coburn, to Miss Mary Adeline Ehney, all of this city.
At Oak Grove, on the 22d of May last, by the Rev. Mr. Leverette, Edward D. Bailey, Esq., Planter of Edisto Island, to Elvira L., fourth daughter of Wm. Reynolds, Esq., deceased, late Planter of Wadmalaw.
At Lexington, S. C., on Thursday 1st of May, by the Rev. Mr. Bachman, Rev. George Washington Muller, to Miss Mary Elizabeth Schwartz, all of this city.
At Lexington, S. C., on Thursday the 8th of May, by the Rev. Dr. Hazelius, Mr. Francis Sebastian Schwarts, of the city, to Miss Mary Ann Hendricks, of Lexington.
Departed this life on the 14th inst., Mrs. Elizabeth Green (widow of the late Edmund Green), in the 63d year of her age....
Died, near Hamilton, Harris Co., Ga., on the Sabbath of 25th ult., Samuel Richard, the only son of Rev. William B. Richards, aged 5 years, 1 month and 8 days....

Issue of June 28, 1834

Married on Thursday evening, 19th inst., by the Rev. Mr. Kennedy, Mr. Paul A. Fripp, of St. Helena, to Miss Jane J. Kugley, of this city.
Departed this life on Saturday the 14th inst., in the 79th year of his age, the venerable Solomon Legare, a Soldier of the Revolution....
In this city on the 5th inst., Mrs. Ann C. Calender, wife of Capt. Joseph Callender, aged 33 years.
On the 21st inst., in this city, Mrs. Ann Matilda Kennedy, wife of Rev. Wm. M. Kennedy, aged 36 years and 3 days.
Departed this life on the 18th inst., in this city, Miss Sarah Ann Valk, daughter of Jacob R. Valk, Esq., in the 16th year of her age....

Issue of July 5, 1834

Married on the 26th inst., by the Rev. Mr. Bachman, Mr. Isaac M'P. Lee, to Miss Anna Maria, second daughter of Paul S. H. Lee, Esq., all of this city.
On Wednesday evening, 18th inst.,by the Rev. Mr. Manley, Mr. E. R. Cowperthwait, of New-York, to Miss Emily A. Collins, of this city.
On the 25th inst., by the Rev. Mr. Manley, Mr. David M. Ross, to Miss Eliza C. Gefkia, all of this city.
Departed this life on the 23d ult., Lionel Chalmers Nowell, of St. John's Parish, Berkley, in the 25th year of his age....
Died at Barnwell C. H., on the 7th inst., aged 13 months, Henry Lee, son of Henry M. and Caroline W. Tompkins....

Issue of July 12, 1834

Married on Sabbath Afternoon, the 29th June, in the 2d Presbyterian Church, by Rev. Mr. Smith. the Rev. John B. Adger, to Miss Elizabeth Keith, daughter of Mr. Edward Shrewsbury, all of this city.
On Tuesday evening, July 1st, by the Rev. T. Smith, Mr. Jesse R. Gary to Mrs. Elizabeth A. J. O'Neale.

On Tuesday evening, July 1st, by the Rev. T. Smith, Mr. Oswell Reeder to Mrs. Louisa Martindale, all of this city.
In Columbia, S. C., on the 1st inst., by the Rev. Dr. Leland, Mr. James P. Caldwell, of Newberry District, to Miss Sarah B., daughter of Mr. G. Chapman, of the former place.
Died on Friday, 27th ult., at his residence in Sumter Dist., Col. Charles Spann, jr., in the 52d year of his age.
In Fayetteville, N. C., on the 26th ult.,Major William L. Hawley, aged 35 years.
In St. Mary's, 30th ult.,Mr. Lewis Bochlott, for many years a respectable merchant at Savannah.
In Cheraw, S. C., on Wednesday morning, 2d inst.,Mrs. Martha Smith, relict of the late Mr. Jno Smith, in the 74th year of his age.

Issue of July 19, 1834

Married on Friday morning, the 11th inst., at the Sand Hills, near Augusta, Ga., by the Rev. S. S. Davis, the Rev. Samuel K. Talmage, Pastor of the Presbyterian Church of Augusta, to Miss Ruth, daughter of Dr. Sterett, deceased, of Louisvilla, Ga.
Died, in Hancock co., Ga., at the house of Mr. Isaac P. Knowles, on the 28th ult, Mrs. Tabitha Marchman, aged 91 years...a member of the Presbyterian Church over 75 years.
At Edgefield , S. C., on the 6th inst., in the 23d year of her age, Mrs. Harriet Hayne Butler, wife of Judge Butler.

Issue of July 26, 1834

Died at London, on the 1st of June last, Mrs. Lydia Lucas, relict of Jonathan Lucas, Esq., late of this city....
In Columbus, Ga., Mr. George C. Shivers, aged 20 years and 6 months.

Issue of August 2, 1834

Died in Pineville, S. C. on the 26th inst., Mr. J. L. Snowden, of this city, aged 38 years.
At Branchville, S. C. on the 25th inst., Mr. Wm. P. Bason, aged 36 years, a native of Philadelphia, but for the last 13 years a resident of this city.
Died on the 28th of June last, in the Chickesaw Nation, whither he had gone for the purpose of examining the country, with a view to removal, Mr. Charles W. Rawson, of Lawrenceville, Ga., in the 42d year of his age. a native of East Haddam, Conn., but for many years had resided in Ga....left a wife and five small children....

Issue of August 9, 1834

Died in this city on the 1st inst., of Country Fever, Mr. Charles O. Duke of Columbia, S. C.
In Georgetown, S. C., 29th ult., Mrs. Graham, wife of Mr. John Graham, of Williamsburgh. At her residence on Pee Dee, 28th ult., Mrs. Grier, wife of Mr. Samuel Grier.
In Columbus, Ga., 28th ult., Mr. Isaac A. Smith of the firm of Bardley & Smith, of that city, and late of New-Haven, Conn., aged 34 years.

Issue of August 16, 1834

Died on Sullivan's Island, on the 17th inst., Mr. Sedgwick Lewis Simons...in the prime of life....
In Columbia, S. C., on the 31st ult., Mrs. Abigail, wife of Dr. A. Fitch, aged 37, leaving an affectionate husband and four interesting children....
On the 28th ult., at the residence of Dr. Scudder, near Princeton, N. J., Mr. Charles B. G. Guild, of Philadelphia, in the 24th year of his age...a graduate of Nassau Hall....

Issue of August 23, 1834

Married on Tuesday evening last, by the Rev. Mr. Manly, Mr. William Clark, to Miss Ann L. Perdriau, all of this city.
Departed this transitory life, on the 13th inst., Mrs. Eliza Wightman, in the 35th year of her age, consort of Mr. John T. Wightman, of this city.

Issue of August 30, 1834

Died, at her residence in Meeting street, on Saturday, Aug. 9th, Mrs. Margaret McClean, in the 62d year of her age...born in the county of Monaghan, Ireland, on 16th March 1773, arrived in this country October 9th, 1792...one of the first member who joined the 2nd Presbyterian Church, under the Rev. Dr. Flinn....
Departed this life on the morning of the 15th inst., Mrs. Josiah Sturgis, aged 70 years, a native of Boston, Mass.,but for 40 years a resident of this city.

Issue of September 6, 1834

Married in Knoxville, Tenn., by E. Nelson, Esq., Dr. Williams, aged 100 years, to Miss Nancy, youngest daughter of Mr. James Israel, all of Knox co., East Tennessee.
Died in this city on the 22d ult., in the 20th year of his age, Edmund Tucker, son of Dr. Edmund H. Tucker, deceased late of Georgetown District.

Issue of September 13, 1834

Departed this life, very suddenly, on the 29th ult., in the 52d year of his age, Mr. John Limbaker, a native of Madmalaw Island, but for many years an inhabitant of James Island, and for several years an Elder in the Presbyterian Church....

Issue of September 20, 1834

Married on the 9th inst., by the Rev. Mr. Manly, Mr. Charles W. Hurst, of this city, to Miss Sarah I. Gregory, of the city of New York.
Died in Montgomery, Ala., on the 4th inst., Mr. Thomas H. Richards, formerly of this city.

Issue of September 27, 1834

Departed this life in this city on the 18th inst., Keating Simons, Esq. in the 82d year of his age....
Died at his residence in Broad street, on the 11th inst., John Black, Esq. in the 81st year of his age. born in Aberdeen, Scotland, on 13 October 1753, went out in early life to Pensacola, West Florida , and on that colony falling into the hands of the Spaniards in 1784, he removed to this city....

Issue of October 4, 1834

Married on Tuesday evening last, 23d inst., by the Rev. Mr. Cobia, Mr. Charles Rogers to Miss Margaret Emeline Miscally, both of this city.
Died on the 31st August last, at the Red Sulpher Springs, Va., Thomas Johnston, Esq., a native of County Down, Ireland, in the 66th year of his age, and a respectable resident of thie City upwards of 44 years.
Died on Wednesday morning, the 24th inst., at her late residence in Charlotte-street, Mazyckborough, aged 75, Miss Mary Porcher, eldest daughter of the late Philip Porcher, Esq.

Issue of October 11, 1834

Married on Thursday evening, 2d inst., by the Rev. Mr. Gilman, Mr. Herbert Roby, to Miss Sophia Oliver, both of this city.
On Saturday evening, 5th inst.,by the Rev. Dr. Gadsden, Mr. John McCauldless, of this city to Mrs. Elenora Bowman, of Sumter District.
Departed this life on the morning of the 1st inst., Thomas W. Bacot, Esq., in the 70th year of his age....

Issue of October 18, 1834

Died on the 11thinst., Mrs. Catharine Macingram, wife of Mr. John Macingram, of New-York, and daughter of Capt. Redmond of Virginia.

Issue of October 25, 1834

Married on Wednesday evening last, by the Rev. Mr. Smith, Thos Kershaw, Esq., to Miss Mary Jane, daughter of Col. Richard Cunningham.
Departed this life on the 20th of August, in Liverpool, Eng., in the 72d year of his age,Robert Harvey, Esq.,formerly a respectable and highly esteemed Merchant of this City.

Issue of November 1, 1834

Married on Thursday the 23d inst.,by the Rev. Mr. Bachman, Dr. W. G. Ramsay, to Miss Elizabeth, eldest daughter of Dr. Samuel Wilson.
On Thursday evening, 23d inst.,by the Rev. Mr. Bachman, Mr. John Carter, to Miss Eliza Main, both of this city.
Departed this life on the morning of the 19th inst., Miss Martha Holmes, aged 16 years and 11 months....
On the 1st ult., Mrs. Mildred M. James, in the 56th year of her age, a native of London, Eng., but for the last 25 years, a resident of this city...leaving five children.
On the 17th inst., at her residence in St. Mathew's Parish, Mrs. Ann Lovell, aged 77 years, 11 months and 10 days.

Issue of November 8, 1834

Married on Wednesday evening, 29th ult., by the Rev. Mr. Hanckel, Simons Lucas, Esq., to Miss Emma S., second daughter of William Johnston, Esq., all of this city.
On the 29th ult., by the Rev. Mr. Pierce, Mr. Wm. P. Gorman, of Georgetown, S. C., to Miss Ann Aurelia Keowin, of this city.
Died of Country Fever, on the 29th ult., Mr. P. P. Marchant, a native of this place, aged 61 years and 29 days...left a widow advanced in years....

Departed this life on the 16th ult., Mrs. Jane C. Woodruff, relict of the late Major Joseph Woodruff...left two interesting orphans....

Died in Greenville, on Monday, the 20th ult., Miss Elizabeth Broughton, in the 53d year of her age. She was a native of St. James, Goose Creek.

Issue of November 15, 1834

Married on Thursday evening, 5th inst., by the Rev.Mr. Cobia, Peter G. Parker, Esq. to Miss Maria L. Brailsford, both of this city.

At St. Paul's Church, on the 6th inst., by the Rev. Mr. Hanckel, Mr. Joseph A. Robinson, of this city, to Miss Eliza M., daughter of the late Isaac Pickling, Esq. of John's Island.

On Thursday evening, 5th inst., by the Rev. Dr. Bachman, J. M. Hudson, to Miss Constantia D., fourth daughter of Mr. J. H. Fastbender, all of this city.

Died in Camden, on the 7th inst., Capt. John Chesnut M'Ra, in the 45th year of his age.

In Columbia, S. C., on the 31st ult.,Mr. Alexander Shinnie, a native of Aberdeen, Scotland, and for the last 12 or 14 years a resident citizen of Charleston, S. C.

Issue of November 22, 1834

Married on Thursday evening last, by the Rev. Bishop Bowen, Mr. Henry Manly Neyle, to Miss Jane, youngest daughter of the late James Miller, Esq.

In Walterborough, on Thursday the 6th inst., by the Rev. Mr. Ledbetter, Mr. J. Porteous Deveaux, of this city, to Mrs. Harriet E. Witsell, of the former place.

On Sunday evening, 16th inst., by the Rev. Mr. Gilman, Mr. Henry Hunt, of Boston, Mass., to Miss Eliza Ann Jenney, of this city.

Departed this life on the 8th inst., in the 79th year of her age, Mrs Elizabeth Bounetheau.

On the 18th Oct., at the U. S. Hospital at Pensacola, in the 26th year of his age, Augustus R. Strong, of the U. S. Navy, of Cincinnati, Ohio.

Issue of November 29, 1834

Married on Thursday evening 20th inst., by the Rev. Dr. McDowall, John B.Girardeaux, Esq., of St. Andrews', to Miss Mary Hughes, of this city.

On Tuesday 18th inst., by the Rev. Mr. Hanckel, W. O. Prentiss, Esq. of Beaufort, to Miss Mary S., eldest daughter of the late Christopher Jenkins, Esq.,of this city.

Departed this life on Sabbath Evening, the 23d inst., Mary Jane, youngest child of Rev. Edward Palmer, of Prince Williams Parish, aged 5 years, 5 months and 22 days.

At his residence in Lexington, S. C., on the 4th inst., Richard Williams, Esq....

At Georgetown, D. C., on the 17th inst., Brevet Brig. Gen. James House, Col. of the 1st Regiment U. S. Artillery.

Issue of December 6, 1834

Married on Tuesday evening last, by the Rev. Dr. Gadsden, Dr. C. C. Pritchard, to Miss Elizabeth, eldest daughter of John F. Knox, Esq. all of this city.

On Wednesday evening, 26th inst., by the Rev. Mr. Smith, Mr. Edward Fogartie, to Miss Mary M., daughter of the late Dr. Montgomery.

On Wednesday evening, 26th inst., by the Rev. Mr. Cobia, Mr. Edward H. Browne, to Miss Mary Ann Doyle, all of this city.

On Wednesday evening, 26th inst., by the Rev. B. Manly, Mr. Joseph Zealy, to Miss Ann J., daughter of Dr. J. L. E. W. Shecut.

On Thursday morning last, by the Rev. Mr. Hanckel, Dr. John S. O'Hear, to Miss Catharine M., only daughter of the late Benjamin Fuller, both of St. Andrew's Parish.

On Thursday evening 27th inst., by the Rev. C. Gadsden, Horatio Allen, Esq. to Miss Mary M., daughter of the late Rev. Dewar Simons.

On the 27th ult., by the Rev. J. Bachman, Mr. Thomas L. Jaques, to Miss Caroline Angeline Lacoste, both of this city.

Died at Milledgeville, Ga., on the 26th ult., the Hon. Jonathan Lewis, Senator from the County of Burke....

In New Orleans, on the 17th inst., in the 24th year of his age, Mr. Thomas C. Jones, a native of Charleston, S. C.

Issue of December 13, 1834

Married on Thursday evening, 4th inst., by the Rev. Mr. Manly, Mr. Joseph Thomlinson, to Miss Ann Lawrence, all of this city.

On Tuesday evening the 9th inst., by the Rev. Mr. Delavaux, Laurent D. Hallonquist, Esq. of Greenville, S. C., to Sophia, youngest daughter of the late John Berney, Esq. of this city.

In this city on the 27th ult., Mr. Benjamin Deye, a native of Hamburg, aged 52 years and a resident of Charleston 37 years.

Departed this life at Somerset, St. John's Berkeley on the 2d November, Thomas Porcher Dwight, aged about 7 years; on the 7th Nov., Francis Marion Dwight, aged 4 years and on the 22d Nov. Isabella Safford Dwight, aged 2 years, and on the 1st December Martha Maria Dwight, aged 6 years--all children of Isaac M. and Martha M. Dwight.

In Tallahssee, Fla., on the 15th ult., Mr. Philip Hilligas, of this city, aged 41 years.

Issue of December 20, 1834

Married on Thursday evening 14th inst., by the Rev. Dr. McDowell, Dr. George Logan to Anna Catherine eldest daughter of the late Capt. George R. Turner, all of this city.

On Thursday evening, 14th inst., by the Rev. Mr. Hanckel, Theodore Gaillard, Esq., youngest son of the late Judge Gaillard, to Emily Rutledge, eldest daughter of John Parker, Esq.

At Augusta, Ga., on the 17th inst., by the Rev. Mr. Talmage, Mr. Joseph Jewitt of this city, to Miss Margaret Jane Stokes, of Augusta.

Died at Ithaca, N. Y., on the 3d inst., the venerable Simeon DeWitt, Surveyor General of the State of N. Y., in the 79th year.

Issue of December 27, 1834

Married in Savannah, Ga., on the 17th inst., by the Rev. Dr. Capers, Mr. Gideon James Cole, of S. C., to Miss Mary Ann Elizabeth Rabb, of that city.

In Washington county, Miss., on the 28th ult., Mr. John Turnbull, Jr., to Miss Mary Ann., eldest daughter of Sinclair D. Gervais, Esq. of Charleston, S. C.

Died in Savannah, Ga., on the 9th inst., Daniel Baker, Esq., of this state, in the 59th year of his age.

Issue of January 3, 1835

Married on the 23d ult., by the Rev. Bazil Manly, Mr. Alexander Walker, to Miss Mary E., eldest daughter of H. Cannaday, Esq., all of this city.
At Waccamaw, on Tuesday the 23d Dec., by the Rev. Mr. Glennie, Col. Thomas O. Elliott, to Miss Irvinia A. Magill, only daughter of Daniel Magill, Esq. deceased.
At Orangeburg, S. C., on the 18th ult., by the Rev. J. A. McKenney, Edmund J. Felder, M. D.,of Alabama, to Sarah Zilpha, third daughter of Washington Potter, Merchant, deceased of Charleston, S. C.
Died in this city on the 22d ult., Mrs. Ann M. Gadsden, relict of the late John Gadsden.
Departed this life in this city on the 22d ult., Miss Mary Inglis. upwards of 74 years....
At Yonge's Island, St. Paul's Parish, on the 6th ult., William Simmons, Es. in the 67th year of his age.
On the 11th Oct. at his residence in Pineville, Dr. Edwin Gaillard, in the 39th year of his age.

Issue of January 10, 1835

Married on Thursday evening, the 1st inst.,by the Rev. Wm. States Lee, Dr. D. J. Townsend, of Edisto Island, to Miss Henrietta Maria, eldest daughter of Dr. Evans, of St. Paul's.
At the Lutheran Church on Thursday evening, the 1st inst., by the Revd. John Bachman, Philip Arthur Strobel to Miss Caroline M. Wilson, both of this city.
On Wednesday evening last, by the Revd. John Bachman, William C. Catewood, Esq. to Miss Mary M., daughter of the late John Schirer, all of this city.
In Lagrange, Geo., on the 11th inst.,by the Rev. Mr. Stanley, Rev. Thomas A. Cook of Beaufort, S. C., to Miss Ann Eliza, eldest daughter of Elias Jones, Esq. formerly of this city.
Death of a father in the gospel and soldier of the Rev. War., Elder Elias Mitchel, of Union District, who died in a Preaching Stand in the Brushy Fork Vicinity, in Chester District, S. C., on the 20th ult., about 84 years of age....Columbia Telescope
At Columbia, S. C. 12th ult., Mr. George L. A. Davis, aged 24.
At Augusta, Ga., 20th ult., Mrs. Cynthia Maria Norton, aged 29, a native of Sheffield, Conn. Same place, 31st ult., Alex. Graham, of the old and extensive firm of Kerrs, Graham & Hope.
In Waynesborough, on the 27th ult., Robert Emmet Bourke, Esq., Attorney at Law, aged about 26 years.

Issue of January 17, 1834

Married on Wednesday evening, 7th inst.,by the Rev. Mr. Manly, Mr. Thomas F. Lebby, of this city, to Miss Sarah Wade, of Smithville, N. C.
On Tuesday evening last, by the Rev. Mr. Kennedy, Mr. Orlando Carter, to Miss Margaret Knox, both of this city.
On Tuesday evening the 30th of December, by the Rev. James S. Adams, the Rev. J. M. H. Adams, to Miss Eliza A. Burton, daughter of Robt. H. Burton, Esq. all of Beatties Ford, N. C.
Departed this life on Saturday morning last, in the 41st year of his age, Mr. James W. Bonnetheau....
In St. Luke's Parish, on the 4th inst., at her residence (Strawberry Hill), Mrs. Ann B. Graham, in the 43d year of her age.

At his residence in St. Matthew's Parish, on the 7th inst., David Rumph, Esq., in the 57th year of his age.

In Augusta, Ga, on the 31st ult., Alexander Graham, Esq., of the extensive firm of Kerrs, Graham & Hope, about 50 years of age. He was a native of Mecklenburgh, N.C.-- for the last 18 years a Merchant in Augusta.

Issue of January 24, 1835

Married on Thursday 15th inst., by the Rev. Mr. Rogers, W. A. Mikell, Esq. of Edisto Island, to Miss Hess Marion Waring, youngest daughter of W. S. Smith, Esq., of this city.

Died at Black River, on the 7th ult., Mrs. Elizabeth L. Keith, consort of Mr. Thomas J. Keith.

At Philadelphia, on the 11th inst., Dr. Philip Moser, a native of that place, and formerly resident of this city, aged 64 years.

At Philadelphia, on the 6th of Consumption, W. B. Schultz, of New York, aged 33 years and formerly a merchant of Charleston.

At Middletown Point, Monmouth county, on the 25th ult., Rev. George S. Woodhull, late of Princeton and Pastor of the Presbyterian Church at Middletown Point.

Died at the residence of Elisha Root, Esq., Greenfield, Mass., Mrs. Lydia Mosely, Relict of Col. David Mosely, aged 93 years, the oldest person except one in that town Mrs. M. for the last 30 years had her grave cltohes on hand....

Issue of January 31, 1835

Married at Bugby, Wadmalaw Island on Thursday 22d inst., by the Rev. Mr. Hanckel, John Townsend Esq. of Edisto Island, to Mary Caroline, only daughter of the late Richard Jenkins, of Johns Island.

In Columbia, on Thursday evening, 22d inst., by the Rev. Dr. Leland, Mr. John Murphy, of Norfolk, Va., to Miss Eliza Byrd, of Charleston, S. C.

Departed this life on the 17thinst., Miss Adeline Miller, in the 19th year of her age....

Died on the 19th inst., in the 33d year of her age, Mrs. Sarah M. Chisolm, consort of Geo. Chisolm, jun.

At his residence in Abbeville, Maj. Andrew Hamilton, in the 94th year of his age. He was a soldier of the Revolution.

Issue of February 7, 1835

Married on the 29th ult., by the Rev. Dr. Palmer, Charles R. Brewster, Esq. to Miss Anna R. Prentiss, all of this city.

On the 29th ult., by the Rev. Mr. Campbell, at the residence of Mr. James Gaillard, St. John's Berkley, Charles Macbeth, Esq., to Henrietta, only daughter of the late Dr. James Ravenel.

Died on the 4th ult., at his late residence in Mount Pleasant Village, Christ Church Parish, Mr. James Hibben, in the 69th year of his age, leaving a numerous family of children...Representative of his native Parish of the Legislative Councils of this State....
(long eulogy)

Issue of February 14, 1835

Married on Tuesday evening last, by the Rev. Dr. Palmer, Mr. John H. Hauck, to Miss Ann Elizabeth, eldest daughter of Mr. John T. Elsworth, all of this city.

On Tuesday evening last, by the Rev. Mr. T. Smith, Mr. R. V. Jones, to Miss Mary Elizabeth, daughter of Robert Wright, Esq. all of this city.

On Thursday Morning, the 5th inst., in St. Philip's Church, by the Rev. Mr. Cobia, Effigham Wagner, Esq. to Miss Emma Barton Fronty; all of this city.

On the 3d inst., at the residence of Charles Bearing, Esq., (Combahee), by the Rev. Mr.Gilchrist, Charles L. Stokes, Esq., to Miss Susan Baring, eldest daughter of the late Dr. Henry Farmer.

In New York, on the 4th inst.,by the Rev. Dr. Berrian, John Ravenel, Esq. of this city, to Eliza, daughter of Charles McEvers, Esq.

Departed this life on the 2d inst., Mr. James C. Courtenay, in the 33d year of his age....

At his residence in Barnwell district, Isaac Rush, Esq., aged 72 years.

On the 4th inst., at Columbia, General Wade Hampton in the 81st year of his age.

In Washington, Ga., on the 2d Jan., Mr. Abner B. Stanley, a licensed Baptist Preacher, in his 32 year....

At Savannah, Ga., 2d inst., Mrs. Caroline Cumming, wife of Joseph Cumming, of that city. At Milledgeville, 9th ult., Mrs. Ann Dixon, aged 88 years.

In Sunbury, Liberty Co., on the 3d of Jan., Mrs. Ann Winn, in the 77th year of her age.

Issue of February 21, 1835

Married on Thursday evening, Feb. 5th, by the Rev. Thomas Smith, Mr. Henry John Raine, to Miss Adaline Eliza Laats, all of this city.

On Wednesday evening, the 11th inst., by the Rev. Mr. Hanckel, John Boyle, Esq. of St. Pauls Parish, to Miss Elizabeth, eldest daughter of the late Nathaniel Farr.

Died in New Orleans, on Saturday the 31st ult., Mr. Edward Welsh, a native of this city, in the 34th year of his age.

Issue of February 28, 1835

Departed this life, in Chesterville, on the 3d inst., Mrs. Sarah, wife of Mr. A. R. Vicholson (sic, for Nicholson), in the 40th year of her age....member of the Baptist Church....

Issue of March 7, 1835

Married on Thursday evening last, by the Rev. Thomas Leadbetter, Mr. David Barsh, of Matthew's, to Miss Agnes, eldest daughter of Mr. John Farley, of this city.

On the 26th inst., by the Rev. C. G. Hill, D. G. Pepper, Esq., to Miss Eliza Y., eldest daughter of Dr. R. Jones, all of St. George Parish, Colleton District.

On the 19th inst., by the Rev. Mr. Bachman, Dr. William A. Hagood, of Barnwell District, to Miss Ann Sophia Martin, of this city.

Died, on Thursday the 17th ult., at the residence of his mother, in Clarendon, Mr. Theodore C. McFaddin....(eulogy)

At his residence in Richland District, on the 14th ult., Mr. Jesse Howell, in the 57th year of his age.

Issue of March 14, 1835

Married on Tuesday last, by the Rev. Mr. Bachman, Mr. Paul Jones, to Miss Margaret, fourth daughter of Mrs. Mary Evans, all of this city.

Departed this life on Thursday the 12th ult., in the 73d year of his age, Mr. Eliab Kingman, Senr., a native of Hingham, Mass.

Departed this life at his residence, Cedar Grove, Prince William's Parish, on the 9th of February, of a dropsy in the chest, William H. Hutson, Sen. aged 58 years....Ordinary of Beaufort District, which he had discharged for 15 years...Congregational Church of Stoney Creek, Prince William's...a Church which was founded and built for his grandfather, the Rev. William Hutson, in the year 1743....(eulogy)

Issue of March 21, 1835

Married on Sunday evening, 15th inst.,by the Rev. Mr. Bachman, Mr. John R. Allman, Merchant of Franklin, Macon Co., N. C., to Miss Mary Ann Isabella M'Donald, of this city.

Died on the 14th inst., Mr. Henry W. Paxton, a native of this city, in the 29th year of his age....left widowed mother.

Died in Georgetown, on the 7th inst., Major William S. Harvey, aged 48 years.

On the 2d inst., at her residence Sans-souci, near Statesburg, Mrs. Mary G. Rutledge, relict of Chancellor Hugh Rutledge.

Issue of March 28, 1835

Died on the 15th of February last, at his residence in St. John's Berkley, Col. Thomas Porcher in the 60th year of his age.

At Wadesborough, N. C., on the 7thinst., Mrs. Rosanna T. Lance, relict of the late Dr. John G. Lance, of Cheraw, S. C., in the 29th year of her age.

In Washington, Wilkes county, Ga., on the 18th inst., Dr. John L. Wingfield, in the 40th year of his age.

Issue of April 4, 1835

Married on Thursday evening, 25th inst.,by the Rev. Mr. Ball, Mr. Benjamin Stiles, to Mrs. Margaret Sandford, of St. Paul's Parish.

On Sabbath Evening last, by the Rev. E. T. Buist, Francis Rivers, Esq., to Miss Martha Caroline Green, both of James Island.

On Wednesday 25th inst., by the Rev. A. G. Brewer, Mr. William G. Mood, to Miss Sarah A. daughter of Thomas Walker, Esq. all of this city.

Died at Washington, on the 26th ult., Mr. Charles Pinkney, Jun., Editor of the Washington Sun, in the 39th year of his age. He was the second son of the late Hon. Wm. Pinkney of Maryland.

In Madison county, Ten., Moses Robeson Sen., and Mary his wife, the former aged 68 years, six months and 20 days, the latter aged 68 years, lacking three days...lived together as husband and wife 47 years and 15 days, raised a large family of children, were baptized the same day, and died within 12 hours of each other, and were interred in the same grave.

Issue of April 11, 1835

Married on Thursday the 19th ult., by the Rev. B. Manly, Timothy B. Folger, of New-York, to Miss Cordelia Rains, daughter of Jacob Henry, Esq. of this city.

On Thursday the 2d inst., by the Rev. Thomas Smith, George Christian Logan, Esq., to Miss Rose Isabella Turner, daughter of the late Capt. George R. Turner of this city.

On Tuesday the 31st ult., by the Rev. Mr. Manly, Mr. Edward Smith, to Miss Sarah eldest daughter of Capt. John Bonnell, all of this city.

Departed this life in this city on the 3d inst., Henry Alston Owens, Esq. of Fairfield district, S. C., aged 22 years and 6 months.

Departed this life at Quinby, St. Thomas' Parish, on the 2d inst., Mrs. Keziah Ann Coward, consort of Mr. Jesse Coward, in the 26th year of her age...left a husband, two small children, a sister and brother....

Issue of April 18, 1835

Married on Thursday evening, 2d inst., by the Rev. Jno Harrington, at the residence of Capt. James H. Wilson, of Sumter District, Mr. Robert L. Wilson, of Sumter, to Miss Emma L. Gray, of this city.

In Grahamville, S. C., on Sunday evening, 5th inst., by the Rev. Mr. Young, S. W. Wilkinson, U. S. Navy, to Miss Evelina C. Allston, of that place.

Died, on the 6th inst., on board the brig Gen. Trotter, on the passage from St. Croix, Charles Augustus Little, of Albany, formerly of Bangor, Me., aged 26.

Death of Mrs. Sarah Bell, consort of David Bell, Sen., of this city, who departed this life on Sabbath morning, 5th inst., in the 56th year of her age...a native of Nova Scotia. Her uncle, Bazil Lanneau, Esq., removed her with a brother, as adopted children....(eulogy)

Issue of April 25, 1835

Married at Whitehall, on the evening of the 16th April, by the Rev. Mr. Campbell, Mr. S. Porcher Gaillard, to Miss Mary M. Peyre, all of St. Stephens Parish.

Died on the 15th inst., in this city, Mrs. Eliza Ross, consort of Major James L. Ross.

At his residence in Cambridge, Dorchester Co., the Hon. Wm. Bond Martin, Chief Justice of the 4th Judicial District in Maryland, in the 66th year of his age.

Issue of May 2, 1835

Married in this city on the evening of the 15th inst., by the Rev. Mr. Barnwell, Capt. James E. Robinson of Barnwell C. H., to Miss Mary Motte, daughter of Thomas L. Dart, of Pendleton Village.

At Whitemarsh, on Thursday evening last, by the Rev. Mr. Delavaux, James O'Hear, Esq., to Mary D., second daughter of Lawrence Witsell, Esq. of St. Bartholomew's Parish.

At South Mulberry, St. John's Berkley, on Wednesday evening, the 22d inst., by the Rev. Mr. Fowler, Dr. Sanford N. Barker, to Miss Christiana Constantia, second daughter of the late Philip Porcher Broughton, Esq.

On Thursday evening, 9th inst., by the Rev. Jos. W. Pharr, Mr. Malichi Martin, to Miss Eliza Jane, only daughter of James and Mary Ann Wilson, of Gwinnette Co., Ga.

Departed this life on the 24th inst., in the 22d year of her age, Mrs. Mary C. Allan, daughter of the late Robert J. Turnbull, and wife of Robert M. Allan.

In Early Co., Ga., on the 16th ult., Mr. Jesse Brown, aged about 75, a soldier of the revolution.

In Upson Co., Ga., on the 6th inst., Mr. W. J. Wayman, aged 40.

Issue of May 9, 1835

Died at his residence near Greenville, on the 20th ult., John Young, Esq. in the 78th year of his age.
Died on the 11th ult., at his residence in Mecklenburg Co., N. C., James Conner, Esq., one of the few remaining soldiers of the revolution.
Of consumption, in Raleigh, N. C., on Saturday the 25th inst., Jonathan P. Cushing, President of Hampden Synden College, Va.
Died in Greenbush, N. Y., at the house of John Vanderzee, Getty Vanderzee, aged 84 years, widow of Teunis Vanderzee, and mother of S. T. Vanderzee, Esq., of Troy. The deceased was the last of four sisters, who together with a number of other ladies, assisted by an ensign, gallantly defended the Middle Fort at Schoharie during the Rev. war....

Issue of May 16, 1835

Married on Wednesday last, by the Rev. Mr. W. Martin, Mr. Richard S. Wish, to Mrs. Elizabeth Braid, all of this city.
Departed this life on the morning of the 7th inst., Mrs. Mary A. Lee, late consort of Mr. Joseph T. Lee, of this city....
Died on Wednesday morning, the 29th ult., Mrs. Rachel Carroll, consort of Mr. Bartholomew Carroll in the 65th year of her age.
Died in Washington, on the 6th inst., Mr. John Egan, Merchant, formerly of Alexandria, but for the last three years of that place ....

Issue of May 23, 1835

Married on the 12th inst., by the Rev. Mr. Bachman, Mr. John H. Steinmyer, to Miss Eliza R. Clarke, all of this city.
On the 14th inst.,by the Rev. Mr. Bachman, Mr. Herman Tracy, to Miss Ann Rivers, all of this city.
in Columbia, S. C., on the 13th inst., by the Rev. Dr. Leland, Albert M. Smith, Esq., of Beaufort to Miss Sarah Taylor, daughter of the late Hon. John Taylor.
Departed this life on the morning of the 6th inst., Mrs. Mary W. Guerard, late consort of Jacob W. Guerard.
Died at his late residence near Pendleton on the 5th inst., Dr. T. L. Dart....
At his plantation, seven miles from Savannah, on Wednesday the 13th inst., in the 53d year of his age, John Hugeunin, Esq... left a widow and family both in this state and S. C.
At Wilmington, Delaware, on the 25th of April, in the 23d year of her age, Mrs. Mary E., wife of the Rev. Arthur Granger, Pastor of the Presbyterian Church in that place...a native of Mendon, Mass....(eulogy)

Issue of May 30, 1835

Departed this life on the 22d inst., in the 26th year of her age, Mrs. Emily C. Mikell, consort of J. Jenkins Mikell, Esq. and only daughter of the late Rev. Thos H. Price, for many years Pastor of the Presbyterian Church, James Island...left an aged mother....
Died on the 12th May, at his residence in Union District, Mr. John Van Lew, an aged and respectable citizen, in the 81st year of his age.
At Chappell Hill, in St. Johns Berkley on Tuesday, 5th inst., Mrs. Charlotte Porcher, consort of Isaac Porcher, Esq., aged 40 years.

At Camden, on the 21st inst., Mr. William N. McCully, in the 22d year of his age, a native of Fairfield District.

Issue of June 13, 1835

Married on the 4th inst., by the Rev. Mr. John Forrest, Capt. George Wilson, to Miss Isabella M'Claren, all of this place.
At Columbia, S. C., on the 4th inst.,by the Rev. Dr. Capers, James Wilson Gibbes, Esq., of this city to Miss Susan P., youngest daughter of James S. Guignard, Esq. of Columbia.
Departed this life on Tuesday the 5th of May last, at her resident in St. John's Berkeley, in the 41st year of her age, Mrs. Charlotte Porcher, late wife of Isaac Porcher, and second daughter of Rene Ravenel of said Parish.
In Fairfield, S. C., 28th ult., Mrs. Alice Williamson, in the 73d year of his age.
At his residence in Jefferson Co., Fla., Capt. Thos Wilkes Seabrook, aged 28 years a native of S. C.

Issue of June 27, 1835

Married on the evening of the 19th inst., by the Rev. Dr. Palmer, Mr. Charles E. Dana, of Cincinnati, Ohio, to Miss Mary S. B. Palmer, second daughter of the Rev. Dr. Palmer, of this city.
On the evening of the 25th inst., by the Rev. Dr. Palmer, the Rev. Erastus Hopkins of Beech Island, toMiss Sarah Bennett, youngest daughter of the late Swinton Bennett, Esq., of this city.
On Thursday evening, 18th inst., by the Rev. Bishop Bowen, Wm. D. Gilliland, Esq. to Miss Mary S., daughter of James O'Neale, Esq., all of this city.
On Wednesday afternoon last, by the Rev. Mr. Hanchell, Dr. Philip S. Postell, to Miss Septema E., youngest daughter of Dr. Joseph Glover, all of this city.
In Hamburg, on the evening of the 21st inst.,Dr. J. R. E. Coutrier, of this city, to Miss Julia Ann, daughter of Milton Antony, M. D.,of Augusta, Ga.
At Beech Island, on the evening of the 9th inst., by the Rev. E. Hopkins, Mr. George Washington Mayson, of Hamburg, to Miss Sarah, daughter of Mr. James Lamar.
At New York, on the 15th inst., by the Rev. Cyrus Mason, Mr. Edmund Hyatt of this city, to Miss Mary E., daughter of the late Stephen Upson, of Oglethorpe Co., Geo.
Died in this city on the 2d inst., Mrs. Mary Parker, wife of Major Charles Parker, aged 33 years.
At St. James, Santee, on the 16th inst., Elias Whilden, Esq., in the 70th year of his age...a native of Christ Church Parish, and for the last 20 years of his life, a member of the Congregational Church at Wappetau, and also a Deacon....

Issue of July 4, 1835

Died near Lawrenceville, Gwinnett Co., Ga., on the 31st May, Mr. John Comine, an Elder of the Presbyterian Church.
Departed this life on the 23d of June, in the 20th year of her age, Miss Louisa M. Tilden, a native of Baltimore City....

Issue of July 11, 1835

Died on the 29th ult., at the residence of Arch. Heggie, of Columbia Co., Ga., Mr. John P. Furr, formerly of Charleston, aged about 30 years.

In Savannah, on the 1st inst., Mr. S. T. Star, son of Mathew Star, of Danbury, Conn., aged 24 years.

Issue of July 18, 1835

Died in this city on the 9th inst., Charles Elliott Rowand, Esq.
In Columbia, S. C. on the 1st inst., Mrs. Mary Ann Thomas, consort of Stephen Thomas, Esq., of this city, in the 68th year of her age.
In Camden Co., Ga., on the 3d inst., Dr. John H. Hardee, in the 33d year of his age.
In Augusta, on the 9th inst., Mr. Charles Blake, aged about 23 years, a native of Woodstock, Shenandoah co., Va.

Issue of July 25, 1835

Married on Wednesday the 22d inst., by the Rev. Mr. Hanckel, Capt. Edward W. Mathewes, to Miss Sarah Antonio Toomer, all of this city.
On Tuesday evening 21st inst., by the Rev. Mr. Gilman, Mr. G. W. Delacrois, to Miss Amanda M., daughter of Mrs. Sarah Wilmans, all of this city.
Died on the 12th inst., in the District of Abbeville, and in the vicinity of Warrington, S. C., Mrs. Sarah Ann Boyd, the wife of John Boyd, and daughter of John Gray, in the 27th year of her age.
Died in Vicksbury, on the 29th inst., the Rev. Alexander Tally, of the Miss Con., leaving a wife and two little daughters. From the best information I have, I think brother Talley was a native of Green co., Ga...in S. C. Conference. (account and eulogy). Benj. A. Horton, Vicksburg, May 30.
At the Walnuts Hills, on July 7th, Mrs. Harriet, wife of the Rev. Dr. Beecher.

Issue of August 1, 1835

Departed this life on Wednesday 22d inst., Mr. Jeremiah J. Miles, of St. Paul's Parish, Planter...left a wife and one child.

Issue of August 8, 1835

Died in Greenville, S. C. on the 26th ult., Mr. Nathaniel Vannoy, in the 87th year of his age...a native of N. C., and the first person born in the Western part of that state.
Same place, 28th ult., Mr. Elisha Hamlin, in the 22d year of his age...graduate of S. C. College.

Issue of August 15, 1835

Died on the 4th inst., Walter Izard Manigault, aged 14, son of the late Major G. H. Manigault, of this city.
In Savannah, on the 28th ult., A. Aldrich, Jr., in the 24th year of his age.
On the 16th ult., at the Red Sulphur Springs, Va., Thomas Alston, son of the late Col. John A. Alston, of Waccamaw, S. C.
At New York, 7th inst., Martin Woodworth, merchant, of Savannah, Ga.
In Mobile, 31st ult., T. J. O'Connor, of the firm of Curran & O'Conner.

Issue of August 22, 1835

Died at New-York, on the 14th inst., in the 55th year of his age, at the residence of Capt. M. Berry, Mr. Joseph Hicks, merchant of Charleston, S. C.
At New-York, on the 13th inst., John Bentley, merchant, of Savannah, Ga.

Issue of August 29, 1835

Died at the residence of Mrs. Shevolett, in Orangeburgh District, S. C., Mr. Louis Britt, a native of Brunswick co., Va., but for the last five or six years a resident of this state.
At Tuscaloosa, Alabama, 6th inst., Mrs. Sarah A. Gayle, consort of Governor Gayle.

Issue of September 5, 1835

Died in Augusta, on the 16th inst., Mrs. Mary Murren, in the 69th year of her age.
In Newport, Rhode Island, on Friday the 21st ult., in the 70th year of her age, Mrs. Honora Pyne, relict of the late John Pyne, of this state.
Married on Tuesday evening last, by the Rev. Mr. Bachman, Mr. John Everett, of Baltimore, to Miss Elizabeth Sigwald, of this city.

Issue of September 12, 1835

Died at her residence on Canonchee Bluff, Liberty Co., Ga., Mrs. Sarah Cassels, aged 66 years....
Near Litchfield, Arkansas, on the 19th ult., Miss M. E. J. Means, aged 21, daughter of J. P. Means, late of Greene Co., Ala.
On the same day, and near the same place, Mrs. E. H. Waddell, aged 26, late of Union District, S. C.
On 25th ult., near the same place, Miss E. White, aged 24, late of Union District.

Issue of September 19, 1835

Died, in Walterboro', on the morning of August 31st, Frances Hayne Stall, aged four years, youngest daughter of Thos D. Stall, Esq....
Death of Mr. Edward Barrett, of Sumter district...on 30th August, in the 60 year of his age. (eulogy)

Issue of September 26, 1835

Married on Sunday morning, 16th Aug. ult., at Harmony Church, by the Rev. James Parsons, Lemuel B. Davis, Esq., to Mrs. Leonora McCleary, all of Sumter District.
Died, in this city, on the 19th ult., Mrs. Mary C. Fishburne, in the 51st year of her age.
In this city, on the 5th inst., Miss Mary Ann Hatfield, aged 19 years.
In Yorkville, S. C., 5th inst., Joseph M'Cosh, aged 80 years.
At his residence, in Clinton, Ga., on Monday evening, 31st ult., General William Flewellen, in the 84th year of his age.
At Baltimore, on the 16th inst., in the 38th year of his age, Rev. William Nevins, D. D., Pastor of the First Presbyterian Church of that city.

Departed this life on the 26th August, at Charleston, Illinois, Dr. William Mitchell, brother of Rev. J. A. Mitchell, of this city, formerly of Elizabethtown, Tenn., leaving a wife and three children....in the 32d year of his age.

Issue of October 3, 1835

Died, in this city, on the 21st ult., Miss Mary Eliza Smith Miles, daughter of John Miles, Esq., of St. Paul's Parish, aged 22.
On Sunday 20th ult., at his summer residence, near the Bradford Springs, in Claremont County, Col. Evan Benbow, in the 71st year of his age.
On the 25th ult., at Erin, near Coosawhatchie, Mr. Henry Gregorie, aged 29.
Died at Hamburg, S. C., on the 8th Sept., Benjamin Chaplin, son of Joseph and Elizabeth F. Milligan, in the 4th year of his age....

Issue of October 10, 1835

Death of Mary Elizabeth, daughter of John and Susan Robinson, who departed this life the 5th inst., in the 22d year of her age....
Died on the 14th ult., in Chester District, Miss Lucretia Knox, in the 25th year of her age...left an aged mother, brothers and sisters.
Died of a painful illness, near Zebulon, Pike Co., Geo., on the 26th inst., at the house of his brother, the Rev. Arthur M. Mooney, Mr. John D. Mooney, formerly of Tennessee, aged 17 years... member of the Presbyterian Church....   J. T. S.

Issue of October 17, 1835

Married on Wednesday evening 7th inst., at Aiken, by the Rev. Mr. Ford, Mr. Horton Hamner, to Miss Leocadia Kennedy, of Charleston.
Married, on Tuesday evening, 6th inst., by the Rev. Dr. Gadsden, Edward Morris, Esq., to Miss Margaret Ann Primrose, eldest daughter of the late Robert Primrose.
Died in Camden, S. C., on the 5th inst., at the Rembert Camp Ground, in the 23d year of his age, Rev. P. W. Clenny, Preacher in charge of the Santee Circuit...Methodist Episcopal Chruch
At Georgetown, S. C., on the 3d inst., Mr. John Coachman, a native citizen of that district, in the 67th year of his age.

Issue of October 24, 1835

Married on the 15th inst.,by the Rev. Bishop Bowen, at St. Michael's Church, Mr. Charles A. Desaussure, to Miss Thomasine Welding, second daughter of the late Wm. W. Fell.
On the 5th of Sept., at St. Bride's Church, London, Ch. Choisy, of Geneva, Switzerland, to Jessie, second daughter of A. M'Dowall, Esq. of Charleston, S. C.
Departed this life on the 8th inst., Mrs. Lucretia Horry, in the 83d year of her age.
At Hampstead, on Monday the 12th inst., Miss Sarah N. Screven, daughter of the late Thomas Screven.
Died at his son's residence in Houston co., on the 11th ult., Thomas Dozier, Sen., in the 84th year of his age. He was formerly of Edgefield District, S. C., but for the last two years of Houston Co., Ga.
Died suddenly on the 28th August, on the road from Castleton to Braemer to Ballater in Scotland, Mary Scott Bryce, of this

city, in the twenty-sixth year of her age, leaving her parents....
   At Marion Court House on the 28th ult., Mrs. A. J. Harlee, consort of Dr. Robert Harlee of that place, aged 16 years and 4 months.
   In Columbia, on the 7th inst., Mr. L. Hardin, aged 83 years.
   At his residence, near Anderson C. H. on the 1st inst., P. Keys, Esq., in the 70th year of his age.
   At his residence in McIntosh Co., on the night of the 7th inst., the Rev. Edward P. Postell, in the 38th year of his age.
   In Abbeville District, on the 15th inst., Rebecca Elizabeth, only daughter of John and Elizabeth Gray, in the 21st year of her age.
   Departed this life on Thursday the 1st inst.,at the house of Mr. Robert Humber, in Butts County, Ulysses M. C. Montgomery, in the 30th year of his age...a citizen of DeKalb Co....left widow and aged parents. (long account and eulogy).

Issue of October 31, 1835

   Married on Thursday evening last, by the Rev. Mr. Mitchell, Mr. Mortimer Calvert, to Miss Ann Naser both of this city.
   In Columbia, S. C., on the 10th inst., in the 33d year of her age, Mrs. Jane Shand Bryce, wife of Mr. Robert Bryce, of that place, and youngest daughter of the late Mr. Robert Shand, of this city.

Issue of November 7, 1835

   Married on Wednesday last, by the Rev. Mr. White, Charles L. Trenhom, of this city, to Miss Portia A., daughter of Kinsey Burden, Sen., Esq. of John's Island.
   In Columbia, on the 29th ult., at the Presbyterian Church, by the Rev. Dr. Leland, Rev. Wm. B. Yates of Charleston, to Mrs. Jane B. Taylor, of that town.
   Died in Georgetown, on the 27th ult., Mrs. Elizabeth Wragg, an old and respectable inhabitant of that town.
   In Fairfield District on the 22d ult., Mr. T. C. Ware, in the 40th year of his age.
   On the 27th, Mrs. Lucy R., consort of John M. Waring, Esq., aged 32.

Issue of November 14, 1835

   Married on the 21st Oct. at St. Paul's Church, by the Rev. Mr. Hanckell, John Rutledge Smith, Esq. of this city, to Sophia Gordon, only daughter of the late James G. Taylor, of Virginia.
   On Tuesday evening, 3d inst., by the Rev. Mr. Mitchell, Mr. Wm. Tennent, to Miss E. S. Hopkins, daughter of the late Jos. Hopkins all of this place.
   On Wednesday last, by the Rt. Rev. Bishop Bowen, Dr. Henry R. Frost, to Miss Mary D., daughter of the late Thos. Lessesne, Esq.
   In Prince Williams Parish, on the 25th inst., by the Rev. Mr. Elliott, Col. Charles C. Gregorie, to Miss Emily, youngest daughter of James Gregorie, Esq.
   Departed this life on the 7th of November last, in the 27th year of his age, Nicholas Harleston Rutledge, youngest son of Edward and Mrs. Jane Rutledge.
   Died on Monday, the 26th ult., Mrs. Esther Lloyd, in the 71st year of her age.

Issue of November 21, 1835

Married on Tuesday evening last, by the Rev. W. States Lee, of Edisto, Mr. Dandridge C. You, to Miss Mary Lee, third daughter of Joshua Lockwood, sen., Esq. all of this place.
Married, on the 19th inst., by the Rev. J. Dickson, in the 2d Presbyterian Church, Mr. Thomas Dixon, to Miss Elvina Long, youngest daughter of the late John Long, all of this city.
On Wednesday morning, the 18th inst., in the second Presbyterian Church, by the Rev. Mr. Manly, Elijah Freeman, Esq., of St. Pauls Parish, planter, to Miss Eliza Ann Simonds, of this City.
On Tuesday evening 10th inst., by the Rev. Mr. Manly, Mr. William Kirk, of London, to Miss Catherine M. Luthern, of this city.
On Wednesday evening, 11th inst., by the Rev. Mr. Manly, Charles H. Bryant, to Miss Emma, eldest daughter of Frederick Naser, Esq., all of this city.
On Thursday evening 12th inst., by the Rt. Rev. Bishop Bowen, William S. Elliot, Esq. to Miss Anna Huger, second daughter of Major John Huger.
Died at his residence, Waxhaw, Lancaster District, on the 24th ult., Thomas McDow, Esq., in the 71st year of his age...in the Revolution...a member of the Presbyterian Church....
Departed this life Mrs. Rachael Woolf, in the 81st year of her age....(eulogy).

Issue of November 28, 1835

Married in Christ Church Parish, on Thursday evening the 27th inst., by the Rev. Mr. Gildersleeve, Mr. James Hibben Leland, to Miss Susan, only daughter of Capt. Richard Morrison.
On Tuesday evening the 24th inst., by the Revd. Mr. Hanckell Dr. Richard Allan, to Miss Ann Allston, only daughter of the late Octavius Cripps.
Died at his residence in Greenville District, on the 30th ult., Ransom Cobb, aged 43 years.
Died at Chaneyville, La., on the 30th of August last, Mr. John B. Jones, in the 28th year of his age, a native of this city...left mother and wife....

Issue of December 5, 1835

Married on Tuesday the 24th ult.,by the Right Rev. Dr. Bowen, John McPherson, Esq. of Prince William's Parish, to Mary Anna, second daughter of Charles Kiddell, Esq. of this city.
On Tuesday evening, 24th ult., by the Right Rev. Bishop Bowen, James K. Anderson, Esq. of Florida, to Harriet Louisa, youngest daughter of the late Joshua Brown, Esq., of this city.
On Wednesday night, 25th ult., by the Rev. Mr. Martin, Mr. James H. R. Washington, of Milledgeville, Ga., to Miss Mary Ann daughter of Col. S. Hammond, of Beach Island.
On Thursday evening, 26th ult., by the Right Rev. Bishop Bowen, Dr. Edward Porcher, of St. Stephens, to Elizabeth Ashby, second daughter of the late Wm. F. Shackelford, of this city.
On Tuesday evening last, by the Rev. Dr. Bachman, Mr. Joseph Prevost, to Miss Margaret Henrietta, eldest daughter of the late Capt. Alexander Taylor, all of this city.
By the Rev. Mr. Brewer, Mr. Samuel M. Gilman, to Miss Annie O. Kugley, youngest daughter of Mrs. Martha Kugley.
Died in Columbia, S. C., on the 5th ult.,Mr. Geo. A. Hillegas, in the 34th year of his age, a native of Charleston.
Departed this life on the 13th inst., in the 44th year of her age, Mrs. Sarah Heron, formerly of Elbert Co., Ga.

Death of Mrs.Elizabeth Ann, consort of the Rev. James DuPre... departed this life at the residence of her mother, Mrs. Monk, on 6th Nov., in the 24th year of her age...member of the Baptist Church at the High Hills of Santee...(long eulogy) Sumter, Nov. 28th,1835.

Issue of December 12, 1835

Married on Monday evening last, by the Rt. Rev. Bishop Bowen, James S. McPherson, Esq., to Cornelia, third daughter of the late Wm. Washington, all of this city.

On Tuesday evening last, by the Rev. Mr. Martin, Mr. S. J. Dickson, to Miss Eliza M., third daughter of Capt. S. Webber, all of this city.

In Wilmington, N. C., on the 31st ult., by the Rev. Thos F. Davis, the Rev. Daniel Cobia, A. M., of Charleston, S. C., to Miss Louisa Hooper, daughter of A. M. Hooper, Esq. of that place.

At Marblehead, Mass., on the 25th ult., by the Rev. Mr. Dana, Mr. Wm. C. Hichborn, of this city, to Louisa, youngest daughter of the late Hon. Nathaniel Hooper, of the former place.

Married, by the Rev. S. J. Cassels, on Monday evening, the 23d ult., Rev. J. B. Cassels to Miss Lucia Magruder, daughter of Judge Thomas Magruder, of Columbia Co., Ga.

Died on the 4th inst., on the Plantation of T. Wigfall, in St. Thomas Parish, Daniel Shepard, in the 28th year of his age.... left wife and two young children.

Issue of December 19, 1835

Married on Thursday evening last, by the Rev. Mr. Buist, Mr. Robert S. Millar, to Miss Caroline J. Pemble, all of this city.

On Wednesday evening, the 9th inst.,by the Rev. W. S. Lee, Dr. Lockwood Alison, of Alabama, to Miss Jane E., youngest daughter of Josiah Taylor, Esq. of this city.

On Wednesday evening last, by the Rev. Dr. Gadsden, Mr. James Fife, Merchant to Isabella M., eldest daughter of Mr. William Timmons, all of this city.

In Wilmington, N. C., on the 1st inst., the Rev. Daniel Cobia, of Charleston, S. C., to Miss Louis (sic) Hooper, eldest daughter of A. M. Hooper, Esq.

At Liverpool, on the 28th Oct., by the Rev. M. Oppenheiner, Major Lazarus, of S. C., U. S. to Phebe, daughter of the late Samuel Yates, Esq. of Liverpol. (sic)

Died on Friday the 4th inst., in the 31st year of her age, Mrs. Elizabeth T. Dunlap, consort of Dr. George Washington Dunlap of Lancasterville...left husband and two infant children....

Died in Beaufort, S. C., on the 6th inst., Mrs. Emma Heyward, aged 29 years, wife of Charles Heyward, of this city, and daughter of the late Col. Edward Barnwell, of Beaufort.

Died, at Chester Court House, on the 9th inst., Mr. Joseph Thornton, of Philadelphia, but for a number of years a resident of the former place.

Issue of December 26, 1835

Married on Wednesday evening, the 9th inst., by the Rev. W. S. Lee, Dr. Lockwood Alison, of Alabama, to Miss Jane E., youngest daughter of Josiah Taylor, Esq. of this city.

On Tuesday evening, the 15th inst., by the Rev. Mr. Bachman, John M. Chisolm, to Ann Jane, second daughter of Dr. Edward W. North.

Also, on the same eveing, Robert Chisolm to Susan Emma, youngest daughter of Dr. Edw. W. North.

On Wednesday evening, 16th inst., by the Rev. Mr. Hanckel, Francis Simons Parker, Esq., to Miss Mary Taylor Lance, eldest daughter of the Rev. M. H. Lance.

On Thursday evening last, by the Rev. Mr. Trapier, Col. Richard Felder, of St. Mathew's Parish, to Miss Jane, eldest daughter of Thomas Duggan, Esq. of this city.

Died in Greensboro', Alabama, on the morning of the 17th ult., in the 47th year of his age, the Rev. James Hillhouse, for several years Pastor of the Presbyterian Church in that place... born in York District, S. C...licensed to preach in 1815... twice married..his first wife was the daughter of Patrick Norris, formerly of Pendleton, S. C.,--his second wife was Miss Emily Richardson, of Vermont. (eulogy)

Died at his residence in Carnesville, on the 2d inst., Col. James C. Terrell, who departed this life last night....

In Philadelphia, Mr. Isaac Snowden, for many years the Treasurer of the General Assembly of the Presbyterian Church.

Issue of January 2, 1836

Married on Thursday evening, 24th inst., by the Rev. Mr. Bachman, Mr. R. J. Eason to Miss Lavinia, youngest daughter of J. Walter, Esq. of this city.

On Thursday evening 17th inst., by the Rev. C. Hanckel, James Simons, Esq. to Sarah L., daughter of Major Samuel Wragg.

Died on the 12th inst., in the 55th year of her age, Mrs. Marianne G. Porcher, relict of the late George Porcher, of St. John's, Berkley.

On the 26th inst., in the 21st year of his age, William T. M. Waring, son of the late Dr. Edmund T. Waring.

In Columbia, on the 3d inst., Mrs. Mary E. Burnap, in the 29th year of her age.

In New York on the 22d inst., Doctor David Hosack, one of the most distinguished physicians of that city.

Issue of January 9, 1836

Married at Camden, on the 31st ult., by the Rev. George Howe, Professor in the Theological Seminary at Columbia, Mr. William D. McDowall, of this city, to MissSusan K. Witherspoon, eldest daughter of the Rev. J. Witherspoon, Pastor of the Presbyterian Church, Camden, S. C.

On the 22d ult., at the residence of Charles Bering, Esq., (Combahee), by the Rev. Mr. DeLaveaux, Charles B. Smith, Esq. to Miss Ann Claiborne, youngest daughter of the late Henry T. Farmer, M. D.

Departed this life on Sunday the 27th Dec., at Almonbury Hill, St. Bartholomews Parish, Mrs. Sophia F. Sheppheard, aged 55 years.

On the 31st Dec. at her place of residence in St. George's, Dorchester, Elizabeth Strobel, in the 75th year of her age, who had been a member of the Methodist Episcopal Church for upwards of 40 years.

Issue of January 16, 1836

Married on the 7th inst., by the Rev. Mr. Yates, Mr. Jas. Johnston, of Columbia, to Miss Jane, daughter of Mr. Whiteford Smith, of this city.

On the evening of the 9th, by the Rt. Rev. Bishop Bowen, Edward Croft Esq., of Greenville, S. C., to Sarah, eldest daughter of the Hon. E. H. Bay, of this city.

In St. Bartholomews Parish, on Wednesday, 30th Dec., by the Rev. Dr. Boyd, John H. Dent, Esq., to Mary Elizabeth, eldest daughter of Robert Morrison, Esq., all of Colleton District.

Departed this life on the 1st inst., Mrs. Caroline Holmes, consort of Henry P. Holmes, and daughter of the late Thos. Drayton.

Died at his residence, on 27th inst., in St. George's Parish, Mr. Thomas Thackam, aged 43.

At Savannah, on the 29th ult., Hon. T. U. P. Charlton, known for many years as a distinguished citizen of the State of Ga.

On the 18th ult., at his residence in Oglethorpe co., Rev. Benj. Pope of the M. E. Church.

In Milledgeville, on the 20th ult., Maj. Wm. W. Carnes, late Comptroller General.

On the 5th ult., at his late residence in Montgomery co, Ala., Col. Benj. B. Lamar, formerly of Georgia.

Issue of January 23, 1836

Married on Thursday evening, 14th inst., by the Rev.Mr. Manly, Mr. E. Cheney, to Miss Martha M. Joye, all of this city.

On Thursday evening, 14th inst., by the Rev. B. C. Webb, Edward J. Webb, Esq., to Miss Mary B., eldest daughter of Capt. F. Fraser, of St. Bartholomew's Parish.

On the 9th inst., by the Right Rev. Bishop Bowen, Edward Croft, Esq. of Greenville, S. C., to Miss Sarah, eldest daughter of the Hon. Judge Bay.

Departed this life on Sunday the 17th inst., Mr. John Odum, a native of Williamsburgh District, but for many years past a resident of St. John's Parish, Berkley.

On the 16th ult., at his residence in Lowndes Co., Ala., Mr. Robert H. Brown, in the 27th year of his age...a native of S. C., and moved to this State about three years ago.

Issue of January 30, 1836

Married on Thursday evening 21st inst, by the Rev. Mr. Hanckel, Dr. John P. Porcher, of St. John's, Berkley, to Anna Ford, second daughter of the late Charles Banks, of Charleston.

Died at Savannah, on the 23d, Mr. William D. Judah, of the house of J. B. Herbert & Co., aged 39 years, formerly of Sagatuck, Con.

On his passage from Charleston to New York, Capt. Allyn Smith, of the latter city.

Issue of February 6, 1836

Married, on Thursday morning, 28th ult., by the Rev. Mr. Trapier, James Kerr, Esq., of Dublin, Ireland, to Miss Elizabeth, only daughter of the late Wm. Wilkie, Esq. of this city.

Died at his residence in Orangeburg District, S. C., Mr. Richard Norton, son of Mr. Daniel Norton, Sen. of Sumter District.

Issue of February 13, 1836

Married on Wednesday evening 3d inst., by the Rev. Mr. J. Bachman, Mr. Andrew Jackson Haupt, of Savannah, Geo., to Miss Caroline, youngest daughter of the late Casper Naser, Esq. of this city.

In Tallahassee, Fla., on the 31st Jan., at the M. E. Church, by the Rev. Mr. Knowles, Robert L. Tillinghast, Esq., to Miss Sophia E. Tillinghast, both of Beaufort District, S. C.

Died in this city on Friday, the 5th inst., in the 55th year of his age, Mr. Thomas Burnham, a native of Georgetown, S. C., and for many years a resident in this city--leaving a large and respectable circle of relatives and friends....

Issue of February 20, 1836

Married at Stoney Creek, Prince Williams, on the evening of the 11th inst., by the Rev. Edward Palmer, W. Ferguson Hutson, Esq., to Miss Sophronia L., daughter of Rev. Edw. Palmer.
Departed this life on the 7th inst., at Pee Dee, Mrs. Elizabeth Collins, in the 67th year of her age.
At Edgefield, on the 6th ult., Jefferson Richardson, Esq., in the 38th year of his age...for many years Clerk of the Court of Common Pleas, and for upwards of a year Judge of the Court of Ordinary.

Issue of February 27, 1836

Died on Wednesday 27th ult., the Rev. Frederick David Schaeffer, D. D., late Pastor of the German Lutheran Congregation in the city of Philadelphia.
Departed this life at San Pedro, near Matanzas, Cuba, on the 3d inst., in the 23d year of his age, Mr. Jacob Lawrence Valk, third son of Jacob R. Valk, of consumption.
Died, on Saturday evening last, Gen. Edward King, of Cincinnati. He was the son of the celebrated Rufus King of New York....
Cincinnati Journal, Feb. 11

Issue of March 5, 1836

Married on Monday evening last, by the Rev. Bishop Bowen, the Rev. B. C. Webb, of St. Luke's Parish, to Miss H. Allison, daughter of Joshua Lockwood, jr., Esq. of this city.
On Thursday 25th ult., at the residence of Capt. D. Townsend, Edisto Island, by the Rev. Mr. Manley, J. Jenkins Mikell, Esq. to Miss Amarapthia J. Townsend.
Died on the 13th Feb., on board the schr. Caleb Goodwin, on a voyage to New Orleans, to which he was going for the restoration of his health, Thos Waring Smith, son of William S. Smith, in the 28th year of his age.
Died, in St. Lukes' Parish, George Washington Morrall, Esq., in the 50th year of his age.

Issue of March 12, 1836

Married, on Sunday evening last, in the Lutheran Church, by the Rev. Dr. Bachman, the Rev. Edwin A. Bolles, to Miss Harriet A., only daughter of the late Wm. Parler, Esq. of this city.
On Tuesday evening last, by the Rev. Mr. Manly, Mr. Peter G. Gerard, to Miss Elizabeth Dupree, all of this City.
At the High Hills of Santee, on Wednesday the 27th Jan., by the Rev. James DuPre, Mr. James C. Little of Benton, Miss., to Miss Sarah W. Denson, of Sumter District.
Departed this life on Friday the 5th ult., at his residence in Orangeburg, S. C., Mr. Samuel Phillips Jones, in the 77th year of his age...born in Colchester, Conn in 1759, removed to S. C. in 1790, and for nearly 40 years has been a resident of this village.
Died at his plantation in Abbeville District on the 17th of Feb., George Brownlee, sen., in the 80th year of his age. He was born in the County of Antrim, Ireland, and the last 65 years a citizen of Abbeville....

At his residence in Abbeville District on the 25th Feb., William McCrone, a native of the County of Antrim, Ireland, in the 93d year of his age.

Issue of March 19, 1836

Married on Wednesday evening, 9th inst., by the Rev. C. Gadsden, Mr. Henry D. Walker, to Miss Jane A. Stewart, all of this city.

On Thursday evening, the 10th inst., by the Rev. C. Hanckell, Alfred Raoul, of Columbia, S. C., to Miss Eliza B. Hasell, eldest daughter of the late Andrew Hasell, Esqr., of this city.

On Thursday evening the 10th inst., by the Rev. C. Hanckell, Thomas Savage Heyward, Esqr., of St. Luke's Parish, to Miss Georgianna Hasell, youngest daughter of the late Andrew Hasell, Esqr., of this city.

Departed this life on Tuesday morning, last inst., Lills Shaw Cousar, consort of the Rev. John Cousar, in the 34th year of her age...left four sons, all in minority.

Departed this life at Mobile, Ala., on Saturday the 20th Feb., last, Mrs. Elizabeth Rogers, in the 73d year of her age... a native of the Parish of St. John's Berkley, but for many years a resident of the town of Camden, S. C...a member of the Presbyterian Church.

Departed this life on the 12th inst., in the 29th year of his age, Col. D. W. Pearson, of Orangeburg District...left a widow, and four young children....

Issue of March 26, 1836

Married on Thursday evening, 17th inst., by the Rev. Dr. Capers, Mr. John G. Fair, to Miss Eliza Brockway, both of this city.

On the 10th inst., by William H. Preston, Esq., Rev. William B. Richards, to Miss Ann L. Lowry, daughter of the Rev. M. Lowry, of Jasper, Ga.

In the Circular Church, on Tuesday evening last, by the Rev. Mr. Post, Isaac Henry Warren, Esq., of Princeton, Mass., to Miss Maria Alexina, daughter of Peter Catonet, Esq. of this city.

Died at Columbia, on the 13th inst., in the 63d year of his age, Dr. Edward Fisher, a native of Virginia, and for more than 30 years one of the most loved and respected citizens of Columbia.

Issue of April 2, 1836

Married at Georgetown, S. C., on the 24th ult., by the Rev. Mr. Walker, Mr. Frederick R. Dixon, of Georgia, to Miss Amanda E., eldest daughter of Richard S. Wish, of Charleston, S. C.

Departed this life on the 12th inst., at the residence of Joseph Longworth, Esq., St. Lukés Parish, Mrs. Ann Beck, relict of the Rev. John Beck, aged 64 years....

In the County of Tuscaloosa, Ala., on the 15th ult., Mr. David Wilson, in the 57 year of his age.

At Washington, D. C., on the 22d ult., Gen. Mount Joe Baily, an officer of the Revolution, in the 82d year of his age.

At Philadelphia, on the 18th inst., Miss Francis Butler, daughter of the late Hon. Pierce Butler, of S. C.

Issue of April 9, 1836

Married on the 5th inst., by the Rev. Dr. Capers, John Jenkins, Esq. of John's Island, to Miss Harriet A. Serjeant, of this city.

Married on Tuesday evening the 5th inst., by the Rev. Dr. Gadsden, Mr. Robert E. Brown, to Miss Amelia Elizabeth, second daughter of Capt. James Welsman, all of this city.

On Thursday evening, 31st ult., by the Rev. A. G. Brewer, Mr. James E. Walker, to Miss Rebecca Brewer, all of this city.

In the 1st Presbyterian Church, Savannah, Ga., on Tuesday evening, 8th inst., by the Rev. R. F. Scott, Rev. Julius J. Dubose, of S. C., to Miss Margaret E. Thompson, of that city.

Died on the 26th ult., Captain Ulmer A. Davis, Member of the House of Representatives for Prince William's Parish.

At Charleston, S. C., on the 4th inst., while on his way to the Island of Cuba, Henry Barber, aged 23 years, eldest son of Mr. William Barber, one of the Editors of this Paper....

Newport, R. I. Mercury, March 19

Issue of April 16, 1836

Married on Wednesday evening 6th inst., by Rev. B. Manly, David B. W. Hard, M. D. of Montgomery, Ala., to Miss Ann Miranda, eldest daughter of Benj. F. Hard, Esq. of this city.

On Tuesday evening last, by the Rev. Mr. Spear, Mr. John Minturn of New Orleans, to Miss Lydia M. Clement of this city.

On the 10th inst., by the Rev. A. G. Brewer, Mr. Alexander Campbell, of Alabama, Merchant, to Miss Jacintha E. C., eldest daughter of Jacint Laval, of this city.

Died at Beach Island, on the 3d inst., Mrs. Sarah R. M. Ardis, in the 63d year of her age....

At Georgetown on the 5th inst., Dr. Edward Gibbes Thomas, aged 61 years and 5 months.

At his residence on South Island, on the 27th ult., Mr. Wm. T. Brown, aged 36 years.

On Pee Dee, on the 7th inst., Mrs. ____ Price, consort of Mr. Isham Price.

In Chester, New Hampshire, on the 21st ult., Hon. John Bell, formerly Governor of that State, in the 71st year of his age.

Issue of April 23, 1836

Married on Thursday evening the 7th inst., by the Rev. Mr. Barnwell, Edwd L. Trenholm, of this city, to Eliza B., youngest daughter of the late J. Holmes, Esq. of John's Island.

On Wednesday evening the 13th inst., in St. Michael's Church, by the Rev. Mr. Spears, Dr. J. D. Dickerson of Virginia, to Miss Eliza L., daughter of the late Dr. Henry Gleize, of this city.

On Thursday evening the 14th inst., in St. Paul's Parish, by the Rev. Mr. Rogers, Lionel C. Boyle, Esq. to Mary Julia, only daughter of the late Josiah Perry, Esq.

Departed this life on Sunday morning the 17th inst., Mrs. Rebecca Folker, consort of the late John Casper Folker, aged 76 years and 1 month.

Died at his residence in St. George's Dorchester, on Saturday the 19th March, Mr. William Murray, Sen. in the 53d year of his age....

In Greenville, S. C., on the 3d inst., Mr. Thos Rowland, in the 88th year of his age.

In Columbia, Co, Ga., on the 18th inst.,Mr. John L. Anderson, in the 42d year of his age, a native of Boston, and for many years a resident of Augusta.

In Hawkinsville, Ga., the Hon. James Polhill, Judge of the Supreme Court of the Southern Circuit.

Died at Fort Barnwell, St. John's River, E. F., on the night of the 1st inst., Private John Rish, of Lexington, S. C., belonging to Capt. Quattlebaum's Company....

On the morning of the 13st ult., Private Matthew Bagle(?) of Colleton, S. C., belonging to Capt. Douein's Company and attached to Capt. Allans Company at that place, March 25th,1836....
Malikiah Clark, mustered in the service of the U. S. under Capt. Douein, and attached to Capt. Allan's Co., March 25th, 1836.
At his residence in Pickens District, S. C., on the 7th inst., Mr. Robert Henry Briggs, in the 47th year of his age...leaving a widow and five children.

Issue of April 30, 1836

Married on Tuesday evening the 26th inst., at the residence of Mrs. Gen. Pinckney in this city, by the Rev. Cotesworth Pinckney, Mr. Daniel Heyward Hamilton to Miss Rebecca Middleton, second daughter of John Middleton, Esq., deceased, late of St. John's Santee.
On Tuesday evening the 26th inst., by the Rev. Mr. Brewer, Mr. R. W. Vanderhorst, to Miss Emeline Amanda, daughter of the late James Mitchell, all of this city.
Died on the 12th inst., in Salem, Sumter District, Mrs. Margaret Frierson Muldrow, consort of Dr. Robt. Muldrow, in the 42d year of her age, leaving a husband and six children....
Died in Columbia a few days since, the Rev. Geo. Reid, a member of Harmony Presbytery.
Died at Onancock, Accomac Co., Eastern Shore of Virginia, on the 8th inst., Rev. Wm. H. Mitchell, of the Protestant Episcopal Church, formerly of Charleston, S. C., aged 36 years.
We learn that Daniel Faust, Esq., an old and respect citizen of Columbia, died at that place a day or two since.

Issue of May 7, 1836

Died onJohn's Island, the 28th April, Miss Susan H. L. White, daughter of Rev. E. White....
Died near Jacksonham, Lancaster, S. C., on the 6th of April, Capt. James Huey, in the 77th year of his age--a soldier of the Revolution.

Issue of May 14, 1836

Married on Tuesday evening, 5th inst., by the Rt. Rev. Bishop Bowen, Henry D. Lesesne, Esq. to Miss Harriette Petigru.
Married on Saturday evening, 7th inst., by the Rev. Dr. Bachman, Benjamin P. Fishburne, of Walterboro, to Miss Martha M. Fishburne, of this place.
On Wednesday evening last, at Trinity Church, by the Rev. Mr. Smith, Mr. Wm. H. Jones, to Miss Catharine Rebecca Scott, youngest daughter of the late Daniel Benoist, all of this city.
Died on the 29th ult., Mary Elizabeth Robinson Buist, only daughter of Rev. E. T. Buist, aged 10 months and 4 days.
On the 8th inst., Wilhelmina Moughan, infant daughter of Rev. John Forrest, Minister of the 1st Presbyterian Church of this city...
Death of Mr. Michael Makensie, who was born in the county of Meath, Ireland, 1799, and departed this life 26th ult., in the 38th year of his age....
In Lincoln Co., N. C., on the 21st ult., Hutchins G. Burton, Esq., formerly Gov. of N. C., and a member of Congress from the same state.
At his father's residence, St. Mary's, Ga., on the 1st inst., Archibald Clark, jun., late of Franklin College, aged 20 years.
At his residence in Warrenton, Ga., on the morning of the 20th inst., Dennis L. Ryan, Esq., in the 54th year of his age....

111

Issue of May 21, 1836

Married on Wednesday evening last, by the Rev. W. A. Gamewell, William F. Simons, of Philadelphia, to Sarah, second daughter of John Thompson, of this city.
On Tuesday evening, 10th inst., by the Rev. W. A. Gamewell, Mr. Manning Reeder, of Newberry, to Miss Louisa M., third daughter of Henry Muckenfuss, of this city.
On the 3d inst., by the Rev. Mr. Postell, Dr. J. S. Shingler, to Miss Elizabeth Ann, daughter of P. W. Frederick, Esq., of Orangeburg, S. C.
Married at Washington City, on the 5th inst., by the Rev. Mr. Hawley, Mr. Andrew P. Calhoun of S. C., to Miss Margaret M. Green, of that city.
Died at St. Augustine, on Saturday night, the 7th inst., John J. Bulow, Jr., Esq. a wealthy planter of Musquitoe Co., East Florida.
At Key West, on Saturday 30th ult., Mr. ____ Douglass, of Lancaster Dist., S. C. On 1st May, J: B. Malphus, 2d Lt. in Col. Brisbane's regiment of volunteers, of Colleton Dist., S. C. On the 3d May, Thomas Bone of S. C. Volunteers for Florida.

Issue of May 28, 1836

Married on the 18th inst., by the Rev. Paul Trapier, Mr. Edward Henry Gay, of Boston, to Mrs. Margaret Summers Merchant, of this city.
On Thursday evening 19th inst., by the Rev. Mr. Gilman, Mr. James Boatwright, of Columbia, to Ellen daughter of Charles H. Miott, Esq. of this city.
Departed this life on the 5th inst., Tuskagee, Alabama, Dr. Thomas Riggs, of this city, in the 25th year of his age...graduated from the Medical College of S. C....

Issue of June 4, 1836

Married at the residence of Mr. S. L. Bennett, Sumter Dist., on Wednesday evening, 30th March, by the Rev. J. Cousar, Samuel J. Montgomery, of Williamsburg Dist., to Miss Caroline A. Wooley, of Charleston.
On Wednesday evening 25th inst., by the Rev. Dr. Bachman, Mr. P. V. Dibble, to Miss Frances Ann Evans.
Died at the Hospital in this city, on Friday 27th inst., Mr. John Yargan, in the 19th year of his age...attached to the company of mounted men from Anderson Dist. in this State, volunteers in the Florida Campaign.

Issue of June 11, 1836

Married in Georgia, by John M'Gehee, Esq., Mr. David Hodge, aged 102 years and 2 months, to Miss Elizabeth Raily, aged 40 years, both of Columbia Co., Ga. Mr. Hodge was at Braddock's defeat, and served throughout the whole period of the Rev. War.
On Tuesday evening, 31st ult., by the Rt. Rev. Bishop Bowen, William Ravenel, Esq. to Miss Eliza Butler, daughter of James R. Pringle, Esq. both of this city.
Departed this life on the 10th of May last, Mrs. Charlotte Ling, in the 48th year of her age.... (eulogy)
Died on the 28th April, at his residence in Clarendon, Col. James B. Richardson, formerly Gov. of this state.

Issue of June 18, 1836

Married on Sunday evening last, 12th inst., by the Rev. Thomas Smith, George W. Patterson, Esq., of Pittsburgh, Pa., Merchant, to Miss Sarah Harris, daughter of Dr. Edward Jones, of this city.
Departed this life on the 28th of May, Mrs. Sarah Lance, relict of Col. Lambert Lance. Bowed with the weight of nearly 77 years....

Issue of June 25, 1836

Married on Wednesday evening, 15th inst., by the Rev. Dr. C. E. Gadsden, Dr. Henry V. Toomer, to Miss Mary Priscilla, second daughter of the late Gen. R. W. Vanderhorst, all of this city.
On Wednesday evening, 15th inst., by the Rev. Mr. Smith, Mr. Simeon S. Roath, of Orangeburg District, to Miss Mary Jane Thompson, of this city.
In Athens, Ga., on Tuesday morning, 14th inst., by the Rev. Mr. Hoyt, Col. Paul J. Semmes of Washington, Wilkes Co., to Miss Emily J. Hemphill, of Athens.
Departed this life in this city on the 1st June, Dr. John L. E. W. Shecut, in the 66th year of his age.
Departed this life on the 3d of June, Michael P. Walsh, in the 31st year of his age....(eulogy)

Issue of July 2, 1836

Married on Sunday evening last, at the Lutheran Church of German Protestant, by the Rev. John Bachman, Mr. Octavious L. Whitney, to Miss Elizabeth Ann Luther, daughter of W. W. Wilbur, all of this city.
Died at the Parsonage House of the Methodist Episcopal Church, in this city, at 5 P. M. on Saturday the 25th inst., Thomas Fletcher, the eldest son of the Rev. James Sewell, in the 15th year of his age.
Departed this life in this city on the 8th inst., William C. Doughty, in the 61st year of his age.
Died at Knoxville, Crawford Co., Ga., on the 18th inst., Mrs. Leonora Caroline Gaillard, wife of D. A. Gaillard, and daughter of the late Wm. J. Huguenin, of St. Lukes Parish, Beaufort District, S. C., aged 22 years and 2 months.

Issue of July 9, 1836

Married on Sunday evening, 3d inst., by the Rev. Thomas Smith, Mr. James Steedman to Miss Deborah, second daughter of William Smith, jr., Esq., all of this city.
On Tuesday morning, 5th inst., by the Rev. Dr. Gadsden, Mr. Laurence Benson, to Mrs. Mary Granby, daughter of Mr. Jacob Sluter.
Died at Mount Pelier, Orange co., Va., James Madison...on Tuesday last--June 28.... United States Telegraph, June 30.
Died on the 18th ult., on North Saluda, Greenville Dist., S. C., William Goodlett, sen. in the 78th year of his age...an officer of the American Revolution.
Departed this life in Henry co., Ga., on the 22d May, Jesse Bentley, a Revolutionary Soldier, aged 87 years.

Issue of July 16, 1836

Died on the morning of the 12th inst., Thomas Young Simons, the youngest son of Rev. Mr. and Mrs. Arthur Buist.
At Walterborough, on the 7th inst., Mrs. Sarah A. Ford, consort of Col. Malachi Ford.

Issue of July 23, 1836

Married on Thursday evening 14th inst.,by the Rev. Mr. Bachman, Mr. Frederick Myers, to Martha Davis Myatt, youngest daughter of the late Edward Myatt, of this city.
Died in this city on the 9th inst., Daniel Whitmore, in the 16th year of his age, a native of Liverpool
Departed this life on Thursday morning, the 7th July 1836, Miss Frances Moore Hasket, aged 23 years....came on some time in the last year from New York at the solicitation of her aunt Mrs. Mary Crawford, a resident in Abbeville Dist., S. C....

Issue of July 30, 1836

Died in this city on the 18th inst., Mrs. Margaret E.,wife of Mr. Russel Middleton, and daughter of the late Henry Izard.
on Friday afternoon, the 22d inst., at his summer residence, Pineville, St. Stevens, Daniel Broughton, Esq., planter of St. John's, Berkley, in the 45th year of his age.
Died at his residence in Marengo Co., Ala., on the 8th inst., Mr. Thomas Witherspoon, a native of Williamsburgh Dist., S. C., in the 60th year of his age....
Gen. Robert Augustus Beall died at Macon, Ga., on the 16th inst., in the 32d year of his age.

Issue of August 6, 1836

Married on Thursday 28th ult., by the Rev. Mr. Hanckel, Mr. Wm. M. Newton to Miss Elizabeth Anna Martha, eldest daughter of the late Julus U. G. Angel, all of this city.
On Sunday evening 31st July, by the Rev. Mr. Gamewell, Mr. John M. Jaudrell, to Miss Margaret A. Minus, third daughter of Mrs. Margaret E. Minus, all of this city.
In Philadelphia, on the evening of the 26th ult., by the Rev. Mr. Boardman, Mr. Robert Adger, of this city to Miss Jane Eliza, eldest daughter of Thomas Flemming, Esq. of Philadelphia.
Died at Columbus, Ga., on the 4th ult., Mr. Joseph Fulker, formerly of this city, aged 49 years.
In New York, on the 13th ult., Mrs. Martha M. Russell, late consort of Mr. R. E. Russell, of Columbia, S. C.
Died at Brandywine Springs, near Philadelphia, on the 27th ult., Mrs. Mary A., wife of the Rev. John Dickson, of this city, and daughter of the late Rev. Andrew Flinn, D. D....

Issue of August 13, 1836

Married on Monday afternoon, 8th inst., by the Rev. Mr. Gadsden, Mr. William Ogden, to Miss Ann Anthony, all of this city.
On Wednesday evening, 3d inst., by the Rev. Mr. Sewell, Mr. A. J. Crews, to Miss Rebecca C., youngest daughter of the late Capt. Wm. Fair, all of this city.
Died in this city on the 4th inst., Mrs. Rebecca Screven, aged 81 years.
Departed this life on Saturday last, Mrs. Elizabeth F. Hayne, wife of Wm. A. Hayne, Esq. in the 42 year of her age.
In this city on the 4th inst., Col. Simon Magwood, in the 74th year of his age.
On the 23d ult., in this city, John T. Robertson, Esq., Navy Agent, aged 37 years.
At Brailsfordville, Prince William's Parish, on the 26th July, Capt. Joseph B. Wilkie, in the 42d year of his age.
At the White Sulphur Spring, Va., on the 20th ult., Mr. Charles H. Tuuls (sic), in the 55th year of his age, Merchant, of this city.

Died on the 5th inst., at Vaucluse, Edgefield Dist., Benj. Postell,infant son of Mr. D. P. Lockwood, of the Vaucluse Factory, aged eight months. (poem)

Issue of August 20, 1836

Married at St. Michael's Church, on Wednesday evening 10th inst., by Rev. Bishop Bowen, Wm. Davidson, Esq. to Julia Emma, youngest daughter of the late James H. Ancrum.

On the 12th inst., bythe Rev. Mr. Post, Mr. Joseph A. Pelot, of Savannah, Ga., to Miss Elizabeth R., second daughter of the late Saml. Parker.

Departed this life on the 13th inst., Mrs. Hannah Revell, at the advanced aged of 83 years. Her native place was Salem, but the greatest portion of her life has been spent in this city....

Died on the 21st July, Mrs. Ann Eliza Campbell, wife of Alexander W. Campbell, in the 38th year of her age.

On the 3d inst., Alexander Henry, Esq. in the 65th year of his age, for many years a respectable merchant of this city.

On the 7th inst., Mr. John J. Frazer, in the 39th year of his age...left a widow and three children.

On the 25th ult., Mrs. Martha Lawton, wife of Col. A. J. Lawton, of Black Swamp, St. Peters Parish, Beaufort Dist., aged 47 years and some months.

Died on the 1st inst., the Rev. Hugh M. Koontz, Pastor of the Presbyterian Church in Amsterdam village, aged 32 years. N. Y. Obs.

In New Jersey, on the 29th of July, the Rev. Wm. R. Burroughs, in the 36th year of his age, and the 4th year of his ministry.

Issue of August 27, 1836

Departed this life on Saturday the 12th inst., Mrs. Ann Purcell, widow of the late Joseph Purcell, in the 74th year of her age...a member of the Protestant Episcopal Church....

Departed this life on the 19th inst., Mr. Theodore J. Townsend, in the 24th year of his age....

Departed this life on the 31st ult., Mr. Elas Meynardie, in the 33d year of his age...fall from the Rail Road Car....

Died on the 5th inst., at Bradford Springs, Sumter District, aged 42 years, Mrs. Drusilla Britton, wife of Henry Britton, and daughter of the late Rev. George G. McWhorter....

Issue of September 3, 1836

Married on Wednesday evening 24th inst., by the Rev. Mr. Manley, Mr. Ezekiel Rice, of Waterville, Maine to Miss Margaret Ann Bunch of this city.

On the 18th inst., at King's Chapel, Boston, by the Rev. Mr. Greenwood, Mr. James W. Bryant, of this city, to Miss Rebecca H., daughter of James Hall, Esq. of Boston.

Died, near Raytown, Warren co., Ga., on the 22d July last, Mrs. Elizabeth Greer...a member of the Presbyterian Church at South Liberty, and one that adorned her profession.

Departed this life on the 22d inst., the Rev. John Howard, of the M. E. Church.... Macon (Ga.) Telegraph.

Died at San Pedro in Florida, on the 10th ult.,Rev. Thomas Alexander, aged about 50 years. He was a native of this county... For several years he was the pastor of Salem Church, S. C....
Charlotte (N. C.) Journal

Issue of September 10, 1836

Married on Thursday evening 1st inst., by the Rev. Dr. Bowen, Mr. William Lindsay, to Miss Ann Elizabeth, daughter of the late Rev. Edmund Mathews, of St. Simons Island, Geo.

On Wednesday evening 31st ult., by the Rev. Dr. Capers, Mr. R. S. Chrietzberg to Miss Joanna Caroline, eldest daughter of the late Conrad Winges, all of this city.

On Wednesday evening 31st ult., by the Rev. Mr.Gamewell, Mr. Samuel B. Webber, to Miss Jane Emma, third daughter of the late Jacob Lord, all of this city.

On Sunday evening last, by the Rev.Mr. Gildersleeve, Mr. William Thompson, to Miss Sarah Mary Naser, eldest daughter of the late Casper Naser, Esq. all of this city.

On the evening of the 1st inst., at Warthourville, by the Rev. Josiah Law, Mr. Saml. Spencer to Miss Harriet McIver, all of Liberty Co., Geo.

Died at his residence in Grahamville, on the 1st inst., Dr. Edward N. Chisolm, in the 32d year of his age.

Departed this life at Mount Pleasant, St. Luke's Parish, on the 25th ult., Mr. Richard Dawson, aged 81 years and 3 months. ...relic of the Revolution.

Died on the morning of the 21st ult., at Jericho Neck, Beaufort Dist., S. C., Mrs. Cynthia Russell, wife of Richard Russell, Esq., of that place, and daughter of the late Mr. Murdock.

Issue of September 17, 1836

Married in the Lutheran Church at Lexington Court House, S. C., on Tuesday evening, Aug. 23d by the Rev. E. L. Hazelius, D. D., the Rev. William Ernenpeutsch, of Dhun, in Germany, and Rector of the Augusta (Ga.) Academy, to Miss Eliza Hayne, eldest daughter of Dr. Thomas H. Simons.

At Barnwell on the evening of the 8th inst., by the Rev. Coln. Howell, Mr. Benjamin Bynum, of Columbia, S. C., to Miss Sarah, eldest daughter of Major Louis and Mrs. Cynthia O'Bannon, of this place.

In Habersham Co., Ga., by the Rev. Dr. Church, of Athens, Richard W.Habersham, Jr., of Geo., to Miss Martha J. Matthewes, third daughter of John R. Matthewes, Esq. of S. C.

Died on the 31st ultimo, Rachael Kiddell, wife of Charles Kiddell, Esq., of this City, in the 54th year of her age.

Departed this life on the evening of the 1st inst.,at his residence, Edingsville, Mr. William Seabrook, sen., in the 64th year of his age...elder of the Presbyterian Church of Edisto Island....

Died on the 4th day of August, near the town of Benton, Miss., Mr. Thomas G. Hodge, in the 24th year of his age...a native of Sumter Dist., S. C....

On the 11th inst., Lemuel James, infant son of Mr. Lemuel B. Davis, of Sumter District, aged 1 year and 6 months.

Issue of September 24, 1836

Married on Tuesday evening 13th inst., by the Rev. Dr. C. E. Gadsden, Mr. John Corby jun. to Miss Ann Eliza, daughter of the late Mr. Daniel Miller, all of this city.

On Wednesday evening, 14th inst., by the Rev. Dr. Bachman, Mr. Carson Dickman, to Miss Elizabeth Hildesheimer, both of Germany.

On Thursday evening, 15th inst., by the Rev. W. Capers, Mr. John F. Gordon, to Miss Elizabeth B. Humphries, both of this city.

On Sunday evening, 18th inst., by the Rev. Wm. Capers, Mr. F. H. Alley, to Miss Elizabeth Jane, daughter of the late Wm. Robison, all of this city.

Departed this life on Thursday 15th inst., in the 21st year of her age, Miss Martha Clementina Water(?), a native of James Island, but for the last 18 months a resident of this city....

Died on Charleston Neck, on the 17th inst., John E. Halsall, a native of this city, in the 35th year of his age.

Departed this life in Columbia, S. C.,on the morning of the 8th inst., in the 20th year of her age, Mrs. Mary Jane Johnston, wife of Mr. James Johnston, Merchant, of that place, and eldest daughter of Mr. Whiteford Smith, of this city.

Died on the night of the 8th inst., at St. Augustine, Mr. Robert J. Zylstra, of this city...a member of Capt. Dummett's company of volunteers....

Issue of October 1, 1836

Married on Thursday evening 22d ult., by the Rev. Mr. Forrest, Mr. A. C. Waugh, to Miss Jane, daughter of the late Mr. David Haig, of this city.

On Tuesday evening last, by the Rev. Mr. Manly, Mr. John D. Miller, to Miss Mary C. Recard, both of this city.

Married, on the 31st August, at Monticello, Ga., by the Rev. C. W. Howard, Rev. J. H. George to Miss Martha Ann, daughter of Capt. W. B. Taylor, all of that place.

Died on the 26th inst., Mrs. Eliza, wife of John C. Pillans, Esq., in the 47th year of her age.

Died in this city on Sunday 25th ult., Mr. Robt Gibbes jr., eldest son of the late John Gibbes, aged 49 years.

On the 21st inst., in this city, Miss Martha Smith, in the 43d year of her age.

In this city on the 23d inst., Miss Amelia De Bow in the 21st year of her age.

At Rockville, S. C., on the 1st inst.,Mrs. Sarah Graves, in the 60th year of her age, a native of this city....

Died, on the 22d ult., on board the steamer Santee, Mr. John Eason, eldest son of Mr. Robert Eason, sen., aged 25 years....

Died in this city on the 19th Sept., Mrs. Mary B. De Bow, in the 53d year of her age; also on the evening previous her eldest son, Mr. Wm. G. DeBow, in the 28th year of his age....

Issue of October 8, 1836

Married on Tuesday evening last by the Rev. Mr. Post, Mr. Joseph T. Zealy, of Beaufort, S. C., to Miss Sarah Bell, eldest daughter of Mr. James Badger, of this city.

On the 29th ult., by the Rev. Mr. Hanckell, Chas. Parker, to Anna Maria, daughter of the late Rober Smith, all of this city.

Departed this life on Monday the 26th ult., in the 17th year of her age, Mrs. Eliza Pillans,consort of Mr. John C. Pillans, and daughter of Mr. John Palmer. (eulogy)

Died on the 2d inst., Mr. William Gray, in the 37th year of his age.

Died in this city, on the 27th Sept. last, Mrs. Sarah J. Harleston, consort of Dr. Summers Haleston.

On the 12th of Sept., Mr. Joseph T. Wells, aged 38 years, a native of Rhode Island, but for the last 13 years a resident of this city.

In Philadelphia, on the 21st ult., Robert Maxwell, Esq., for many years a very respectable resident and merchant of this city, but latterly a citizen of Philadelphia.

Died on the 10th Sept. last, at the house of William Morgan, near Greenville, Merriwether co., Ga., a young man who said his name was Reuben Burriss...said he came from Charleston, S. C....
Departed this life, in Tallahassee, on Tuesday 20th inst., Major Washington, of the Tenn. Volunteers.
At Abbeville Court House, on the morning of the 20th ult., James Nicholson, Esq. of this city, in the 78th year of his age.

Issue of October 15, 1836

Married on the 29th ult., by the Rev. Mr. Hanckel, Charles Parker, Esq. to Miss Anna Maria, daughter of the late Roger Smith, all of this city.
Married on Thursday 6th inst., by the Rev. Mr. Gamewell, Mr. Jesse Wiggins, of St. James, Goose Creek, to Miss Mary Syfan, of this city.
Married on Sunday evening last, by the Revd. Dr. Bachman, Mr. Henry Gaigler, to Miss Christeener Loner, both of Hanover, Germany.
On the 4th inst., at New York, by the Rev. A. Maclay, Henry Hone, Esq. to Miss Hannah H. Hayward, daughter of Wm. Hayward, Esq. of S. C.
Departed this life in this city on the 26th Sept., Miss Charlotte Huger, in the 63d year of her age, the last surviving daughter of the late Col. John Huger....
Departed this life on the 8th inst., Mrs. Louisa Enslow, consort of Mr. Joseph Enslow, in the 27th year of her age.
Departed this life in the 68th year of her age, Mrs. Catharine Poyas, relict of the late Dr. J. E. Poyas.
Died in this city on the 5th inst., Mr. Joshua Lockwood, aged 57 years and 11 months.
Died, at his residence in Middle Salem (Sumter District) on the 3d Sept., Mr. James Hervey Wilson, in the 38th year of his age....
Died on Wadmalaw Island on the evening of the 4th inst., in the   year of her age, Mrs. Rebecca G. Youngblood, daughter of Col. Wm. Cotesworth Pinckney, and consort of Richard S. Youngblood, Esq.
At her residence in Beaufort, on the 19th of Sept., Mrs. Elizabeth F. Verdier, in the 32d year of her age, leaving an affectionate husband, six children....
At Columbia, S. C., on the 6th inst., Mr. Richard E. Hammer, in the 23d year of his age.
At his residence in St. Matthew's Parish, Orangeburg, on the 27th ult., Mr. James S. Miles, Clerk of the House of Representatives of this State, in the 43d year of his age.

Issue of October 29, 1836

Married on Tuesday evening 18th inst., by the Rev. Mr. Trapier, Mr. J. F. Alderson, of Iberville, La., to Miss Elizabeth Mary, youngest daughter of the late Aaron Barton of this City.
On Monday, 24th inst., by the Rev. Dr. Hanckle, Allston L. White, M. D., to Miss Ann Eliza, youngest daughter of the late Wm. Simmons, Esq., of St. Paul's Parish.
On Thursday evening 20th inst., by the Rev. Dr. Capers, Mr. John L. Bod(?), to Miss Dorinda Burnham, all of this city.
Died in this city on the 2d inst., Mrs. Ann Reid, aged 69 years, relict of Major George Reid.
Departed this life at Beaufort on the 15th inst., Mrs. Martha Perryclear, relict of the late Mr. John Perryclear, aged 33 years.
Departed this life at Legrange, near Hamburgh, S. C., on the 15th Oct. 1836, in the 26th year of her age, Mrs. Amelia Ann,

consort of Mr. James C. Broome, and daughter of the late Abraham Giles and Rebecca Dozier of Abbeville Dist., S. C. (eulogy)
Died, at Bath, Richmond Co., Ga., on the morning of the 12th inst., Mrs. Angela Dwight, wife of the Rev. Theodore M. Dwight, aged 26 years.

Issue of November 5, 1836

Married on Thursday evening the 26th inst., by the Rev. Mr. Hanckle, Mr. Samuel H. Mortimer, to Harriet Constantia, eldest daughter of the late D. Jennings Waring, of this city.
On Sunday evening 23d inst., by the Rev. Mr. John Bachman, Mr. John C. Koch, to Mrs. Ann F. Carpenter, all of this city.
On Thursday evening 27th inst., by the Rev. Mr. John Bachman, Mr. Augustus Abbs, of Germany, to Miss Margarette Wright, of this city.
Died in this city, on the 27th inst., Col. George Warren Cross....
Departed this life on Saturday afternoon, the 29th inst., James Drummond, a native of Alloa, Scotland, aged 67 years and a resident of this city 40 years.
Died at St. Augustine, on the 26th inst., George I. F. Clarke, Esq. a native Floridian and for many years Lt. Gov. and Surveyor General of the Province of East Florida, under the Spanish Government.
In Providence, Rhode Island, Rev. Asa Mercer, D. D. LL. D., formerly President of Brown University.
At Bath, Richmond Co., Ga., on the 12th inst., Mrs. Angela Dwight, wife of Rev. Theodore M. Dwight, aged 29 years...leaves husband and child.....(eulogy)

Issue of November 12, 1836

Married on Thursday evening 3d inst., by the Rev. Mr. White, Warren W. Clements, Esq. to Miss Eliza S., fourth daughter of the late Francis S. Legare, of St. Pauls Parish.
On Thursday evening, 3d inst., by the Rev. John Forrest, Dr. John L. Dawson, to Jane Fullerton, eldest daughter of Dr. Thomas Y. Simons, of this place.
On Thursday evening 3d inst., by the Rev. Mr. Yates, James W. Gray, Esq. to Miss Anna E. Porter, eldest daughter of Mr. Wm. L. Porter, all of this city.
On Thursday evening 2d inst., at St. Phillip's (temporary) Church, by the Rev. Mr. Kaufman, Mr. Wm. N. Simmons, to Miss Eliza L. Folker, both of this city.
On Wednesday evening 9th inst., by the Rev. Mr. Capers, Mr. L. P. Speissegger, to Miss Agnes Shepherd, both of this city.
In the vicinity of Warreton, Abbeville, on the 1st inst., by the Rev. Mr. A. Gray, Mr. John H. Gray, to Miss Jane Clementina, eldest daughter of J. B. Huey, deceased.
Died on Monday evening the 7th inst., in the 72d year of her age, Mrs. Elizabeth Holmes, relict of the late John Bee Holmes.
Departed this life on the morning of the 30th of October, Miss Charlotte E. Cochran....
Departed this life on Thursday morning 27th ult., Mr. William George Armstrong, in the 40th year of age...leaving a widow, two sons, an affectionate sister and other relatives....
On the 25th ult., in the 54th year of his age, Mr. Alexander Howard, a native of this city.
Departed this life in Sumter District, on the 4th inst., Mrs. Harriet Russell, consort of the Rev. John A. Russell, in her 63d year.

Issue of November 19, 1836

Married on the morning of the 16th inst., by the Rev. Dr. Bachman, Mr. Robert Muirhead, to Miss Ann Caroline Hauck, only daughter of the late John S.Hauck, Esq.
On Thursday evening 19th inst., by the Rev. Mr. Rodgers, Mr. John W. Caldwell, to Miss Martha Coates, both of this city.
On Thursday evening 19th inst., by the Rev. J. Bachman, Mr. C. Panknin, to Miss Martha Fasbender, both of this city.
Died Nov. 2, 1836, at his father's residence in Marion Dist., Henry Smilie Gregg, in the 21st year of his age.
Died on the 13th of June, of the present year, at the house of Mr. D. Boyd, in Wilcox Co., Ala., Mr. Hugh Gaston, Sen., in the 86th year of his age, and on the 21st of Oct., his partner, Mrs. Martha Gaston, aged 81...Mr. and Mrs. Gaston were married on the 14th day of May 1776...Mr. Gaston was ordained a ruling elder in the Presbyterian Church in Purity congregation, Chester Dist., S. C., more than 40 years ago...a soldier in the Rev. war... interred in the burying ground at Shell Creek Church, six miles from Prairie Bluff, Wilcox Co., Alabama.

Issue of November 26, 1836

Married on Friday morning, 18th inst.,by the Right Rev. Dr. Bowen, J. P. Clement., to Isabella H., youngest daughter of the late Edward Mortimer, Esq.
On Tuesday evening the 15th inst., by the Rev. Mr. Hanckel, W. Gilmore Simms, to Miss Chevillette Eliza, only daughter of N. Roach, Esq. all of this city.
On Thursday evening 17th inst., by the Rev. Dr. Gadsden, Philip A. Neyle, to Mary J., eldest daughter of B. D. Roper, Esq.
On Tuesday evening, 15th inst., at St. Paul's Church, by the Rev. Mr. Hanckel, Dr. Charles C. Spann, of Sumter Dist., to Miss Mary Gertrude, daughter of Mr. John Glen, of this city.
On Sunday morning, 6th inst., at St. Joseph's, Fla., by Robert Beveridge, Esq., Mayor, Theodore L. Smith of Charleston, S. C., to Mrs. Elvira B. Bulloch, of the former place.
Died on the 14th inst., Mary Blackwood Chapman, wife of Thomas Chapman, and daughter of the late Thomas Blackwood.
Died on Sabbath morning, 13th inst., at the residence of Judge William Magruder, Columbia Co., Ga., the beloved infant of Rev. J. B. and Mrs. Laera(?) Cassels, aged 2 months and 6 days.
Departed this life the 3d Nov., at the residence of Capt. Thomas Gordon, St. Luke's Parish, William Grierson, in the 34th year of his age, leaving an affectionate wife and two children....
Died, on the 10th of this month, Mrs. Ann Garden, consort of John E. Burrell, and third daughter of James Shoolbred, in the 36th year of her age...left husband and five children.
On the 22d ult., in Hinds Co., Miss., in the 22d year of his age, Edmund Gregorie, son of James Gregorie.
On the 12th inst., at his residence in Marlborough District, Col. Benjamin Rodgers, aged 73 years...a soldier in the rev. war.

Issue of December 3, 1836

Married on Thursday evening the 24th Nov., by the Rev. Mr. Sewell, Mr. Andrew Fur, to Miss Caroline V. Laats, both of this city.

Issue of December 10, 1836

Married on Thursday evening 1st inst., by the Rev. Mr. Manly, Rev. J. L. Reynolds to Miss Charlotte Mary, eldest daughter of B. Smith, Esq, all of this city.

On Tuesday evening last, by the Rev. Saml Gilman, Mr. Thomas C. Oxlade, of England, to Miss Emely Smith, of Charleston.

Died two miles south of Cassville, on Tuesday evening 1st inst., Rachael Adarine, aged between 45 and 50 years...a member of the Presbyterian Church....(eulogy)

Issue of December 17, 1836

Married on Thursday evening, 15th inst., by the Rev. Mr. Forrest, Mr. Franklin M. Bartlett, to Miss Elizabeth Mary Scott.

Married on Wednesday evening 7th inst.,by the Rev. Mr. Cobia, Dr. Hopson Pinckney, to Louisa, youngest daughter of Bartholomew Gaillard of St. Johns Berkley.

On Tuesday evening 13th inst., by the Rev. Dr. Bachman, Mr. Henry S. Griggs, to Miss Juliana M. Elsworth, both of this city.

On Thursday evening the 8th inst., by the Rev. Mr. Bachman, Benjamin Swan Munn (formerly of Greenfield, Mass.), to Miss Ann Maria, daughter of Mr. John Parkerson, of this city.

On Thursday evening 8th inst.,by the Rev. John Forrest, William S. Dower, Esq., to Miss Isabella Blair, both of this city.

On Wednesday evening last, by the Rev. John Honour, Mr. Samuel Burk, to Miss Atharine Burnham, both of this city.

On Tuesday morning 6th inst., near Decatur, DeKalb co., Ga., by the Rev. M. Dickson, Rev. Wm. Quillin, of Chattooga, Walker Co., to Miss Eliza Frances Davis.

Died on the 19th Oct., in the 40th year of his age, Capt. James Geddes, a native of this place.

Departed this life on Sunday 4th inst., at his residence in Barnwell Dist., William H. Cannon, in the 27th year of his age.

Died at St. Marks, Fa., on Thursday Nov. 2d, Major Bethel Durant Bellamy, in the 25th year of his age...born in S. C., All Saints Parish, Waccamaw, and he became a resident of Florida in 1820.

Issue of December 24, 1836

Married on Tuesday evening the 20th inst., by the Rev. Mr. T. Smyth, Mr. J. H. Ragan, jr., of Sumter Dist., to Miss Mary Elizabeth, eldest daughter of Wm. C. Dukes, Esq. of this city.

Married on the 4th inst.,at Walnut Grove, Rutherford, N. C., by the Rev. Mr. Bell, Mr.Thomas A. Hayden of this City, to Mrs. Nancy M. Walker, daughter of Francis Alexander, of the former place.

In this City on the 17thinst., by the Rev. C. Hanckel, Samuel S. Mills, to Mary, eldest daughter of the late John Egleston.

On Thursday evening the 15th inst., in St. Stephen's Chapel, by the Rev. Mr. Trapier, Joseph Morrison, Esq. of Prince Williams Parish, to Frances Charlotte, third daughter of the late Mr. Timothy Sullivan of this City.

Died at his residence in St. Mathew's Parish, on the morning of the 15th inst., Dr. V. V. Jamison, in the 72d year of his age.

Issue of January 7, 1837

Died at his residence in Horry Dist., S. C., Capt. Edward Conner, aged 80 years, an officer of the Revolution.

At his residence in Monroe st., N. Y., December 14th, Rev.

John Robert McDowell, aged 35 years....
Married on the morning of the 28th inst., by the Rev. Mr. Manly, Dr. Albert G. Mackay, to Sarah Pamela, only daughter of Capt. Sears Hubbell, all of this city.
On the 29th inst., by the Rev. B. Manly, Mr. Daniel Billings, to Miss Julia Harpoldt, both of this city.
At Vaucluse on the 6th inst., by the Rev. Mr. Axon, Dr. S. Way, to Miss O. T. Axon, all of Liberty Co., Ga.

Issue of January 14, 1837

Married on Thursday evening last, by the Rev. Wm. W. Spears, Dr. D. F. Nardin, to Miss Eleanor S., eldest daughter of Wm. Walker, Esq. all of this city.
Married by the Rev. R. Quarterman, on Monday the 19th ult., the Rev. Professor Howe, of the Theological Seminary, at Columbia, to Mrs. Sarah Ann McConnell, of Walthourville, Ga.
Died, in St. Pauls Parish, Colleton Dist., on the 24th Dec., Mrs. Charlotte S. Price, widow of the late Thomas W. Price, aged 67 years and 4 months.
Died on the 25th day of Dec. last, in the 88th year of her age, Mrs. Mary Cudworth, widow of the late Major Nathaniel Cudworth...born in the city of Bocton, but had resided in this city for the last 50 years. None of her children proceded her to the grave.

Issue of January 21, 1837

Married on Tuesday evening, 10th inst., by the Rev. Mr. Hanckle, Samuel W. Gibbes, Esq. to Miss Eleanor C., eldest daughter of the late Chas. Banks.
On Thursday evening 12th inst., by the Rev.Dr. Gadsden, John Ward, Esq. to Miss Mary G., only daughter of David Johnston, decd.
On Tuesday evening 17th inst., by the Rev. Mr. Manly, Mr. George N. Reynolds, jr. to Miss Jane Thompson, both of this city.
Married at Dungeness, on Cumberland Island, on the 27th ult., by the Rev. H. S. Pratt, George H. Johnston, Esq. of St. Catharines, to Miss Emily Turner of the former place.
At. St. Mary's on the 1st inst., by the Rev. H. S. Pratt, Archibald Clarke, Esq. of St. Mary's, to Miss Sarah Bramford Gist, of Charleston, S. C.
At the South Point, Cumberland Island, on the 7th inst.,by the Rev. H. S. Pratt, Mr. Cribb, to Miss Mary Ann Latham.
At. St. Marys on the 15th ult., by the Rev. H. S. Pratt, M. Helverston, of Camden Co., to Miss Engruia Demott, of the former place.
Departed this life on Thursday 12th Jan. 1837, in the 33d year of her age, Mrs. Susan E. Frazer, wife of Mr. Charles P. Frazer, of this city....
Died at Beech Island on the 18th Sept. last, Mrs.Sarah Jones, in the 53d year of her age...a member of the Presbyterian Church.

Issue of January 28, 1837

Married on Thursday evening 19th inst., by Rev. Mr. Hopkins, Mr. J. B. Campbell, to Miss Anna Margaret, youngest daughter of Hon. Thomas Bennett, all of this city.
Departed this life in this city on the 20th inst., Richard William Yeadon (eldest son of Col. William Yeadon) aged 36 years.
Died, at his fathers residence, St.Luke's Parish, on the 18th inst., Mr. Philip C. Besselen, in the 32d year of his age.

Issue of February 4, 1837

Married on Sunday evening 29th inst., by the Rev. Dr. Bachman, Mr. Richard Bell to Miss Caroline C. Leibrandt, all of this city.

On the 18th inst., by the Rev. Dr. Gadsden, Mr. Charles G. Branford, of Grahamville, Beaufort Dist., to Miss Susan Elizabeth, fourth daughter of Robert Limehouse, Esq. of this city.

At Frogmore, Edisto Island, on Wednesday 25th ult., by the Rev. Mr. Leverette, Wm. Whaley, Esq., to Miss Rachel Louisa, second daughter of Dr. Edward Mitchell, all of that place.

In Hamburgh, S. C., on Thursday evening 26th inst.,by the Rev. Whitefoord Smith, Mr. J. W. Stoy, of Augusta, to Miss Mary Louisa Cole, of Charleston.

Died in this city on the 28th inst., Edward Mitchell, a native of Kentucky....

Departed this life on the 29th ult., Col. Richard Cunningham, in the 57th year of his age.

At his place, near Charleston, on the 25th inst., Arthur Middleton, Esq., in the 52d year of his age.

At his plantation, St. Thomas' Parish, on the 16th Dec., D. C. Edwards, Esq., in the 39th year of his age.

Issue of February 11, 1837

Died, at Barnwell, Abbeville District, Mr. Wm. Petigur, aged 78 years.

Issue of February 18, 1837

Died on the morning of the 14th inst., Joseph Milligan Sillman, aged 16 years 7 months and 16 days....

Died at his residence at Marion Court House, S. C.,on the 19th ult., Maj. James C. Bellune, last Post Master at that place, in the 44th year of his age.

Departed this life on the night of the 10th inst., in the 34th year of her age...Mrs. Eugenia Michel, wife of Dr. Wm. Michel.

Issue of February 25, 1837

Married on Wednesday evening 15th inst., by the Rev. Mr. Manly, Mr. A. J. Burke, to Miss Agnes T., youngest daughter of the late Mr. Thomas Burnham, all of this city.

On Tuesday evening, 16th inst., by the Rev. Dr. Bachman, Mr. John B. Martin, to Miss Catherine M., eldest daughter of Mr. Abraham Jones, all of this city.

On the 16th ult.,Major Jessee F. Davis, late of Florida, to Miss Emma Simons, of St. Bartholomew's Parish.

At Combahee, on the 9th inst., by the Rev. Mr. Delavaux, Thomas Pinckney Rutledge, Esq. to Miss Fanny Middleton, youngest daughter of the late Daniel Blake, Esq.

At Aiken, On the 14th inst., by the Rev. William Tucker, Mr. Nathaniel Prothro, to Miss Emeline, second daughter of Henry Canady, Esq. all of Aiken, S. C.

On Monday evening 13th inst., by the Rev. T. Smyth, Capt. William Ham, to Miss Elizabeth Moore, both of this city.

At Fair Hope, Combahee, on the 12th inst., by the Rev. E. Palmer, Mr. Jonah Collins, to Miss Mary Hutchinson, all of Beaufort District.

Departed this life on the 21st inst., Mrs. Sarah A. Axson, daughter of Mr. Job Palmer, in the 52d year of her age....

Died, at Oakland, Jefferson Co., Ga., on the morning of the 29th January, Mrs. Catharine J. Berrien, wife of James W. M. Berrien, aged 25; and on the 10th of Feb., Frances Pamela, their daughter, aged 2 years....

Issue of March 4, 1837

Married on Wednesday evening 15th inst., by the Rev. Dr. Bachman, Mr. Daniel Molean, of Sweden, to Mrs. Anna Caroline Christie, of Charleston.
In Washington, Ga., on the 16th inst., by the Rev. Mr. Goulding, the Rev. John W. Baker, of Milledgeville, to Miss Charlotte W. Sheppard, of the former place.
Died at Georgetown, S. C., on the 21st inst.,Mr. John Hawkins, sen.
At Jacksonville, on the 15th inst., Squire Streeter, Esq., in the 49th year of his age.

Issue of March 11, 1837

Married on the 22d ult., by the Rev. Mr. Spears, Benj. T. Gibbes, Esq. to Miss Ann W. Roper, second daughter of Benj. D. Roper, all of this city.
On Tuesday evening last, by the Rev. Mr. Spear, Mr. James M. Wilson, to Mrs. Ann J. Howe, all of this city.
In Columbia, S. C., on the 28th ult., by the Rev. Dr. Ernest Hazelius, Edward Horlbeck, of Charleston, to Miss Ainsley H. Rives, of Richland District, S. C.
Died on Monday morning last, 6th inst., on board ship Charleston, on the passage from Boston to this port, John H. Manning, M. C. in the 24th year of his age.
Died at Fort Heileman, Garey's Ferry, Fa., on the 20th Feb., Kennedy Glisten, a valuable Private from Marion Dist., S. C., belonging to the company of Capt. J. H. Pearce....

Issue of March 18, 1837

Married on the 8th March by the Rev. Mr. Post, Dr. Lawrence Lee, to Miss Sarah, youngest daughter of the late Col. Francis Dickinson, all of this city.
On the 30th Jan. by Judge Allison, in Appalachicola, Fla., D. E. Kittelband, Esq. of Charleston, S. C. to Miss Mary Smith, of Warren Co., Ga.
Died on Monday morning 6th inst., on board the ship Charleston, on the passage from Boston to this port, John H. Manjing, M. D., in the 24th year of his age.
Departed this life in Oglethorpe co., Ga., on the 18th Dec. last, Mr. Matthew Ramey, in the 80th year of his age...a rev. soldier, and a member of the Baptist Church for 56 years.

Issue of March 25, 1837

Died in this city on the 26th ult., Maria Wilkinson, aged 26 years, wife of Mr. David W. Leland, and daughter of Hezekiah Howe, Esq. of Cohoes Falls, New York.
At his residence in Greenville District, on the 21st ult., Mr. Martin Ayres, aged 71 years.

Issue of April 1, 1837

Married on Monday evening the 27th ult., by the Rev. Mr. Spears, Joseph W. Faber, Esq., to Miss Isabella, second daughter of the Right Rev. Dr. Bowen, all of this city.
On Tuesday evening the 21st ult., in St. Peter's Church, by the Rev. Mr. Barnwell, Mr. Francis S. Holmes, to Miss Elizabeth S., daughter of Henry B. Toomer, Esq. all of this city.

On Tuesday evening the 21st ult., in St. Peter's Church by the Rev. Mr. Barnwell, Dr. John D. Hall, of Alabama, to Miss Septima Thayer, of this city.
On the 9th ult., by the Rev. Dr. Backman, Mr. Abraham Dantzler, to Miss Eliza F. Speissegger, all of this city.

Issue of April 8, 1837

Married on Thursday evening 30th ult., by the Rev. B. Manley, Mr. George M. Savage, of Henrico Co., Va., to Miss Mary E.,eldest daughter of G. N. Reynolds, Esq. of this city.
On the 25th ult.,by the Rev. Dr. Bachman, Mr. J. D. Tolck, of this city, to Miss Weilhelmina Frederica Elderbrook, of Germany.
On Monday the 3d inst., by the Rev. Mr. Sewell, Mr. William Rode, to Miss Sarah Ann Evans.
Died at Montpelier Springs, nearMacon, Geo., 19th inst.,the Rev. Robert M. Laird...pastor of a Presbyterian Church at Princess Ann, Maryland....   S. J. Cassels, March 27, 1837
Died in Harris Co., Ga, on the 3d inst., in the 29th year of her age, Mrs. Elizabeth Blake Holsey, consort of Hon. Holpins Holsey.
At Darien, Ga., on the 19th March, Mrs. Maria Brailsford, aged 70 years, relict of the late Wm. Brailsford, formerly of this city.

Issue of April 15, 1837

Married on the 9th inst., by the Rev. Thomas Smyth, Mr. T. V. Holmes, to Miss Lavinia Sweeny.
On Wednesday evening 12th inst., by the Rev. Thomas Smyth, Mr. Thomas Fitzpatrick to Miss Cecilia Louisa Crovat.
At Beaufort, S. C., on the 4th inst., by the Rev. D. Bythewood, Mr. Benjamin F. Smith, of this city to Miss Susan Elizabeth Cole, of Beaufort.

Issue of April 22, 1837

Married on Sunday last, the 19th inst., in this city, by the Rev. B. Manly, Mr. P. H. Belin, Merchant of Savannah, Geo., to Miss Olivia Ann., eldest daughter of Mr. Geo. A. C. Rivers.
On Wednesday evening 12th inst., by the Rev. Dr. Capers, Mr. Phinehas Matthews to Miss Elizabeth Ann, daughter of Nathaniel Johnson, all of this city.
On Tuesday evening 11th inst., by the Rev. John H. Honour, James H. Myrover, Esq., Merchant of Fayetteville, N. C., to Miss Amanda C., Duhadway, of this city.
On Thursday the 13th inst., in St. Andrew's Parish, by the Rev. Mr. Hanckle, Henry M. Manigualt, to Miss Susan M. Lining, daughter of Edward B. Lining, Esq.
By the Rev. Mr. Sewell, on Thursday evening, the 13th inst., Mr. Edward Welling, to Miss Ann Simmons, both of this city.
On Thursday evening last, at the German Lutheran Church, by the Rev. Mr. Ring, Mr. William Petsch, to Miss Ann America M' Cleish, all of this city.
Married on the 29th ult., by the Rev. Wm. B. Richard, Mr. Thomas N. Griffen, of Newton,Ga., to Miss Elizabeth, eldest daughter of William Robinson, Elder in the Presbyterian Church, McDonough, Ga.

Issue of April 29, 1837

Married in Augusta, Ga., on the 18th inst., by the Rev. Dr. Anderson, one of the Secretaries of the A. B. C. F. M., Mr.

125

Leonard Bostwick, merchant in that place, to Miss Eliza B. Meigs, eldest daughter of the Rev. Benjamin C. Meigs, of the Ceylon Mission.

Married on Tuesday evening, 25th ult., Mr. J. T. James of Claramount, to Miss Julia Carter, of Clarendon, all of Sumter Dist.

Died on the 1st inst., at the residence of Mrs. Childs, Charleston, S. C., on his way to the West Indies, Mr. James MacFie, merchant of Columbia...aged 37 years.

Issue of May 6, 1837

Married on Thursday evening last, by the Rev. P. A. Strobel, the Rev. E. Hawkins, of Newbury (sic) District, to Miss Anna C. Wilson, of this City.

On Tuesday evening 2d May, by the Rev. Mr. Post, Mr. Nathaniel Hunt, to Miss Ann Rivers, only daughter of Geo. K. White, Esq., all of this city.

On Sunday evening last, by the Rev. Dr. Bachman, Mr. George Riecke, to Miss Elizabeth V. D. Lippe.

Died in this city on the 20th ult., at the Merchant's Hotel, Mr. George Cooper Welch, of Darlington District, a private in Capt. William's Company, Major Harllee's Regiment of S. C. Volunteers serving in Florida....

Died in Milledgeville, on the 22d inst., Gen. D. B. Mitchell, an emigrant from Scotland in his early youth....

Issue of May 13, 1837

Married on Thursday last, by the Rev. Mr. Backman, J. S. Steads, to Miss Ella, eldest daughter of Joseph Legg, all of this city.

On Thursday evening last, by the Rev. Mr. Sewell, Stephen Danniels, to Elizabeth Haden, of this city.

In Barbourville, Wilcox co., Ala., on Tuesday evening, 25th ult., Mr. John A. Evans, to Miss Elizabeth M., second daughter of James Caldwell, Esq.

Died at Greenville, on the 22d ult., Mr. Danl. Ford, in the 79th year of his age, a revolutionary soldier.

Died at Philadelphia, on the 4th inst., at the advanced age of 76, Louis Clapier, Esq., one of the oldest and most eminent merchants of that city....

Issue of May 20, 1837

Departed this life on the morning of the 1st inst., at her residence in King-street, Mrs. Margaret Cochran, aged 73 years, a native of Argyleshire, Scotland.

It becomes our duty (says the Georgetown Union, of Saturday) to announce the death of Dr. Samuel P. Dunbar, Intendant of Georgetown...died in this place on Monday afternoon last, 8th inst...we believe a native of New York....

Married on Tuesday evening the 9th inst., by the Rev. Mr. Kaufman, Charles Wm. Simons to Miss Elizabeth S.Mazyck, daughter of the late Nathaniel B. Mazyck.

On Wednesday evening last, the 17th inst., by the Rev. Mr. Spears, Edward Adams, of Edgefield Dist., S. C., to Miss Mary, eldest daughter of Capt. S. Alexander, of this city.

On the 16th inst., by the Rev. Mr. Kaufman, Mr. E. Hilton Williams, to Mrs. Harriet H. Thorn.

On Tuesday evening 9th inst., by the Rev. B. English, Mr. Josias G. DuPre, to Miss Jane R., eldest daughter of the Rev. Christian A. Mood, all of this city.

At Columbus, Miss., on the 27th ult., by the Rev. H. Reed, Mr. F. G. Bobo, to Miss Sarah Louisa, eldest daughter of Rob Eager, Esq., late of Charleston, S. C.

On Thursday evening 11th inst., by the Rev. Mr. Sewel, Mr. Christopher Rouse, to Mrs. Amelia Elmore, all of this city.

Issue of May 27, 1837

Death of Mr. Horatio Leavitt, wife and two children...Mr. Leavitt was a native of Greenfield, Mass., and came to this city about 35 years ago. Mrs. Leavitt, was a native of this city, and a daughter of John King, Esq. Her parents and several brothers and sisters still survive her...member of the Circular Church long before their marriage...(eulogy and account)

Married on the evening of the 18th inst., by the Rev. Mr. Barnwell, Col. W. E. Martin, of Beaufort Dist., to Miss Eloise M., eldest daughter of Wm. Ed Hayne, Esq. of this city.

On the same evening, by the Rev. Mr. Barnwell, Col. A. R. Taylor, of Columbia, to Miss Sarah, second daughter of Wm. Ed. Hayne, Esq.

Departed this life on the 18th inst., Mrs. Rebecca Giles, relict of Mr. Othniel J. Giles in the 49th year of her age....

Died at her father's residence in Jackson county, Ga., on the 14th May, Miss Martha Eliza, second daughter of Mr. James Montgomery, in her 14th year....

Issue of June 3, 1837

Married on Wednesday 24th ult., by the Right Rev. Bishop Bowen, Dr. Thomas Means, of Beaufort, S. C., to Miss Ann Stuart, daughter of the Rev. Charles Hanckel, of this City.

On Sunday the 28th inst., by the Rev. Mr. Gilman, at the Unitarian Church, Mr. Henry T. Street, of this city, to Miss Martha E. Nichols, of Charlestown, Mass.

In Columbia, on the 20th inst., by the Rev. Mr. Birmingham, Mr. Oni Allison of York, to Margaret P., third daughter of Mr. James Johnston, of Charleston, S. C.

At Philadelphia, on the 23d inst., by the Rev. Albert Barnes, Capt. Daniel Turner, of the U. S. Navy to Catharine M. Bryan, daughter of the late Arthur Bryan of Charleston. SC.

Died in this city on the 29th ult., in the 68th year, Miss Margaret Swinton, daughter of the late Hugh Swinton, Esq.

On the 12th inst., Mrs. Matilda, wife of Rev. R. Chamberlain of Butts Co., Ga...a member of the Presbyterian Church about 12 years.

Issue of June 10, 1837

Married on the 20th May last, by the Rev. Joseph Wallace, Mr. George Rivers of Madmalaw, to Mrs. Martha Seabrook, of St. Helena Island.

On Thursday evening 1st inst.,by the Rev. W. B. Yates, Mr. Ferdinand S. Joye, to Mrs. Ann Eliza Roach, all of this city.

Died at New York on the 28th ult., inthe 22d year of her age, Jane Keith Palmer, daughter of Rev. B. M. andMrs. M. S. Palmer, late of this city.

Issue of June 17, 1837

Married on Wednesday 7th inst., by the Rev.F. H. Rutledge, Mr. Allen Sloan, to Mrs. Mary Guyton, all of St. Thomas Parish.

Departed this life on the morning of the 14th January last, in the vicinity of Warrenton, Abbeville, David Ramsay Gillcopic,

only son of Andrew Gillespie, sen., aged 12 years 4 months and 22 days.
Departed this life on the 5th of April last, in the 85th year of her age, Mrs. Margaret Holmes, a native of Ireland,but for the last 40 years of her life a member of this community... member of the Second Presbyterian Church.
Died in Columbus, Miss., on the 24th of May, Hugh Wilson, aged 7 years.
On the 29th Jane Erwin, aged 5 years.
And, on the 30th Thomas Reese, aged 2 years, children of Mr. Thomas Rees, and Mrs. Margaret Witherspoon. In addition to these, on the 31st, Mr. Witherspoon aged 45 years, leaving a wife, seven surviving children....
On the 24th of May last, at his residence in Abbeville District, S. C., Capt. Reuben Starcke, aged 77 years...the last of six brothers who were all soldiers of the Rev. He served under Gen. Greene in N. C., was wounded in Georgia, and fought in several battles in N. C.

Issue of June 24, 1837

Married on the 16th inst., in St. Paul's Church, Norfolk, by the Rev. Mr. Atkinson, Walter Blake, Esq. to Miss Ann S. Izard, of Charleston.
Died at Greenville, S. C., on the 23d ult., Mrs. Laodicea Springfield, aged 71, wife of Capt. Thomas Springfield, and daughter of Solomon Langston, of revolutionary memory...the mother of 22 children, and has left about 140 grandchildren and great-grandchildren.
Death of Elisha Franklin McCutchen...died on his way home from school, on Friday the 26th of May when his horse became affrighted,threw him off, and killed him instantly.... born 28th June 1824....   A. G. Brewer, Principal Mechanicsville Academy June 16, 1837.

Issue of July 1, 1837

Married on Wednesday evening last, by the Rev. Dr. Bachman, John W. Audubon, Esq. to Miss Maria R. Bachman.
Died at Barnwell C. H. on the 20th inst., Mrs. Eliza C., consort of Col. Barnet M. Brown...left a husband and several children...member of the Baptist Church....

Issue of July 8, 1837

Married on Sunday evening last, by the Rev. Mr. Sewell, Mr. Clark Mills, to Miss Eliza S. F. Valentine, all of this city.
Died at his farm, on Jackson's Creek, Fairfield Dist., Capt. Hugh Milling, an Officer in the army of the revolution, born in Drumbo County Down, Ireland, on the 21st Feb. 1752; emigrated to America in the year 1771, resident in Charleston in the year 1774...died 7th May 1837, aged 85 years 2 months and 16 days. (long account).
Died at Coldstream, the seat of his father, on the 18th June, Thomas M. Witherspoon, in the 20th year of his age....(eulogy)

Issue of July 15, 1837

Married on Thursday evening, 6th inst., by the Rev. Mr. Barnwell, Mr. Nathaniel Hayden, to Miss Theodosia P. Walter, all of this city.
On Tuesday 4th inst., by the Rev. Mr. Sewel, Mr. Frederick Wittpen, to Mrs. Johana Schriber, both of this city.

Died, on Sunday morning last, John Francis Lanneau, infant son of Bazile and Sarah Lanneau, aged 4 months and 13 days.

Issue of July 22, 1837

Died in this city on the 15th inst., Francis Malbone Waring, eldest son of Dr. Edward T. Waring, aged 33 years, 1 month and 7 days.

At New Haven Conn., on the 3d inst., Joseph Bennett, Esq., aged 49, a native of Charleston.

Died on the morning of the 9th of June, Mrs. Hannah Anderson, wife of David Anderson, Esq., and eldest daughter of Dr. Charles West....(eulogy)

Issue of August 5, 1837

Died on the 18th July, in the 36th year of her age, Mrs. Elizabeth Montgomery, late consort of Joseph Montgomery, of Sumter District, S. C. (eulogy)

At Athens, Ga., on the 13th inst., Mr. William Eheny, aged 62 years and 9 months...a native of this city, until he removed to the former place about 18 months since.

Died on the 29th July, George Haunbaum, aged 3 years and 4 months; and on the 1st August, Edward Payson aged 1 year and 2 months, son of Mr. A. P. Gready....

At Pendleton, on the 19th inst., Miss Harriet C. Hamilton, youngest daughter of the late Major James Hamilton.

At Georgetown, S. C., on the 24th inst., Dr. Edward Lowndes.

Issue of August 12, 1837

Died in this city on the 18th ult., Mrs. Catharine L. Dennehy, aged 45 years, a native of this city, late consort of Mr. Jeremiah Dennehy....

Issue of August 19, 1837

Married on the 15th inst., by the Rev. Thomas Smyth, Mr. William Harral, to Miss Anna Vardell, both of this city.

Died at the residence of Capt. Wm. Harris, in Salem, Sumter Dist., Miss Mary Madeline Wilson, in the 17th year of her age. (eulogy)

Departed this life on the 23d of July, at the residence of his father (Professor Adams of Dartmouth N. H.), Mr. Ebenezer Adams, Jun., late of the S. C. Female Collegiate Institute....

Died at the Cataraet Hotel, Niagara Falls, on Wednesday, 26th July 1837, David G. Coit, Esq., of Marlborough District, S. C., aged 36 years...a native of New London, Conn., but for the last 16 years had resided in S. C...and elder in the Presbyterian Church....

Issue of August 26, 1837

Mr. M. Burke was born in Ireland, Dec. 8, 1772, left there in his 14th or 15th year for America, has resided in Jefferson Co., Ga., ever since the year 1804...brought up by Presbyterian parents (his father was a Minister of that denomination)...died 30th of May...left a wife and six children.

Issue of September 9, 1837

Died at her residence in St. Paul's Parish, on 20th August last, Mrs. Martha C. Delgar, in the 51st year of her age...left a large circle of relatives and friends.
Departed this life at Warrenton Post Office, Abbeville Dist., S. C., on the 27th inst., Mrs. Mary Huey, in the 32d year of her age...a native of Waxhaw, Lancaster Dist., S. C., leaving a husband and four children....
Died at his residence in Elbert Co., on the 30th ult., George Cook, Esq. He was, with an exception of two, the oldest lawyer in the State of Georgia. He was born 18 Nov 1764.
Died in Macon, Ga., August 28, 1837, Jno Winn, youngest child of Rev. Samuel J. and Mary H. Cassels, aged 20 months.

Issue of September 16, 1837

Married on Tuesday evening 12th inst.,by the Rev. Mr. Manly, Mr. Philip M. Douein, to Miss Emily R. Brown, all of this city.

Issue of September 23, 1837

Married on the 7th inst., by the Rev. Dr. Capers, Mr. Charles P. Landershine, to Miss Susan A. M. Fordham, all of this city.
Died in Greenville, S. C., on the 2d inst., Miss Hannah Hayden Porter, a native of this city, in the 19th year of her age.
Departed this life on the 31st August last, at Staunton, Va., George Chisolm, Esq., eldest son of the late George Chisolm, aged 40 years.
Died at New York, on the 12th inst., William Gaston, of Savannah....
Departed this life on May River, St. Luke's Parish, on the 12th inst., Mrs. Martha H. Bealer, consort of Charles Junius Bealer, and youngest daughter of Bethel Threadcraft, Esq., deceased, late of Charleston, in the 24th year of her age...left a husband and mother....

Issue of September 30, 1837

Married on Wednesday evening, 20th inst.,by the Rev. Thomas Smyth, Mr. Samuel Robinson to Miss Sarah Jane, eldest daughter of the late Dr. I. A. Johnson, all of this city.
Eulogy and account of George Chisolm.
Died in New York, on the 19th inst., A. T. Gaillard, of this city, aged 39 years.

Issue of October 7, 1837

Married at Pendleton Village, S. C. on the 13th of Sept., by the Rev. Wm. Potter, Paul Hamilton, Esq. to Miss Catharine A. Campbell, daughter of the Rev. J. B. Campbell.
Died at Point Hope, St. Thomas' Parish, on the 23d ult., aged about 73 years, Mrs. Mary Guerin, a pious member of the M. E. Church for the last half century.
Died at his residence in Fayetteville, N. C. on the 5th inst., Rev. James W. Douglass, Pastor of the Presbyterian Church in that place...a native of Virginia, born in Loudon co., Nov. 5, 1979... (eulogy)

Issue of October 14, 1837

Married on the 4th inst., by the Rev. G. Hanckle, Mr. Benjamin John Parker, to Miss Sarah Howe, daughter of the late George Peters, Esq. all of this city.

On Thursday the 5th inst., by the Rev. Dr. Gadsden, Dr. Wm. T. Wragg, to Miss Ann, daughter of J. W. Toomer, Esq.

On the 26th ult., at New York, by the Rev. H. Chase, Capt. M. Weeb, of Portland, to Mrs. Mary Ward, of Charleston.

Issue of October 21, 1837

Married on Tuesday evening 10th inst., in St. Paul's Church, by the Rev. C. Hanckle, Mr. F. William Sweet, to Miss Ann M. Muggride.

On Tuesday evening 10th inst., by the Rt. Rev. Bishop Bowen, Thomas Lessene, Esq. to Ann Horry, daughter of Henry Deas, Esq.

On Tuesday evening 10th inst., by the Rev. Dr. Gadsden, Mr. Otis J. Chafee, to Miss Mary A., daughter of Mr. Geo Kinloch, all of this city.

On the 12th inst., by the Rev. Dr. Gadsden, Doctor William Yates, to Miss Caroline Lawrence, daughter of Oliver O'Hara, Esq.

On Wednesday evening the 4th inst., by the Rev. Mr. Barnwell, George Henry Smith, Esq. of St. George's Dorchester, to Miss Eliza Fishburne, eldest daughter of Capt. Thomas P. Lockwood, of this city.

At the residence of her father, near Clarksville, Ga., on the 5th inst., by the Rev. S. G. Hillyer, Miss Harriett E., daughter of John R. Matthews, to Barnard Elliott Habersham, Esq. formerly of Savannah.

At Lancaster, Pa., on the 3d ult., by the Rev. Richard W. Dickinson of New York, the Rev. H. M. Blodgett, of S. C., to Miss Catharine O. Hall, of Lancaster, Pa.

In Sumter District, on the 4th inst., by Rev. D. McQueen, Rev. J. L. Bartlett, to Miss Agnes P. White, daughter of Mr. Leonard White.

Issue of October 28, 1837

Married in Green Co., Ga., on the evening of the 12th inst., by the Rev. John B. Cassels, Mr. John F. Huke, of Talliaferro Co., to Miss Mary A. Culbreath of the first mentioned County.

In Milledgeville, Ga. on the morning of the 10th inst., D. A. Gaillard, formerly of Charleston, to Mrs. Ann A. Floyd, daughter of Col. Robert W. Alston, of Florida.

Died in this city on the 26th Sept., William Smith, in the 61st year of his age, a native of Scotland.

Issue of November 4, 1837

Married on Wednesday evening the 25th ult.,by the Rev. Dr. Manly, Wm. B. Heriot, Esq. to Miss Catharine Yates, all of this city.

On Tuesday evening the 17th ultimo, by the Rev. Mr. Smyth, George Cannon Jr., to Miss Mary R., eldest daughter of the late Thomas Smith Taylor, Esq.

Also, on the same evening, by the Rev. Mr. Pool, Wm. B. Moore, to Miss Eleanor R., second daughter of the late T. S. Taylor, all of this city.

Died at his residence in Salem, Sumter Dist., on the morning of the 11th ult., Mr. Robert Witherspoon, in the 71st year of his age...in the revolutionary war under Marion....a member of the Presbyterian Church..left widow and four children.

At Spring Hill, Alabama, at the residence of Maj. John Mayrant, on Sunday 22d, Mrs. Mary Reese, in the 87th year of her age...born on James River, in Virginia, but lived 80 years of her life in Sumter Dist., S. C.
Departed this life on the 30th ult., at his residence in Summerville, Col. Charles Bayle, of St. Paul's Parish.

Issue of November 11, 1837

Married on the 25th Oct. by the Rev. Dr.Baxter, Dr. I. S. K. Palmer, of Charleston, S. C. to Miss Margaret C. Williams, of Prince Edward Co., Va., adopted daughter of Samuel Anderson, Esq., of said county.
On Sunday evening 5th inst., by the Rev. Dr. Bachman, Mr. Samuel R. Lopez, to Miss Thankful B. E. King, both of Providence, R. I.
On Friday evening, 3d inst., by the Rev. Dr. Bachman, Mr. H. Stegen, to Miss Catharine E. Nicolai, all of Germany.
Died in this city on the 3d inst.,Mrs. Mary Huger, aged 85 years, 4 months and 6 days.

Issue of November 25, 1837

Married on Thursday evening the 16th inst., by the Rev. Mr. Dana, Mr. William R. Sanders of Abbeville to Miss Frances Henrietta Simonds, of this city.
In this city on the 15th inst., by the Rev. Mr. Rogers, William Simmons, Esq. to Miss Anna Maria, youngest daughter of the late William Clement, Esq. all of St. Paul's Parish.
On Monday 13th inst., by the Rev. P. A. Strobel, Benjamin C. Hard, to Emma B., youngest daughter of John Strobel, all of this city.
On Thursday evening 16th inst., by the Rev. Mr. Gilman, Thomas C. Glen, to Margaret Eliza second daughter of the late Peter Artman, all of this city.
On Tuesday evening the 14th inst.,by the Rev. Mr. Kaufman, Henry F. Faber, Esq. to Mrs. Mary Ann Kirkland,both of this city.
On Wednesday evening last, by the Rev. Mr. Forest, Mr. Stephen Lee Alison, to Miss Lavina W., daughter of Mr. Samuel W. Corrie, both of this city.
At Grahamville on the 15th of Nov., by the Rev. Mr. Young, Thomas C. Dupont, Rector of the Church of the Holy Trinity, to Miss Constantia, daughter of the late Col. M'Nish.
Died at Plain Hill, in Claremont County, Sumter District, S. C., on the 4th inst.,Capt. Francis L. Kennedy, in the 46th year of his age.

Issue of December 2, 1837

Married on Thursday evening 23d inst.,by the Rev. Mr. Hanckel, Cornelius M. Huguenin, Esq. of St. Luke's Parish, to Adelaide Maria, second daughter of Thos Barksdale, Esq. of this city.
On Thursday evening the 23d inst.,by the Rev. Mr.Hanckel, Mr. Benjamin P. Ravenel, of St. John's Berkley, to Miss Sarah E., daughter of the late Francis Marion, Jr.
Died on Monday morning, Nov. 27th, Sarah Ann Magee Smyth, eldest daughter of Rev. Thomas Smyth, aged 4 years and 7 days....

Issue of December 9, 1837

Married on the 14th Nov., by the Rev. Mr. Hanckel, Mr. Francis W. Johnson, to Miss Eleanor B., eldest daughter of the late Sedgwick L. Simons.

On Tuesday afternoon, the 5th inst., by the Right Rev. Dr. Jasper Adams, Gilbert C. Geddes, Esq. to Miss Caroline, youngest daughter of Thos B. Seabrook, Esq. both of this city.

Died on Saturday morning, Dec. 2, 1837, Susan Adger Smith, second and only remaining daughter of Rev. Thomas Smith aged 2 years, 8 months and 10 days....

Issue of December 16, 1837

Married on Tuesday evening, 5th inst., by the Rev. Dr. Bachman, Mr. Laurens Benson, to Mrs. Isabella C. Schafner, third daughter of John H. Fasbender.

On Thursday evening 7th inst., by the Rev. Dr. Jno Bachman, Mr. Wm. H. Schirmer, toMiss Ann E. Prible, both of this city.

On Thursday evening 7th inst., by the Rev. T. F. Montgomery, Capt. John M. Panible, to Miss Martha P. Buchanan--all of Talbot Co., Ga.

On Sunday evening, the 10th inst., by the Rev. T. F. Montgomery, Dr. James T. Gardner, to Miss Nancy G. Gullet, all of Talbotton,Ga.

Died in Greenville District, on the 23d ult., Mrs. Martha Wallace, consort of Mr. J. B. Wallace, and daughter of the late Capt. Wm. Young.

At Montgomery, Ala., on the 23d ult., William D. Pickett, Judge of the Eighth Judicial Circuit of that State.

Died Nov. 27th, near Riceboro., Liberty Co., Ga., Miss Ann Caroline, daughter of Nathaniel and Ann Varnedoe. (poem)

Issue of December 23, 1837

Married in this city on the 19th inst., at St. Philips Church, by the Rev. C. Gadsden, Mr. Allen F. Owen, of Georgia, to Miss Emeline L. Matthews, daughter of the late Mr. Robert Matthews, of this State.

Married in Norfolk, Va., on Thursday evening, the 23d Nov., by the Rev. Dr. Webb, Wm. R. Webb, Esq. of Portsmouth, Va., to Sophronia Elizabeth, eldest daughter of the late David P. Bingley, of Charleston, S. C.

Issue of December 30, 1837

Married on Monday evening last, by the Rev. Mr. Hanckel, Mr. Laurence A. Edmondston, to Miss Sarah, youngest daughter of the late Mr. Jno. Egleston.

At Grove Hill, near Statesburg, on the 20th inst., by the Rev. Mr. Converse, Mr. James M. Nelson, to Miss Sarah Robinson, daughter of Samuel J. Murray, Esq.

Died, suddenly, at Prairie Bluff, Wilcox Co., Ala., in Nov. last, Dr. Francis Witherspoon, formerly of Charleston, leaving a mother and two sisters....

Died at his residence in Barnwell Dist., on the 23d inst., William R. Bull, Esq...left a wife and eight children.....

Issue of January 13, 1838

Married at Warrenton, Abbeville Dist., S. C., by the Rev. Ebenezer E. Pressley, Mr. John B. Brooks, to Miss Jane Caroline Huey, daughter of James Huey, Esq., both of Abbeville.

Died in Augusta, Ga., on the morning of the 28th of Dec. last, Mrs. Jeanette Amelia Starke, aged 35 years, consort of Wyatt W. Starke, of Hamburg, S. C.

Issue of January 20, 1838

Married on Monday evening, 8th inst., by the Rev. Dr. Brantly, Mr. Thomas Chapman, to Miss Rachel, daughter of the late Thomas Blackwood, Esq.
Married on Thursday evening, 14th inst., by the Rev. Mr. Forrest, Charles Edmondston, Jr., Esq. to Miss Mary Maria Chisolm.
On Thursday 11th inst., by the Rev. Mr. Hanckel, Mr. Edward J. Walker, to Miss Ellen B., only daughter of the late James Wilkie, Esq.
On Monday evening 15th inst., by the Rev. Dr. Capers, Capt. Benj. M. Donnell, of Bath, to Miss Sarah H., youngest daughter of the late Capt. S. Webber, of this city.
On Tuesday evening 16th inst., by the Rev. Dr. Post, Mr. Samuel C. Wilson, of Augusta, Ga., to Miss Elizabeth J. Gillett, eldest daughter of the late Wm. S. Gillett, Esq. of Barnwell Dist., S. C.
In New York, on the 28th Dec., by the Rev. Mr. Nichols, Mr. Peter Hood, of Charleston, to Miss Mary, eldest daughter of James B. Oakley, of New York.
Died, in this city on the 29th Dec., Tilson Tipley, infant son of Thomas S. and Elizabeth C. F. Jones, aged 3 months and 15 days.
Died in Merriweather Co., Ga., Mr. Wm. Perry and two sons-- Thos J. Perry on the 5th ult., in the 17th year of his age; Francis A. Perry on the 13th ult., in his 16th year. Mr. William Perry on the 14th ult., in his 57th year.

Issue of January 27, 1838

Married on Sunday evening, 21st inst., by the Rev. Mr. Trapier, Mr. Joseph T. Smith, to Mrs. Elizabeth A. Allen--all of this city.
On Thursday evening, 11th inst., by Rev. Chas. W. Martin, Col. James H. Witherspoon, of Lancasterville, S. C., to Mrs. Francis E. H. McCaw, of Abbeville Dist, S. C.
On the 1st inst., William Bacon Stevens, M. D.,to Miss Alettea, eldest daughter of Dr. Edward Coppee, all of Savannah.
Died in this city on the morning of the 19th inst., Mr. J. G. Bell, of Darien, Ga., aged 35 years.
In this city on the 1st inst., Mrs. Eliza L. Simons, wife of Benj. P. Simons.
Died on the 16th inst., at Barnwell Court House, S. C., Brig. Gen. Gasper J. Trotti, in the 39th year of his age....

Issue of February 3, 1838

Married in this city on Thursday evening, 25th ult., by the Rev. Dr. Bachman, Mr. Daniel T. Ryan, of Columbia, to Miss Mary A. E., only daughter of Col. James S. Shingler, of St. James, S. C.
On Thursday evening 25th ult., by the Rev. Dr. Capers, Rev. Jehu G. Postell, of the S. C. Conf., to Miss Rebecca Ann, eldest daughter of Wm. Bird, Esq. of this city.
Died at Spartanburgh C. H., a few days since, Capt. Wm. Evans, formerly of this ctiy.
At Savannah, on the 18th ult., in the 65th year of his age, Capt. John Hutson of McIntosh Co., Ga. On the 6th inst., in the 73d year of his age, Dr. Wm. Parker, one of the oldest native inhabitants of Savannah.
At Velasco, Texas, sometime in Nov. last, Mrs. Henrietta W. Parker, formerly of this city...left a husband and four children.

On Monday the 22d ult., died at his residence on Edisto Island, Mr. Ephraim Mikell, aged 64 years and 5 months...(eulogy)

Issue of February 10, 1838

Married on Wednesday evening the 31st ult., by the Rev. Mr. Kaufman, James Brown to Miss M. C. daughter of the late Isaac Bennett.

In this city on Wednesday evening last, by the Rev. Mr. Yates, Capt. Robert Campbell, to Miss Regenia H. Holmes, all of New York.

On Thursday evening the 1st of Feb., by the Rev. Dr. Gadsden, Mr. Thomas P. Gough, to Miss Rebecca, daughter of Col. Edward H. Edwards.

Departed this life at his residence in Barnwell Dist., S. C., on the 25th Dec., William Vance, in the 35th year of his age. And, on the 12th Nov. preceding, his infant daughter Susan Dart, aged 2 years. And on the 7th Dec. yet another daughter, Mary Moncrief, aged 7 years. Also, in this city, on the 17th ult., Frances Lawson Vance, infant daughter of Mrs. James Nicholas, and niece of Mr. Vance, deceased.

Departed this life on the 25th Dec.,Mrs. Obedience Ryan, in her 93d year, a native of Hanover Co., Va. In 1809, her family moved to Georgia, where she has remained ever since....

Issue of February 17, 1838

Married on Tuesday evening 6th inst., by the Rev. Dr. Gadsden, Mr. Benjamin Archer of N. Y. to Miss Elizabeth Mary Hammett, of this city.

At Liberty Hall, on Wednesday the 7th inst.,by the Rev. Mr. E. Leverett, Edward Mikell Esqr. to Miss Elizabeth M., eldest daughter of Whitemarsh B. Seabrook, Esq. all of Edisto Island.

Died on the 22d Jan., Ellen A. Millar, in the 2d year of her age; and, on the 31st Jane Childs, in her 5th year; and on the 1st Feb., Martha Linn, in her 9th year--only children of William and Jane Boyd.

At his residence in Orangeburgh District, S. C., on the night of the 2nd inst., Gen. William Rowe.

Issue of February 24, 1838

Married on Tuesday evening 13th inst., by the Rev. Dr. Brantley, Mr. Daniel H. Silcox, of New York, to Miss Martha S., second daughter of the late Mr. John Myce, of this city.

On Thursday evening 15th inst, by the Rev. Mr. Forrest, Dr. John Ashby Wragg, to Miss Caroline, eldest daughter of Andrew McDowall, Esq. all of this city.

On Thursday morning the 15th inst.,by the Rt. Rev. Bishop Bowen, Dr. Mitchell C. King, to Miss Elizabeth L., third daughter of the late Mr. John Middleton, all of this city.

Died at Anderson District, S. C., on the 9th ult.,Mrs. Nancy M. Cunningham, wife of Mr. Thomas Cunningham, in the 26th year of her age...left husband and two little children (eulogy)

Issue of March 3, 1838

Married on Wednesday evening, 21st int., by the Rev. Thomas Smyth, Rev. D. J. Auld, to Miss Adeline H. Hughes, both of this city.

On Thursday evening, 22d inst., by the Rev. Dr. Gadsden, Dr. E. Horry Deas, to Miss Ann, youngest daughter of the late John Ball, Esq.

On Wednesday evening by the Rev. Mr. Barnwell, Thomas F. Drayton, of this City, to Miss Emma C. Pope, of Hilton Head.
On Wednesday evening, 14th inst.,by the Rev. Mr. Bachman, Capt. L. M. Porter, of Summerville, to Mrs. Ann W. Burie, of this city.

Issue of March 10, 1838

Married on Thursday 1st inst., by the Right Rev. Bishop Bowen, Joseph Allan Smith to Emma, daughter of Daniel Elliott Huger.
On Wednesday evening 28th ultimo, by the Rev. Mr. Hanckel, Mr. H. C. Bissell, to Miss Glorvina, daughter of Mr. L. La Rouseliere, all of this city.
On Thursday evening the 1st inst., by the Rev. D. M. Brown, Allen Madison Odom, Major of the 1st Bat 43d Regt. of S. C. Militia, to Miss Eliza, eldest daughter of Mr. and Mrs. James Hagood, of Ball Pond, Barnwell District.
Died, in Boston, on the 22d ultimo, Benjamin Dearborn, Esq., in the 83d year of his age....
At Savannah, on the 3d inst., Mr. Robert Malone, of Augusta.

Issue of March 17, 1838

Married on Wednesday evening last, by the Rev. Dr. Brantley, Col. G. W. Brown of Nicholasville, Ky., to Mrs. C. L. Blackwood, daughter of the late Geo. Gibbs, Esq., of this city.
On Thursday 1st inst., by the Rev. Dr. Gadsden, William Nayler, Esq. to Miss Harriett G., youngest daughter of Richard Lord, Esq., deceased.
Death of Mr. James Badger, who died on the 14th ult., in the 45th year of his age...(eulogy)

Issue of March 24, 1838

Married on Thursday evening 15th inst.,by the Rev. C. K. Ketchum, Mr. John J. Boyce, of this city to Miss Catharine H., eldest daughter of the Hon. Job Johnston, of Newberry.
Died on Thursday 15th inst., at the residence of her father in St. Bartholomew's Parish, in the 22d year of her age, Mrs. Mary D. O'Hear, wife of Jas. O'Hear, of this city.
In Hamburg, S. C., on Saturday 10th inst., in a fit of apoplexy, Charles B. Pennington, in the 32d year of his age, a native of this city.

Issue of March 31, 1838

Married on Thursday the 22d inst.,by the Rev. Mr. Barnwell, Mr. Frederick A. Porcher, to Miss Emma C., eldest daughter of the late Dr. John P. Gough.
On Wednesday night last, by Rev. Wm. C. Dana, Mr. Belah H. Jacobs, Merchant, to Miss Julia Ann Davis, daughter of Capt. Thomas Davis,all of this city.
Departed this transitory life, on March 4th, at her residence on John's Island, Mrs. Ann Eliza Legare, consort of Thomas Legare, Esq., aged 61 years...(eulogy)....
Died at his residence in Lower Salem, Sumter Dist., S. C., on the 12th of March, Richard Rollins, in the 98th year of his age. a member of the Presbyterian Church about 50 years..a soldier of the Rev. (eulogy)...left widow, children, and grandchildren.

Issue of April 7, 1838

Married on Monday evening 26th ult.,by the Rev. Mr. Adams, William F.Colcock, to Miss Emeline L. Huguenin.
On the 3d inst., by the Rev. Thomas Smyth, Mr. James Mack, to Mrs. Mary Walsh, all of this City.
On Thursday evening the 29 inst., by the Right Rev. Bishop Bowen, Mr. Alonzo J. White, to Miss Eliza M. Ingraham.
On Tuesday the 27th ultimo, by the Rev. Dr. Gilman, Col. John Schnierle, to Miss Elizabeth eldest daughter of Thomas J. Horsey, Esq.
At Columbia, on the evening of the 28th March, by the Rev. Dr. Witherspoon, the Rev. Edwin Cater of Anderson, S. C. to Sarah Margaret eldest daughter of the Rev. Dr. Leland.
On Tuesday the 27th March, by the Rev. Paul Trapier, Mr. John Dawson, to Miss Susan McClintoch.
In Williamsburg Dist., on Thursday evening, the 22d inst., by the Rev. Mr. Peden, Mr. Samuel E. Bigham, of Darlington, to Miss Sarah A. B. Singletary, of the former District.
Died, at the residence of his nephew, Major Charles M. Hart, in the town of Raymond, Miss., on the 8th inst., Stephen D. Miller, Esq., one of the former Governors of S. C.
Departed this transitory life, at her residence in Kingstree, on the 11th inst., Mrs. Susan A. Staggers, consort of Mr. Wm. Staggers, in the 30th year of her age.

Issue of April 14, 1838

Married on Thursday the 5th inst., by the Rev. Mr. Spear, Mr. Robt L. Baker, to Miss Sarah Ann, eldest daughter of the late Capt. Wm. Brow(sic), all of this city.
On Sunday evening 8th inst., by the Rev. Dr. Bachman, Mr. J. R. Wood, to Miss Ann Disher, all of this city.
On Thursday evening, 5th inst.,by the Rev. Dr. Bachman, Mr. John Wn. Evans, of Baltimore, to Miss Ann Amanda, second daughter of Abraham Jones, of this city.
On the 4th inst., in Walterboro, by the Rev. Adam Gilchrist, Mr. Arthur A. Gilling, of Edisto Island, to Mrs. Mary Nohr of the former place.
Departed this life on the 1st inst.,at her residence, Poplar Grove, in St. Paul's Parish, Mrs. Henrietta Rowand, in the 63d year of her age, relict of the late Charles E. Rowand.
Died, at Columbia, S. c., on the 3rd inst.,in the 34th year of his age, Richard L. Ludlam, of New York City, and for many years a merchant at Lima, in Peru....

Issue of April 21, 1838

Married on Tuesday evening last, by the Rev. Thomas Smyth, Mr. Charles P. Frazer, of this city, to Miss Hannah P., youngest daughter of Capt. N. Raymond, of Brooklyn, N. Y.
On the morning of the 7th inst., at St. Helena Church, Beaufort, by the Rev. Jos. R. Walker, Nathaniel Heyward, Jr. to Eliza B. Smith, daughter of the late James Smith.
Death of Miss Margaret J. Crosby, who died on the 11th March 1838...youngest daughter of the late Capt. Crosby....
Died on the 5th inst., in Knoxville, Ga., Mr. William S. Harrison, of Chittenden, Vt.,aged about 32....
Departed this life on the 2d of April at the house of her son, H. H. Means, Esq. in Marshall Co., Miss., Mrs. Hannah Means, consort of the late Gen. Hugh Means, of Union District, S.C., in the 72 year of her age...for 53 years a member of the Presbyterian Church.

Issue of April 28, 1838

Married on Thursday evening the 19th inst., by the Rev. Mr. Spear, Mr. L. C. Clifford, to Miss Caroline McPherson, only daughter of the late Samuel Colleton Graves, all of this city.
On Tuesday evening, 17th inst., by the Rev. Mr. Trapier, Mr. Frederick P. Elford, to Miss Maria A., only daughter of Mr. Jacob Burn, all of this city.
On the 12th inst., at Washington, D. C., by Rev.Mr. McClain, Rev. James Stratton, Pastor of the Presbyterian Church in Irwinton, Alabama, to Miss Elizabeth R. Floyd, only daughter of the late Rev. L. Floyd, of St. Bartholomew's Parish, S. C.
In Hartford, Conn., on the 12th inst., at Christ Church, by the Rev. Mr. Burgess, Chauncy Barnard, Esq. of that place, to Mrs. Harriet Barnard, of this city.
Died at Athens, Ga., on Sunday, the 15th inst., Stevens Thomas, Esq., one of the oldest and most respectable citizens of that place.
At Matanzas, on the 13th inst., Lieut. A. Ury, a native of Tennessee, and a graduate of West Point Academy.

Issue of May 5, 1838

Married on Tuesday, April 24th by the Rev. Thomas Smyth, Mr. Charles J. Sparks, to Miss Susan V., youngest daughter of the late John Ruberry.

Issue of May 12, 1838

Married in Beaufort District, on Thursday evening, 3d inst., by Bishop Bowen, Col. Isaac B. Ulmer, of Prince Williams Parish, Beaufort District, to Miss Abby Johnson, third daughter of the late Oliver Cromwell, Esq. of this place.
Married on the 1st inst., by the Rev. Mr. Smyth, Moses Whitesides, Esq., of Christ Church, to Mrs. Mary Barnes, of this city.
Died, in Greenville district, S. C., on the 17th ult., Mrs. Elizabeth Wright, widow of the late Asa Wright, aged about 68 years....

Issue of May 19, 1838

Married on the 9th inst.,by the Rev. Dr. Brantley, Mr. W. T. Purdy, to Mrs. Eliza Merrett, both of this city.
On Thursday evening the 10th inst., by the Rev. Dr. Gadsden, Mr. Nathl. Hyatt, to Charlotte Augusta, daughter of the late John Simons Bee, Esq., all of this city.
On the 10th inst., by the Rev. Dr. Brantley, Capt. Levin Stott, of Fairhaven, Mass., to Miss Harriet Fredeburg, of this city.
In Troup Co., Ga.,on the 3d inst., by the Rev. J. Y. Alexander, the Rev. Lyman W. Corbin to Miss Elizabeth H. Boyd, eldest daughter of Joseph H. Boyd.
Departed this life on Saturday evening, 5th inst., Elizabeth Hahnbaum, only daughter of Mr. and Mrs. Joseph T. Zealy, aged 6 months and 7 days. (poem)
Died, in this city, on the 12th inst., Capt. John S. Walker, of Columbia, S. C.
Departed this life on the 24th March last, at his residence in Monroe Co., Ga., Matthew Thompson Caldwell, aged 45 years and 6 months, nearly...Elder in the Presbyterian Church....
James C. Patterson

Issue of May 26, 1838

Married on Thursday evening 17th inst., by the Rev. Mr. Sheppard, Mr. Theodore C. Tharin, to Miss Caroline Julia, only daughter of the late Nathaniel W. Marrion, Esq.

Died on the 15th inst., Mrs. Jane O'Riley Veitch, aged 36 years.

On the 20th inst., Mr. George F. Keckley, aged 27 years and 11 months.

Died, at Beach Island, Edgefield District, Ann Helena, infant daughter of Mr. and Mrs. Samuel Clarke, aged 3 months and 16 days.

Issue of June 2, 1838

Married at New York, on the 26th inst., at St. Thomas Church, by the Rev. F. L. Hawks, D. D., James Alexander Ashby, Major 2d Regt. Dragoons, to Harriet Eliza, daughter of Christopher Williman, Esq., of this city.

In Columbia, on Wednesday evening 23d inst.,by the Rev. Mr. McPherson, Mr. Isaac C. Morgan, formerly of this city, to Miss Frances Bynum, of Columbia.

On the evening of the 25th inst., by Rev. John B. Cassels, Mr. William A. Curry to Miss Martha M. Bunkley, all of Green co., Ga.

Died at Troy, N. Y., on the 3d inst., Mrs. Sarah H. Hopkins, wife of Rev. Erastus Hopkins, of that place, and daughter of the late William Swinton Bennett, Esq., of this city....

Issue of June 9, 1838

Died at the residence of her husband, in Newton co., Ga., on the 14th inst., 28 minutes before 1 o'clock A. M., in her 27th year, Mrs. Harriet M. Levingston, wife of Alfred Levingston, Esq. and daughter of Felix Symington, Esq., of Troup County...left husband and five small children.

Married on Thursday evening 26th April, by the Rev. Mr.Dana, Thomas Lehre, Esq., to Miss Caroline Jane Swinton.

On the 24th May by the Rev. Dr. Gadsden, Mr. Alex. Inglis, to Maria Schmidt, daughter of Christopher Williman, all of this place.

On Tuesday evening the 5th June, by the Rev. John Forrest, Dr. Thomas Y. Simons, to Mary Elliott, eldest daughter of the late Charles E. Rowand, Esq.

Issue of June 16, 1838

Married on Wednesday evening 6th inst., by the Rev. Mr. Brantley, Mr. James Crose, of Bourbon Co., Ky., to Miss Caroline S., second daughter of the late John Casten, of this city.

On Tuesday 5th inst.,at Philadelphia, by the Rev. Mr. Furness, Mr. Thomas J. Kerr, of Charleston, S. C. to Miss Elizabeth C., daughter of M. L. Hurlbut, Esq. of the former place.

Departed this life, suddenly on Thursday the 7th inst.,in the 65th year of his age, William Timmons, esq., for many years, a respectable merchant in this city.

Died at Mobile, Alabama, on the 21st of March last, Mr. William Lacey, aged 28 years, a native of this city.

Died, in Liberty township, Columbia Co., Pennsylvania, on the 28th April last, Michael Dearmond, a Soldier of the Revolutionary war, aged one hundred and five years.

Issue of June 23, 1838

    Married on Tuesday evening the 19th inst.,by the Rt. Rev. Dr. Bowen, Dr. Richard L. North, to Miss Martha P. Gervais.
    Died at Walterboro', on Monday, the 11th inst., Samuel G. Sanders, in the 22d year of his age....
    At Milledgeville, Ga., on the 10th inst., Charles L. Bradley, in the 37th year of his age...a native of New Haven, Conn., but for the last 11 years a resident of Ga.
    At Montgomery, Ala., on the 3d inst., Mr. William Crosby, of this city, aged 31 years, 6 months and 20 days.

Issue of June 30, 1838

    Died on the 26th of May, in Talifero co., Ga., Mr. James Morgan...left a wife and three small children...a member of the Presbyterian Church....

Issue of July 7, 1838

    Died at N. Y., on the 5th ult., Mr. Wm. Brown, for many years a resident of Georgetown, S. C....
    In Lincolnton Co., N. C.,on the 18th ult., Mr. John Wilfong, Sr., aged 78 years. He was an officer in the Rev. war.
    Married on Thursday evening 26th inst.,at the First Presbyterian Church of this city, by the Rev. John Forrest, Mr. Samuel A. Suydam, of New York city, to Maria Caroline Augustine, of Augusta, Ga.
    Married on the morning of the 26th inst., in Salem Church, by the Rev. John B. Cassels, Charles W. Gresham, Elder of the Church, to Miss Easter Wright, all of Wilkes Co., Ga.

Issue of July 14, 1838

    Married at Spring Hill, Arkansas, on Tuesday 5th June by the Rev. Elisha Battle, Rev. A. R. Banks, formerly of Fairfield, S. C. to Miss Elizabeth Pratt, formerly of Troy, N. Y.
    On Thursday evening, the 7th inst., by Rev. A. R. Banks, Mr. _____ Nobles, to Miss Ann Pettigur, all of Spring Hill, Arkansas.
    Died at Spring Hill, Ark., on Monday 21st May, by descending into a well full of Carbonic Acid Gas, in order to draw up his negro man who had just fallen from the bucket in descending, from the same cause, Mr. Thomas C. Dupree, a worthy citizen formerly of Alabama....
    Died, also at the same place, on Saturday, 25th May, Mrs. Helen Tarwater, formerly of Clarksville, Va....left husband and two little children....

Issue of July 21, 1838

    Married on Tuesday evening 10th inst., by the Rev.. Dr. Gadsden, Mr. Milton W. Leach, of Rochester, Mass.,to Miss Isabell C. Hamett, of this city.
    On Thursday evening 12th inst., by the Rev. Mr. Evans, Mr. George B. Dyer, to Miss Ann L. Hurst, all of this city.
    Departed this life on the 5th inst., aged 71 years, Capt. Joseph Young, a native of North Yarmouth, Me., and for the last 22 years a resident of this city.
    Died on the 24th ult., near Pontotoc, Miss., in the 59th year of his age, Col. Andrew Pickens, late of S. C.

Issue of June 28, 1838

Married on Thursday evening, 12th inst.,by the Rev. Dr. Post, Mr. Edward J. Jones, to Miss Abigail, second daughter of John T. Elsworth, all of this city.
On the 28th June, by the Rev. Hansford D. Duncan, Col. B. H. Brown, to Mrs. C. H. Charlton, relict of Judge T. U. P. Charlton, of Savannah.
Departed this life on the 21st inst., John Criffs Ravenel, in the 24th year of his age, son of Daniel Ravenel, Esq. of this city.
Died, in this city, on Monday evening, 23d inst., Mr. James Taylor, a native of Bordentown, N. Y., aged 28 years.
On the 17th inst., Helen Yancey, daughter of James W. Gray, aged 11 months and 5 days.

Issue of August 4, 1838

Married on Tuesday evening last, by the Rev. Dr. Brantley, Capt. Wm. P. Rose to Miss Sarah Ann, eldest daughter of Richard Bringloe, all of this city.
Departed this life on the evening of the 27th inst.,Mrs. Jane Holland, in the 78th year of her age....
Died in St. Augustine, on Tuesday morning, 17th inst., Capt. William Levingston, in the 61st year of his age, a native of Ga., but for the last 20 years a resident of St. Augustine....He served with great credit at the battle of New Orleans.
In Morgan Co., Ga., on the 9th ult., Major John Floyd, in the 67th year of his age.

Issue of August 11, 1838

Died on the 30th of June last, Mrs. Mary Huger, in the 76th year of her age.
Departed this life, on Tuesday, the 7th inst.,Mr. Wm. Mason Smith, and on Wednesday his remains were consigned to the tomb in the Cemetery of St. Philip's Church.
On the night of the 27th ultimo, Benjamin J. Grimball, eldest son of P. C. Grimball, of John's Island, in the 19th year of his age.
Departed this life at her residence near Church Hill, Abbeville Dist., S. C., on the 22d July, Mrs. Jane Younge, aged 77 years. She was the widow of Samuel Younge, who died at the same place in 1824...in the Presbyterian Church of Rocky River upwards of 50 years ago....
Died at Lagrange, Troup Co., Ga., on the 21st of July, Rebecca Jane, eldest daughter of Mr. Daniel and Mrs. Elmyra McMillen, aged 4 years, 10 months and 24 days....
In Crawford county, Ga., on the 26th ult., Rev. Daniel Duffey, a native of Ireland, in the 76th year of his age. He was a member of the Methodist Episcopal Church 36 years, and a local preacher most of that time.

Issue of August 18, 1838

Married on Thursday evening 2d inst., by the Rev. Samuel Gilman, Mr. Joseph Walker, to Miss Ellen S., daughter of the late Wm. B. Wilkie, all of this city.
Died in Fairfield District, S. C., on the 4th inst., Dr. James Davis, for nearly thirty years an eminent physician of Columbia.
At Walterborough, S. C. on the 4th inst., in the 19th year of his age, Lawrence Sanders, youngest son of Capt. Lawrence Fishburne.

Issue of August 25, 1838

Departed this life on the 1st inst., Alexander Sinclair, Esq., a native of Perthshire, Scotland, for the last forty years a merchant of Charleston.
Departed this life in Salem, Sumter Dist., on the evening of the 5th inst., Mrs. Sarah Ann English, consort of the Rev. T. R. English...On 1st November last she was joined in marriage with the Rev. Mr. E....Mr. E. having had four children by a former marriage. (long eulogy)

Issue of September 1, 1838

Died, suddenly, at New Haven, Conn., on the 19th inst., Theodocia P. Hayden, aged 21 years, wife of Mr. Nath'l Hayden, merchant of this city.
Departed this life on the 14th day of August, Abraham S. Dantzler, a native of Orangeburg, in the 25th year of his age....
Died at Mobile, on the 17th inst., after a few days confinement, Mrs. Ann Matilda Heard, formerly of Augusta, Geo.
Died, in Salem, Sumter district, S. C., on the 5th inst., Mrs. Sarah Ann English, consort of Rev. T. R. English.

Issue of September 8, 1838

Departed this life on the 30th August, in the 30th year of his age, William Cripps Fayssoux, eldest son of the late Dr. James H. Fayssoux.
Died at his summer retreat, near McPhersonville, on the 16th August, 1838, in the 44th year of his age, Col. James Cuthbert.
Died on the 16th inst., at his residence in Oglethorpe Co., Geo., David McLaughlin, a native of Maryland, in the 76th year of his age...a member of the Presbyterian Church in N. C. in 1792. spent a small portion of his life in Pennsylvania. From 1797 to the day of his death he resided at the place where he died.... (eulogy).

Issue of September 15, 1838

Departed this life on the 26th ult., in Calhoun's Settlement, Abbeville District, Mrs. Caroline A. Lee, consort of Dr. Thomas Lee, of that district....
Departed this life, June 12th,1838, at "The Pas," near Matagorda, Texas, Mr. Hugh Davies Gaston, son of Captain Gaston, of Pendleton, S. C. and lately a resident of Kemper Co., Miss., in the 29th year of his age...(eulogy)   AN ONLY BROTHER.
Died, in Gainesville,Ga., August 28th, Miss Jane A. Nesbitt, daughter of Mrs. A. A. Nesbitt, and of the late Allen Nesbitt, of Beach Island, S. C....

Issue of September 22, 1838

Died on the 24th ult., Andrew, son of Andrew and Anna Moffett, aged 15 years, 8 months and 22 days.
Died in Beaufort, S. C., on the 28th August last, Mrs. Elizabeth H. Verdier, relict of John M. Verdier, Esq., in the 72d year of her age...member of the Episcopal Church....

Issue of September 29, 1838

Died in this city on the 17th inst.,Eliza Stanyarne Mazyck, in the 29th year of her age, eldest daughter of Dr. Philip P. Mazyck.

In Columbia Co., Ga., on the 23d ult., Mrs. Sarah Whittington, aged 74 years.

Issue of October 6, 1838

Married on Tuesday evening last, by the Rev. Mr. Gildersleeve, Mr. Wm. P. Bond, of Baltimore, Md., to Mrs. Mary E. Keaton, of Alexandria, D. C.
 Died on the 4th inst., in the 49th year of his age, Mr. Charles S. Simonton, one of the Ruling Elders of the Second Presbyterian Church....
 In Union District, near Pacolet river, on the 30th July, Miss Margaret E. Foster. Onthe 6th August, Mrs. Rebecca Foster. On the 7th Sept., infant son. On the 11th Sept., William G. Foster. On the 12th Sept., Samuel G. Foster. On the 14th Sept. Miligan P. Foster, wife and children of Mr. Nathaniel Foster.
 Departed this life on the 17th Sept., at his residence in Union District, Davis Goudelock, Esq.,in the 74th year of his age...served in the revolutionary army in the latter part of the war.
 Death of Sir John Nicholl; Sir William Maxwell; Dr. Barns, from the London papers.

Issue of October 13, 1838

Married on Sunday evening 7th inst., by the Right Rev. Dr. Bowen, Mr. James Smith, to Miss Elizabeth Don, daughter of the late Alexander Don, both of this city.
 Died on the 20th inst.,in the 7th year of her age, Jane Eliza Badger, of this city....
 Departed this life on the 1st inst., at Georgetown, S. C., Mrs. Mary E. Magill, aged 35 years and 5 months, consort of Dr. Wm. Magill, formerly of this city...left husband and children.
 At Macon, Ga., on the 30th ult., Major Thomas Napier, one of the oldest citizens of that place, aged 71 years.

Issue of October 20, 1838

Married on the 11th inst., by the Rev. Mr. Gildersleeve, Mr. G. L. Warren to Miss Mary R. Vardell, all of this city.
 On Wednesday evening last, by the Rev. C. Hanckel, George M. Coffin, Esq., to Miss Sarah L. second daughter of Thos Grange Simons, Esq.
 Married, in St. Peter's Parish, on Thursday the 4th inst., by the Rev. Isaac Nichol, Dr. Henry W. Richardson, of Beaufort, to Mary, daughter of Major John S. Manor.
 Died at Mount Pleasant Village, Christ Church Parish on the night of the 12th inst., Susan Ella, second daughter of Henry C. and Julia Tovey, aged 3 years, 11 months and 7 days.
 Died on Wednesday the 10th October, at the residence of his brother, on Sullivan's Island, James Hamilton, eldest son of Gen. Hamilton of this city.
 In Burke co., Ga., on the 26th ult.,Rev. Lawson B. Clinton, in the 41st year of his age....a member of the Presbytery of Hopewell....

Issue of October 27, 1838

Married on Thursday evening, the 11th inst., at St. Luke's Church, New York, by the Rev. J. M. Forbes, the Rev. Robert Howard, of this city, to Hester M., daughter of B. B. Seamon, Esq.
 On the 23d inst., by the Rev. Mr. Gilman, Mr. L. A. Shecut, to Alvina Eliza, youngest daughter of the late A. J. Brown, both

143

of this city.
Departed this life on the 2d inst., in the 31st year of his age, Thomas Pinckney Lowndes....
Died on the 12th inst., in Mobile, Ala., in the 24th year of his age, Thomas Savage Deas, son of Mr. Henry Deas, of this city.
Departed this life in Northampton, Mass., on the 10th inst., Mrs Rebecca Theus, aged 33, wife of James Hibben, Esq.,late of Charleston...left seven young children.

Issue of November 3, 1838

Married on Thursday evening 25th inst., by the Rev. Mr. Evans, Mr. Henry G. Guerry, to Miss Catharine E., daughter of John M. Happoldt, deceased, all of this city.
Married on Tuesday evening last, by the Rev. Dr. Gilman, Mr. Henry S. Tew, to Miss Sarah R., daughter of the late Mr. Bethel Treadcraft, all of this city.
Married on the 25th inst., by the Rev. Mr.Dupont, Mr. John Fenebee, of Grahamville, S. C., to Miss Margaret Eikerenkoetter.
Married on the 18th inst., by the Rev. J. C. Posthill, Dr. William E. Dargan, to Miss Sarah T., second daughter of Isaiah Dubose, Esq., all of Cheraw, S. C.
Died on the 5th inst., William Vincent Hutchings, formerly of Boston, Mass., aged about 30.
Died at Carlowville, Dallas Co., Alabama, on the 11th ult., Harriet Rebecca, youngest daughter of Maj. Paul S. H. Lee, aged 16 years.

Issue of November 10, 1838

Married on Thursday evening, 1st inst.,by the Rev. Mr. Barnwell, Mr. Nicedemus Aldrich, to Miss Elizabeth D., third daughter of John Strobel, Esq., all of this city.
On Thursday evening, 1st inst.,by the Rev. Dr. Capers, Mr. Andrew Doty, of Courtlandville, N. Y., to Miss Ellen Hayden, of St. Augustine, E. F.
Died in this city on the 26th ult.,in the 24th year of his age, John McPherson, Esq....
Departed this life at his residence near Darien, Ga.,on the 23d ult., Mr. John G. Bell, in the 41st year of his age.
Died in the Town of Mount Pleasant, C. C. Parish, on Friday, the 2d inst., Elizabeth Fosbury, infant daughter of Henry C. and Julianna Tovey, aged 2 months and 27 days.

Issue of November 17, 1838

Married on Thursday evening 1st inst. by the Rev. Dr. Gadsden, Mr. Daniel Lesesne, to Miss Sarah Lewis, daughter of the late Col. Keating L. Simons, all of this city.
On the 8th inst.,by the Rev. Mr. Trapier, Mr. Joseph Torlay, to Miss Elizabeth Palmer, of this city.
On Thursday evening 8th inst.,by the Rev. Dr. Gadsden, Mr. Charles Kerrison to Miss Mary Ann, daughter of Capt. Mullings, all of this city.
Died, on Tuesday night, 30th ult., Thomas Smyth, third son of Thomas R. and Amelia A. Vardell, aged 11 months and 15 days.
Died on the 12th ult., Wlliam H., second son of the late William H. Gray, aged 7 years, 7 months and 9 days.

Issue of November 24, 1838

Married on Wednesday evening 14th inst., by the Rt. Revd. Bishop Bowen, Richard Wainwright Bacot to Miss Maria Ramsey, eldest daughter of William Lance, Esq.

On Thursday evening, the 15th inst., by the Rev. Mr. Armstrong, Mr. William M. Eager, to Mrs. Eliza D. Bythewood, all of this city.

On James Island, 14th inst., by Rev. C. Taylor, Capt. John Rivers, to Mrs. Sarah Rivers, all of James Island.

Died at Edingsville, on the 19th Sept., Dr. Francis Y. Simmons, late State Senator from St. Paul's Parish....

Issue of December 1, 1838

Married in this city on the evening of the 5th inst., by the Rev. Mr. Talley, Mr. Norborne Radcliffe, late of Mobile, Alabama, to Miss Julia E. Wells, daughter of the late Col. Nathan Huggins, of Winyaw, Prince George Parish.

On Thursday evening 22d inst., by the Rev. Dr. Gadsden, Dr. George Gibson, to Miss Sarah H., daughter of Daniel Huger, Esq.

On Wednesday the 21st inst., by the Rev. C. Hanckle, Dr. Summers Harleston, to Miss Elizabeth P., youngest daughter of the late Dr. Robert M. Haig.

On Thursday evening 22d inst., by the Rev. Dr. Capers, Mr. Henry Casey, to Miss Sarah Catharine, eldest daughter of the late Mr. John E. Burdell, all of this city.

In Philadelphia, on the 13th inst., by the Rev. Mr. Moreton, Lieut. K. Hoff, U. S. Navy, of this city, to Louisa A. W., daughter of the late Commodore Wm. Brainbridge.

Died in this city on the 17th inst., Martha W., wife of Christopher P. Walter, of St. Paul's Parish, aged 22 years.

Departed this life on Thursday last, 22d inst., Mrs. Mary Brewton Alston, wife of Col. Wm. Alston, in the 79th year of her age.

Died in Chester Dist., S. C., Nov. 22, Mrs. Mary P., wife of Mr. John Walker, and second daughter of John and Elizabeth Douglas, in the 39th year of her age...member of the Presbyterian Church.....

Died in St. Bartholomew's Parish, on the 10th inst., Mrs. Sarah S., wife of Col. Walker.

Issue of December 15, 1838

Married on Wednesday evening 28th ult., by the Rev. Mr. Brantley, Mr. Robert Aldrich, to Mrs. Frances S. Lebby, both of this city.

On Thursday evening 6th inst., by the Rev. Dr. Post, Mr. Peter C. Gaillard, to Miss Ann L., youngest daughter of Wm. E. Snowden, of this city.

At Savannah, on the 29th ult., by the Rev. T. C. Dupont, Rev. Edward Neufville, Rector Christ Church, to Mary Fenwick, daughter of the late Lemuel Kollock, M. D.

Departed this life on the 4th inst.,Miss Martha Reynolds Bascom, within five days of the completion of her 12th year....

Issue of December 29, 1838

Married on Thursday 20th inst., by the Rev. Dr. Capers, Mr. Mortimer W. Venning, to Miss Martha Elizabeth Dickson, all of this city.

At Gillisonville, on Thursday, December 20th, John D. Williamson, to Miss Sarah Jane Beard, both of Beaufort Dist., S. C.

On Wednesday evening the 19th inst, by the Rev. Mr. Howard, Mr. John W.Johnson, to Miss Louisa Amelia, youngest daughter of Mr. John N. Martin, all of this city.

On the 27th Nov.,by the Rev. Mr. Converse, Major Abraham Van Buren, oldest son of the Pres. of the U. S. to Miss Sarah Angelica Singleton, youngest daughter of Mr. Richard Singleton, at her fathers residence, Sumter Dist., S. C.

Departed this life at his residence in Chester Dist., S. C., on the 11th day of December, Charles Walker, in the 60th year of his age...an elder in the Presbyterian Church...left wife and nine children.

Departed this life, on the morning of the 1st inst., Miss Margaret Catharine Martin, daughter of Mr. Alexander Martin, decd., and Mrs Lauretia Martin, aged 40 years....

Died at Walterboro, on the night of Dec. 16th, Hester Maria, second daughter of Rev. Adam Gilchrist, aged 2 years, and 3 months.

Died on the night of December 22d, at Walterboro, William Edward, youngest son of Dr. William Webb, aged 4 years, 11 months. (eulogy)

Issue of January 29, 1839

Departed this life at his residence in Sumter Dist., on Tuesday morning, the 8th inst., Mr. Amos Chandler, in the 63d year of his age...Presbyterian Church of Concord....

Died in Boston, on Saturday 5th inst., Mrs. Isabella Nott Perkins, wife of Mr. Daniel Perkins, formerly a native of this city.

From the Hudson Republican:
Died in the city of Hudson, on the evening of the 13th inst., Capt. Alexander Coffin, in the 99th year of his age...born 21st Sept. 1749, on the Island of Nantucket...(eulogy and account)

Issue of February 2, 1839

Married in Grahamville, on Wednesday evening, 23d ult., by the Rev. Mr. Dupont, Dr. Wm. M. Bailey, of Edisto Island, to Miss Julia Laura, youngest daughter of the late Capt. John Graham, of St. Luke's Parish.

In Macon on the 15th inst., by the Rev. Mr. Baker, of Milledgeville, the Rev. Samuel J. Cassels, pastor of the Presbyterian Church in Athens, to Mrs. Sarah Ann Wallis.

Departed this life on the 29th Dec. last in Spartanburg Dist., S. C.,Capt. Martin Cole, an officer of the Rev...aged 83 years, 4 months and 9 days...one of Gen. Washington's Life Guard for two years.

Died on the 7th inst., at the house of the Rev. Henry Brown, 40 miles north of Wilmington, N. C.,the Rev. Thomas Dickson Baird, late editor of the Pittsburgh Christian Herald, in the 66th year of his age.

Issue of March 9, 1839

Married on Thursday evening, Feb. 28 by the Rev. Mr. Trapier, Mr. F. A. Baker to Miss Mary Ann White, both of this city.

On the 6th inst.,by the Rev. Dr. Post, Edgar G. Stoney, Esq., to Miss Ann Octavia, daughter of Col. John Bryan.

On Wednesday evening 27th ult., by the Rev. Samuel Gilman, Mr. George W. Eason, to Miss Amelia Verone, all of this city.

On Wednesday 27th ult., at Macon, Ga., by the Rev. Mr. Bragg, Dr. Edward E. Strohecker, of Charleston, S. C., to Miss Sarah Ann Williams, youngest daughter of the late Drury Williams, of Ga.

On Wednesday 20th ult., by the Rev. W. Capers, Mr. Eugene Hatchet, of this city, to Miss Floride Esdra, of Bordeaux, France.
At New York, on Tuesday evening 29th ult., by the Rev. Mr. Taylor, and afterwards by the Right Rev. Mr. Power, Robert Berney Esq. of Charleston, S. C., to Miss Louise Chebec, of France.
Died in Havana, Green co., Alabama, on the 10th ult., and in the 26th year of his age, Dr. S. Keith Palmer, only son of the Revd. B. M. Palmer, of this city. (eulogy)
Departed this life in this city, on the 4th of Feb last, Mrs. Rebecca H. Magwood, consort of Charles A. Magwood, Esq., in the 39th year of her age....

Issue of March 16, 1839

Married on the 7th inst, by the Rev. Dr. Post, Dr. F. Jay Hay, of Barnwell District, to Miss Caroline A. Hasell, of this city.
Departed this life on the 18th ult., in Spartanburg Dist., S C., on the 18th ult., Mr. Henry Cole a Soldier of the Rev., aged 85 years 6 months and 5 days.
Died near Ognawka, Ill., Mr. Daniel McMillan, in the 87th year of his age. He was a native of Ireland, but came to S. C., and joined the Patriotic Army.

Issue of March 23, 1839

Married on the 2d inst., by the Rev. Dr. Post, Mr. P. F. Smith, to Miss Harriet Yeadon, daughter of Col. Richard Yeadon, of this city.
On the 26th ult., by the Rev. Mr. Dana, Dr. John Dickson, to Miss Louisa O'Hear, of this city.
On the 2d inst., by the Rev. Mr. Tally, Mr. Wm. P. P. Patterson, of Baltimore, Md.,to Miss Lydia C. Clark, of this city.
In Wilcox Co., Ala., on the 7th Feb.,last, by the Rev. Mr. Sibly, Mr. Green Lee Yongue, formerly of Fairfield Dist., S. C., to Miss Margaret Rebecca Brown Burke, formerly a resident of this city.

Issue of April 13, 1839

Married on Wednesday evening, 3d inst.,by the Rev. Dr. Brantley, Mr. T. A. Whitney, to Miss Elizabeth Ann, eldest daughter of the late Robert C. Brown, Esq. all of this city.
On John's Island, on Tuesday evening, 2d inst, by the Rev. Thomas J. Young, Mr. Thomas W. S. Chrietzberg, to Miss Jane B. Addison, youngest daughter of the late Wm. Addison, Esq.
On Tuesday evening, March 12, at Middleton Place, in the Parish of St. George, Dorchester, by the Rev. Mr. Trapier, Mr. J. Francis Fisher, of Philadelphia, to Miss Eliza, daughter of the Hon. H. Middleton.
In Lexington, Oglethorpe Co., Ga., on the 26th March, by the Rev. Mr. Hoyt, William H. Crawford, Eq., son of the late Hon. W. H. Crawford, to Miss Caroline L. Thomas, daughter of the late Mr. John Thomas.
In the same place and by the same, on the 28th March, Mr. William L. C. Gerardine, son of the late Dr. John Gerardine, to Miss Lucy Lumpkin, second daughter of Col. Joseph H. Lumpkin.
Departed this life on the 23d Feb., Elizabeth, consort of Rev. Daniel Sheppard, of St. John's, Berkley.
Departed this life on the 1st day of Feb., Mr. John Lewis, in the 63d year of his age, for many years a respectable merchant of this city....

Died suddenly at his residence in Barnwell Dist., on Thursday the 4th inst., Mr. James Hagood, aged 58 years....
Death of Chancellor Desaussure...departed this life on Friday 30th ult in this city, at the advanced age of 75 years...(long account)

Issue of April 20, 1839

Married in Maddison Co., Middle Florida, on the 14th ult., by the Rev. Mr. Cooper, John C. Pillans, Esq. of this city, to Mrs. Angelina Alexander, of the former place.
Died, in this city on the 7th inst.,Mrs. Ann Neufville, in the 72d year of her age, consort of Isaac Neufville, deceased.
Departed this life at Henderson, Kentucky, on the 26th Feb., in the 44th year of her age, Mrs. Ann Caroline Gill, daughter of the late Mr. John Rudolph Switzer, of this city.

Issue of April 27, 1839

Married at Bethel, near Pocotaligo, on Tuesday 16th inst., by Rev. Mr. Elliott, Mr. John Webb, to Miss Elizabeth H. Heyward, daughter of the late Thomas Heyward, Esq.
Departed this life on the 17th inst., Mrs. Sophia C. Egleston, wife of G. W. Egleston, Esq.
Died on the 14th inst., George Edward, infant son of William and Ann Harral, aged 9 months and 26 days. (poem)

Issue of May 11, 1839

Married on Thursday evening 2d inst., by the Rev. Dr. Brantley, Mr. Daniel O'Leary, to Miss Mary Ann, youngest daughter of the late John Burke, all of this city.
Married at the residence of Col. Crosby, in Washington, Texas, on the 11th ult., by the Rev. Mr. Wilson, Major Henry R. Cartmell, of Nashville, Tenn., to Mrs. MaryA. Crosby, of Charleston, S. C.
Died in Philadelphia, on Saturday morning, 14th inst., in the 41st year of his age,Rev. Albert Jueson, Pastor of the 1st Presbyterian Church in Southwark....

Issue of May 18, 1839

Married on Tuesday evening 7th inst., by the Rev. Mr. Smyth, Mr. William H. Ellison of Fairfield, S. C., to Miss Elizabeth Ann, only daughter of the late Mr. Robert Adger, of this city.
In this city on Tuesday evening 7th inst., by the Rev. Mr. Hanckle, Mr. Henry Tilton, of Portland, Me., to Miss Ellan Virginia Johnson, of Middletown, Conn.
On Wednesday evening 8th inst., by the Rev. C. Hanckle, William Jervey, Esq. to Miss Catharine R. Stevens, daughter of the late Charles Stevens.
On Sunday evening 12th inst.,by the Rev. Dr. Bachman, Dr. George Caulier, to Miss Jane Halliday, both of this city.
Died, on Thursday evening, May 2d, at the residence of Col. Billups, in Lexington, Oglethorpe County, Mrs. Sarah Jane, wife of Major William Rembert, and daughter of the late Dr. Joel Abbot, of Washington, Wilkes Co., Ga., aged 29 years.
Departed this life on the 27th April last, in Prince Williams Parish, Beaufort Dist., Mr. Paul A. Fripp...left two small children....

Issue of May 25, 1839

Married on Wednesday evening the 15th inst., by the Rev. Bishop Bowen, John F. Blacklock, Esq., to Miss Mary, daughter of the late William Robertson.
At St. Helena Island, on the 16th inst., by the Rev. Joseph Wallace, Mr. William P. Perry, of that place, to Miss Arabella Amanda, youngest daughter of the late Garrett Debow, of this city.
Departed this life on the 23d ult., at her residence in Summerville, S. C.,Mrs.Susan S. Hamilton, aged 25 years and 8 months. left a husband and two children....

Issue of June 1, 1839

Married in this city on the 28th inst., by the Rev. Mr. Gildersleeve, Mr. W. B. Beazley, of Abbeville, S. C., to Miss Martha, second daughter of John McMaster, of this place.
On Thursday evening 23d inst.,by the Rev. Dr. D. Davies, Mr. Philip B. Maull, to Miss Margaret E. Gruber, all of this city.
Departed this life on the 8th of April last, Maria Ainslie; on the 9th, Margaret Deas; and on the 24th May, Mary Mathewes, children of Robert D. and H. Anslie Lawrence.
Died on the 7th inst., Mr. William B. Legare, aged 40 years. (eulogy)

Issue of June 8, 1839

Married on Tuesday evening the 28th ult., by the Rev. Mr. Smith, Mr. William Crawford, to Miss Rebecca, eldest daughter of the late Alexander Berry.
On Wednesday evening 29th ult., by the Rev. Mr. Rogers, Mr. Charles Stillman, to Miss Josephine Louise, only daughter of H. Monjoy, all of this city.
On Thursday evening 30th ult., by the Rev. Mr. Trapier, Mr. Thos Morrison, to Miss Agness, eldest daughter of the late Mr. George Thompson, both of this city.
Died in this city on the 20th ult., Mrs. Elizabeth Brown, consort of Mr. Alexander Brown, merchant of this city, in the 39th year of her age....
Departed this life at his residence near Sparta, Ga., on the 24th ult.,in the 79th year of his age, Gen. Henry Mitchell... a soldier of the Revolution; a native of Sussex co., Va., but for more than 50 years resided in this and the adjoining county of Warren.
Died on the 20th May last, at her residence in Colleton Dist., Mrs. Mary Emeline Youg (sic), eldest daughter of the late Dr. J. L. E. W. Shecut, in the 41st year of her age.

Issue of June 15, 1839

Married at St. Matthew's Church, Jersey City, on the 2nd inst., by the Rev. Dr. Barry, Charles B. C. Bacot, of Charleston, S. C., to Sarah, third daughter of the late John Von Vorst, of New Jersey.
Departed this life at Sullivan's Island on Monday evening last, Charles Henry, youngest son of Mr. Bazil and Mrs. Sarah L. B. Lanneau, of this city, aged 5 years and 10 months....
Died at her residence in Walker Co., Ga., on the 26th March, Mrs. Lydia Dickson, in the 51st year of her age...a member of the Presbyterian Church...left family of children.

Issue of June 22, 1839

Married on Wednesday last,the 12th inst., in Sumterville, S. C., by the Rev. James Duprie, Mr. Samuel McBride, of Salem, Sumter Dist., to Miss Martha M. Ruberry, of Charleston.
Married on Tuesday 11th inst., by the Rev. Charles P. Elliott, Mr. George Robertson of this city to Miss Anna M. C., youngest daughter of the late John P. Richardson, of Clarendon, Sumter District.
Died at his residence in Wilkes Co., Ga., on the 22d of April last, Mr. Cunningham Daniel, aged 70 years. (eulogy)....
Died at Walterboro, Colleton, on Thursday 13th inst., Richard Henry Fishburn, infant son of Bernjamin P. Fishburn, Esq., of that place, aged five months and 14 days.

Issue of June 29, 1839

Married on the 17th inst., by the Rt. Rev. Bishop Bowen, Dr. Thomas W. Hutson, of Prince Williams Parish, to Miss Eliza Ferguson Bacot, of this city.
Departed this life on the 28th of May last, at her residence in St. Matthews, Mrs. Susannah Clayton, relict of the late Daniel Clayton, aged about 76 years.
Died at her residence on Flat Creek, Lancaster Dist., on the 5th inst.,Mrs. Catharine Hale in the 102d year of her age...born on the Rappahannock, Virginia in March 1738, and removed to her residence on Flat Creek before the Rev. War...member of the Baptist Church. (long account)

Issue of July 6, 1839

Another Patriot of the Revolution gone. The venerable Col. William Alston died in this city on 25th ult in the 83d year of his age...(eulogy and account)
Another. Departed this life in Laurens District, S. C., on the 13th day of June, Mr. John Cummins, aged about 85 years....
And Another. Died in Oglethorpe Co., Ga., on the 28th May, Mr. Michael Buff, in the 102 year of his age.
Died at his residence in Athens Ga., on Friday night 21st inst.,the Hon. Augustin S. Clayton. Judge Clayton was born in the State of Virginia, on the 27th Nov 1783. He completed his education at the University of Ga. in 1804...In 1835 he was elected a representative in Congress for the State of Ga....
Southern Banner
Died in this city on the 14th inst., William Y. Mitchell, aged 26 years and six months.

Issue of July 13, 1839

Married in Beaufort S. C. on the 7th inst., by the Rev. Mr. Walker, William Henry Heyward, to Esther, only daughter of the late Nathaniel Heyward Jr.
On Wednesday the 3d inst., by the Rev. Christopher Gadsden, Mr. Frederick Richards, to Miss Ann Eliza Walker, all of this city.
Died on the 4th inst., Mary Pringle, a daughter of John J. Pringle, Esq.
At Macon, Ga., on the 6th inst., Robert W. Fort, of this city, aged 38 years....

Issue of August 3, 1839

Died at her residence near Darlington C. H. on the 14th inst., in the 29th year of her age, Mrs. Elizabeth A. Law, wife of Capt. Wm. Law...member of the Presbyterian Church. (eulogy)
Died at Marietta, Cobb Co., Ga., on the 17th ult., Mrs. Hannah Simpson, wife of Leonard Simpson sen., formerly of S. C., aged 68 years....(eulogy) a Presbyterian.

Issue of August 10, 1839

Married in St. Paul's Church on Wednesday afternoon, 1st inst., by the Rev. C. Hanckle, Edward Melrose Whiting, to Elizabeth Ann only daughter of the late Wm. Pritchard, Jr.
Died in this city on the 21st ult., in the 76th year of her age, Mrs. Mary S. Grimke, the relict of the late Hon John F. Grimke, one of the Judges of the State of S. C....(long eulogy)
<u>Gospel Messenger</u>
Departed this life on Sabbath morning, the 4th inst., in the 27th year of his age, Mr. Peter Lanneau, Merchant of this city, of the firm of Bannister & Lanneau....left wife and three children. (eulogy)

Issue of August 17, 1839

Married on the 8th inst., by the Rev. Dr. Post, Mr. Samuel Schivers, of New Jersey, to Mrs. S. Kittleband, of this city.
Died on Tuesday the 30th July, Mrs. Sarah, wife of Mr. William Miller...leaving a husband, sisters and a brother, and a widowed mother....
Died in this city on the 27th July, John J. Daily, from Portland, in the State of Maine, aged 29 years....
Died, at Naples, Italy, on the 7th May last, Mrs. Mary Ann Olin, wife of the Rev. Stephen Olin, D. D., late President of Randolph Macon College, Va.
Died at her residence near Columbia, in the 39th year of her age, Mrs. Emeline McCord, consort of Col. D. McCord, and daughter of George Wagner, Esq. deceased.

Issue of August 31, 1839

Married in Paris at the residence of the British Embassador, on the 22d July last, by the Right Rev. Bishop Luscomb, William Young, Esq.,of London, youngest son of Rear Admiral Young, of the British Navy, to Miss Harriet Elizabeth, only daughter of A. S. Willington, Esq. of Charleston, S. C.
Died in this city on the 17th inst., Mrs. Ann McCants, widow of the late Wm. McCants, Esq. of St. Bartholomew's Parish, in the 83d year of her age....
Departed this life on the 14th inst., Mr. Benjamin Granger, a native of Suffield, Conn., in the 37th year of his age.
On the 23d inst., Mr. John F. Wheat, a native of Marlborough Co., Va., aged 33 years.
In Lawrence Co., Ga., on the 20th ult., aged about 80 years, Col. Harmon Runnels, father of Ex Gov. Runnels, of the State of Miss....for about 30 years a member of the Legislatures of Ga. and Miss.

Issue of September 14, 1839

Married on Wednesday evening 4th inst., by the Rev. Mr. Capers, Mr. Peter S. Smith, to Miss Mary D., daughter of Wm. Bird, esq., all of this city.

151

Died in this city on the 27th of August, Mr. Henry Charlton Tovey, in the 37th year of his age...left parents, widow and children, and an only sister....
Died in this city on Friday morning the 6th inst., Mrs. Nancy McCall, wife of Mr. Thomas A. Hayden, and daughter of Major Francis Alexander, of Rutherford, N. C....(eulogy)
Died on the 6th inst., Benjamin Chauncey Cady, in the 21st year of his age, a native of Greenville, S. C. (eulogy)
Died at the residence of his parents (Paul and Martha M. Fulton), Samuel Davis Fulton, aged 16 years, 4 months and 20 days. a member of the Presbyterian Church....died 1 August 1839.

Green County, Alabama, August 30

Issue of September 21, 1839

Married on Sunday evening the 14th inst., on Sullivan's Island, by the Rev. Mr. Forrest, Capt. Daniel Wells, to Miss Jane P. Scoular, all of Charleston.
At Guilford, Chenango Co., N. Y., on the 7th inst., Mr. G. J. Westcott, of Charleston, S. C., to Miss Lucie Knapp, daughter of Colby Knapp, M. D.,of the former place.
Died on the 9th inst., Mr. Copeland W. Stiles, a native of this city, aged 19 years and 6 months....(eulogy)
Died in Williamsburg District, S. C., August 26th, Mrs. Agnes Shaw, wife of Henry Shaw, in the 56th year of her age...a member of the Presbyterian Church. (eulogy)

Issue of September 28, 1839

Married in this city on Wednesday evening, 18th inst., by the Rev. John H. Honour, Mr. Asa J. Muir, of Wilmington, N. C., to Miss Martha P. Curtis, eldest daughter of Joseph and Mary Curtis, of this city.
Married at Pleasant Valley, Chester District, on the 29th August, by the Rev. Mr. Johnson, Rev. D. McNeill Turner, Pastor of the Presbyterian Church at Fayetteville, N. C., to Harriet Davis, third daughter of Capt. John Stringfellow of the former place.
Died at his residence at Abbeville C. H., S. C., on the evening of the 17th inst., John M'Laren, Sen., a native of Scotland....
Died at Darlington C. H., S. C., on the 19th Sept., Mr. Samuel Harris, a native of England, and a resident of the U. S. for the last 8 or 10 years...an Engineer...(eulogy)

Darlington C. H., September 21, 1839.

Died at his residence near Boston, Lowndes Co., Ala., on the 2d inst., John Wilton Frierson, late of Charleston, S. C., in the 25th year of his age....

Issue of October 5, 1839

Married on Thursday evening 26th inst., by the Rev. Mr. Rogers, James B. Betts, to Emily M., only daughter of the late Capt. John H. Silliman, both of this city.
Married at M'Phersonville, on the 3d of September, by the Rev. Edward Palmer, Mr. William S. Townsend, of Ira, N. Y., to Maria P. Hutson, of the former place.
Married by the Rev. J. N. Coons, in Nicholasville, Ky., on the 19th ult., Moreau Brown, Esq. of that place to Miss Charlotte Endora, eldest daughter of the late Major John Blackwood, of Charleston, S. C.
Died on Sabbath the 22d inst., 1839, Miss Gardenia Garden Gibbes, daughter of Mrs. Robert Gibbes, aged 24 years and 10 months....(eulogy)

Departed this life in the city of New York, on the 11th ult., Miss Harriet B. McCay, of this city(eulogy)

Death of Urben J. Rice, son of Col. Jesse Rice, who departed this life at Barnwell Court House in the 16th year of his age, on the 10th inst....

Died at Georgetown, S. C., the place of his nativity, on the 1st inst., Mr. John Chapman, President of the Bank of that place, aged 37 years.

Issue of October 12, 1839

Married on the 29th ult., by the Rev. Mr.Barnwell, Mr.Jabez Norton, to Miss Elizabeth I. Brodie, both of this city.

On Thursday evening the 26th ult., by the Rev. C. W. Martin, Mr. William N. Martin of Tallihatchie Co., Miss., to Miss Ann eldest daughter of John Wier, Esq. of Abbeville Dist., S. C.

Died at his residence in Marion District, S. C., on the morning of the 26th inst., Capt. Gregg, in the 58th year of his age...a ruling elder in the Presbyterian Church of Hopewell.... (eulogu)

Died on the 23d inst.,at the residence of her grandfather, Capt. John Gregg, in the fifth year of her age, Emma Eliza, eldest daughter of Moses and Mary M'Call, of Darlington District. (poem)

Issue of October 19, 1839

Married in McDonough, Ga., on the 8th inst., by the Rev. James H. Saye, Mr. William Markham, to Miss Amanda D. Berry.

Died on the 6th ult.,Susan Quimby, aged 37 years, eldest daughter of Mrs. Elizabeth Quimby.

Died, at North Santee, on the 3d inst., Mrs. Elizabeth Q. Graham, consort of Hugh Graham, aged 19 years and 10 months eldest grand daughter of Mrs. E. Quimby.

In Greenville, S. C., on the 3d inst., Mrs. Susan E. Leland, wife of Dexter Leland, and eldest daughter of the late Elias Smerdon of this city.

Died in Chambers Co., Ala., in the vicinity of West Point, on the 22d inst., Margaret Reese...member of the Presbyterian Church.

In the vicinity of West Point, Chambers Co., on the 4th inst., Gavin Reese, aged ten yers, son of George and Mary Ann Reese....

Departed this transitory life in Columbia, S. C.,on the 23d ult.,in the 54th year of his age, the Hon. Thomas Dugan, for 8 years a member of the Legislature of this State, and for the last 12 years a member of the Senate from Sumter District.

Drowned, in the Savannah River, on the 8th inst., opposite Purysburg, Mr. Douglass Stoner, a native of New York....

Issue of October 26, 1839

Married in Beaufort, S. C., on the 7th inst.,by the Rev. Richard Fuller, N. P. Danner, to Sarah, daughter of the late John Porteous, all of that place.

Died on Friday morning the 18th inst., Miss Eliza Ann, adopted daughter of Mr. William and Mrs. Eliza Thompson of this city, at the age of 28 years....(eulogy)

Died at Edingsville, on the 9th inst., Mrs. Frances A. Wilson, consort of John H. Wilson in the 48th year of her age....

Died, in Lafayette, Walker Co., Ga., on Friday night, 11th inst., in the 29th year of her age, Mrs. Margaret J. Barry, wife of Dr. A. L. Barry...member of the Presbyterian Church....

Died in Laurens County, Alabama, on the 30th of August last, in the 26th year of her age, Eliza L. Jackson, daughter of James Jackson, Professor of Natural Philosophy and Chemistry in the University of Ga....(eulogy) member of the Presbyterian Church.

Issue of November 2, 1839

Married on the 10th inst., at the Golden Grove, Greenville District, the residence of her grandfather, Dr. Yore, by the Rev. Mr. Pinckney, Dr. P. Gadsden Edwards, to Miss Ann M. Coffin, both of this city.
At Darlington Court House, S. C., on Thursday evening the 24th inst., by the Rev. JohnO. B. Dargan, Mr. James Donegan, of England, to Miss Jane Milling, of Winnsboro, Fairfield District, S. C.

Issue of November 16, 1839

Married on Tuesday evening last, by the Rev. C. Hanckel, Mr. Henry Honarth, to Miss Caroline Virginia, daughter of the late Mr. Richard F. Howare--all of this city.
Married on Wednesday evening, 13th inst.,by the Rev. Mr. Forrest, Mr. J. W. Wilder of Savannah, to Miss Georgiana, daughter of Capt. George Easterby, of this city.
Married on Thursday 7th inst., by Rev. Mr. Yates, Mr. Louis N. Vidal, recently of Toulon, in France, to Miss Maria Therese Vidal, of the sam place.
Married at Bethal, in Prince William's Parish, on the evening of the 4th inst., by the Rev. Stephen Elliott, Mr. Charles Jones Colcock, to Miss Mary Caroline, daughter of the late Thos. Heyward, of St. Lukes Parish.
Died, in this city, on Wednesday morning, 16th inst., in the 25th year of her age, Mrs. Martha Ann Smith, wife of Rev. Whiteford Smith, of the M. E. Church. (eulogy)

Issue of November 23, 1839

Married on Thursday evening, 14th inst.,by the Rev. William State Lee, Mr. Edward N. Fuller, of this city, to Miss Mary Ann, daughter of the late Ephraim Mikell, Esq. of Edisto Island.
At Cheraw, S. C.,on the 12th inst.,Mrs. C. K. Pritchard, in her 55th year, formerly of Charleston, S. C., but for many years a resident in Cheraw.
Died at his residence near Pensacola, on the 9th inst., Hugh Wilson Nesbit, Esq., formerly of Beech Island, near Augusta, leaving a wife and numberous relations....
Died at Ashford, Conn., Jebediah Amidon, aged 86 years... in the battle on Bunker Hill....

Issue of November 30, 1839

Died at Summerville, on the 7th inst., William McDow, Esq., in the 69th year of his age,formerly of this city.
Married on the 20th inst.,by the Rev. C. Hanckel, Mr. Henry T. Peake, to Miss Ann S. Gilbert, all of this city.
On Thursday evening the 21st inst.,by the Rev. Dr. Brantly, Mr. L. D. Dinkins, to Miss Camilla W.,eldest daughter of James Holmes.
At Walterborough, on Thursday evening the 21st inst., by the Rev. Francis F. De La Vaux, Mr. Simon John Magwood, to Miss Susan Sarah Pinckney, youngest daughter of the late Hon. William C. Pinckney, of St. Bartholomew's Parish.

Issue of December 7, 1839

Married on Tuesday evening last, 25th ult.,by the Rev. Dr. J. Bachman, Mr. J. J. Martin, to Miss Agnes, eldest daughter of James Calder, Esq.,all of this city.
On Wednesday evening 26th ult.,by the Rev. P. Trapier, Mr. James W. Gros, to Miss Emeline Louisa, the only daughter of Mr. Peter Hernandes, deceased.
In Abbeville Village, on Tuesday morning 19th inst., by the Rev. Dr. Barr, Col. John Cunningham of Laurens District, to Miss Floride C. Noble, of Abbeville Village, daughter of HIs Excellency the Governor.
Died at Sullivan's Island, on Tuesday 19th ult., Henry P. Holmes, in the 51st year of his age.

Issue of December 14, 1839

Married on Tuesday evening 3d inst., by the Rev. Dr. Bachman, Mr. Robert W. Burdell, to Miss Eleanor Francis, eldest daughter of Mr. B. T. Gitsinger, all of this city.
On Wednesday evening 4th inst., by the Rev. Dr. Bachman, Victor G. Audubon, Esq., of New York, to Miss Eliza Bachman, of this city.
Married in the village of Orangeburg, on Thursday evening, 5th inst., by the Rev. I. S. Legare, the Rev. T. F. Montgomery, of Talbot Co., Geo., to Miss Emily, daughter of Mr. Samuel Felder of the former place.
Married in McDonough, Ga., on the 21st of Nov., by the Rev. James H. Saye, Mr. Daniel L. Gordon, to Miss Catharine Johnson.
Died at Baton Rouge, La., on the 26th ult., Col. Wm. S. Foster, Lieut. Col. of the 4th Regt. U. S. Infantry.
Died on the 15th inst., at his residence in Claremont, Sumter Dist., S. C., Mr. John J. Frierson, in the 48th year of his age...left a widow and two sons....

Issue of December 21, 1839

Died at his residence in Lowndes Co., Miss., on the 5th ult., Capt. William Ervin (formerly of Sumter District in this State) in the 60th year of his age.
Married on the 10th inst., by the Rev. Paul Trapier, Mr. Benjamin Lucas, to Miss Augusta Dawson, all of this city.
On Tuesday evening the 10th inst.,by the Rev. Mr. Clayton, Mr. Adolphe Beckman, to Miss Elenora P. Withers, all of this city.
On Wednesday evening the 11th inst., by the Rev. Dr. Capers, Joseph H. Long, of Northboro', Mass., to Miss Mary White of this city.
On Thursday evening the 12th inst.,by the Rev. Mr. Forrest, Mr. Wm. Boineau Taylor to Miss Isabella Corrie, daughter of Samuel Corrie.
On Thursday evening the 12th inst., by the Rev. Thomas Smyth, Mr. Jos. Wienges(?), to Lucinda Ann, daughter of the late John Martin, Esq.,of St. Thomas's Parish.
On the 17th inst., by the Rev. Mr. Tally, Mr. Lyttleton R. Brewer, of Monroe, Walton Co., Ga., to Miss Martha E., daughter of Mr. William Humphreys, of this city.

Issue of December 28, 1839

Lost overboard from the barque Valhalla, from Boston for this port, Reuben Whitney, seaman, of Thomaston, Me.
Died near Lancasterville, S. C., on the 2d inst., Abraham Perry, in the 66th year of his age.

155

Died at his residence (Wild Cat), Lancaster Dist., S. C. on the 1st inst., Mr. Jacob Funderburk in the 77th year of his age, leaving a wife and a numberous family of grandchildren, etc., 140 in number....

Died in Winnsboro., S. C., on Saturday 4th inst., Mrs. Melinda R. B. Woodward, consort of Joseph Woodward, Esq., in the 32d year of her age...member of the Presbyterian Church. (eulogy)

Issue of February 22, 1840

Just before our paper went to press, we received the intelligence through the Rev. E. Palmer, of the deceased of the Rev. John B. Van Dyck, Pastor of the Saltcatcher Church, and Principal of the Academy at Walterboro'--who died at Walterboro' on Monday night the 17th January.

At the village of Newberry, S. C.,on the 10th inst., Maj. F. Nance, in the 70th year of his age.

At Camden, S. C., on the 13th inst., Mr. John Clyde, aged about 28 years, a native of New York, but for the last two years a residence of the former place.

At Macon, Ga.,on the 10th inst., Mr. Rodman Church, formerly of Durham, Con.

Issue of February 29, 1840

Married on Tuesday evening 18th inst., by the Rev. Thomas Smyth, Dr. J. Louis Gervais, to Miss Louisa, second daughter of Hugh Wilson, all of this city.

On Thursday evening the 20th inst., by the Rev. Mr. Tally, Mr. Lewis L. Sibley, to Miss Maria Theresa, only daughter of William H. Rivers, all of this city.

Rev. J. B. Van Dyck...a native of New York. For the last ten or 12 years he has resided in Colleton Dist., of this State....

Died at Beech Island, on the 19th inst., Edward Payson, infant son of Samuel Clarke, Esq.,aged 5 months and 4 days.

Departed this life at the residence of his father in Columbia, on the night of the 17th inst., Robert Wallace Shand, only son of the Rev. Peter J. Shand, in the 14th year of his age....

Issue of March 14, 1840

Married, on Wednesday evening 4th inst.,by the Rev. Dr. Bachman, Mr. Samuel Chapman, to Miss Amelia youngest daughter of the late Dr. John S. Trescott.

On Thursday evening 5th inst.,at Springwood, by the Rev. John Forrest, the Hon. Thomas Bennett, to Mrs. Jane M. Fordon, both of this city.

On Tuesday evening 10th inst., by the Rev. Paul Trapier, Mr. Robert H. Waterman, of Philadelphia, to Mrs. Mary Ann M'Clintock, of this city.

At Winnsboro', S. C., on Thursday evening 5th inst., by the Rev. William Brearly, Rev. Thomas R. English of Sumter, S. C. to Miss Eliza Ann Brearly, of Trenton, N. Y.

Died at Savannah, on the 1st inst., S. G. Threadcraft, Esq., a native of S. C., but for the last fifty years a resident of Ga.

Issue of March 28, 1840

Married on Thursday evening 19th inst., by the Rev. Mr. Barnwell, Dr. H. W. DeSaussure, to Miss Mary Coffin, daughterof H. W. Peronneau, Esq.

On the 19th inst., by the Rev. Mr. Gilman, Wilson, Glover, Esq., to Miss Caroline Harwood, daughter of the Rev. Samuel Gilman.

On Thursday evening, 19th inst.,by the Rev. Dr. Brantley, Mr. Horace E. Nichols, of Middleburgh, Vt., to Miss Mary H., youngest daughter of the late Rev. Joel Kethcum, of New York.

On the 19th inst., by the Rev. Dr. Bachman, Mr. W. J. McAllister of Tallahassee, Florida, to Miss Elizabeth Christina Stopplebein, of this city.

On Tuesday evening 24th inst., by the Rev. J. H. Honour, Mr. Albert Nye, of Falmouth, Mass., to Miss Henrietta M., eldest daughter of the late John Forbes, of this city.

On Wednesday evening 25th inst., by the Rev. Mr. Forest, Mr. Dunbar Paul, to Mrs. J. W. Bacon.

At Camden, on the 8th inst., by the Rev. Mr. Phillips, Mr. Robert Fletcher, of Charleston, to Miss Charlotte M., daughter of Paul F. Villepigue, of the former place.

Issue of April 4, 1840

Married on Tuesday evening last, 31st ult., by the Rev. Dr. Brantley, Charles Merrick, Esq., of Jacksonville, E. F., to Miss Sarah Margaret, youngest daughter of Roger Heriot, Esq. of this city.

At Walnut Grove, Ga., on the 19th inst.,by the Rev. James C. Patterson, the Rev. Stanhope W. Erwin, of Irwinton, Ala., to Miss Jane Marion, only daughter of John Dunwoody, Esq.

Died at Walterboro, on the 20th inst., Mrs. Margaret D. W. Webb, aged 35 years, 2 months and 22 days....(eulogy)

Issue of April 11, 1840

Married on Thursday evening 2d inst., by the Rev. Dr. Brantley, Mr. James Lawrence Gantt, to Miss Mary Eliza, eldest daughter of the late James H. Merritt, Esq.

On Thursday evening 2d inst., by the Rev. Dr. Post, Dr. William F. Percival, of Columbia, S. C., to Emma, second daughter of Sandiford Holmes, Esq., of this city.

On Tuesday evening 31st ult., by the Rev. Dr. Galman, Mr. Newman Kershaw, to Miss Ann Elizabeth, eldest daughter of Mr. Chas. Graves, all of this city.

Died in Greensboro', Ga., on Tuesday, the 3d of March, Mr. Eralbon Seymour, in the 43d year of his age...a native of Conn., and removed to Greensboro, about 20 years ago....(eulogy)

Issue of April 18, 1840

Married on Tuesday evening, 7th inst., by the Rev. Dr.Post, Mr. Charles D. Frierson, of Lowndes County, Alabama, to Miss Susan Mary, youngest daughter of the late Samuel Parker, of this city.

On Tuesday the 7th inst., by the Rev. C. C. Pinckney, at Christ Church, Greenville, S. C., Mr. Henry Morris to Anterisia C., second daughter of the late Elias Smerdon, of Charleston, S. C.

On Thursday evening, the 9th inst.,by the Rev. C. Martin, Mr. James H. Giles to Miss Anna Hamilton, all of Abbeville Dist.

Issue of April 25, 1840

Married on Thursday evening 16th inst.,by the Rev. Dr. Capers, Mr. H. N. Sprague, formerly of Buffalo, N. Y., to Miss Elizabeth Thompson, of this city.

Married, at Mildwood, on Wednesday, 15th inst., by the Rev. Richard Johnson, William H. Colcock, Esq.,to Miss Mary Ellen, daughter of Col. Wm. L. Lewis, of St. Matthew's Parish.

Died at the residence of Mr. George McMichael, near Poplar Spring, Orangeburg District, .S C.,on the 16th inst., Rufus King, Esq.

Issue of May 2, 1840

Married on Tuesday morning 21st inst.,by the Rev. T. Smyth, Mr. Charles Graves to Miss Julia M. M., only daughter of the late Stephen Thomas--all of this city.

On Wednesday evening 22d inst., by the Rev C. Hanckel, Rev. J. Stuart Hanckel, to Miss Fanny Eliza, eldest daughter of Lewis Trapman, Esq., all of this city.

Died, at the Gwinnett Institute, near Lawrenceville, Ga., on Sabbath morning, the 19th of April, Augustin Sloan, eldest son of Samuel F. and Mahulda Alexander, aged 5 years, 10 months and 14 days. (lines)

Issue of May 9, 1840

Married on Wednesday evening 29th inst., at St. Phillip's Church, by the Rev. Dr. Gadsden, William W. Kunhardt, Esq., to Julia Adelaide, eldest daughter of Dr. William Hall.

On the 5th inst., by the Rev. C. Hanckel, George W.Egleston, Esq., of this city, to Mrs. Martha Porcher, daughter of the late Samuel Dubose, Senior, Esq., deceased of St. Stephen's Parish.

Married in Williamsburgh, on the 21st ult., by the Rev. Mr. Peden, Mr. James Augustus Burgess, to Miss Eliza Adams, daughter of the late Mr. Samuel Adams, of Kingstree.

Departed this life on the 29th of April, William Govan Steele, Esq., in the 49th year of his age....(account and eulogy)

Died in Sumter Co., Ga., on the morning of the 4th inst., Mr. John C. Daniel, in the 32d year of his age...a member of the Presbyterian Church about 7 years....(eulogy)

Issue of May 16, 1840

Married, on Wednesday evening, 6th inst., by the Rev. Dr. Bachman, John D. Forst, Esq.,of Richland District, to Miss Sophia Naser, daughter of Mr. Frederick Naser, of this city.

Died, at Beech Island, Edgefield Dist., on the 7th inst., Miss Sarah Ann Reddick.

Issue of May 23, 1840

Married on Tuesday evening, 12th inst., by the Rev. C. Hanckel, Thomas R. Waring, Esq.,to Miss Anna, daughter of the late Major Perry, of St. Paul's Parish.

Married at Walnut Grove, St. John's Berkley, by the Rev. David J. Campbell, on Thursday, 30th ult., Isaac Porcher, Jr., to Miss Elizabeth L., daughter of Mr. James Gaillard.

Departed this life, at Aiken, on Friday, the 8th May, in the 29th year of his age, Wm. Savage Elliott, eldest son of the late Benjamin Elliott, Esq.

Died in Fairfield Dist., S. C.,on Monday 11th inst., Mrs. Eliza P., wife of Robert B. Caldwell, and only daughter of Major John and Elizabeth Walker, of Chester Dist., leaving behind her two children--the youngest only a few hours old--aged 23 years and two months...member of the Presbyterian Church....

Issue of May 30, 1840

Married on Tuesday 19th ult., by the Rev. Mr. Barnwell, Charles Davis, M. D., Professor of Chemistry, to Miss Sarah Mitchell Waring, daughter of the late Dr. Thomas Waring, of All Saints Parish, Waccamaw.
On the 20th inst., at Lang Syne, St. Matthew's Parish, by the Rev. Richard Johnson, D. J. M'Cord, Esq., to Miss Louisa Cheves, daughter of the Hon. Langdon Cheves.
On the 21st inst., at Pendleton, by the Rev. Mr. Potter, Joseph A. Huger, to Mary E., daughter of Col. F. K. Huger.
In Newbern, N. C., on the 20th inst., by the Rev. Mr. Stratoon, the Rev. Richard M. Baker, to Mrs. Mary E. Horne, both of Florida.
Died at New Orleans, on the 20th inst., James Bowman Anderson, editor of the New Orleans Sun, a native of New York, in the 29th year of his age.

Issue of June 6, 1840

Married, on Thursday evening, 28th ult., by the Rev. Mr. Spear, Col. Wm. W. Harllee, of Marion,S. C., to Martha S.,daughter of the late Wm. F. Shackelford, of this city.

Issue of June 13, 1840

Married on the 28th of May, by the Rev. A. G. Peden, Dr. Richard Jarrott, of Kings-Tree, to Miss Louisa Eleanor, daughter of Henry D. Shaw, Esq. of Williamsburg Dist., S. C.
Died, on Thursday afternoon, 4th inst., Mrs. Ann Suder, in the 62d year of her age....
Died, at his pine land residence, near Walterborough, on the 6th inst., Dr. Joseph Glover, of this city.

Issue of June 20, 1840

Married on Wednesday evening, the 10th inst., by the Rev. Dr. Brantley, Walter Finney, Esq., of this city, to Rebecca Cecelia, eldest daughter of Mr. Hamilton Slawson, of Beaufort, S. C.
Married, on Wednesday evening,the 11th inst., by the Rev. Dr. Gilman, Octavius B. Heriot, Esq., to Miss Decima Mary, daughter of Jeremiah A. Yates, Esq., all of this city.
On Thursday, the 11th inst., by the Rev. William Barnwell, Capt. Henry Johnson, to Elizabeth, only daughter of Capt. Thomas H. Jervey.
On Wednesday evening, the 17th inst., by the Rev. John H. Honour, Mr. Daniel L. Glen, to Miss Mary Laura Nelson, both of this city.
Died at Russell Place, Kershaw, early in June, Dr. David George, Postmaster at the place, and an Elder of the Presbyterian Church....
Died at the residence of her husband, in Union District, S. C., on the 10th inst.,Mrs. Susan Thomson, wife of Richard Thomson, Esq....

Issue of June 27, 1840

Married on Tuesday evening the 16th inst.,by the Rev. Dr. Brantley, Mr. William T. Hieronymous, to Elvina S.,only daughter of the late J. G. Bowles, Esq. of this city.
On Thursday evening the 18th inst., by the Rev. Whiteford Smith, Mr. E. J. Rodgers, to Miss Ann L. Pelzer, all of this city.
Departed this life on the 6th of June, Dr. David George, of Russell Place, S. C., in the 48th year of his age...Ruling Elder

of the Presbyterian Church of Beaver Creek....
    Departed this life on the 1st of June, in Lagrange, Troup
Co., Ga., John Likens, aged 76 years....(eulogy) the father of
Rev. John Glenn Likens....

Issue of July 4, 1840

    Married on Wednesday evening the 24th inst., by the Rev. Mr.
Campbell, James H. Gager, to Julia Selma, daughter of the late
J. Simmons Bee, Esq., all of this city.
    On the 30th ult., by the Rev. Dr. Capers, Mr. Andrew J. Buckner, to Miss Sarah Clements, all of this city.
    Died in this city on the 20th inst., Ann Elizabeth, wife of
W. Lindsay, Jr., and daughter of the late Rev. Edmund Matthews,
of Georgia.
    Died, in Beaufort, S. C., on the 7th inst., Col. Middleton
Stuart, of the 12th Regt., S. C. Militia, in the 34th year of
his age.

Issue of July 11, 1840

    Married on Tuesday evening 7th inst., by the Rev. Whiteford
Smith, Mr. William Logan, jun., to Miss Henrietta, eldest daughter
of the late William R. Thorne--all of this city.
    Died at the family residence in Athens, on the __ of June
1840, Mrs. Elizabeth Bolling, wife of Major Robert Taylor...
entombed in the family vault, in the burying ground at Madison,
Morgan County...born in McIntosh co., Ga., on the 26th March
1800, daughter of the late William Delony, Esq., of that county,
formerly of Virginia....(eulogy)
    Died at Savannah, Geo., Mrs. Lucy Patterson, wife of Capt.
William Patterson, in the 50th year of her age...member of the
Methodist Church...
    Died, in Macon, Ga.,at the house of Mr. Jerry Cowles, Remembrance Chamberlain Saunders, aged 30 years...a native of Vermont,
and nephew of the Rev. Mr. Chamberlain....

Issue of July 18, 1840

    Married on Thursday 2d July by the Rev. R. W. James, Rev.
D. J. Auld, to Miss Leah Ann, daughter of M. H. Plowden, Esq.,
all of Sumter District, S. C.
    Died at the residence of Capt. Thomas Kilpatrick, in Fairfield Dist., on Saturday the 6th day of June, Mr. Robert Kilpatrick,
a Revolutionary soldier, aged 105 years...a native of Ireland...
Sumter was his general, and Nixon and Adams his Captains.

Issue of July 25, 1840

    Married on Thursday evening, the 16th inst., by the Rev. Dr.
Brantley, Benjamin C. Pressley, Esq., to Louisa M., second daughter of the late Henry Wheeler, Esq. of this city.
    Married on Wednesday evening, 15th inst., by the Rev. Dr.
Post, Mr. William Adger, to Miss Margaret Hall, eldest daughter
of Andrew Moffett, Esq., all of this city.

Issue of August 8, 1840

    Died, in this city on the 1st inst.,John Adams, in the 20th
year of his age....
    Died on Tuesday the 21st of July, in Gwinnett Co., Ga., Mrs.
Margaret Knox, wife of William Knox, in the 44th year of her age.

Issue of August 15, 1840

Died on Sunday the 9th inst., William Johnston, Esq.,in the 64th year of his age.
On the 6th August, Lewis S. Mathews, the eldest son of William Mathews, Jr., of James Island.
At Summerville, on the 22d of July, Mrs Dorothy S. Mitchell, in the 48th year of her age....

Issue of August 22, 1840

Married at Withersville, on Thursday the 13th inst., by the Rev. Mr. William, Arthur Vanderhorst, Esq., of this City, to Miss Susan E. F., eldest daughter of the late William Shackelford, of Georgetown District.
Died at his residence in Jasper Co., Geo., Aug. 11th, James McKemie, Esq.,aged 49 years...an Elder of the Presbyterian Church at Monticello....

Issue of August 29, 1840

Married on Monday evening 17th inst., by the Rev. Dr. Brantley, Mr. Thomas Watson, to Miss Johanna, eldest daughter of the late John Burke--all of this city.
Married at Portobello, Scotland, on the 23d June last, Mr. Adam E. Gibson, to Miss Antonia B. Weston, and on the same evening, Mr. Hugh Fraser, to Miss Margaret J. Weston, daughter of the late Dr. Paul Weston--all of S. C.
Died in Sumter Co., Ala., on the 23d of June last, Mr. William Irvin Stocker, in the 29th year of her age, and
On the 12th July, Mrs. Abigail Brown, grand-mother of the above, aged 78 years, all formerly of this city.
Died at her father's residence, Butts Co., Geo., on the 23d August, Mrs. Jane Dougherty, only daughter of Mr. Robert Grier, aged 31 years...left husband and four children.... (lines)

Issue of September 5, 1840

Died on the 24th August, at the residence of his father, John McClenaghan, in Darlington District, S., C., Mr. George McClenaghan, in the 19th year of his age.... (eulogy)
Died at Manchester, England, on the 21st July, George Street, Esq., aged 34 years....(eulogy)   Boston Post.

Issue of October 3, 1840

Died on the 8th inst., at the residence of his father, Williamsburg District, in the 25th year of his age, Doctor James H. Frierson....(long eulogy)
Died at St. Mary's, Ga., on the 11th Sept., Miss Letitia Jane Atkinson,eldest daughter of Mrs. M. J. Geer, aged 19 years, 10 months and 19 days....(eulogy, lines)

Issue of November 14, 1840

Married on Wednesday evening 4th inst.,by the Rev. Mr. Barnwell, Mr. J. Ward Motte, to Miss Elizabeth second daughter of the late Robert Primrose, Esq., all of this city.
On Thursday evening 5th inst., by the Rev. Mr. Trapier, C. C. P. Chapman, of this city, to Mrs. Isabella Gray, second daughter of T. Shore, Esq., of Bath, England.

Issue of November 21, 1840

Married, on Wednesday evening 11th inst., by the Rev. Dr. Gilman, Mr. W. B. Smith, to Miss F. S. second daughter of Wiswall Jones, Esq., all of this city.
On Thursday evening 12th inst., by Rev. Mr. Forrest, Mr. David Mustard, of Augushire, Scotland, to Miss Caroline Anne H., daughter of Mr. Daniel W. Miscally, of this city.
At Beaufort, S. C., on Tuesday 19th inst.,by the Rev. Richard Johnson, Mr. Henry G. Loper, of this city, of this city, to Miss Mary Whaley, daughter of Wm. Johnson, Esq., of the former place.
Died at his residence in Fairview, Greenville District, S. C., Mr. Robert Montgomery Morton, in the 29th year of his age....
Departed this life on the 14th inst., Joseph W. Trescot, in the 16th year of his age....

Issue of November 28, 1840

Married on the 8th inst., by the Rev. Dr. Bachman, Mr. Otto Tietyan, to Miss Matta, daughter of Mr. John Stagman, both natives of Hanover, Germany.
On Tuesday evening, 17th inst., by the Rev. Dr. Hanckel, J. Harleston Read, Jr., Esq., to Miss Esther Jane Lance, daughter of the Rev. Maurice H. Lance.
On Tuesday evening 17th inst., by the Rev. J. B. Campbell, Mr. Orrin Taylor, of Westport, Conn., to Miss Susan, youngest daughter of the late M. Muggridge, of this city.
On Wednesday evening, 18th inst., by the Rev. John H. Honour, Mr. R. W. Burnham, to Miss Ann D., daughter of Mr. A. Beckman, all of this city.
On Tuesday evening, 19th inst., by the Rev. Hanckel, Capt. Samuel H. Mortimer, to Miss Elizabeth L. LaBruce, both of this city.
Departed this life on the 24th ultimo, at Sumterville, Mrs. Ann Mayrant, relict of the late Hon. Wm. Mayrant, in the 70th year of her age....

Issue of December 5, 1840

Married on Tuesday evening the 24th ult., by the Rev. Dr. Palmer, Mr. Francis L. Phelps, to Miss Helen A. Fraser, both of this city.
On the 6th Sept. last, by the Rev. Mr. Connel, George Washington Gelzer, of Charleston, S. C., to Miss Martha Ann Hutchins, only daughter of Daniel Spaulding Graham, Esq.,of Monticello, Fla.
On Thursday evening 26th ult., by the Rev. T. C. Clayton, Mr. Edwin Welling, to Miss Susan Disher, both of this city.
On Thursday evening 26th ult., by the Rev. J. Stuart Hanckel, John Laurens Toomer, Esq., to Mary Ellen, daughter of Dr. H. Boylston.
Departed this life on the 10th November in the parish of St. John's Berkley, Mrs. Mary Villo Pontoux, having completed her 70th year on that day...for more than 30 years a member of the M. E. Church....
Departed this life on the 21st ult., in Anderson Dist., S. C., Capt. Hugh Robinson in the 61st year of his age....
Departed this life in Orangeburg on Thursday evening 26th ult., Julia Isadora, daughter of Mr. and Mrs. Joseph T. Zealy, aged 18 months and 13 days. (poem)

Issue of December 12, 1840

Married on Tuesday evening 1st inst., by the Rev. Thomas A. Cook, Mr. Thomas T. Windsor, to Miss Martha Elizabeth, second daughter of Mr. Elias Jones, all of this city.

Married, on Thursday evening the 3d inst., by the Rev. Whiteford Smith, Mr. James Tinsely, of Augusta, Geo., to Miss Christiana Cregner, of this city.

Died on the 10th of Nov., in the 46th year of his age, the Rev. Dexie J. Campbell, late Rector of St. Stephen's Parish, and of the churches at Black Oak and the Rocks in St. John's Parish....

Died on the 29th ult., at his Plantation on Pon Pon, in St. Paul's Parish, James King, Sen. in the 75th year of his age...a native of the city of Norwich, England, and for about 53 years a resident of this State....

Died at his father's residence near Hayneville, Ala., on the 22d of Octo., in the 4th year of his age, Simon Magwood, youngest son of Thomas S. and Ellen Coburn, formerly of S. C.

Died, near Hayneville, Ala., on the 15th of Oct., at the residence of John L. Coburn, Sarah Ann Caroline, in the 8th year of her age, youngest daughter of the late Col. Richard Appleby, formerly of S. C.

Issue of December 19, 1840

Married on Thursday evening 10th inst. by the Rev. Dr. Bachman, C. W. Bingley, Esq., to Miss Jane Gano, youngest daughter of Jacob Martin, Esq., all of this city.

On Thursday evening 10th inst., by the Rev. Dr. Palmer, Mr. John B. Welling, to Mrs. Sarah Ann Strobel, both of this city.

Died, on Charleston Neck, on the 2d inst., Mr. Francis Good, aged 92 years.

Issue of December 26, 1840

Married on Sunday evening last, by the Rev. W. Smith, Mr. Henry W. Schroder, to Miss Ann Eugenia Chitty, all of this place.

On Tuesday evening 15th inst., by the Rev. Mr. Smith, Mr. Thomas Kelly, to Miss Louisa, second daughter of Mr. Henry Bradley, both of this city.

Married at Beaufort, S. C., on the 15th inst., by the Rev. Mr. Walker, Dr. J. A. Bewers, of Russel co., Ala., to Mary, eldest daughter of Edward Butler, Esq.

Died in Tuscaloosa, Ala., on the 2d Dec., Mr. C. W. Cozens, late of Columbia, S. C., in the 37th year of his age.

Issue of January 2, 1841

Departed this life on Monday the 21st inst., from a wound received by the accidental discharge of a gun, Mr. Paul Walter Witsell, of St. Bartholomew's Parish, in the 29th year of his age....(eulogy)

Married in Spartanburgh District, on the 17th inst., by the Rev. James H. Saye, Mr. Thomas G. Mayes, to Miss Celia Shields.

Married at Lexington C. H., on Wednesday evening Dec. 23, by the Rev. E. L. Hazelius, the Rev. John P. Magart of this city, to Miss Ann(?), eldest daughter of Mr. Samuel Treadwell, of St. Matthews Parish, Orangeburg District, S. C.

On the 24th inst., by the Rev. Nicholas Talley, Dennis J. Simons, of Charleston to Miss Sarah C., youngest daughter of Mr. Edward R. Taylor, deceased of Georgetown, S. C.

Issue of January 9, 1841

Departed this life in Charleston, on the 14th Dec., Mrs. Harriet Gillard, in the 67 year of her age....
Died, on the 3d ult., at Talofa, Madison Co., Fla., in the 68th year of her age, Mrs. Jennett Broome, wife of Rev. John Broome, and daughter of the late David Witherspoon of S. C...a descendant of one of the oldest and most respectable families of her native State....
Married on Wednesday evening the 30th inst.,by the Rev. Thomas Smyth, Mr. Frederick H. Whitney, of Boston, Mass., to Miss Sarah C., eldest daughter of the late Capt. J. C. Anthony of this place.
On Thursday evening the 31st ultimo, by the Rev. Whiteford Smith, Mr. Charles Whittemore, of England, to Miss Ellen C. Jordan, of this city.
On Thursday evening, 24th ultimo, by the Rev. Dr. Gilman, Mr. Joseph Walker, to Miss Cornelia M., daughter of the late Wm. B. Wilkie, Esq., all of this city.
On the 23d ultimo, by the Rev. Handsford D. Duncan, Wm. H. Thomson, Esq., to Miss Adeline Elizabeth, eldest daughter of Mr. Charles Rice, all of Barnwell District.
On the 15th of December last, by the Rev. James Gamble, Mr. John Knox, to Miss Mary Agnes Boyll, both of Chatooga Co., Ga.

Issue of January 16, 1841

Married on Thursday evening 7th inst., by the Rev. W. Williams, Mr. Elijah Brownlee, of this city, to Miss Sarah Catharine, eldest daughter of the Hon. J. S. Murry, of St. George's Parish, S. C.
Departed this life on the 4th inst.,in St. Andrew's Parish, at the residence of his father, Robert Heriot, Sen., William Heriot, in the 25th year of his age.
Died in Limestone county, Alabama, Capt. Thomas West, in the 79th year of his age, formerly an inhabitant of this city.

Issue of January 23, 1841

Married on Sunday evening 17th inst., by the Rev. Dr. Post, Mr. Peter Caw, to Miss Jane, daughter of Mr. David Bell, all of this city.
Married on the 14th inst., by the Rev. Dr. Gilman, Samuel Frothingham, Jr., Esq., of Boston, Mass., to Miss Maria Louisa, eldest daughter of Dr. J. B. Whitridge, of this city.
Married, in this city, on the 19th inst., by the Rev. Stewart Hankle, Dr. George E. Harrall, of Mobile, Alabama, to Miss Anna C. Righton, of Edenton, N. C.
Departed this life on the 6th inst., Mr. John J. Reardon, a resident of St. James, Goosecreek, aged 26 years and 3 months.
Died, in St. John's, Berkley, on the 4th inst., Mr. William Meree, sen., in the 57th year of his age.

Issue of February 6, 1841

Died, in Greene county, Ala., on the 5th Sept., at the residence of her son in law, Mr. Robert Craig, Mrs. Nancy Hutton, relict of Gen. Joseph Hutton, aged 67 years. The deceased was born in Abbeville District, S. C., and emigrated to Alabama in April 1822...attached herself to the Presbyterian Church...left seven children, and grandchildren.
Departed this transitory life on the morning of the 5th of Jan., Georgianna M. Nicholson, consort of Major B. F. Nicholson, in the 28th year of her age....left husband, five children, a mother, sister and brother.

Issue of February 13, 1841

Died at his residence near Pendleton C. H., Mr. William Walker, in the 77th year of his age...left a widow and seven children....a Ruling Elder in the Presbyterian Church.

Died in Wilcox Co., Ala., on the 3d of Sept., 1840, at the residence of his father, Mr. John Gaston, Jun., in the 23d year of his age...a member of the Presbyterian Church....

Died at his residence in Wilcox Co., Ala., on the 21st of Sept., 1840, Mr. Samuel S. Gambie, in the 52d year of his age, a native of S. C...left a wife and six children....

Died on the 7th of Oct., 1840, near Prairie Bluff, Wilcox Co., Ala., Mrs. Sarah D. Gaston, consort of William Gaston, and daughter of Daniel and Sarah Key, of Chester District, S. C... the mother of seven children, three of whom are left....

Died at his residence in Wilcox Co., Ala., on the 17th Oct., 1840, Mr. William Gaston, in the 55th year of his age....

Issue of February 20, 1841

Married on Wednesday evening 10th inst., by the Rev. J. Bachman, Mr. William Walter, to Miss Mary G., second daughter of James Calder, Esq., all of this city.

Married on Wednesday evening 10th inst., by the Rev. Mr. Forrest, Mr. David Leekie, to Miss Ellen A. Millar, both of this city.

On Thursday evening 28th ult., by the Rev. John Forrest, Capt. William Robertson, of the town of Aiken, to Miss Mary Macbeth of this city.

On Thursday 11th inst., by the Right Rev. C. E. Gadsden, Mr. Peter Gaillard of St. John's Parish, to Miss Henrietta C. Barker, of this city.

On Thursday evening by the Right Rev. Dr. Gadsden, William E. Jenkins, Esq., to Miss Ann B., youngest daughter of the late H. S. Poyas.

On the 16th inst., by the Rev. C.Hanckel, J. Chapman Huger, to Henrietta, second daughter of James Lynah, Esq.

On Sunday evening, the 14th inst., by the Rev. W. Smith, Mr. John P. Griner, of Philadelphia, to Mrs. Ann Fash, of this city.

On Monday evening 1st inst., at Hilton Head, by the Rev. Mr. Neufville, the Rev. A. Woodward, Rector of St. Luke's Parish, to Miss Eliza C., only daughter of the Hon. Wm. Pope, Senr., all of Beaufort District, S. C.

At Beaufort, on the 11th inst., by the Rev. Joseph R. Walker, Mr. Robert Chisolm, to Miss Louiza Scriven Guerard, eldest daughter of Dr. J. D. Guerard, all of Beaufort.

Married, on Tuesday the 2nd inst., by Rev. Mr. Woodruff, Mr. Thomas Austin, to Mary, daughter of John T. Peden, of Fairview--both of Greenville District.

On Thursday 4th inst., by the Rev. William Carlile, James Anderson, of Lawrence, to Miss Rachael Stines, of Fairview, S. C.

Departed this life at his residence in this district, on the morning of the 31st January, John Simonton, Sen., in his 81st year ...an elder in the Associate Reformed Church. (eulogy)

Issue of February 27, 1841

Married on the 18th inst., by Rev. Mr. Forrest, the Rev. Firmin Prud Homme, to Madame D'Orval, both of France.

On Wednesday evening last, by the Rev. Dr. Post, Mr. George Elfe, to Miss Eliza, second daughter of the late William Clement.

Married on Wednesday 17th inst., by the Rev. Dr. Hanckel, Mr. J. G. Milnor to Miss Agnes, youngest daughter of John Dixon,

Esq., all of this city.
Died on the 11th inst., Thomas Addison Vardell, infant son of William and Anna Harrall, aged 2 months and 16 days.

Issue of March 6, 1841

Married on Thursday evening 25th ult.,by the Rev. Mr. Forrest, George Fryer, Esq., to Mrs. Julia Francis, both of this city.
At Greenville, on Tuesday evening 16th ult., by the Rev. A. M. Spalding, Robert Berry Duncan, Esq., to Miss Susan Drodie, eldest daughter of Mr. P. G. Gerard.
In Athens, Geo., on the 18th ult., by the Rev. Nathan Hoyt, William H. Lee, Esq. of Charleston, S. C. to Miss Elvira A. Church, daughter of the Rev. Dr. Church, President of Franklin College.
At Hopewell, Geo., on the 18th ult., by the Rev. C. C. Jones, Rev. John Jones, of Bryan co., Ga., to Miss Jane A. Dunwody, daughter of Col. James Dunwody, late of McIntosh Co., Ga.,
Died in Kingstree, Williamsburg District, S. C., on Wednesday the 17th ult., in the 22d year of her age, Mrs. Jane S. Matthews, consort of Mr. Samuel Patterson....(eulogy)

Issue of March 13, 1841

Died at his residence in Charlotte Co., Va., on the 14th Feb., the Rev. Clement Read, aged 72 years....(eulogy)

Issue of March 20, 1841

Married on THursday evening 11th inst., by the Rev. Mr. Barnwell, Capt. W. O. P. Fripp of St. Helena Island, to Miss Thomas Ann, youngest daughter of the late T. S. Taylor, Esq., of Charleston, S. C.
Married in Hayneville, Ala., on the 15th of Feb., by the Rev. Mr. Rice, Mr. G. W. O. Harbin, to Miss Elizabeth G., youngest daughter of John Coburn, deceased, and formerly of Charleston, S. C.
Died on the 3d inst., in the 44th year of his age, William George Rout, a native of Charleston. He was an excellent citizen, and an honest man.

Issue of March 27, 1841

Died in Kingstree, Williamsburg, S. C., on Wednesday the 17th ult., in the 22nd year of her age, Mrs. Jane S. Matthews, consort of Mr. Samuel P. Matthews....left husband and two infant children.
Died, at Pleasant Green, Chattooga Co., Ga., on the 4th of March, in the 75th year of his age, David Rounsaval, late of Clark County, known as the exemplary Christian, and valuable ruling elder.

Issue of April 3, 1841

Married on Thursday evening 25th ult., by the Rev. Bishop Gadsden, Mr. Joseph W. Harrison, of New Bedford, Mass., to Miss Eliza A., eldest daughter of Mr. Thomas Meacher, of this city.
On Wednesday morning, the 31st ult., by the Rev. Trapier Keith, J. Motte Middleton, Esq., to Elizabeth, only daughter of Gen. James Hamilton.
On Wednesday evening last, 31st ult., by the Rev. Mr. Sewell, Mr. Edward G. Heriot, to Miss Emma Eliza, only daughter of Thomas D. Fell, Esq., all of this city.
Died, in Laurens District, S. C., on the 8th inst., Rev. William Howard, in the 63d year of his age.

In Pickens District, S. C., on the 17th inst., Major James McKinney, in the 78th year of his age.

Issue of April 10, 1841

Married by the Rev. Wm. K. Patton, on the evening of the 25th inst., the Rev. G. W. McCoy, of West Point, Troup Co., Ga., to Miss Susan Caroline, daughter of Mr. Jno. and Mrs. E. Fitten, of Oak Bowery, Chambers Co., Alabama.

Married on Thursday evening, 1st inst., by the Rev. Dr. Brantley, Mr. B. A. Coachman, of Georgetown, S. C. to Miss E. O. Taylor, of this city.

Married on Wednesday 31st ult., by the Rev. Dr. Gadsden, John M. Harleston, Esq., to Mrs. Eleanor E. Gourdin, daughter of B. Gaillard, Esq.

Died in this city on the 28th ult., John Hume, aged 78 years and 5 months...left 7 children, 44 grandchildren, and 4 great-grandchildren.

Departed this life on the 27th Feb., Mrs. Susan McCalla (widow of Maj. John McCalla, late of Abbeville District, decd.), aged 45 years...a member of the Presbyterian Church. (eulogy)

Issue of April 17, 1841

Married in the city of New York, by the Rev. Mr. White, Henry Black, Esq., of Orange County, to widow Eliza Gray, of Green County, daughter of Henry Brown, of Bluehill, Maine.

Died at her residnece in Greene Co., Alabama, on the 31st ult., Mary C., consort of Abner A. Steele, Jr., and daughter of Col. Samuel Bigham, formerly of S. C., in the 28th year of her age....(eulogy)

In Harden Co., Ky., on the 3d inst., Rev. Alexander M'Dougall in the 102d year of his age.

Issue of April 24, 1841

Married on Wednesday evening 14th inst., by the Rev. Mr. Dupont, Mr. Edward P. Leman, to Martha Catharine, eldest daughter of the late Mr. Archibald Armstrong, all of this city.

Married on Wednesday evening the 14th inst., by the Rev. Philip A. Strobel, Mr. Robert L. Stewart, to Miss Mary Elizabeth Strobel, all of this city.

Died in Lincoln Co., Ga., on the 24th of March, 1841, Mrs. Thurza Fleming, wife of Robert Fleming, Esq., in the 62nd year of her age....a member of the Presbyterian Church for about 37 years.

Issue of May 1, 1841

Married, in Walterboro', on Thursday 15th inst., by the Rev. E. P. De La Vaux, Mr. William C. P. Bellinger, to Miss Jane E., third daughter of Col. E. W. Rice.

Died on the 24th inst., Mrs. Sarah A., wife of Edward W. Matthews, and youngest daughter of the late Anthony Toomer, aged 27 years and 7 months.

Issue of May 8, 1841

Married on Tuesday evening 27th ult., by the Rev. Dr. Bachman, Benjamin F. McKensie, Esq. of Greenville, S. C., to Mrs. Sarah Ann Cohrs, of this city.

On Tuesday 27th ult., by the Rev. Thos Smyth, John J. Seibel, Esq., of Columbia, S. C., to Miss Phillipa Berney, of this place.

On Thursday 29th ult., by the Rev. Mr. Forrest, Mr. Thomas E. Addy, to Miss Martha Detart, second daughter of the late Isaac Rembert, Esq.
Departed this life near Warrenton, Abbeville District, Mrs. Jane Caroline Brooks, in the 20th year of her age...leaving a husband, father, one brother and two sisters...a daughter of James Huey, Esq., Post Master, at Warrenton, S. C.

Issue of May 15, 1841

Married on the 4th inst., by the Rev. Mr. Keith, Mr. E. Mills Beach, to Miss Roseann Vandine, both of this city.
Died in York District, S. C., at her son-in-law (Mr. Jasper S. Naginses), Mrs. Susanna Dunlap, wife of William Dunlap, on her birth-day, being 65 years old....(eulogy)
Died, at his residence in Spartanburg District, S. C., Matthew Mayes, in the 57th year of his age...a member of the Fairforest Presbyterian Church, and for the last 17 or 18 years, a ruling elder of the same....
Died at the residence of her daughter, Mrs. Mary Black, in Union District, S. C.,Mrs. Barbara McDowell, wife of Mr. John McDowell, on the 2nd inst...a native of Ireland, came to this country more than 50 years ago with her husband...a member of the Fairforest Presbyterian Church. She lived to be upwards of 90 years of age....

Issue of May 22, 1841

Married on the evening of the 13th inst., by the Rev. Mr. Stacey, Mr. Nelson O. J. Staley, of Orangeburg District, to Miss Caroline Hoff, of this city.
Departed this life on the 7th inst., Mrs. Hester Tulyman, in the 85th year of her age....
Departed this life on the 8th inst., Mr. John B. Brown, in the 36th year of his age....

Issue of May 29, 1841

Departed this life on the 18th inst., Charles Henry, the infant son of Jonah M. and Elizabeth Venning, aged 9 months and 21 days....
Died in Salem, Sumter District, on the 5th inst., Mrs. Susan V. Sparks, aged 24 years 1 month and 15 days....2d Presbyterian Church in this city, as Teacher of the Infant Class....
Departed this life in Bishopville, S. C., on the 18th inst., Hester M'Crea Durant, infant daughter of Dr. James and M. E. Durant, aged 11 months and 7 days...

Issue of June 5, 1841

Married on Wednesday evening the 26th ult., by the Rev. Mr. Barnwell, Josiah Bedon Perry of Walterborough, to Fanny, eldest daughter of the late Newman Kershaw of this city.
On Thursday evening 27th ult.,by the Rev. Dr. Bachman, Mr. James Ballantine, of Norfolk, Va., to Miss Martha Cruikshands, of this city.
On Tuesday evening last, by the Rev. John H. Honour, Mr. Robert R. Kugley, of Charleston, to Mrs. Martha E. Keals, of Santee.
On Tuesday evening the 25th ult., by the Rev. Dr. Samuel Gilman, Joseph Aquilla Enslow, to Martha Ann Artman, both of this city.

Died suddenly on the 7th ult., Mr. James Harper, aged 67 years, a native of England, and for more than 40 years a resident of this city...member of the Baptist Church. (long eulogy)

On the afternoon of the 22d May, Dr. John Wagner, Professor of Surgery in the Medical College of S. C.

In the city of New-York, on the 21st inst., Mrs. Mary Eliza, wife of Victor G. Audubon, and daughter of the Rev. Dr. John Bachman.

Issue of June 12, 1841

Married on Wednesday morning 19th May, by the Rev. Mr. Dupont, Mr. George Calder of Edenboro', Scotland, to Miss Jane H. Gray, of this city.

On Tuesday evening 1st inst., by the Rev. James Sewell, Mr. Edmund Freeman, of Middletown, Conn., to Martha A. Henry of Baltimore, Md.

On Tuesday 1st inst., by the Rev. H. B. Cunningham, Mr. Lemuel W. Nesmith, to Miss Sarah Heddleston, all of Williamsburg Dist., S. C.

Died in this city on the 1st inst., Mrs. Eleanor F. Gitsinger, in the 80th year of her age.

On the 4th inst., in the 81st year of her age, Mrs. Jane Thurston, a meek and pious Christian.

Died in this city on the 4th inst., Mrs. Sarah, wife of Edward Gamage, and youngest daughter of the late Thomas Barksdale, Esq., aged 55 years and 11 months.

At his residence on Twelve Mile, Pickens District, S. C., the Rev. Philip Porter, in the 77th year of his age.

Died on the 18th ult., at the residence of Capt. James Gaston, in Spartanburgh District, Amzy Williford Gaston, aged 27 years... left widow and two infant children, one of which was only a few hours old...a member of the Presbyterian Church. His only grief was that he was called to leave a helpless family destitute of a father's care.

Departed this life on the 29th ult., in the 15th year of his age, James W. Bacon, only son of Mrs. Mary J. Bacon, of Hinesville, Liberty Co., Ga....(eulogy)

Issue of June 19, 1841

Married at Aberfoil, Alabama, on the 10th inst., by the Rev. A. M. Mooney, A. McNeil, Esq. to Miss Eliza J. Laslie, all of this place

Died on the 10th inst., aged 69 years, Mr. William Thompson, a native of England, but for 37 years a resident of this city.

Died at his residence on Lynch's Creek, Darlington Dist., on Sunday evening the 6th inst., Col. William Timmons in the 43d year of his age.

Departed this life on the 28th ult., at the residence of his father in Greene Co., Ala., Abner A. Steele, Jr., aged 31 years, 6 months and 13 days...member of the Presbyterian Church (eulogy)

Issue of June 26, 1841

Married on Thursday evening 17th inst., by the Rev. Mr. Furman, Mr. T. C. Hubbell, to Miss Mary M., eldest daughter of Mr. E. G. Sass, all of this city.

Died, near Edgefield C. H. on the 1st inst., Capt. Wm. Robertson, in the 72d year of his age.

Issue of July 3, 1841

Died in this city on the 23d ult., Mrs. Susan S. Haskell, wife of William E.Haskell, of St. Matthew's Parish, S. C., in the 31st year of her age.

Issue of July 10, 1841

Married in this city on the 23d ult., by the Rev. Wm. Brooker, Mr. Joshua Prothro of Orangeburg District, to Mrs. Elizabeth Redman, of this city.
Married on the 22d ult., at Woodland, six miles below Spartanburg village, S. C., by the Rev. C. C. Pinckney, Major G. W. H. Legg, to Mrs. Clementena Sarah, daughter of Maj. L. H. Kennedy, all of Spartanburg District.

Issue of July 24, 1841

Married on Thursday the 8th inst., by Rev. C. C. Pinckney, the Rev. Edward T. Buist, to Mrs. E. R. Lowndes, all of Greenville District.
Died, at the residence of her husband, in Sparta, Ga.,on the 13th inst., Louisa Caroline, wife of Wm. H. Sayre, in the 34th year of her age.

Issue of July 31, 1841

Departed this life at his residence in Gwinnett Co., Ga., on the 24th inst., John Newton Alexander, Esq., in the 34th year of his age, leaving a wife and two infant daughters....

Issue of August 21, 1841

Death of the Rev. Dr. John Breckenridge...departed this life on the 4th inst., at the residence of his mother, in Kentucky...

Issue of August 28, 1841

Married at Rome, in April last, Arthur Middleton jr., Esq., late American Cearges at Madrid, to the Countess, daughter of the Count of Bentivoglis, of the former place....Mercury.
Died on the 30th of July, in Calhoun's settlement, Abbeville, S. C., Mrs. Elizabeth Lee, consort of Stephen Lee, Esq...for years a member of the Presbyterian Church....

Issue of September 4, 1841

Married on Thursday evening 26th inst., by the Rev. Mr. Forrest, Mr. George Garrett, to Mrs. P. Storm, all of this city.
Died on the 10th ult., Miss Mary King, in the 81st year of her age.
Departed this life in Sumter District on the 22d inst.,James Summers, son of Dr. Thos. M. and Mrs. Mary E. Dick, aged 2 months and 6 days. (poem)

Issue of September 18, 1841

Died on the 6th inst., at his residnece in Cannonsboro, James McElhenney, in the 40th year of his age.
Died on Friday morning Aug. 27th, Andrew Moffett, infant and first born son of William and Margaret H. Adger.....

Issue of September 25, 1841

Died on the 15th inst.,Henrietta Martha, daughter of Dr. and Mrs. Thomas Y. Simons, aged 2 years, 5 months and 22 days.
Died on Muddy Creek, Williamsburg District, S. C. on Thursday the 9th inst., Jennet Barr, aged 50 years, 1 month and 9 days, daughter of James and Martha Daniel...member of the Presbyterian Church at Indiantown about 35 years....

Issue of October 2, 1841

Died, at Branchville, on the 12th inst., Mrs. Lavenia, consort of Mr. Phillip Chartran, in her 30th year....(lines)
Died at Glenn's Springs, on the 18th inst., Capt. Benjamin Thomas Elmore, in the 51st year of his age, leaving a bereaved wife, six children....
Departed this life on the 29th Aug last, at the residence of her mother, Mrs. Elizabeth Sanders, in Crawford Co., Miss Susan Lucinda Sanders, in the 27th year of her age....
Departed this life at Saratoga Springs on the 18th August, Col. John Russel Spann, in the 61st year of his age...left a wife and two children....

Issue of October 9, 1841

Married on the 3d inst., by the Rev. W. H. Smith, Mr. William Millar, Jr., to Miss Mary Henwood Dillon, both of this city.
On the 7th ult., near Danville, Va.,by the Rev. John Ker, Rev. William T. Brantley Jr., to Miss Mary Ann Turpin, both of Augusta, Geo.
Departed this life on the 8th ult., at her residence in Beech Island, Mrs. Elizabeth Miller, consort of John Miller, in the 48th year of her age, leaving a husband and five affectionate children....
Departed this life at the residence of Dr. Brice, Fairfield District, on the morning of the 18th of Sept., Mr. James Walker, a Licentiate of 1st Presbytery of the Associate Reformed Synod of the South...a native of Canonsburp, Pa., and a graduate of Jefferson College....minister in Chester District....
Died at Aberfoil, Miss Catharine Bethune, aged 10 years, 1 month and 1 day....
Died in Middle Salem, Sumter District, S. C., on the 9th ult., Cornelia Carter, aged 2 years, 6 months and 9 days. Also on the 12th ult.,Sarah Eliza, aged 4 years 11 months and 12 days, daughters of Ezra M. and Mrs. Susan J. Gregg.
Died at Aberfoil, Alabama, Mrs. Christian McLean, aged 77, a member of the Presbyterian Church from the age of a little girl.
Also, Miss Louisa Emeline Hickson, aged 18 years, a member of the Presbyterian Church for several years....
Died in Haynesville, Ala., Sept. 19th, in the 31st year of her age, Mrs. Caroline Anna Woods, widow of Mr. Moses Woods, formerly of Charleston, S. C...Second Presbyterian Church, Charleston.

Issue of October 16, 1841

Departed this life on the 30th ult., Mrs. Elizabeth B. Keckley, consort of John C.Keckley, aged 50 years and 7 days.
Died, at his residence in Washington City, on the 6th inst., in the 61st year of his age, Lieut. Col. Robert D.Wainwright, of the U. S. Marine Corps, a native of this city.
Died on the 11th inst., John Lanneau, only child of John L. and Dorinda Bell, aged 2 years and 1 month....
Died in Barbour Co., Alabama, on Saturday the 11th ult., Richard Morrison, son of Mr. and Mrs. Hibben Leland, aged two years

two months and 23 days.

Issue of October 23, 1841

Married on Tuesday the 12th inst., by the Rev. Thomas Smyth, William Walker Leman, to Catharine Ann, eldest daughter of the late Isaac Rembert, Esq., of St. Thomas Parish.

On Wednesday evening 13th inst., by the Rev. Mr. Honour, Mr. Daniel G. Wayne, to Miss Mary E., daughter of Mr. John Kingman, all of this city.

On Wednesday evening 13th inst., by the Rev. Mr. Sewell, Mr. Samuel A. Duffin, of Sumter District, S. C., to Mrs. Margaret E. Villineuve, of this city.

Died, in Walterborough, on the 12th inst., Lawrence Witsell, Esq., aged 71 years.

Died at her residence on Waccamaw sea shore, on the 7th of October, Mrs. Mary Allston, wife of the late Gen. Joseph W. Allston....left two sons....

Departed this life on the 8th inst., Wm. McDuffie, aged 25 years. He was of a respectable Presbyterian family....

Died on the 30th Sept., at Mine La Motte, Missouri, Mr. Charles McIntire, formerly of this city, and extensively known as a Merchant....

Issue of October 30, 1841

Married on Wednesday evening 20th inst., by the Rev. Dr. Post, Mr. Peter B. Simons, of Philadelphia, to Miss Margaret Thompson, youngest daughter of the late Geo. Thompson.

On the 14th inst., at Edingsville, by the Rev. C. E. Leverett, Robert B. Jenkins, Esq., of John's Island, to Miss Elizabeth L., third daughter of the late Capt. Benjamin Bailey, of Edisto.

At Society Hill, S. C., on the 21st inst., by the Rev. Mr. Furman, Dr. Henry H. Bacot, to Mary E., daughter of Major D. R. W. M'Iver, of that place.

At Jersey City, N. J., on the 16th ult., by the Rev. Mr. Leesk, Mr. Robert Cochran Bacot, to Mary, daughter of Robert Gilchrist, Esq., of that city.

At St. Ann's Church, Morrisania, New York, onthe 14th inst., by the Rev. Mr. Cox, H. Heyward Manigault, to Miss Charlotte M., daughter of Col. Lewis Morris.

Died in this city on the 20th inst., Mr. John Neufville, aged 46 years, 6 months and 24 days.

On the 11th inst., at Society Hill, S. C., Rev. E. M. Wheeler, late Rector of the Episcopal Church in that place....

Issue of November 6, 1841

Married in Columbia, on the 7th Oct.,by the Rev. Dr. Howe, Miss M. A. McConnell, daughter of Mrs. Howe, to Mr. B. M. Palmer, of Beaufort District.

Marriedon the 21st ult., by the Rev. Joseph Walker, in Beaufort, James Moore Rhett, Esq., to Miss Eliza M. Means, of Beaufort.

Died at Walterborough, on Friday 29th inst., Mrs. Youngblood, wife of Dr. Isaac Youngblood, leaving sevenlittle children...a member of the Presbyterian Church.

Died, at Columbia, on the 27th Oct., George, eldest son of Rev. Dr. Howe, aged 3 years and 6 months....

Issue of November 13, 1841

Married on Tuesday evening 4th inst.,by the Rev. Mr. Keith, Mr. James Ravenel, to Miss Augusta, daughter of Joseph Winthrop, Esq., all of this city.
On Wednesday morning 27th ult., by the Rev. James Sewell, E. Thayer, to Elodia Sarah, only daughter of the late Thomas Moer, Esq., all of this city.
On Wednesday evening last, by the Rev. J. Stuart Hanckel, Dr. J. Hume Simmons, to Miss Eliza, youngest daughter of Thomas Wigfall, Esq., all of this city.
Married, in St. Peters Church, on the 4th inst., by the Rev. Mr. Barnwell, James B. Heyward, to Mariah, daughter of the late Wm. M. Heyward.
Died at his residence in Bishopville, Sumter District, S. C., on the 31st ult., Capt. James W. English, in the 44th year of his age...a member of the House of Representatives and a Senator. (eulogy)...left widow and children.
Died on the 3d inst., at his Fathers residence in St. Thomas Parish, William Moore Wigfall, in the 41st year of his age.
Died at his residence on the 3rd inst., Dr. John Oswald, nearly 61 years of age...a Trustee of the Bethel Presbyterian Congregation...lft a wife and sister also--now both widows....
Departed this life Oct. 27, in Decatur Ga., J. Alfred Clark, aged 24 years, a native of Columbia county....

Issue of November 20, 1841

Married on Tuesday evening 9th inst., in St. Peter's Church, by the Rev. Mr. Barnwell, Mr. George A. Locke, to Miss Lucretia O. Bowker, both of this city.
Married on the 4th inst., by the Rev. B. C. Webb, Mr. Laurence J. Witsell to Miss Elizabeth W., youngest daughter of the late Charles Webb, of Ashepoo.
Died on Wednesday morning the 17th inst., Augustine, infant son of the Rev. Thomas Smyth, aged 11 months and 7 days.
Departed this life on the 9th inst., Col. Richard Yeadon, in the 69th year of his age, leaving a widow and family....
Death of James D. Moore, on the 18th of October, in the 34th year of his age...a native of S. C., and had within the past year settled as a merchant in Tallahassee....
Died in Chesterville, S. C.,Nov. 10th, Mrs. Ann T. McLure, wife of Thomas McLure, and daughter of Mrs. Phebe R. Eagle, of New Ark (sic), New Jersey, aged 37 years, and 2 months...a member of the Presbyterian Church....
Died in Fairfield Dist., S. C.,near Youngsville, Nov. 5th, Mr. Robert Caldwell, aged 57 years...a member of the Presbyterian Church and for more than 15 years a Ruling Elder in the Church of Concord.

Issue of November 27, 1841

Married on Thursday evening the 18th inst., by the Rev. Mr. Stacy, Mr. James Dunning, to Miss Rebecca W. Fulmer, both of this city.
Married on Thursday the 18th inst., by the Rev. Dr. Frederick Beecher, Mr. Henry Van Glahn, to Miss Margrettia Schmidt, both of Hanover, Germany.
On the evening of the 16th inst., by the Rev. H. B. Cunningham, Mr. Robert H. Wilson, to Miss Margaret Jane Gotes.
Died at Mobile, on the 18th inst., Duke Goodman, Esq., for several years past a merchant of that city, and formerly of Charleston.

Died on the 28th ult., in Fairfield Dist., Mr. William Roseborough, son of John Rosborough, aged 33 years...Presbyterian Church...Ruling Elder in Aimwell Church, but declined....

Issue of December 4, 1841

Married on Thursday evening 25th inst., by the Rev. Dr. Post, John W. Lewis, Esq.,to Miss Julia E., daughter of Dr. Francis Y. Porcher.

Married on Wednesday evening 24th ult., by Rev. Mr. Stacy, Mr. Joseph T. Sanders, of Baltimore, to Miss Susan Baker, of this city.

Married on Thursday evening 25th inst., by the Rev. Edwin Carter, Mr. James M'Cracken, of Abbeville District, to Miss Eliza Harriet, eldest daughter of Mr. Robert Anderson, of this city.

Married on Thuesday (sic) evening last, by the Rt. Rev. Bishop Gadsden, William N. Lucas, Esq.,to Miss Ann S., eldest daughter of Wm. Mazyck, Jr., Esq., all of this city.

Died in Chesterville, S. C.,Nov. 10th, Mrs. Ann F. McLure, wife of Thomas McLure, and daughter of Mrs. Phebe R. Goble, of New Ark (sic) New Jersey, aged 37 years and 2 months...member of the Presbyterian Church....

Died at the residence of his father, in the vicinity of Macon, Ga., on Monday the 22nd inst., John Patterson Smith, Esq.,only son of Mr. Joseph Smith, in the 22d year of his age.

Issue of December 11, 1841

Died on the 1st inst., at Double Branches, Anderson Dist., Mrs. Elizabeth, wife of William McElmoyle, Esq...a native of Londonderry, Ireland, where she united with the Presbyterian Church, emigrated to this country more than 40 years ago...Her four daughters living and her husband, are all members of the same Church.

Died in Andersonville, Cobb Co., Ga., on the 17th Nov., Mrs. Margaret Eccles, aged 74 years...a member of the Presbyterian Church....

Issue of December 18, 1841

Married on Thursday 16th inst., by the Rev. Mr. Paul Trapier, William Augustus Carson, to Caroline, eldest daughter of James L. Petigure, Esq.

Married at Richmond, Va., on Tuesday 2d inst., by the Rev. Mr. Norwood, W. J. Bennett, Esq., of Charleston, S. C., to Miss Sarah Frances Rutherford, daughter of Col. John Rutherford.

Died on Tuesday the 7th inst., William Henry, infant son of the Hon. Thomas Bennett.

Issue of December 25, 1841

Married in Walterboro, on Thursday evening last, by the Rev. Mr. Huggins, Mr. James Douglass Barns, to Miss Margaret A., second daughter of Dr. Richard Jones.

Issue of January 1, 1842

Married on Thursday evening 16th ult.,by the Rev. Mr. Trapier, Theodore Debon Wagner, to Esther Constance, second daughter of the late William Trenholm, Esq.

On Tuesday evening 21st ult., in Trinity Church, by the Rev. A. R. Danner, Mr. Benjamin Ford, to Miss Harriet H. D. Wilcox, both of this city.

On Thursday morning 24th ult., at the Circular Church, by the Rev. Dr. Post, John Artman, to Mary Gibson, second daughter of Mr. Elisha Whilden, both of this city.

On Friday evening 24th ult., at the Baptist Church, by the Rev. Dr. Brantley, Franklin Robbins, to Miss Sarah L. Dawson, both of this city.

Died in Fairfield District, on the 5th ult., in the 69th year of her age, Mrs. Ann C. Rosborough, consort of John Rosborough... member of the Presbyterian Church for 41 years.

Departed this life on the 1st Dec., in Madison Co., Ga., Mr. James D. Montgomery, a member of the M. E. Church.

Departed this life on the 25th ult., Miss Sarah Anna Mayers, in the 53d year of her age.

On the 13th ult., Miss Sarah E. Ward, aged 76 years and 10 months.

Issue of January 8, 1842

Married in Union District, S. C., on the 16th ult.,by the Rev. James H. Saye, Jesse Gordon, Esq., of Greene Co., Alabama, to Miss Dorcas N. Means. (poem)

Died at his residence in Milledgeville, on Monday morning, the 3d inst., Col. Thomas Haynes, for many years Treasurer of the State of Georgia, and Editor of the "Standard of Union," published in this place...left a large family....

Issue of January 22, 1842

Married on Tuesday evening 11th inst., by the Right Rev. Dr. Gadsden, Dr. Alexander E. Gadsden, to Mrs. Mary Anna Axson, all of this city.

On the 18th inst., by the Rev. Dr. Bachman, Cleland Kinloch Huger, to Mary Augusta, eldest daughter of Chancellor Dunkin.

Died at her residence Barnwell C. H., aged 79 years, on the 6th January 1842, Mrs. Hannah Duncan, wife of the late Capt. Joseph Duncan...a native of Fauquier Co., Va....(eulogy)

Issue of January 29, 1842

Married on Thursday evening the 20th inst., by the Rev. Dr. Bachman, Mr. Optimus E. Hughes, to Mrs. Mary W. Edings, daughter of John R. Matthews, Esq.,of Edisto Island, S. C.

Died at the residence of her brother, S. H. N. Dickson, in Autauga Co., Alabama, on the 8th inst., Miss Sarah Ann Dickson, aged 31 years and some months, daughter of Samuel H. Dickson, formerly of Pendleton, S. C....a member of the Presbyterian Church.

Departed this life on the 15th inst., at St. Augustine, Fla., Thomas Getty, a native of New York, and for several years a resident of this city....

Issue of February 5, 1842

Married on Thursday evening last, 27th inst.,by the Rev. J. S. Hanckel, T. M. Hume, to Georgianna, only daughter of the late G. T. Spear.

Married on the 27th inst., at St. Peter's Church, by the Rev. Mr. Trapier, George W. Cooper, Esq., to Miss Sophia Shaffer.

Married on Thursday evening 27th inst., by the Rev. Mr. Marshall, Mr. Wyatt C. Leak, to Miss Ursula R. Lloyd, all of this place.

Issue of February 12, 1842

Married on Tuesday 8th inst., by the Rev. J. S. Hanckel, William J. Ball, to Miss Julia, daughter of John Cart, Jr., Esq., all of this city.
On Thursday 27th ult., by the Rev. Dr. Gadsden, John G. Shoolbred, Jr., to Miss Jane, only daughter of the late Isaac Ball, Esq.
On Tuesday evening 1st inst., by the Rev. Dr. Bachman, Mr. John H. Rennecker, to Miss Louisa C., Weyman, both of this city.
Departed this life on the 12th of June, 1841, at her residence in Fayette Co., Alabama, Mrs. Margaret Harris, consort of Edwin Harris, in the 42d year of his age...member of the Presbyterian Church...left children.
Died, Miss Rachel H. Harris, daughter of Adlar and Rebecca Harris on the 5th of Sept 1840(?)...(cut off)

Issue of February 19, 1842

Married on Thursday 10th inst., by the Rev. P. T. Keith, William Mason Smith, to Eliza Middleton, youngest daughter of the Hon. D. E. Huger.
In Philadelphia on the 8th inst., Wm. Lowndes, Esq., to Miss Mary Middleton.

Issue of February 26, 1842

Married on Tuesday evening the 22d inst., by the Rev. Mr. Gildersleeve, Mr. Ira Brown, of Littlefield, Conn., to Miss Mary E. Badger, of this city.
Married on Tuesday evening last, the 22d inst., in St. Matthews Parish, by the Rev. Richard Johnson, Thomas Pinckney Huger, to Anna, youngest daughter of the Hon. Langdon Cheves.
In the Town of Irwinton, Alabama, by the Rev. Dr. Brown, on the 23d January, the Rev. R. C. Smith, to Miss Mary A. P. Woods, both of this place.
Died in this city on the 14th inst., Erasmus Darwin Merriman, M. D., a native of Elbridge, Onondaga Co., N. Y.
Died in this city, on the 19th inst., in the 30th year of her age, Mrs. Elizabeth J. Fripp, wife of Mr. Edward Fripp, of St. Helena, and a native of Beaufort, S. C...left a husband and children....

Issue of March 5, 1842

Married on Wednesday evening the 23d ult., by the Rev. J. Bachman, B. B. M'Call, Esq. to Miss Ann S. Woddrop, both of this city.
On Thursday evening the 24th ult., by the Rev. J. Stuart Hanckel, Henry Wigfall, to Elizabeth M. L., eldest daughter of William Blamyer, Esq. of this city.
Married in the neighborhood of Aberfoil, by Rev. Arthur M. Mooney, Thomas M'Clure, to Miss Sarah Barsden. Also, Ignatius Cade, to Miss Jane Bine, all of this place.
Married in Union District, on the 22d of Feb 1842, by the Rev. J. H. Saye, Mr. J. E. Meng, to Miss Emily Jeffries.
Departed this life on the 9th ult., Dr. Alexander L. Barron, in the 33d year of his age.
Died at Philadelphia, on the 23d ult., in the 17th year of his age, Mr. John A., third son of George Pringle, Esq. of this city. (poem)

Issue of March 12, 1842

Married on Wednesday evening the 2d inst., by the Rev. Dr. Post, Mr. James P. Thomson, to Miss Angelina A. Carter, both of this city.
Died at his residence in Chester Dist., on Tuesday the 8th inst., Major Robert G. Mills, in the 55th year of his age.

Issue of March 19, 1842

Death of the Mayor. The Hon. Jacob F. Mintzing, Mayor of the City, departed this life on Tuesday morning last...interred in the cemetery of the German Lutheran Church....
Married on Tuesday evening last, by the Rev. Mr. Keith, Mr. Richard Caldwell, to Miss Maria B., second daughter of Capt. Samuel Alexander, all of this city.
On Tuesday evening last, by the Rev. Bishop Gadsden, Mr. James R. Gready, to Miss Sarah E., daughter of the late Capt. George Croft, all of this city.
On the evening of the 6th inst., by the Rev. W. B. Yates, W. B. Thompson, to Miss Marion Anderson, both of this city.
Died on the 5th inst., Eleanor Jane, wife of Wm. Hume, aged 31 years and 6 months.

Issue of March 26, 1842

Married on Tuesday evening 19th inst., by the Rev. Dr. Gadsden, George W. Stow, to Susan A., youngest daughter of Benjamin Fairchild, Esq. of Stratford, Con.
Married in Beech Island, Edgefield Dist., S. C., on the 17th inst., by the Rev. A. N. Cunningham, of Augusta, Ga.,the Rev. John Francis Lanneau, of this city, Missionary of the A. B. C. F. M., Jerusalem, and Miss Julia Helena, second daughter of the late John J. Gray, Esq. of said District.
Died in Spartanburgh Dist., S. C., on the 19th ult., Major Samuel Morrow, aged 81 years, 11 months and 2 days, a soldier of the Revolution.
Died in Lowndes Co., Ala., on the 22d ult., Mrs. Sarah Broughton, relict of Col. Peter Broughton, late of S. C., in the 67th year of her age....

Issue of April 2, 1842

Married on the 23d ult., at the 2d Presbyterian Church by the Rev. Thomas Smyth, Mr. William Brockleback, to Mrs. Margaret E. Carter, both of this city.
Married in Walterboro, on the 24th March, by the Rev. James Fowls, Mr. James C. McCants, to Miss Adeline, youngest daughter of Mrs. Jane Mey.
Death of W. W. Gordon, Esq...last evening at 10 o'clock.
Savannah Republican

Issue of April 9, 1842

Married on Tuesday evening last, by the Right Rev. Bishop Gadsden, Oliver L. Dobson,Esq. to Mrs. Naomie Rose Timmons, daughter of the late Col. Charles O'Hara.
Departed this life on Monday afternoon, the 4th inst., Peter Caw, infant son of Peter and Sarah Gowan, aged 1 year, 6 months and 18 days. (poem)

Issue of April 16, 1842

Married on Tuesday morning last, the 12th inst., by the Rev. Mr. Trapier, Capt. John Williamson, of the U. S. Army, to Miss Louisa E., daughter of the late James H. Ancrum, Esq.

Issue of April 23, 1842

Married in Walterborough, on Thursday evening, the 14th inst., by the Rev. G. W. Boggs, Mr. George W.Oswald, to Miss Jane S., daughter of Capt. Benjamin S. and Mrs. Sarah Ann Rivers, all of St. Bartholomew's Parish.
Died on the 10th inst., William James, only child of Ann and William Harral, aged 2 years and 6 months.

Issue of April 30, 1842

Married on Wednesday evening 20th inst.,by the Rev. C. Hanckel, Mr. John Hanckel, to Miss Susan Henrietta, eldest daughter of Mr. George Wagner, all of this city.
On Thursday evening the 21st inst., by the Rev. C. Hanckel, Benjamin W. Warren of this city, to Miss Mary Elizabeth, daughter of the late John A. Warren, Esq., of Colleton District, S. C.
On Thursday evening 21st inst., by the Rev. Mr. Furman, Mr. Amos Pettingell, of Salisbury, Mass., to Miss Mary Louisa, eldest daughter of R. B. Lawton, of this city.

Issue of May 7, 1842

Married at Camp Vere, on the 27th April, by the Rev. Dr. Post, Dr. John Hall, to Miss Mary Swinton, daughter of Col. John Bryan.
Married on Tuesday evening 3d inst., at St. Peters' Church, by the Rev. Mr. Barnwell, Edward W. Mathewes, to Mrs. Ann Claiborn, both of this city.
On Tuesday evening 26th ult., by the Rev. Dr. Bachman, Mr. Thomas J. Cumming, of England, to Miss Fredricka Elizabeth Mary Richards, youngest daughter of the late Frederick Richards, Esq., of this city.
Died at Fairlawn, St. John's Berkley, on the 21st of April, Mrs. Emma Caroline Blacklock, relict of the late Wm. Blacklock.
Departed this life on the 11th April, in St. Matthew's, Orangeburg Dist., where she had lately gone to reside, Mrs. Sarah A. Welling, in the 85th year of her age, a native of this city, and consort of John B. Welling.

Issue of May 14, 1842

Married at Waccamaw, on Wednesday evening the 4th inst., by the Rev. Mr. Glennie, Dr. S. Deas, to Mary Ashe, daughter of Col. William A. Alston.
At Liberty Hall, Edisto Island, on the 4th inst., by the Rev. Edward Leveret, Josiah E. Smith, Esq., of Columbia, to Mrs. E. M. Mikell, eldest daughter of the Hon. Whitemarsh, B. Seabrook.
Died at the Warrior, Ga., on the 11th Mrs. Margaret Cason, consort of Mr. Seth Cason, in the 58th year of her age...for 21 years a member of the Presbyterian Church....

Issue of June 4, 1842

Married at St. Peter's Church, on the 26th ult., by the Rev. Mr. Barnwell, Col. Allard H. Belin, of Georgetown, to Miss Virginia Wilkinson, daughter of Willis Wilkinson, of this city.

Died, April 17th, 1842, William Kelso, aged 78, for nearly 40 years an Elder of North Pacolet Church, Spartanburg District....

Issue of June 11, 1842

Married in this city on the 2d inst., by the Rev. Mr. English, Mr. John Clark, formerly of Spartanburg Dist., to Mrs. Mary Ann Bowers, of Colleton Dist., S. C.
At Walterborough, on the 2d inst., by the Rev. Mr. Fowles, Mr. Edward Edmund Bellinger, to Miss Eliza, daughter of the late Col. Peter Girardeau.
Died at his residence in Sumter Dist., on the 21st May, Thomas Rose, Jun., in the 35th year of his age...a member of the Presbyterian Church. (eulogy)...left wife and eldest son, about 4 years old....

Issue of June 18, 1842

Married at Midway, near this city, on the 9th inst., by the Rev. Mr. Baker, R. M. Orme, Esq. one of the Editors of the Milledgeville Recorder, to Mrs. A. A. Egerton.
Died in Savannah, on Thursday morning, the 19th of May, Mary Emma Evans Rees, aged 15 years, 11 months and 8 days,youngest daughter of Ebenezer S. and Mary D. Rees, of Darien, Ga...(long account and eulogy)
Died in De Kalb Co., Ga., on Sabbath May 29th, 1842, Mrs. Ann W. Watson, wife of James Watson, and only daughter of Elder Thomas Harris, aged 34 years and 20 days....(eulogy)

Issue of June 25, 1842

Married on Wednesday evening the 5th inst.,by the Rev. Dr. Bachman, Commander Richard S. Pinckney of the U. S. Navy, to Miss Susan L. Cochran, youngest daughter of the late Thomas Cochran, all of this city.

Issue of July 2, 1842

Died, on Saturday evening 11th June, at hom near Harper's Ferry, in Abbeville district, Mrs. Henrietta Harris, wife of Rev. William H. Harris, and only daughter of James Anderson, Esq.,of Spartanburg District....They were married on the first day of March, and died on the 11th June following. Both his first and last wives were well known to the writer ofthis notice...Both went to the grave in the prime of line, about 27 years of age....

Issue of July 9, 1842

Married on Thursday evening 30th ult., by the Rev. Mr. Dupont, Mr. Albert J. Roberts, to Miss Agness M. Amesburg, both of this city.
Died on Saturday the 11th ult.,at the residence of his uncle, William Ellison, Esq. near Winsboro, William Law Adger, aged a few days over 20 years.
Died on the 22d inst., in Spartanburg Dist.,Mrs. Jane Peden, consort of Andrew yeden, sen. in the 59th year of his age...a native of Iredell Co., N. C...At an early period in life, she connected herself with the Seceding Church, of which she continued a member until her marriage; at which time she removed without the bounds of that Church, and connected herself with Nazareth Church....(eulogy)

Issue of July 16, 1842

Married on Wednesday evening 6th inst., by the Rev. Dr. Post, Mr. Elijah Augusta King, of New Orleans, La.,to Miss Mary Ann King, of this city.
Married at Oak Wood, July 7th, by the Rev. E. Cater, Rev. Wm. H. Davis, to Miss Mary Elizabeth, eldest daughter of Mr. Isaac Morague, all of Abbeville District.
Died at Pineville, on the 3d inst., Samuel Palmer, M. D., in the 26th year of his age.
Died at Savannah, on the 9th inst., John T. Lamar, Esq. of Macon.

Issue of July 23, 1842

Death of Mrs. Eliza Catharine Bryan, who on the 28th ult., passed from time to eternity, aged 48 years and 26 days....
Died in this city on the 14th inst., Dr. Joseph Burroughs Ponce, in the 35th year of his age...born in Savannah, Ga., Aug. 31, 1807.

Issue of July 30, 1842

Departed this life on the morning of the 19th inst., in Savannah, Ga., John B. Cumming, M. D., in the 32d year of his age, a native of Galway, Ireland.

Issue of August 6, 1842

Departed this life on the 18th of July, George Washington, infant son of Thomas M. and Harriet Clyde, aged 10 months and 21 days.
Died in Sumterville on the 21st July, Thomas McCrea McDowell, in the 5th year of his age,son of the late Davison McDowell, Esq.

Issue of August 13, 1842

Departed this life on the 27th ult., at her residence at the Standing Peach Tree in Dekalb Co., Ga., Mrs. Nancy F. Montgomery, wife of Col. J. M. C. Montgomery, in the 62d year of her age....(eulogy)

Issue of August 20, 1842

Died on the 13th inst., Victoria Alexina, youngest child of Charles and Hannah P. Frazer, aged 2 years and 6 months...
Died on the 29th of July, Mrs. Susan Taylor Shaw, consort of Henry D. Shaw, in the 25th year of her age....left an afflicted husband (in charge of an infant sons), as well as her aged parents.
King's Tree, August 11.

Issue of August 27, 1842

Departed this life, June 11th, at the residence of her son, Alexander Peden, Fayette County, West Tennessee, Mrs. Mary Peden, aged about 80 years. Early in life she connected herself with the Presbyterian Church at Catholic, in Chester District, .. C. She was the consort of William Peden. They moved from Chester to Fairview, in Greenville Ditrict, where their family, three sons and three daughters were raised. In the year 1817, she was left a widow....
Died at his residence in the town of Winnsboro, on the 15th of August, Mr. Andrew Crawford, in the 72d year of his age...a

native of Antrim County, Ireland, from whence he removed to S. C., and settled in the town of Winnsboro, in the year 1802...a member of the Presbyterian Church. About 19 years ago, Mr. Crawford lost his wife, who accompanied him in his emigration from Ireland, and the care of a large family of children devolved on him....
    Died on the 4th inst., Dr. Christopher C. Johnson, of Fairfield District, son of Chancellor David Johnson.

Issue of September 3, 1842

    Died at his residence in Fairfield District on the 15th inst., Dr. James T. Rosborough, aged 39 years....
    Died at Bethel Church, in the neighborhood of Aberfoil, Ala., Mrs. Francis M. Bethune, aged 27 years...a native of Sumpter Dist., S. C....

Issue of September 10, 1842

    Died, in Williamsburg Dist., S. C., in the neighborhood of Indiantown, on the 7th of August, Mr. Hugh Hanna, in the 83d year of his age..the last survivor of that noble band of patriots who fought under Marion....

Issue of September 17, 1842

    Married at Lynch's Creek, S. C., on the 3d ult.,by John Baker, Esq., Dr. James H. Benton, to Miss Nelly, youngest daughter of John Keels.
    Married in the vicinity of Lebanon, Cobb Co., Ga., on Wednesday evening the 31st ult., by the Rev. Philip Grover, Judge James Berry, to Miss Mahala Shockley, both residents of Cobb.
    Death of Mr. William Smith Sen. who departed this life on Saturday Sept. 10th, in his 71st year...Since the year 1776, Mr. Smith ahs been an esteemed and valued member of this community...(eulogy, poem)
    Death of Mrs. Margaret Elder, who departed this life on Tuesday, Sept. 13th, 1842, in the 42d year of her age....
    Death of Mrs. Tyler, wife of President Tyler, 51 years of age.
    Died on the 2d inst., in Long Cane, Troup Co., Geo., Mr. Robert Curtis, a Ruling Elder of the Presbyterian Church....
    Departed this life at Carlowville, Ala., on the 19th of August, in the 31st year of her age, Mrs. Jane Eliza, wife of Dr. Lockwood Allison, and youngest daughter of Mr. Josiah Taylor of this city.
    Death of Alexander Lowry, of Sumter, who departed this life on the 4th ult.

Issue of September 24, 1842

    Departed this life on the morning of the 25th of August, Mrs. Elizabeth Johnson, in the 65th year of her age...a member of the Independent or Congregational Church in this city.
    Departed this life in Fairfield Dist., on the 7th inst., James Nelson, Esq. in the 53d year of his age...an Elder in the Associate Reformed Church at Ebenezer...left wife and eleven children.
    Died, at Darlington C. H., on the 17th inst.,Rev. Josiah B. Furman, pastor of the Baptist Church at that place.
    In Columbia, S. C., on the 12th inst.,Mrs. Frances Myers, aged 39 years, consort of Mr. Philip Myers.
    In Greenville, on the 8th inst., Mrs. Harriet C. Dawkins, wife of Col. Thomas N. Dawkins.

In Fairfield Dist., on the 3d inst., Mr. Alexander Wylie Hamilton, in the 26th year of his age.
At his residence near Sumterville, on the 12th inst., Col. William M. Miller, son of Col. John B. Miller, in the 27th year of his age.

Issue of October 1, 1842

Died on the 12th ult., Mrs. Eliza Crocker, wife of Doddridge Crocker, Esq., in the 72d year of her age.

Issue of October 8, 1842

Died, on the 5th Sept., at her residence in Cannonsborough, Mrs. Harriet Ward, aged 65 years, relict of hte late Major James M. Ward.
Departed this life on the 22d Sept., inCharleston, at the residence of Col. Robert Howard, Miss Sarah D. Lee, in the 54th year of her age...youngest daughter of the late Col. Wm. Lee, of this city.
Died, at Sumterville, S. C., Dr. Isaiah DuBose Barrett, aged 36 years....(eulogy)

Issue of October 15, 1842

Died, at his residence, Standing Peachtree, DeKalb Co., Ga., on the 6th Oct. inst., inthe 73d year of his age, Col. James M. C. Montgomery...About the close of the Rev. war, he accompanied his father (a firm Whig, and Captain of a militia company), in an expedition against the Tories. He served as a private at Dean's Station, East Tenn., during the Indian distrubances in 1791 and 1792.... He was the school-mate, the personal friend and for a time the army companion of Gen. Andrew Jackson... had thirteen children. (long account)

Issue of October 29, 1842

Married on Tuesday evening 18th inst., by the Rev. J. Forest, Robt. More, Esq., to Miss Isalla J., youngest daughter of Robt. Downie, Esq. of this city.
Died on the 6th ult., in the 65th year of her age, Miss Henrietta Bacot.
And on the 21st ult., Mr. Thomas Bacot McCay, in the 29th year of his age.
Also on the 10th inst., Mrs.Elizabeth S. W. Bacot, in the 65th year of her age.
Sister, Nephew and Relict of the late Thomas W. Bacot, of this city.
Died on the 17th inst.,in Georgetown, Mrs.Louisa Mathews, relict of the late John Mathews, aged about 30 years.
Died at his residence in the Fork of Savannah and Rocky Rivers, on the 30th July last, Mr. James Caldwell, in the 58th year of his age...for 20 or 21 years a ruling elder in the Presbyterian Church....

Issue of November 5, 1842

Died, at St. George's, Dorcheter, on the 28th Oct., Mr. Edwin T. Moor, in the 20th year of his age,eldest son of the late Thomas Moore, planter of that place...left mother, brother, sister, and relations....

Issue of November 12, 1842

Died in Chambers Co., Ala., on the night of the 18th inst., the Rev. George W. M'Coy, a native of N. C., and a graduate of Franklin College, Ga., and a Student of the Theological Seminary, Columbia, S. C....(account and eulogy

Issue of November 19, 1842

Married onThursday evening 10th inst., by the Rev. C. Hanckel, S. W. Palmer, Esq. of St. Stephen's Parish, to Mrs. Maria H. Cooper, of this city.
Died in St. John's Berkley, on the 6th inst., J. Sanford Barker, of this city in the 72nd year of his age.

Issue of November 26, 1842

Married on Thursday the 10th inst., by the Rev. F. Palmer, the Hon. John E. Frampton, to Miss Harriet J. Hay, all of Beaufort Dist., S. C.
On the 15th inst., by the Rev. Mr. Barnwell, Winthrop B. Williams, to Miss Catharine Jones, daughter of the late Charles Banks.
On Thursday morning the 17th inst., by the Rev. William H. Barnwell, James S. Bigges, of this city to Mary, daughter of the late Dr. Evans, of St. Paul's Parish.
On Thursday eveming, the 17th inst.,by the Rev. Mr. English, Mr. Richard N. Lord, of this city, to Miss Susan A. Taylor, of Georgetown, S. C.
On Tuesday morning the 22d inst., by the Rev. Dr.Hanckle, Keating Simons, to Eliza Read, daughter of the late Edward Simons, Esq.

Issue of December 3, 1842

Married on Tuesday the 29th inst., at the house of Wm. Adger, Esq., by the Rev. B. Gildersleeve, Mr. Robert Jas. Griffiths, to Miss E. Nelson.
Married in Hinesville, Liberty Co., Ga., on the 17th inst., by the Rev. R. Quarterman, Simon A. Fraser, Esq., to Miss Mary W. J. Bacon, daughter of Mrs. Mary J. Bacon--all of that place.
Died in LaGrange, Troup Co., Ga., on the 7th of Nov., Mrs. Aley R. Smith, consort of Doctor Nathaniel N. Smith, in the 25th year of her age. (long eulogy)

Issue of December 10, 1842

Married at Rocky Mount, Fairfield District on Tuesday evening, the 8th ult.,by the Rev. John Douglas, Mr. Robert Douglas, of Chester, to Miss Jane, duaghter of Major James Berkley.
Departed this life on the 22nd inst., Mrs. Mary Yeadon, relict of the late Col. Richard Yeadon, of this city....(long eulogy)
Departed this life Oct. 26th, at her residence on Lynches Lakes, Williamsburg Dist., S. C., Samuel Singletary, aged 57 years, 10 months and 15 days...born on Lynches Creek in said district, near seven miles from the place of his departure-...

Issue of December 17, 1842

Married on the 6th inst., by the Rev. W. M. Reid, Rev. George C. Gregg, to Miss Jane, daughter of Capt. Wm. Harris, all of Sumter Dist.

Died, on the 5th inst., at her residence in Walterborough, Mrs. Jane Glover, in the 81st year of her age, widow of Joseph Glover, Esq., and daughter of Capt. Peter Sinkler, of Santee.

Issue of December 24, 1842

Married on Thursday evening 15th inst., by the Rev. Mr. Forrest, Mr. Charles D. Wood, to Miss Isabella R. Anderson, both of this city.

On Thursday evening, 15th inst.,by the Rev. Dr. Gilman, Mr. F. J. Porcher, to Miss Abby Louisa, eldest daughter of the Rev. Dr. Gilman.

On Wednesday evening 7th inst.,by the Rev. Dr. Hanckel, Mr. Thomas A. Fuller, to Miss Harriett Anne, daughter of the late Andrew G. Hasell, Esq. all of this city.

Departed this life on Monday morning the 12th inst.,Peter Gowan, infant son of Peter and Jane Caw, aged 13 months and 15 days....

Issue of December 31, 1842

Married at Pineville, on Thursday 22d inst., by the Rev. C. Wallace, Charles B. Cochran, Esq., of this city, to Miss Charlotte Lavinia Cordes, of the former place.

Died on the 3d inst., at his residence at Pine Hill, St. Bartholomew's Parish, Mr. Stiles Rivers, aged 47 years...one of the Trustees of the united Presbyterian congregation of Bethel and Walterboro' Churches....

Issue of January 7, 1843

Married on Wednesday evening 28th ult., by the Rev. Mr. Wightman, Capt. James Craton Nichols, of Maine, to Miss Charlotte Gibbs, daughter of H. J. Slawson, of Beaufort, S. C.

Married on Thursday evening 29th ult.,by the Rev. Dr. Brantley, Mr. Simeon Hyde, jr. of N. York, to Miss Ann Eliza, eldest daughter of T. Tupper, Esq. of this city.

Died in this city on the 4th inst., the Rev. Arthur Buist, in the 44th year of his age...son of the Rev. Dr. Buist, formerly Pastor of the First Prsbyterian Church in this city, and President of Charleston College....

Died at Pleasant Valley, Hancock Co., Ga.,on the 8th Dec. last, Anna Maria, wife of Mr. Francis J. Ponce, aged 21 years....

Died, at Liberty Hill, Kershaw District, S. C., on Tuesday the 27th ult., Rosa Turner, elder daughter of Rev. George C. and Rose J. Logan, formerly of Charleston, aged 15 years 3 months and 7 days....

Issue of January 14, 1843

Married on the 5th inst., at Beach Island, Edgefield Dist., by the Rev. Thos Smyth, William Miller, Esq. of Charleston, to Caroline Louisa, daughter of the late John J. Gray, of the former place

Married on Tuesday evening 10th inst., by the Rev. Dr. Brantley, Mr. William Wescoat, of Edisto, to Miss Ellen G., daughter of the late Stephen West Moore, Esq., of this city.

Died at Washington, D. C., on the 1st inst., Mrs. Mary S. Legare....

Died at the Presbyterian Camp ground, near Marietta, Cobb Co., Ga., on Sunday 25th Sept., 1842, Mrs. Damaris Simpson, wife of David Simpson, and daughter of Joseph D. and Amelia S. Shumate, in the 22d year of her age....

Issue of January 21, 1843

Died, at the residence of her son, Col. William Turk, near Bushville, Franklin Co., Ga.,on the 30th of Nov. last,Mrs. Margaret Turk, in the 83d year of her age....born in 1760, joined the Presbyterian Church at Bethany, Iredell Co., N. C. She married in 1784, removed to Abbeville Dist., thence to Elbert Co., Ga.... (Long account & eulogy) Charlotte, N. C.,Jan. 7, 1843

Issue of January 28, 1843

Married on Tuesday 17th inst., by the Rev. Dr.Brantley, Mr. J. Hobson to Miss Margaret J. Smith, adopted daughter of the late Judge Lee, all of this city.
Died on the 9th inst., at her son's residence in Pickens Dist., Mrs. Jane Hamilton...in the 84th year of her age....
Died at his residence in Sumter Dist., on the 9th inst., Redden McCoy in the 86th year of his age...served his country faithfully during the struggle for independence...fought under Marion....

Issue of February 4, 1843

Married on the 24th Jan., by the Rev. Mr. Barnwell, Mr. John Bryan Jr., to Miss Harriet Edwards, third daughter of the late Charles Banks.
On Thursday evening by the Rev. R. T. Howard, of Georgetown, S. C., Wm. E. Snowden, Esqr., to Miss Mary Lee, second daughter of Col. Robert Howard--all of this city.
On the 12th ult.,by Rev. Dr. Humphreys, Mr. Baylies Crayton, to Miss Emeline Benson, both of Anderson Village, S. C.
Died at Newberry, S. C., on the 23d ult., Mrs. Eliza M. Johnston wife of Chancellor Job Johnston.
Mrs. Charlotte Victoria Coxe was the daughter of Matthew James, of Sumpter District, S. C.,where she was born Oct. 9, 1798. She was married March 6, 1817 to Mr. Edward Coxe, of Lexington, Ga., in which place she resided from her marriage...died 17 Jan 1843....(eulogy)

Issue of February 11, 1843

Married on Thursday evening 7th Feb., by the Rev. Mr. Barnwell, T. Heyward Thayer, Esq. to Miss Catharine Barnwell Livingston, second daughter of the late P. P. Livingston, of New York.
On Tuesday evening last, by the Rev. Mr. Baker, Dr. G. W. Taylor, of Columbia, S. C., to Miss Emily C., second daughter of the late Dr. Anderson, of St. Augustine, E. F.
Died at her residence in this city on the 29th ult.,Mrs. Lydia Bryan, aged 86 years and 16 days....
Departed this life on the 24th ult., in this city, Mrs. Catharine Cleary, in the 87th year of her age.

Issue of February 18, 1843

Married on Wednesday evening the 8th inst., by the Rev. Dr. Bachman, Dr. Daniel D. Graves, to Ann E., daughter of Frederick Wesner, Esq.
On the 24th ult.,at Walthourville, Liberty Co., Ga.,by Rev. John Jones, Mr. Joseph A. Anderson, to Miss Evelyn E. Jones.
On the 26th ult., at Walthourville, Liberty Co., Ga., by Rev. I. S. K. Axson, Mr. Charles Berrien Jones, to Miss Marian S. Anderson.
Died at Columbia, S. C., on the 23d ult., Mr. Alexander Kirk, aged 64 years, but has resided in Columbia for the last 24 years.

Died on the morning of the 2d inst., in Lawrenceville, Ga., Richard Henry Harrison, youngest son of Dr. William J. and Mrs. S. Russell, aged 5 years, 11 months and 4 days....

Issue of February 25, 1843

Married on Thursday evening the 16th inst., by the Rev. Dr. Bachman, Edward J. Jones to Catharine Maria, second daughter of William Jones, both of this city.

Departed this life on the 21st ult., at his residence, Wilton Bluff, John H. Wilson, in the 50th year of his age.

Died, on Waccamaw, on the 16th inst., at Rice Hope Plantation, Samuel Fraser, Esq., inthe 56th year of his age, a native of Darlington District.

Issue of March 4, 1843

Married on Tuesday evening 21st inst., by the Rev. W. H. Barnwell, Isaac Wilson, Esq., to Miss Eleanor Schoolbred, eldest daughter of Joseph S. Gibbs, both of this city.

On Monday 27th ult., by the Rev. Thos. Smyth, Mr. Robert Church, of Charleston, to Miss Eliza James, third daughter of the late John James Stewart, of Aberdeen, Scotland.

Married on Lynches Lake, at Graham's Cross Roads, on the 16th ult., by the Rev. Mr. Trapier, Mr. Robert Graham, to Miss Adaline only daughter of Capt. A. F. Graham, of Williamsburg, S. C.

Died, at the Parsonage, John's Island, on the 20th inst., Miss Charlotte D. L. Young, aged 30 years.

Died at the residence of William Gordon, near Lawrenceville, Gwinnett Co., Ga., on the evening of the 17th ult., Miss Margaret Teresa Peden, second daughter of Mr. James Peden, late of Greenville, S. C....

Issue of March 11, 1843

Married on the 16th Feb. by Bishop Peden, Mr. John Graham, to Miss Martha Jane, only daughter of Mr. George Gibson, all of Black Mingo, Williamsburg, S. C.

On the 1st inst., by Bishop Peden, Mr. William Hannah, to Miss Sarah Snowden, all of Indiantown, Williamsburgh, S. C.

Died in Lawrenceville, Ga., on Friday morning, 3d Feb., 1843, John M., youngest son of Col. K. L. and Mrs. Mary Hutchins.

Issue of March 18, 1843

Married on Thursday evening the 23d ult.,by the Rev. H. B. Cunningham, Mr. Austin Stone to Miss Mary Elizabeth Barr, all of Williamsburg District, S. C.

Issue of March 25, 1843

Death of Hon. John Julius Pringle...on Friday the 17th inst., having nearly reached his 90th year...born in this city, about 1754, was son of Hon. Robert Pringle, who was appointed Assistant Judge of the Prov. of S. C. 3 March 1760....Courier.

Death of Dr. North...Dr. Edward W. North Senr died on Tuesday last.... Mercury.

Died at his residence in St. Peter's Parish, Beaufort Dist., on Saturday the 18th inst., Capt. Jonas Johnston, in the 77th year of his age.

Issue of April 1, 1843

Married on the 23d inst., by the Rev. Mr. White, Mr. Charles Rutledge Parker to Miss Susan Jane, youngest daughter of the late James Holmes.
Died, at Liberty Hill, Kershaw District on the 8th of Feb., Woodford Ussery, in the 57th year of his age...Presbyterian Church of Beaver Creek. (eulogy)

Issue of April 8, 1843

Married on Sunday evening 26th March, by the Rev. Dr. Bachman, Mr. Alexander Calder, to Miss Anna Isabella--And on the same evening, Captain GeorgeF. Trescott, to Miss Mary Elizabeth daughters of the late Wm. Cross, Esq., all of this city.
On Thursday 30th March, by the Rev. Paul Trapier, Henry C. King, to Susan M., youngest daughter of James L. Petigrue, Esq.
On Thursday evening 30th ult., by the Rev. Dr. Bachman, Mr. Addison Beach, of Orangeburg, S. C., to Miss Maria L., second daughter of the late C. D. Happoldt, of Charleston, S. C.
On Thursday evening, 30th ult., by the Rev. Dr. Bachman, Mr. Edward H. Carsten, to Miss Caroline P.,daughter of the late A. J. Browne, Esq. all of this city.
Married in the neighborhood of Aberfoil, Ala., by the Rev. A. M. Mooney, Mr. Andrew Bruce, to Miss Rebecca Corley. Also, by the same, Mr. Jno. Smyth, of Monticello, to Miss Jane McLain, of Pike.
Departed this life on the 30th of August last, at Koo-long-Soo, near Amoy, China, Mrs. Sarah Amelia Boone, consort of Rev. William J. Boone, missionary of the Protestant Episcopal Church.
Died, in the vicinity of Darlington Village,on the 4th inst., Mrs. Mary Adeline Dargan, consort of G. W. Dargan, Esq.,and daughter of Samuel Wilson, in the 33d year of her age....

Issue of April 15, 1843

Died on Saturday 8th inst., in the 48th year of her age, Mrs. Mary B. Dawes, daughter of the late David Alexander and wife of H. P. Dawes.
Died on the 28th March, at her residence in the Town of Eufaula, Ala., Mrs. Sarah Elizabeth Hunter, wife of Col. Jno. L. Hunter, formerly of S. C. the daughter of James Henry and Sarah Bradwell Bowler, and was born 26 Aug 1798, in Colleton Dist., S. C. Being deprived in infancy of her mother, Mrs. H. was committed to the guardianship of an affectionate grandmother....

Issue of April 22, 1843

Married on Tuesday evening 18th inst., at St. Philip's Church, by the Rev. Maurice H. Lance,Mr. Robert Dewar Bacot, to Miss Amelia Amanda Huger, daughter of Daniel Huger, Esq.
Departed this life on Saturday 8tb inst.,Miss Elizabeth Pinckney Quash, in the 54th year of her age.
Died in this city on Sunday evening 9th inst., Thomas Chapman, late Cashier of the Bank of S. C.,aged 44 years and 7 months.
Died, in Edgartown, Mass., Mr. Joseph Huxford, a rev. soldier, aged 94.

Issue of April 29, 1843

Married on Wednesday evening 19th inst., by the Rev. Dr. R. Post, Mr. Hugh Legare Bryan, to Miss Louisa Ward, daughter of the late Major James M. Ward.

Died at his plantation in St. John's Berkley, on the 21st inst., Elias O. Ball, Sen., in the 34th year of his age.

Issue of May 6, 1843

Married on Monday evening by the Rev. Dr. J. Bachman, Mr. J. D. Gray, of Macon, Ga., to Miss Ann Amelia Grech, of this city.

Married on Tuesday eveing 18th ult., by the Rev. Dr. Post, William McLeish, of Perth, Scotland, to Miss Margaret Jane Kennedy, of this city.

Died in All Saints Parish, S. C., on the 19th of March, Mrs. Hannah Rice, consort of the late Mr. Charles Rice, of Marion Dist., aged about 90 years.

Departed this life on his Plantation in St. Paul's Parish, April 23d 1843, in the 50th year of his age, Samuel King, Esq....

Died at his residence in Coweta Co., Ga., on the 19th of March, Mr. William M. Stokes, in the 73d year of his age.

Died at his residence at Princeton Factory, near Athens, Ga., on the 15th ult., Mr. Wllliam Williams, in the 58th year of his age.

On Friday the 14th ult.,at the residence of Benjamin W. Walker, Esq., at Mount Meigs, Alabama, Gen. James C. Watson, of this city, (Columbus), breathed his last, in the 56th year of his age.

Issue of May 13, 1843

Married on Thursday evening the 4th inst., by the Rev. William Capers, D. D., Isaac Dodd, Esq., of N. C., to Mrs. Harriet Crow, of this city.

At McPhersonville, on Thursday evening the 4th inst., by the Rev. Stephen Elliott, R. W. Colcock, Esq.,to Miss Mellicent J. Bacot, all of Prince William's Parish.

In Beaufort, S. C., on the 25th ult., by the Rev. Mr. Walker, T. H. Spann, Esq.,of Sumter District, to Caroline B., eldest daughter of Stobo R. Perry, of the former place.

Issue of May 20, 1843

Married on Tuesday evening 16th inst., by the Rt. Rev. Dr. Gadsden, Mr. John Ashe Livingston, of New York, to Miss Charlotte Smith, youngest daughter of the late Col. Philip S. Postell, of this city.

Married on Tuesday evening the 16th inst.,by the Rev. Mr. Gilman, R. F. Coates,to Mary Ann,daughter of the late Thos. Price, all of Charleston.

Married on Thursday evening the 4th inst., by the Rev. George C. Gregg, Mr. Warren A. Muldrow, of Sumter Dist., to Miss Martha Ann Brockinton, of Williamsburgh District.

Re-Married "In this village," says the Glenn Falls Clarion, on the 22d April by the Rev. J. Wells of the Baptist Church, Mr. Joseph Francis, to his own faithful spouse, with whom he has lived for 21 years...former marriage was solemnized in the Roman Church ....

Issue of May 27, 1843

Married by the Rev. J. L. Reynolds, on Wednesday evening, 17th inst., William Y. Leitch, to Harriet Perrink youngest daughter of George N. Reynolds, Esq.

Married on Thursday evening last, 18th inst., by the Rev. Mr. Barnwell, Mr. Robert James, to Miss Eady, second daughter of the late John Redfern, both of this city.

Married in Chesterville, on the 17th inst., by the Rev. John
Douglass, James Hemphill, Esq. to Miss Rachel E. Brawley.
 Died in York Dist., S. C., on the 27th ult., Dr. John S.
Bratton, in the 54th year of his age....

Issue of June 3, 1843

Died at the residence of John R. Slaughter, in Tallapoosa
Co., Ala., on the 13th of April, Martha Emily Frances Slaughter,
aged 4 years, 7 months and 5 days....
 Died in Rothesay, Scotland, on the 8th of April last, in
the 74th year of his age, Mr. James M'Dowall, for many years a
respectable merchant of Charleston, S. C.

Issue of June 10, 1843

Married on the morning of the 26th ult., by the Rev. John W.
Reid, Dr. D. Watts McJunkin, of Wilkes Co., Ga., to Miss Jane
McHange, of Greene Co.
 Departed this life on the morning of the 1st of June, in
the 26th year of her age, Julia P. Parker, consort of R. Lawrence
Parker and eldest daughter of Casimer and Julia Patrick.

Issue of June 17, 1843

Married on the 15th inst., by the Rev. B.Gildersleeve, Mr.
A. M. Lee, to Miss Susan, youngest daughter of John Robinson,
Esq., all of this city.
 Married on Tuesday evening 8th inst., by the Rev. Dr. Leland,
Mr. James Harral, to Miss Emma P. Vardell, both of this city.
 Married on Tuesday evening 8th inst.,by the Rev. Mr. Barnwell,
Robert L. Baker, Esq., to Mrs. Isabel C. Field, of St. Bartholo-
mew's Parish, daughter of the late Capt. John C. Field, of the
same Parish.
 Married on Tuesday morning June 8th, by the Rev. Nathan Hoyt,
D. D., L. S. Craig, of Richmond, Va. 1st Lt. U. S. Infantry,
stationed at Jefferson Barracks, Missiouri, to Miss Elizabeth
W. H., third daughter of the Rev. Alonzo Church, D. D., President
of Franklin College, Ga.
 Died on Tuesday May, 30, Mrs. Ann Elizabeth Elsworth, consort
of Mr. John Elsworth, of this city, aged 61 years, 5 months and
19 days....
 Died in Spartanburg Dist., on the 9th ult., Miss Elmina Peden,
daughter of Andrew Peden, Sen, aged 23 years and 9 months....

Issue of June 24, 1843

Married on Thursday evening 15th inst.,by the Rev. Dr. Bachman,
Mr. William Catherwood Maine, to Miss Emily Mousseau, all of this
city.
 Departed this life on the 16th ult., Mrs. Elizabeth A. Moore,
in the 53d year of her age...Second Presbyterian Church of this
city...
 Departed this life at his residence in Springville, near
Darlington, on the 20th of May ult., Mr. Hugh Lide...died on the
70th anniversary of his birth....

Issue of July 1, 1843

Death of the Hon. Hugh S. Legare...cpied from the Courier of
the 26th June....
 Departed this life on the 17th inst., near Rocky Mount, S.
C., Mr. John Doig, a native of Forfarshire, Scotland, in the 50th

year of his age...for the last 18 years resided in Ga. and S. C.

Issue of July 15, 1843

Married in this city on the 8th inst., by the Rev. Dr. Hanckel, Edward Gamage, Esq. to Mrs. Esther Ball.

Departed this life on the 8th inst., at his residence in this city, the Hon. Thomas Lowndes, in the 78th year of his age. received the rudiments of his education under Mr. Pillins, then a teacher of reputation in Charleston.

Died in Marion Dist., S. C., on the 27th ult., Mr. Wm. Richardson, aged 80 years...served with Gen. Greene in the Revolution.

Died at her residence in Columbia Co., Ga.,on the 28th of June, Mrs. Elizabeth Hardwick, in the 50th year of her age....

Issue of July 22, 1843

Married on the 19th inst.,by the Rev. B.Gildersleeve, Mr. Archibald Cameron, to Miss Jane McFarlane.

Married on the 4th inst.,by the Rev. Dr. Bachman, Mr. L. A. Rose, to Mrs. Isabella Matthews, both of this city.

Died at her residence in Walterborough, on the evening of the 10th inst., Mrs. Mary Witsell, relict of the late Mr. John Witsell, in the 69th year of her age....

Died in Sumter Dist., on the 1st inst., Mrs. Sarah Shaw, consort of Mr. David Shaw, in the 42d year of her age....

Died in Sumter Dist., on the 11th inst., Mr. David Shaw, in the 64th year of his age....

Died in Sumter Dist., on the morning of the 11th inst., Mrs. Sarah Pringle, relict of the late Mr. William Pringle, in the 43d year of her age....

Departed this life at his residence on Ashepool, Col. O'-Brien Smith Price, in the 48th year of his age.

Issue of July 29, 1843

Married on Sunday evening, 23d inst., by the Rev. H. Bass, George W. W. Stone, Esq., Professor of Mathematics in Emory College, Ga., to Miss Susan Bethia, second daughter of Rev. William Capers, both of this city.

Married on Tuesday evening 25th inst., by the Rev. Dr. Curtis, Mr. Wm. T. Rives, to Miss Margaret H. Sass.

Died in Lagrange, on the evening of the 8th of July,Mrs. Martha Moore, wife of J. Moore, in the 32d year of her age....

Issue of August 5, 1843

Married on the 3d inst., by the Rev. B. Gildersleeve, Mr. Wm. S. Carpenter, to Miss Margaret E. Enslow, all of this city.

Died in Pike Co., Ala., on Sabbath the 10th inst., Mr. John McKinnon, in the 63d year of his age...a native of Cumberland Co., N. C....(long account and eulogy)

Issue of August 12, 1843

Married on Tuesday the 25th ult., by the Rev. Mr. Hanckel, James Heriot to Miss Eliza La Rousselliere, both of this city.

On Tuesday the 25th ult.,by the Rev. Thomas C. Dupont, Mr. Charles Gyles, to Miss Cecilia Harth, youngest daughter of William Harth, Esq., formerly of this city.

On Thursday the 3d inst., by the Rev. C. Hanckel, William Hamilton, Esq., to Miss Louisa M., daughter of William S. Wahley, Esq., all of this city.

Died at his residence at Summerville, on the 21st ult., Cornelius Dupont, M. D., inthe 58th year of his age.
Departed this life at the residence of his mother in Crawford Co., Ga., on the morning of the 21st ult., Billington M. Saunders, in the 31st year of his age...member of the Presbyterian Church.

Issue of August 19, 1843

Died, on the 5th inst., at her father's residence in Talbot Co., Ga., Miss Susannah, second daughter of James and Jane McRory. member of the Presbyterian Church for 12 years....

Issue of August 26, 1843

Departed this life on the morning of the 7th inst., Mrs. Maria L. Parker, and in the evening of the same day, Sarah Elizabeth, consort and only child of Peter G. Parker....

Issue of September 2, 1843

Married on Tuesday 22d Aug., by the Rev. Wm. H. Barnwell, Benj. H. Wilson, Esq.,of Geertown, to Maria Julia, eldest daughter of Wm. L. Maxwell, Esq.,of this city.
Death of Thomas W. Moer (who died at Aiken on the 22d inst.), in the 15th year of his age....

Issue of September 9, 1843

Married on Tuesday evening 28th ult., by the Rev. J. Forrest, Dr. David R. Williams, of Wadmelaw, to Miss Isabella J., eldest daughter of John White, Esq., of this city.
Died on the 23d ult., Mrs. Ann Catharine Logan, consort of George Logan, M. D.,of this city in the 39th year of her age.... (eulogy)
Died on Thursday Aug. 34th (sic), 1843, in Sumter Dist., Martha Frances, only daughter of Rev. D. J. and Mrs. Anne P. Auld, aged 1 year and 14 days.

Issue of September 16, 1843

Died on the 11th April last, on his voyage from Calcutta to Liverpool, on his return home, Mr. George Wagner, Jr., aged 27 years, a native of this city.

Issue of September 23, 1843

Married on Thursday evening, 14th inst., by the Rev. Dr. Palmer, Dexter Leland, to Miss E. S. B. Axson, daughter of Mrs. Ann Axson, all of this city.
Died at Double Branches, S. C., on the 23d of August, in the 44th year of his age, Mr. Isaac Sentor Bailey, a native of Middleton, R. I., for many years a resident of this city, leaving a wife and two children....
Died at his residence in Dooly County, on the 3d instant, Arthur A.Morgan, Esq.,late Judge of the Southern Circuit...

Issue of September 30, 1843

Died on the 18th inst.,Mr. Anthony Savage, in the 71st year of his age...an Elder of Fairview Church, Greenville Dist., S. C.
Died in Mobile, on the 21st inst.,the Rev. Jacob Henry Schroebel, Pastor of the Baptist Church in this city...born March 17, 1801, in the city of Charleston, S. C., where he married July

10, 1823....

Issue of October 7, 1843

Died on the 2d Sept., at his residence near Monticello, Col. John A. Cuthbert, in the 44th year of his age, a native of Beaufort Dist., S. C.,and moved to Florida in 1828...left a wife and seven children of tender age....

Issue of October 14, 1843

Married on Thursday evening 5th inst., by the Rev. H. Bass, Mr. J. Blakely Smith, to Miss Ann K. Morgan, daughter of the late Rev. Asbury Morgan.
In Washington, Geo., on the 28th ult., by the Rev. G. H. W. Petrie, Jonathan Bryan, Jr., of this city to Miss Georgia A., daughter of the late Archibald H. Sneed, Esq., of the former place.
Died at South Island, on the 1st inst., Emma Septima, wife of Simons Lucas, in the 28th year of his age.

Issue of October 21, 1843

Married on the 5th inst., by the Rev. Dr. Bachman, Mr. Isaiah Purse, of Augusta, Ga., to Miss Caroline H. Naser.
On Tuesday evening 10th inst., by the Rev. Paul Trapier, Mr. Edward Addison to Miss Frances Louisa, second daughter of Mr. Brossier Rene all of this city.
On Thursday evening 12th inst., by the Rev. A. R. Danner, Mr. John Carr, formerly of Baltimore, Md., to Miss Dalcedia L. Thomas, recently of Smithville, N. C.
On the 6th of Oct., in the city of New-York, by the Rev. Dr. Hutton, Mr. James J. McCarter, to Miss Mary Caroline Bryan, daughter of J. Bryan, Esq., of Charleston.
Died, Mr. Daniel Lyle, on the 15th of Sept., at Mr. F. L. J. Prides, York Dist., S. C....
Died in Fairfield Dist., on Tuesday the 19th ult.,Mary Hope, only daughter of Dr. A. M. and M. Carothers, aged 11 months and 8 days.

Issue of October 28, 1843

Married on the 18th inst.,by the Rev. Dr. Brantly, Mr. Perry E. Chapman, to Miss Julia Ellen Anderson, all of this city.
Died in this city on the 3d inst.,Maria M. Denoon, wife of Mr. Campbell Douglas, in the 45th year of her age.
Departed this life on the 14th inst.,in the 73d year of her age, Isabella Timmons, relict of the late Wm. Timmons.
Died, in this city, in the 43d year of his age, on the 13th inst., Martin L. Wilkins....

Issue of November 4, 1843

Married onWednesday evening 25th inst., by the Rev. Mr. Nipper, Mr. James E. Withington, to Miss Martha W., only daughter of the late Charles J. Henry, Esq., both of this city.
Married on the evening of the 26th inst., by the Rev. Mr. Campbell, John Barnwell Gibbes, Esq., to Miss Sarah Ann, youngest daughter of P. McOwen, Esq.,all of this city.
Died in this city on the 20th ult., Joseph Tyler, a native of Mass.,but a resident in Charleston,for the last 30 years, aged 68.
Died at Oakland, near Cheraw, on the 13th ult., Ellen Phebe, wife of the Rev. J. C. Coit, and daughter of Dr. Elisha North, of New London, Conn....

Died in Fairfield Dist.,on the 20th ult., Joseph Caldwell, Esq., in the 68th year of his age...a member of the Presbyterian Church....

Issue of November 11, 1843

Married on the 31st ult., by the Rev. Mr. Honor, Mr. Robert S. Wright, to Miss Catharine R., daughter of John Kingman, Esq., all of this city.

Died, at Walterborough, on the 5th inst.,Mrs. Martha Eliza Fishburne, in the 52d year of her age....

Died, on Fishing Creek, Chester Dist., S. C., on the morning of the 3d inst.,Mrs. Rebecca B., wife of the Rev. James R. Gilland and daughter of David Hutchison, Esq. of York Dist...just entered her 24th year....left husband and two small children, the youngest is but little more than a week old....

Issue of November 18, 1843

Married on Tuesday evening 7th inst.,by the Rev. Dr. Bachman, Mr. James R. Bee, to Miss Anna Margaret, eldest daughter of Mr. Wm. Jones, all of this city.

Married on the evening of the 9th inst.,by the Rev. Dr. T. Smyth, Mr. Edward R. Poole, to Miss Victoria B., youngest daughter of the late Mr. Robert R. Gibbes, both of this city.

Issue of November 25, 1843

Married on Thursday evening 23d inst.,at the Circular Church, by the Rev. Dr. Post, Mr. William G. Armstrong, to Miss Emma, daughter of the late Wm. Cudworth, all of this city.

On Thursday evening, 16th inst., at St. Michael's Church, by the Rev. Mr. Trapier, Thomas B. Bennett, Jr., Esq. to Miss Fanny, youngest daughter of the late Right Rev. Bishop Bowen, all of this city.

On the 15th inst., by the Rt. Rev. Dr. Gadsden, Dr. Wm. L. Moultrie of St. John's Berkley, to Miss Juliet H., daughter of the late Nathaniel Ingraham, Esq.

In this city on Wednesday morning, 15th inst., by the Rev. Philip Gadsden, Mr. Thomas B. Miles to Miss Elizabeth S. Waring, only daughter of the late John Waring, all of St. Paul's Parish.

On Wednesday evening, 15th inst., by the Rev. Mr. Nipper, Mr. Wm. J. H. Stewart, to Miss Jannett C. McMillan, both of this city.

At Society Hill, S. C., on Thursday evening, 9th inst., by the Rev. Mr. Furman, Mr. Etsel L. Adams, of this city, to Miss Mary M., daughter of David Gregg, Esq., of Society Hill.

Died at her residence in St. Stephen's Parish, on the morning of the 17th inst., Mrs. Henrietta Porcher, wife of Maj. Samuel Porcher, in the 72d year of her age.

Issue of December 2, 1843

Married on Wednesday evening 22d ult., by the Right Rev. C. E. Gadsden, Walter M. Otis, to Maria Catharine, daughter of Capt. James Welsman, all of this city.

On the 23d ult.,by the Rev. Mr. Forrest, Mr. William Lebby, to Miss Anne, daughter of James Smith, Esq., all of this city.

Died at his residence in Anderson Dist., on the 7th of Nov., 1843, Capt. Hugh McLin, in the 81st year of his age...raised a large family, lived to see them all grown...He came over with his parents from Ireland when very young--settled in N. C., Shortly after the Rev. J. McLin, an elder brother of his, came to Abbeville Dist...Rocky River Church....

Died, in Monroe, Walton Co., Ga., on the 10th Nov., Sarah
Octavia Rosamond, second (but only surviving) daughter of James
and Elsa Rosamond, aged 2 years, 1 month and 3 days....
Died at the same place, on the 13th inst., only son of Josiah
A., and Mary Clark, aged 5 weeks and 3 days.

Issue of December 9, 1843

Departed this life on the 24th of June, in St. James'
Parish, Martha Cecelia, youngest daughter of Samuel M. and A. H.
Timmons, aged 9 months and 23 days.
Died in St. James Parish, on the 15th of Oct., Rectina
Ophilus second daughter of Samuel M. and Agness Theturah Timmons,
aged 2 years, 4 months and 8 days.
Departed this life on the 18th of July, at Muddy Creek,
Williamsburg Dist., S. C.,Martha Elizabeth, eldest daughter of
James Daniel and Martha M. Singeltary, aged 2 years, 9 months and
20 days.
Died at his residence in Pickens Co., Ala., on the 17th of
Nov., Capt. David Morrow, in the 53d year of his age...a native
of S. C.,and emigrated to Alabama in the fall of 1818.... elder
in Hebron Church.

Issue of December 16, 1843

Married at St. Phillip's Chruch, on Tuesday evening, 5th
Dec., by the Right Rev. Bishop Gadsden, Mr. J. F. Edwards, Jr.,
to Miss Sarah A. Scriven, all of this city.
Died in this city on the 23d ult., William Scott, eldest son
of Franklin M. and Elizabeth M. Bartlett, aged 5 years and 10
months.
Also on the 27th ult.,Maria Theresa, only daughter of Franklin
M. and Elizabeth M. Bartlett, aged 1 year and 9 months.
Died at the Boiling Springs, Barnwell Dist.,on the 19th of
Nov., Lewis S. Hay, son of Col. Fred J. Hay, in the 22d year of
his age. (eulogy)

Issue of December 23, 1843

Married on Wednesday 20th inst., by the Rev. Mr. Bachman, Mr.
T. W. Speisegger, to Miss Rebecca Taylor.
Died on the 13th inst.,Arthur, youngest son of Mr. John
Robinson of this city, aged 19 years, 1 month and 19 days....
(eulogy)
Died on the 20th ult., Lewis Gervais, aged 3 years, 8 months
and 8 days--son of Stephen T. and Mary Robinson.
On the 25th ult., James Kirk, aged 6 years, and 13 days. And
on the 9th inst.,John Brownlee, aged 3 years, 5 months and 24
days. Also, on the 17th inst., Henry Dickson, aged 4 years, 10
months and 27 days, all children of James K. and Mary T. Robinson.
On the 23d ult.,John Bainbridge, aged 3 years and 19 days.
and on the 4th inst., Stephen Thomas aged 18 days--both children
of James M. and Ann T. Caldwell. These were all grandchildren of
Mr. John Robinson.
Died at Darlington Village, on Thursday the 23d ult.,Isaac
Henderson Rosser, in the 26th year of his age....

Issue of December 30, 1843

Married in Augusta, Ga.,on Tuesday 19th Dec., by the Rev.
President Talmage, John H. Fitten, Professor of Mathematics in
Oglethorpe University, to Ann S., daughter of Mr. Alexander
Martin, of ths former place.

Died on Fishing Creek, Chester Dist.,S. C. on the morning of the 3d inst., Mrs. Rebecca B.,wife of the Rev. James R. Gilland, and daughter of David Hutchison, Esq.,of York Dist...She is the third of her family that has been called away during this year....

Issue of January 6, 1844

Married on Thursday 28th ult., by the Rev. Mr. Stacy, Mr. Richard M. Butler, to Miss Catharine Spencer, eldest daughter of the late Paul C. Gibbs, all of this place.

On the 13th ult., by Rev. A. J. Peden, Mr. A. Murfee, to Miss A. McGill, all of Cedar Swamp, Williamsburg Dist., S. C.

On the 14th ult., by the Rev. A. J. Peden, Mr. R. Shaw, of Black River, to Miss Barnett, of Santee.

On the 21st ult., by the Rev M. Peden, Capt. R. B. Caldwell, of Fairfield Dist.,to Miss Mary Neeley, of Mecklenburg, N. C.

At Philadelphia, on the 26th ult., by the Rev. S. B. Wylie, D. D., William Milliken, of Charleston, S. C., to Mary Jane, daughter of the late William Milliken, of the former place.

Departed this life om the 1st Dec., 1843, Mr. John M'Clure, Senr., aged nearly 88 years...member of the Presbyterian Church at Beaver Creek...in the Rev. war....

Died in Monroe Co., Ga.,on the 22d Nov., Aaron Jordan, Esq., aged 82 years, a soldier of the revolution.

Issue of January 13, 1844

Married on Thursday evening, 4th inst., by the Rev. Dr. Bachman, Capt. R. N. Bullen, to Miss Catharine Ryburn, all of this city.

In Savannah, Geo., on the evening of the 18th ult., at the residence of her brother, by the Rev.Charles B. Jones., Benjamin Franklin of Camden, S. C., to Maria Elizabeth, third daughter of Mr. Abraham Jones, of this ctiy.

Died at Beech Island (Edgefield Dist.), on the 29th ult., Mrs. Catharine A., wife of Dr. U. B. Clarke, and daughter of the late Major George Watkins, of Greene Co., Ga., in the 86th year of her age.

Also on the 5th inst., George Bender, infant son of Samuel Clarke, Esq.,aged 1 year and 26 days.

Died at his residence in Dekalb Co., Ga., on Thursday evening, the 21st ult., Mr. Robert Lemon, in the 75th year of his age...a native of Antrim, Ireland, from whence he emigrated with his parents when seven years of age...a resdient of Pendleton Dist., S. C., and came to this state about 15 years since...a member of the Presbyterian....

Issue of January 20, 1844

Married in Union District, on the 2d inst., by the Rev. James H. Saye, Mr. David C. Judd to Miss Catharine Foster.

Departed this life on Saturday morning, 6th inst.,Mrs. Martha Drennes, a native of this city, aged 82 years, 2 months and 26 days....

Issue of January 27, 1844

Married on Thursday evening 18th inst., by the Rev. Dr. Bachman, Mr. Conrad Wienges, to Miss Caroline E.,eldest daughter of Henry Willis, Esq., all of this city.

Departed this life, on the 16th inst., Mrs. Isabel H. DeSaussure, wife of Dr. Louis M. DeSaussure, of Beaufort District.

In Chester Dist., on the morning of Dec. 23d, 1843, Mrs. Patience Stringfellow ended her mortal career...made a profession of faith prior to her marriage while on a visit to her eldest sister who was the wife of the Rev. John B. Davies, the pastor of Fishing Creek Church.... (eulogy)

Issue of February 3, 1844

Married on Wednesday evening 24th ult., by the Rev. John Douglas, of Chesterville, S. C., John H. Blake, to Miss Elizabeth W., eldest daughter of Jas. Legare, Esq.

On Thursday evening the 11th ult., in Cullodenville, by the Rev. T. P. Montgomery, Mr. James W. Carsten, of Talbotton, to Miss Ann V. Oliver of the former place.

On Thursday morning, the 18th ult., at 9 o'clock, A. M. at Talbotton, by the Rev. T. F. Montgomery, A. C. Van Epps, Esq., of Eufaula, Alabama, to Miss Caroline, daughter of Gen. N. Howard of the former place.

Departed this life on Saturday last, 27th ult., Mrs. Caroline Ravenel, wife of Daniel Ravenel, aged 51 years, and 5 months.

Died, on the 26th inst., in the 75th year of his age, Mr. William S. Parsons....

Died in Chester Dist., near Chesterville, S. C., John Douglas, Esq., in the 73d year of his age...left an aged companion and an affectionate family....

Issue of February 10, 1844

Married on the 30th ult., by the Rev. Dr. Bachman, Mr. John Rose(?), to Miss Harriet C. Belser, of this city.

Died in McPhersonville, on the 4th of Jan., Mrs. Eliza Mary Colcock, wife of Thomas H. Colcock, in the 41st year of her age....

Died on the 12th ult., Anna Kerrison, aged 4 years, 4 months and 18 days. And on the 4th inst., William Kerrosn, aged 2 years, 10 months and 28 days, two eldest children of Mr. and Mrs. Charles Kerrison of this city.

Issue of February 24, 1844

Married in this city on Wednesday evening, 14th inst., by the Rev. W. S. Lee, William Edings, Esq., to Mrs. Wm. A. Mikell, both of Edisto Island.

Married on the 15th inst., by the Rev. Paul Trapier, Mr. Murdoch P. Matheson, to Miss Eugenia L., youngest daughter of the late John Stoney, Esq., of this city.

Died at the residence of Hugh Wilson, Esq., in Cannonsboro', on Thursday last, the 15th inst., Ann Eliza eldest daughter of Hugh and Eliza Wilson, aged 12 years and 6 months....

Died at his residence in Marion Dist., S. C., on the 1st inst., Mr. Thomas M'Call, aged about 45...a member of the Presbyterian Church of Hopewell.

Died at his residence in Darlington Dist., S. C., on the 8th inst., Mr. John M'Clenaghan, a native of Ireland, born in the County of Antrim, aged 51 years and 10 months....

Issue of March 2, 1844

Married on Wednesday 28th Feb., by the Right Rev. Bishop Gadsden, at St. Michae's Church, Edward Lynah, to Eliza, daughter of the late Col. John Heyward Glover, of this state.

On Wednesday evening 28th Feb., by the Right Rev. Dr. Gadsden, Mathew R. Singleton, Esq., of Sumter Dist., to Miss Martha Rutledge Kinloch, of this city.

Married on Thursday evening 22d inst., by the Rev. Dr.Hanckel, James Perry, Esq., of St. Paul's Parish, to Miss Sarah E., daughter of the late D. Jennings Waring of this city.

Married by the Rev. A. M. Mooney, M. M. Dennis, Esq., of China Grove, to Miss Mary M'Clure, all of Pike Co., Alabama.

Died on the 21st Jan., at Mount Zion, Geo., Mrs. Maria Connel,, wife of Dr. Connel and daughter of Joseph Bryan, Esq....

Died on the 15th of Feb., in the 56th year of her age, Mrs. Catharine Stokes, wife of Mr. Archibald Stokes, of Petersburgh, Ga...daughter of Col. James and Mrs. Hannah Patton, of Woodbridge, N. J....

Died in Sumter Dist., on the evening of the 16th inst., of a wound caused by the accidental discharge of his gun, James Dickey, eldest son of M. Hampton and Martha L. Plowden, aged 17 years and 8 months....

Died in Baltimore, on the 16th inst., the Rev. Daniel Davies, M. D., late Pastor of the Methodist Protestant Church in this city.

Issue of March 9, 1844

Married on Wednesday the 28th Feb., by the Rev. T. Keith, George S. Bryan, Esq., of Charleston, to Rebecca Louisa, daughter of the late Dr. S. Dwight, of St. John's Berkley.

On Tuesday evening 27th ult.,by the Rev. Dr. Bachman, Mr. Henry Williams, to Mrs. Mary Ann Evans, both of this city.

On Wednesday 28th ult.,by the Rev. Mr. Chapman, Mr. J. P. Joy, to Miss Margaret Berry, both of this city.

Died, Feb. 10th, Mrs. Elizabeth Frost, aged 74 years, widow of Thomas Frost, former Rector of St. Philips Church, and mother of Thomas Frost late assistant minister of the same church....

Issue of March 16, 1844

Married on Tuesday evening last, 5th inst., by the Rev. Mr. Kirkland, Mr. Theodore Roberts to Miss Emma C. Biggs, both of this city.

Married on Wednesday morning 6th inst., at St. Philip's Church, by the Rev. Mr. Campbell, Thomas L. Bulow, Esq., of St. Andrew's Parish, to Martha Caroline, only daughter of the late Alvyn Ball, of St. John's Berkley.

On Wednesday evening 6th inst., by the Rev. Dr. Post, Mr. James E. Thwing, to Mrs. Isabella C. Benson, all of this city.

On the 14th of Feb., by the Rev. T. R. Montgomery, Mr. James Sheridan to Miss Catharine Forbes, all of Talboton, Ga.

On the 5th inst., by the Rev. T. F. Montgomery, Mr. A. F. Owen, to Miss Sarah A., youngest daughter of Robert Gamble, Senr., all of Talbot Co., Ga.

On the 10th inst., in Ephesus Presbyterian Church, by the Rev. T. F. Montgomery, Mr. John M. Bruce, of Meriwether Co., to Mrs. Martha Buchanan, of Talbot Co.

Died on the 23d Jan. last, Margaret, youngest daughter of the late David Haig, aged 21 years and 5 months.

Died on the 22d ult., at the house of Mr. William Gray, near Macon, Ga., Mrs. Eliza Maria Gnech, of Charleston, S. C., in the 63d year of her age.

Departed this life on the 15th Feb., Miss Martha H. L. Ramsey, second daughter of the late Dr. David Ramsay, the historian, and of Mrs. Martha L. Ramsay....(eulogy)

Died on the 11th Oct. last, in Florida, Mr. John Miller, in the 40th year of his age...a native of this city....

Died at Richmond, Bryan Co., Ga., on the 27th of Feb., Mrs. Mary Clay....in a ripe old age.

Issue of March 23, 1844

Married on Tuesday evening 19th inst., by the Rev. Dr. Bachman, Peter W. Knapp, Esq., formerly of New York to Cecilia Louisa, youngest daughter of the late Peter Crovat, Esq., of this city.
Married in Spartanburg Dist., S. C.,on the 12th inst., by the Rev. James H. Saye, Dr. Samuel Means to Miss Nancy V. Whetstone.
Died in Prince William's Parish, on the 9th inst., Mrs. Charlotte M. Heyward, in the 71st year of his age.
Died in Madison, Morgan Co., Ga., on the 6th inst., Robert Cleveland, aged 4 years, 10 months and 23 days; on the 16th inst., Cynthia Evelina, aged 2 years, 6 months and 15 days--both the children of Daniel and Cynthia A. Killian.

Issue of March 30, 1844

Married in Christ Church, Macon Geo., on Thursday evening, 21st inst., by the Rev. Mr. Bragg, Mr. James M. Jeannerett, of this city, to Catharine Dalton, daughter of the late Dr. Fitzgerald Bird, of Columbus, Ga.
On the 9th of Jan., by the Rev. James Thompson, Mr. William F. Boyd, to Miss Eleanor M. Rodgers, both of the County of Wilcox, Alabama.
Died at the residence of Mrs. Mary S. Wilson, Middle Salem, Sumter, S. C., on the morning of the 13th inst., in the 34th year of her age, Mrs. Lydia Arthurs, wife of Joseph W. Arthurs, and daughter of the late James Morrison, of Iredel Co., N. C. (eulogy)
Departed this life on the 16th inst., at Jefferson Hall, in Greene Co., Mrs. Sophia P. J. Russell, the wife of Dr. William J. Russell, of Lawrenceville, Ga....

Issue of April 6, 1844

Married in the 2d Presbyterian Church on the 28th ult., by the Rev. Dr. Smyth, Henry King M'Clintock, of Walterboro', to Mrs. Julianna Tovey, daughter of the late Thos. A. Vardell, of this city.
On Sunday evening 31st ult., by the Rev. James Stacey, Mr. Alexander John Ballantine, to Mrs. Caroline DeVeaux, widow of the late Thos. E. DeVeaux, all of this city.
Died at her residence in York Dist., S. C., on the morning of the 21st ult., Mrs. Erixene Adams, relict of aev. James S. Adams, daughter of Rev. James McEwin, of N. C. and was in the 65th year of her age....
Died at his residence in Darien, McIntosh Co., on the 2d Feb., Hon. Allen B. Powell, in the 61st year of his age.

Issue of April 13, 1844

Married in this city on Wednesday evening 3d inst., by the Rev. Dr. Hanckel, Mr. John C.Mikell, of Edisto Island, to Miss Mary H. Frazer, only daughter of the late J. J. Frazer, Esq.
On Tuesday evening last, by the Rev. Mr. Kirkland, Mr. James P. M. Lord, of this city, to Miss Catherine Ann Brock, of Greenville, S. C.
Departed this life on the 4th inst.,Mrs. Harriott Elliott Maxwell, in the 78th year of her age.

Issue of April 20, 1844

Married on Thursday evening, 11th inst., at St. Michael's Church, by the Rev. Paul Trapier, Mr. William N. Barnett, to Miss Mary S., daughter of the late Paul Pritchard, Senr., Esq., all of this city.
In Macon, on the 8th inst., by the Rev. Mr. Payne, Mr. George R. Frazer, of Augusta, Ga., to Mrs. Malvina C. Jackson, of the same place.
Departed this life on Tuesday the 9th inst., Mrs. Elizabeth Hemphill, wife of Maj. P. W. Hemphill, of Floyd Co., and daughter of Capt. J. T. Cunningham, of Jackson Co., Ga....left father and mother, brothers and sisters, a husband and three little daughters. aged 34 years and 24 days.

Issue of April 27, 1844

Married on the 17th inst., in St. Paul's Church, by the Rev. J. S. Hanckel, Mr. Louis F. Klipstein, lately of Virginia, to Miss Allston C., daughter of the late Hon. James G. Jerman, of St. James, Santee.
Died on the 17th inst., at Edgewood, the residence of Col. F. W. Pickens, Mrs. Maria E. Calhoun, wife of Col. J. Edward Calhoun, of Abbeville District, in the 28th year of her age.

Issue of May 4, 1844

Married on Thursday evening last, in St. Philip's Church, by the Right Rev. C. E. Gadsden, D. D., Henry B. Bonnetheau, Esq., to Miss Julia C. Dupre, both of this city.
On Wednesday morning last, 24th inst., by the Rev. Dr. Post, Mr. John T. Syme, Jr., to Miss Sarah D. Simmons, both of this city.
Died in the Village of Anderson, on the 1st inst., Mrs. Mary Prince, wife of Mr. C. J. Prince, formerly of Charleston, though the last 11 years a resident of this Village....(eulogy)
Died at the residence of her son, Dr. R. W. Gibbes, in Columbia, on the 21st April, Mrs, Mary P. Gibbes, aged 71 years, 10 months and 17 days....

Issue of May 11, 1844

Married on Wednesday 1st inst., in this city by the Rev. Dr. Post, Charles J. Moore, Esq., to Miss Eliza Susan, only daughter of the late Robert D. Lawrence.
Married on Wednesday 1st May, at the Episcopal Church on Edisto Island, by the Rev. Mr. Walker, Wm. G. B. Mitchell, Esq., to Miss Mary S., youngest daughter of Gen. W. C. Wayne.
Died in this city on Friday, April 12, Mrs. Sarah Croft, of Greenville, S. C.

Issue of May 18, 1844

Died, at his residence in Pike Co., Alabama, on the 3d ult., John Bethune, Esq., in the 49th year of his age...made a profession of religion in Sumter Dist., S. C., and attached himself to Salem Church...later moved to the vicinity of Bishopville Church.
Died, at Rotherwood, Carroll Co., Ga., 6th May, Mrs. Elizabeth Baxter, formerly of Hancock Co., in the 79th year of her age....

Issue of May 25, 1844

Married on Wednesday 15th inst., by the Rev. Dr. Hanckel, Mr. James J. Clark, of Edisto Island, to Josephine Felicea, only daughter of the late E. Liepman, of St. John's, Berkley.
Died on the 19th ult., near Waterloo, Laurens Dist., S. C., Capt. Andrew Burnside, a veteran soldier of the revolution, in the 82d year of his age.

Issue of June 1, 1844

Married on Wednesday evening 22d inst., by the Rev. Dr. Gilman, Thomas M. Horsey, Esq., to Miss Emily S. Fisher, both of this city.
On Thursday evening 23d inst.,by the Rev. Wm. B. Yates, Mr. John A. Rose, to Miss Harriet E. Gitsinger, all of this city.
At Beaufort, on the 23d inst., by the Rev. Mr. Walker, G. Henry Guerard of this city, to Alice L., daughter of the late Dr. Edward Cuthbert of Beaufort.
Died in this city on the 12th May, Isabel Miller, fourth daughter of George and Alison Moffitt, aged 6 years, 6 months and 13 days.

Issue of June 8, 1844

Died in Columbia, S. C.,on Sabbath evening last, the 2d inst., Benjamin Blakely, only child of Rev. B. M. Palmer, Jr., aged 1 year, and 10 months.
Died in this city on the 17th May, James Marion M'Caffrey, aged 1 year and 28 days.
Died on the 24th of April last, in the 51st year of her age, Mrs. Mary McKay, wife of John McKay, of Pike Co., Alabama...born in Scotland,; when an infant, her parents emigrated and settled in North Carolina...member of Pinetree Church....

Issue of June 15, 1844

Died at the residence of Dr. John E. Dubose in Salem, Sumter Dist., on the 23d ult., Mrs. Rebecca Dubose...(eulogy)
Died, in Augusta, on the 1st inst., in the 27th year of her age, Miss Margaret L. Gamble, only daughter of the Hon. Roger L. Gamble...(long eulogy)

Issue of June 22, 1844

Married on the 12th inst.,by the Rev. J. Forrest, James Hopkinson,of Philadelphia, to Miss Carolina Lafayette, daughter of the late William Seabrook, of Edisto Island, S. C.
On Wednesday evening the 12th inst., at Darlington C. H., S. C., by the Rev. Allen M'Corquedale, Mr. James S. Gibson, to D. Amarintha Dubose, third daughter of Capt. John Dubose.
In Philadelphia, where he had gone for the benefit of his health, on the 4th inst., Dr. James Stuart, a native of Beaufort, S. C., and for many years a summer resident of Pendleton Village.
Died at Greensboro, Alabama, on the 8th inst., Mrs. Ann Eliza, consort of Rev. Thomas S. Witherspoon, and daughter of Hon. Samuel W. Goode.... Greensboro, Ala., June 12, 1844.

Issue of June 29, 1844

Married in England, on the 23d May last, at St. John's Church, Margate, Kent, by the Rev. C. R. Carroll, the Baron Elphege Van Zuylen Van Nyevelt De Gaesebeke, a native of Bruges, to Ellen

Clairborne, a native of Charleston, and eldest daughter of Thomas Higham, Esq., of this city, and of Margaret, Kent.

Departed this life on the 22d inst., in the city of New York, Alexis S. Bessent, a native of St. Mary's, Ga., in the 31st year of his age.

Died at her husband's residence in Talbot Co., Ga., Mrs. Sophia C., wife of Capt. James G. Gamble, and daughter of the Rev. John B. Kennedy, of S. C....left no children....

Issue of July 6, 1844

Married on Thursday evening 27th ult., by the Rev. Mr. Bachman, George W. Willey, Esq. of Savannah, Ga., to Miss Sarah Ann Revel, of this city.

Departed this life on the 12th ult., at his residence in this city, Dr. Philip Gendron Prioleau, having nearly completed the 68th year of his age.

Died at his residence in Abbeville Dist., in the 56th year of his age, Mr. William Giles, for more than 30 years a consistent member of the Presbyterian Church....

Issue of July 13, 1844

Departed this life on the 29th ult., Mrs. Rebecca Humphreys, wife of the Rev. David Humphreys, and daughter of S. Cunningham Esq., in the 39th year of her age....(long eulogy)

Died at Bluffton, S. C., on the 27th ult., Wm. P. Guerard, in the 26th year of his age.

Issue of July 20, 1844

Departed this life on the 5th inst., in St. Paul's Parish, Mrs. Anna M. Doyle, consort of Mr. Thomas E. Doyle, in the 29th year of her age, leaving a husband and three children....

Died in York Dist., on the 2d inst., Samuel Melville Crenshaw, youngest child of Rev. William B.Davies and Mrs. Eliza A. Davies, aged 1 year, 9 months and 18 days....

On the 10th inst., at the residence of John P. Anderson, in Lexington Dist., in the 26th year of her age, Mrs. Sydney Ann Anderson, wife of Wm. F. Anderson, of Columbia, and daughter of Geo. Knight, Esq., of Winchester, Virginia.

At his residence in Richland Dist.,on the night of the 2d inst., Mr. James Hopkins, in the 71st year of his age....

Issue of July 27, 1844

Married on Wednesday evening 17th inst., by the Rev. Dr. Hanckell, John J. Hanahan, of Edisto Island, to Eugenia Olivia, eldest daughter of Thomas Gelzer, Esq.

On Thursday evening 18th inst., by the Rev. Benjamin M. Palmer, D. D., Ralph Bailey, Esq. of St. John's, Colleton, to Miss Constantial Clementina, second daughter of J. B. Whitridge, Esq., of this city.

In Newnan, Geo., on the evening of the 4th inst.,by the Rev. J. Y. Alexander, William McBride, Esq., of Fayetteville, to Miss Sophia McKenzie, of the former place.

On the 16th inst., by the Rev. J. Barr, at Lancaster, Pa., Robert A. Pringle, Esq. of this city to Clara M., daughter of the late Rev. William Ashmead, of Philadelphia.

Died on the 8th inst.,in this city, Dr. John Turnbull Pratt, in the 46th year of his age...He was a native of this place, but for the last 12 years resided in Alabama...left a widow and widowed mother....

Departed this life on 3d April last, in Marengo Co., Ala., Mrs. Mary Ann Price, wife of Dr. William S. Price, aged 34 years and 8 months...born in Sumter Dist., S. C....joined the M. E. Church at age 15....
On the 4th inst., in Eatonton, Ga., Major Albert Jones, in the 40th year of his age.
On the 7th inst., at his residence near Columbus, Geo., Milton Williams, Esq.,Solicitor General of the Chattahoochee Circuit.
In Jasper Co., Ga., on the 23d ult.,the Rev. David L. Adams, in the 46th year of his age.

Issue of August 3, 1844

Married at Columbia, on the 13th June last, by the Rev. Dr. Leland, his second daughter Miss Hannah Napier, to the Rev. Abner A. Porter, of Greene Co., Alabama.
Married at Legareville, on the 25th inst., by the Rev. Dr. White, Dr. Charles Tennent, to Mary Julia, daughter of John A. Fripp, Esq.
Departed this life on the 27th ult., Mrs. Eliza Berkley Flinn, relict of the late Rev. Dr. Andrew Flinn, of this city, in the 80th year of her age....
Died on the 11th July, Mary Ellen Postell, infant daughter of James R. and Sarah E. Gready, aged 6 months and 24 days....
Died at his residence in Fairfield Dist.,near Winnsboro', on the 5th of March, John Mushatt, in the 66th year of his age... a native of Cambridge, New York, but removed to Charleston, S. C., and resided at that place for many years....

Issue of August 10, 1844

Died at the U. S. Hotel, Augusta, Ga.,on Wednesday 21st ult., Mr. James Laurence Frazer, in the 31st year of his age, a native of this city, but for several years past a resident of that state.
Died in Sumter Dist.,on the 25th ult., Mary Jane, only daughter of Mrs. Mary Hudson, aged 11 years....
Died at Tuscaloosa, Ala., on the 8th July, aged 9 months, Jane Bavden, daughter of Rev. J. B. and Mrs. Laleah G. Dunwody.

Issue of August 17, 1844

Married on THursday the 1st inst., by the Rev. John Forrest, Mr. Samuel Wiley, to Miss Ann Knox, daughter of the late Walter Knox, all of this city.
On the 7th inst., at Newbury, by the Rev. Mr. Cater, Chancellor J. Johnston, to Miss Aurelia DeWalt.
Died, on the 30th ult., at the residence of her uncle, Dr. E. R. Henderson, St. Bartholomew's Parish, Sarah Webber Smith, in the 11th year of his age....

Issue of August 24, 1844

Married on Thursday 15th inst., by the Rev. Dr. Hanckel, Capt. Daniel B. Vincent to Josephine F., daughter of the late Richard F. Howard.
Died in Georgetown, S. C., on the 16th inst.,Miss Sarah Cannon Wakefield, in the 75th year of her age.
Departed this life on the 26th of July 1844, in Sumpter Dist., S. C., Mrs. Naomi Plowden, wife of Mr. James Plowden, aged 27 years 9 months and 23 days...M. E. Church.

Issue of August 31, 1844

Died in this city on Wednesday evening the 21st inst., Mr. George Modett, in the 44th year of his age...a native of Dunse, Berwickshire, Scotland...Ruling Elder in the 2d Presbyterian Church.....

Died at her residence in Union Dist., S. C., on the 19th inst., Mrs. Mary Tomson...member of Fairforest Presbyterian Church.

(Two obits very dim in this issue--one appears to be a Thomas W. Baxter.)

Issue of September 7, 1844

Married on Thursday 29th inst., at St. Peters' Church, by the Rev. Mr. Barnwell, Mr. William G. Hunting, of this city, to Miss Alzada Susan, daughter of the late Ezekiel Wood, Esq., of Savannah, Ga.

Died on Monday 26th ult.,at the residence of Mr. J. B. Rhame, Wassamasaw, St. James, Goose Creek, Dr. James S. Shingler, in the 30th year of his age.

Issue of September 14, 1844

Death of Joseph Ellison, Esq., a citizen and merchant, of the firm of Law & Ellison, at his residence in this city on Tuesday evening last, aged 54.   Columbia So. Carolinian.

Departed this life on the 31st Aug., Mary Crawford, the elder daughter of the Rev. A. G. and M. E. Peden, aged 6 years and 3 months....

Died in Athens, Ga., on Sunday the 1st inst., Charles Coppee second son of Dr. Edward Coppee, of Savannah, a member of the Jr. class of Franklin College, aged 17 years and 3 months.

Issue of September 21, 1844

Died in this city on the 7th inst., William Henry Ogier, second son of the late Thomas Ogier.

In Richmond, at the residence of Col. John Rutherford, on the 7th inst., in the 7th year of his age, James Butler, only son of James B. and Anna Margaret Campbell, of this city.

Issue of October 19, 1844

Married on Thursday the 10th inst., by the Rev. Mr. Forrest, Mr. Augustus P. Wilmans, to Miss Jane M. Ferguson, both of this city.

On Thursday evening 10th inst., by the Rev. Dr. Post, Mr. Davis Taft, to Miss Julia Ann, daughter of the late Nathaniel Green Hillard, all of this city.

On Thursday 10th inst., by the Rev. Mr. Stacey, Mr. James W. McMillan, to Miss Amelia Eliza, second daughter of the late James Fincklea, Esq., all of this city.

On the 8th inst., in Spartanburg Dist., S. C., by the Rev James H. Saye, Mr. Ramsom Tinsly to Miss Isabella J. Foster, second daughter of Mr. Andrew Foster.

Also, by the same on the 10th inst., in Union District, Mr. Francis Hobson, to Miss Margaret Ann, only surviving daughter of Col. Samuel Beaty.

On the 13th inst., in Laurens Dist., S. C., by the Rev. E. F. Hyde, Mr. Thomas J. Newman, to Miss Jane Anderson.

Died on Indian River, E. F., in September last, Dr. Moses Holbrook, formerly of Charleston, S. C., aged about 60 years.

Died at Hudsonville, Miss., on the 20th ult., Mrs. Mary W. Gray, wife of Rev. Daniel L. Gray...a native of S. C.,born May 28, 1813, and joined the Presbyterian Church at the age of 16... married Rev. Daniel L. Gray but a few years afterwards....left husband and children (long eulogy)

Issue of October 26, 1844

Married on Tuesday evening 15th inst., by the Rev. Dr. Bachman, Mr. Samuel P. Bennet, of this city, to Miss Grimball P., third daughter of the late Robert S. Jenkins, of Edisto Island.

On Thursday morning 24th inst., by the Rev. Mr. Gildersleeve, Mr. Peter A. Horn, merchant, to Miss Amelia M. K. Webb, all of this city.

Died on the 27th ult.,at Davidson College, Mr. Samuel J. Fraser, in the 10th year of his age...son of Mr. Thomas Fraser, of Sumter Dist., and a member of the Jr. Class in College....

Issue of November 2, 1844

Married on the 24th ult., by the Rev. Mr. Barnwell, Dr. W. Michel, to Miss Anne Loughton Smith, daughter of the late Capt. David Campbell.

On Tuesday 22d ult., by the Rev. Dr. Bachman, Mr. Edmund Bull, to Miss Evelina Bruen, all of this city.

In Chesterville, S. C.,on Tuesday evening 22d ult., by the Rev. John Douglas, Mr. Davis Melton, of Yorkville, to Miss Dary Bufort of the above place.

In Chester Dist., on Thursday evening 24th ult., by the Rev. John Douglass, Rev. James R. Gilland, to Miss Caroline, second daughter of Mr. Wilmot and Frances Gibbes, all of Chester Dist.

Died on Monday last, Mr. Charles Kiddell, one of the U. S. appraisers for the port of Charleston...left a large family....

Issue of November 9, 1844

Married on Wednesday evening, Oct. 30, by the Rev. Mr. Stacey, Capt. Daniel Wells, to Mrs. Frances A. Quinby, all of this city.

Died on the 3d inst., Mr. Edward C. Burch, of this city, in the 48th year of his age.

Died on the 22d Sept. last, at Galveston, Texas, Mrs. Eliza Franklin, daughter of William T. Brantly, D. D. of this city.

Died on the morning of the 28th of Oct., near Laurenceville, Gwinnett Co., Ga.,Mrs. Jane Peden, consort of James Peden, in the 72d year of her age...left husband and children.

Departed this life in his 17th year at the residence of his father in Upper Salem, Sumpter Dist., Thomas Drayton Fraser, son of Thomas Fraser, Esq...(long eulogy)

Issue of November 16, 1844

Married on Tuesday evening 28th inst., by the Rev. Geo. C. Gregg, Dr. Junius A. Mayes, to Miss Mary Frances Muldrow, all of Sumpter Dist.

In Dallas Co., Ala., on the 30th ult., by the Rev. F. B. Lee, Mr. George Haig, formerly of Charleston, to Miss Eugenia V., daughter of William Bower, Esq. of Mobile.

Died in Marion Dist., S. C., on Wednesday 6th inst., Mrs. Eliza C. Brown, wife of Rev. Joseph Brown, in the 36th year of her age....

Issue of November 23, 1844

Married on the 13th inst., by the Rev. Mr. Gildersleeve, Mr. Joseph Coppinberg, of Westphalia, to Miss Eliza Marshall, of this city.

On Thursday evening 14th inst., at the Lutheran Church, by Dr. Bachman, Wm. E. Haskell, Esq. to Miss Harriet E. Bachman, all of this city.

On Thursday evening 14th inst., by the Rev. Mr. Trapier, at St. Michael's Church, Mr. Jacob K. Sass, to Octavia, daughter of the late Jeremiah Murden, of this city.

On the 8th ult., by the Rev. Julius J. DuBose, Mr. Joseph A. Scott, to Miss Jane M. Thompson, both of Sumter Dist., S. C.

Departed this life Nov. 6th, 1844, Mr. Henry Tovey, aged 73 years and 8 months, a native of Rhode, Somersetshire, England, and for nearly 50 years a resident of this city...left aged widow, and an only daughter, with several grandchildren.

Died on the 27th ult., at his residence in Talbot Co., Ga., William Ratchford, in the 80th year of his age...born and raised in York Dist., S. C., but for the last 40 or 50 years a resident of Ga....

Issue of November 30, 1844

Married on the 19th inst.,at the 2d Presbyterian Church by the Rev. Dr. Smyth, Mr. James Shoolbred Drayton, to Miss Louisa Eleanor, youngest daughter of the late Capt. James M. Elford, all of this city.

On Tuesday evening 19th inst., by the Rev. Mr. Bachman, Mr. Thomas J. Burdell, to Miss Catharine Fuller Wilson of St. Paul's parish.

On Wed., the 20th inst.,at the 1st Baptist Church by the Rev. William Royall, Dr. N. V. Bailey of James Island, to Miss Ann Boyce, only daughter of the late George Henry, Esq. of this city.

On Thursday evening 21st inst.,by the Rev. Dr. Curtis, James M. Kennedy, Esq.,of Columbia, S. C., to Miss Mary Ann Williams, of this city.

On the 22d inst., by the Rev. Dr. Post, E. Sharpe, Esq., of Pendleton, S. C. to Miss Frances H., daughter of the late Gen. R. Y. Hayne.

In Milledgeville, Ga.,on the 19th inst., by the Rev. J. W. Baker, Rev. Charles A. Stillman, of Eutaw, Alabama, to Miss Martha Hammond, of Mildedgeville, Ga.

Died on the 19th inst., at the Parsonage, on John's Island, Mrs. Dinah Young, in the 76th year of her age.

Issue of December 7, 1844

Married on Tuesday eveing 26th ult., by the Rev. Dr. Bachman, John J. Foran, of Ireland, to Mary Adeline, eldest daughter of John H. Schreiner, Esq., of this city.

On Tuesday evening 26th ult., by the Rev. Mr. Keith, James Reid Pringle, Esq.,to Miss Sarah Gilmor, daughter of James H. Ladson, Esq.,both of this city.

On Wednesday evening 27th ult., by the Rev. Dr. Bachman, William G. Carrere, to Anna, only daughter of William Roper Brailsford, Esq., all of this city.

On Thursday 28th ult., by the Rev. Dr. Post, Mr. Michael Bryan, to Miss Harriet Marion, youngest daughter of the late Samuel Dwight, of St. John's, Berkley.

On Thursday evening 28th ult.,by the Rev. Dr. Post, E. N. Miller, to Sarah Maria, daughter of the Joseph S. Coates, of

Philadelphia.

Issue of December 14, 1844

Married on the 5th inst., by the Rev. Mr. C. Hanckel, Mr. Thomas Waring, junr. to Miss Harriet E., daughter of the late Mr. John Mauger, both of this city.

Married on Wednesday eveing 11th inst., in St. Philip's Church, by the Rev. J. B. Campbell, Mr. Benjamin Johnson, of Edisto Island, to Miss Mary Jane Coleman, of this city.

In Savannah, Ga., on Thursday evening 6th inst.,by the Rev. Mr. Wyer, Lieut. William M. Wilson, U. S. R. M., to Miss Elizabeth L., youngest daughter of the late Samuel B. Webb of that city.

Died at his residence on Little River, Fairfield Dist., S. C., on the 27th ult., Charles Bell, Esq.,in the 61st year of his age.

Died on the 16th ult., at his place, well known as the "Big Spring," in the 63d year of his age, Major William Henry Robinson, a native of Barnwell Dist., S. C., but for about the last 20 years a resident of the country.

Issue of December 21, 1844

Married on Thursday 12th inst., by the Rev. John Campbell, William Ward Davenport, of Boston, Mass., to Miss Julian Emelia Monefeldt, of this city.

On the 14th inst., by the Rev. W. Hoemsooth, Mr. Johannes Eckerd, from the Kingdom of Bavaria, to Mrs. Maria Bertram from Marringen, Kingdom of Hanover.

Another Revolutionary Patriot Gone. Died in this city, on the 23d ult.,in the 81st year of his age, Capt. Napthali Raymond ...native of Norwalk, in Conn....

Issue of January 4, 1845

Married on Wednesday evening 25 Dec.,by the Rev. Wm. T. Brantley, Jr., James R.Addison to Adeline E.,daughter of James English, Esq., all of this city.

Married on Tuesday evening the 17th ult., by the Rev. Dr. Hanckel, Dr. P. C. Gaillard, to Henrietta E., daughter of the late Samuel Wragg.

Departed this life on the evening of the 20th ult., Robert J. Howard, aged 27 years.

Died in Greenville Dist., S. C., on the 27th of Oct. last, Mr. Runnell Dill, aged 87 years a native of North Carolina, and a soldier of the Revolution.

Issue of January 11, 1845

Married on the 31st of Dec., by the Rev. P. McNab, Rev. M. A. Patterson, of Barbour Co., Ala., to Miss Ann McRae, of Early Co., Ga.

On Thursday 2d inst., by the Rev. Dr. Gilman, William Henry Swinton, to Josephine G., youngest daughter of Philip Moore, Esq., all of this city.

On the 5th inst., at Mr. A. Rayser's by the Rev. R. J. Limehouse, Mr. J. W. Sleigh, to Mrs. Harriet Barns, all of Colleton Dist., S. C.

Died at Ebenezer, Ga., on Saturday 38th (sic) ult., Mrs. Caroline M. Strobel, consort of the Rev. P. A. Strobel....

Died at the residence of her father (Dr. Charles West) in Haynesville, Houston Ga., on Friday 29th Nov., Miss Elizabeth M. West....

Died of Cholera Infantum, on the 28th of Dec. 1844, at Monroe Church, six miles from Pontotoc, Miss., Catharine Mary Elder, second daughter of Rev. M. and E. C. Peden, aged 1 year, 6 months and 8 days....

Issue of January 18, 1845

Married on Wednesday evening 8th inst., by the Rev. Dr. Bachman, Mr. Horace Massot, jr., to Jane Ann, second daughter of John Andrew Blum, Esq., all of this city.

In this city on the 9th inst.,by the Rev. Nathan Hoyt, D. D., of Athens, Ga., the Hon. F. W. Pickens of Abbeville Dist., to Miss Marion A., second daughter of Mr. Wm. Dearing.

In St. Paul's Parish, on Thursday evening the 9th inst., by the Rev. Philip Gadsden, Robert H. Garden, Esq., to Miss Susan M., daughter of Thomas W. Boone, Esq. of St. Paul's Parish.

On Thursday evening 14th Nov. last, by the Rev. James P. McMullen, Dr. John G. McKeme, of West Point, Ga., to Miss Margaret H., only daughter of Robert and Susannah McKeme, Tuscaloosa Co., Carthage, Ala.

Another Revolutionary Soldier gone. Departed this life on the 5th December, Mr. William Purse, aged 84 years....

Issue of February 8, 1845

Married on the 3d inst., by the Rev. John Forrest, Francis J. Betts, of this city to Miss Horatia Ellenor, daughter of the late Mr. B. M. Haigir(?) of New York.

Died at Beech Island, Edgefield Dist., on the 16th Jan., Mrs. Mary, relict of Benjamin Bowers, in the 60th year of her age, leaving three children....

Departed this life at Warrenton, Abbeville Dist., S. C., on the 21st ult., John Thompson Huey, in the 20th year of his age, leaving a father and two sisters.....

Issue of February 15, 1845

Married on Thursday evening 6th inst., at St. Phillips Church, by the Right Rev. Bishop Gadsden, Wm. Alston Pringle, to Emma P., daughter of Robert Smith, Esq.

On Thursday 6th inst., at Strawberry Chapel, St. John's Berkley, by the Rev. Mr. Wallace, Keating Lewis Simons, Esq., to Miss Augusta Melanie, youngest daughter of Augustus Taveau, Esq.

At James Island, on Thursday evening last, 6th inst., by Rev. Mr. Fleming, Joseph M. Mikell, to Cornelia, second daughter of Croskeys Royall, Esq., both of that Island.

Issue of February 22, 1845

Death of Judge Eckhard...Hon. George B. Eckhard, Judge of the City Court...died on Tuesday morning last, in the 51st year of his age....

We learn (says the Columbia Chronicle of the 19th inst.,)that the Rev. Ferdinand Jacobs, his wife, child and nurse, all died on the night of the 31st ult. at Yorkville in this State. Mr. Jacobs was the Pastor of the Presbyterian Church and principal of the Female Academy of that village.

Married on Tuesday morning last, by the Rev. Mr. Capers, Mr. Rufus K. Evans of Macon, Ga.,to Mrs. Eleanor P. R. Burdell, eldest daughter of B. R. Gitsinger, of this city.

Issue of March 1, 1845

Died in Edgefield Dist., S. C., on the 12th inst.,Mr. John Culbreath, in the 70 year of his age.
At Key West, on the 11th inst., Dr. J. H. Williamson, aged 36 years, a native of S. C.
Departed this life on the 6th ult., at Guinea in the Island of Cuba, Francis D. Hort, fo the firm of Gadsden & Nephew, in the 27th year of his age....

Issue of March 8, 1845

Married on Thursday 27th ult., by the Rev. Dr. Post, Mr. Thomas Roper, of John's Island, to Miss Elizabeth C. Lewis, of this city.
On Thursday 27th ult., by the Rev. Dr. Bachman, Mr. Ralph Earle to Miss Amanda N., youngest daughter of the late Dr. John Mackey, of this city.
On the evening of the 5th inst.,by the Rev. Mr. Keith, William Henry Peronneau to Martha Blake, youngest daughter of the late William Washington.
On Tuesday 4th inst., by the Rev. Mr. Pritchard, Dr. F. T. Matthews, to Miss Sarah D. Richbourg, both of this city.
On Tuesday evening 4th inst., by the Rev. Mr. Keith, at St. Michael's Church, Lieut. J. Stewart, U. S. Army, to Octavia, daughter of the late Dr. Jas. H. Gayssoux.
On Monday evening 3d inst., at Eutaw, by the Rev. Mr. Dehon, Richard J. Manning, Esq.,to Miss Eliza A., daughter of Wm. Sinkler, Esq.
At Silverton, Barnwell, on the 26th ult., by the Rev. B. Gildersleeve, Rev. E. F. Hyde, to Miss Caroline A. Hammond.
Died in this city on the 26th ult.,Mrs. Mary Hayes Lucas, wife of Col. Jonathan Lucas, aged 40 years and 6 months....
At Augusta, Ga., on the 24th ult., Mrs. Mary Ann Olivia Longstreet, wife of William Longstreet, Esq., in the 38th year of her age.
At Ashville, N. C.,on the 17th ult., Mr. Jacob Martin, a soldier of the Revolution, aged about 82 years.

Issue of March 15, 1845

Married on Tuesday evening 4th inst., by the Rev. T. Huggins, Mr. Charles M. Jefford, to Miss N. Matilda Barnes, of this city.
On the 13th ult., by the Rev. W. H. Davis, Sandford Holmes, Jr., of this place, to Susan Amelia, second daughter of Philip LaRoy, of Abbeville Dist., S. C.
Departed this life on the 8th ult.,in York Dist., S. C., Dr. J. F. Watson, a native of that District, and a successful practitioner.
Died in Savannah, on the 26th ult., on the 69th anniversary of her birth day, Mrs. Clarissa Shellman, relict of the late Col. John Shellman

Issue of March 22, 1845

Married on Tuesday evening 18th inst.,by the Rev. Dr.Hanckel, Mr. J. Hume Lucas, to Miss Eleanor B., third daughter of Thomas G. Simons, Esq.
Married on the 17th inst., by the Rev. Dr. R. Post, Mr. B. Franklin DeBow, to Josephine E. Q. Bell, all of this city.
At Montrepos, St. Luke's Parish, on the 13th inst., by the Rev. Mr. Reid, Col. Isadore Lartigue, of St. Peters, to Miss Adela G., eldest daughter of Samuel R. Gillson, Esq.

Died on the morning of the 4th inst., Mr. Samuel N. Stevens... recently attained his 49th year. (eulogy)

Issue of March 29, 1845

Married on Tuesday the 18th inst., by the Rev. C. H. Pritchard, Mr. Charles Smith, to Miss Frances, daughter of the late William Hamlin.

On the 6th inst., at Bluffton, by the Rev. Joseph R. Walker, John J. Stoney, to Agnes M., daughter of James Kirk, Esq.

Died at his residence near Clinton, Greene co., Ala., on the 19th ult., Mr. Charles M. Barry, in the 69th year of his age... the death of his daughter Miss Margaret Rosanna, who departed this life on 24th Sept last, in the 21st year of her age. She died in an adjoining county....a native of S. C., removed to Perry Co., in 1830....

Died in this city on Friday the 21st inst., Catharine Dalton, wife of James M. Jeannerett, of Charleston, and daughter of the late Dr. Fitzgerlad Bird, of Columbus, Geo....

Departed this life on the 12th inst., Mrs. Elizabeth Miller, consort of Mr.William B. Miller of Crawford County, leaving a husband, four children a widowed mother, brothers and sisters... member of the Presbyterian Church at Hopewell, Crawford County....

Issue of April 5, 1845

Died, in this city on the 20th of March, Mrs. Amelia, wife of Mr. Thomas R. Vardell, and only daughter of the late Henry Tovey, Esq., in the 27th year of her age....

Died on the 26th ult., while on a visit in Anderson Dist., George I., son of the late Isaac S. Bailey, of this city, having just entered his 9th year....

Issue of April 12, 1845

Married on Thursday evening 3d inst., by the Rev. Wm. C. Dana, Edward Mallory Burch, Esq., to Miss Rosamond Susan, eldest daughter of Copeland Stiles, Esq. all of this city.

Died at Aiken, S. C., on the 27th March last, Mr. William W. Williams, in the 59th year of his age.

Died in Pickens Dist., S. C.,on the 25th ult., Mr. David W. Hamilton, in the 65th year of his age, leaving a wife and 15 children.

Issue of April 19, 1845

Died at his residence in St. Thomas Parish, on the 8th inst., Maurice Simons, in the 60th year of his age....

Died at Mt. Zion, Geo. on the 5th inst.,at an advanced age, Mrs. Deborah, wife of Dr. Timothy W. Rossetter (Eulogy).

Issue of April 26, 1845

Married on Thursday evening 10th inst., by the Rev. S. H. Hay, Dr. Thomas T. Hay, to Miss Rhoda Marion Furse, all of Barnwell Dist.

Issue of May 3, 1845

Married on Wednesday 23d inst., by the Rev. Daniel DuPre, John A. Leland, Esq.,to Miss Ann Allston, eldest daughter of Rev. Daniel DuPre.

Married on Tuesday evening the 29th of April, by the Rev. Mr. Gildersleeve, Mr. James McElmoyle, to Miss Eliza, daughter of Wm. McElmoyle, Esq. of this city.
Died, very suddenly, in Greene Co., Ala., on the 20th of Apr., Mrs. Hannah, wife of the Rev. A. A. Porter, and daughter of the Rev. Dr. Leleand of Columbia, S. C....left husband, infant daughter and parents, brothers and sisters....

Issue of May 10, 1845

Died in Columbia, S. C., on Thursday morning, 24th ult., Mrs. Harriet Jane Crawford, wife of Mr. Andrew Crawford, and daughter of Dr. George W. Glenn, of Newbury Dist., in the 29th year of her age....
Died, at Ashepoo, on the 1st inst., Edward Pinckney, youngest son of Daniel S. and Caroline R. Henderson of Walterborough, aged 2 months and 4 days.

Issue of May 17, 1845

Married in Mecklenburg Co., N. C. on Wednesday evening, the 16th April, by the Rev. B. H. Morrison, D. D., the Rev. H. B. Cunningham, to Miss Dovey Adelaide Winslow, eldest daughter of the late D. M. W. Alexander, M. D.
Died in this city on the 26th ult., Mrs. Mary Brisbane, relict of the late Wm. Brisbane, Esq., in the 71st year of her age....
On Saturday evening the 10th inst, Mrs. Harriet B. Pain, in the 49th year of her age.
Died at Warrenton, Abbeville, S. C., on Wednesday morning, 7th inst., about 4 o'clock, in the 49th year of his age, Mr. James Huey, Esq., Post Master. a native of Lancaster Dist., S. C., Waxhaw settlement, removed to Abbeville Dist.,about 1820.

Issue of May 24, 1845

Married on the evening of Wednesday 14th May, in the 2d Presbyterian Church by the Rev. Dr. Thomas Smyth, Mr. Robert Man, to Miss Eliza J., Whitaker, all of this place.
Died on the 1st inst.,at the Grove, the residence of her uncle, Dr. J. S. Reid, Abbeville Dist., S. C., Mrs. L. M. W. Gibert, wife of Mr. S. F. Gibert, and daughter of the Rev. R. B. and Mrs. L. M. Cater, aged 22 years, leaving a husband and other relatives....

Issue of May 31, 1845

Married on Thursday evening last, the 22d inst., by the Rev. Dr. Gilman, William L. Webb, to Miss Mary E., eldest daughter of George Gibbon, Esq., all of this city.
Died in this city on the 18th inst. Lawton Cooper, son of George W. and Sophia Cooper, aged 2 years 6 months and 5 days.

Issue of June 14, 1845

Married on the 4th inst., by the Rev. Mr. Barnwell, the Rev. Stephen Elliott, of Beaufort Dist., to Sarah G. Baron, daughter of H. A. DeSaussure, Esq.
Departed this life on the 29th of May, 1845, Mrs. Mary Mazyck, widow of Stephen Mazyck, deceased at the advanced age of 81 years and six months.
Death of Dr. James Durant who departed this life at his

residence in Sumterville, S. C., on the 2d inst., in the 33d year of his age....left wife and three small children.

Issue of June 21, 1845

Married at St. Paul's Church, on Thursday evening the 12th inst.,by the Rev. Dr. Hanckell, Major William Postell Ingraham, to Hannah Harleston, daughter of Robert H. Quash, Esq.,both of this city.
On Thursday evening 12th inst.,by the Rev. Paul Trapier, Mr. William J. Smith, to Miss Mary C., daughter of Wm. Lindsey, Esq., all of this city.
On the morning of the 18th inst., by the Rev. Mr. Dupon, Mr. George A. Hyde, of Bridgeport, Conn., to Miss Amanda D. Groves, of this city.
On the 19th inst., by the Rev. C. H. Pritchard, J. B. N. Hammet, Esq., of Sumter Dist., to Miss Anna W., daughter of John Clark, Esq. of this place.
The Knoxville (Tenn.) Register announced the marriage in Jefferson Co., to Mr. Frederick Pulse, age 102 years to Miss Dorcass Mannon aged 30 years.
Departed this life on the 12th inst., Mrs. Mary Enslow, in the 75th year of her age, a native of Nova Scotia, but for the last 50 years a resident of this city. She was of a family, a part of whom suffered severely in what is known as the Old French war....
Died on Monday morning 9th inst., at the residence of the Hon. B. F. Porter, in the vicinity of Tuscaloosa, Ala., Joseph J. Porter, Esq.,Attorney at Law, aged 25 years...a native of this city and resided here until 1836....

Issue of June 28, 1845

Married in this city on the 18th inst., by the Rev. Dr. Gilman, Col. W. Gates, U. S. Army, to Miss Harriet Louisa, daughter of Mr. Artemus Carter, of Portland, Me.
Died at his residence near Abbeville, S. C., on the 14th inst., Mr. John Gillespie, in the 81st year of his age.
At Calcutta, on the 26th of March last, Thomas Bennett, Jr., of this city.

Issue of July 5, 1845

Married on the 24th ult., by the Rev. Dr. Post, Dr. John S. O'Hear, of St. Andrews Parish, to Miss Anna B., daughter of John B. Legare, Esq.
Married, on Thursday evening last, by the Rev. Dr. Bachman, Mr. Granville M. Bugby, of Burlington, N. J., to Miss Sophronia Matilda Dixon, of Charleston, S. C.
Died at Abbeville, S. C., on Tuesday night, the 17th ult., Mrs. Sarah B. Wardlaw, consort of Hon. D. L. Wardlaw, aged 38 years.
At Walterboro, on Tuesday the 24th ult., Maria A. Glover, wife of Dr. J. Edward Glover, formerly of this city.
Died at his residence in Morgan Co., Ala., on the 7th ult., Samuel Morrow, Esq., in the 70th year of his age...a native of S. C., emigrated to Alabama in 1817...one of the founders of the church at Somerville, and a Ruling Elder....

Issue of July 12, 1845

Married at Haddrell's Point, on Wednesday evening, 2d inst., by the Rev. Dr. Gadsden, Rev. J. R. Fell, of this city, to Miss Sarah, eldest daughter of John Hamlin, Esq. of Christ Church.
At Scottsboro, Ga.,on the 25th ult., by the Rev. Mr. Baker, Dr. John Howard Furman, of S. C., to Catherine Eliza, daughter of Col. F. Carter.
Died in the 70 year of his age, Wm. McElmoyle, Esq., a native of Ireland, County Antrim, but for the greater part of the last 45 years a resident of this city. A few years previous to his death, he removed to Double Branches, Anderson, and received the appointment of Post Master....
Died in this city on the 25th ult., Mrs. Mary F., wife of George Cannon, Jr., in the 30th year of her age...member of the Presbyterian Church 6 years....
Died in Union Dist., S. C., on the 24th ult., in the 60th year of her age, Mrs. Margaret McJunkin, wife of Abraham McJunkin, sen...native of Union Dist., and the oldest daughter of Capt. John and Sarah Savage...a member of Cane Creek Church....

Issue of July 19, 1845

Married at McPhersonville, on the 1st inst., by the Rev. Mr. James Dunwoodie, Mr. A. F. Gregorie, Jun., to Miss E. L. Bacot, both of Prince William's Parish.
Died on the 25th ult., Mrs. Mary Mathewes, relict of the late George Mathewes, Esq.,deceased....
Died on the 26th day of May 1845, in Tallapoosa Co., Ala., at the residence of Mr. Zechariah James, Matthew Harris, a revolutionary soldier, aged 100 years...a native of North Carolina, Mecklenburg County....one of the member who constituted Bethany Church, Greene Co., Alabama....

Issue of July 26, 1845

Married at St. Michael's Church, on Thursday 17th inst., by the Rev. Mr. Keith, Mr. Isaac Lesasen, to Miss Mary Louisa, daughter of Edward Blake, Esq.
On the 24th ult.,by the Rev. Mr. Colburn, Mr. D. H. Farmer, to Miss Charlotte Smith, eldest daughter of Dr. Wm. S. Price, all of St. Paul's Parish.
In Gillisonville, on Thursday evening the 17th ult.,by the Rev. Stephen Elliott, of McPhersonville, Dr. Thomas H. Gregorie, to Miss Martha H., second daughter of Mr. Samuel R. Gillison, all of Beaufort District, S. C.
Departed this life in McPhersonville, on the 14th inst., Col. James S. McPherson, in the 36th year of his age.
Departed this life at his residence in Fairfield Dist., on the 2d inst., Mr. William Bell, in the 70th year of his age....

Index prepared by Mary Elizabeth Phillips

Aarons, Maj. John 22
Abbot, Dr. Joel 148
Abbs, Augustus 119
Abernathy, Henry G. 14
  Lecy 8
Aborn, Sarah R. 5
Adair, Sally 19
Adams, Capt. ___ 160
  Rev. David L. 202
  Ebenezer Jr. 129
  Edward 126
  Eliza 158
  Erixene 198
  Etsel L. 193
  Frances Elizabeth 51
  Rev. J.M.H. 93
  James S. 198
  Rev. James S. 93
  Jane 4
  Jane E. 15
  Rev. Dr. Jasper (off.) 133
  John 15,160
  Joseph 51
  Professor ___ 129
  Rev. Dr. (off) 73
  Rev. Mr. (off) 137
  Rev. Rt. (off) 17
  Samuel 158
  Susan 22
  Thomas K.J. 68
  William M. 72
Addison, E.A. 47
  Susannah 2
  William 2
Adarine, Rachael 121
Addison, Edward 192
  James R. 206
  Jane B. 147
  William 147
Addy, Thomas E. 168
Adger, Andrew Moffett 170
  Elizabeth Ann 148
  Isabella W. 63
  James 64
  Rev. John B. 87
  Margaret H. 170
  Margaret M. 64
  Robert 114,148
  William 160,170,183
  William Raw 179
Adrian, William 40
Aggnew, Susan A.M. 9
Agnew, Mary Nelson 69
Aiken, Henrietta 75
  William 49
Aikman, Rev. Mr. Alexander 52
Airey, Mary E. 23
Alderson, J.F. 118
Aldrich, A. Jr. 100
  Letitia 54

Aldrich (cont'd)
  Nicedemus 144
  Robert 145
  Dr. Whipple 54
Alexander, Agnes 16
  Dr. Amvi 31
  Amanda C. 54
  Angelina 148
  Augustin Sloan 158
  D.M.W. 210
  David 187
  Dovey Adelaide Winslow 210
  Eli O. 18
  Elizabeth 7
  Francis 121,152
  J.Y. 59
  Rev. J.Y. (off.) 138,201
  James 7
  Maj. John 38
  John G. 13
  John Newton 170
  Joseph Houston 59
  Mahulda 158
  Maria B. 177
  Mary 126
  Rachel 8
  Rev. Mr. (off.) 81
  Capt. S. 126
  Capt. Samuel 177
  Samuel F. 158
  Rev. Thomas 115
Alison, Caroline 63
  Jacob H. 63
  Dr. Lockwood 105(2)
  Stephen Lee 132
  see Allison
Allan, Capt. ___ 111(2)
  Mary K. 63
  Mary C. 97
  Dr. Richard 104
  Robert M. 97
  Susan M. 82
  Thomas 6
  William 63,82
Allen, Rev. D.O. 58
  Eliza 58
  Elizabeth A. 134
  Elizabeth C. 18
  Harriett S. 45
  Harris 29
  Horatio 92
  Rev. James 47
  James R. 48
  John C. 45
  Mary 58
  Mary M. 62
  Samuel 62
  Sarah 47
  Sarah M. 44
  Thomas 16
  William 44

Alley, F.H. 117
Allison, Jane Eliza 181
  Judge ___ 124
  Dr. Lockwood 181
  Oni 127
  see Alison
Allman, John R. 96
Allston, Evelina C. 97
  Joseph W. 63,172
  Margaret H. 29
  Mary 172
  see Alston
Ally, Sarah 48
Alston, Col. Absalom 21
  Charlotte A. 15
  Henrietta 24
  Col. J.A. 19
  J.H. 9
  Col. John A. 100
  Julianna Ellen 9
  Mary Brewton 145
  Col. Robert W. 131
  Sarah M. 19
  Thomas 100
  Col. William 145,150
  Col. William A. 178
  see Allston
Amesburg, Agness M. 179
Amidon, Jebediah 154
Ancrum, Ann W. 82
  James H. 82,115,178
  Julia Emma 115
  Louisa E. 178
  William 3
  Capt. William 55
  Wm. Washington 66
Anderson, David 129
  Dr. ___ 185
  Eliza Harriet 174
  Emily C. 185
  Hannah 129
  Isabella R. 184
  James 55,165,179
  James Bowman 159
  James K. 104
  James M. 55
  Jane 203
  John 37,55
  John L. 110
  John P. 201
  Joseph A. 185
  Julia Ellen 192
  Marion 177
  Marion S. 185
  Rev. Dr. (off.) 125
  Robert 174
  Samuel 132
  Sydney Ann 201
  Thomas J. 15
  William F. 82,201
Andrews, Edwin R. 53
  Samuel R. 29
  Sarah N. 8

Angel, Elizabeth Anna Martha 114
  Julius U.G. 114
Annely, Felix L. 58
Anthony, Ann 114
  Elizabeth C. 21
  Isaac 6
  James 21
  Capt. J.C. 164
  Martha 12
  Capt. J.C. 164
  Martha 12
  Sarah C. 165
Antony, Julia Ann 99
  Milton 99
Appleby, Col. Richard 163
  Sarah Ann Caroline 163
Appleton, Ann 2
  Dr. ___ 45
  William 45
Archer, Benjamin 135
Archibald, Samuel 43
Ard, Eliza 43
Ardis, Sarah R.M. 110
Area, Caroline Elizabeth 30
Ariail, John 21
Armstrong, Anne 14
  Elizabeth 40
  Martha Catharine 167
  Rev. Mr. (off.) 145
  Capt. W. 2
  William George 119
  William G. 193
Arnau, Michael 38
Arnold, Joseph 32
  Kezia 39
Arthur, Julia 3
  Susan 7
Arthurs, Joseph W. 198
  Lydia 198
Artman, John 174
  Margaret Eliza 132
  Martha Ann 168
  Peter 132
Ashby, James Alexander 139
Ashe, Mary J. 54
  Maj. Richard 54
Ashley, William Sr. 20(2)
Ashmead, Clara M. 201
  Rev. William 201
Askew, Amanda J. 26
Atkins, Dr. Charles 69
  Ellen 16
  James 15
Atkinson, Edmund C. 32
  Rev. Mr. (off.) 128
Audubon, John W. 128
  Mary Eliza 169
  Victor G. 155,169
Augustine, Maria Caroline 140
Auld, Anne P. 191
  Rev. D.J. 135,160,191

Auld, Martha Frances 191
Austin, Chelaty 29
　Green Deberry 29
　Thomas 165
Avinett, Tabitah 9
Axon, Rev. I.S.K. (off.) 185
　O.T. 122
　Rev. Mr. (off.) 122
Axson, Ann 191
　E.S.B. 191
　Mary 67
　Mary Anna 175
　Sarah A. 123
Ayres, Martin 124

Bachlot, John Sr. 74
Bachman, Eliza 155
　Harriet E. 205
　Rev. Dr. John 169
　Rev. J. (off.) 92,107,120,165, 176,188,
　Rev. Dr. J. (off.) 155
　Rev. Dr. Jno. (off,) 133
　Rev. John (off.) 33,84,93(2), 113,119(2),
　Maria R. 128
　Rev. Dr. (off.) 80,91,104,108, 111,112,116,118,120,121,123(2), 124,125(2),126,128,132(2),133, 134,137(2),148,155(2),156,157, 158,162,163,167,168,175(2),176, 178,179,185,186,187(3),189,190, 192,193,195(2),196,197,198,204 (2),205(3),207,208,211
　Rev. Mr. (off.) 15,20,34,37, 39,40,45,46,47,49,52,55,59,61, 63,64,66,71,79,82,83,86,87(2), 90(2),95(2),96,98(2),101,105, 106,114,121,126,136,194,201,205.
Bacon, Mrs. J.W. 157
　James W. 169
　John B. 15
　John M. 9
　Mary J. 169,183
　Mary W.J. 183
　William 81
Bacot, Charles B.C. 149
　E.R. 212
　Eliza Ferguson 150
　Elizabeth S.W. 182
　Henrietta 182
　Col. Henry H. 77,172
　Mellicent J. 188
　Richard Wainwright 145
　Robert Cochran 172
　Robert Dewar 187
　Capt. Samuel 78
　Thomas W. 90,182
Badger, Elizabeth 10
　James 117,136
　Mary E. 176
　Sarah Bell 117

Bagby, A.P. 32
Bagge, Mrs. ___ 45
Bagle, Pvt. Matthew 111
Bagley, Mary Ann 31
Bailey, Ann C. 6
　Capt. Benjamin 172
　Edward D. 87
　Elizabeth L. 172
　George I. 209
　Isaac S. 209
　Isaac Sentor 191
　J.S. 37
　Lucy C. 69
　Margaret C. 50
　Dr. N.V. 205
　Dr. R.S. 6
　Rev. R.W. 69
　Rev. R.W. (off.) 78
　Rachel M. 81
　Ralph 201
　Dr. William M. 146
Baily, Gen. Mount Joe 109
Bainbridge, Elbridge 7
　Louisa A.W. 145
　Commodore Wm. 145
Baird, Col. A. 15
　Eliza C. 13
　Rev. Thomas Dickson 146
Baker, Maj. Benjamin 10
　Calvin 82
　Daniel 92
　F.A. 146
　Rev. J.W. (off.) 181
　John (off.) 181
　John N. 38
　Rev. John W. 124
　Martha E. 84
　Mosely 29
　Rev. Mr. (off.) 146,179, 185,212
　Rev. Richard M. 159
　Robert L. 137,189
　Sarah 23
　Susan 174
Balch, Stephen B. 77
Baldwin, Ann 11
　Mrs. R. 23
　Russell 63
　Capt. Samuel 13
　Dr. William 11
Ball, Alvyn 197
　Ann 135
　Elias O. Sr. 188
　Esther 190
　Isaac 176
　Jane 176
　John 66,135
　Lydia Catharine 66
　Martha Caroline 197
　Rev. Mr. (off.) 96
　William J. 176
Ballantine, Alexander John 198
　James 168

Ballow, Mary 33
Ballund, Caroline 55
Balst, Rev. Mr. (off.) 61
Bankhead, James 81
Banks, Rev. A.R. 140
  Rev. A.R. (off.) 140
  Anna Ford 107
  Catharine Jones 183
  Charles 107,122,183,185
  Eleanor C. 122
  Harriet Edwards 185
Bannister, ___ 151
Barber, Henry 110
  William 110
Bardley, ___ 88
  see Bradley
Barker, Amanda A.B. 50
  Henrietta C. 165
  J. Sanford 183
  Dr. Sanford N. 97
Barksdale, Adelaide Maria 132
  Thomas 132,169
Barnard, Chauncy 138
  Harriet 138
Barnes, Rev. Albert (off.) 127
  Elizabeth P. 17
  Joseph 44
  Mary 138
  N. Matilda 208
  see Barns
Barnet, Mary Anna 24
Barnett, Elizabeth 49
  Miss ___ 195
  Robert C. 14
  William N. 199
Barney, Mary Anna 23
Barnillon, Christopher 17
Barns, Dr. ___ 143
  Harriet 206
  James Douglass 174
  Capt. Samuel 47
  William 47
  see Barnes
Barnwell, Col. Edward 105
  Maj. Michael 17
  Rev. Mr. (off.) 97,110,124,
  125,127(2),128,131,136(2),144,
  153,156,159,161,166,167,173(2),
  173(2),183,185(2),188,189,203,
  204,210
  Rev. W.H. (off.) 185
  Rev. William (off.) 158
  Rev. Wm. H. (off.) 183,191
Baron, Dr. ___ 68
  Isabel Ann 68
  Laura Louisa 53
Barr, Rev. J. (off.) 201
  John 61
  Mary Elizabeth 186
  Rev. Dr. (off.) 33,155
Barrett, Edward 101
  Ellen S. 48(2)

Barrett (cont'd)
  Dr. Isaiah DuBose 182
  Thomas 43,48(2)
Barringer, Mary 20
Barron, Dr. Alexander L. 176
Barry, Dr. A.L. 153
  Charles M. 209
  Margaret J. 153
  Margaret Rosanna 209
  Rev. Dr. (off.) 149
  see Berry
Barsden, Sarah 176
Barsh, David 95
Bartlett, Elizabeth M. 194(2)
  Franklin M. 121,194
  Rev. J.L. 131
  Maria Theresa 194
  Dr. Myron 54
  William Scott 194(2)
Barton, Aaron 118
  Elizabeth Mary 118
  Willoughby 27
Bascom, Martha Reynolds 145
Baskin, James 14
Baskins, Mary Stewart 22
Bason, William P. 88
Bass, Rev. H. (off.) 190,192
  Rev. Mr. (off.) 82(2)
  Sarah Eaton 41
Bates, Anna D. 17
  Thomas G. 17
Battey, Cynthia Ann 63
Battle, Rev. Elisha 140
  Uriah 26
Baudry, Dr. Augustus 35
Baugh, Virginia 16
Baxter, Elizabeth 199
  Rev. Dr. (off.) 132
  Thomas W. 203
Bay, Andrew 83
  E.H. 106
  Judge ___ 107
  Martha D. 10
  Sarah 106,107
Bayard, Andrew 64
Bayle, Col. Charles 132
Beach, Rev. Abraham 29
  Addison 187
  E. Mills 168
  Rev. Dr. 11
Bealer, Charles Junius 130
  Martha H. 130
Beall, Narcissa 2
  Maj. Robert A. 29,30,73
  Gen. Robert Augustus 114
  Susan Ann 73
  Z. 2
Beard, Moses 71
  Sarah Jane 145
  Sarah M. 31(2)
Bearing, Charles 95
Beasley, Rev. (off.) 56

Beasley (cont'd)
  Robert C. 31
  see Beazley
Beasly, Philip T. 15
Beattie, Fountarin F. 84
Beatty, Robert R. 14
Beaty, Margaret Ann 203
  Col. Samuel 203
Beaver, Benjamin 27
  Dawalt 20
Beazley, W.B. 149
  see Beasley
Beck, Ann 109
  Rev. John 109
Beckham, Lydia 8
Bechman, A. 162
  Adolphe 155
  Ann D. 162
Bedell, Mary 41
Bedford, Bridget 41
Bee, Ann 80
  Charlotte Augusta 138
  Elizabeth 32
  J. Simmons 160
  James R. 193
  John Simmons 80,138
  Julia Selma 160
  Robert R. 46
  William H. 67
Beecher, Rev. Dr. Frederick
  (off.) 173
  Harriet 100
  Rev. Jacob 55
  Rev. Dr. 100
  Samuel T. 54
Beeman, Joshua 23
Beeks, Hannah 47
Belin, Col. Allard H. 178
  P.H. 125
Bell, Charles 206
  David 164
  David Sr. 97
  Dorinda 171
  Elizabeth 73
  J.G. 134
  Jane 164
  John 110
  John J. 144
  John L. 171
  John Lanneau 171
  Josephine E.Q. 208
  Rev. Mr. (off.) 121
  Richard 123
  Sarah 97
  William 212
  William Neilson 60
Bellamy, Maj. Bethel Durant 121
Bellinger, Edward Edmund 179
  Joseph 34
  William C.P. 167
Bellune, Maj. James C. 123
Belser, Harriet C. 196

Belvin, Capt. Wilie 54
  Capt. Wille 54
Beman, Henry D. 12
Benbow, Col. Evan 102
Benedict, Rev. A. 48
Benjamin, Susanna M. 18
Bennet, Samuel P. 204
Bennett, Ann Hayes 40
  C.C. 68
  Henry 14
  Isaac 135
  Joseph 129
  M.C. 135
  Martha 14
  S.L. 112
  Samuel L. 61
  Sarah 99
  Swinton 99
  Thomas 40,122,156,174
  Thomas Jr. 211
  Thomas B. Jr. 193
  W.J. 174
  William Henry 174
  William Swinton 139
Benoist, Catharine Rebecca
  Scott 11
  Daniel 11
Benson, Abner 13
  Emeline 185
  Emily 11
  Grace 11
  Isabella C. 197
  Laurence 113
  Laurens 133
  Spencer 21
  William 76
Bentham, Capt. James 33
Bentivoglis, Count 170
  Countess 170
Bentley, Jesse 113
  John 101
Benton, Dr. James H. 181
Bering, Charles 106
Berkley, Maj. James 183
  Jane 183
Bernie, Edward 75
Berney, John 92
  Phillipa 167
  Robert 147
  Sophia 92
  Susan 67
Berrian, Rev. Dr. (off.) 95
Berrien, Catharine J. 123
  Eliza 28
  Frances Pamela 123
  James W.M. 123
  John McPherson 54
  L.M. 54
  Valeria G. 24
Berry, Alexander 47,149
  Amanda D. 153
  Caroline Elizabeth 19

Berry (cont'd)
  E. 51
  Henry H. 71
  Judge James 181
  James B. 2,51
  Joel H. 61,80
  Capt. M. 101
  Margaret 197
  Maria 47
  Martha E. 80
  Rebecca 149
Berthelot, Mary Antoinette 25
Berton, D.V. 75
Bertram, Alexander 13
Besselen, Philip C. 122
Bessent, A.J. 62
  Alexis S. 201
Bethune, Catharine 171
  Mrs. Francis M. 181
  John 199
Betts, Francis J. 207
  James B. 152
Beveridge, Robert 120
Beverly, William 44
Bigelow, Samuel 39
Bewers, Dr. J.A. 163
Biggens, Matthew 7
Bigges, James S. 183
Biggs, Emma C. 197
Bigham, John 4
  Samuel 167
  Samuel E. 137
  William 76
Billings, Daniel 122
Billups, Col. ___ 148
Bine, Jane 176
Bingley, C.W. 163
  David P. 133
  Sophronia Elizabeth 133
Birch, Charles 47
Bird, Catharine Dalton 198
  Dr. Fitzgerald 198,209
  John JR. 20
  Mary D. 151
  Rebecca Ann 134
  Dr. Thompson 25
  William 134,151
Birdsong, Col. Isaac 15
Birmingham, Rev. Mr. (off.) 127
Bishop, John 31
  Lucy 24
Bison, Abner F. 14
Bissell, H.C. 136
Bitting, Mary 8
Black, Ann 46
  Charles 32
  Henry 167
  Jane 18
  John 89
  John W. 8
  Mary 168
  Rebecca D. 59

Blacklock, Emma Caroline 178
  John F. 149
  William 178
Blackman, Elias 13
  James A. 9
Blackmon, Col. John P. 56
Blackwood, Rachel 134
  Thomas 134
Blackshear, Anne 35
  Gen. David 41
  Edward 35
  James Hamilton 25
  Col. Joseph 41
Blackwell, Mary 45
Blackwood, Mrs. C.L. 136
  Charlotte Endora 152
  Maj. John 152
  Thomas 120
Blaine, Mary 62
Blair, Horace 4
  Isabella 121
Blake, Charles 100
  Daniel 123
  Edward 212
  Mary Louisa 212
  Fanny Middleton 123
  John H. 196
  John Haig 72
  Walter 128
Blamyre, Elizabeth M.L. 176
  William 176
Blasingame, Parthena 21
Blocker, James 52
Blodgett, Rev. H.M. 131
Blois, Peter 47
Blount, Elizabeth 57
  John G. 70
  Maj. John G. 28
  Lavinia E.H. 30
  Maj. Stephen W. 57
  Thomas M. 10
Blum, Caroline D. 59
  Jane Ann 207
  John Andrew 207
Blythe, Rev. James 31
Boardman, Rev. Mr. (off.) 114
Boatwright, James 112
Bobo, F.G. 127
Bochlott, Lewis 88
Bod, John L. 118
Boger, Sally 30
Boggs, Rev. George W. 63
  Rev. G.W. (off.) 178
  Mrs. ___ 75
  Rober 48
Boinest, Sarah S. 54
Boies, Rev. Artemas 10
Bolan, James 85
  Rachael 85
Bold, William H. 86
Bolles, A. 80
  Rev. Edwin A. 108

Bolles (cont'd)
  Eliza R. 80
Bollough, Catharine 74
Bond, Ann 9
  Mary E. 38
  William P. 143
Bone, Thomas 112
Bones, Malinda R. 80
Bonham, Elizabeth J. 10
Bonnell, Capt. John 96
  Sarah 96
Bonnetheau, Henry B. 199
  James W. 93
  see Bounetheau
Boone, Sarah Amelia 187
  Susan M. 207
  Thomas 45
  Thomas W. 207
  Rev. William J. 187
Booth, Anna 68
  James 17
Boroughs, A. Bryan 18
  see Burroughs
Borum, Elizabeth 48
Bostick, Mary Ann 3
Bostwick, Leonard 126
Bottom, David 36,37
Bouchelle, Laurinda E.D. 37
Bounetheau, E.W. 68
  Edward 68
  Elizabeth 91
  see Bonnetheau
Bourke, Robert Emmet 93
  see Burk
Bourquin, Adeline Elizabeth 50
  William H. 50
Bourreus, Joseph M. 86
Bouyer, Elois Therese 21
Bouyson, Augustus 23
Boyssou, Augustus 22
Bowdre, Hays 14
Bowen, Ann H. 30
  Bishop (off.) 138
  Fanny 193
  Isabella 124
  Margaret B. 6
  Capt. Owen J. 20
  Rt. Rev. Bishop 30,193
  Rt. Rev. Bishop (off.) 18,19,
    23,34,36,71,91,99,102,103,
    104(3),105,106,107,108,111,112,
    115,127,131,135,136,137,145,
    149,150
  Rt. Rev. Dr. 6,124
  Rt. Rev. Dr. (off.) 63,72,79,
    82(3),104,116,140,143
  Rev. Dr. (off.) 120
Bower, Eugenia V. 204
  William 204
Bowers, Benjamin 207
  Caroline 79
  Mary 207
  Mary Ann 179

Bowker, Lucretia O. 173
Bowler, James Henry 187
  Sarah Bradwell 187
Bowles, Elvina S. 159
  J.G. 159
  John Taylor 39
Boyce, John J. 136
  Lydia 44
Boyd, Caroline S.M. 82
  D. 120
  Elizabeth H. 138
  Ellen Millar 135
  Jane 135
  Jane Childs 135
  John 100
  Dr. John 42
  John L. 14
  Joseph H. 138
  Martha Linn 135
  Reuben 13
  Rev. Dr. (off.) 107
  Sarah Ann 100
  Susannah 42
  William 135
Boyle, Col. Charles 84
  John 3,79,95
  Lionel C. 110
  Margaret E. 84
  Rosa S. 79
Boyll, Mary Agnes 164
Boylston, Dr. H. 162
  Mary Ellen 162
Bozeman, James 9
  James N. 12
Bradford, Rev. Henry 72
Bradley, Charles L. 140
  Henry 163
  Louisa 163
Brady, Nathan Jr. 50
Bragg, Rev. Mr. (off.) 146,198
Braid, Elizabeth 98
Brailsford, Anna 205
  Maria 125
  Maria L. 91
  William 125
  Dr. William M. 84
  William Roper 205
Brame, Miss ___ 22
Brandon, Margaret 53
Branford, Charles G. 123
Branham, Capt. H. L. 61
Brantley, Amos 20
  Rev. Dr. (off.) 135,136,
    138(2),141,147,148,157(3),
    159(2),160,161,167,175,
    184(2),185
  Rev. Mr. (off.) 39,145
  Thirza Ann 68
  Rev. William T. 171
  Rev. William T. (off.) 206
Brantly, Rev. Dr. (off.) 134,
  154,192

Brasch, Catharine A. 9
Bratton, Dr. John S. 189
Brawley, Rachel E. 189
Brazeal, David R. 22
  Williamson 31
Brearly, Eliza Ann 156
  Rev. William (off.) 63,80,156
Breckenridge, Dr. John 170
Brenan, Charles 7
  Mary Lavinia 65
  Richard 65
Brevard, Capt. Alex. 21
  Caroline Anne 22
  Mary M. 21
  Sarah 12
Brewer, A.G. 128
  Rev. A.G. (off.) 96,110(2)
  Lyttleton R. 155
  Rebecca 110
  Rev. Mr. (off.) 104,111
Brewster, Charles R. 94
  Margaret B. 14
  Sarah Ann 14
  William 14
Brian, Council S. 23
  see Brien, Bryan
Brice, Dr. ___ 171
Brickle, Susan M. 32
Bridges, Charlotte 44
Bridgewood, Thomas 39
Brien, John Macpherson 68
  see Brian, Bryan
Briggs, Jemima 54
  Robert Henry 111
  Sarah 26
Bringloe, Richard 141
  Sarah Ann 141
Brinkle, John 54
Brisbane, Col. ___ 112
  Mary 210
  William 210
  Rev. Wm. H. (off.) 65
Britt, Louis 101
Britton, Drusilla 115
  Henry 115
Broadfoot, William 18
Broadwater, Clementine C. 72
Brock, Catherine Ann 198
Brocker, Georgiana 46
Brockinton, Martha Ann 188
Brockleback, William 177
Brockman, Susannah 20
Brockway, Eliza 109
Brodie, Elizabeth I. 153
Broer, Martha C. 36
  see Brower
Bronson, Martha 61
Brooker, Rev. Wm. (off.) 170
Brooks, George G. 15
  Jane Caroline 168
  John B. 133
  Martha 36,37

Brooks, (cont'd)
  Mary Julia 76
  R.I. 52
Broome, Amelia Ann 118-119
  James C. 119
  James E. 81
  Jennett 164
  Rev. John 164
Broughton, Alexander 84
  Christiana Constantia 97
  Daniel 114
  Elizabeth 91
  Elizabeth Damaris 84
  Col. Peter 177
  Philip Porcher 9,97
  Sarah 177
  Thomas 9,14
Brow, Sarah Ann 137
  Capt. William 137
Brower, Eliza W. 47
  William N. 25
  see Broer
Brown, Mrs. A. 79
  A.J. 143
  Abigail 161
  Alexander 149
  Alexander H. 68
  Alvina Eliza 143
  Col. B.H. 141
  Col. Barnet M. 128
  Charles J. 8
  Rev. D.M. (off.) 136
  Eliza C. 128,204
  Elizabeth 149
  Elizabeth Ann 147
  Emily H. 6
  Emily R. 130
  Gen. Epps 9
  Col. G.W. 136
  Dr. George A. 54,58
  Grace 48
  Harriet Louisa 104
  Henry 167
  Rev. Henry 146
  Isabella 3,77
  Ira 176
  James 135
  James D. 10
  James W. 80
  Jesse 97
  Rev. John 7
  John B. 168
  John Davies 20
  Jonathan 72
  Joseph 19
  Rev. Joseph 6,7,204
  Joshua 65,104
  Laura P. 54
  Maria H. 6,7
  Mary Lavinia 57
  Peter M. 15
  R.W. 79

Brown (cont'd)
  Rev. Dr. (off.) 52,176
  Rev. Mr. (off.) 61,62
  Robert C. 147
  Robert E. 110
  Robert H. 107
  Thomas 15
  William 140
  William S. 48
  William T. 110
  William W. 6
Browne, A.J. 187
  Caroline P. 187
  Edward H. 92
Browning, Lavenia W. 27
Brownlee, Elijah 164
  George Sr. 108
Brownlow, Rebecca E. 15
Bruce, Andrew 187
  John B. 33
  John M. 197
Bruckner, Elizabeth 51
Bruen, Evelina 204
Bruikshank, Daniel 16
  Jane 16
Brumby, Richard T. 21
Bruns, Henry M. 79
  see Burns
Brunson, Deniel D. 24
Bryan, Ann Octavia 146
  Arthur 127
  Catharine M. 127
  Eliza Catharine 180
  Elizabeth 71
  George S. 197
  Hugh Legare 187
  Col. John 79,146,178
  John Jr. 185
  Jonathan 71
  Jonathan Jr. 192
  Joseph 52,197
  Lydia 185
  Lydia Ball 79
  Maria M. 52
  Mary Caroline 192
  Mary Swinton 178
  Michael 205
  see Brian, Brien
Bryant, Charles H. 104
  James W. 115
Bryce, Alexander 31
  Jane Shand 103
  Mary Scott 102
  Robert 103
Bryson, Rev. Henry 31
Buchanan, Martha P. 133
Buchannan, Barnet 16
  Martha 197
Buckner, Andrew J. 160
Budd, Lt. Charles A. 3
Buff, Michael 150
Buford, Lucy V. 24

Bufort, Dary 204
Bugg, Edmund 58
  Mrs. ___ 35
Buis, Alexander W. 54
Buist, Rev. A. (off.) 85
  Mrs. Arthur 113
  Rev. Arthur 113,184
  Rev. Arthur (off.) 69
  Rev. E.T. 69,111
  Rev. E.T. (off.) 96
  Rev. Edward T. 170
  Dr. Henry 47
  Mary Elizabeth Robinson 111
  Rev. Dr. 184
  Rev. Mr. (off.) 16,42,46,
    68,105
  Thomas Young 113
Bull, Andrew G. 38
  Edmund 204
  William Izard 79
  William R. 133
Bullen, Capt. R.N. 195
Bulloch, Charles 17
  Elvira B. 120
  Hetty A. 49
  James S. 49
  Mary M. 23
  William 23
  William B. 74
Bullock, David 28
Bulow, Caroline Amelia 11
  John J. Jr. 112
  Maj. John J. 11
  Thomas L. 197
Bunch, James 75
  Margaret Ann 115
Bunkley, Martha M. 139
Burch, Edward C. 204
  Edward Mallory 209
Burchard, James 14
Burdell, Eleanor P.R. 207
  John E. 145
  Robert W. 155
  Sarah Catharine 145
  Thomas J. 205
Burden, Kinsey 103
  Portia A. 103
Burdett, Rev. S.S. (off.) 20
  Rev. Staunton S. 34
Burger, David Devose 49
  Elizabeth B. 70
  Capt. Robert 22
  Samuel 70
Burgess, James Augustus 158
  Rev. Mr. (off.) 138
Burgoine, Mary M. 84
Burie, Ann W. 136
  Daniel Sr. 86
  Elizabeth Ann 86
Burk, Samuel 121
Burke, A.J. 123
  Henrietta 38

Burke (cont'd)
  Johanna 161
  John 148,161
  M. 129
  Margaret Rebecca Brown 147
  Mary Ann 148
  Capt. William 56
Burks, Charles S. 40
Burleson, Susan E. 52
Burn, Jacob 138
  Maria A. 138
  William 64
  see Bruns
Burnap, Mary E. 106
Burnet, James 28
Burnett, Elizabeth W. 1
  Sally 10
  Thomas 45
Burnham, Agnes T. 123
  Atharine 121
  Dorinda 118
  R.W. 162
  Richard 16
  Thomas 108,123
Burnside, Capt. Andrew 200
Burrell, Ann Garden 120
  John E. 120
Burriss, Deliah 20
  Reuben 20,118
Burroughs, Joseph 24
  Reuben 68
  Rev. William R. 115
  see Boroughs
Burrows, Sam'l. 65
  see Boroughs
Burt, Maj. Armistead 19
  Rev. Federal 18
  Francis Jr. 51
  Martha B. 24
  Dr. William 30
Burton, Edward M. 19
  Eliza A. 93
  Hutchins G. 111
  Robert H. 93
  Sarah R. 46
Bush, Richard 18
Bushnull, Rev. Jedediah 67
Bussy, Charles 35
Buswell, Thomas G. 9
Butler, Col. A.P. 39
  Anna Maria 61
  David B. 40
  Edward 163
  Francis 109
  Col. Frank 9
  Harriet Hayne 88
  Judge ___ 88
  Col. Leontine 10
  Mary 163
  Pierce 109
  Richard M. 195
  Sophia B. 17
  Susan Ann 38,39

Butts, Eliza 14
Buzzard, Louisa 20
Byrd, Eliza 94
  see Bird
Bynum, Benjamin 116
  Frances 139
Byron, Elizabeth 31
Bythewood, Rev. D. (off.) 125
  Rev. Daniel (off.) 79
  Eliza D. 145
  Mary 35

Cabot, Elizabeth 9
  George 9
Cade, Ignatius 176
Cady, Benjamin Chauncey 152
Cahill, Daniel 58,59
  Elizabeth 59
Calder, Agnes 155
  Alexander 187
  George 169
  James 155,165
  Mary G. 165
  Nancy 47
Caldwell, Ann T. 194
  Catharine 12
  Eliza P. 158
  Elizabeth A. 28
  Elizabeth M. 126
  Elsy 34
  James 126,182
  James M. 194
  James P. 120
  John Bainbridge 194
  John W. 120
  Joseph 193
  Lucy 21
  Dr. Lawson 46
  Mary A-n 76
  Matthew Thompson 138
  Capt. R.B. 195
  Rebecca Amanda 14
  Richard 177
  Robert 173
  Robert B. 158
  Stephen Thomas 194
  Col. William H. 34
  Col. William R. 70
Calhoun, Andrew P. 112
  Caroline 26
  Col. J. Edward 199
  John 68
  Lucretia Ann 2
  Maria E. 199
  Martha Catharine 19
  Sarah Ann 68
  William 2,19
Callaway, Rev. Francis (off.) 22
Callender, Ann C. 87
  Capt. Joseph 87
  Thomas 28

Callier, Susan 29
Calvert, Mortimer 103
Cam, Emily C. 55
Cameron, Archibald 190
  John 59
  Samuel D. 82
  Susan 82
Cammel, Dr. ___ 41,47
  Nancy A. 41
Campbell, Alexander 110
  Alexander W. 115
  Ann Eliza 115
  Anna Margaret 203
  Anne Loughton Smith 204
  Catharine 130
  Rev. D.J. (off.) 158
  Capt. David 204
  Rev. David Erving 12
  Rev. David J. (off.) 158
  Rev. Dexie J. 163
  Col. Duncan G. 26
  Fanny 10
  Frances 17
  Henrietta 42
  J.B. 122
  Rev. J.B. 130
  Rev. J.B. (off.) 162,206
  James B. 203
  James Butler 203
  John 30
  Rev. John 206
  Mrs. ___ 42
  Margaret 42
  McMillan 42
  Rev. Mr. (off.) 94,97,160, 192,197
  Rebecca Ann 40
  Robert 76
  Capt. Robert 135
  Sarah G. 29
  Susan 32
Campfield, Horace T. 56
Canady, Emeline 123
  Henry 123
Candee, E.B. 12
Candler, Capt. Edward 55
Cannaday, H. 93
  Mary E. 93
Cannon, Amelia 27
  Caroline E. 28
  George Jr. 131,212
  Mary F. 212
  W.H. 46
  William H. 121
Cantey, Gen. Z. 49
Cantley, Capt. Henry T. 49
Cantwell, P. 82
Capers, Rev. Charles William 50
  Rev. Dr. (off.) 65,69,77(2), 79,92,99,109(2),116,118,125, 130,132(2),144,145(2),155, 157,160

Capers (cont'd)
  Rev. Mr. (off.) 80,119,151, 207
  Rev. Samuel Wragg
  Susan Bethia 190
  Rev. W. (off.) 116,147
  Rev. William 190
  Rev. William (off.) 33, 117,188
  William H. 6
Cardwell, Theodocia 57
Carleton, Agale 84
  Henry 84
Carlile, Rev. William (off.) 61,76,165
Carlisle, Isaac 16
  Maria 21
  Rev. Mr. (off.) 80
Carlile, Rev. William 50
Carmell, J.R. 56
Carmichael, Gilbert 72
  Maria A. 14
Carnes, Thomas P. 49
  Maj. William W. 107
Carothers, Dr. A.M. 192
  James N. 22
  M. 192
Carpenter, Dan 57
  William S. 190
Carr, Charles D. 44
  Cynthia 75
  John 192
  Mary 22
  Susan G. 8
  Maj. Gen. Thomas 6
  Col. Thomas D. 40
  William 16
  William A. 75
Carre, Eugenie 73
Carrere, William G. 205
Carroll, B. Rivers 79
  Bartholomew 98
  Rev. C.R. (off.) 200
  Ellen H. 7
  Rachel 98
Carson, Elizabeth 56
  John 52
  Mary Eliza 52
  Seth P. 13
  William A. 65
  William Augustus 174
Carsten, Edward H. 187
  James W. 196
Cart, John Jr. 176
  Julia 176
Carter, Rev. Abiel 11
  Angelina A. 177
  Angus 26
  Ann 28
  Artemus 211
  Catherine Eliza 212
  Rev. Edwin (off.) 174

Carter (cont'd)
  Col. F. 212
  Rev. Mr. Hampden C. 72
  Harriet Louisa 211
  John 90
  Julia 126
  Margaret E. 177
  Maria B. 11
  Martha G. 16
  Mary 39
  Nelson 35
  Orlando 93
  S. 61
Cartmell, Maj. Henry R. 148
Cartwright, Capt. Paul 4
Caruthers, Col. John 25
Carwile, John H. 72
Cary, Eliza 22
Casey Henry 145
Cason, Margaret 178
  Seth 178
Cassels, Rev. J. B. 105,120
  Rev. John B. (off.) 131,139,
  140
  Jno. Winn 130
  Laera 120
  Mary H. 130
  S.J. 125
  Rev. S.J. (off.) 105
  Rev. Samuel J. 130,146
  Sarah 101
Cassin, Margaret 40
  Com. Stephen 40
Casten, Caroline S. 139
  John 139
Caswell, Alexander 51
Cater, Benj. F. 14
  Rev. E. (off.) 180
  Rev. Edwin 137
  Mrs. L.M. 210
  Rev. R.B. 210
  Rev. Mr. (off.) 78,202
  Richard B. 66
  Rev. Richard B. 7-8
  Rev. Richard B. (off.) 84
Catewood, William C. 93
Cathey, Margaret 15
Catonet, Maria Alexina 109
  Peter 109
Cauble, Frierny 14
Caught, Thomas 26
Caulier, Dr. George 148
Caw, Jane 184
  Peter 164,184
  Peter Gowan 184
Chadbourn, Isabella 40
  Jacob 30
Chafee, Otis J. 131
Chamberlain, Mary H. 46
  Matilda 127
  Rev. Mr. 160
  Rev. R. 127

Chambers, Rev. J.W. (off.) 34
  Dr. William 7
Champion, Henry 10
  Isabella 30
Chandler, Amos 146
  Daniel 29
  Mary Ann 43
  Rev. Mr. (off.) 41
Chapman, C.C.P. 161
  Edward W. 57
  G. 88
  James 3
  John 153
  Mary Blackwood 120
  Perry E. 192
  Rev. Mr. (off.) 197
  Sarah B. 88
  Thomas 120,134,187
Chappel, John 33
Charles, Hopkins G. 78
Charlton, Mrs. C.H. 141
  John K.M. 20
  T.U.P. 30,107,141
Chartran, Lavenia 171
  Phillip 171
Chase, Rev. H. (off.) 131
Chastain, Stephen Sr. 39
Chatburn, Mary 80
Chebec, Louise 147
Cheney, E. 107
  Sarah A. 44
Chesnut, Harriet 57
  Col. James 81
  Col. John 57
  Mary 81
Cheves, Anna 176
  Langdon 46,159,176
  Louisa 159
  Sophia L. 46
Chew, B.F. 24
Chifelle, Ann Alicia 62
  Thomas P. 62
Childers, Elizabeth 2
Childs, Mrs. ___ 126
Chisolm, Dr. Edward N. 116
  Dr. Edward Neufville 59
  George 130(2)
  George Jr. 94
  John M. 105
  Martha 27
  Mary Maria 134
  Robert 106,165
  Sarah M. 94
Chitty, Ann Eugenia 163
  Edward Hollinshead 8
  John W. 72
  Thomas J. 59
Choisy, Ch. 102
Chrietzberg, Martha T. 65
  Mr. ___ 65
  R.S. 116
  Thomas W.S. 147

Christian, Mary Saltus 49
Christie, Anna Caroline 124
  John 49
  Margaret F.G. 49
Church, Rev. A. (off.) 18
  Rev. Alonzo 189
  Elizabeth W.H. 189
  Elvira A. 166
  Rev. Dr. 166
  Rev. Dr. (off.) 116
  Robert 186
  Rodman 156
Churchill, Charles 29
Claiborn, Ann 178
Clapier, Louis 126
Clapp, Rev. Mr. (off.) 62
Clark, Abigail M. 33
  Anna W. 211
  Archibald Jr. 111
  Gen. Elijah 9
  Eliza Ann 21
  Emma Cornelia 63
  Hannah 9
  J. Alfred 173
  James Sr. 33
  James J. 199
  James L. 11
  Jerome 63
  Capt. Jerome 71
  John 179,211
  Rev. Joseph 13
  Josiah A. 194
  Lydia C. 147
  Malikiah 111
  Mary 194
  Mary E. 29
  Rev. Orin 19
  William 89
Clarke, Mr. ___ 44
  Ann Helena 139
  Ann Margaret 21
  Archibald 122
  Catharine A. 195
  Edward Payson 156
  Eliza R. 98
  George Bender 195
  George I.F. 119
  John M. 43
  Leonora Agnes 21
  Mary Ann 43
  Nathaniel 14,21
  Samuel 139,156,195
  Mrs. Samuel 139
  Sophia L. 23
  Dr. U. B. 195
Clarkson, Catharine 65
  Rev. William 65
Clay, Mary 197
Clayton, Augustin S. 150
  Caroline V. 6
  Daniel 150
  C.R. 6

Clayton (cont'd)
  Philip Augustin 30
  Rev. Mr. (off.) 155
  Susannah 150
  Rev. T.C. (off.) 162
Cleapor, John 22
Cleary, Catharine 185
Cleaveland, George 37
Clemence, Charles P. 23
Clement, Anna Maria 132
  Eliza 165
  J.P. 120
  Jesse A. 15
  Lydia 110
  William 132,165
Clements, Emily 51
  Sarah 160
  Warren W. 119
Clendinnen, Robert 43
Clenette, Amanda M. 74
Clenny, Rev. P. W. 102
Clifford, L.C. 138
Clifton, Algeron S. 23
Clinch, Capt. J.J. 11
Cline, Elizabeth 38
  Sarah 5
Clinton, Gov. DeWitt 18
  Rev. Lawson 57
  Rev. Lawson B. 143
Clough, Benjamin 79
Clurkey, Charles B. 56
Clutts, Jacob 14
Clyde, George Washington 180
  Harriet 180
  John 156
  Thomas M. 180
Coachman, B.A. 167
  Francis G. 79
  John 15,79,102
Coates, Joseph S. 205
  Martha 120
  R.F. 188
  Sarah Maria 205
Cobb, Mary W. 51
  Ransom 104
  Thomas W. 35
Cobia, Rev. Daniel 105(2)
  Rev. Mr. (off.) 90,91,92,
    95,121
Cobourn, John C. 34
Coburn, Anna 66
  Eliza M. 54
  Elizabeth G. 166
  Ellen 163
  John 66,166
  John L. 54,163
  Philip Girhan 54
  Peter K. 87
  Simon Magwood 163
  Thomas S. 163
  see Colburn

Cochran, Charles B. 184
  Charlotte E. 119
  Margaret 126
  Robert E. 62
  Rosa Adeline 37
  Susan L. 179
  Thomas 37,179
Cocke, William 57
Coe, Francis Caroline 78
  William H. 43
Coffin, Ann M. 154
  Capt. Alexander 146
  George M. 143
  Robert S. 4
Cogdell, James Gorden 65
  Mary A.E. 6
Coghlan, Mary 6
Cogswell, H. 30
  Dr. Mason F. 48
Cohen, Celia 42
Cohrs, Henry A. 6
  Sarah Ann 167
Coit, David G. 129
  Ellen Phebe 192
  James 7
  Rev. J.C. 192
Colburn, Benjamin Prince 83
  Rev. Mr. (off.) 212
  see Cobourn, Coburn
Colclough, Col. William A. 42
Colcock, Charles Jones 154
  Eliza Mary 196
  R.W. 188
  Thomas H. 196
  William F. 137
Cole, Ann D. 72
  Gideon James 92
  Henry 147
  Ira 24
  Capt. Martin 146
  Mary Louisa 123
  Susan Elizabeth 125
Coleman, Capt. John 23
  Mary Jane 206
  see Colman
Coley, Eugene 18
Colley, James 23
Collidge, Samuel Judson 29
Collins, Elizabeth 108
  Emily A. 87
  Jonah 123
  Nicey 44
Colman, Robert 11
  see Coleman
Comine, John 99
Conant, Elizabeth 21
  Thatcher 21
Condit, John 85
Connel, Dr. ___ 197
  Maria 197
  Rev. Mr. (off.) 162
Connell, Elizabeth 32

Conner, Capt. Edward 121
  James 98
Connolly, Elizabeth 33
  Richard 33
Converse, Rev. Mr. (off.) 133, 146
Conyers, Capt. Daniel 53
Cook, Benjamin 37
  D.P. 12
  Francis 24
  George 130
  Rev. Joseph B. 76
  Rev. Thomas 93
  Rev. Thomas A. (off.) 163
Coons, Rev. J.N. (off.) 152
Cooper, A. Milton 17
  Charlotte 42
  Eliza 12
  Rev. Fleet 17
  George W. 175,210
  Lawton 210
  Maria H. 183
  Mary 27
  Martha 34
  Mary M. 5
  Rev. Mr. (off.) 148
  Sophia 210
  Thomas B. 80
  William H. 15
Cope, Mary E. 21
Coppee, Alettea 134
  Charles 203
  Dr. Edward 134,203
Coppinberg, Joseph 205
Coquillon, Francis B. 5
Corbett, Sarah E. 74
Corbin, Rev. Lyman W. 138
Corby, John Jr. 116
Cordes, Charlotte Lavinia 184
Corl, Sarah 14
Corley, Rebecca 187
Cornwall, Nathaniel 13
Corrie, Isabella 155
  Lavinia W. 132
  Margaret 55
  Samuel 55,155
Corss, Philip 4
Cotton, George 71
  Joseph 37
  Roderick 7
Coturier, Emma 3
Cousar, Rev. John 109
  Lills Shaw 109
Courson, Benjamin 33
Courtenay, James C. 95
Cousar, Rev. J. (off.) 112
Coutrier, Dr. J.R.E. 99
Covington, Gen. B.H. 12
Cowan, Benjamin Sr. 32
  J.T. 6
  Mary C. 12
Coward, Jesse 97
  Keziah Ann 97

Cowen, Elizabeth 4
  Thomas L. 4
Cowles, Jerry 160
  Maj. Wm. Marstern 33
Cowling, John G. 20
Cowperthwait, E.R. 87
Cox, George W. 67
  Rev. Mr. (off.) 172
Coxe, Charlotte Victoria 185
  Edward 185
Cozart, William M. 53
Cozens, C.W. 163
Crabtree, Lydia Maria 51
Craft, Hugh 19
  Martha E. 19
  Nathan 14
Craig, Capt. Allen 5
  L.S. 189
  Robert 164
  S.E. 13
Crane, Joseph 54
  Mary E. 3
Crask, Caroline E. 15
Crawford, Andrew 180-181,210
  Ann Catharine 39
  Arthur 83
  Harriet Jane 210
  John 41
  Julia A. 50
  Mary 114
  Mary R. 15
  Peter 44
  W.H. 147
  William 149
  William H. 147
Crayton, Baylies 185
Cregner, Christiana 163
Crews, A.J. 114
Cribb, Mr. ___ 122
Cripps, Ann Allston 104
  Esther 39
  Octavius 104
Crocker, Doddridge 182
  Eliza 182
  Dr. William 28
Croft, Edward 106,107
  Capt. George 177
  Sarah 199
  Sarah E. 177
Cromwell, Abby Johnson 138
  Oliver 138
Cronn, William 31
Crook, Rev. Mr. (off.) 69
  Rev. William (off.) 51
Crosby, Capt. ___ 137
  Col. ___ 148
  Jane 16
  Margaret J. 137
  Mary A. 148
  William 140
Crose, James 139
Cross, Anna Isabella 187

Cross (cont'd)
  Col. George Warren 119
  Rt. Rev. John 65
  Mary Elizabeth 187
  William 187
Crovat, Cecilia Louisa 125,198
  Peter 198
Crow, Harriet 188
Crowder, Adeline E.A. 32
  Hannah 29
Cruger, Catharine DeNully 19
  Nicholas 19
Cruickshanks, Daniel 46
  Martha 168
  see Bruikshank
Cudworth, Emma 193
  Mary 22,122
  Maj. Nathaniel 122
  Sarah 74
  William 193
Culbreath, Mary A. 131
Cullens, Miles D. 32
  Myles W. 32
Culloden, William 35
Culp, Dr. Wm. A. 30
Cumming, Caroline 95
  John B. 180
  Joseph 95
  Thomas J. 178
Cummins, Francis 74
  John 150
  Joseph 10
  Matilda Ann 10
  Sarah 74
Cunningham, Rev. A.N. (off.) 177
  Arthur 27
  Catharine 36
  Eliza 53
  Esquire 47
  Rev. H.B. 210
  Rev. H.B. (off.) 169,173, 186
  Capt. J.T. 199
  Col. John 155
  Mary Jane 90
  Nancy A. 47
  Nancy M. 135
  Rev. Paxton 17
  Rebecca 3
  Col. Richard 90,123
  Rt. 53
  S. 201
  Samuel 3
  Susan M.J. 25
  Thomas 41,47,135
Cureton, Elizabeth 7
  Everard 77
  Mary S. 77
  Thomas T. 5
Curran, ___ 100
Currence, John 8

Curry, Mary A. Johnson 19
  William A. 139
Curtis, Joseph 152
  Martha P. 152
  Mary 152
  Rev. Dr. (off.) 205
  Robert 181
Cushing, Jonathan P. 98
Cushman, Rev. Ralph 56
  Xerzes H. 17
Cutbreath, John 208
Cuthbert, Alice L. 200
  Dr. Edward 200
  Col. James 142
  Col. John 192
Cutting, Brockholst 6
Cuyler, Judge ___ 46
  Margaret 46
Cyers, Joseph 31

Daily, John J. 151
Dalcho, Rev. Dr. (off.) 30,33, 64,68
Dalton, Jane 32
Cana, Charles E. 99
  Rev. Mr. (off.) 105,132,139, 147
  Rev. William C. (off.) 136,209
Danan, Rev. Joseph 13
Dane, Euphemia 46
Danelly, Ann Eliza 67
  Louisa 55
  Capt. William J. 17,53
Danforth, Samuel 13
Daniel, Asberry 44
  Cunningham 150
  David 64
  Elisha 9
  Francis Eliza 22
  James 171
  Jennet Barr 171
  John 12
  John C. 158
  John W.L. 71
  Joshua 73
  Martha 171
  Sarah 57
  Sarah Ann 71(2)
  Serena M. 28
  see Danniels
Daniell, John 24
  Martha 83
  Dr. W.C. 83
Danielly, Col. Andrew 9
  see Danelly
Danner, Rev. A.R. (off.) 174,192
  N.P. 153
Dannery, Jean Germain Samuel Adams 40
Danniels, Stephens 126
  see Daniel
Dans, Dr. James Freeman 3

Dantzler, Abraham 125
  Abraham S. 142
Darby, Dr. A. 84
  Mary E. 5
  Capt. R.A. 5
Dargan, G.W. 187
  Rev. John O.B. (off.) 154
  Mary Adeline 187
  William E. 144
Darling, Capt. G. 19
  Capt. Gamaliel 17
Darnell, Henry 26
Darrell, Ann S. 59
Dart, Mary Motte 97
  Dr. T.L. 98
  Thomas L. 97
Dasher, Susan 162
  Thomas J. 23
Dauce, P. Harriet 56
Daugherty, Rebecca 11
  see Dougherty
Dauvergne, A.P. 67
Davenport, Dr. James S. 22
  Thomas M. 16
  William Ward 206
Davidson, James 81
  Priscilla E. 17
  William 115
Davies, Rev. Dr. D. (off.) 149
  Rev. Daniel 197
  Eliza A. 201
  Rev. John B. 196
  Samuel Melville Crenshaw 201
  Thomas W. 54
  Rev. William B. 201
Davis, Charles 159
  Eliza Frances 121
  Rev. G.W. 18
  George L.A. 93
  Dr. Henry W. 10
  Lt. Jackman J. 18
  Jacob 66
  Dr. James 141
  Maj. Jessee 123
  John R. 71
  Joseph 77
  Julia Ann 136
  Lemual B. 101,116
  Lemuel James 116
  Loton 26
  Nathan 7
  Rev. Noah 41
  Piety 64
  Rev. S.S. (off.) 88
  Siney Ann 25
  Capt. Thomas 136
  Rev. Thomas F. (off.) 105
  Capt. Ulmer A. 110
  Rev. W.H. (off.) 208
  Rev. William 59
  Rev. William H. 180

Davitt, Dr. Hugh 5
Dawes, H.P. 187
  Mary B. 187
Dawkins, Elizabeth 13
  Harriet C. 181
  Col. Thomas N. 181
Dawsey, Mary 16
Dawson, Augusta 155
  George A. 24
  Harriet Horry 66
  J. Drayton 81
  John 137
  Dr. John L. 118
  Laurens M. 66
  Margaret Mary 63
  Richard 116
  Sarah L. 175
Day, Elizabeth 29
  Moses 15
  Nancy 11
Deal, Polly 12
Dean, Seaborn L. 25
Dearborn, Benjamin 136
Dearing, Marion A. 207
  William 207
Dearmond, Michael 139
Deas, Ann Horry 131
  Dr. E. Horry 135
  Henry 131,144
  Dr. S. 178
  Thomas Savage 144
DeBow, Amelia 117
  Arabella Amanda 149
  B. Franklin 208
  Garrett 149
  Mary D. 117
  William G. 117
Decker, John 55
DeGaesebeke, Baron Elphege Van Zuylen Van Nyevelt 200
Dehon, Bishop 72
  Sarah Russell 72
  Rev. Mr. (off.) 208
Dejarnat, Elias 22
Delacrois, G.W. 100
Delameter, Abraham 9
DeLancey, Eliza 77
  John 77
Delavaux, Rev. E.P. (off.) 167
  Rev. Francis (off.) 154
  Rev. Mr. (off.) 92,97,123
Delaveaux, Rev. Francis P. (off.) 83
  Rev. Mr. (off.) 106
Deleon, Jacob 30
Delgar, Martha G. 130
Deliesseline, F.G. 39
Deloach, Charles 16
Delony, Dr. Edward 32
  William 160
Demott, Engruia 122
Dennehy, Catharine L. 129

Dennehy (cont'd)
  Jeremiah 129
Dennis, M.M. 197
Denson, Sarah W. 108
Dent, John H. 107
Denton, Joshua 9
Desaussure, Chancellor 148
  Charles A. 102
  H.A. 210
  Dr. H.W. 156
  Isabel H. 195
  Dr. Louis M. 195
  Sarah G. Baron 210
Deveaux, Caroline 198
  J. Porteous 91
  Thomas E. 198
Devereux, Frances A. 39
DeWalt, Aurelia 202
Dewees, William Sr. 7
Dewell, Zachariah 20
  see Dewill
Dewett, Charles 46
  see Dewitt
Dewill, Zachariah 20
  see Dewell
DeWitt, Simeon 92
  see Dewett
Dews, Eliza 45
  John I. 22
Deye, Benjamin 92
Dibble, Andrew C. 20
  P.V. 112
Diliac, Antoine P. 32
Dick, James Summers 170
  Mary E. 170
  Dr. Thomas M. 170
Dickens, Jane 41
Dickerson, Dr. J.D. 110
Dickey, Rev. Ebenezer 53
Dickinson, Col. Francis 124
  Rev. Richard W. (off.) 131
  Sarah 124
Dickman, Carson 116
Dickson, Gen. David 41
  Rev. J. 104
  Col. John 50
  Dr. John 147
  Rev. John 114
  Rev. John (off.) 79,83
  Lydia 149
  Rev. M. (off.) 121
  Malachi 49
  Martha Elizabeth 145
  Mary A. 114
  S.H.M. 175
  Dr. S. Henry 83
  S.J. 105
  Samuel H. 175
  Sarah Ann 175
  William 83
  see Dixon
Dill, Eliza 29

Dill (cont'd)
  Runnell 206
Dillon, Keziah 48
  Mary Henwood 171
Dimbar, Robert 46
Dimon, Jane Adelaide 75
Dinkens, Mary 8
Dinkins, Elizabeth C. 11
  Harris E. 18
  James Jr. 129
  L.D. 154
  Lewis 18
Disher, Ann 137
Dismukes, Dr. George W. 22
Dixon, Agnes 165
  Ann 43,86,95
  Frederick R. 109
  John 86,165
  Mary C. 26
  Nancy H. 11
  Robert H. 11
  Sophronia Matilda 211
  Thomas 104
  see Dickson
D'Lyon, Abram 3
Dobbins, James 7,16
  Milas 10
  Rebecca 14
Dobson, Oliver L. 177
Dodd, Isaac 188
Doig, John 189
Doles, Jesse Sr. 56
Dollar, Sarah 16
Dolly, John M. 5
Don, Alexander 143
  Elizabeth 143
Donaldson, Rt. 19
  D John 57
Donegan, James 154
Donnell, Capt. Benj. M. 134
Dopson, Jane Rebecca 67
Dorman, Allen 57
Dorrill, Angeline 70
  R. 70
Dorsey, Clement 34
  Sally Maria 34
D'Orval, Madame 165
Doty, Andrew 144
Douein, Capt. 111(2)
  Philip M. 130
Dougherty, Jane 161
  John 18
  see Daugherty
Doughty, John M. 23
  William C. 113
Douglas, Campbell 192
  John 196
  Rev. John (off) 183,196,204
  Maria M. Denoon 192
  Robert 183
Douglass, ___ 112
  Alanson 53

Douglass (cont'd)
  Elizabeth 145
  Rev. James W. 130
  John 3,145
  Rev. John (off.) 189,204
  Rev. Sutherland 53
Douthit, Susannah Eleanor 27
Dove, Sarah Pritchard 64
  Capt. William P. 64
Dower, William S. 121
Dowling, Daniel Sr. 42
Downie, Isalla J. 182
  Robert 182
Dowse, Abbey E. 25
  Samuel 25
  Col. Samuel 6
Doyle, Anna M. 201
  Elizabeth 40
  Mary Ann 92
  Thomas E. 201
Dozier, Agram Giles 81,119
  Amelia Ann 81
  Bartlett M. 55
  Rebecca 119
  Thomas Sr. 102
Drake, Harvey 68
Drayton, Alfred Y. 68
  Hannah 73
  James Shoolbred 205
  Thomas 107
  Thomas F. 136
  William 73
Drennan, Joseph 20
Drennes, Martha 195
Drew, William 4
Drisdale, Eliza 10
Drummond, James 119
  John 43
  Margaret 43
Drysdale, Isabel 60
Duboc, Azelie 61
  Francis 61
DuBose, D. Amarintha 200
  Dorcas 34
  Isaiah 144
  Capt. John 200
  Dr. John E. 200
  Capt. Jno. 34
  Rev. Julius J. 110
  Rev. Julius J. (off.) 205
  Louisa M. 78
  Rebecca 200
  Samuel Sr. 158
  Sarah T. 144
Duckett, Miss ___ 22
Dudley, Jane D. 15
Duffey, Rev. Daniel 141
Duffin, Samuel A. 172
Duffus, J.A. 85
Duffy, Edward 39
Dufore, E. 63
Dugan, Thomas 153

Duggan, Jane 106
  Thomas 106
Duhadway, Amanda C. 125
Duhun, James 21
Duke, Charles O. 89
  Marg. 19
Dukes, Mary Elizabeth 121
  William C. 121
Dummett, Capt. 117
Dunbar, Rebecca 14
  Dr. Samuel P. 126
Duncan, Hannah 175
  Rev. Hansford D. (off.) 141, 164
  Capt. Joseph 175
  Robert Berry 166
  see Dunkin
Dunham, Col. W.H. 38
Dunkin, Chancellor 175
  Mary Augusta 175
  see Duncan
Dunlap, David 40
  Elizabeth T. 105
  George Hamilton 46
  Dr. George Washington 105
  Mary M. 46
  Maj. Robert 34
  Samuel 68
  Sarah C. 68
  Susanna 168
  William 168
Dunn, John 25
Dunning, James 173
Dunwoodie, Rev. Mr. James (off.) 212
Dunwoody, Caroline S. 86
  Hetty Augusta 33
  Rev. J.B. 202
  Col. James 86,166
  Jane A. 166
  Jane Bavden 202
  Jane Marion 157
  John 157
  Laleah G. 202
Dupon, Rev. Mr. (off.) 211
Dupont, Charles 14
  Charles C. 59
  Cornelius 191
  Dr. John 47
  Rev. Mr. (off.) 144,146,167, 169,179
  Susan Baker 14
  Rev. T.C. (off.) 145
  Thomas C. 132
  Rev. Thomas C. (off.) 190
DuPre, Ann Allston 209
  C.P. 3
  Rev. Daniel 209
  Rev. Daniel (off.) 209
  Elizabeth Ann 105
  Rev. James 105
  Rev. James (off.) 108

DuPre (cont'd)
  Josias G. 126
  Julia C. 199
Dupree, Elizabeth 108
  Dr. Ira E. 55
  Nancy 55
  Thomas C. 140
Duprie, Rev. James 150
Durand, Victor 61
Durant, Hester McCrea 168
  Dr. James 168,210
  M.E. 168
  Dr. Robert 31
Durell, Zechariah 11
Durisoe, William F. 36
Duryea, E.S. 62
Duval, Edward W. 45
  Elizabeth 82
  P. 82
Duyckinck, Benjamin T. 1
Dwight, Angela 119(2)
  Francis Marion 92
  Harriet Marion 205
  Isaac M. 92
  Isabella Safford 92
  Martha M. 92
  Martha Maria 92
  Rev. Nathaniel 53
  Rebecca Louisa 197
  Dr. S. 197
  Samuel 205
  Theodore M. 119(2)
  Thomas Porcher 92
  Timothy 53
Dyer, George B. 140
Dyson, John H. 67

Eager, Rob 127
  Sarah Louisa 127
  William 145
Eagle, Phebe R. 173
Earle, Harriet 27,28
  Maria 13
  Ralph 208
  Samuel 79
  Sarah Ann 24
Eason, George W. 146
  John 117
  R.J. 106
  Robert Sr. 117
Eastburn, Rev. Joseph 16
Easterby, Capt. George 154
  Georgiana 154
Eaton, Joseph C. 26
Eccles, Margaret 174
Echols, Olive Ann 18
  Philip Henry 54
Eckerd, Johannes 206
Eckford, Henrietta 17
  Henry E. 17
Eckhard, George B. 207
Ector, Martha 29

Edings, Mary W. 175
  William 196
Edmonson, Drusilla 10
Edmonston, Charles Jr. 134
  Laurence A. 133
Edwards, Alexander L. 35
  Alexander M. 18
  Ambrose 11
  D.C. 123
  Col. Edward H. 135
  George 75
  J.F. Jr. 194
  Jennetta 70
  Malakiah 15
  Mary W. 58
  Dr. P. Gasden 154
  Rebecca 135
Egan, John 98
Egerton, A.A. 179
Egleston, G.W. 148
  George W. 158
  John 121,131
  Mary 121
  Sarah 131
  Sophia C. 148
Eheny, William 129
Ehney, Mary Adeline 87
  Peter 79
  William H. 78
Eikerenkoetter, Margaret 144
Elder, Margaret 181
Elderbrook, Weilhelmina Frederica 125
Elfe, Benjamin C. 26
  George 165
  George Jr. 33
Elford, Frederick P. 138
  Capt. James M. 205
  Louisa Eleanor 205
Ellemore, Capt. William 38
Elliott, Benjamin 158
  Rev. Charles P. (off.) 150
  Rev. Charles Pinckney 82
  Elizabeth R. Hahnbaum 10
  Jane E. 21
  John 8,49
  John W. 50
  Dr. Ralph E. 40
  Rev. Mr. (off.) 103,148
  Col. Stephen 34
  Rev. Stephen 210
  Rev. Stephen (off.) 154,188, 212
  Dr. Thomas A. 10
  Col. Thomas O. 93
  William S. 104
  William Savage 158
Ellis, Austin 14
  Thomas M. 53
  Jane M. 72
  William D. 66
Ellison, Joseph 203

Ellison (cont'd)
  Margaret 18
  Margaret M. 24
  William 63,179
  William Sr. 179
  William H. 148
Elmore, Amelia 127
  Capt. Benjamin Thomas 171
  Col. T.H. 5
Elsworth, Abigail 141
  Ann Elizabeth 94,189
  John 189
  John T. 62,94,141
  Juliana M. 121
Ely, John W. 16
Emanuel, Sarah 27
Emberson, Sarah 17
Emmett, Thomas Addis 13
England, Bishop (off.) 19,20
  Rev. Bishop (off.) 21
English, Adeline E. 206
  Rev. B. (off.) 126
  James 206
  Capt. James W. 173
  Rev. Mr. (off.) 73,179,183
  Sarah Ann 142(2)
  Rev. T.R. 142(2)
  Rev. Thomas R. 156
Enloe, Nathaniel 26
Enslow, Charlotte E. 49
  Joseph 118
  Joseph Aquilla 168
  Joseph L. 49
  Louisa 118
  Margaret E. 190
  Mary 211
Ernenpeutsch, Rev. Wm. 116
Erskine, Taliaferro 17
Ervin, Capt. William 155
Erwin, Elizabeth 71
  Leander A. 71
  Levin 14
  Rev. Stanhope W. 157
  see Irwin
Esdra, Floride 147
Espey, Rev. Thomas 73
Estes, Rev. Elliott 47
Eustis, Col. ___ 77
Evans, Benjamin J. 31,67
  Rev. Charles 44
  Dr. ___ 93,183
  Frances Ann 112
  Harris Smith 37
  Henrietta Maria 93
  John 22
  John A. 126
  John William 137
  Margaret 95
  Martha 38
  Mary 95,183
  Mary Ann 197
  Rev. Mr. (off.) 140,144

Evans (cont'd)
  Rufus K. 207
  Sarah Ann 125
  Thomas 10
  Capt. William 134

Faber, Henry 8
  Henry F. 132
  Joseph W. 124
  Sarah 8
Fair, Eliza 62
  John G. 109
  Rebecca C. 114
  Capt. William 62,114
Fairchild, Benjamin 177
  Susan A. 177
Fairlie, James 44
Falconer, A. Joshua 50
Fall, Eliza J.C. 15
Fannin, James W. 21
Farley, Agnes 95
  John 95
  Louisa 54
Farmer, Ann Claiborne 106
  D.H. 212
  Dr. Henry 95
  Dr. Henry T. 106
  Susan Baring 95
Farr, Catherine S. 84
  Elizabeth 95
  Nathaniel 84,95
  Nathaniel J.S. 82
Farrington, Maj. Rufus M. 28
Fasbender, John H. 133
  Martha 120
Fash, Ann 165
Fastbender, Constantia D. 91
  J.H. 91
Faust, Daniel 81,111
  Dr. Edwin D. 61
  Jane Arabella 81
  Gen. J.J. 114
Fauster, William 34
Fayssoux, Dr. James H. 142
  Peter 74
  William Cripps 142
Felch, Dr. Cheve 3
Felder, Capt. Abram 66
  Edmund J. 93
  Emily 155
  R. 34
  Col. Richard 106
Fell, Emma Eliza 166
  Frederick S. 14
  Rev. J.R. 212
  Thomas D. 166
  Thomasine Welding 102
  William W. 102
Fenebee, John 144
Fenet, Joseph 37
Ferguson, Barkley 5
  Jane M. 203

Ferguson (cont'd)
  John 46
  Mary 46,47
  William H. 83
Ferrill, James 23
Few, Col. William 26
Field, Isabel C. 189
  Capt. John C. 189
  Rev. Mr. (off.) 50
Fielder, Lewis 13
Fife, James 105
Fincklea, Amelia Eliza 203
  James 203
Finney, Lucretia 19
  Lucretia A. 19
  Walter 159
Firth, Mary H. 15
Fishburn, Benjamin P. 150
  Mary E. 13
  Richard 13
  Richard Henry 150
Fishburne, Benjamin P. 111
  Capt. Lawrence 141
  Lawrence Sanders 141
  Martha Eliza 193
  Martha M. 111
  Mary C. 101
Fisher, Dr. Edward 109
  Emily S. 200
  J. Frances 147
Fisk, Rev. Dr. 80
Fiske, Rev. Nathan W. 31
Fitch, Dr. A. 89
  Abigail 89
Fite, Eve 20
Fithina, Capt. Isaac 70
Fitten, E. 167
  John H. 194
  Jno. 167
  Susan Caroline 167
Fitts, Mary B. 35
Fitzpatrick, Thomas 125
Fitzsimons, Christopher 70,71
Fleming, Elizabeth Howard 30
  Francis F. 73
  Laird 80
  Rev. Mr. (off.) 207
  Robert 167
  Thurza 167
Flemming, Elizabeth 4,39
  Jane Eliza 114
  Ruth Almira 29
  Thomas 4,114
Fletcher, Delphia 23
  Robert 157
Flewellen, Gen. William 101
Flinn, Rev. Andrew 114
  Rev. Dr. Andrew 202
  Eliza Berkley 202
  Rev. Dr. 89
Flournoy, Marcus A. 55
  Mary M. 38

Flournoy (cont'd)
   Rev. Robert 84
   Susannah 55
   William 53
Floyd, Andrew 18
   Ann A. 131
   Caroline E.L. 25
   Elizabeth R. 138
   Fountain R. 35
   Gen. John 58
   Maj. John 141
   Rev. L. 138
   Gen. William 65
Flud, Col. Augustus 41
Fogartie, Edward 91
Folger, Timothy B. 96
Folk, Rev. Joseph 3
Folker, Eliza L. 119
   John Casper 110
   Rebecca 110
   Rev. Mr. (off.) 84
Footman, Eliza 39
Foran, John J. 205
Forbes, Catharine 197
   Henrietta M. 157
   Rev. J.M. (off.) 143
   John 157
   William P. 79
Forbs, Adelai 68
Ford, Benjamin 174
   Danl. 126
   Julia Ann 52
   Malachi 76
   Col. Malachi 113
   Margaret 79
   Margaret Ann 76
   Rachel M. 35
   Rev. Mr. (off.) 102
   Sarah A. 113
   Stephen 48
   Maj. William P. 52
   Wyatt 50
Fordham, John G. 44
   Susan A.M. 130
Fordon, Jane M. 156
Forest, Rev. J. 182 (off.) 182
   Rev. Mr. (off.) 132,157
   see Forrest
Forman, Owen 45
Forney, Fatima E. 16
Forrest, Rev. J. (off.) 191,200
   Rev. John 85,111
   Rev. John (off.) 202,207
   Rev. Mr. John (off.) 81,99,
   119,121,139,140,156,165
   Rev. Mr. (off.) 78,117,121,
   134,135,152,154,155,162,165(2),
   166,168,170,184,193,203
   Wilhelmina Moughan 111
   see Forest
Forst, John D. 158
Forsyth, John 3,51

Forsyth (cont'd)
   Julia 51
   Rebecca 25
Fort, Charlotte M.C. 77
   John E. 77
   Minerva D. 21
   Moses 56
   Robert W. 150
   Sophenia Matilda 34
   T.V. 35
Forten, Harriet Davy 56
   James 56
Fortune, Betsey 42
Foster, Rev. A. 63
   Rev. A. (off.) 6,48
   Altona H. 13
   Andrew 203
   Rev. Anthony 13
   Catharine 195
   Elizabeth 37
   George Leavitt 63
   Isabella J. 203
   Rev. J. (off.) 3
   Col. John 37
   Margaret E. 143
   Miligan P. 143
   Nathaniel 143
   Rebecca 143
   Samuel G. 143
   William G. 143
   Col. William S. 155
Foullen, Maria J. 19
Fowke, Dr. Richard C. 45
Fowler, John James 1
   Rev. Mr. (off.) 97
Fowles, Rev. Mr. 179
Fowls, Rev. James 177
Fox, George W. 43
   John 16
Fraley, Malinda 54
Frampton, John 4
   John E. 183
Francis, Joseph 188
   Julia 166
Franklin, Benjamin 195
   Eliza 204
   Q.L.C. 2
Fraser, Caroline Georgiana 56
   Capt. F. 107
   Helen A. 162
   Hugh 161
   Mary B. 107
   Samuel 186
   Samuel J. 204
   Simon A. 183
   Thomas 204(2)
   Maj. Thomas 56
   Thomas Drayton 204
   see Frazer
Frayssee, John A. 86
Frazer, Charles 180
   Charles P. 122,137

Frazer (cont'd)
  George R. 199
  Hannah P. 180
  J.J. 198
  James Laurence 202
  James Laurens 80
  John J. 115
  Mary H. 198
  Rebecca 45
  Susan E. 122
  Victoria Alexina 180
  see Fraser
Fredeburg, Harriet 138
Frederick, Elizabeth Ann 112
  P.W. 112
Freeman, Edmund 169
  Elijah 104
  Mary 53
  Michael 53
  William 29
Freer, John 61
Frierson, Charles D. 157
  Dr. James H. 161
  James Madison 53,63
  Jennet Emeline 38
  John 79
  John J. 155
  John Wilton
  William V. 38
Fripp, Edward 176
  Elizabeth J. 176
  John A. 202
  Isaac Perry 60
  Mary Julia 202
  Paul A. 87,148
  Capt. W.O.P. 166
Fronty, Emma Barton 95
Frost, Elizabeth 197
  Dr. Henry R. 103
  Thomas 197
Frothingham, Samuel Jr. 164
Fry, George 166
Fulker, Joseph 114
Fuller, Benjamin 92
  Benjamin Jr. 16
  Catharine M. 92
  Edward N. 154
  Rev. Richard (off.) 153
  Thomas A. 184
Fullwood, Nancy 29
  William 10
Fulmer, Rebecca W. 173
Fulton, Martha M. 152
  Paul 152
  Samuel Davis 152
Funderburk, Jacob 156
Fur, Andrew 120
Furman, Jessy Rosalia 8
  John G. 44
  Dr. John Howard 212
  Rev. Josiah B. 181
  Rev. Dr. 41,44

Furman (cont'd)
  Rev. Mr. (off.) 169,172,
  178,193
Furness, Jesse 25
  Rev. Mr. (off.) 139
Furr, John P. 99
  see Fur
Furse, Rhoda Marion 209
Furst, Mary 16
Futerell, Catharine 54

Gachet, Caroline S.M. 22
Gadsden, ___ 108
  Dr. A.E. 84
  Dr. A.F. 58
  Dr. Alexander E. 175
  Ann M. 93
  Rt. Rev. Bishop (off.)
  194,196,207
  Rev. C. (off.) 92,109,133
  Rev. C.E. (off.) 87,165,
  199
  Rev. Dr. C.E. (off.) 113,
  116
  Rt. Rev. E.C. (off.) 193
  Rev. Christopher 150
  Fisher 4
  James W. 86
  John 93
  Mary W. 84
  Rev. Philip (off.) 193,207
  Rebecca 87
  Rev. Bishop (off.) 166,174,
  177(2)
  Rev. Dr. (off.) 4,30,38(2),
  51,58,62(2),75,83,84,86,
  90,91,102,105,110,113,120,
  122,123,131(3),135(3),136,
  138,139,140,144(2),145,
  158,165,167,175,177,193,
  196,212
  Rev. Mr. (off.) 68,79,84,
  114
  Rt. Rev. Dr. (off.) 175,
  188
Gage, John 12
  John Jr. 5
  Nancy 5
Gager, James H. 160
Gaigler, Henry 118
Gailard, Alfred S. 43
Gaillard, A.T. 130
  Anne D. 69
  B. 58,63,167
  Bartholomew 121
  Dr. Charles L. 69
  D.A. 113,131
  David 69
  Dr. Edwin 93
  Eleanor E. 63
  Elizabeth L. 158
  Emma Anna 58
  James 94,158

Gaillard (cont'd)
  Judge 92
  Leonora Carolina 113
  Louisa 121
  Dr. P.C. 206
  Peter 165
  Peter C. 145
  S. Porcher 97
  Theodore 92
  Theodore Jr. 43
Gains, Rev. Henry 42
Gaither, Margaret 23
  Sarah Ann 11
Galliber, Isabella 66
  Samuel 66
Galman, Rev. Dr. (off.) 157
Gamage, Edward 169,190
  Sarah 169
Gambie, Samuel S. 165
Gamble, Elizabeth 6
  Capt. James G. 201
  Rev. James (off.) 164
  Margaret L. 200
  Robert Sr. 197
  Roger L. 200
  Sarah A. 197
  Sophia C. 201
Gambold, Rev. John 18
Gambrell, Larkin 27
Gamewell, Rev. Mr. (off.) 114, 116,118
  Rev. W.A. (off.) 112(2)
Gantt, James Lawrence 157
  Richard Allen 70
Garden, Robert H. 207
Gardiner, John 52
Gardner, Anna 25
  Dr. James T. 133
  Jane 30
Garner, Lydia 15
Garnett, Deborah 4
Garreston, Rev. Freeborn 11
Garret, Catharine 57
  George 170
  Mary 25
Garrison, Maria 26
Garvin, Capt. James 47
  James M. 28
Gary, Jesse R. 87
Gassaway, John 8
Gaston, Amzy Williford 169
  Capt. 142
  Hugh Davies 142
  Hugh Sr. 120
  Capt. James 169
  John Jr. 165
  Martha 120
  Sarah D. 165
  Susan Jane 19
  William 19,130,165(2)
Gates, Col. W. 211
Gaulding, Emily J. 11

Gay, Edward Henry 112
Gayer, William J. 35
Gayle, Gov. ___ 101
  Sarah A. 101
Gayssoux, Dr. Jas. H. 208
  Octavia 208
Gazaway, William 77
Geddes, Gilbert C. 133
  Capt. James 121
Gee, John 84
Geer, Letitia Jane Atkinson 161
  Mrs. M.J. 161
  Willia 17
Gelzer, Eugenia Octavia 201
  George Washington 162
  Thomas 201
Gefkia, Eliza C. 87
George, Dr. David 159
  Rev. David 159
  Rev. J.H. 117
Gerard, P.G. 166
  Peter G. 108
  Susan Drodie 166
Gerardine, Dr. John 147
  William L.C. 147
Germany, Elizabeth Olivia 18
Gervais, Dr. J. Louis 156
  Martha P. 140
  Mary Ann 92
  Sinclair D. 92
Getty, Thomas 175
Geyer, Frederick A. 6
Ghen, Thomas 26
Gibbes, Rev. Allston (off.) 58,64
  Ann Isaklen 53
  Benjamin T. 124
  Caroline 204
  Edwin 53
  Frances 204
  Gardenia Garden 152
  Rev. Henry 53,73
  James Wilson 99
  John 117
  John Barnwell 192
  Lewis L. 31
  Mary P. 199
  Dr. R.W. 199
  Rev. Mr. (off.) 39,44
  Robert Jr. 117
  Mrs. Robert 152
  Robert R. 59,193
  Robert Wilson 14
  Samuel W. 122
  Victoria B. 193
  William Hasell 82
  Wilmot 204
  see Gibbs
Gibbon, George 210
  Mary E. 210
Gibbons, Mary 35

Gibbs, Catharine Spencer 195
  Eleanor Schoolbred 186
  George 136
  Joseph S. 186
  Paul C. 195
  Rev. Mr. (off.) 22
  see Gibbes
Gibert, Mrs. L.M.W. 210
  S.F. 210
Gibson, Adam E. 161
  Alexander 5
  George 186
  Dr. George 145
  Capt. Henry 59
  James S. 200
  Judge ___ 8
  Margaret 36
  Martha Ann 8
  Martha Jane 186
  Sarah A. 59
  see Gipson
Gidiere, Philip N. 46
Gieger, Ann G. 11
Gifford, William 3
Gilbert, Ann S. 154
  J.G. (off.) 21
  Maj. Washington G. 52
Gilchrist, Rev. Adam 62,146
  Rev. Adam (off.) 86,137
  Hester Maria 146
  Mary 172
  Rev. Mr. (off.) 80,95
  Robert 172
Gildersleeve, Rev. B. 26
  Rev. B. (off.) 6,76,84,183,
  189,190(2),208
  Mary Frances 45
  Rev. Mr. (off.) 24,31,36,52,
  59,60(2),64,68,69,70,73,104,
  116,143(2),149,176,204,205,
  210
Gildon, Sophia 10
Giles, James H. 157
  Othniel J. 127
  Rebecca 127
  William 201
  see Gyles
Gilfillin, Alexander 82
Gilham, Thomas 59
Gill, Ann Caroline 148
Gilland, Rev. James R. 193,195,
  204
  Rebecca B. 193,195
Gillard, Harriet 164
  Rev. Mr. (off.) 59
Gillaspie, J. 47
  Nancy R. 47
Gilleland, Ann Eliza 61
  William H. 61
  see Gilliland
Gillespie, Alexander 18
  Andrew Sr. 128

Gillespie (cont'd)
  Daniel 16
  David Ramsey 127
  John 211
  Samuel 42
Gillett, Elizabeth J. 134
  William S. 134
Gilliland, Ann Eliza 60
  William D. 99
  see Gilleland
Gilling, Arthur A. 137
Gillis, Angus 29
Gillison, Martha H. 212
  Samuel R. 212
  Thomas S. 76
Gillson, Adela G. 208
  Samuel R. 208
Gillups, Capt. Thomas A. 16
Gilman, Abby Louisa 184
  Abigail H. 13
  Caroline Harwood 157
  Rev. Dr. 184
  Rev. Dr. (off.) 137,144,
  159,162,164(2),184,200,206,
  210,211
  Rev. Mr. (off.) 20,46,64,
  83,86,90,91,100,112,127,
  132,143,157,188
  Rev. Samuel 157
  Rev. Samuel (off.) 121,141,
  146
  Rev. Dr. Samuel (off.) 168
  Samuel M. 104
Gilmer, Capt. John 5
  Mary 55
Gilstrap, Angelina 57
Gipson, Benjamin 23
  see Gibson
Girardeau, Maria Pinkney 12
  Col. Peter 179
Girardeaux, John B. 91
Gist, Louisa 39
  Sarah Bramford 122
Gitsinger, B.R. 207
  B.T. 155
  Eleanor F. 169
  Eleanor Francis 155
  Harriet E. 200
Gitzinger, John R. 8
Givens, Charles 85
  Emeline S. 86
  Mary 85
  Stephen 86
  see Givins
Givhan, Eliza M. 34
  Job P. 34
Givins, Martha 62
  see Givens
Gladney, Jennet 78
  Richard S. 59
Glass, Doda 31
  Salina Ann 12

Glascock, Mary Savannah 43
  Gen. Thomas 43
Gleize, Eliza L. 110
  Dr. Henry 110
Glen, Anna 70
  Daniel L. 159
  Henrietta Amanda 70
  James S. 70
  John 120
  Mary Gertrude 120
  Thomas C. 132
Glenn, Dr. George W. 210
Glennie, Rev. Mr. (off.) 93,178
Glisten, Kennedy 124
Glover, Alethe Ann 22
  Charles 40
  Eliza 196
  Dr. J. Edward 211
  Jane 184
  Col. John Heyward 196
  Joseph 184
  Dr. Joseph 99,159
  Maria A. 211
  Septema E. 99
  William 17
Gnech, Eliza Maria 197
Gobel, Phebe R. 174
Goddard, Bailey 24
  Thomas M. 26
Gold, Thomas 2
Golding, R.D. 8
Goddard, Thomas F. 47
Godfrey, James T. 77
Good, Francis 163
Goode, Samuel W. 200
Goodlett, William Sr. 113
Goodman, Duke 173
Goodrich, Luthern 21
Goodwin, Maj. Charles 10
Gookin, Richard 37
Gordon, Alexander 16
  Daniel L. 155
  Jesse 175
  John F. 116
  Capt. Thomas 120
  W.W. 177
Gore, Christopher 2
Gorman, Mary S. 32
  William P. 90
Goss, Anne 17
Gotes, Margaret Jane 173
Goudelock, David 143
Gough, Emma C. 136
  Dr. John P. 136
  Thomas P. 135
Gouldine, Rev. T. 59
Goulding, Rev. Dr. (off.) 60,69,73
  Rev. Mr. (off.) 124
Gourdin, Ann R. 23
  Eleanor E. 167
  Louis J. 68

Gourdin (cont'd)
  Maj. Samuel 23
  William D. 63
Gowan, Peter 177
  Peter Caw 177
  Sarah 177
Gowdey, Margaret 69
Graham, Mrs. 88
  Capt. A.F. 186
  Adaline 186
  Alex. 93,94
  Ann B. 93
  Daniel Spaulding 162
  Elizabeth Q. 153
  Fergus 23
  George W. 29
  Hugh 153
  James 35
  Jane 35
  John 88,186
  Capt. John 146
  John P. 71
  Julia Laura 146
  Martha Ann Hutchins 162
  Robert 186
Granby, Mary 113
Grand, Elizabeth 26
Granger, **Rev. Arthur** 98
  Benjamin 151
  Capt. Benjamin 44
  Mary E. 98
Grant, Alexander 8
  Eugenia 52
  Kenneth M. 29
  Thomas 32
  William 52
  William A. 77
Grantland, Eliza A. 16
Granville, Charles 37
Grave, Mary 32
  Sarah 117
Graves, Ann Elizabeth 157
  Caroline McPherson 138
  Charles 157,158
  Dr. Daniel D. 185
  Samuel Colleton 138
Gray, Rev. Mr. A. (off.) 119
  Caroline Louisa 184
  Rev. D.L. (off.)36
  Rev. Daniel L. 203
  Eliza 86,167
  Elizabeth 103
  Emma L. 97
  Harriet E. 47
  Helen Yancey 141
  Isabella 161
  J.D. 188
  Rev. J.H. (off.) 69
  James 38
  Dr. James A. 82
  James W. 119,141
  Jane H. 169

Gray (cont'd)
  John 100,103
  John H. 119
  Rev. John H. 32
  John J. 177,184
  John M. 8
  Julia Helena 177
  Mary Ann 13
  Mary W. 204
  Rebecca Elizabeth 103
  William 78,117,197
Green, Dr. B.F. 14
  Benjamin D. 10
  Christopher R. 26
  Edmund 87
  Elizabeth 87
  F.W. 26
  James 85
  Maj. John Thompson 26
  Margaret M. 112
  Maria Sophia 51
  Martha Caroline 96
  Mary Ann 26
  Richard 9
  Samuel 79,80
  Sarah 80
  Thomas F. 30
  Thomas P. 51,68
Grayson, Dr. C.W. 7
  Maria Willard 78
  William J. 78
Gready, A.P. 11,73,129
  Edward Payson 129
  Emily 73
  George Haunbaum 129
  James R. 177,202
  Mary Ellen Postell 202
  Sarah Adeline 11
  Sarah E. 202
Grech, Ann Amelia 188
  see Gnech
Greene, General ___ 128,190
  Herman D. 12
  Nath. T. 12
  Sarah Cornelia Coleman 12
  William H. 29
Greenwood, Maj. Benjamin L. 24
  Carolina M. 7
  Mary Ann 31
  Rev. Mr. (off.) 115
Greer, Elizabeth 115
  Thomas 17
  see Grier
Gregg, Capt. ___ 153
  Cornelia Carter 171
  David 193
  Ezra M. 171
  Rev. George C. 183
  Rev. George C. (off.) 188,204
  Henry Smilie 120
  Capt. John 153
  John G. 60

Gregg (cont'd)
  Mary M. 193
  Sarah Eliza 171
  Susan J. 171
Gregorie, A.F. 81,212
  Ann Ladson 84
  Caroline Sarah 85
  Col. Charles C. 103
  Edmund 120
  Emily 103
  Henry 102
  James 103,120
  Dr. Thomas H. 212
Gregory, Sarah I. 89
Greiner, John P. 23,24
  see Griner
Gresham, Charles W. 140
  Lucinda 51
Grier, Col.Aaron W. 2
  James M. 7
  Mrs. ___ 88
  Robert 161
  Samuel 88
  Sarah 60
  see Greer
Grierson, William 24,120
Griffen, Thomas N. 125
Griffin, Ariana B. 25
  Ira 35
  James C. 10
  James S. 52
Griffiths, Robert Jas. 183
Grigg, Sarah 18
Griggs, Caroline H. 20
  Henry S. 121
  Isaac 20
Grimball, Benj. J. 141
  John Berkley 36
  P.C. 141
Grimes, Charity 63
  Thomas W. 63
Grimke, John F. 151
  Mary Augusta 23
  Mary S. 151
Grinage, Josephine O. 56
Griner, John P. 165
  see Greiner
Grisham, Col. Joseph 6-7
  Martha Jane 6
Gros, James W. 155
  John H. 83
Grover, Rev. Philip (off.) 181
Groves, Amanda 211
  Martha Hannah 35
Gruber, Margaret E. 149
Guerard, Elizabeth M. 82
  G. Henry 200
  Dr. J.D. 165
  Jacob W. 98
  John 66,79
  John B. 80
  Joseph 82

Guerard (cont'd)
  Louisa Scriven 165
  Mary Lucia 79
  Mary W. 98
  William P. 201
Guerin, Mary 130
Guerry, Henry G. 144
  James 55(2)
  Mary A.K. 14
Guffey, Elizabeth 42
Guffy, Henry 30
Gugel, Harriet 22
Guignard, Caroline 14
  James S. 99
  Susan P. 99
Guild, Charles B.G. 89
Gullet, Nancy G. 133
Gulmarin, John 66
  Sarah 66
Gurvin, Jane 31
Guthrie, Amos 39
  James 39
Guy, Theodore B. 74
Guyton, Charles S. 41
  Mary 127
  William W. 44
Gwyn, Amelia 14
Gyles, Charles 190
  see Giles

Habersham, Ann 34
  Barnard Elliott 131
  Joseph 59
  Richard W. Jr. 116
Hacker, George S. 61
Hadden, Rev. J. 61
Haddon, Rev. J. (off.) 61
Haden, Elizabeth 126
Hagan, Eleanor Virginia 71
Hagnod, Harriet A. 15
Hagood, Eliza 136
  Elvira A. McPherson 47
  Rev. Gideon 6,47
  James 136,148
  Mrs. James 136
  John W. 43
  Dr. William A. 95
Hague, Thomas A. 13
Haig, David 77,117,197
  Elizabeth P. 145
  George 204
  Dr. George 82
  Jane 117
  Margaret 197
  Dr. Robert M. 145
Haigir, B.M. 207
  Horatia Ellenor 207
Hale, Catharine 150
Hall, Catherine O. 131
  Cynthia 17
  Eliza 12
  George Ann 51

Hall (cont'd)
  James 115
  Dr. John 178
  Dr. John D. 125
  Josephine C. 81
  Josiah Q. 53
  Julia Adelaide 158
  Laura 41
  Dr. Philo C. 16
  Rebecca H. 115
  Rev. Robert 50,51
  Maj. Thomas 27
  William 21
  Dr. William 158
Halliday, Jane 148
Hallonquist, Laurent D. 92
Hallum, Eliza Ann 4
  John 3
Halsall, John E. 117
Halsey, David F. 38
Ham, Capt. William 123
Hambleton, Dr. Samuel Henry 33
Hamill, Charlotte Frances 48
Hamilton, Alexander Wylie 182
  Maj. Andrew 94
  Anna 157
  Caroline W. 65
  Daniel Heyward 111
  David W. 83,209
  Capt. Duke 69
  Elizabeth 166
  Emma Eliza 166
  Frances 3
  Gen. ___ 143
  Harriet C. 129
  Maj. J.W. 13
  James 166,143
  Gen. James 166
  Maj. James 129
  Jane 185
  John 64
  Mary 64
  Moses B. 38
  Paul 130
  Susan S. 149
  Walter 6
  William 190
Hamlet, John G. 58
Hamlin, Cornelius 85
  Elisha 85,100
  Emily Edgeworth 84-85
  Frances 209
  John 212
  Mary Gibson 85
  Sarah 212
  William 209
Hammer, Richard E. 118
Hammet, J.B.N. 211
Hammett, Elizabeth Mary 135
  Isabell C. 140
  Mar. Caroline 75

Hammond, Caroline A. 208
  Eliza 27
  Martha 205
  Mary Ann 104
  Col. S. 104
Hamner, Horton 102
Hampton, Ann 71
  Evelina 41
  Gen. ___ 64
  Mary 13
  Col. Wade 71
  Gen. Wade 95
Hanahan, J.C. 8
  John J. 201
Hanchell, Rev. Mr. (off.) 99
Hanckel, Ann Stuart 127
  Rev. C. (off.) 84,106,109(2), 121,143,154(2),158(3),165,178(2),183,190
  Rev. Charles 127
  Rev. J.S. (off.) 175,176,199
  Rev. J.Stuart 158
  Rev. J.Stuart (off.) 162,173, 176,
  John 178
  Rev. Dr. (off.) 162,165,184, 190,197,198,200,201,202,206, 208,211
  Rev. Mr. (off.) 1,21,47,66,67, 78,79(3),80,81(2),82,85,86, 90,91(2),92(2),94,95,100,103, 104,106,107,114,117,118,120(2) 132(3),133,134,136,162,190,206
Hanckle, Rev. C. (off.) 131,145, 148,151
  Rev. Dr. (off.) 118,183
  Rev. G. (off.) 131
  Rev. Mr. (off.) 58,61,69,119, 122,125,148
  Rev. Stewart 164
Hane, John W. 49
Hanks, Thos. 17
Hanna, Britain 18
  Hugh 181
Hannah, William 186
Happoldt, Adeline C. 69
  C.D. 187
  Catharine E. 144
  John M. 144
  Maria L. 187
Harbin, G.W.O. 166
  James 23
Harby, Isaac 3,33
  Rachel 3
Hard, Ann Miranda 110
  Benjamin C. 132
  Benj. F. 110
  David B.W. 110
Hardaway, Robert S. 23
  see Hardway
Hardee, Dr. John H. 100
Hardey, Rev. Charles 29
  see Hardy

Hardin, L. 103
Hardman, Ann 25
Hardway, Capt. Robert S. 22
  see Hardaway
Hardwick, Elizabeth 190
Hardy, Rev. Charles 30
  Elizabeth 44
  Miles 34
  see Hardey
Harford, Wm. Henry 52
Hargrave, Almira 31
  Jesse 28
Hargraves, Joseph 26
Harleston, Edward 56
  Elizabeth 56
  Hugh A. 32
  James Burn 28
  Col. John 56, 167
  Sarah J. 117
  Dr. Summers 117, 145
Harlee, Mrs. A.J. 103
  Dr. Robert 103
Harllee, Maj. ___ 126
  Col. Wm. W. 159
Harlow, Sarah 14
  Dr. Southworth 71
Harmon, Noah Simpson 30
Harn, John B. 22
Harper, James 169
  Martha 38
Harpoldt, Julia 122
  see Happoldt
Harral, Ann 148,178
  George Edward 148
  James 189
  William 129,148,178
  William James 178
Harrall, Anna 166
  Dr. George E. 164
  Thomas Addison Vardell 166
  William 166
Harrington, Desdemona 26
  Harriet 34
  Rev. Jno. (off.) 97
Harris, Adlar 176
  Capt. ___ 74
  Charles 2
  Edmund S. 55
  Edwin 176
  Rev. Elezaur 15
  Francis 55
  Hanna Caroline 80
  Henrietta 179
  James 8
  James W. 48
  Jane 36,183
  Jane Agnew 15
  Margaret 176
  Mary Delia 31
  Mary W. 37
  Matthew 212
  N. 55
  Rachel H. 176

Harris (cont'd)
  Rebecca 3,176
  Robert 42
  Samuel 152
  Dr. Samuel S. 36
  Thomas 179
  Thomas C. 80
  Capt. William 129,183
  William H. 76
  Rev. William H. 179
  William L. 38
Harrison, Amanda Emerson 52
  Elizabeth 34
  Rev. J. (off.) 81,83(3)
  Rev. Jeptha 85
  John Cleves Symms 46
  Joseph W. 166
  Dr. Richard 50
  Sarah 14
  William S. 137
Hart, Caroline 27
  Charles G. 84
  Maj. Charles M. 137
  William 57
Harth, Cecilia 190
  William 190
Hartley, Sarah 56
  Thomas 56
Hartman, Henry 21
Hartt, Gen. Davies 15
  Margaret P. 15
Hartwell, Rev. Jesse (off.)34
Harvey, Dr. Henry Olin 44
  Robert 90
  Tabitha Napier 54
  Thomas Pinckney 61
  William M. 4
  Maj. Wm. S. 96
Hasell, Andrew 109(2)
  Andrew G. 184
  Bentley 19
  Caroline A. 147
  Eliza B. 109
  Georgiana 109
Haskell, Charles T. 46
  Susan S. 170
  William E. 170,205
Hasket, Frances Moore 114
Hatch, Reuben 69
Hatcher, Robert 43
Hatchet, Eugene 147
Hatfield, James 21
  Mary Ann 101
Hathaway, Thomas 10
Hathorn, William 51
  see Hawthorn
Hauck, Ann Caroline 120
  John H. 94
  John S. 120
Haupt, Andrew Jackson 107
Havis, Col. Jesse 9
Hawes, Mary Bonneau Lee 50
  Dr. Oliver 50

Hawkins, Rev. E. 126
  Dr. Hamilton S. 62
  John Sr. 124
  Col. Joseph 9
Hawks, Rev. F.L. (off.) 139
Hawley, Rev. Mr. (off.) 112
  Maj. Wm. L. 88
Hawthorne, Jane 39
  see Hathorn
Hay, Dr. F. Jay 147
  George 44
  Harriet J. 183
  Lewis S. 194
  Maria Louisa 70
  Martha L. 33
  Rev. S.H. (off.) 209
  Dr. Thomas T. 209
Hayden, Ellen 144
  Emma C. 33
  Nancy McCall 152
  Nathaniel 128,142
  Theodocia P. 142
  Thomas A. 69,121,152
Hayne, Elizabeth F. 114
  Eloise M. 127
  Frances H. 205
  Col. Isaac W. 85
  Paul H. 57
  Gen. R.Y. 205
  Sarah 127
  William A. 114
  William Ed 127(2)
Haynes, Dr. C.E. 53
  Elizabeth Frances 21
  Mary Ann McKinley 53
  Col. Thomas 175
Hays, Capt. James 28
  Minerva 15
Hayward, Hannah H. 118
  John 21
  William 118
  see Heyward
Hayword, John 13
Hazelius, Rev. Dr. (off.)87
  Rev. E.L. (off.) 116,163
  Rev. Dr. Ernest 124
Hazzard, Mary Elizabeth 59
Head, Eliza H. 24
  Maj. Robert M. 4
Heard, Ann Matilda 142
  Elezaer F. 39
  Elizabeth 23
  Elizabeth A. 63
  Faulkner 40
  John J. 63
  Col. Thomas J. 21
Heath, Rev. Henry H. 56
Hecklin, Capt. Reuben N. 57
Heddleston, Sarah 169
Heggie, Arch. 99
  Mary Emily 63
Helms, Rela F. 55
Helverston, M. 122

Hembree, Joel 20
Hemingway, John 50
Hemphill, Elizabeth 199
   Emily J. 113
   James 189
   Maj. P.W. 199
   Wade 73
Henderson, Caroline R. 210
   Daniel S. 83,210
   Dr. E.R. 202
   Edward Pinckney 210
   Eliza 31
   Elizabeth 33
   John 25
   Rev. Mr. (off.) 19
   Richard Bullock 36
Hendricks, Mary Ann 87
   Sally 10
Henley, Capt. Robert 29
Hennis, John 14
Henry, Alexander 115
   Ann 23
   Ann Boyce 205
   C.S. 5
   Charles J. 192
   Cordelia Rains 96
   Dr.))) 22
   George 205
   Jacob 96
   James Edward 25
   Martha A. 169
   Martha W. 192
   Patrick 57
Henson, Rebecca 25
Herb, Cathrine 23
Herbemet, Alexander 10
Herbert, J.B. 107
   Joseph B. 59
Hernandes, Emeline Louisa 155
   Peter 155
Heriot, Edward G. 166
   James 190
   Octavius B. 159
   Robert Sr. 164
   Roger 157
   Sarah Margaret 157
   William 164
   William B. 131
Heron, Sarah 104
Herrick, Rev. Claudius 53
Herring, Dr. William A. 33
Herron, Daniel 37
   Rachel 37
Hertz, J. 73
   Rebecca 73
Hester, Sarah 57
Heyward, Ann Markoe 6
   Charles 105
   Charlotte M. 198
   Daniel 58
   Elizabeth H. 148
   Emma 105
   Esther 150

Heyward (cont'd)
   James B. 173
   Mariah 173
   Mary Caroline 154
   Nathaniel Jr. 137,150
   Thomas 148,154
   Thomas Savage 109
   William 6
   William Jr. 23
   William Henry 150
   William M. 173
   see Hayward
Hibben, James 94,144
   Rebecca Theus 144
   Sarah 7
Hichborn, William C. 105
Hickerton, Maj. L. 14
Hicks, Joseph 101
   Capt. William 13
Hickson, Louisa Emeline 171
Hieronymous, Wm. T. 52,159
Higham, Ellen Clairborne 200-201
   Thomas 201
Hildesheimer, Elizabeth 116
Hill, Ann B. 40
   Rev. C.G. (off.) 95
   George 40
   John 51
   Col. John 51
   Mary 8
   Robert 28
   Sarah A. 51
   Starkey 20
   Maj. Uel 67
   Walter A. 48
Hillard, Ann E. 51
   Julia Ann 203
   Nathaniel Green 203
   see Hilliard
Hillegas, George A. 12,104
   Sarah 47
   see Hilligas
Hillhouse, Rev. James 40,106
   Nancy 40
   Sarah 15,51
Hilligas, Philip 92
Hilliard, H.W. 41
   Louisa M. 36
   see Hillard
Hillyer, Rev. S.G. (off.)131
Hitchcock, James M. 58
Hobbs, John 20
   Rebecca 20
Hobby, Alfred M. 67
Hobson, J. 185
Hodge, David 112
   Thomas G. 116
Hodges, Rev. Mr. (off.) 27
Hoemsooth, Rev. W. (off.)206
Hoff, Caroline 168
   John 24
   Lt. K. 145

Hoff (cont'd) Margaret 41
Hoffman, George 3
Hogan, William 1,15
Hoge, Dr. Moses 1
   Rev. Samuel Davis 1
Holbrook, Dr. Moses 203
Holcombe, Rev. Dr. Henry 24
   James W. 10
Holland, J.W.T. 20
   Jane 141
Holler, Mary 12
Holley, Dr. Horace 8
Holloway, Penelope H. 31
   Dr. S.M. 26
   Silas 22
   Utincy W. 22
Holman, Rev. R. (off.) 18,19
   Rev. Robert 21
Holmes, Camilla W. 154
   Caroline 107
   Eliza B. 110
   Elizabeth 119
   Emma 157
   Francis S. 124
   Henry P. 107,155
   J. 110
   J.T.W. 21
   James 154,187
   Jane H. 38
   John Bee 119
   John L. 86
   Margaret 128
   Martha 90
   Rebecca 55
   Regina H. 135
   Sandford Jr. 208
   Sandiford 157
   Susan Jane 157
   T.V. 125
   Venon 31
   Viveon 31
Holsey, Elizabeth Blake 125
   Holpins 125
Holson, Richard G. 83
Holt, Cicero 45
   Dr. Samuel D. 41
Honarth, Henry 154
Hone, Henry 118
Honor, Rev. Mr. (off.) 193
Honour, Rev. J.H. (off.) 157
   Rev. John (off.) 121
   Rev. John H. (off.) 125,152,
     159,162,168
   Rev. Mr. (off.) 172
Hood, John 2
   Peter 134
Hooper, A.M. 105(2)
   Maj. John W. 1
   Louisa 105(3)
   Nathaniel 105
Hope, ___ 93,94
Hopkin, Charles 85

Hopkins, Rev. E. (off.) 99
   E.S. 103
   Edward 63
   Rev. Erastus 99,139
   Isabella Melinda 58
   J. Albert 61
   James 201
   Joseph 103
   Mary T. 12
   Maj. P. 58
   Rev. Mr. (off.) 122
   Samuel 54
Hopkinson, James 200
Hopping, Ephraim S. 14
Horlbeck, Edward 124
Horn, Elmina 41
   Peter A. 204
Horne, Mary E. 159
Horry, Lucretia 102
Horsey, Elizabeth 137
   Thomas J. 137
   Thomas M. 200
Hort, Francis D. 208
Horton, Maj. Alfred M. 55
   Benj. A. 100
   George 23
Hosack, Dr. David 106
Houghton, Jane 44
House, Brevet Brig. Gen. James 91
Houston, Caroline 30
   Mary Ann 3
   William H. 60
Houze, Thomas Y. 30
Howard, Alexander 119
   Dr. Alfred 25
   B. 17
   Rev. C.W. (off.) 117
   Caroline 68,196
   Charles B. 27
   Mrs. E. 36
   Homer 22
   John 49,68
   Rev. John 115
   John Eager 11
   John L. 39
   Josephine F. 202
   M. 36
   Mary Lee 185
   Gen. N. 196
   Nancy 17
   Rev. R.T. (off.) 185
   Richard F. 64,202
   Col. Robert 182,185
   Rev. Robert 143
   Robert J. 206
   Rev. Mr. (off.) 146
   Rev. William 166
Howare, Caroline Virginia 154
   Richard F. 154
Howe, Ann C. 71
   Ann J. 124

Howe (cont'd),
    Charles 71
    George 172
    Rev. George (off.) 106
    Hezekiah 124
    Mrs. ___ 172
    M.A. McConnell 172
    Mary 67
    Rev. Dr. 172
    Rev. Dr. (off.) 172
    Rev. Professor 67,122
Howell, Jesse 95
    Rev. Thomas D. 9
Howland, John 51
Hoxey, Sarah 22
Hoyle, Margaret H. 24
Hoyt, Rev. A. 19
Hubbell, Andrew 10
    Sarah Pamela 122
    Capt. Sears 122
    T.C. 169
Huber, Dr. J.A. 37
Huckaba, Rev. B. 12
Hudson, Emeline 31
    Irby 71
    J.M. 91
    Jane F. 71
    Mary 202
    Mary Jane 202
    Sophia 14
    Col. Thos. 14
Huey, J.B. 119
    James 133,168,210
    Jane Caroline 133
    Jane Clementina 119
    John Thompson 207
    Mary 130
Huff, T.D. 72
Huffman, Jacob 11
Huger, Amelia Amanda 187
    Anna 104
    Charlotte 118
    Cleland Kinloch 175
    D.E. 176
    Daniel 145,187
    Daniel Elliott 136
    Daniel Elliott Jr. 62
    Elizabeth Middleton 176
    Emma 136
    Col. F.K. 159
    J. Chapman 165
    John 68
    Col. John 118
    Maj. John 104
    Joseph A. 159
    Judge ___ 74
    Margaret Heyward 68
    Mary 132,141
    Mary E. 159
    Sarah H. 145
    Thomas Pinckney 176
    William Elliott 74

Hugeunin, Cornelius M. 132
    John 98
    see Huguenin
Huggins, Charles 34
    Julia E. Welts 145
    Louisa Blake 34
    Col. Nathan 145
    Rev. Mr. (off.) 174
    Rev. T. (off.) 208
Hughes, Adeline H. 135
    Mary 91
    Optimus E. 175
Hughs, Elizabeth 71
Huguenin, Emeline L. 137
    Eugenia Amanda 19
    James D. 32
    Julius G. 80
    William J. 113
    see Hugeunin
Huie, Harvey 47
    see Huey
Huke, John F. 131
Huling, Andrew 41
Hull, Ann 59
    Rev. Hope 59
Humber, Robert 103
Hume, Eleanor Jane 177
    Henrietta 35
    John 167
    William 177
Humming-bird, Gen. 19
Humphreys, Rev. D. (off.)14,38
    Rev. David 3,201
    Rev. David (off.) 1
    Martha E. 155
    Rebecca 201
    Rev. Dr. (off.) 185
    Rev. Mr. (off.) 16,34
    William 155
Humphries, Elizabeth B. 116
Humphrys, Rev. D. (off.)41,50
Hunt, Dr. George 82
    Hannah 67
    Henry 91
    Capt. Joseph 67
    Nathaniel 126
    Dr. Thomas 84
    Col. William 72
    William H. 45
Hunter, Alex 2
    Rev. Humphrey 10
    Col. John G. 40
    Col. Jno. L. 187
    Lewis 44
    Sarah Elizabeth 187
Hunting, William G. 203
Hurlbut, Elizabeth C. 139
    M.L. 139
Hurst, Ann L. 140
    Charles W. 89
Hussey, Mary S. 44
Hutcherson, Richard W. 46

Hutchings, William Vincent 144
Hutchins, John M. 186
  Col. K.L. 186
  Mary 186
  Rev. Mr. (off.) 20
Hutchinson, Ann 6
  Ann S. 5
  Elizabeth L. 83
  Mary 123
  Thomas Leger 71
  William 16
Hutchison, David 193,195
Hutson, Ann 56
  Capt. John 134
  Maria P. 152
  Nancy 11
  Dr. Thomas W. 33,150
  W. Ferguson 108
  Rev. William 96
  William H. 96
Hutton, Gen. Joseph 164
  Nancy 164
  Rev. Dr. (off.) 182
Huxford, Joseph 187
Hyatt, Edmund 99
  Nathl. 138
Hyde, Rev. E.F. 208
  Rev. E.F. (off.) 203
  George A. 211
  Simeon Jr. 184

Inge, Dr. Ricard 15
Inglis, Alex. 139
  Mary 93
Ingraham, E.D. 8
  Eliza M. 137
  Henry 35
  Juliet H. 193
  Lt. 38
  Nathaniel 193
  Maj. William Postell 211
Ingram, Bartholomew 18
Irvine, Dr. Mathew 9
Irwin, James 21
  see Erwin
Israel, James 89
  Nancy 89
Iverson, Col. Alfred 51
Izard, Alice 62
  Ann S. 127
  Henry 114
  Ralph 62

Jack, Mary 24
Jackson, Eliza L. 154
  James 154
  Malvina C. 199
  Mary P. 18
  Orra 10
  Rachel 14
  Col. Samuel 10,46
Jacobs, Belah H. 136
  Rev. Ferdinand 207

James, Ann R. 45
  Holloway 43
  J.T. 126
  Jane Isabella 59
  John 48
  Joshua 33
  Mary N. 48
  Matthew 185
  Mildred M. 90
  Rev. R.W. (off.) 16,18,78,
    85,160
  Robert 188
  Sarah 48
  Sarah A. 85
  William E. 46
  William F. 59
  Zechariah 212
Jamison, Iby 45
  Dr. V.V. 121
Jaques, Thomas L. 92
Jardoe, Walter 68
Jarratt, Martha Bibb 22,23
Jarrott, Dr. Richard 159
Jastice, Eliza 32
Jaudrell, John M. 114
Jayroe, Nancy 8
Jeannerett, Catharine Dalton
  209
  James M. 198,209
Jeffers, Rev. John F. 30
Jefford, Charles M. 208
Jeffries, Emily 176
Jenkins, Christopher 91
  Grimball P. 204
  John 23,109
  Dr. John J. 66
  Maria Eliza 78
  Mary Caroline 94
  Mary S. 91
  Micah Sr. 35
  Richard 94
  Robert B. 172
  Robert S. 204
  Susan 66
  T.C. 64
  William E. 165
Jenks, Frederick A. 7
Jenney, Eliza Ann 91
Jennings, Nancy 43
Jerman, Allston C. 199
  James E. 46
  James G. 199
Jernigan, Henry 22
Jerry, Rev. John L. 17
Jervey, Elizabeth 159
  Dr. James Postell 69
  Thomas 70
  Capt. Thomas H. 159
  William 148
Jeter, Capt. Andrew 22
  Sabra 41
Jewitt, Joseph 92

Johns, Rev. Mr. (off.) 68
Johnson, B.R. 61
  Benjamin 206
  Catharine 155
  Dr. Christopher C. 181
  Daniel 57
  Chancellor David 181
  Eliza 13
  Elizabeth 181
  Elizabeth Ann 125
  Ellan Virginia 148
  Francis W. 132
  Gabriel 16
  Capt. Henry 159
  Dr. I.A. 130
  Dr. Isaac A. 77
  James 12,84
  John W. 146
  Jonathan 11
  Letitia Jane 84
  Lotta 18
  Maria 57
  Mary 16
  Mary A. 18
  Mary Whaley 162
  Nathaniel 125
  Rev. Mr. (off.) 152
  Rev. Richard (off.) 158,159, 162,176
  Sarah Jane 130
  William 162
  Rev. William B. 47
Johnston, Anna Eliza 7
  Dr. Benjamin 32
  Catharine H. 136
  David 122
  Elizabeth 9,70
  Emma S. 90
  George H. 122
  Chancellor J. 202
  James 106,117,127
  James C.A. 80
  Job 136
  John 10,58
  Capt. Jonas 186
  Margaret P. 127
  Mary 58,70
  Mary Campbell 83
  Mary G. 122
  Mary Jane 117
  Matilda 29
  Sarah 32
  Sophia C. 10
  Thomas 9,83,90
  William 90,161
Joiner, John A. 45
Jones, Abraham 123,137,195
  Maj. Albert 202
  Ann Amanda 137
  Ann Eliza 25,93
  Anna Margaret 193
  Dr. Bartlett 49

Jones (cont'd)
  Rev. C.C. (off.) 166
  Catharine M. 123
  Catharine Maria 186
  Rev. Charles B. (off.) 195
  Charles Berrien 185
  Gen. Edmund 25
  Dr. Edward 113
  Edward J. 141,186
  Edwin H. 36
  Elias 93,163
  Eliza M. 185
  Eliza Y. 95
  Elizabeth C.F. 134
  Elizabeth Creswell 45
  Evelyn E. 185
  F.S. 162
  Frances 26(2)
  George 39
  Gershon 52
  Dr. Harris Graham 27
  Jabez 22
  James 27
  James L. 13
  Chancellor Job 185
  Rev. John 166
  Rev. John (off.) 185
  John B. 104
  John C. 34
  Mrs. ___ 32
  Margaret A. 174
  Maria Elizabeth 195
  Martha 15,22
  Martha Elizabeth 163
  Paul 95
  Dr. R. 95
  R.V. 94
  Rev. Mr. (off.) 34
  Dr. Richard 174
  S.P. 25
  Samuel Phillips 108
  Sarah 122
  Sarah H. 22
  Sarah Harris 113
  Col. Thomas 13
  Thomas C. 92
  Thomas H. 24
  Thomas L. 56
  Mrs. Thomas L. 43
  Thomas Legare 13
  Thomas S. 82,134
  Tilson Tipley 134
  William 33,80,193,186
  Rev. William 9
  William C. 69
  William H. 111
  William R. 86
  Wiswall 162
Jordan, Aaron 195
  Ellen C. 164
  John 27
  Joshua 27

Jordon, Uriah 18
Joseph, Henry 11
  Jacob J. 27
Joudon, Elizabeth 7
Joy, J.P. 197
Joye, Ferdinand S. 127
  Martha M. 107
Judd, David C. 195
Judson, Isaac 20
  Mrs. 3
Judah, William D. 107
Jueson, Rev. Albert 148

Katchler, John F. 19
Kaufman, Rev. Mr. (off.) 119, 126(2),132,135
Keals, Martha E. 168
Kearney, Lawrence 81
Keaton, Mary E. 143
Keckeley, Dr. Edward C. 36
Keckley, Elizabeth B. 171
  George F. 139
  John C. 171
Keels, John 181
  Nelly 181
Keith, Elizabeth L. 94
  James C. 15
  Mariette 37
  Rev. Mr. (off.) 168,173,177, 205,208(2),212
  Rev. P.T. (off.) 19,196
  Rev. Dr. Reuel 37
  Rev. T. (off.) 197
  Thomas J. 94
  Rev. Trapier (off.) 166
Kelly, Thomas 163
  Col. William T. 11
Kelogh, Thomas 41
Kelso, William 178
Kemp, Rt. Rev. Bishop 12
Kendrick, Col. J.W. 29
  John B. 54
  see Kindrick
Kennan, Dr. Lewis H. 31
  see Kennon
Kennedy, A.A. 13
  Aaron A. 14
  Ann Matilda 87
  Clementena Sarah 170
  Eliza Ann 17
  Capt. Francis L. 132
  George 5
  Hannah 5
  Rev. J.L. (off.) 73
  Rev. J. Leland (off.) 73
  James M. 205
  John 5
  John B. 201
  Maj. L.H. 170
  Leocadia 102
  Miss ___ 22
  Margaret Jane 188

Kennedy, (cont'd)
  Martha M. 22
  Rev. R.W.B. (off.) 47
  Rev. Mr. (off.) 84,87,93
  Rev. W.M. (off.) 77
  Rev. William M. 87
  Rev. William M. (off.) 85
Kenney, Rachel 43
Kennon, Augustus 24
  Dr. John 55
  see Kennan
Keowin, Ann Aurelia 90
Ker, Rev. John (off.) 171
Kerr, Alexander M. 16
  James 107
  Thomas J. 139
  Whitfield 28
Kerrison, Anna 196
  Charles 144,196
  William 196
  Capt. William 65
Kers, ___ 93,94
Kershaw, Fanny 168
  Newman 157,168
Ketchum, Rev. C.K. (off.) 136
  Rev. Joel 157
  Mary H. 157
Key, Daniel 165
  Sarah 165
Keys, Caroline 17
  Ellenor Frances 6
  P. 103
Kiddell, Charles 104,116,204
  Mary Anna 104
  Rachel 116
Kilgore, Joseph 21
Killian, Cynthia A. 198
  Cynthia Evelina 198
  Daniel 198
  Robert Cleveland 198
Kilpatrick, Robert 160
  Capt. Thomas 160
Kimberly, Anon 56
Kindrick, William O. 25
  see Kendrick
King, Amanda D. 10
  Catharine 36
  Charles M. 10
  Dr. Edmund T. 10
  Gen. Edward 108
  Elijah Augusta 180
  Elizabeth S. 59
  Capt. George 7
  Henry C. 187
  James Sr. 163
  John 2,52,127
  Lucinda Sophronia 52
  Maria C. 58
  Mary 170
  Mary Ann 180
  Priscilla 24
  Mitchell 28,42

King (cont'd)
  Rufus 4,108,158
  Samuel 188
  Sarah 41
  Thankful B.E. 132
Kingman, Catharine R. 193
  Eliab Sr. 96
  John 172,193
  Mary E. 172
Kinloch, George 131
  Martha Rutledge 196
  Mary A. 131
Kirk, Agnes M. 209
  Alexander 185
  James 209
  Lucy 29
  William 104
Kirkland, Rev. John T. 9
  Mary Ann 132
  Rev. Mr. (off.) 197,198
Kirkly, Thomas 45
Kirkpatrick, Benjamin 30
  John 14
  Rev. Josiah James 41
Kissiah, Susan 55
Kitchings, Elizabeth 27
Kittleband, D.E. 124
  David 56
  Margaret 58
  Mrs. S. 151
Kittles, Louisa 33
Klipstein, Louis F. 199
Knapp, Colby 152
  Lucie 152
  Peter W. 148
Knight, George 201
Knowles, Isaac P. 88
  Rev. Mr. (off.) 107
Knox, Ann 202
  Elizabeth 91
  George W. 48
  John 164
  John F. 91
  Johnson J. 78
  Lucretia 102
  Margaret 93,160
  Samuel B. 7
  Rev. Samuel 66
  Sarah Eugenia 18
  Walter 202
Kollock, Lemuel 145
  Mary Fenwick 145
  Sarah B. 26
  Rev. Shepherd K. 26
Koontz, Rev. Hugh M. 115
Krider, Margaret 12
Kugley, Annie O. 104
  Jane J. 87
  Martha 104
  Robert R. 168
Kunhardt, William W. 158
Kuypers, Rev. Girardus A. 74

Laats, Adaline Eliza 95
  Caroline V. 120
LaBruce, Elizabeth L. 162
Lacey, William 139
Lachicotte, Julius 85
Lackey, Elizabeth 24
Lacoste, Caroline Angeline 92
  Sarah E. 84
  William 60
  William C. 65
Ladson, James H. 205
  Sarah Gilmor 205
  William F. 38
Laird, Rev. Robert M. 125
Lamar, Basil Sr. 12
  Col. Benjamin B. 107
  James 99
  Jefferson J. 27
  John T. 180
  Mary Ann 73
  Rebecca Ann 27
  Sarah 99
  Dr. Thomas R. 29
Lamkin, Helen 51
Lampkin, Mary 44
Lamson, Susan 10
Lancaster, Martha 86
Lance, Esther Jane 162
  Dr. John G. 96
  Col. Lambert 113
  Rev. M.H. 106
  Maria Ramsey 145
  Mary Taylor 106
  Rev. Maurice H. 162
  Rev. Maurice H. (off.) 187
  Rev. Mr. (off.) 69
  Rosanna T. 96
  Sarah 113
  William 145
Lanchester, Elizabeth A. 14
Landers, C. 23
Landershine, Charles P. 130
  Martha Ann 35
Landrum, Rev. J. 12
  Lucinda 12
Lane, Benjamin 70
  Mark A. 39
  Martha M. 70
  Mary S. 39
Laney, Rev. Noah (off.) 18
Langdon, Elizabeth 31
Langston, Solomon 128
Lanneau, Bazil 97,149
  Bazile 78,129
  Charles Henry 149
  Emma Louise 26
  Fleetwood 69
  John Francis 129
  Rev. John Francis 177
  Peter 151
  Peter Jr. 70
  Sarah 129
  Sarah L.B. 149

Lanos, Charles 23
Lapsley, Rev. Joseph 31
　Sarah W. 31
LaRoche, Eliza S.M. 35
LaRouseliere, Glorvina 136
　L. 136
LaRousselliere, Eliza 190
Lartigue, Col. Isadore 208
LaRoy, Philip 208
　Susan Amelia 208
Laslie, Eliza J. 169
Lasseter, John 40
Latham, Mary Ann 122
Lattimer, Alfred R. 16
　Margaret Ann 3
Laughton, Rev. Winborn A.12
Laurens, Caroline Olivia 32
　Frederick 4
　Harriet Horry 38
　Henry 38
　John Ball 32
Laval, Catharine Ann 45
　Jacint 110
　Jacint Jr. 45
　Jacintha E.C. 110
　Louisa H. 16
Law, ___ 203
　Ann 32
　Elizabeth A. 151
　Dr. John S. 21
　Rev. Josiah (off.) 116
　Rev. Mr. Josiah S. 48(2)
　Maria Matilda 32
　Capt. William 151
Lawrence, Alexander R. 38
　Ann 92
　Eliza Susan 199
　H. Anslie 149
　Margaret Deas 149
　Maria Ainslie 149
　Mary Mathewes 149
　Robert D. 149,199
Lawry, John 47
　Lycia 47
　see Lowry
Lawson, Col. Roger 43
Lawton, Col. A.J. 115
　Joseph M. 51
　Margaret M. 40
　Martha 115
　Mary Ann 41
　Mary Louisa 178
　R.B. 178
　Winborn 40
Lazarus, Maj. 105
Lea, Henry Clinton 28
　Mary Amanda Adeline 69
　see Leigh, Lee
Leach, Milton W. 140
Leadbetter, Rev. Mr. (off.) 62
　Rev. Thomas (off.) 95
Leak, Rev. Samuel 36
　William P. 11

Leak (cont'd). Wyatt C. 175
Leavitt, Horatio 58,127
　Mrs. Horatio 127
　Jonathan 38
Lebby, Francis S. 145
　Thomas F. 93
　William 193
Ledbetter, Rev. Mr. (off.) 64,91
　William 17
Lee, A.M. 189
　Abijah 2
　Anna Maria 87
　Caroline A. 142
　Elizabeth 170
　Rev. F.B. (off.) 204
　George W. 40
　Harriet 73
　Harriet C. 40
　Harriet Rebecca 144
　Isaac McP. 87
　Joseph T. 98
　Judge ___ 185
　Dr. Lawrence 124
　Mary A. 98
　Mary C. 74
　Paul S.H. 87,144
　Rev. Mr. (off.) 79
　Sarah D. 182
　Stephen 170
　Dr. Thomas 63,142
　Thomas Y. 45
　Rev. W.S. (off.) 105(2),196
　William 73
　Col. William 182
　Rev. W. States 104
　Rev. Wm. S. (off.) 33
　Rev. Wm. States 74
　Rev. Wm. States (off.) 93, 154
　see Lea,Leigh
Leefe, Benjamin 85
　John B. 53
　Louisa 85
　Mary Jane 77
Leeke, David 165
Lees, William Sr. 18
Leesk, Rev. Mr. (off.) 172
Lefevre, Clementine Helen 30
Legare, Ann Eliza 136
　Anna B. 211
　Eliza S. 119
　Elizabeth W. 196
　Francis S. 119
　Hugh S. 189
　Rev. I.S. (off.) 155
　I.S. Keith 80
　James 34,196
　James C.W. 79
　John B. 211
　Joseph 17
　Mary S. 184
　Sarah 17

Legare (cont'd) Solomon 87
  Thomas 136
  William B. 149
Legay, Rebecca S. 4
Legg, Ella 126
  Maj. G.W.H. 170
  Joseph 126
Lehre, Thomas 139
  Col. Thomas 11
Leibrandt, Caroline C. 123
Leigh, Benjamin 36
  see Lea, Lee
Leitch, Duncan 23
  William Y. 188
Leland, Rev. Dr. A.W. (off.) 21
  David W. 124
  Dexter 77,153,191
  Dr. ___ 210
  Hannah Napier 202
  Hibben 171
  James Hibben 104
  John A. 209
  Joseph 54
  Maria Wilkinson 124
  Rev. Dr. 137
  Rev. Dr. (off.) 73,88,94,98,
    103,189,202
  Richard Morrison 171
  Sarah Margaret 137
  Susan E. 153
Leman, Edward P. 167
  William Walker 172
Lemmon, Dr. Sheldon 12
Lemon, Robert 195
Lequex, Capt. Peter 11
Lesasen, Isaac 212
Lesesne, Daniel 144
  Henry D. 111
Lessene, Thomas 131
Lessesne, Mary D. 103
  Thomas 103
Leverett, Rev. Edward (off.) 178
  Rev. Mr. E. (off.) 135
Leverette, Rev. C.E. (off.) 172
  Rev. Mr. (off.) 87,123
Levingston, Alfred 139
  Harriet M. 139
  Capt. William 141
Levy, Col. Chapman 24
  Rosina 24
Lewers, Rev. Mr. (off.) 85
Lewis, Caroline M. 32
  Elizabeth C. 208
  John 147
  John W. 174
  Jonathan 92
  Mary Ellen 158
  Smith L. 38
  Col. William L. 158
Liddell, Andrew Sr. 73
  George W. 3
Lide, Hugh 189

Liepman, E. 200
  Josephine Felicea 200
Likens, John 160
  Rev. John Glenn 160
Limbaker, John 89
Limehouse, Rev. R.J. (off.) 206
  Robert 123
  Susan Elizabeth 123
Linder, Mary M. 37
Lindsay, Ann E. 82
  Ann Elizabeth 160
  Betsy 16
  Esther 28
  Robert 3,45
  W. Jr. 160
  William 82,116
Lindsey, Mary C. 211
  William 211
Ling, Charlotte 112
Lining, Edward B. 125
  Susan M. 125
Linster, John W. 11
Linton, Dr. A.B. 81
  Mary H. 81
Lippe, Elizabeth V.D. 126
Liston, H.S. 11
Little, Andrew 42
  Charles Augustus 97
  James C. 108
  Rev. Robert 8
  William 42
Liverman, Conrad Sr. 30
Livingston, A. 12
  Catherine Barnwell 185
  John Ashe 188
  Madison C. 25
  P.P. 185
  Thomas 61
  see Levingston
Lloyd, Esther 103
  Susan Pickering 78
  Ursula R. 175
  William 8
Locke, George A. 173
  George B. 76
  Matthew B. 36
  Zilpah 76
Lockwood, Allison 108
  Benj. Postell 115
  D.P. 115
  Eliza Fishburne 131
  Joshua 118
  Joshua Jr. 108
  Joshua Sr. 104
  Mary Lee 104
  Capt. Thomas P. 131
Lofton, John 4
Logan, Ann Catharine 191
  Dr. George 92,191
  Rev. George C. 184
  George Christian 96

Logan (cont'd), Mary 51
  Rosa Turner 184
  Rose J. 184
  Tyre J. 51
  William Jr. 160
  William Daniel 70
Loner, Christeener 118
Long, Elvina 104
  Felix 14,67
  Maj. Gabriel 2
  John 104
  Joseph H. 155
  Louisa 46
  Sarah 71
  William 71
Longstreet, Mary Ann Olivia 208
  William 208
Longworth, Joseph 109
Loomis, Flavel 8
Loper, Henry G. 162
Lopez, Samuel R. 132
Lord, A.B. 83
  Fanny 17
  Harriett G. 136
  Hezekiah 50
  Jacob 116
  Jane Emma 116
  Mary Proctor 83
  P.M. 198
  Richard 136
  Richard N. 183
  S. 50
Love, Sarah 22
  Thomas W. 22
Lovell, Ann 90
Lowe, Henry W. 51
Lowndes, Mrs. E.R. 170
  Dr. Edward 129
  Edward Rutledge 79
  James Sr. 79
  Rawlins W. 69
  Thomas 190
  Thomas Pinkkney 144
  William 69,176
Lowrance, Sarah 35
Lowrey, Charles Sr. 75
Lowry, Alexander 181
  Dr. Alexander 40
  Ann L. 109
  Rev. M. 109
  Mary 79
  see Lawry
Loyless, Ally Caroline 23
Lubbock, Capt. Henry W. 35
Lucas, Benjamin 155
  Emma Septima 192
  J. Hume 208
  John 57
  Jonathan 88
  Col. Jonathan 208
  Jonathan Sr. 71
  Lydia 88

Lucas (cont'd) Martha 57
  Mary Hayes 208
  Robert 57
  Simons 90,192
Ludlam, Richard L. 137
Lumpkin, George W. 38
  John B. 32
  Col. Joseph H. 147
  Lucy 147
Luscomb, Rt. Rev. Bishop (off.) 151
Luther, Mary 55
Luthern, Catherine M. 104
Lyle, Daniel 192
Lynah, Edwqrd 196
  Henrietta 165
  James 165
Lynn, John S. 43
Lyon, Rosina 46
Lyons, Isabella 17
  Martha 10

McAdams, Thomas 34
McAllister, W.J. 157
  see McCallister
McAlpin, William C. 54
McBee, Silas 11
McBride, Jane 14
  Samuel 150
  William 201
McCaffrey, James Marion 200
McCalin, Tilla 11
McCall, B.B. 176
  Emma Eliza 153
  Hext 81
  John G. 67
  Louisa 60
  Mary 153
  Moses 153
  Sarah Georgiana 22
  Thomas 60,196
  William 81
McCalla, Maj. John 167
  Susan 167
McCallister, James 48
  see McAllister
McCann, Maj. Hampdon 78
  Robert 53
McCants, Ann 151
  James C. 177
  William 151
McCarter, James J. 71,192
  Walter 76
McCauldless, John 90
McCaw, Francis E.H. 134
McCay, Harriet B. 153
  Thomas Bacot 182
  see McKay
McClain, Rev. Mr. (off.) 138
  see McLean
McClaren, Isabella 99
McClary, David 12
  Samuel 57

McClean, Margaret 89
  William Sr. 31
  see McLean
McCleary, Leonora 101
McCleish, Ann America 125
McClelland, Jackson 62
  Mary 68
McClenaghan, George 161
  John 161,196
McClintoch, Susan 137
McClintock, Henry King 198
  Mary Ann 156
McClure, John Sr. 195
  Mary 197
  Thomas 176
  see McLure
McCombs, Robert 36
  Sarah W. 36
McConnell, M.A. 172
  Sarah Ann 122
  Tirza 10
McCord, Col. D. 151
  D.J. 159
  Maj. David 19
  Emeline 151
McCorley, Peggy 14
McCorquedale, Rev. Allan (off.) 200
McCosh, Joseph 101
McCoy, Rev. G.W. 167
  Rev. George W. 183
  Redden 185
  William 14
McCracken, James 174
McCrea, Esther Louisa 16
  Mary E. 60
  Thomas 60,75
  see McRa
McCreight, Margaret 11
  Nancy 5
  Col. William 5
Mc Mary A. 67
McCrone, William 109
McCulloch, Canzada 83
  Mary 21
McCullough, Martha 76
  William 76
McCully, William N. 99
McCutchen, Elisha Franklin 128
McDaniel, Sarah Ann Frances 83
McDermont, P. 25
McDill, Nancy 4
McDonald, Flora 24
  Mary Ann Isabella 96
McDougall, Rev. Alexander 167
McDow, Sarah 8
  Thomas 104
  William 154
McDowall, A. 102
  Andrew 76,135
  Caroline 135
  James 189

McDowall (cont'd), John 76
  Jessie 102
  William D. 106
McDowell, Barbara 168
  Davison 180
  John 168
  Rev. John Robert 121-122
  Mary D. 48
  Rev. (off.) 65
  Rev. Dr. (off.) 23,26,64,
    66,70,71,91,92
  Rev. Mr. (off.) 4,5,66
  Thomas McCrea 180
McDuffie, George 43
  Mary Rebecca 43
  William 172
McElhenney, James 170
McElmoyle, Eliza 210
  Elizabeth 174
  Hannah Jane 37
  James 210
  William 37,174,210,212
McEvers, Charles 95
  Eliza 95
McEwin, Rev. James 198
  Rev. Mr. (off.) 60
McFaddin, Capt. John 5
  Martha 45
  Mary 31
  Capt. Robert 31
  Theodore C. 95
McFarland, Rev. Asa 2
  Rev. John 27
  William 86
McFarlane, Jane 190
McFie, James 126
McGann, Patrick 84
McGarrity, Martha Howell 73
McGehee, John 112
  John C. 81
McGill, A. 195
  see Magill
McGinn, Elizabeth 57
McGowen, Ann 26
McGran, Margaret 68
McGregor, Capt. William 11
McHange, Jane 189
McIntire, Charles 172
McIntosh, Barbara 32
  Charlotte J. 66
  Daniel 65
  Henrietta 65
  Sarah 28
McIver, Maj. D.R.W. 172
  Harriet 116
  Mary E. 172
McJunkin, Abraham 212
  Dr. D. Watts, 189
  Margaret 212
McKay, John 200
  Mary 200
  see McCay, Mackay

McKee, Margaret 85
McKeen, Louisa 27
McKelvey, Margaret 45
McKeme, Dr. John G. 207
  Margaret 207
  Robert 207
  Susannah 207
McKemie, James 161
McKenney, Rev. J.A. (off.) 93
McKenny, John 16
McKensie, Benj. F. 167
McKenzie, James 8(2)
  Mary 26
  Sophia 201
  see Makenzie
McKey, Francis 50
McKinney, Maj. James 167
McKinnon, John 190
McKnight, Ann 29
  James 10
McLain, Jane 187
  see McClain, McClean, McLean
McLaren, John Sr. 152
McLaughlin, David 142
McLean, Mrs. Christian 171
  Mary 25,55
  Gen. Richard D.S. 4
  Gen. R.D. 75
  see McClain, McClean, McLain
McLeish, William 188
McLin, Rev. J. 193
  Capt. Hugh 193
McLure, Ann F. 174
  Ann T. 173
  Thomas 173,174
  see McClure
McMahen, Mary 14
McMasters, John 149
  Martha 149
McMath, John H. 23
McMeens, Margaret 33
  Matilda 33
McMichael, George 158
McMillan, Daniel 147
  James W. 203
  Jane A. 59
  Jannett C. 193
  John 10
  Rev. John 80
McMillen, Daniel 141
  Elmyra 141
  Rebecca Jane 141
McMullen, Archibald 31
  Hannah 31
  Rev. James P. (off.) 207
McMurray, Hugh 8
McNabb, Rev P. (off.) 206
McNarr, D. 84
McNeal, Augustus 22
McNeel, Samuel 20
McNeely, Andrew 20,21
  Samuel 21

McNeil, A. 169
McNeill, Capt. Daniel 74
  see McNeal, McNeel
McNish, Col. ___ 132
  Constantia 132
  Jane D. 26
McOwen, P. 192
  Sarah Ann 192
McPherson, Col. James E. 83
  James S. 105
  Col. James S. 212
  John 104,144
  Rev. Mr. (off.) 139
McQueen, Dr. Alexander 30
  Dr. Archibald 7
  Rev. D. (off.) 131
  Eliza 11
McQuerne, Samuel 17
McRa, Capt. John Chesnut 91
  Margaret 5
McRae, Ann 206
  see McCrea
McRory, James 191
  Jane 191
  Susannah 191
McTyre, Judge 54
McWhorter, Andrew 10
  Rev. George G. 115
  Mary Ann 10

Macaulay, Daniel 9
  George 71
  Lydia Julia 71
  Mary Ann 9
Macbeth, Charles 94
  Mary 165
Macbride, Henrietta 64
  Dr. James 64
Macell, Caledonia C. 23
Macin, Elenor H. 38
  see Macon
Macingram, Catharine 90
  John 90
Mack, James 137
Mackay, Dr. Albert G. 122
  Margaret C. 40
  Pphraim Mikell 61
  Robert 40
  see McCay, McKay
Mackey, Amanda N. 208
  Franklin Payne 3
  Dr. John 3,208
Maclay, Rev. A. (off.) 118
Macon, Capt. H. 17
  Nathaniel 14
  see Macin
Madison, James 113
  Mrs. ___ 57
Magart, Rev. John P. 163
Magarth, John 9
Magill, Daniel 93
  Irvinia A. 93

Magill (cont'd), Mary E. 143
  Dr. William 143
Magrauder, Sophronia J. 39
Magruder, George M. 63
  Lucia 105
  Judge Thomas 105
  Judge William 120
Maguire, Catharine 27
Magwood, Charles A. 147
  Rebecca H. 147
  Col. Simon 114
  Simon John 154
Main, Amelia 5
  Eliza 90
  J. 26
Maine, Wm. Catherwood 189
Makensie, Michael 111
  see McKenzie
Mallard, Thomas 47
Mallory, John 3
Malone, Robert 136
Malphus, J.B. 112
Man, Robert 210
  see Mann
Maner, Major ___ 67
Mangham, Henry 49
Manigault, Maj. G.H. 100
  H. Heyward 172
  Henry M. 125
  Louisa M. 57
  Peter 57
  Walter Izard 100
Manjing, John H. 124
Manley, Rev. B. (off.) 33,92,
  110,122,125
  Rev. Mr. B.(off.) 39,96
  Rev. Bazil (off.) 93
  Rev. Dr. (off.) 131
  Rev. Mr. (off.) 44,46(2),61,
  67(3),71,74,78,80,87(2),89(2),
  92,93,96,104(3),107,108(2),
  115,117,121,122(2),123,130
Mann, Peter D. 59
  see Man
Manning, John H. 124
  Richard J. 208
Mannon, Dorcass 211
Manor, Maj. John S. 143
  Mary 143
Mansfield, John 23
Manson, George R. 71
Marchant, P.P. 90
Marchman, Tabitha 88
Mariano, Ann C. 11
Marion, F.B. 58
  Francis 73
  Gen. Francis 73
  Francis Jr. 132
  Sarah E. 132
  see Marrion
Markham, William 153
Marks, Dr. Elias 6,60
  Jane 6

Marrion, Caroline Julia 139
  Nathaniel W. 139
  see Marion
Marshall, Rev. Alexander W. 34
  Eliza 205
  Rev. Jabez P. 62
  John 70
  Rev. Mr. (off.) 175
Martin, Alexander 146,194
  Ann 51
  Ann Eliza 86
  Ann S. 194
  Ann Sophia 95
  Betsey K. 14
  Rev. C. (off.) 157
  Rev. C.W. (off.) 153
  Rev. Charles W. (off.) 134
  Edmund 56
  Elizabeth B. 43
  J.J. 155
  Jacob 163,208
  James 26
  Rev. James 47
  James B. 123
  Jane Gano 163
  John 155
  John N. 86,146
  Julia Ann 5
  Julius M. 3
  Lauretia 146
  Louisa Ann 155
  Mrs. ___ 56
  Malichi 97
  Margaret 34
  Margaret Catharine 146
  Rev. Mr. (off.) 104,105
  Robert 28
  Thomas F. 28
  Rev. Mr. W. (off.) 98
  W.D. 34
  Col. W.E. 127
  William Bond 97
  William N. 153
Martindale, Louisa 88
Mason, Rev. Cyrus (off.) 99
  Polly 10
  see Mayson
Massey, Enos 14
Massot, Horace Jr. 206
Maston, Jefferson 16
Matheson, Murdoch P. 196
Matthewes, Capt. Edward W. 100
  Edward W. 178
  Eliza Ann 49
  George 212
  J.R. 49
  Mary 212
Mathews, Ann Elizabeth 116
  Caroline 30
  Rev. Edmund 116
  Emma Catharine 80
  Dr. J. Holmes 49
  John 102

Mathews (cont'd), John R. 45
  Lewis S. 161
  Louisa 182
  Rev. Moses 76
  Sarah 13
  Susan 45
  William 80
  William Jr. 161
Matthewes, Ann Asby 83
  John R. 116
  Martha J. 116
  William 83
Matthews, Rev. Edmund 160
  Edward W. 167
  Emeline L. 133
  Dr. F.T. 208
  Harriet E. 131
  Isabella 190
  Jane S. 166
  John 18
  John R. 131,175
  Phinehas 125
  Robert 33,133
  Samuel P. 166
  Sarah A. 167
  Susan 33
Mauger, Harriet E. 206
  John 206
  Maria Ann 47
Maull, Philip B. 149
Maverick, Samuel 86
Maxey, Col. Esek H. 11
  Samuel T. 84
Maxwell, Eliza 23
  Harriott Elliott 198
  Maria Julia 191
  Mary T. 7
  Robert 117
  Sir William 143
  William L. 191
May, Sibyl H. 44
Mayarant, Isabella 70
  see Mayrant
Maybank, Maj. Andrew 81
Mayers, Sarah Ann 175
Mayes, Dr. Junius A. 204
  Matthew 168
  Thomas G. 163
  see Mays
Mayhon, Minerva 11
Maynard, Elizabeth Ann 34
  Dr. Richard 34
Mayo, Frederick 21
Mayrant, Ann 162
  Charles 84
  John 70
  Maj. John 132
  William 162
  see Mayarant
Mays, Col. Samuel Warren 64
  see Mayes
Mayson, Elizabeth G. 63
  George Washington 99

Mazyck, Alexander H. 58
  Ann S. 174
  Eliza Stanyarne 142
  Elizabeth S. 126
  Mary 210
  Nathaniel B. 126
  Dr. Philip P. 142
  Stephen 33,210
  William Jr. 174
Meacher, Eliza A. 166
  Thomas 166
Mealy, Rev. A. Stephen 9
  Rev. Mr. (off.) 19
  Rev. S.A. (off.) 22
Means, Dorcas N. 175
  Eliza M. 172
  Elizabeth 17
  H.H. 137
  Hannah 137
  Gen. Hugh 137
  J.P. 101
  M.E.J. 101
  Dr. Samuel 198
  Dr. Thomas 127
Medlin, Richard 12
Meers, Jane Eves 26
Meigs, Rev. Benjamin C. 126
  Eliza B. 126
Meiklejohn, Rev. Dr. 55
Melton, Davis 204
Melvin, Robert 46
Memminger, Col. C.G. 67
Meng, J.E. 176
Mercer, Rev. Asa 119
  Daniel 36
  Silas 22
Merchant, Margaret Summers 112
Mercheson, Isabell 45
  see Murchison
Meree, Thomas H. 85
  William Sr. 164
Meriam, Charlotte 54
  Joseph 54
Meriwether, Dr. T. 29
  see Merriwether
Merrett, Eliza 138
Merrick, Charles 157
Merriman, Erasmus Darwin 176
Merritt, Elizabeth 27
  Hester B. 76
  James H. 157
  Mary Eliza 157
Merriwether, Dr. George Matthews 28
  Thomas 51
  see Meriwether
Mershon, Arden R. 26(2)
Messeeh, Abdool 17
Mey, Adeline 177
  Jane 177
Maynardie, Elas 115
Michau, Laura W. 4
  Mary C. 5

Michel, Eugenia 123
  Dr. W. 204
  Dr. William 123
Middleton, Arthur 123
  Arthur Jr. 170
  Eleanor Isabella 3
  Eliza 147
  Elizabeth L. 135
  H. 147
  Henry 3,73
  J. Motte 166
  John 34,72,111,135
  John Izzard Jr. 19
  Margaret E. 114
  Maria Henrietta 73
  Mary 176
  Nancy P. 21
  Rebecca 111
  Russel 114
Mikell, Mrs. E.M. 178
  Edward 135
  Eliza Adeline 79
  Emily C. 98
  Ephraim 79,135,154
  J. Jenkins 98,108
  John C. 198
  Joseph M. 207
  Mary Ann 154
  William A. 196
Miles, Ann E. 16
  James S. 118
  Jeremiah J. 100
  John 102
  Mary Eliza Smith 102
  Thomas B. 193
  William 12
Millar, Ellen A. 165
  J.C. 68
  Robert S. 105
  William Jr. 171
Miller, Adeline 94
  Ann 44
  Ann Eliza 116
  Daniel 116
  E.N. 205
  Edward W. 75
  Elizabeth 171,209
  Elizabeth Steed 8
  Rev. G.B. (off.) 63
  J.P. 26
  James 91
  Jane 91
  Job P. 80
  John 171,197
  Col. John B. 182
  John D. 117
  Joseph 27
  Mary 15
  Rev. R.J. 15
  Rev. Robert 86
  Sarah 151
  Sarah Jane 18
  Stephen D. 137

Miller (cont'd)
  William 151,184
  William B. 209
  Capt. William H. 46
  Col. William M. 182
Mil**lig**an, Benjamin Chaplin 102
  Elizabeth F. 102
  Joseph 102
Milliken, Mary Jane 195
  William 195
Milling, Hugh 128
  Jane 154
Millner, Pitt W. 11
  see Milner
Mills, Clark 128
  Drake 60
  Rev. E.J. (off.) 4,6,15
  H.G.O. 18
  J.L.F. 48
  Jacob 4,10
  James A. 15
  John Anderson 74
  Maj. Robert G. 177
  Samuel S. 121
  Sarah 60
  Dr. Thomas S. 67
  William 4
  William H.C. 13
Milner, Elizabeth 17
  Martha W. 11
  Susan 11
  see Millner
Milnor, J.G. 165
Milstead, Sally 23
Milton, Ranson 2
Mims, Henry 13
  Nancy E. 29
Minton, Avis 12
Minturn, John 110
Mintzing, Jacob F. 34,177
Minus, Margaret A. 114
  Margaret E. 114
Miott, Charles H. 112
  Ellen 112
Miscally, Caroline Anne H.162
  Daniel W. 162
  Margaret Emeline 90
Mitchel, Elias 93
Mitchell, Anne F. 84
  Byrd B. 31
  Charles 30
  Gen. D.B. 126
  Dorothy S. 161
  Edward 123
  Dr. Edward 123
  Ellen E. 17
  Elizabeth Martha 80
  Emeline Amanda 111
  Gen. Henry 149
  Rev. J.A. 102
  James 49,61,80,111
  Maria Sutherland 61
  Martha 26

Mitchell (cont'd), Mary S. 199
  Rachel Louisa 123
  Rev. Mr. (off.) 44,68,103(2)
  Stephen 7
  Dr. William 102
  William G.B. 199
  Rev. William H. 111
  William Y. 150
Mobley, William 55
Modett, George 203
Moer, Elodia Sarah 173
  Thomas 173
  Thomas W. 192
Moffat, S. 68
Moffett, Andrew 142,160
  Anna 142
  Margaret Hall 160
Moffitt, Alison 200
  George 200
  Isabel Miller 200
Molean, Daniel 124
Monefelot, Julian Emelia 206
Mongin, John David 79
Monjoy, H. 149
  Josephine Louise 149
Monk, Mrs. ___ 105
  Stephen P. 39
Monroe, James 44
Monteith, Galloway 44
  Rev. Walter 86
Montgomery, Dr. ___ 92
  Elizabeth 129
  Col. J.M.D. 180
  James 127
  James D. 175
  Col. James M. C. 182
  Maj. John 8
  Joseph 129
  Martha Eliza 127
  Mary M. 92
  Nancy 16
  Nancy F. 180
  Narcissa 48
  Samuel J. 112
  Sarah C.H. 57
  Rev. T.F. 155
  Rev. T.F. (off.) 133(2),196, 197(2)
  Rev. T.P. (off.) 196
  Rev. T.R. (off.) 197
  Ulysses M.C. 103
Mood, Rev. Christian 126
  Jane R. 126
  William G. 96
Moodie, Louis Alexander Edward 42
Moody, James G. 37
Mooney, Rev. A.M. (off.) 169,187
  Rev. Arthur M. 102
  Rev. Arthur M. (off.) 176
  John D. 102
Moore, Alfred 50

Moore (cont'd) Amanda 64
  Ann C. 82
  Augusta L. 61
  Bryson 11
  Catherine C. 82
  Charles A. 199
  David Jr. 17
  Edwin T. 182
  Elizabeth 123
  Elizabeth A. 189
  Ellen G. 184
  J. 23,190
  James 37
  James D. 82,173
  John 39
  Josephine G. 206
  Martha 190
  Mary 19
  Mary Ann 20
  Mary Jane 36
  Capt. Matthew S. 7
  Philip 206
  Dr. Robert 25
  Stephen West 184
  Thomas 182
  William A. 30
  William B. 131
Moorhead, Cynthia 81
Moorman, Lemuel 29
Morague, Isaac 180
  Mary Elizabeth 180
Morcock, William 9
Mordecai, M.C. 17
More, Nancy 51
  Robert 182
  William 51
Morehead, William 42
  see Moorhead
Moreland, Lydia 23
Moreton, Rev. Mr. (off.)145
Morgan, Ann K. 192
  Arthur A. 191
  Rev. Ashbury 28,192
  Catherine Ann Louisa 16
  Capt. Charles W. 16
  Isaac C. 139
  James 140
  Rev. N.R. (off.) 60
  Richard 69
  William 118
Moring, John Jr. 19
Morison, Agnes 81
  see Morrison
Morrall, George Washington 108
Morrell, George W. 80
  Eliza Louisiana 80
Morris, Charlotte M. 172
  Edward 102
  Henry 157
  Col. Lewis 36,172
  Mary W. 2
  Meta A. 36
  Robert 2

Morrison, Rev. B.H. (off.) 210
  Elizabeth S. 38
  Isabella 70
  James 198
  John M. 17
  Joseph 121
  Margaret 13
  Mary Elizabeth 107
  Mary F. 46
  Capt. Richard 104
  Robert 107
  Susan 104
  Thomas 149
  see Morison
Morrow, Capt. David 194
  Samuel 211
  Maj. Samuel 177
Mortimer, Edward 7,120
  Isabella H. 120
  Samuel H. 119,162
Morton, Henry 66
  Robert Montgomery 162
Mosely, Col. David 94
Moser, Dr. Philip 51,94
Moses, Isaac 56
  Solomon Sr. 24
Moss, Eliza B. 15
  J.B. 15
  John B. 11
Motte, J. Ward 161
Moughon, William 17
Moultrie, Dr. William L. 193
Mourton, Penelope E. 57
Mousseau, Emily 189
Mouzon, Charles 30,85
  Esther Susan 30
  Martha Ann 85
Muckenfuss, Henry 112
  Louisa M. 112
Muggride, Ann M. 131
Muggridge, M. 162
  Susan 162
Muir, Alexina Jessie 73
  Asa J. 152
  William 73
Muirhead, Robert 120
Muldrow, Margaret Frierson 111
  Mary Frances 204
  Dr. Robert 111
  Warren A. 188
Mulheron, Mary Ann 58
Muller, Rev. Geo. Washington 87
Mullings, Capt. ___ 144
  Mary Ann 144
Munn, Benj. Swan 121
Munroe, Nathan C. 24
Munsell, Rev. Saber 65
Murat, Joachim 56
  Prince Lucien 56
Murchison, E.E. 26
  Jane M. 26
  see Mercheson

Murden, Jeremiah 205
  Octavia 205
Murdock, ___ 116
Murfee, A. 195
Murphy, Amanda Margaret 62
  E.F.Thomas 50
  John 16,61,94
  Peter 62
  Rev. Mr. (off.) 61
Murrah, Rev. W. 77
Murray, Col. D. 53
  Hilary M. 25
  James L. 33
  Samuel J. 133
  Sarah J. 53
  Sarah Robinson 133
  Col. Thomas W. 66
  William Sr. 110
  William C. 82
  see Murry
Murren, Mary 101
Murrill, Benjamin 45
Murry, J.S. 164
  Sarah Catharine 164
  see Murray
Mushatt, John 202
Mustard, David 162
Myatt, Edward 114
  Martha Davis 114
Myce, John 135
  Martha S. 135
Myers, Frances 181
  Frederick 114
  Henry 23
  Philip 181
Myrick, Capt. Goodwin 50
Myrover, James H. 125

Naginses, Jasper S. 168
Nail, Barbara T. 16
  Malinda 15
Nance, Maj. F. 156
  Sarah 34
Napier, Col. Thomas 48
  Maj. Thomas 143
  Tabitha E. 24
Nardin, Dr. D.F. 122
Naser, Ann 103
  Caroline 107
  Caroline H. 192
  Casper 107,116
  Emma 104
  Frederick 104,158
  Sarah Mary 116
  Sophia 158
Nash, Elizabeth 13
Nayler, William 136
Neagle, Dr. R.C. 12
Neal, Mary Ann 54
Nealy, Rev. Richard 19
Neel, Samuel J. 38
Neeley, Mary 195

Neely, Eleanor 58
Capt. Nathan 21
Samuel 58
W.C. 58
William N. 29
see Nealy, Neeley
Nelson, Ann Eliza 14
 E. 89,183
 James 181
 James M. 133
 Mary Laura 159
 Mathew 42
 William 84
Nephew, ___ 208
 James I
Nesbit, Mrs. A.A. 142
 Allen 142
 Hugh W. 37
 Hugh Wilson 154
 Dr. James 63
 Jane A. 142
 Robert 64
Nesmith, Lemuel W. 169
Neufville, Ann 148
 Benjamin S. 47
 Rev. Edward 23,75,145
 Isaac 148
 John 172
 Mary Martha 75
 Rev. Mr. (off.) 165
Nevins, Rev. William 101
Newcomb, Lemuel 15
Newman, Thomas J. 203
Newsom, Anthony 6
Newton, Elizabeth 33
 William M. 114
Neyle, Henry Manly 91
 Philip A. 120
Nichol, Rev. Isaac (off.) 143
Nicholl, Sir John 143
Nichols, Horace E. 157
 Capt. James Craton 184
 Martha E. 127
 Rev. Mr. (off.) 134
Nicholson, Maj. B.F. 164
 Benjamin F. 46
 Georgiana M. 164
 James 118
 Dr. John O. 48
 see Vicholson
Nickerson, Mary Ann 38
Nicolai, Catharine 132
Nipper, Rev. Mr. (off.) 192,193
Nixon, Capt. ___ 160
Noah, M.M. 14
Noble, Floride C. 155
 Mr. ___ 140
 William 30,83
Nohr, Mary 137
Nolls, Parmelia J. 75
Nopie, William A. 84
Norman, Selina S. 33

Norment, Rev. John H. 25
Norris, James C. 33
 Patrick 106
 Phoebe 20
 William J. 22
North, Ann Jane 105
 Dr. Edward W. 105,106,186
 Dr. Elisha 192
 John G. 8
 Dr. Richard L. 140
 Susan Emma 106
Norton, Cynthia Maria 93
 Daniel Sr. 107
 Jabez 153
 Richard 107
Norwood, Rev. Mr. (off.) 174
Nowell, Lionel Chalmers 87
Nurser, Jacob 2
Nutting, Mary 47
Nye, Albert 157

Oakes, Charlotte H. 49
 Samuel 49
 Z.B. 49
Oakley, James B. 134
 Mary 134
O'Bannon, Cynthia 116
 Maj. Louis 116
 Sarah 116
O'Callaghan, Francis 48
O'Connor, T.J. 100
O'Dina, John E. 82
Odom, Allen Madison 136
Odum, John 107
Ogden, William 114
 Mrs. Wm. S. 65
Ogier, Sarah J.K. 85
 Thomas 76,85,203
 Dr. Thomas L. 78
 William Henry 203
O'Hara, Caroline Lawrence 131
 Col. Charles 177
 Mary Jane 33
 Oliver 131
O'Hear, James 97,136
 John S. 92
 Dr. John S. 211
 Louisa 147
 Mary D. 136
O'Leary, Daniel 148
Olin, Mary Ann 151
 Rev. S. 3
 Rev. Stephen 151
Oliver, Ann V. 196
 Sophia 90
Onderdonk, Rev. Bishop (off.) 56
 Rev. Dr. (off.) 12
O'Neal, Charles 72
O'Neale, Elizabeth A.J. 87
 James 99
 Mary S. 99
O'Neil, Jane J. 17

Onis, Don ___ 7
Oppenheiner, Rev. M. (off.) 105
O'Riley, Caroline 6
Orr, Capt. Jehu 3
Orme, R.M. 179
Orurute, Kingatara 86
Osborn, Rev. Mr. (off.) 60
   Richard 56
   Rev. Thomas 1
Osborne, Adeline L. 26
Oster, Martin 14
Oswald, Gen. ___ 6
   George W. 178
   Dr. John 173
   Robert Sr. 82
   William 6
Otis, Walter M. 193
Overstreet, William 7
Owen, A.F. 197
   Allen F. 133
   George 16
Owens, Dr. Benj. F. 31
   Henry Alston 97
Oxlade, Thomas C. 121

Pace, Col. Thomas 49
Paden, Mary 8
Padget, Polly 14
Page, John 6
   John Wesley 6
   Margaret Honour 6
   Thomas Mason 6
Pain, Harriet B. 210
Paine, Capt. Joseph B. 7
   Thomas 18
   see Payne
Paisley, Robert A. 41
Palmer, B.M. 172
   Rev. B.M. 127,147,200
   Benjamin Blakely 200
   Rev. Benj. M. (off.) 201
   Catharine 85
   Rev. E. 156
   Rev. E. (off.) 123
   Rev. Edward 91,108
   Rev. Edward (off.) 50,108,152
   Elizabeth 144
   Esther 64
   Rev. F. (off.) 183
   Harriet Jerman 60
   Dr. I.S.K. 132
   Jane Keith 127
   Jeffrey 35
   Job 64,123
   John 60,73,117
   Joseph 11
   L. 85
   M.S. 127
   Martin 68
   Mary Jane 91
   Mary S.B. 99
   Dr. Peter P.P. 60

Palmer (cont'd), Rev. Dr. 99
   Rev. Dr. (off.) 14,31,33
   37,47,49,51,52,58,61,62,63,
   64,78,87,94(2),99(2),162,
   163,191
   S.W. 183
   Dr. S. Keith 147
   Samuel 180
   Sophronia L. 108
   William G. 60
Panible, Capt. John M. 13
   Panknin, C. 210
Parish, Gary F. 14
Park, James 21
   Mary C. 24
Parker, Ann S. 83
   Benjamin John 131
   Charles 117,118
   Maj. Charles 99
   Charles Rutledge 187
   Elisha 54
   Elizabeth R. 92
   Emily Rutledge 92
   Francis Simons 106
   Henrietta 134
   Isaac 41
   John 24,92
   Julia P. 189
   Maria L. 191
   Noah 18
   Peter G. 91,191
   R. Lawrence 189
   Samuel 115,157
   Sarah Elizabeth 119
   Susan Mary 157
   Trena 12
   William Henry 27
   William McKenzie 42
Parkerson, Ann Maria 121
   John 121
Parks, Capt. Hugh 35
Parler, Harriet A. 108
   William 108
Parrot, Nancy 10
Parson, Henry 23
Parsons, Caroline E. 10
   Henry 24
   Rev. James (off.) 101
   William S. 35,196
Parter, Margaret 45
Paslay, Edward 59
Pasmore, Delanore B. 22
Pass, Mathew J. 25
Passman, Margaret 8
Patillar, James 31
Paton, Catharine 2
   see Peyton
Patrick, Casimer 189
   Julia 189
Patterson, George W. 113
   James 85
   James C. 138

Patterson (cont'd)
  Rev. James C. (off.) 157
  Jane L. 66
    Jane S. Matthews 166
    Josiah 3
    Lucy 160
    Margaret Euphemia 79
    Mary 47
    Samuel 79,166
    Sarah 3
    Simeon H. 45
    Capt. William 160
    William Jr. 47
    William P.P. 147
Patton, Hannah 197
  Col. James 197
  James W. 16
  Rev. William K. (off.) 167
Paul, Dunbar 157
Pawley, Elizabeth Francis 86
Paxton, Henry W. 96
Payne, Emma R. 62
  John B. 6
  Rev. Mr. (off.) 199
  William 62
  see Paine
Peack, Richard 10
Peacock, R. 12
Peake, Henry T. 154
Peale, Charles W. 2
Pearce, Capt. J.H. 124
  Rev. Theophilus 8
  see Peirce, Pierce
Pearson, Col. D.W. 109
  I.M. 78
Pease, Peter 5
Peck, Ephraim 74
Pecket, Eliza W. 29
Peden, Rev. A.G. 203
  Rev. A.G. (off.) 159
  Rev. A.J. (off.) 195(2)
  Alexander 180
  Andrew 179,189
  Bishop (off.) 186
  Catharine Mary Elder 207
  E.C. 207
  Elmina 189
  James 186,204
  Jane 179,204
  John T. 165
  Rev. M. 206
  Rev. M. (off.) 195
  M.E. 203
  Margaret Teresa 186
  Mary 165,180
  Mary Crawford 203
  Rev. Mr. (off.) 137,158
  William 180
Peeler, Michael 11
Pegues, Mary S. 22
Peirce, Marcus T. 84,85
  see Pearce, Pierce

Peixotta, Rev. Mr. (off.) 17
Pelot, Joseph A. 115
  William 12
Pelzer, Ann L. 159
Pemble, Caroline J. 105
Penfield, Josiah 28,29
Pennington, Ann Elizabeth 66
  Charles B. 136
Penny, George 29
Penot, R. 56
Pepper, D.G. 95
Percival, Dr. Wm. F. 157
Perdriau, Ann L. 89
  Lydia Ann 67
  Martha 31
Perkins, Benjamin 81
  Daniel 146
  Elisha 17
  Henrietta 81
  Isabella Nott 146
  Capt. William 4
Peronneau, Edward C. 83
  H.W. 156
  Mary Coffin 156
  William Henry 208
Perony, Louisa G. 67
Perry, Abraham 155
  Ann D. 46
  Anna 158
  Caroline B. 188
  Edward D. 47
  Maj. Edward Drayton 79
  Elizabeth 2
  Francis A. 134
  James 197
  Josiah 110
  Josiah Bedon 168
  Maj. ___ 158
  Mary Julia 110
  Stobo R. 188
  Terril 43
  Thomas J. 134
  William 134
  William P. 147
Perryclear, John 118
  Martha 118
Peters, George 82,131
  Jane 81
  Mary 82
  Sarah Howe 131
Petete, John 22
Petigrue, James L. 187
  Susan M. 187
Petigur, James 8
  Jane G. 8
  William 23
Petigure, Caroline 174
  James L. 174
  see Pettigur
Petigru, Harriette 111
  see Petigrue
Petrie, Rev. G.H.W. (off.) 192
  George 54

Petsch, William 125
Pettibone, Chauncey 32
Pettigur, Ann 140
  see Petigur
Pettingell, Amos 178
Pettus, Cynthia 7
Peyre, Mary M. 97
Peyton, Edward W. 16
Pharr, Rev. Henry N. 10
  Rev. Henry N. (off.) 21
  Rev. Jos. W. (off.) 97
Phelps, Francis L. 162
  Dr. H.C. 22
Phifer, Barbara 51
  Col. Caleb 51
Philips, William 5
Phillips, Rev. Mr. (off.) 82,157
Pickens, Col. Andrew 140
  F.W. 207
  Col. F.W. 199
  Francis W. 11
  Israel 5
  Capt. Joseph J. 6
Pickett, Frances 30
  William D. 133
Pickler, Garrett 20
Pickling, Eliza M. 91
  Isaac 91
Pierce, Lydia 5
  Rev. Mr. (off.) 82,86,90
  Susan J. 56
  see Pearce, Peirce
Pigott, Joseph 19
  Rachael 9
Pillans, Eliza 117(2)
  John C. 117(2),148
Pillins, Mr. ___ 190
Pillsbury, Samuel 52
Pilsbury, Samuel 25
Pinckard, Charlotte F. 25
Pinckney, Rev. C.C. (off.) 157, 170(2)
  Charles Jr. 96
  Rev. Cotesworth (off.) 11
  Edward 20
  Dr. Hopson 121
  Mrs. Gen. 111
  Rev. Mr. (off.) 154
  Commander Richard S. 179
  Susan Sarah 154
  Maj. Gen. Thomas 30
  William 96
  Dr. William 86
  William C. 154
  Col. Wm. Cotesworth 118
Pinkston, Tabitha 45
Player, Maj. Joshua 79
Pledger, William M. 75
Plowden, James 202
  James Dickey 197
  Leah Ann 160
  M.H. 160
  M. Hampton 197

Plowden (cont'd), Martha L. 197
  Martha L. 197
  Mary M. 28
  Naomi 202
  William 28
Player, Col. ___ 64
  Mary 64
Poe, Washington 33
Poindexter, Thomas B. 43
  Col. William 14
Poinsett, Joel R. 77
Polhill, James 110
Polk, Ann Formentin 23
  Rev. Leonidas 39
  M.T. 12
  Marthall T. 51
Pomeroy, Rev. Thaddeus 62
Ponce, Anna Maria 184
  Francis J. 184
  Dr. Joseph Burroughs 180
Pond, Charles 24
Pontoux, Mary Villa 162
Pool, Edlizabeth 15
  Rev. Mr. (off.) 131
Poole, Edward R. 193
Pope, Rev. Benjamin 107
  Caroline 14
  Daniel 12
  Eliza C. 165
  Emma C. 136
  Thomas H. 34
  William Sr. 165
Porcher, C.R. 49
  Catharine 7
  Charlotte 98,99
  Dr. Edward 104
  F.J. 184
  Dr. Francis Y. 174
  Frederick A. 61,136
  George 106
  Henrietta 193
  Isaac 98,99
  Isaac Jr. 158
  Dr. John P. 107
  Julie E. 174
  Marianne G. 106
  Martha 158
  Mary 90
  Philip 77,90
  Maj. Samuel 193
  Col. Thomas 96
Post, Ralph 44
Porter, Rev. A.A. 210
  Rev. A. 202
  Anna E. 119
  B.F. 211
  Caroline A. 14
  Dr. ___ 76
  E.W. 24
  Joseph J. 211
  Hannah 210
  Hannah Hayden 130
  Col. John Jr. 30

Porter (cont'd), Col. John S. 31
  Joseph J. 211
  Capt. L.M. 136
  Mary Ann 23
  Rev. Philip 169
  Ruth B. 21
  William L. 119
Porteous, John 153
  Sarah 153
Post, Rev. Dr. (off.) 134,141,
  145,146,147(2),151,157(2),160,
  164,165,172,174,175,177,178,
  180,188,192,197,199(2),203,
  205(3),208,211
  Rev. Dr. R. (off.) 187,208
  Rev. Mr. (off.) 109,115,117,
  124,126
Postell, Charlotte Smith 188
  Rev. Edward P. 103
  Rev. Jehu G. 134
  John 62
  Col. Philip S. 188
  Dr. Philip S. 99
  Rev. Mr. (off.) 112
Posthill, Rev. J.C. (off.) 144
Potter, John 4,40
  Obediah 29
  Priscilla 25
  Rev. Mr. (off.) 159
  Sarah Zilpha 93
  W.H. 4
  Washington 57,93
  Rev. William (off.) 130
Potts, Henry 29
  James 13
  Thomas H.D. 82
Powell, Allen B. 198
  Lewis 49
  Sarah Ann 54
Powelton, Col. Near 15
Power, Caroline A. 12
  Elizabeth H. 13
  Rev. Dr. (off.) 40
  Rt. Rev. Mr. (off.) 147
Powers, Rev. Mr. (off.) 13
  Rev. Urias 81
Powledge, Lucy V. 10
Poyas, Ann B. 165
  Catharine 118
  H.S. 165
  Dr. J.E. 113
Prater, Lydia 17
Pratt, Col. David 25
  Elizabeth 140
  Rev. H.S. (off.) 122(4)
  Rev. Horace S. 60
  Dr. John Turnbull 201
  Rev. Nathaniel 36
  Rev. Mr. (off.) 8,86
Prentiss, Anna R. 94
  W.O. 91
Presley, William 6

Pressley, Benjamin C. 160
  Rev. Ebenezer E. (off.) 133
Pressly, Rev. John T. (off.)
  31
Preston, Sarah H. 76
  Rev. W. 76
  William H. 109
Preval, J.C. 38
Prevost, Joseph 104
  Margaret Emma 44
Pribble, Ann E. 133
Price, Ann Eliza 87
  Charlotte S. 122
  Charlotte Smith 212
  Isham 110
  John B. 10
  Mary Ann 188,202
  Mrs.   110
  Col. O'Brien Smith 190
  Thomas 183
  Rev. Thomas H. 98
  Thomas W. 122
  William Jr. 52,87
  Dr. William S. 202,212
Prides, F.L.J. 192
Primrose, Elizabeth 161
  Margaret Ann 102
  Robert 102,161
Prince, Aylwin Lawrence 82
  C.J. 199
  Mary 199
Pringle, Edward J. 73
  Eliza Butler 112
  George 65,176
  James R. 112
  James Reid 205
  John A. 176
  John J. 150
  John Julius 186
  Louisa C. 65
  Mary 77,150
  Robert 186
  Robert A. 201
  Sarah 190
  William 190
  William Alston 207
Prioleau, Cahterine 67
  Dr. Philip Gendron 201
  Samuel 67
Prior, Richard 16
  Maj. Seth T. 46
Pritchard, Agnes Taylor 53
  Dr. C.C. 91
  Rev. C.H. (off.) 209
  Mrs. C.K. 154
  Cashal F. 12
  Constantia Smith 21
  Elizabeth Ann 151
  Mary S. 199
  Paul 53
  Paul Sr. 199
  Rev. Mr. (off.) 208

Pritchard (cont'd)
  William 75
  William Jr. 151
  William Sr. 21
Propst, Jacob 21
Proctor, Carolina Matilda 62
  John B. 4
  Col. Stephen 62
Prothro, Joshua 170
  Nathaniel 123
Provost, Joseph 69
Prud Homme, Rev. Firmin 165
Pullig, Anthony 30
Pulse, Frederick 211
Purcell, Ann 115
  Joseph 115
Purdy, W.T. 138
Purse, Isaiah 192
  Julia A. 72
  William 207
Purvis, Robert 56
  William 86
Putnam, Adeline M. 11
  Maj. Gen. Israel 12
  Schuyler 12
Pye, Benier 50
Pyne, Honora 101
  John 101

Quarles, Maj. R.F. 69
  Robert G. 32
Quarterman, Col. Joseph 45
  Rev. R. (off.) 122,183
  William 16
Quash, Elizabeth Pinckney 187
  Hannah Harleston 211
  Robert H. 211
Quattlebaum, Capt. ___ 110
Quillin, Rev. William 121
Quimby, Elizabeth 153
  Mrs. E. 153
  Susan 153
Quinby, Frances A. 204

Rabb, Mary Ann Elizabeth 92
Rabun, John W. 15
Radcliffe, Norborne 145
Ragan, J.H. Jr. 121
Raily, Elizabeth 112
Raine, Henry John 95
Raines, Lucien H. 35
Ramey, Matthew 124
Ramsay, Dr. David 197
  Martha H.L. 197
  Martha L. 197
  Dr. W. G. 90
Randal, Elizabeth 42
Randall, Wm. Washington 47
Randle, Susan 44
Randolph, Dorothy 8
  Jane C. 62
  Capt. Richard 8
  Sabra J. 10

Randolph (cont'd)
  Thomas M. 24
  Thomas E. 62
Rankin, William 11
Ransom, Reuben Sr. 72
Raoul, Alfred 109
Ratchford, William 205
Ratcliffe, Mary F. 65
  Norborne 64,65,70
  Thomas Campbell 65
  William Preston 64
  see Radcliffe
Ravenel, Benjamin P. 132
  Caroline 196
  Daniel 141,196
  Dr. Edward 75
  Henrietta 94
  James 173
  Dr. James 94
  John 95
  John Criffs 141
  Rene 99
  William 112
Ravenscroft, Rt. Rev. John
  Stark 36
Rawls, John I. 11
Rawson, Charles W. 38
Ray, Mary 85
  Capt. Peter 85
  Capt. William D. 21
Rayfield, W.J. 30
Raymond, Hannah P. 137
  Capt. N. 137
  Capt. Napthali 206
Read, Rev. Clement 166
  Gen. ___ 16,40
  Harleston Jr. 162
  Jacob 40
  Sarah W. 74
  Dr. William 74
  see Reed, Reid, Ried
Rearden, Ellen 34
Reardon, John J. 164
Reaves, Elizabeth Martha 35
  Thomas 35
Rebb, Mary 8
Recard, Mary C. 117
Rector, Rev. Lewis 4
Reddick, Sarah Ann 158
Redfern, Eady 188
  John 188
Redfield, Isaac 22,55
Red Jacket 35
Redman, Elizabeth 170
Redmond, Capt. ___ 90
Reed, Rev. H. (off.) 127
  Susan B. 13
  see Read, Reid, Ried
Reeder, Manning 112
  Oswell 88
Reeks, Mary Ann 11
Rees, Ebenezer S. 179
  Emma Evans 179

Rees (cont'd), Louisa M. 44
  Mary D. 179
  Talbot S. 47
Reese, Gavin 153
  George 153
  H.D. 48
  Horatia 38
  Margaret 153
  Maria 49
  Mary 132
  Mary Ann 153
Reeves, Maria 15
  Thomas 15
  see Reaves
Reid, Andrew 55
  Ann 118
  Elizabeth 1
  Maj. George 118
  Rev. George 111
  Rev. H. (off.) 19
  Rev. Henry 24
  Dr. J.S. 210
  Janet Joanna 32
  John 11,29
  Rev. John W. (off.) 189
  Maria 28
  R.R.R. 32
  Rev. Mr. (off.) 208
  Sarah 24
  Rev. W.M. (off.) 183
  see Read, Reed, Ried
Reimer, John 20
Reinhardt, John 30
Rembert, Andrew 7
  Catharine Ann 172
  Harriet L.C. 7
  Isaac 168,172
  Martha Detart 168
  Sarah Jane 148
  Maj. William 148
Rene, Brossier 192
  Frances Louisa 192
Rennecker, John H. 176
Rennie, Rev. Mr. (off.) 7,16
Revel, Sarah Ann 201
Revell, Hannah 115
Reynolds, Ann 2
  Elizabeth 15
  Elvira L. 87
  Emily 29,30
  G.N. 125
  Dr. George 81
  George N. 188
  George N. Jr. 122
  Harriet Perrink 188
  Rev. J.L. 121
  Rev. J.L. (off.) 188
  Mrs. Joshua 85
  Mary E. 125
  Reubin Sr. 30
  Richard 85
  William 87

Rhame, J.B. 203
Rhett, James Moore 172
Rhodes, Dr. Nathaniel 61
  Rebecca B. 61
  Rev. Thomas 70
Rhodus, John S. 60
Rice, Adeline Elizabeth 164
  Caroline 14
  Charles 164,188
  Col. E.W. 167
  Ezekiel 115
  Hannah 188
  Jane E. 167
  Col. Jesse 153
  Nancy 21
  Rev. Mr. (off.) 166
  Urben J. 153
Rich, Christopher 12
  George Jones 19
Richard, Rev. Wm. B. (off.)125
Richards, Frederick 150,178
  Fredricka Elizabeth Mary
    178
  Mary Rowan 59
  Samuel Richard 87
  Thomas H. 89
  William B. 59
  Rev. William B. 87,109
Richardson, Maj. A. 32
  Anna M.C. 150
  Cecelia J. 81
  Dr. ___ 81
  Emily 106
  Dr. Henry W. 143
  Hezekiah 66
  Col. James B. 41,112
  Jefferson 108
  John P. 150
  Matilda M. 41
  William 190
Richardsone, Dr. Cosmo P. 50
Richbourg, Sarah D. 208
Richmond, Rev. Leigh 7
Riddle, Capt. Cato 15
Riecke, George 126
Ried, Mary 29
  see Read, Reed, Reid
Riggs, Dr. Thomas 112
  Capt. William 81
Riley, Robert 20
Ring, George E. 80
  Rev. Mr. (off.) 125
Ripley, Elizabeth C.F. 82
Rish, Private John 110
Righton, Anna C. 164
Rivers, Ann 98
  Capt. Benjamin S. 178
  Francis 96
  George 127
  George A.C. 125
  Jane S. 178
  Capt. John 145
  Joseph B. 9

Rivers (cont'd),
  Maria Theresa 156
  Olivia Ann 125
  Sarah 9,145
  Sarah Ann 178
  Stiles 184
  William H. 156
Rives, Ainsley H. 124
  William T. 190
Riviere, Vincent E. 54
Roach, Ann Eliza 127
  Chevillette Eliza 120
  N. 120
Roath, Simeon S. 113
Robards, Samuel 16
Robb, James 28
  Lilly 28
Robbins, Franklin 175
Roberson, Nancy 16
Roberts, Adelena A.V. 71
  Albert J. 179
  Elias C. 8
  Mary Anne 38
  Theodore 197
Robertson, Ann 37
  Elizabeth 8(2)
  George 150
  James 16,81
  Jane 83
  Jane B. 32
  John 18
  John T. 114
  Martha A. 69
  Mary 149
  Mary E. 32
  Capt. Robert 169
  Robert L. 19
  Samuel 83
  William 45,149,165
Robeson, Dr. John W. 12
  Margaret 18
  Mary 96
  Moses Sr. 96
  see Robison
Robinson, Arthur 194
  Cuzziahr 50
  Elizabeth 18,125
  Henry Dickson 194
  Capt. Hugh 162
  Capt. James E. 97
  James K. 194
  James Kirk 194
  Jane 26
  John 27,69,102,189,194(2)
  John Brownlee 194
  John T. 27
  Joseph A. 91
  Lewis Gervais 194
  Margaret 69
  Mary 194
  Mary K. 194
  Stephen T. 194

Robinson (cont'd)
  Susan 102,187
  William 125
  Dr. William 13
  William Henry 206
Robison, Elizabeth Jane 117
  William 117
  see Robeson
Roby, Herbert 90
Rockwell, Hester Ann 48
Rockwood, Rev. M. (off.) 66
Rode, William 125
Rodgers, Col. Benjamin 120
  E.J. 159
  Eleanor M. 193
  James 17
  Rev. Mr. (off.) 120
  see Rogers
Roe, Ann H. 32
  Ann Henrietta 32
Rogers, Anna 1
  Charles 90
  Rev. Daniel 1
  Elizabeth 109
  John 9
  Rev. John 1
  Martha F. 9
  Nancy 14
  Rev. Nathaniel 1
  Rev. Mr. (off.) 55,94,110,
    132,149,152
  Dr. William B. 38
  see Rodgers
Rolfe, Rev. Mr. 49
Roll, Luthern 12
Rollins, Richard 136
Root, Alvira 66
  Rev. David 66
  Elisha 94
Roots, Serena 28
Roper, Ann W. 124
  B.D. 120
  Benjamin D. 124
  Mary Ann E. 36
  Mary J. 120
  Sarah Ann 24
  Thomas 208
Rosamond, Elsa 194
  James 194
  Sarah Octavia 194
Rose, Ann 4
  Arthur G. 45
  Elizabeth W. 45
  Hugh 19
  John A. 200
  L.A. 190
  Rebecca Ann 55
  Simri 30
  Thomas 4
  Thomas Jr. 55,179
  Capt. William P. 141
Rosborough, Ann C. 175

Rosborough (cont'd)
  Dr. James T. 181
  John 174,175
  William 174
Rose, John 196
  see before Rosborough
Ross, Ann 2
  Eliza 97
  David M. 87
  James 23
  Maj. James L. 97
  Louisa 38
Rosser, Isaac Henderson 194
Rossetter, Deborah 209
  Dr. Timothy W. 209
  Capt. White 19
Rothrock, Lydia 15
Rounsaval, David 166
Rountree, George R. 13
Rouse, Christopher 127
Rout, William George 166
Rowand, Charles E. 68,139
  Charles Elliott 100
  Martha Sommers 68
  Mary Elliott 139
Rowe, Gen. William 135
Rowell, William 76
Rowland, Charles E. 137
  Henrietta 137
  Isaac B. 17
  Thomas 110
  see Rowand
Royal, Ferriby 60
Royall, Cornelia 207
  Croskeys 207
  Rev. Wm. (off.) 205
Ruberry, Harriet R. 62
  John 138
  Martha M. 150
  Susan V. 138
Ruddell, Andrew 24
Rudisil, Dr. James C. 54
Ruffin, Col. Robert R. 42
Ruger, Valentine 78
Rumph, David 94
Runnels, Ex. Gov. 151
  Col. Harmon 151
Rush, Isaac 95
Rushin, Maj. Joel 10
Russell, Cynthia 116
  Elijah P. 24
  Eliza D. 17
  George 72
  Harriet 119
  James B. 24
  Rev. John A. 119
  Kezia H. 56
  Maria F. 24
  Martha M. 114
  Mrs. ___ 64
  R.E. 114
  Richard 116

Russell (cont'd)
  Richard Henry Harrison 186
  Mrs. S. 186
  Sophia P.J. 198
  Dr. William J. 186,198
Rutgers, Col. Henry 35
Rutherford, Adolphus S. 40
  Col. John 174,203
  Sarah Frances 174
Rutledge, Edward 103
  Rev. F.H. (off.) 85,127
  Hugh 96
  Jane 103
  Mary G. 96
  Nicholas Harleston 103
  Rosa 17-18
  Thomas Pinckney 123
Ryan, Daniel T. 134
  Dennis L. 111
  Capt. John 10
  Lawrence 20
  Obedience 135
Ryburn, Catharine 195
Ryerson, George 11

Sackett, Leonard 21
  Rebecca 21
Sadler, Elizabeth 38
  Henry Sr. 23
  Jane 13
  Margaret 50
Sage, Cyprean 27
  Mary Louisa 40
St. Andre, Durant 40
  Marie Alexandrine 40
Sally, Capt. W.C. 83
Salter, Elizabeth 57
  James 74
Saltonstall, Emily 9
Sampson, Joseph 33
Sams, Ariana H. 58
  Elizabeth M. 58
Samuel, Joseph 16
Sanches, Ramon Leon 59
Sanders, Eliaabeth 171
  Joseph T. 174
  Samuel G. 140
  Susan Lucinda 171
  Thomas 37
  Thomas Mr. 14
  William R. 132
Sandford, Margaret 96
Sanford, Jesse 25
  John W. 25
Sarye, P.D. 6
  see Sayre
Sass, E.G. 169
  Jacob K. 205
  Margaret H. 190
  Mary M. 169
Saunders, Billington M. 190
  Remembrance Chamberlain 160

Savage, Ann 25
 Anthony 191
 Daniel 55
 George M. 125
 John 212
 Sarah 212
Sawyer, Enoch 4
Saye, Rev. J.H. (off.) 176
 Rev. James H. (off.) 153,155,
 163,175,195,198,203
 Mary 40
Sayre, Louisa Caroline 170
 William H. 170
 see Sarye
Schaeffer, Rev. Frederick David 108
 P.C. 15
Schafner, Isabella C. 133
Scheck, Rev. John D. 28
Schenk, Catharine Ann 28
Schilpp, Ferdinand 26
Schirer, John 2,93
 Mary M. 93
Schirmer, William H. 133
Schivers, Samuel 151
Schmidt, Margrettia 173
Schnell, John Jacob 43
Schnierle, Col. John 137
Schollebarger, Sophia 20
Schreiner, John H. 205
 Mary Adelaine 205
Schriber, Johana 128
Schroder, Henry W. 163
Schroebel, Rev. Jacob Henry 191
Schudy, Rev. Mr. (off.) 63
Schultz, W.B. 94
Schulz, John 77
Schutz, Wade Hampton 79
Schwarts, Francis Sebastian 87
Schwartz, Mary Elizabeth 87
Scott, Elizabeth Mary 121
 George 20
 Joseph A. 205
 Martha S. 11
 Peter 14
 Rev. R.F. (off.) 109
 Capt. William F. 15
 William R. 56
Scoular, Jane P. 152
Screven, Rev. Charles O. 41
 Maj. John 83
 Rebecca 114
 Sarah N. 102
 Thomas 74,102
Scriven, Sarah A. 194
Scudder, Dr. 89
Scurry, Elizabeth M.M. 24
Seaborn, Maj. George 24
Seabrook, Carolina Lafayette 200
 Edward S. 11
 Elizabeth M. 135
 Col. George W. 33
 Harriet S. 7

Seabrook (cont'd), Martha 127
 Thomas B. 133
 Capt. Thomas Wilkes 99
 Whitemarsh B. 135,178
 William 200
 William Sr. 116
Seals, Martha T. 15
 Thomas 15
Seamon, B.B. 143
 Hester M. 143
Secress, Jane 86
Seibel, John J. 167
Selah, William W. 33
Semmes, Andrew 38
 Maj. Andrew J.T. 68
 Frances 38
 Col. Paul J. 113
Sergeant, Thomas H. 69
Serjeant, Harriet A. 109
Sewel, Rev. Mr. (off.)127,128
Sewell, Rev. James 113
 Rev. James (off.) 169,173
 Rev. Mr. (off.) 114,120,
 125(2),126,128,166,172
 Thomas Fletcher 113
Seyle, Samuel F. 46
Seymour, Eralbon 157
 Isaac G. 32
Shackelford, Clara E. 5
 Elizabeth Ashby 104
 Francis R. 5,36
 Martha S. 159
 Susan E.F. 161
 William 161
 William F. 104,159
Shackleford, Rev. Edmund 43
 William Jr. 9
Shad, Col. Solomon 73
Shadd, John R. 14
Shaffer, Sophia 175
Shand, Nancy W. 57
 Peter J. 57
 Rev. Peter J. 156
 Robert 103
 Robert Wallace 156
Shannon, Esther 18
Shapter, James M. 28
Sharp, Caroline 38
Sharpe, E. 205
Shaw, Agnes 152
 David 190(2)
 George W. 18
 Henry 152
 Henry D. 158,180
 Lt. J.B. 50
 Jane 35
 John 37
 Louisa Eleanor 158
 R. 195
 Sarah 190
 Susan G. 37
 Susan Taylor 180
 William 15

Sheaver, William F. 47
Shecut, Ann J. 92
  Dr. J.L.E.W. 92,149
  Dr. John L.E.W. 113
  L.A. 143
Sheehan, Rev. Godfrey 10
Sheftall, Hannah 3
Shelleto, John 33
Shellman, Clarissa 208
  Col. John 208
Shelton, Clough 49
Shepard, Daniel 105
  W.F. 41
Shepherd, Agnes 119
  Maj. Andrew 27
  J.C. 28
  Mary 9
  Piannah 32
  Susan P. 36
  Thomas J. 36
  Thomas P. 36
  William 23
Sheppard, Charlotte W. 124
  Rev. Daniel 147
  James 28
  Rev. Mr. (off.) 139
  Thomas C. 77
Sheppheard, Sophia F. 106
Sherer, Eli 19
Sheridan, James 197
Sherill, Elizabeth L. 17
Sherman, Hestor Ann 3
Sherrard, Manisia Ganer Mcnetta
  Sylvester Malvina Llewellen 21
Sherrell, Dorcas 53
Sherrill, Elizabeth 25
Sherrod, Maj. Felix A.M. 68
Shevolett, Mrs. ___ 101
Shick, Mary C. 14
  Peter T. 38
Shields, Celia 163
Shingler, F.M. 85
  Dr. J.S. 112
  Col. James S. 134
  Dr. James S. 203
  Mary A.E. 134
Shinnie, Alexander 91
Shipley, Russell 17
Shive, Dr. Caleb P. 48
Shiver, William 61
Shivers, George C. 88
Shockley, Mahala 181
Shook, Susan 11
Shoolbred, James 120
  John G. Jr. 176
Shore, T. 161
Shrewsbury, Edward 87
  Elizabeth Keith 87
Shuman, George 20
Shumate, Amelia S. 184
  Joseph D. 184
Siau, Lewis 75
Sibley, Lewis L. 156

Sibly, Rev. Mr. (off.) 147
Sigwald, Ann Catharine 79
  Elizabeth 101
  Thomas 79
Silcox, Daniel H. 135
Sill, Dr. Edward 7
Silliman, Emily M. 152
  Capt. John H. 152
  Rev. Mr. (off.) 16
Sillman, Joseph Milligan 123
Simison, James H. 18
Simkins, Col. ___ 11
  Col. Eldred 39,59
  Capt. John 76
  Margaret Eliza 11
Simmerl, James 17
  Vilet 17
Simmons, Ann 125
  Ann Eliza 118
  Dr. Francis Y. 145
  Dr. J. Hume 173
  Rev. John 24
  Sarah D. 199
  William 93,118,132
  William N. 119
Simms, W. Gilmore 120
  William Gilmore Sr. 37
  see Sims
Simonds, Eliza Ann 104
  Frances Henrietta 132
Simons, Benj. Bonneau 44
  Benjamin P. 134
  Charles William 126
  Dennis J. 163
  Rev. Dewar 92
  Edward 183
  Eleanor B. 132,208
  Eliza Hayne 116
  Eliza L. 134
  Eliza Read 183
  Emma 123
  Dr. F. Yonge 49
  Hannah 83
  Henrietta Martha 171
  James 106
  Jane Fullerton 119
  Julia Augusta 44
  Keating 2,89,183
  Keating Lewis 207
  Martha 20
  Mary M. 92
  Maurice 209
  Mrs. ___ 2
  Peter B. 172
  Sedgwick L. 132
  Sedgwick Lewis 89
  Thomas B. 208
  Thomas Grange 143
  Dr. Thomas H. 116
  Dr. Thomas Y. 44(2),119,
    139,171
  William F. 112

Simonton, Charles S. 143
  John Sr. 165
Simpson, Archibald 80
  Damaris 184
  David 184
  Elizabeth Dunham 69
  Hannah 151
  John 69
  Leonard Sr. 151
  Martha 46
  Martha E. 61
Sims, David W. 26
  Fred 67
  Henry Lightfoot 51
  James W. 9
  Margaret 9
  Mathew 8
  William 23
  see Simms
Sinclair, Alexander 142
  Commodore Arthur 49
Singes, Sarah 32
Singletary, Isaac J. 5
  James Daniel 194
  Martha 194
  Martha Elizabeth 194
  Samuel 183
  Sarah A.B. 137
Singleton, Mathew R. 196
  Richard 43,146
  Sarah Angelica 146
Sinkler, Eliza A. 208
  James 68
  Capt. Peter 184
  William 208
Sipe, John 12
Skennal, Margaret 77
Skinner, Alfred 40
  Nancy 40
Slade, Ann Eliza 17
Slappey, Hannah 17
Slaughter, Martha Emily Frances 189
  John R. 189
Slawson, Charlotte Gibbs 184
  H.J. 184
  Hamilton 159
  Rebecca Cecelia 159
Sledge, Wiley 10
Sleigh, J.W. 206
  John 84
  John William 52
Sloan, Allen 127
  Hiram L. 12
  Jane 13,14
  William D. 22
Slone, John 36
Sluter, Jacob 113
Smerdon, Anterisia C. 157
  Elias 58,77,153,157
  Mary Ann S. 58
  Susan E. 77

Smith, Agnes 82
  Albert M. 98
  Aley R. 183
  Capt. Allyn 107
  Anna Maria 117,118
  Anne 193
  Archibald 38
  Asa T. 25
  B. 121
  B. Burgh 84
  Benjamin F. 125
  Lt. D.G. 10
  Caroline 29,30
  Charles 209
  Charles B. 106
  Charlotte Mary 121
  Cynthia 30
  David 57
  Deborah 113
  Edward 96
  Dr. Edward D. 69
  Capt. Edward N. 33
  Eliza 7
  Eliza B. 137
  Elizabeth 10
  Emely 12
  Emma Gough 69
  Emma P. 207
  Frederick 64
  George Henry 131
  G. Laurens 10
  Henry W. 77
  Hess Marion Waring 94
  Horace 22
  Lt. Horace 16
  Rev. Hugh (off.) 23
  Isaac A. 88
  J. Blakely 192
  James 137,143,193
  Dr. James B. 66
  James S. 48
  Jane 22,106
  John P. 62
  John Patterson 174
  John Rutledge 103
  Jno. 88
  Joseph 174
  Joseph Allan 136
  Joseph T. 134
  Josiah E. 178
  Col. Keating L. 144
  Louisa C. 54
  Margaret J. 185
  Martha 88,117
  Martha A. 41
  Martha Ann 154
  Mary 68,69,124
  Michael 45
  Dr. Nathaniel N. 183
  P.F. 147
  Peter S. 151
  Rev. Mr. (off.) 70,87,90,
    92,111,113,149,163

Smith (cont'd), Rev. R.C. 176
　Rober 117
　Robert 207
　Robert Barnwell 1
　Roger 69,118
　Samuel 26
　Sarah Lewis 144
　Sarah Webber 202
　Simon 44
　Susan 28
　Susan Adger 133
　Sybil 6
　Rev. T. (off.) 87,88,94
　Theodore L. 120
　Rev. Thomas 64,133
　Rev. Thomas (off.) 64,133
　Thomas Waring 108
　Rev. W. (off.) 163,165
　W.B. 162
　Rev. W.H. (off.) 171
　W.S. 94
　Whiteford 106,117
　Rev. Whiteford 85,154
　Rev. Whiteford (off.) 123,159,
　　160,163,164
　William 10,33,36,131
　Maj. William 36
　William Jr. 113
　William Sr. 181
　Rev. William B. 42
　William J. 211
　William Mason 141,176
　William R. 34
　William S. 108
Smyth, Augustine 173
　Jno. 187
　Rev. Dr. (off.) 198,205
　Rev. Mr. (off.) 131,138,148
　Sarah Ann Magee 132
　Rev. Dr. T. (off.) 193
　Rev. Mr. T. (off.) 121,123,158
　Rev. Thomas 132,173
　Rev. Thomas (off.) 125(2),129,
　　130,135,137(2),138,155,156,164,
　　167,172,177,184,186
　Rev. Dr. Thomas (off.) 210
　William W. 65
Sneed, Archibald H. 192
　Emily C. 67
　Georgia A. 192
Snow, George H. 10
　Margaret 64
　Martha 15
　Pheldon R. 13
　Samuel N. 64
　Capt. William 64
Snowden, Ann L. 145
　Charles 69
　Eliza 7
　Eliza Jane 9
　Gilbert T. 9
　Isaac 106
　Dr. Isaac B. 26

Snowden (cont'd), J.L. 88
　Sarah 186
　Selina K. 68-69
　William E. 145,185
Solomon, William 28
Sondley, Narcissa 72
　Richard 72
Souleay, John 29
Sowell, William 45
Spaight, Charles G. 56
Spalding, Rev. A.M. (off.)166
　Elizabeth S. 36
Spann, Augusta L. 16
　Col. Charles Jr. 88
　Dr. Charles C. 120
　Col. John Russel 171
　T.H. 188
Sparks, Charles J. 138
　Susan V. 168
　Thomas 53
　William H. 14
Spear, G.T. 175
　Georgiana 175
　Mary Ann 25
　Rev. Mr. (off.) 110(2),
　　124,137,138,159
Spears, George W. 30
　Rev. Mr. (off.) 124(2),126
　Rev. Wm. W. (off.) 122
　see Speer, Spiers
Speed, G.W. 23
Speer, Eliza 34
　see Spear
Speissegger, Eliza F. 125
　John Sr. 75
　L.P. 119
　T.W. 194
Spencer, Samuel 116
Spicer, John F. 41
Spiers, Martha 7
　see Spears
Spivey, Col. E.B.W. 22
Spooner, Capt. Charles 86
Sprauge, H.N. 157
Sprigg, Elijah 5
Springfellow, Laodicea 128
　Capt. Thomas 128
　William 22
Sprout, Mary 6
Stacey, Rev. James (off.) 198
　Rev. Mr. (off.)168,203,204
Stacy, Rev. Mr. (off. 173,
　　174,195
Staggers, Susan A. 137
　William 137
Stagman, John 162
　Matta 162
Staley, Nelson O.J. 168
Stall, Frances Hayne 101
　Thomas D. 101
Stammire, B.H. 13
Standback, Marth 20
Stanley, Abner B. 95

272

Stanley (cont'd)
  Rev. Mr. (off.) 93
Stapler, Louisa J. 28
Star, Mathew 100
  S.T. 100
  see Starr
Starcke, Capt. Reuben 128
Stark, Robert 42
Starke, Jeanetta Amelia 133
  John W. 17
  Samuel 17
  Wyatt W. 133
Starks, Eliza C. 25
Starr, Caroline 63
  Samuel G. 12
  see Star
Statham, William R. 41
Stavall, Louisa 9
  Pleasant 9
Steadman, Horace 69
Steads, J.S. 126
Steedman, Col. Charles J. 79
  Col. Charles John 34
  Elizabeth 79
  James 113
Steele, Abner A. Jr. 167,169
  John 28
  Mary C. 167
  Rachel C. 52
  William G. 52
  William Govan 158
Stegen, H. 132
Steinmyer, John H. 98
Stennis, John 8
Stephenson, John H. 27
Sterett, Dr. ___ 88
  Ruth 88
Stevens, Ann 86
  Caroline S. 80
  Catharine R. 148
  Charles 77,148
  Hannah 14
  Harriette E. 45
  Jacob 80,86
  Dr. James D. 71
  Jervis Henry 25
  Maj. John 45
  Mrs. S. 23
  Samuel N. 64,209
  William Bacon 134
Stevenson, Mary 16
Stewart, Eliza James 186
  Lt. J. 208
  James 14
  Jane A. 109
  John James 186
  Margaret 79
  Mary 27
  Mary J. 5
  Naomi J. 12
  Parmelia 14
  Robert 27,79
  Robert L. 167

Stewart (cont'd), Samuel 75
  William J.H. 193
  see Stuart
Stiles, Benjamin 96
  Copeland 209
  Copeland W. 152
  Rev. Mr. (off.) 6
  Rosamond Susan 209
  Samuel 47
Stillman, Charles 149
  Rev. Charles A. 205
  James 78
  Mary 78
Stilwell, Abigail M. 43
Stines, Rachael 165
Stirewalt, John 30
Stitt, James 26
Stock, John F. 30
Stocker, James M. 49
  William Irvin 161
Stocking, Stephen H. 9
Stockton, Richard 2,19
Stoddard, Solomon 15
Stokes, Archibald 2,197
  Catharine 197
  Charles L. 95
  E.R. 86
  Eliza 8
  M. 63
  Margaret Jane 92
  William M. 188
Stokey, Elizabeth 40
Stoll, William 15
Stone, Austin 186
  Charles R. 12
  George W.W. 190
Stoner, Douglass 153
Stoney, Edgar G. 146
  Eugenia L. 196
  John 196
  John J. 209
Stopplebein, Elizabeth Christina 157
Storke, Rev. Charles A.G. 50
Storm, Mrs. P. 170
Stott, Capt. Levin 138
Stoue, Lucy 28
Stovall, Jane E. 43
  Mrs. ___ 43
  Stephen 43
Stow, Abram 31(2)
  George W. 177
  Nelson L. 58
Stoy, Henry W. 14
  J.W. 123
  Pierre 13
Stratford, George 37
  Sarah 37
Stratoon, Rev. Mr. (off.) 159
Stratton, Rev. James 138
Street, George 161
  Henry T. 127
  Sarah 56

Street (cont'd), Timothy 76
Streeter, Squire 124
Stribling, Rebecca C. 30
Stringfellow, Harriet Davis 152
  J.M. 38
  Capt. John 152
  Patience 196
Strobecker, Charles C. 53
Strobel, Dr. Benjamin B. 5
  Caroline M. 206
  Elizabeth 106
  Elizabeth D. 144
  Emma B. 132
  Emma Cornelia 71
  Jacob 47
  John 132,144
  Mary Elizabeth 167
  Rev. P.A. 206
  Rev. P.A. (off.) 126,132
  Rev. Philip A. (off.) 167
  Philip Arthur 93
  Sarah Ann 163
  Rev. William D. 63,71
Strohecker, Dr. Edward E. 146
  H.F. 49
Strong, Augustus R. 91
Strother, Mary 21
Stroub, Serena 44
Stuart, Dr. James 200
  Mary 15
  Col. Middleton 160
  see Stewart
Studwick, Dr. Samuel 13
Sturges, Abbey E. 6
Sturgis, Daniel Sr. 20
  Mrs. Josiah 89
Subers, Amos 50
Suder, Ann 159
  Peter J. 68
Suit, Mary Ann 44
Sullivan, Elizabeth G. 82
  Frances Charlotte 121
  Dr. James C. 56
  Mary 49
  T. 49
  Timothy 121
Summers, Mary 37
  Z. 10
Sumter, General ___ 160
Sutherland, John 41
Suttle, Irena 42
Suydam, Eliza M. 7
  Samuel A. 140
Swartworth, Gen. Jacobus 5
Sweeny, Helen L. 86
  James 86
  Lavinia 125
Sweet, F. William 131
Swift, Ann H. 32
  Lavina 22
Swinton, Caroline Jane 139
  Hugh 127
  Margaret 127

Swinton (cont'd)
  William Henry 206
Switzer, John Rudolph 148
Syfan, Margaret L. 64
  Mary 118
Symes, John T. Jr. 199
Symington, Felix 139
Symmes, Daniel 18
  Rev. R.S. 51

Taggart, Mary 7
Tait, Antoinette 68
  Gen. James M. 68
  see Tate
Talbot, Capt. Mathew 10
Talley, Rev. Mr. (off.) 22, 35,145
  Rev. Nicholas (off.) 163
  William H. 27
Tally, Rev. Alexander 100
  Rev. Mr. (off.) 147,155,156
Talmage, Rev. Mr. (off.) 33,92
  Rev. President (off.) 194
  Rev. S.K.(off.) 60
  Rev. Samuel K. 88
Tamoree, George 4
Tankersley, Nehemiah 10
Tarbox, Thomas 56
Tarrant, Frances 10
Tarver, Absalom 57
  William M. 17
Tarwater, Helen 140
Tate, Hannah 79
  Hugh A. 16
  see Tait
Taveau, Augusta Melanie 207
  Augustus 207
Taylor, Col. A.R. 127
  Adeline S. 77
  Agnes M. 77
  Capt. Alexander 104
  Rev. C. (off.) 145
  E.O. 167
  Edward R. 163
  Eleanor R. 131
  Elizabeth Bolling 160
  Gov. ___ 5
  Dr. G.W. 185
  Harriet C. 5
  Col. Henry F. 63
  James 141
  James F. 25
  James G. 103
  James H. 66
  Jane B. 103
  Jane E. 105(2)
  John 98
  John Jr. 48
  Capt. Joseph 77(2)
  Josiah 105(2),181
  Justina M.H. 48
  Lavinia 3
  Margaret Henrietta 104

Taylor (cont'd), Martha Ann 117
  Mary B. 11
  Mary Louisa 18
  Mary R. 131
  Orrin 162
  R.A. 22
  Rebecca 194
  Rev. Mr. (off.) 25,68,147
  Maj. Robert 160
  Sarah 98
  Sarah C. 163
  Sophia Gordon 103
  Susan A. 183
  T.S. 131,166
  Thomas Ann 166
  Thomas Smith 131
  Capt. W.B. 117
  William 3
  Capt. William 24
  General William 24
  William Boineau 155
  William Jesse 73
Tebbetts, Moses 28
Teimarsch, George 7
Telfair, Edward 11
  Sarah 11
Temple, Lt. William T. 41
Tennent, Dr. Charles 202
  Mary S. 64
  William 103
Tennessee, W. 31
Terrell, Buffon D. 45
  Col. James C. 106
Terry, James 5
Tew, Catharine Burdick 61
  Henry 61
  Henry S. 144
  see Thew
Thackam, Thomas 107
Tharin, Theodore C. 139
Tharm, Edward C. 51
Thaxter, Rev. Joseph 7
Thayer, E. 173
  Septima 125
  T. Heyward 185
Thew, George M. 63
  see Tew
Thomas, Anna H. 70
  Caroline L. 147
  Dalcedia L. 192
  Drury 9
  Rev. E. (off.) 49
  Dr. Edward Gibbes 110
  Jacob T.H. 20
  John 147
  Maj. Jonathan 3
  Col. Joseph D. 33
  Julia M.M. 158
  Juliana 25
  Mary Ann 100
  Richard J. 2
  Stephen 69,100,158
  Stevens 138

Thomlinson, Joseph 92
Thompson, Agness 149
  Ann 22
  Dr. Asa 16
  Eliza 153
  Eliza Ann 153
  Eliza B. 35
  Elizabeth 10,157
  George Washington 44
  Hedge 26
  Rev. James (off.) 198
  James Hamden 75
  Jane 122
  Jane M. 205
  John 21,112
  Margaret 84,172
  Margaret E. 110
  Mary Jane 113
  Nancy 85
  Ramalia Louisa 46
  Rebechah M. 44
  Robert Clark 27
  Samuel M. 85
  Sarah 112
  Col. Willim A. 75
  William 15,31,62,116,153,
    169
  William N. 44,46
  Y.B. 177
Thomson, Benjamin 51
  Elizabeth A. 51
  James P. 177
  Richard 159
  Susan 159
  William H. 164
  see Tomson
Thorn, Harriet H. 126
Thorne, Henrietta 160
  William R. 160
Thornton, Abthiah Harvey 48
  Joseph 105
  Phineas 48
Threadcraft, Bethel 130
  S.G. 156
  see Treadcraft
Threewits, Elizabeth Julia 48
Thurmond, Willis 25
Thurston, Jane 169
Thweatt, Elizabeth 22
  Susan R. 40
Thwing, Edward 34
  James E. 197
  Louisa 34
Tibbets, N.H. Israel 7
Tidwell, Greuman 17
Tietyan, Otto 162
Tigner, Young F. 14
Tilden, Louisa M. 99
Tillinghast, Robert L. 107
  Sophia E. 107
Tilton, Henry 148
Timme, Elizabeth 60

Timmons, A.H. 194
  Agness Theturah 194
  Isabella 192
  Isabella M. 105
  Martha Celcelia 194
  Naomie Rose 177
  Rectina Ophilus 194
  Samuel M. 194(2)
  William 105,139,192
  Col. William 169
Tinsley, James 163
  Sarah F. 14
  Ramsom 203
Tipley, Rev. Hezekiah 60
Tipps, Jacob 12
Todd, James E. 13
  Margaret 13
Tolck, J.D. 125
Tommer, Henry B. Jr. 87
Tompkins, Caroline W. 87
  Henry Lee 87
  Henry M. 65,87
  Stephen 68
  Thomas B. 65
Tomson, Mary 203
  see Thompson, Thomson
Toney, William Hopson 67
Toomer, Ann 131
  Anthony 167
  Elizabeth C. 52
  Elizabeth S. 124
  Henry B. 124
  Dr. Henry V. 113
  J.W. 131
  John Laurens 162
  Sarah Antonio 100
Torlay, Joseph 144
Torrence, John 7
  Nancy 12
  Susan 12
Tovey, Amelia A. 60
  Elizabeth Fosbury 144
  Henry 205,209
  Henry C. 59,143,144
  Julia 143
  Julianna 144,198
  Susan Ella 143
Towns, Dr. Henry 2
Townsend, Amarapthia J. 108
  Capt. D. 108
  Dr. D.J. 93
  John 94
  Rev. S.B. 65
  Theodore J. 115
  William S. 152
Tracy, Maj. D. 32
  Herman 98
Tramble, William 36
Trapier, Alicia Palina 85
  Paul 85
  Rev. P. (off.) 55
  Rev. Paul 72

Trapier (cont'd)
  Rev. Paul (off.) 112,137,
    155,156,174,187,192,196,
    199,211
  Rev. Mr. (off.) 68,83,85,
    106,107,118,121,134,138,
    144,146,147,149,161,174,
    175,178,186,193,205
Trapman, Fanny Eliza 158
  Lewis 158
Traylor, Paschall 30
Treadcraft, Bethel 144
  Sarah R. 144
  see Threadcraft
Treadwell, Ann 163
  Samuel 163
Trenholm, Edward L. 110
  Esther Constance 174
  William 174
Trenhom, Charles L. 103
Trescott, Amelia 156
  Capt. George F. 187
  Dr. John S. 156
  Joseph W. 162
Trexler, Lawrence 11
Trimble, Robert 28
Trisdale, Joseph W. 36
Trott, Rev. James 19
Trotti, Gen. Gasper J. 134
Troup, Col. G.M. 23
  Mrs. ___ 23
Truetlin, Joseph C. 10
Tucker, Charles S. 6
  Edmund 89
  Dr. Edmund H. 89
  Eliza 14-15
  Frances H. 24
  Dr. Henry Wm. 17
  Dr. N. 15
  Thomas Tudor 21
  Rev. William (off.) 123
Tufts, Gardner 29
Tuggle, Thomas 55
Tulyman, Hester 168
Tupper, Ann Eliza 184
  Frederick A. 79
  Holmes 51
  T. 184
Turk, Margaret 185
  Col. William 185
Turman, John 28
Turnbull, Gracia C. 79
  James 78
  John Jr. 92
  Robert J. 79,97
  Sabina Elliott 78
Turner, Anna Catherine 92
  Capt. Daniel 127
  David 79
  Rev. D. McNeill 152
  Emily 122
  Capt. George R. 92,96

Turner (cont'd)
  Capt. George R. Sr. 52
  Henry 33
  Hiram 23
  Louisa W. 79
  Miss ___ 20
  Reuben 60
  Rose Isabella 96
  Dr. W.W. 15
  William 20
Turpin, George P. 21
  Mary Ann 171
Tuttle, Jos. 12
  Gen. Robert 74
Tuuls, Charles H. 114
Twiggs, Maj. George L. 70
  Louisa Sarah 70
Twirewalt, Capt. John 30
Twiss, Thomas S. 25
Tyler, Elizabeth Ann 66
  John M. 59
  Joseph 66,192
  Mrs. ___ 181
  President 181

Ulmer, Col. Isaac B. 58,138
Upson, Mary E. 99
  Stephen 99
Ury, Lt. A. 138
Usher, Catharine R. 24
Ussery, Woodford 187
Utzman, Albertine 12

Valentine, Eliza S.F. 129
Valk, Jacob Lawrence 108
  Jacob R. 87,108
  Sarah Ann 87
Vanbrackez, John 49
VanBuren, Maj. Abraham 146
Vance, Frances Lawson 135
  Mrs. James 135
  Mary Moncrief 135
  Susan Dart 135
  William 135
Vanderhorst, Arthur 161
  Mary Priscilla 113
  R.W. 111
  Gen. R.W. 113
Vanderzee, Getty 98
  John 98
  S.T. 98
  Teunis 98
Vandine, Roseann 168
Vandiver, Rev. George 75
  Rev. S. (off.) 22
Van Dyck, Rev. J.B. (off.) 35
  Rev. John B. 50,156(2)
  Rev. John B. (off.) 47(2),58
Van Epps, A.C. 196
Van Glahn, Henry 173
Vanie, Dr. Robert B. 13
  see Vance
Van Lew, John 98

Vann, Rev. James 38
Vannoy, Nathaniel 100
VanRansselmer, Gen. John J. 29
VanVleck, Rev. Jacob 54
Vardell, Amelia 209
  Amelia A. 144
  Anna 129
  Emma P. 189
  Julia Ann 59
  Mary 64
  Mary R. 143
  Thomas A. 198
  Thomas R. 60,144,209
Varnedoe, Ann 133
  Ann Caroline 133
  Nathaniel 133
Vason, Nancy A. 41
Veitch, Jane O'Riley 139
Venning, Charles Henry 168
  Elizabeth 168
  Jonah M. 73,168
  Mortimer W. 145
Verdier, Elizabeth F. 118
  Elizabeth H. 142
  John M. 142
Verone, Amelia 146
Vicholson, A.R. 95
  Sarah 95
  see Nicholson
Vickers, Theresa 16
  Vinson Ellis 22
Vidal, Louis N. 154
  Maria Therese 154
Villepique, Charlotte M. 157
  Paul F. 157
Villineuve, Margaret E. 172
Vincent, Capt. Daniel B. 202
Vinel, Deborah M. 31
Vining, Samuel 14
Vinson, Elvira 21
Vinyard, Eliza E. 57
VonVorst, John 149
  Sarah 149

Waddel, Mrs. E.H. 101
  Elizabeth Woodson 37
  Rev. Isaac 57
  John N. 69
  Rev. Moses 32
  Rev. Dr. 37
  Sarah E. 32
  Dr. W. W. 36
  Rev. Moses (off.) 66
Waddell, Sarah 13
Wade, Sarah 93
Wagnen, George 55
Wagner, Effigham 95
  George 151,178
  George Jr. 191
  Henrietta M.H. 20
  Dr. John 169
  S.J. 20
  Susan Henrietta 178

Wagner (cont'd),
  Theodore Debon 174
Wainwright, Col. Robert D. 171
Wakefield, Martha 23
  Sarah Cannon 202
Waldo, Horace 57
Walk, Charles 15
Walker, Rev. A.C. (off.) 72
  Maj. Abraham 82
  Alexander 93
  Ann Eliza 150
  Benjamin W. 188
  Charles 146
  Col. ___ 145
  Edward J. 134
  Edward M. 50
  Eleanor S. 122
  Elizabeth 30,158
  Maj. Freeman 10
  Henry D. 109
  James 171
  Dr. James B. 43
  James E. 110
  James M. 39
  Jane 8,40
  John 145
  Maj. John 5,158
  John H. 6
  Capt. John S. 138
  Joseph 141
  Rev. Joseph (off.) 69,164,172
  Rev. Joseph R. (off.) 86,137,
    165,209
  Julius H. 7
  Margaret E.G. 22
  Mary P. 145
  Nancy M. 121
  Narcissa 78
  Rev. Mr. (off.) 59,77(2),78,82,
    85,109,150,163,188,199,200
  Robert T. 23, 58
  Samuel 9
  Sarah A. 96
  Sarah S. 145
  Thomas 96
  William 78,122,165
  William Sr. 48
Walkup, Nancy 8
Wall, Arthur 82
  Jesse 82
Wallace, B.A. 34
  Rev. C. (off.)184
  John 13
  John F. 33
  Rev. Joseph (off.) 127,149
  Lydia 18
  Margaret 13
  Martha 133
  Rev. Mr. (off.) 207
  Sarah 33
Wallis, Mortimer R. 65
  Sarah Ann 146

Walpole, Lady Georgina Mary 3
Walsh, Joanna E. 56
  M.P. 64
  Mary 137
  Michael P. 113
  Patrick 56
  Rev. Mr. (off.) 76
Walter, Christopher P. 145
  E. Wilmot 64
  J. 106
  Lavinia 106
  Martha W. 145
  Theodosia P. 128
  William 165
Walton, Alfred Y. 4
  Dorothy 67
  Elizabeth T. 24
  George 67
  Col. George 67
  Jane Clarissa 16
  Thomas 16
Ward, Harriet 182
  Henry 11
  Maj. James M. 182,187
  John 122
  Louisa 187
  Mary 131
  Sarah E. 175
  Dr. Seth 32
  Thomas 55
Ware, Maj. Gen. Edward 73(2)
  T.C. 103
Warham, Mary 62
Waring, Ann Ball 20
  D. Jennings 66,119,197
  Dr. Edmund T. 106
  Dr. Edward T. 129
  Elizabeth S. 193
  Francis Malbone 129
  Harriet Constantia 119
  John 193
  John M. 103
  Lucy R. 103
  Sarah E. 197
  Sarah Mitchell 159
  Thomas 66
  Dr. Thomas 159
  Thomas Jr. 206
  William T. 106
Warley, Felix Bruneau 37
Warne, Julia Pierpont 60
Warner, John 7
  Col. Nathan 20
Warnock, Dobson 17
Warren, Benjamin W. 178
  G.L. 143
  Isaac Henry 109
  John A. 178
  Mary Elizabeth 178
  T. 78
  William B. 46
Warson, Samuel 14
Washburn, Col. Asabel 1

Washington, Cornelia 104
  James H.R. 104
  Major   118
  Martha Blake 208
  Martha F. 44
  William 36,44,105,208
  Gen. William 36
Wateman, Sarah 19
Water, Martha Clementina 117
Waterman, Robert H. 156
Waties, Thomas 25
Watkins, Dr. Anderson 29
  Dr. C.A. 8
  Catharine 76
  Maj. George 195
  J.D. 77
  Martha 48
Watson, Ann 54
  Ann W. 179
  Dr. J.F. 208
  James 179
  Gen. James C. 188
  Jonathan 11
  Robert 32
  Thomas 161
  Col. William C. 31
Waugh, A.C. 117
Waul, Thomas 15
Way, Quarterma 47
  Dr. S. 122
  Sarah 47
Wayman, W.J. 97
  see Weyman
Wayne, Daniel G. 172
  Gen. W.C. 199
Weathers, Jenkins D. 27
Webb, Amelia M.K. 204
  Rev. B.C. 108
  Rev. B.C. (off.) 107,173
  Caroline R. 33
  Charles 59,83,173
  David Sr. 19
  Daniel C. Jr. 46
  Edward J. 107
  Elizabeth L. 206
  Elizabeth W. 173
  John 148
  Margaret D.W. 157
  Nathaniel B. 26
  Rev. Dr. (off.) 133
  Samuel B. 206
  Stephen 4
  Dr. William 146
  William Edward 146
  William L. 210
  William R. 133
Webber, Eliza M. 105
  Capt. S. 105,134
  Samuel B. 116
Webster, Rev. A.H. 51
  Daniel 16
  Eliza 51

Webster (cont'd)
  Grace 16
  Stephen 2
Weeb, Capt. M. 131
Weeks, John 16
  Margaret 14
Weems, Lock 41
Weir, Silas E. 22
  see Wier
Welch, Daniel C. Jr. 46
  George Cooper 126
  Isaac 24
Welling, Edward 125
  Edwin 162
  John B. 163,178
  Sarah A. 178
  William 63
Wells, Capt. Daniel 152,204
  Rev. J. (off.) 188
  Joseph T. 117
  Susan 67
  Thomas F. 15
  Willis 8
Welsh, Edward 95
  Hannah 16
Welsman, Amelia Elizabeth 110
  Capt. James 110,193
  Maria Catharine 193
Wescoat, William 184
Wesner, Ann E. 185
  Frederick 185
West, Dr. Charles 129,206
  Elizabeth M. 206
  Michael 84
  Capt. Thomas 164
Westbury, Thomas 9
Westcott, G.J. 152
Weston, Antonia B. 161
  Margaret J. 161
  Paul 81,161
  Penelope Bentley 81
Weyman, Catharine 76
  Edward B. 76
  Joseph T. 86
  Louisa C. 176
  see Wayman
Whaley, Benjamin 62
  Louisa M. 190
  William 123
  William S. 190
Wheat, John F. 151
Wheaton, Daniel F. 11
  Dr. Sterling 66
Wheeler, Rev. E.M. 172
  Henry 160
  Louisa M. 160
  Simeon 25
Whetstone, Nancy V. 198
Whilden, Elias 99
  Elisha 175
  Mary Gibson 175
  William 83
Whipple, Lt. P.M. 4

Whishert, John H. 37
Whitaker, Rev. Daniel K. 15
　Eliza J. 210
White, Agnes P. 131
　Alonzo J. 137
　Alston L. 118
　Andrew 29
　Ann 126
　Captain ___ 36
　David 26
　Miss E. 101
　Rev. E. 111
　George K. 61,126
　H. 72
　Isabella J. 191
　James G. 60
　Leonard 131
　John 191
　M.A. 31
　Mary 155
　Mary Ann 43,146
　Mary Ann Belinda 69
　Mary Ann Sarah 14
　Rev. Dr. (off.) 202
　Rev. Mr. (off.) 79,80,103,119, 167,187
　Robert 51
　Susan H.L. 111
　Maj. Thomas 64
　Thomas J. 29
　Col. Thomas 35
　Mrs. R. 61
Whitehead, Amos P. 16
　Mary Susan 24
Whiteside, Ann J. 85
　Eliza Martha Emeline 60
　Mary 15
　Moses 60,85,138
Whiting, D.H.W. 69
　Edward Melrose 151
Whitlock, Eulalia 32
　Rev. Henry 32
Whitmore, Daniel 114
Whitner, Gen. Joseph N. 34
Whitney, Archibald 68
　Elvira 68
　Frederick H. 164
　Octavious L. 113
　Reuben 155
　T.A. 147
Whitridge, Constantial Clementina 201
　J.B. 201
　Dr. J.B. 164
　Maria Louisa 164
Whittemore, Amos 20
　Charles 164
　William Jr. 164
Whittington, Sarah 143
Wienges, Conrad 195
　Jos. 155
Wier, Ann 153
　John 153

Wigfall, Eliza 173
　Henry 176
　Samuel 44
　T. 105
　Thomas 173
　William Moore 173
Wigg, William Hazard 79
Wiggins, Jesse 118
Wightman, Eliza 89
　John T. 89
　Rev. Mr. (off.) 43,184
　Rev. Wm. (off.) 81
Wilbur, Elizabeth Ann Luther 113
　W.W. 113
Wilcox, Rev. Carlos 6
　Harriet H.D. 174
Wilder, J.W. 154
Wiley, Joseph 18,19
　Moses 1
　Samuel 202
　see Wylie, Wylly
Wilfong, John 140
Wilkie, Col. Adam 4
　Cornelia M. 164
　Elizabeth 107
　Ellen B. 134
　Ellen S. 141
　James 134
　Capt. Joseph B. 114
　William 107
　William B. 141,164
Wilkins, Jane Mary 71
　Martin L. 192
　Paul H. 71
　Capt. Wm. F. 36(2)
　Dr. William 39
Wilkinson, Dr. ___ 67
　Mary 67
　Pamelia Ann 75
　Reuben 25
　S.W. 97
　Virginia 178
　Willis 178
Willard, Maj. Charles 54
Willey, George W. 201
Williams, Albert P. 43
　Dr. Alexander 13
　Capt. ___ 126
　Dr. David R. 191
　Dr. ___ 89
　Drury 146
　E. Hilton 126
　Frances Lavinia C. 82
　Henrietta B. 8
　Henry 197
　James M. 68
　John 36
　Lucy J. 57
　Margaret 36
　Margaret C. 132
　Martha S. 3
　Mary Ann 205

Williams (cont'd)
  Mary Walton 44
  Milton 202
  Nancy 68
  Rachel S. 19
  Rev. Mr. (off.) 34,161
  Richard 91
  Samuel 55
  Sarah Ann 146
  T. 32
  Rev. W. (off.) 164
  William 187
  William W. 209
  Winthrop B. 183
  Col. Zachariah 44
Williamson, Alice 99
  Dr. Charles 30
  Elizabeth Ann 30
  Dr. J.H. 208
  James E. 17
  Capt. John 40,178
  John D. 145
  Col. John N. 17
  Louisa 17
  Mary 12
Williman, Christopher 139(2)
  Harriet Eliza 139
  Maria Schmidt 139
  see Willman
Willington, A.S. 151
  Harriet Elizabeth 151
Willis, Caroline E. 195
  Henry 195
  Julia Dunham 86
  Mary H. 86
Willman, F.A. 3
  Mary 3
  see Williman
Willy, Elisha 12
Wilmans, Amanda M. 100
  Augustus P. 203
  Sarah 100
Wilmer, Rev. Dr. 7
Wilson, Ann Eliza 196
  Anna C. 126
  Benjamin H. 191
  Col. Benjamin 17
  Caroline M. 93
  Catharine Fuller 205
  David 72,109
  Eliza 23,24,196
  Eliza Jane 97
  Elizabeth 90
  Elizabeth E. 12
  Elizabeth W. 42
  Elmira R.A. 81
  Frances A. 153
  Capt. George 99
  H. 48
  Hugh 18,128,156,196
  Isaac 186
  James 97
  Rev. James 12

Wilson (cont'd)
  Capt. James H. 42,97
  James Hervey 118
  James M. 124
  James S. 74
  Jane I. 46
  Jennet Cooper 74
  John 27
  John G. 9
  John H. 153,186
  John L. 73
  Rev. John M. 55
  Maj. Josiah 42
  Laura T. 12
  Louisa 156
  Maria Louisa 28
  Mary Amelia 36
  Mary Ann 97
  Mary Madeline 129
  Mary S. 198
  Dr. P.H. 2
  Robert 78,81
  Robert H. 173
  Robert L. 97
  Robert William 48
  Rev. Mr. (off.) 148
  Dr. Samuel 2,90
  Rev. Samuel B. (off.) 85
  Samuel C. 134
  Susan Elizabeth 18
  Thomas 10
  Thomas M. 12
  William 42,178
  William M. 27,206
  Rev. William S. 36
Wimberly, Dr. Joshua R. 63
Windsor, Gracey 69
  Thomas T. 163
Wingard, Rev. Jacob 48
Winges, Conrad 116
  Joanna Caroline 116
  see Wienges
Wingfield, Elizabeth 14
  James 19
  John L. 96
  Mary R. 19
Winn, Ann 95
  Olivia 31
  see Wynn
Winslow, Rev. Miron 53
  Nathaniel 53
Winston, Nancy 35
Winthrop, Augusta 173
  C. 72
  Charles Jr. 72
  F. 72
  Joseph 25,173
Wise, John T. 25
Wiseman, Rebecca L. 4
Wish, Amanda E. 109
  Richard S. 98,109
Withers, Elenora P. 155
  Francis 62

Witherspoon, Ann Eliza 200
  David 164
  Dr. David Ramsay 76(2)
  Dr. Francis 133
  Rev. J. 106
  Rev. J. (off.) 81(2)
  Col. J.H. 68,81
  James Edmond 18
  Col. James H. 134
  Jane 81
  Jane Erwin 128
  John 31,53
  Capt. John M. 52,55
  Dr. John R. 16
  Margaret 128
  Mary 53
  Rev. Dr. (off.) 137
  Robert 78,131
  Sarah 52
  Sarah Ann 78
  Susan K. 106
  Thomas 31,38,114
  Thomas M. 128
  Thomas Reese 128
  Rev. Thomas S. 200
Withington, James E. 192
Witsell, Harriet E. 91
  John 190
  Laurence J. 173
  Lawrence 97,172
  Mary 190
  Mary D. 97
  Paul Walter 163
Witter, Benjamin 21
  Elizabeth Zephryne Amanda 21
  Malvina 14
Wittich, Ernest L. 13
Wittpen, Frederick 128
Woddard, Martha 21
Wolfe, Mary C. 13
Wolfolk, John 43
  Louisa Matilda 43
  see Woolfolk
Womack, Abraham 85
Womble, Angelina T. 12
Wood, Alzada Susan 203
  Benjamin 66
  Charles D. 184
  Ezekiel 203
  Florinda B. 66
  J.R. 137
  James 66
  Joseph 39
Woodhull, Rev. George S. 94
Woodrop, Ann S. 176
Woodruff, C.C. 35
  Jane C. 91
  Maj. Joseph 91
  Rev. Mr. (off.) 165
Woods, Caroline Ann 171
  Mary A.P. 176
  Moses 171
  Maj. William 41

Woodson, Eliza 37
Woodward, Rev. A. 165
  A.B. 6
  Hiram P. 44
  Joseph 156
  Melinda R.B. 156
  Isaac C. 42
Woodword, Joseph 80
Woodworth, Martin 100
Wooley, Caroline A. 112
Woolf, Rachael 104
Woolfolk, Louisa 49
  Parmelia W. 13
  see Wolfolk
Woolfook, Austin 7
Woolley, Charles C. 74
  Martha Frances 61
Woolworth, Aaron 13
Wooten, Mourning 66
Word, Sarah A. 1
  Robert 1
Worsham, Dr. Richard W. 33
Worthington, Edward 7
  Gen. T. 6
Wragg, Elizabeth 103
  Henrietta E. 206
  John Ashby 135
  Samuel 206
  Lt. Samuel 32
  Maj. Samuel 106
  Sarah L. 106
Wray, Thomas 57
  Dr. William T. 131
Wright, Asa 138
  David 1
  Duncan 11
  Easter 140
  Elizabeth 138
  Frances 35
  Francis 54
  Josiah 5
  Lucinda 1
  Margaretta 119
  Mary Elizabeth 94
  Nancy 26
  Robert 94
  Robert S. 193
  William 48
Wyatt, Joseph 12
Wyer, Rev. Mr. (off.) 19,206
Wylie, Mary B. 8
  Rev. S.B. (off.) 195
  see Wiley, Wylly
Wylly, Alexander C. 36
Wynn, Charles R. 17
  Olivia 31
  Rev. Thomas L. 45
  see Winn

Yancey, Bartley 28
Yarborough, Deborah Anne 31
  Washington 31

Yarbrough, Washington 16
Yargan, John 112
Yates, Catharine 131
  Decima Mary 159
  Jeremiah 159
  Joseph C. 77
  Phebe 105
  Rev. Mr. (off.) 106,119,135, 154
  Samuel 105
  Rev. W.B. (off.) 127,177
  Dr. William 131
  Rev. William B. 103
  Rev. Wm. B. (off.) 200
Yeadon, Harriet 147
  Mary 183
  Col. Richard 147,173,183
  Col. William 79,122
Yeaman, Mary Ann 25
Yeatman, James 11
Yongue, Green Lee 147
  Jemima M. 8
  Rev. Samuel W. 8
  see Young
Yore, Dr. 154
You, Dandridge C. 104
Youg, Mary Emeline 149
Youmans, Rev. Mr. (off.) 86
Young, Asa G. 19
  Charlotte D.L. 196
  Dinah 205
  Harriet E. 14
  Jacob 56
  John 15,98
  John P. 2
  Capt. Joseph 70,140
  Joseph H. 68
  Lucy 29
  Mary Ann 70
  N. 29
  Rear Admiral ___ 151
  Rev. Mr. (off.) 97,132
  Rev. T.J. (off.) 52
  Rev. Thomas (off.) 30
  Rev. Thomas J. (off.) 147
  Rev. Thomas John 23
  William 50,151
  Capt. William 133
  Rev. William 57
  William Cox 61
  see Yongue, Younge
Youngblood, Emeline 6
  Dr. Isaac 172
  Mrs. ___ 172
  Rebecca G. 118
  Richard S. 118
Younge, Jame 141
  Samuel 141

Zackman, Ann 45
  Selena C. 83
Zealy, Elizabeth Malmbaum 138
  Joseph 92

Zealy, (cont'd)
  Joseph T. 117,138,162
  Mrs. Joseph T. 138,162
  Julia Isadora 162
Zimmerman, Mary E. 43
Zipperor, Lucretia 22,23
Zylstra, Robert J. 117

www.ingramcontent.com/pod-product-compliance
Lightning Source LLC
Chambersburg PA
CBHW062005220426
43662CB00010B/1236

Marriage and Death Notices from the Charleston Observer 1827-1845

Brent H. Holcomb

HERITAGE BOOKS
2008

HERITAGE BOOKS
AN IMPRINT OF HERITAGE BOOKS, INC.

Books, CDs, and more—Worldwide

For our listing of thousands of titles see our website
at
www.HeritageBooks.com

Published 2008 by
HERITAGE BOOKS, INC.
Publishing Division
100 Railroad Ave. #104
Westminster, Maryland 21157

Copyright © 1980 Brent H. Holcomb

Other books by the author:
Bute County, North Carolina Land Grant Plats and Land Entries
Kershaw County, South Carolina Minutes of the County Court, 1791-1799
Winton (Barnwell) County, South Carolina Minutes of County Court and Will Book 1, 1785-1791
Early Records of Fishing Creek Presbyterian Church, Chester County, South Carolina, 1799-1859, with Appendices of the visitation list of Rev. John Simpson, 1774-1776 and the Cemetery roster, 1762-1979
CD: Marriage and Death Notices from The Charleston [SC] Observer, 1827-1845
CD: South Carolina, Volume 1
CD: Winton (Barnwell) County, South Carolina Minutes of County Court and Will Book 1, 1785-1791
CD: Early Records of Fishing Creek Presbyterian Church, Chester County, South Carolina, 1799-1859
CD: Kershaw County, South Carolina Minutes of the County Court, 1791-1799

All rights reserved. No part of this book may be reproduced or transmitted in any form or by any means, electronic or mechanical, including photocopying, recording or by any information storage and retrieval system without written permission from the author, except for the inclusion of brief quotations in a review.

International Standard Book Numbers
Paperbound: 978-1-55613-419-7
Clothbound: 978-0-7884-7070-7